Electric and Electronic Systems for Automobiles and Trucks

Robert N. Brady

Department Head
Diesel Mechanic/Technician Program
Vancouver Vocational Institute
Vancouver Community College
Vancouver, British Columbia
Canada

A RESTON BOOK
PRENTICE-HALL, INC., Englewood Cliffs, New Jersey 07632

Library of Congress Cataloging in Publication Data

Brady, Robert N.

   Electric and electronic systems for automobiles and trucks.
   Includes index.
   1. Motor vehicles—Electric equipment.   2. Motor vehicles—
Electronic equipment.   3. Motor vehicles—Electric equipment—
Maintenance and repair.   4. Motor vehicles—Electronic equipment—
Maintenance and repair.
I. Title.
TL272.B6177   1983   629.2′54   82-18528
ISBN 0-8359-1610-3

© 1983
by Prentice-Hall, Inc.
A Division of Simon & Schuster
Englewood Cliffs, New Jersey 07632

10   9   8

Printed in the United States of America

Contents

x / Contents

Preface

Any mechanic or apprentice in the automotive or heavy equipment industry today is expected to possess a good theoretical and working knowledge of electrical systems related to this equipment. Without this knowledge and ability, his or her skills will be sadly lacking, and the individual will most certainly encounter day-to-day problems in his everyday service and maintenance of such equipment.

The industry today employs and trains many personnel who become certified automotive electricians, whose main task is to install, service, troubleshoot, and, if necessary, to design and to wire systems specifically required for special equipment that may not be readily available from a manufacturer. If one is employed by a company which has one or more of these automotive electricians on staff, then the mechanic will seldom have to become involved with the day-to-day repairs of electrical equipment. However, this situation is not always the same throughout the industry. More often than not, the automotive or heavy equipment mechanic must by necessity be prepared to undertake the job normally expected of the automotive electrician.

The intent of this book is not to train the reader as a first-class automotive electrician, since a variety of training programs are readily available through such equipment manufacturers as Delco-Remy Division of General Motors Corporation, Leece-Neville Company, Motorola, Robert Bosch, and Lucas C.A.V. Training is offered by automotive and equipment manufacturers, such as Ford, who produce and use Prestolite electrical accessories on their finished equipment. Other manufacturers use accessories produced by one of the companies already listed. In addition to these manufacturers, many Japanese vehicles are fitted with electrical accessories from Nippondenso Co. Ltd.

The present-day electrical systems on vehicles and equipment employ many solid-state devices which minimize possible problem areas, yet cannot be overhauled due to their design parameters. Because of these features, the job of the mechanic or automotive electrician in fleet maintenance is more one of knowing how to effectively analyze and rectify a problem through the use of a wide variety of test tools and special equipment, rather than attempting to repair a major component on site.

The sales and service of automotive electrical and heavy equipment accessories is a multi-billion dollar business today. Many service shops around the country cater to the many needs of this business. These specialty shops are equipped to handle any job of repair at short notice and, because of the large turnover in both sales and service, can remanufacture and sell to the end user any component used in the electrical system at a much cheaper rate than the small fleet or individual user.

The majority of automotive and equipment fleets today do not spend a lot of man-hours in attempting to overhaul electrical componentry on the vehicle. Instead, they have their service personnel exchange the faulty component for a new or exchange unit, if tests indicate that a major problem exists.

Many problems that occur on vehicles or equipment today are the direct result of very minor causes. However, service personnel, lacking understanding of basic electrical theory and operating principles, will remove components and replace them with new or exchange units, when simple tests and repairs could have quickly rectified the problem area. Many personnel tend to shy away from such electrical repairs mainly because they just do not understand the system, cannot actually see the internal workings of a component, and are afraid of either receiving an electrical shock, or doing additional harm or damage to the system. Although it may be necessary to undertake a major repair to an electrical component, the majority of automotive or heavy-duty equipment mechanics will seldom have to become involved in such repairs. As mentioned earlier, it is cheaper and faster to replace a failed component with a new or exchange unit from a local supplier when a major problem is discovered.

Therefore, the purpose of this book is not to duplicate the readily available and excellent manufacturers' service manuals and literature, but to provide one source of general information concerning typical repair jobs that confront the average service mechanic working with automotive or heavy diesel-powered equipment.

Chapter

1

Fundamentals of Electricity

The modern electrical system used on passenger cars, commercial, and heavy-duty equipment is an intricate system that supplies the necessary electrical energy to operate lights, horns, radios, stereo tape decks, heaters, windshield wipers, defrosters, air-conditioning systems, power-seats, and the vehicle ignition system on gasoline engines. In addition, the electric starter would not be possible without the use of a battery, which itself requires a generator or alternator to keep it in a state of charge. All of the other fancy factory options, or after market add-ons, would be of little use without the electrical system.

Considering the little attention that it often receives, the electrical system does a remarkable job in maintaining trouble-free operation throughout its life. When electrical problems occur, they can usually be traced to a lack of maintenance, or improper service procedures.

Although the reader may have a limited knowledge of electricity, most people do understand the typical freshwater system that is found in the normal family home and office. Everyone has probably used a garden hose at some time, and found that with no nozzle on the end of the hose outlet, when you turn the hose tap on, a large volume or quantity of water will flow from the hose, but with little pressure. This can be likened to quantity or volume in an electrical system, only it is commonly called amperes or amps when discussing electricity. In the water system we commonly refer to this quantity or volume as gallons per minute, or liters per minute.

If we were to place our thumb over the end of the garden hose, or to screw an adjustable nozzle onto the hose end, then we would be able to effectively control the quantity or volume flowing from the end of the hose by manipulation of this adjustable nozzle. In either instance, what we actually achieve is a reduction in quantity or volume, but a definite increase in the force of the water leaving the hose. This then is pressure, which in an electrical system is known as *voltage* or *volts*.

We can still have pressure in water flow without placing our thumb or the nozzle over the hose end. However, this pressure remains reasonably constant, and is developed at a city pumping station in your community by the use of mechanically driven water pumps. It is not variable as with the adjustable nozzle on the hose end.

City water pressure will force water through the street pipes until it meets a resistance at your house such as a closed water tap or faucet. This water flow (volume) is the same as the current pushed through an electrical circuit which will also meet resistance in the form of lights or other electrical accessories in the system. All substances offer resistance to flow whether it be water pipes or electrical wires. The size and length of these pipes and wires will vary the amount of resistance present in any given circuit. This resistance in an electrical circuit is known as ohms.

Therefore the main properties that we are concerned with at this time are:

- Quantity or volume expressed as amperes or amps
- Pressure expressed as voltage or volts
- Resistance expressed as ohms

When considering any electric system, remember these three properties.

The water pump at the pumping station supplies the pressure and in effect, becomes the battery in the electrical system. The battery stores electrical energy both in the form of amperes and volts, in quantities determined by the actual physical size and design of the battery. We will discuss this later in the chapter dealing with batteries.

An understanding of the actual relationship between the three properties listed so far—current (amps), pressure (volts), and resistance (ohms)—will assist you in future discussions related to any electrical system.

Common electrical terms include:

Volts Unit of measure for electrical pressure or force, commonly measured by the use of a voltmeter.

Amps Unit of measure for current flow, measured by an ammeter.

Ohm Unit of electric resistance that opposes current flow, and causes heat to be created by this resistance (friction) to flow. Measured by the use of an ohmmeter.

CONDUCTORS

In the typical water system, we use pipes to carry the flow throughout the system; in an electrical system, we use wires for this same purpose. These wires are usually made of copper, since it is reasonably inexpensive and plentiful in supply. Aluminum wiring has also been used, especially in house wiring and commercial buildings. However, in automotive and heavy equipment, copper is used extensively for wiring, since it has proven to be less troublesome than aluminum, and stands up better under the types of operation encountered by these electrical systems.

Most metals, in fact, are good conductors of electricity, with silver, copper and aluminum being the most widely used. When flexibility is desired in a wire, copper wiring may be composed of a large number of very small strands of wire.

The size of the wire used can have an adverse effect on the resistance created when electricity flows through the wire. This can best be explained by considering Fig. 1-1.

In Fig. 1-1., water is directed through pipes of two different diameters, namely Pipe 1 and Pipe 2. You can appreciate that since Pipe 2 is larger than Pipe 1, the tank immediately under Pipe 2 will fill up much

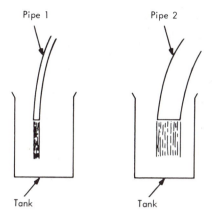

Fig. 1-1. Pipe size versus flow rate and resistance.

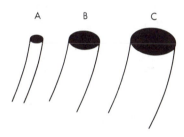

Fig. 1-2. Wire size versus flow rate and resistance.

flow will be in a given time period, similar to the gallons or liters per minute flowing through the water pipe. The electrical flow, as you may remember, is measured in amps.

If we now consider Fig. 1-2, which of the three wires shown would have the greatest resistance to current or amp flow?

If you said Wire 1, you were correct. Which wire in Fig. 1-2 would allow the greatest current or amperage flow? If you said Wire 3, you were correct.

USE OF ELECTRICAL ENERGY

To systematically evaluate how electrical energy can be used in a system or circuit, let's compare the simple water wheel system to that of the electrical one through the use of basic line diagrams.

One of the easiest ways in which water power can be used to provide work output, is that of the old mill wheel, where water from a river or stream was used to drop over an embankment and drive a large water wheel or paddle wheel. A shaft running from the center of the wheel was then connected to a mill stone, which was continually rotated by the water wheel.

If work was required from a water wheel, however, with no river or stream close by, the only way to achieve this was to use a pump driven by some means to direct water to and against an impeller which was then continually rotated by the water pressure produced in the pump. Such an example is shown in Fig. 1-3.

Although Fig. 1-3 shows a sealed system, it is only because this system requires less water than an open system, which would continually require a steady water supply.

In the simple Fig. 1-3, the pump creates the flow within the system to drive the

faster than the tank under Pipe 1. The reason for this is that obviously we can direct a greater volume or quantity of water through Pipe 2 in the same time as that for Pipe 1 due to the larger diameter of Pipe 2.

Both pipes will create a resistance to water flow. Because Pipe 1 has a smaller diameter than Pipe 2, Pipe 1 will have a higher resistance to the flow of water through it.

The flow of electricity is caused by the movement of electrons within the wire. The greater the electron flow within the wire, the greater the quantity or volume

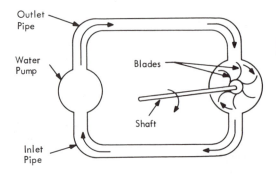

Fig. 1-3. Sealed water pump system. (Courtesy of Caterpillar Tractor Co., Peoria, IL)

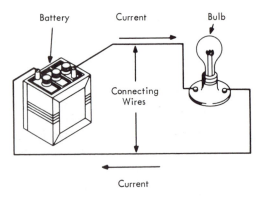

Fig. 1-4. Basic electrical system. (Courtesy of Caterpillar Tractor Co., Peoria, IL)

shaft. As the pump rotates it will create not only flow (quantity or volume), but also pressure because of the sealed system, and resistance is created through the effort required to drive the shaft, and by the size of the piping.

If we now substitute a similar arrangement, but use electrical components, we would have the view shown in Fig. 1-4.

In Fig. 1-4, we have substituted wires for the water pipes, a storage battery in place of the pump, and a light bulb in place of the shaft connected to the load. In Fig. 1-3, the water flow and pressure rotated the

shaft, while in Fig. 1-4, the current being pushed through the wires by the voltage causes the light bulb to glow. Remember that the battery contains both quantity (amps) and pressure (volts); therefore, the battery has replaced the water pump. The system shown in Fig. 1-4 is also a sealed system similar to Fig. 1-3, with no means of recharging the battery at this time. Current flows out of the battery to the light bulb, and then returns to the battery.

In Figs. 1-3 and 1-4 we called the systems a sealed system; however, in an electrical system, the more common term used is closed circuit because there can be direct loss of electrical energy other than that which is used to light the bulb.

If we were to break a water pipe, or cut a wire, then there would be a loss of energy. When such a condition existed, the shaft in Fig. 1-3 would no longer rotate and, in Fig. 1-4, the light bulb would no longer glow. Such a condition in an electrical circuit, is commonly called an open circuit, meaning that there is a loss of electrical energy.

The word circuit is derived from the simple word circle. In other words, in order to complete the circuit, the current must be capable of flowing around the circle from the point of origin and back again to that same point.

In Fig. 1-4, the light bulb is an energy-absorbing device, since it requires current to keep it lighted. In turn, the current or amps are forced through the circuit by the electrical pressure or voltage. Anything wired into an electrical circuit that uses current is, therefore, part of the electrical load placed upon that circuit. The greater the number of accessories wired into the circuit, the greater will be the current requirements or amperage needed to operate them all.

In addition, as we add accessories to the circuit, these current-carrying devices will offer greater resistance to the flow of electricity, requiring additional voltage to overcome this added resistance in many instances.

BASIC ELECTRICAL SYMBOLS

In Fig. 1-4, we showed a battery, wires and a light bulb. This was done for clarity and for ease of instruction. However, this is not the way that such a circuit would be shown in normal electrical terminology and layout.

An easier and less involved method is shown in Figure 1-5.

Note that the battery terminals are shown by two different symbols. These are used to differentiate between the positive and negative terminals.

The positive battery terminal can be a large ⊤ or a plus sign (+).

The negative terminal is shown as either a short ⊥ or a minus sign (−).

Other commonly accepted and used electrical symbols are shown in Table 1-1.

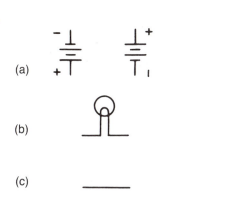

Fig. 1-5. Electrical symbols: (a) battery, (b) light bulb, (c) wire.

Table 1-1
Commonly Used Electrical Symbols

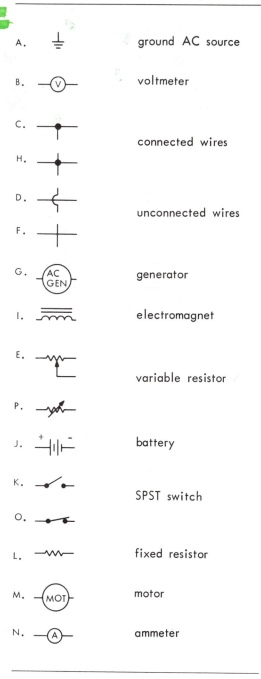

A.	⏚	ground AC source
B.	—Ⓥ—	voltmeter
C.		connected wires
H.		
D.		unconnected wires
F.		
G.	(AC GEN)	generator
I.		electromagnet
E.		variable resistor
P.		
J.	+∣∣∣−	battery
K.		SPST switch
O.		
L.	—⋀⋀⋀—	fixed resistor
M.	—(MOT)—	motor
N.	—Ⓐ—	ammeter

RESISTORS

All conductors will offer some form of resistance to the flow of electrons (current/amps) through the wire. This resistance is caused by the resistance of both the wire and the circuit resistance. A resistor therefore is an electrical component that can be used to add or alter a fixed amount of resistance to any electrical circuit.

By adding a resistor to a circuit, therefore, we decrease the current flow. For example, Fig. 1-6 shows a simple circuit with no resistance other than that offered by the wiring and a single light bulb. This arrangement allows four amps to flow through the closed circuit. However, in Fig. 1-6b, we have installed a fixed resistor to the closed circuit, which will therefore decrease the current flow from the previous four amps shown in Fig. 1-6a, to only two amps as shown in Fig. 1-6b.

Resistors which have more or less resistance can be used to suit the situation as desired in the circuit. Therefore, in Fig. 1-6b, the light bulb will not glow as brightly as it did in Fig. 1-6a because of the lower current (amperage) flow. As the value or amount of resistance is increased, the current flowing through the circuit must decrease. Thus, by employing different resistors in a circuit, we can change the value of a fixed resistor, change the voltage source, and control the amount of current (amps) flowing in that circuit.

The symbols for resistors are shown in Table 1-1.

The fixed (non-variable) resistor is used throughout automotive and heavy equipment circuits to limit the current flowing at any given point. However, there are resistors available that can be adjusted in position by use of a sliding contact to provide variable resistance to suit a variety of con-

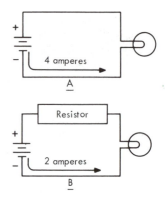

Fig. 1-6. Resistance versus current flow.

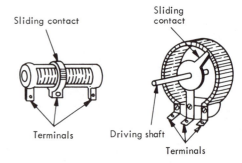

Fig. 1-7. Variable resistance.

ditions. To vary the resistance of a variable resistor, a sliding contact connected to an insulated hand-adjusted sliding contact allows you to dial in the resistance to suit almost any condition within the circuit. A simple variable resistance is shown in Fig. 1-7.

INSULATORS

When it is necessary to prevent a loss of electrical energy by a bare wire (for example, one touching a metal object), the wire must be covered by a material that will not allow any external flow of current. Materials such as rubber, plastic, glass and wood are examples of good insulators, since all of these materials have a very high resistance to the flow of current.

Without this insulation in an electrical circuit, you would get a severe shock when you touched or handled wiring. The insulator also protects other components from short-circuiting, or creating an open-circuit through coming into contact with one another.

GENERAL THEORY OF ELECTRICITY

In its simplest statement, electricity can be said to be the flow of electrons from one atom to another atom within a conductor. All matter is composed of atoms, and these atoms are so small that they are invisible to the naked eye, and even to powerful microscopes. The atom is the smallest particle into which one of the elements can be divided, while retaining its properties. The elements combine in many different combinations to form various kinds of matter found on earth. The elements hydrogen and oxygen for example, combine to produce water. Again, combined, sodium and chlorine combine to produce salt. All atoms have a center or core made up of particles known as protons around which rotate other particles called electrons. Both of these types of particles become extremely important in our more detailed study of electricity.

Let's start with what is known as the simplest of all elements, hydrogen. We will compare this hydrogen element with the very complex one of uranium.

Fig. 1-8 shows the typical arrangement of both of these elements.

The uranium element contains 92 protons (+) in its core, and 92 electrons (-) in an orbit about its core. Between these two

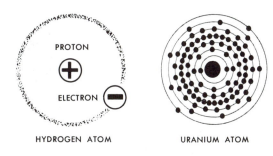

Fig. 1-8. Hydrogen and uranium elements.

are the remaining elements, each having an atomic structure that differs from its two neighbors by one proton (+) and one electron (-). Other well-known elements are nickel with an atomic number of 28, copper with an atomic number of 29, and zinc with an atomic number of 30.

Since we frequently deal with copper in the electrical systems in wiring, connectors, etc., let's look a little more closely at this element. Within the copper atom are 29 protons (+) and 29 electrons (-), with the protons concentrated at the core, while the electrons are distributed in four separate shells or rings, with each shell or ring located at a different distance from the core of the atom.

Figure 1-9 shows the basic core of the

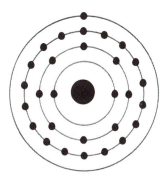

Fig. 1-9. Copper atom.

copper atom with the 29 electrons clustered around it. You will notice that the two electrons in the ring closest to the core remain equally spaced from one another, while the eight electrons in the second ring from the core are equally spaced, and the 18 electrons in the third ring also remain equally spaced from the core. The outer ring, however, only contains one electron.

Any element that has less than four electrons contained within its outer ring is a good conductor of electricity, while elements with more than four electrons in this outer ring are known to be poor conductors of electricity. From our earlier discussions, you may recollect that any element that is a poor conductor of electricity is called an insulator. Those elements that contain four electrons exactly in the outer ring are classified as semiconductors, which we will deal with later in this book. Any conductor with less than four electrons in its outer ring makes it rather easy to dislodge these electrons from their orbits by use of a low voltage. This action will therefore create a flow of current (electron flow) from atom to atom.

In summation, remember that the proton is positively charged, while the electron is negatively charged. Opposite charged particles are attracted to one another, therefore opposing electric charges will always attract. Thus, the negatively charged electron (-), will be pulled towards the positively (+) charged proton.

Because of the electron movement that exists around the core of the atom, it is not at all uncommon for an atom to lose some of its electrons. These electrons that leave the atom's outer rings are generally called free electrons, and they tend to gather in the same place, creating what is known as a charge of electricity. When these free electrons begin to move, say along a cop-

per wire, a certain number of these electrons pass a given point on the wire in a set time period; in other words, we have a certain quantity or volume flowing or moving within the wire. The electrical term for quantity or volume, from our earlier discussion, is current, which is measured in amperes or amps. Electricity, therefore, is flowing in the wire at this time. The free electrons moving along the copper wire will always move away from areas of many electrons into areas where there are less electrons.

ELECTRON FLOW IN A COPPER WIRE

If a negative (-) charge were placed at one end of a copper wire, while a positive (+) charge were located at the other end, the condition shown in Fig. 1-10 would result.

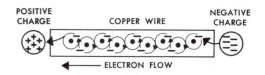

Fig. 1-10. Electron flow in a copper wire.

As we already know, when electrons (-) flow through a wire, a current is created which is measured in amperes. The number of electrons required to produce one ampere is 6.28 billion billion past a given point in one second.

Figure 1-10 illustrates the flow of these electrons within a typical copper wire. For simplicity, we will show only the single electron contained within the outer ring of the atom.

The positive charge at the left side of the wire will create an attraction to the electron, thereby causing it to leave its atom. The loss of the electron now makes the atom become positively charged, and the atom will exert an attractive force on the outer ring electron of its neighboring atom. This reaction causes a chain-reaction to occur along the length of the copper wire, with each succeeding atom giving up its electron to another atom. Because of the great number of electrons flowing, electricity is created.

The negative charge at the right-hand side of the wire shown in Fig. 1-10 provides a repelling force equal to the attractive force created by the positive charge at the other end. Electron flow will continue within the wire as long as the positive and negative charges are maintained at each end of the wire.

VOLTAGE

In earlier discussions, we described the voltage as being similar to water pressure. It is this electrical pressure, then, that pushes the current or amperes (electron flow) through the wire.

In Fig. 1-10 we saw how electron flow was initiated in a wire; the unlike charges at each end of the wire have potential energy due to their capability to move these electrons through the wire caused by the forces of attraction and repulsion.

The potential energy between the wire ends is called voltage or electromotive force (emf). We can produce voltage by various means. In automobiles or heavy equipment, we generate this voltage by chemical means within a battery. Voltage can also be produced through friction and mechanical energy as in a generator or alternator which will be explained later in these chapters.

A typical vehicle battery of 12 volts has a potential voltage of 12 volts between the positive and negative terminals (posts). With no current absorbing devices connected to the battery posts, there is still a potential energy of 12 volts. Voltage can exist on its own without the presence of current (amperes), but current cannot exist if there is no voltage present to push it along through the wiring.

In a battery, the voltage is limited by the strength of the charges between the positive and negative terminals or posts. Therefore, the greater the lack of electrons (-) existing at the positive (+) end or post, and the greater the excess of electrons at the negative post, the higher the voltage will be.

In Fig. 1-4 earlier we showed a battery supplying power to a light bulb. If we were to substitute a generator in place of the battery, the generator when driven would supply a continuous flow of current (amperes) through the light bulb. In effect, the battery or generator pumps electrons through the wiring to the light bulb and back to the source of supply which can be either the battery or generator.

RESISTANCE

Earlier we discussed that if water is forced through a pipe, some resistance to flow would exist because of the friction created between the surface of the pipe and the water. When electrons are forced through a conductor such as a copper wire, resistance will also be created because of two conditions. First, each atom resists the removal of an electron due to the attraction exerted upon the electron by the protons (+) in the core of the atom. Second, collisions are always taking place between the electrons and atoms as the electrons (-) are moving through the wire.

Such collisions create resistance which leads to heat within the conductor as the current is flowing.

We mentioned earlier that the electrical term for resistance is the ohm. An ohm can be defined as the resistance that will allow one ampere to flow under the force or pressure of one volt. The electrical symbol for the ohm is Ω, which is similar in shape to a horseshoe. The number preceding the horseshoe indicates the total number of ohms, therefore 10Ω indicates a total resistance of ten ohms. The symbol for resistance is defined by the Greek letter omega (ω) in addition to the horseshoe shape shown.

TYPES OF ELECTRICAL CIRCUITS

The basic types of electrical circuits that we are concerned with in automotive and heavy equipment are either series or parallel circuits. Certain applications, however, sometimes employ a combination of both of these, and are therefore known as series/parallel circuits. One example of the series/parallel circuit is the use of batteries for both starting and charging; through the use of a series/parallel switch, two 12 volt batteries can be tied together in series to produce 24 volts of cranking power to the starter. Once the engine starts, the automatic operation of the series/parallel switch allows the generator to charge the batteries at a rate of 12 volts.

Prior to looking at several examples of series and parallel circuits, Fig. 1-11 depicts the simplest form of a basic electrical circuit. A battery supplies the energy for the system (volts and amperes), and a resistor (load) offers a fixed resistance in the circuit.

Also shown in Fig. 1-11 are an ammeter

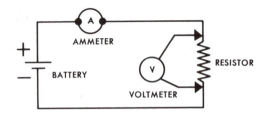

Fig. 1-11. Basic electrical circuit. (Courtesy of Delco-Remy Div. of GMC)

and a voltmeter to measure both the current (amperes), and voltage in the circuit respectively. Take careful note that the ammeter is placed into the circuit, and not across the battery. If the ammeter were placed across the battery, damage to the ammeter would result. The voltmeter, however, can be placed across the circuit at any two points to obtain a voltage reading.

CURRENT FLOW

In the early years of electricity, it was assumed that current in a wire flowed from the positive source of the voltage, to the negative terminal of the source after having passed around the circuit. However, in the year 1897, this theory was proven to be totally incorrect. Scientists discovered and proved that in reality, the current flowed from the negative terminal, through the circuit, and back to the positive source.

Since that time, both theories have been used. For example, some companies in the industry choose to use one theory, while others choose to use the other theory. These two theories are known as:

1. The conventional theory in which the current flow is considered to be from positive to negative.

2. The electron theory in which the cur-

rent flow is considered to be from negative to positive.

The conventional theory is widely used and accepted within the automotive industry, although some major manufacturers of heavy duty equipment prefer to use the electron theory. Again, either theory can be used.

BASIC ELECTRICAL FLOW

There are two theories commonly used to answer the often-asked question, Does electricity flow from the positive battery terminal to the negative battery terminal or is it the other way around?

1. What is referred to as the conventional theory depicts the electrical flow as from the positive to the negative battery terminals. This theory is most often used in discussions and accepted as standard practice.

2. The electron theory, however, maintains that the flow is from the negative battery terminal to the positive battery terminal; this fact was discovered as long ago as 1897.

Since either theory can be used, although the conventional theory is most often followed, most manufacturers state in their manuals which of the two should be used when studying their electrical systems. History records that 2500 years ago the ancient Greeks knew that amber rubbed on cloth would attract feathers, cloth fibers, etc. Since the Greek name for amber was elektron, the term electron was coined in our language, meaning basically the property of attraction. Electrons are negatively charged.

Many manufacturers of heavy-duty trucks, etc. prefer however to use positive ground systems over negative ground systems for reasons given in the following section.

POSITIVE VERSUS NEGATIVE GROUND ELECTRICAL SYSTEMS

A discussion of electrical systems invariably involves the question of why one system is a negative ground system, and another is a positive ground system. Most North American built cars are negative ground, while many imported vehicles are positive ground. Similarly, many trucks and heavy equipment are positively grounded.

The main reason that positive ground electrical systems are more widely used on heavy-duty trucks is that in the electroplating of the vehicle during manufacturing, the plating material is attracted from the positive anode to the item to be plated which is the negative cathode.

If, for example, during manufacture of a heavy-duty truck you could dip a negative ground vehicle into the electrolyte in a plating tank, the positive electrical system consisting mostly of copper (wiring, etc.) would immediately start to plate itself over to the negative structural and steel portion of the vehicle. You would end up with a copper-plated chassis, but no electrical system!

If we were, however, to dip a positive ground vehicle into the same plating tank, the material flow would be from positive to negative; but you would not end up with steel plated copper. When you removed the positive ground vehicle from the tank, it would certainly be nice and clean, but otherwise undamaged.

The situation just described can be compared with the conditions that the average heavy-duty highway truck is exposed to in wet and winter-type weather. Salt placed on the highways to melt snow and ice becomes a very efficient electrolyte. During high-speed winter driving, this spray totally envelopes the entire vehicle in a manner similar to the tank situation described herein. Severe corrision will result to the electrical accessories on the vehicle if the negative pole of the battery is grounded.

Heavy-duty truck manufacturers have found that the positive ground electrical system practically eliminates the worst types of corrosion or electrolysis affecting the electrical system. To further explain the disadvantages of the negative ground system, consider that all of the steel structural parts of the truck are negative or cathodic. The energized electrical system, copper wires, terminals and switches, solenoids, motors, etc. are positive or anodic. The voltage differential between the steel parts and the copper electrical system is approximately 14 volts.

When the negative ground vehicle is exposed to moisture (in particular to salt-laden moisture through salt de-iceing) the condition that exists is similar to that of an electroplating bath in which steel items are being copper-plated. The positive copper anode in the electrolyte bath is ionized and attracted to the negative steel. The same situation exists on the negative ground vehicle with the result that the electrical system deteriorates.

On a positive ground vehicle the action is reversed. However, due to the large mass of steel in comparison to the small amount of energized copper in the electrical system, the effect is insignificant. The advantage of the negative ground system is that if you can totally seal out any entrance of moisture to the electrical system and accessories, then the system will function extremely well. However, the configuration of heavy-duty, on-and-off highway trucks is such that this approach becomes rather impractical due to their operating environments. Many generators and alternators on such trucks are open in order to allow the passage of cooling air through them. The salt fog, drawn through the radiator by the vehicle movement or the engine fan, circulates through these devices, causing electrolytic corrosion of all energized surfaces that it comes into contact with.

When two dissimilar metals meet at a junction in the presence of salt-laden moisture or liquid, a galvanic action will result which generates a voltage which will electrolytically cause ionic material transfer. The voltage generated is dependent upon the electrode potential between the two metals. In the case of a typical truck, copper has a voltage potential of plus 0.347 volts, and steel has a voltage potential of minus 0.340 volts. Therefore, the voltage generated at the junction point becomes in effect 0.687 volts.

Electrolytic activity supported by the typical 14 volts of the vehicle electrical system is 20 times the galvanic 0.687 volts, or 20 times as severe.

The negative ground electrical system was developed because, years ago, few electrical accessories were in use on vehicles other than the basic ignition system and some running lights. However, with the advent of the transistor, research was increased to apply it to automotive use. The car radio was an ideal place in which to use this device. The first transistors were of the germanium PNP type which were more easily applied to a negative ground system than a positive ground system because of their makeup. This generated a swing away from the previously positive ground systems on both cars and trucks. Little information was available as to the problems that could develop with the negative ground system.

Since the PNP germanium transistor was developed, major advances have been made, and silicon transistors are now widely used.

The negative ground system on passenger cars and low mileage vehicles presents no major problem and may be economically impractical to change over to positive ground. However, on high-mileage trucks that are in operation 24 hours a day, seven days a week, where high maintenance-free mileage is expected, and where road failures caused by electrical system problems must be kept to a minimum, many heavy-duty truck manufacturers favor the positive ground electrical system, rather than the negative system.

OHM'S LAW

There are a variety of calculations and formulas that are needed and used when designing electrical circuits and components; however, it is not necessary for the automotive or heavy-duty mechanic to be familiar with these.

It is extremely helpful, though, to know the relationship between amperes, voltage and resistance within an electrical circuit, because if any two of these are known, one can calculate the value of the third. This is advantageous when adding components to an existing circuit, or when wiring a new circuit, to ensure that each component within the circuit will receive the current necessary to operate at peak efficiency.

For example, if the resistance within a circuit was too high, then certain compo-

nents would not operate properly, or operate at reduced efficiency. In addition, one must know the total current draw (load) in the circuit in order to calculate what size battery is required, and also what capacity of generator is required to ensure that the battery will maintain its full-state of charge under varying conditions of load. The wrong size wiring can also produce a high resistance to current flow. If we know how to calculate the necessary current (amperes), voltage, and resistance demands of the circuit, we can establish all the demands to be placed on the circuit. We can accurately establish this through the application of Ohm's law.

Ohm's Law is an expression of the relationship between the current, voltage and resistance in any circuit. The formula for Ohm's Law is arrived at by substituting the letter I for amperes, the letter E for voltage, and the letter R for resistance. Sometimes the letter V is used in place of the letter E for voltage. We will use the more common E designation.

From these letters, we establish the following formula:

1. amperes $= \dfrac{\text{volts}}{\text{ohms}}$ or $I = \dfrac{E}{R}$

2. volts $=$ amperes x ohms or $E = I \times R$

3. ohms $= \dfrac{\text{volts}}{\text{amperes}}$ or $R = \dfrac{E}{I}$

To demonstrate how effective the application of this formula is, let's look at some examples of simple circuits, both series and parallel.

SERIES CIRCUITS

In a series circuit, all current leaving the source of supply, such as a 12 volt battery, must flow through each component of the circuit one at a time. A simple example of this would be to connect three light bulbs as shown in Fig. 1-12, where the current leaving the negative battery terminal would return to the positive battery terminal by one direct path through the circuit, having of course first passed through each light bulb in series.

In the arrangement shown in Fig. 1-12, no switches are shown, therefore the light bulbs would glow constantly. In order to be able to switch them on and off at will, it would be desirable to insert a switch somewhere in the circuit. Fig. 1-13 shows how this could be done.

To re-emphasize the difference between an open and a closed circuit, Fig. 1-12 would be known as a closed circuit, be-cause current can continually flow to and through the light bulbs, and back to the battery.

In Fig. 1-13, the control switch is shown in the open position which will prevent current from flowing to and through the light bulbs; however, the battery still has a potential voltage (electromotive force, or emf) of 12 volts, although no current is flowing.

As mentioned earlier, each accessory or electrical component in a circuit uses current, but it also creates a resistance to current flow. This resistance will vary between accessories, therefore Ohm's Law allows us to calculate just what this resistance is.

To show the Ohm's Law formula at work, the following examples are given.

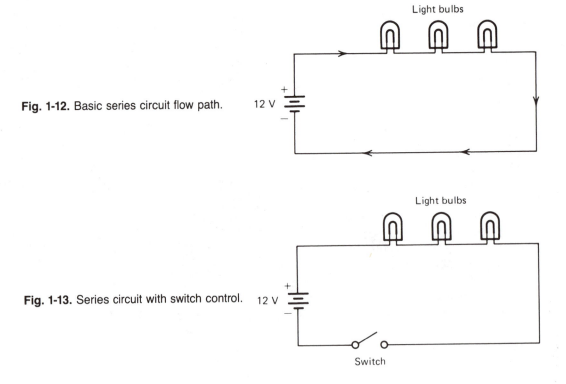

Fig. 1-12. Basic series circuit flow path.

Fig. 1-13. Series circuit with switch control.

Example 1 (series circuit)

Calculate the amount of current flowing in the circuit shown in Fig. 1-14.

The ohm's law formula for finding current is amperes = volts/ohms or I = E/R therefore, I = 12/3 or 4 amps of current.

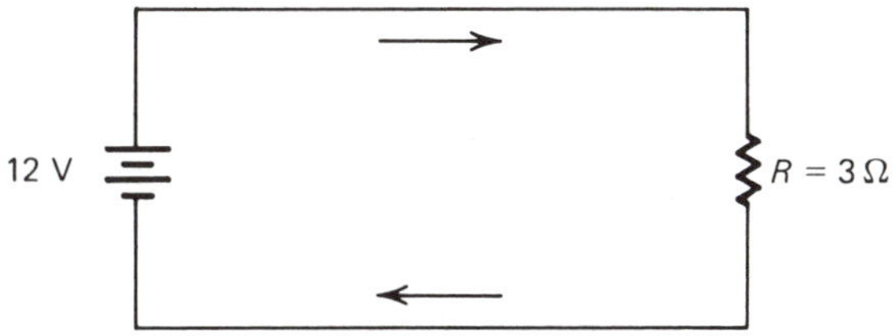

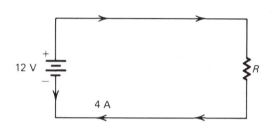

Fig. 1-14. Example 1—series circuit current flow.

Example 2 (series circuit)

Calculate the total resistance in the following circuit shown in Fig. 1-15.

The Ohm's Law formula for finding resistance is: ohms = volts/amperes or more simply, R = E/I (R = 12/4) equals 3 ohms.

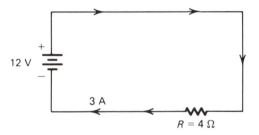

Fig. 1-15. Example 2—series circuit resistance.

Example 3 (series circuit)

Calculate the total voltage in the following circuit shown in Fig. 1-16.

The Ohm's Law formula for finding voltage is: volts = amps x ohms; therefore, volts = 3 x 4 which equals 12 volts.

When more than one resistance is present in a series circuit, the total resistance is simply the sum total of all of the resistors. If three different light bulbs were wired into a series circuit, and they all had 4 ohms of resistance to current flow, then the total resistance would be 12 ohms. If one light bulb had a resistance of 3 ohms, the other a resistance of 4 ohms, and the last one a resistance of 5 ohms, then the total resistance to current flow would be 12 ohms.

In a series circuit, regardless of the number of accessories wired into the flow path, the current flowing is the same at all points of the circuit. If two light bulbs of 4 ohms resistance each, were wired into a series circuit, then with a voltage source of 12

Fig. 1-16. Example 3—series circuit voltage.

volts, one and one-half amps would flow through each light bulb: I = E/R or I = 12/8 = 1.5 amps.

If we were to double the voltage, yet use the same two light bults, then the current flowing would now be 3 amps.

In each of the two situations just mentioned, the same amperage that flows through the light bulbs, will also flow through the battery.

When more than one accessory is used

or wired into a series circuit, the voltage (electrical pressure) must give up some of its potential energy to force the current through the resistance of the accessory, therefore a percentage of the source voltage is used up as it passes through each accessory (load). An example of this is given in Fig. 1-17.

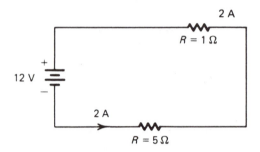

Fig. 1-17. Volts, amperes, and resistance relationship in a series circuit.

The source voltage or potential energy of the battery is 12 volts, with 10 volts being required to force the 2 amp current through the accessory resistance of 5 ohms, and the remaining 2 volts being used to force the 2 amp current through the accessory with 1 ohm of resistance.

The previous examples characterized the value of using Ohm's Law; however, in addition to calculating what an unknown quantity is in a series circuit, we can also use:

• an ammeter to measure current
• a voltmeter to measure voltage
• an ohmmeter to measure resistance

These gauges can be used independently, or can be bought in what is known as a VAR (volts/amps/resistance) meter, or what is more commonly called a multimeter. By use of a selector switch on the face

of the meter, either amps, volts, or resistance can be measured.

Figure 1-18 shows a simple series circuit; with the placement of both the ammeter and voltmeter into the circuit; the ohmmeter can be placed across any two points in the circuit to establish a given resistance at any point.

Figure 1-19 shows a series circuit with four resistors (accessories) wired into the system. Total circuit resistance is established by adding all of the resistance together; the current flowing is I = E/R which is 12/12 which provides a current flow of one amp. An increase in resistance through an accessory will cause a higher voltage drop to occur in the circuit, while a lower resistance through an accessory re-

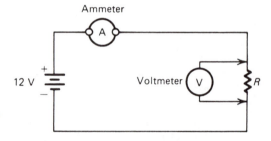

Fig. 1-18. Voltmeter and ammeter placement in a series circuit.

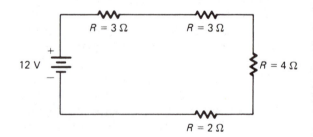

Fig. 1-19. Series circuit with four resistors.

sults in a smaller loss or drop in voltage through the respective accessory.

From the basic information we have learned so far about a series circuit, we can state three known facts related to this type of electrical circuit:

1. The current (amps) that flows through each resistor (accessory load demand) will remain the same.

2. The amount of voltage required to force the current through each resistor will be proportional to the actual resistance within that resistor (accessory); therefore the voltage drop across each resistor or accessory will be different if the resistance through each accessory is different.

3. The amount of voltage loss or drop through the circuit will always equal the source voltage; for example, if a 12 volt battery is the source voltage, then the voltage drop in the circuit will be 12 volts.

In addition to the three facts listed above, we can also list several other known specifics about the series circuit that we have learned about so far. These will quickly allow you to recall some major aspects of these earlier discussions.

1. Total circuit resistance is the total of all resistors in the system.

2. Total series resistance must be more than the largest individual resistance.

3. If an open exists at any one component, then the entire circuit will be open, and no current can flow.

4. A short across part of the circuit will cause increased current in the wire between the short circuit and the voltage source.

PARALLEL CIRCUITS

In the series circuits that we just looked at, the current flowing in the circuit followed one path only from the battery post, through the accessories, and back to the opposite polarity battery post.

In a parallel circuit the current leaving the battery can flow through more than one path prior to returning back to the opposite polarity battery post or terminal.

Figure 1-20 shows the layout for a simple parallel circuit.

The three main facts related to a parallel circuit that distinguish it from the series circuit are:

1. The voltage across each resistor (accessory) is the same.

2. The current (amps), through each ac-

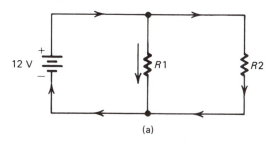
(a)

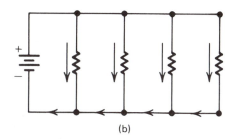
(b)

Fig. 1-20. (a) Simplified parallel circuit, (b) parallel circuit with four resistors.

cessory or resistor will be different if the resistance values are different.

3. The total of the separate currents (amperes) equals the complete circuit current.

To calculate the amps, volts and resistance in a parallel circuit, we can always refer to Ohm's Law. However, let's look at some typical examples of calculating various unknown quantities in a parallel circuit.

Example 1 (parallel circuit)

In a parallel circuit with two resistors, you find the total resistance by using the following formula:

$$R = \frac{R_1 \times R_2}{R_1 + R_2}$$

where R represents resistance.

What is the total resistance of Fig. 1-21?

By application of the formula shown above, we simply replace the R_1 and R_2 portion of the formula with the values of each resistor. We therefore have resistance

$$R = \frac{40 \text{ ohms} \times 10 \text{ ohms}}{40 \text{ ohms} + 10 \text{ ohms}}$$

the result is now 400/50 = 8 ohms, therefore what we have proven, is that the total resistance in a parallel circuit is less than that of any individual resistor.

Example 2 (parallel circuit)

What is the total resistance of Fig. 1-22?

Fig. 1-22 shows four resistors (accessories) in parallel. These accessories will each require a given current to operate them, so we can refer to these as branch currents since they are all attached to the main supply as branches are attached to a tree trunk.

Ohm's Law for finding current is

$$\text{amps} = \frac{\text{volts}}{\text{resistance}} \text{ or } I = \frac{E}{R}$$

therefore in Fig. 1-22, with four branch currents, we would in effect have I = E/R four times, or 12/6 = 2 amps, 12/3 = 4 amps, 12/4 = 3 amps, and 12/4 = 3 amps to give us a total battery current of 2 + 4 + 3 + 3 to equal 12 amperes. The circuit resistances together however, would only be equivalent to one ohm because Ohm's Law for resistance is R = E/I which would be 12 volts/12 amps = 1 ohm. We can calculate this actual circuit resistance by the following method:

$$\frac{R_1 \times R_2}{R_1 + R_2}$$

for the first two resistors, and repeat this same formula for the next two resistors. We therefore have

$$R = \frac{6 \times 3}{6 + 3} = \frac{18}{9} = 2$$

ohms for the first two resistors. In the next two resistors, we have

$$R = \frac{4 \times 4}{4 + 4} = \frac{16}{8} = 2 \text{ ohms.}$$

The total circuit resistance remember in a parallel circuit is always less than that of any individual resistor, therefore the two-ohm equivalent resistor in parallel with the other two-ohm equivalent resistor will be equal to

$$R = \frac{R_1 \times R_2}{R_1 + R_2} = \frac{2 \times 2}{2 + 2} = \frac{4}{4} = 1 \text{ ohm}$$

Total circuit resistance then in Fig. 1-22 is one ohm.

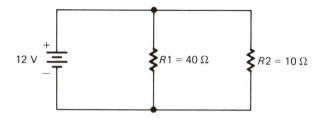

Fig. 1-21. Calculation of total resistance in a two-resistor parallel circuit.

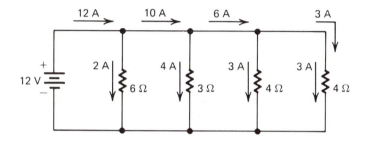

Fig. 1-22. Calculation of parallel circuit resistance with four resistors.

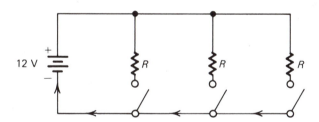

Fig. 1-23. Parallel circuit resistance with three switches controlling resistors.

As we have seen so far, parallel circuits provide more than one path for the current to flow. Therefore, a break in one path (open circuit) will not prevent current from flowing through other parts of the circuit, unless the break existed in the wire before the current reached the individual branch wires. If, however, each branch circuit was to be fitted with a switch as shown in Fig. 1-23, then each circuit or branch could be opened or closed when desired.

Remember that in a series circuit, since the current only has one path of flow, a break in the wire (or the installation of a switch) would result in all accessories losing current flow because of the wire break (or if the switch were to be placed in the off or open position).

Because it is desirable in automotive and heavy equipment installations to have independent control of each accessory to suit conditions, the parallel circuit is usually used. The series circuit is used for certain circuitry to provide, for example, greater starting voltage by wiring two 12 volt batteries together. Parallel circuit wiring is also commonly used in house wiring.

VOLTAGE DROP

The total voltage drop in a series circuit must equal the source voltage. In a parallel circuit, the voltage drop across any component is the same as the source voltage.

To ensure that you understand this concept, look at Fig. 1-24, and establish the source voltage for both the series and parallel circuits shown.

In Fig. 1-24 (a), we see a series circuit with two resistors or accessories. What is the source voltage?

Fig. 1-24 (b) shows a parallel circuit; what is the source voltage?

The correct answer to Fig. 1-24(a) is 16 volts. The answer for Fig. 1-24 (b) is 6 volts.

Example 3 (parallel circuit)

From Fig. 1-25, establish the total resistance in the circuit; also find the current flowing.

Remember that total resistance in a parallel circuit, is less than the resistance of either of the resistors; therefore to solve Fig. 1-25, we simply use the formula for resistance calculation in a parallel circuit:

$$R = \frac{R_1 \times R_2}{R_1 + R_2}$$

$$R = \frac{12 \times 12}{12 + 12} = \frac{144}{24} = 6 \text{ ohms}$$

To find the battery current we refer to Ohm's Law which states that current = volts/ohms, or I = E/R; therefore, I = 24/6 = 4 amps.

SERIES/PARALLEL CIRCUITS

As mentioned earlier, series/parallel circuits are used in certain instances, rather than a straight series or single parallel circuit.

Figure 1-26 shows a typical series/parallel circuit.

Note that Fig. 1-26 shows current flowing from the battery through a series (one path) accessory first, where it then flows to two other accessories in parallel.

The total current flowing in the circuit, is equal to the total voltage divided by the resistance total. To find the total resistance of Fig. 1-26, follow the same sequence as you would in finding the resistance in a parallel circuit first, plus the sequence required to find the resistance in a series circuit.

We would therefore have

$$R = \frac{R_1 \times R_2}{R_1 + R_2}$$

$$R = \frac{6 \times 3}{6 + 3} = \frac{18}{9} = 2 \text{ ohms}$$

for the parallel part of the circuit.

The resistance for the series part of the circuit is shown as 2 ohms, therefore if we add these two resistances together, we have a total circuit resistance of 4 ohms.

From Ohm's Law we can now find the current flowing in this series/parallel circuit; current = volts/ohms is I = E/R or I = 12/4 = 3 amps.

The circuit is therefore arranged as follows. The voltage drop across the series resistor is, voltage = amperes x ohms, or E = I x R which is E = 3 x 2 = 6 volts.

Source voltage remaining after passing through the series resistor or accessory is six volts, which will pass through both branches of the parallel part of the circuit.

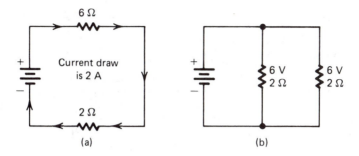

Fig. 1-24. (a) Series circuit resistance calculation review; (b) parallel circuit resistance calculation review.

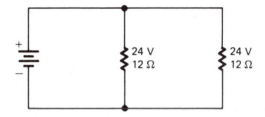

Fig. 1-25. Establishing resistance and current flow in a parallel circuit.

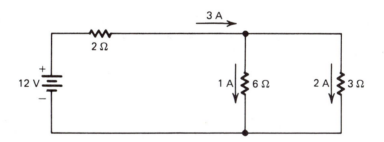

Fig. 1-26. Typical series/parallel circuit.

The current flow through both of these branches is arrived at simply by Ohm's Law where, current = volts/ohms or I = E/R to give I = 6/6 = 1 amp. Current flow in the second branch is also shown, and is arrived at in the same fashion: I = E/R or I = 6/3 = 2 amps.

Total current flow through the parallel branches is therefore the sum of both, which is 1 + 2 = 3 amps.

COMPARISON OF CIRCUITS

Having now looked at and studied the series, parallel, and series/parallel circuits, we can conclude from the examples and calculations that each system would offer a different resistance to current flow because of individual design. In summation, we can say that the resistance to current flow in similarly designed circuits of the three types discussed would be as follows:

1. Series circuits offer the highest resistance to flow.
2. Parallel circuits offer the lowest resistance to flow.
3. Series/parallel circuits offer medium resistance to flow.

CONDUCTOR PROPERTIES

Earlier in this chapter, we discussed the basic makeup of what is classified as a conductor of electricity. Because some degree of flexibility is required in the conductor (wire) used in both automotive and heavy-duty equipment applications, we mentioned that instead of using a solid strand of wire, we most often find a large number of very small strands of wire.

Small strand wire is generally used because current flows on the surface of the conductor; therefore, more surface area is exposed than that of a one-piece solid wire with the net result that there is lower resistance with the stranded wire than with a solid one.

Based on the earlier discussion of how resistance is created, it makes sense to select a conductor that will offer a minimum amount of resistance to the flow of current in the electrical circuit. Selection of a wire with too high a resistance can dramatically affect the current flow to the accessories, and can cause heat buildup within the wiring leading to potential fire damage.

Because of its plentiful supply and relative low cost, copper is widely used for wiring in electrical systems.

The amount of resistance in any copper wire is caused by the following:

1. Wire length
2. Wire diameter
3. Wire temperature

Using a length of wire that is unusually long is not only a waste of wire and money, but also increases the circuit resistance to current flow. Doubling the length of a wire will double its resistance. Also, using a wire that is too small in diameter will similarly create added resistance to current flow. Again, if the cross-sectional area of a wire is doubled by using a wire twice as large, the resistance will be cut in half for the same length of wire. Therefore, select a wire of the smallest size that will not cause excessive voltage drop throughout the circuit.

Let's consider a typical example of a circuit with a given wire size. Figure 1-27 shows a simple electrical circuit with a parallel wire arrangement to two headlights.

The wires shown have a known resistance of .25 ohms each; each headlight has a known resistance of 2 ohms. What is the effective circuit resistance?

To calculate the circuit resistance, we substitute the formula given earlier in parallel circuits:

$$R = \frac{R_1 \times R_2}{R_1 + R_2}$$

Therefore the effective resistance through the two headlights is:

$$R = \frac{2 \times 2}{2 + 2} = \frac{4}{4} = 1 \text{ ohm.}$$

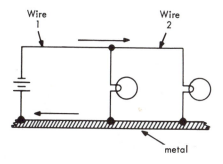

Fig. 1-27. Establishing circuit resistance in a parallel light circuit.

The total resistance of this circuit, however, is the 1 ohm through the headlights plus the resistance of each piece or length of copper wire. Each wire has a resistance of .25 ohms, for a total circuit resistance of .25 + .25 + 1 ohm + 1.5 ohms. The current flow is I = E/R or I = 12/1.5 = 8 amperes.

We mentioned that voltage drop is a factor in an electrical circuit due to resistance, and can cause problems. Let's calculate what the voltage drop would be in this circuit. Ohm's Law for voltage is, volts = current x resistance, therefore we have E = I x R or E = 8 x .25 = 2 volts, or a total of 4 volts for both wires. This is a poorly designed circuit, because having started with a 12 volt source at the battery, we have left to operate our vehicle headlights only 8 volts, because the sum of the voltage drops must equal the source voltage, and we have 8 + 2 + 2 for a source voltage of 12.

Eight volts would provide a very dim headlight indeed. The answer to our problem would be to select a wire having resistance values to allow adequate voltage across the load (accessory) for proper operation; in this case, a high enough voltage for proper illumination of the headlights. The size and resistance of wire can again

be likened to the size or diameter of a water pipe shown in Fig. 1-1 and water pressure.

Although you may not be thoroughly familiar with wire sizes yet, consider that the wires used from the vehicle battery to the starter motor and vehicle frame (ground or earth) are much larger than the wiring used for the accessories. This explanation is easy to understand, when we consider that the starter motor requires very high amounts of current or amperes to crank the engine for starting.

Remember that current or amperes in electricity is the equivalent of gallons or liters per minute in a water system. Therefore the smaller the wire, the smaller the flow rate at the other end for a given pressure (voltage).

We would be unable to supply the high amperage requirements to the starter motor with small gauge wiring, plus we would burn out the smaller wire through overheating (electron bombardment and heat buildup).

TEMPERATURE EFFECT ON WIRE

An increase in temperature creates a similar increase in resistance. One example would be to consider a length of wire ten feet long having a known resistance of 0.4 ohm at 70°F (21°C).

At a temperature of 170°F (76.6°C), the resistance has increased to 0.05 ohm from 0.04 ohm.

Wire Gauge Sizes

Copper wiring used in both automotive and heavy-duty equipment is classified by a wire gauge number which denotes its size, resistance, etc. This is shown on page 24.

WIRING RECOMMENDATIONS

Copper wiring used in automobiles, trucks, and heavy-duty equipment is basically broken into two categories: wire used to carry current for lighting and accessories, and wire required to carry larger currents such as that required for starting motors from the battery.

The following tables show the recommended SAE (Society of Automotive Engineers) and AWG (American Wire Gauge) stranded wire specifications.

Recommended Conductor Construction (AWG Strands)

SAE Wire Size	Class I No. Strands/ AWG Size (in)	Class II No. Strands/AWG Size (in)
6	37/21 (.0285)	7 x 19/27 (.0142)
4	61/22 (.0253)	7 x 19/25 (.0179)
2	127/33 (.0226)	7 x 19/23 (.0226)
1	127/22 (.0253)	7 x 37/25 (.0179)
0	127/21 (.0285)	7 x 37/24 (.0201)
2/0	127/20 (.0320)	7 x 37/23 (.0226)
3/0	-	7 x 37/22 (.0253)
4/0	-	19 x 22/23 (.0226)

Note: The lower the wire number, the larger its size.

Metric Wire Strand Size

SAE Wire Size	Metric Size, mm²	Class I No. Strands/mm Size	Class II Size
6	13.0	37/.66	
4	19.0	61/.63	
2	32.0	127/.57	7 x 19/.57
1	40.0	127/.63	7 x 19/.63
0	50.0	127/.71	7 x 19/.71
2/0	62.0	127/.79	7 x 19/.79
3/0	81.0	-	7 x 37/.63
4/0	103.0	-	7 x 37/.71

Wire gauge sizes from 4/0 up to 6 are generally used on vehicles and equipment that require large current-carrying capacities, although size 4 is generally the minimum size that would be used for battery cables.

The following tables show the accepted wire size recommendations required for vehicle lighting and accessories.

Recommended Construction

SAE Wire Size	Class III No. Strands/ AWG Size (in)	Class IV No. Strands/AWG Size (in)
20	7/28 (.0126)	
18	16/30 (.0100)	65/36 (.0050)
16	19/29 (.0113)	
14	19/27 (.0142)	
12	19/25 (.0179)	
10	19/23 (.0226)	
8	19/21 (.0285)	
6	37/21 (.0285)	7 x 19/27 (.0142)
4	61/22 (.0253)	7 x 19/25 (.0179)

Metric Sizes

SAE Wire Size	Metric Wire Size mm²	Class III No. Strands/mm Size
20	0.5	7/.31
18	0.8	19/.23
16	1.0	19/.28
14	2.0	19/.36
12	3.0	19/.45
10	5.0	19/.57
8	8.0	19/.71
6	13.0	37/.66
4	19.0	61/.63

Wire gauge Size 14 is widely used on automotive applications for lighting and accessories. Refer to Chapters 17 and 32 for additional wiring information.

WIRE COLOR CODE

The recommended colors of wire cable should match as closely as possible the following colors as set forth by *The Color Association of the U.S. Inc.* 9th Edition.

Stripes can be used where additional color combinations are required. The stripes shall be applied longitudinally along the cable. Black or white stripes are recommended but other colors may be specified.

TECA Colors 9th Edition

Color	Nom.	Dark	Light
White	70003	70004	
Red	70180	70082	70189
Pink	70098	70099	70097
Orange	70072	70041	70071
Yellow	70205	70068	70067
Lt Green	70062	70063	70061
Dk Green	70065	70066	70064
Lt Blue	70143	70144	70142
Dk Blue	70086	70087	70085
Purple	70135	70164	70134
Tan	70093	70094	70092
Brown	70107	70108	70106
Gray	70152	70153	70185
Black	None	-	-

In addition to the wire sizes and color codes, wires are further identified as to their specification types by the following abbreviations:

Type GPT	General Purpose, thermoplastic insulated
Type HDT	Heavy Duty, thermoplastic insulated
Type GPB	General Purpose, thermoplastic insulated, braided
Type HDB	Heavy Duty, thermoplastic insulated, braided
Type STS	Standard Duty, synthetic rubber insulated
Type HTS	Heavy Duty, synthetic rubber insulated
Type SXL	Standard Duty, crosslinked polyethylene insulated

ELECTRICITY AND MAGNETISM

In an automobile or piece of heavy-duty equipment, the battery or batteries can supply the reservoir of electrical energy required to operate all of the electrical loads (accessories), including supplying adequate power to the starter motor to crank the engine.

The battery alone, however, can only supply this source of energy as long as it retains a sufficient state of charge to overcome the circuit resistance. If some means is not used to recharge the battery as it is supplying this electrical load on the circuit, eventually the battery would lose this source of energy. We all know what then happens—the battery in our car goes flat!

Batteries today are constantly kept in a state of charge by the action of either a d.c. generator or, more commonly, an alternator which develops a.c. current. The letters d.c. mean direct current and the letters a.c. mean alternating current. Both systems are used, and are explained in detail in Chapters 4 and 5.

Both the generator and alternator rely heavily on the principles of magnetism to produce the necessary electrical energy required to keep the battery or batteries in a constant full charge condition.

Because the theory of magnetism is so important to these two units, let's study how magnetism and electricity are related to the needs of the system.

MAGNETISM

For well over a thousand years, sailors have used the compass as a means of knowing their approximate location. The basic use of the compass was derived from the fact that fragments of iron ore called lodestone were found to attract other pieces of ferrous metals such as other pieces of iron ore. Furthermore, if a long piece of iron ore or an iron bar were to be suspended in the air, one end would always point towards the Earth's North Pole. Naturally, this end was therefore called the north pole while the opposite end was referred to as the south pole. In a compass, the needle will always swing into a north/south pole position because the earth itself is basically a giant magnet.

An iron bar that exhibits magnetic properties is commonly called a bar magnet. You may recall from basic science tests that you conducted at school with bar and horseshoe-shaped magnets that they are both capable of attracting other metal objects to them without having to come into actual physical contact with these objects. A good demonstration of this fact may be given by sprinkling iron filings onto a table top, then placing the magnet in the vicinity of these metal filings. The result is that the metal filings are pulled against the magnet as by some unseen force. This attraction occurs because a magnetic field of force exists around all magnets.

A simple method of establishing what these unseen lines of force look like can be done with the use of a magnet placed underneath a sheet of paper, then sprinkling iron filings onto the paper. By lightly tapping the paper, the iron filings will arrange themselves into a clear pattern around the bar magnet as shown in Fig. 1-28.

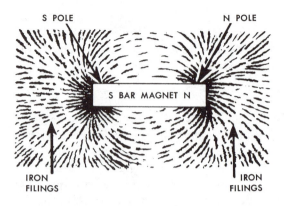

Fig. 1-28. Magnetic attraction of iron filings. (Courtesy of Delco-Remy Div. of GMC)

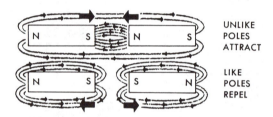

Fig. 1-29. Like and unlike magnetic poles. (Courtesy of Delco-Remy Div. of GMC)

The area around the bar magnet that attracts the iron filings is called the field of force or magnetic field. The strongest field of force is created next to the two poles of the magnet, with the lines of force leaving the north pole and entering the south pole. When two bar magnets are placed opposite one another as shown in Fig. 1-29, unlike poles will attract one another, while like poles will tend to repel one another.

MAGNETIC THEORY

Magnetism can be further simplified by the use of two commonly known theoretical models:

1. Any magnet consists of a very large number of minute magnetic particles, which will align themselves with one another to form the magnet. This concept is shown in Fig. 1-30 (b). If, however, these particles have no particular arrangement, then the bar will be non-magnetic, and the minute particles will not be aligned as shown in Fig. 1-30 (a).

2. The second theory of magnetism deals with the electron which we discussed in some depth earlier in this chapter. You may recall that the electron has a circle of force around it; therefore, anytime that the electron orbits align themselves in a bar of iron so that these circles of force are added together, the bar of iron will also become magnetized.

UNMAGNETIZED IRON

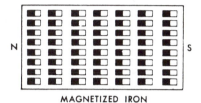

N ⟷ S

MAGNETIZED IRON

Fig. 1-30. Unmagnetized and magnetized iron. (Courtesy of Delco-Remy Div. of GMC)

CREATING A MAGNET

Not all iron bars are magnetic, and of course we would not want them to be. How can we create a magnetic bar from one which is not magnetic?

One simple method is to stroke the non-magnetic iron bar with one which is magnetic to induce the necessary realignment of the particles within the non-magnetic iron bar.

Another method is to place an iron bar into a strong magnetic field so that the lines of magnetic force within the field will pass through the iron bar and will induce the particles to realign themselves so that the bar will become magnetized. Figure 1-31 shows this process of magnetic induction.

In Fig. 1-31, the north and south poles of the magnet can be readily identified by placing the large magnet in suspension on a piece of string which would allow it to rotate of its own free will to the north and south poles of the earth.

Fig. 1-31. Magnetic induction. (Courtesy of Delco-Remy Div. of GMC)

Although we can magnetize an iron bar by these two methods, the specific composition of the iron bar will determine just how much of the induced magnetism will remain after it is removed from the force field of the original magnet.

If the iron bar retains this magnetic force with no loss over time, it would be known as a permanent magnet.

Uses of permanent magnets are very common, one example being in a generator. Other uses of such magnets are in starter motors, and in meters such as voltmeters and ammeters.

ELECTROMAGNETISM

Although magnetism has been used for well over a thousand years, it was not until the year 1820 that some relationship was found to exist between both magnetism and electricity.

A small experiment showed that when electricity flowed through a wire, and a compass was placed over the wire, the needle of the compass automatically swung around to place itself perpendicular or crosswise to the wire. From such an experiment, it was concluded that as the only force that could cause the compass needle to move would be magnetism, then the current flowing in the wire obviously created a magnetic field around the wire.

To obtain a more positive understanding of how these lines of magnetic force emanated from a current-carrying wire, a further simple test was conducted, in which the wire was placed through a hole in a piece of cardboard as shown in Fig. 1-32.

With iron filings sprinkled onto the cardboard, current was then induced through the wire; the result was that the iron filings arranged themselves into concentric circles around the wire.

The concentric circles of iron filings were very heavy near the wire, but became less heavy the further away from the wire they were. This allows us to conclude that the force of the magnetic field decreases as you move away from its center or core. Magnetism produced by passing a current through a wire is known as electromagnetism. This electromagnetic field will exist along the total length of the wire.

If we were to wind a length of wire into a coil, then pass a flow of current through the wire, we would create a magnetic field around the coil of wire with both a north and south pole similar to a bar magnet. Figure 1-33 shows such an arrangement.

The strength of the magnetic field around the coil would be dependent upon the number of turns in the coil, and upon the amount of current flowing in the wire. Therefore, the strength of the magnetic field depends on the ampere-turns of the coil. In order to establish the polarity of the coil ends, we can use what is known as the right-hand rule for coils. This is done by holding your hand as shown in Fig. 1-34 with the thumb extended in the normal direction of current flow which will also be the north pole of the coil. Should the current flow through the coil be reversed, then the polarity of the coil ends will also be reversed.

One additional method which is often

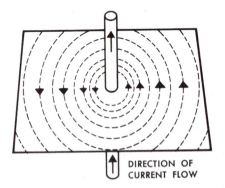

DIRECTION OF
CURRENT FLOW

Fig. 1-32. Field strength (magnetic) versus distance. (Courtesy of Delco-Remy Div. of GMC)

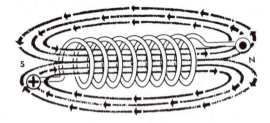

Fig. 1-33. Current flow of magnetism in a coiled wire. (Courtesy of Delco-Remy Div. of GMC)

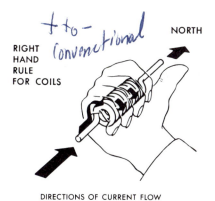

RIGHT HAND RULE FOR COILS

+ to - Convenctional

NORTH

DIRECTIONS OF CURRENT FLOW

Fig. 1-34. Establishing polarity by the right-hand rule method. (Courtesy of Delco-Remy Div. of GMC)

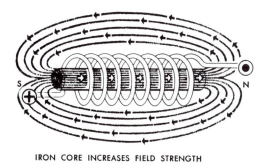

IRON CORE INCREASES FIELD STRENGTH

Fig. 1-35. Iron core increases magnetic field strength. (Courtesy of Delco-Remy Div. of GMC)

used to increase the magnetic field of a coil of wire is to simply insert an iron core into the middle of the coil windings as shown in Fig. 1-35. The use of iron in a magnetic path can increase the magnetic strength by as much as 2500 times over a coil that simply has air in the center.

Because iron is a much better conductor of magnetic lines than is air, the addition of the iron core to the coil shown in Fig. 1-35 creates a considerable increase in the magnetic field when current flows through the wire.

In effect, the coil with the iron core has

now been transformed into an electromagnet. Such an arrangement is typical of the system used in a generator to create the strong magnetic fields required to produce a steady output of electricity. (For general information, a coil without an iron core is usually referred to as a solenoid.)

The resistance that a magnetic circuit offers to lines of force, or flux is commonly called reluctance. The effect of an air gap on the total reluctance of a circuit is very important. As we mentioned earlier, air has a poor conductibility compared to iron, therefore air will also have a higher reluctance than iron. Doubling the size of the air gap in a magnetic circuit will also double the reluctance of the circuit, and the field strength will be reduced by half.

One common application of the electromagnet is the use of the large steel circular weight used on the end of a crane for picking up scrap steel. When current is directed through the coils within the weight, the steel weight becomes magnetized and allows steel to be picked up. When the current through the coils is cut off, the reduced magnetic field allows the scrap steel to be deposited or dropped from the end of the weight.

CREATING ELECTRICITY FROM MAGNETISM

With a good understanding of magnetism, we can now look at how electricity can be produced in a wire through the use of magnetic lines of force. If we move a conductor, for example a piece of copper wire, through a magnetic field, this causes a voltage to be induced in the wire. Such a condition is called electromagnetic induction, and is commonly defined as the induction of voltage in a conductor that moves across any magnetic field. (This induced voltage is also known as electromotive force, as was mentioned in the early part of our discussion on basic electricity.)

Figure 1-36 shows a simple horseshoe magnet with magnetic lines of force passing between the ends of the north and south poles. If a length of copper wire were placed at the right-hand end of the horseshoe magnet and moved parallel to the magnet in order that the wire would be forced through the magnetic field, then a small voltage would be induced in the wire. This voltage could be measured by placing the ends of a voltmeter across the ends of the wire.

The wire must be moved so as to cut the magnetic lines of force. If the wire is moved up and down or parallel to the magnetic lines of force, we would not cut these lines of force and no voltage would be induced in the wire.

From previous discussions, we indicated that the magnetic lines of force always originate from the north pole to the south pole of the magnet. For this reason, when the wire is moved from the right to the left in Fig. 1-36, the end of the wire closest to the north pole will be the negative end, while the end of the wire closer to the south pole will become the positive end. The positive and negative ends of the wire are reversed once we move the wire from the left-hand side of the magnet to the right-hand side.

Although we have shown the conductor (wire) as the moving object, there are instances whereby it may be easier to move the magnetic field rather than the wire. We shall see both conditions later in the chapters on generators and alternators.

In summation, the factors that determine the magnitude or amount of induced voltage are:

- How strong the magnetic field is
- How quickly the magnetic lines of force are cutting across the conductor (wire)

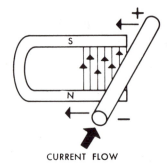

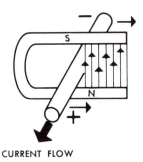

CURRENT FLOW

Fig. 1-36. Inducing voltage flow in a wire. (Courtesy of Delco-Remy Div. of GMC)

- The total number of conductors (wires) that are cutting across these magnetic lines of force.

One other important point to consider is that when a straight wire is wound into a coil and moved across a magnetic field, all the loops of wire are in a series circuit arrangement, so that the induced voltage of all the loops will be added together to produce a higher voltage.

INDUCING VOLTAGE BY ELECTROMAGNETIC INDUCTION

Since the induction of voltage in a wire is necessary in any electrical circuit to produce current flow, how can we actually do this successfully? Three methods are commonly employed to induce voltage flow in a wire conductor.

One of the most widely used methods is that of using the magnetic field in a generator to produce current to keep the vehicle's battery in a permanent state of charge. This method is generated voltage. Figure 1-37 shows a simple line diagram of the basic components required to produce this voltage flow in the wire. This generator produces direct-current (d.c.) by moving a wire through a stationary magnetic field.

There is only one single loop of wire shown rotating through the magnetic field. In reality, a generator uses many loops of wire; however, the principle remains the same. These wires are wrapped around an iron core called an armature, with the ends of the wires attached to individual segments of the armature. These segments are known as a commutator.

As the loop of wire in Fig. 1-37 rotates (driven by a belt drive from the engine to the armature pulley), the current flow in the wire loop is from the negative to the positive terminals. The voltage induced in the wire loop produces a coil voltage at the two commutator segments attached to the wire ends. Spring loaded brushes which are in contact with the rotating commutator/armature pick up the current generated and feed this to the external circuit. The current flowing through the wire loop is established by applying the right-hand rule for induced voltage, which was shown in Fig. 1-34. This method establishes the direction of current flow.

A second method which is used to create generated voltage is that used in the alternator or alternating-current generator. The main difference between this unit and the d.c. generator just discussed is that, in the alternator, the magnetic field is rotated, while in the d.c. generator the magnetic field was stationary.

The principle of voltage generation within a simplified alternator is shown in Fig. 1-38.

In Fig. 1-38, the magnetic field is rotated by a shaft connected to a pulley or gear drive on the engine. The wire or windings of wire are attached to the stationary alternator body or frame. Applying the right-hand rule, current will flow through the wire loop as shown in Fig. 1-38. We have demonstrated in Fig. 1-37 and Fig. 1-38 that voltage can be induced in a wire loop either by moving the wire through the stationary magnetic field, or by rotating the magnetic field past a stationary wire loop.

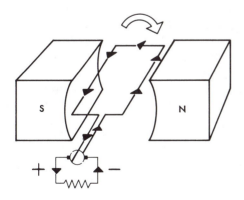

Fig. 1-37. Basic generator principle. (Courtesy of Delco-Remy Div. of GMC)

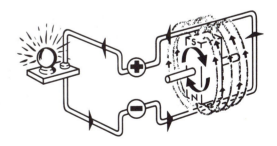

Fig. 1-38. Basic alternator principle. (Courtesy of Delco-Remy Div. of GMC)

SELF-INDUCED VOLTAGE

Another way in which we can induce voltage in a conductor is by self-induction in which no separate magnetic field is used. Instead, by changing the current flowing through a wire which is wrapped around an iron core, the magnetic lines of force around the wire are caused to increase or decrease. The changing current through the wire will induce a voltage in the wire; therefore, the voltage is self-induced.

A good example of self-induced voltage is the standard ignition system coil that produces the high voltage surge to fire the spark plugs. Basically, the coil consists of an iron core with two sets of wire coils wrapped tightly around the iron core. One set of these coils is of a larger heavy wire, while the other coil is made up from much smaller and finer wire. The large coil is known as the primary coil, while the smaller coil is known as the secondary coil.

An increase in current flow through one loop will cause an increase in the strength of the magnetic field around the wire of the coil. This magnetic field will cut across the neighboring loops of wire, thereby inducing a voltage in these loops.

Current flowing from the battery of the vehicle through the primary coil winding will set up a magnetic field which is absorbed by the secondary windings in the coil. When the distributor contacts open, the current will drop to zero, since the energy from the battery flowing through the primary winding of the coil can no longer return to the battery circuit.

Since the secondary winding of the coil has not only a smaller diameter of wire than the primary, but contains a much greater number of turns, the making and breaking of the contact breaker points transfers by mutual induction of the magnetic field within the coil an increase in voltage through the secondary winding. This voltage increase induced in the secondary winding of the coil will be proportional to the ratio of the number of turns between the primary and secondary coil windings.

For example, if the primary winding had ten turns, and the secondary winding had one hundred turns, then the voltage induced in the secondary windings will be one hundred times greater than that developed in the primary windings. The battery voltage of 12 volts flowing through the primary coil windings, will create a magnetic field which induces a voltage of approximately 250 volts. This 250 volts of energy will be boosted to 25,000 volts in the secondary winding which forms the arc at the spark plug to fire the mixture in the cylinder.

MUTUAL INDUCTION

Another method of inducing voltage in a wire is mutual induction, whereby a voltage is induced in one coil due to the changing current in another coil. The changing magnetic flux created by the current flow in one coil links or cuts across the windings of the second coil, thereby inducing voltage in proportion to the number of turns in both coils. This mutual induction follows the same pattern as that of self-induction.

REVIEW QUESTIONS

The following questions are simple, but are designed to allow you to quickly ascertain to what degree you remember the material that was discussed.

Q1 Water flow through a pipe is measured in gallons per minute, or liters per minute; what is the electrical term for capacity or volume?

Q2 Electricity is made up of many small particles called _____?

Q3 The pressure or force that causes electrons to move is known as _____?

Q4 Electrical pressure or voltage is similar to water pressure in a pipe; this pressure or voltage causes what to flow through a wire?

Q5 The resistance in a wire is affected by its _____ and its _____?

Q6 If two wires of equal length were placed in a circuit and one wire were smaller in diameter than the other, which wire would create the greater resistance to current flow?

Q7 Electrical resistance can be compared to the size of what item in a simple water system?

Q8 Write down the electrical term or measurement that expresses current, pressure and resistance?

Q9 The amount of electrons flowing past a fixed point in a given time period is actually a measurement of _____?

Q10 The load on any electrical circuit is established by the current draw of the _____?

Q11 Each accessory in an electrical circuit offers some resistance to current flow; how would you measure this resistance?

Q12 Current can only flow in a _____ circuit?

Q13 Current will not flow in an _____ circuit?

Q14 A pump in a water system produces the energy for the system to operate; what do we use in an electric circuit to provide the source of energy?

Q15 In order to have a complete electric circuit, we must allow current to flow from the battery through a wire, and allow it to return through another wire back to _____?

Q16 What are the names of the terminals on a battery?

Q17 Sketch the symbol commonly used to illustrate the terminal names in Q16.

Q18 A break in the wiring of an electrical circuit creates an _____?

Q19 The word circuit is derived from the word _____?

Q20 State the two theories used to describe the direction of current flow in an electrical circuit.

Q21 What is a conductor?

Q22 What is a resistor?

Q23 What is the difference between a fixed and variable resistor?

Q24 Sketch the symbol used to show both a fixed and a variable resistor.

Q25 What is an insulator?

Q26 Which has the greatest resistance to current flow; a conductor, a resistor, or an insulator?

Q27 To increase the current flowing in a circuit, you must increase the _____?

Q28 To decrease the current flow in a circuit, we could decrease the voltage. What else could we do?

Q29 To increase current flowing in a circuit, you must decrease the _____?

Q30 Write the formula to show Ohm's Law.

Q31 Write the three combinations available from Ohm's Law, stating not only the transposed formula but also what each letter in the formula means.

Q32 What are the three types of circuits that we looked at in Chapter 1?

Q33 Briefly describe a series circuit.

Q34 Briefly describe a parallel circuit.

Q35 Briefly describe a series/parallel circuit.

Q36 Sketch a simple line diagram depicting a series circuit.

Q37 Sketch a simple line diagram depicting a parallel circuit.

Q38 Sketch a simple line diagram showing a series/parallel circuit.

Q39 To determine the value of the total resistance in a series circuit, 1) you add all resistances, 2) you multiply all resistances, 3) you subtract all resistances, or 4) you divide all resistances by the total number in the circuit?

Q40 What is voltage drop in an electrical circuit?

Q41 What is the total amount of voltage drop that can occur in a series circuit?

Q42 How would you establish the total resistance of a parallel circuit?

Q43 Is the total resistance in a parallel circuit greater or less than that of any individual resistor?

Q44 With respect to magnets, like poles _____ and unlike poles _____?

Q45 Do the lines of magnetic force flow from the north pole to the south pole, or opposite?

Q46 What is the basic difference between a d.c. generator, and an alternating current (a.c.) generator?

Q47 What are the two basic methods of producing electron flow in a wire?

Q48 What is an electromagnet?

Q49 How would you determine the direction of the lines of force around a wire?

Q50 Why is an iron core used with a coil?

ANSWERS

A1 The term used is current.

A2 Electrons.

A3 Electromotive force or voltage.

A4 Current.

A5 Length and Diameter.

A6 The smaller one.

A7 The size of the water pipe.

A8 Current is called amperes, pressure is called voltage, and resistance is called ohms.

A9 Current or ampere flow.

A10 Components or accessories.

A11 By the use of an ohmmeter.

A12 Closed circuit.

A13 Open circuit.

A14 The battery is the source of electrical energy.

A15 The source of supply, which is the battery.

A16 The positive terminal or post, and the negative terminal or post.

A17 Positive (+), and negative (-).

A18 Open circuit, therefore no current flow.

A19 Circle (circuit: to complete the path around the circle or more commonly, the circuit).

A20 Theory 1 is the conventional theory, in which the direction of current flow is assumed to be from the positive terminal of the voltage source, through the external circuit, and then back to the negative terminal of the source.

Theory 2 is the electron theory of current flow in which flow is from the negative terminal, through the external circuit, and then back to the positive terminal of the source.

A21 A conductor allows a flow of electricity with a minimum of resistance. Good conductors are those elements with less than four electrons in the outer ring of the atom.

A22 A resistor is an element containing four electrons in the outer ring of its atom; it is the resistance of a wire that slows down the current flow.

A23 A fixed resistor has a specific amount of resistance, therefore its value doesn't change; a variable resistor has a sliding contact that allows you to change the value of the resistance.

A24

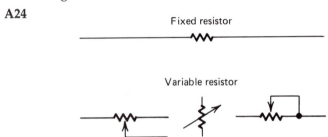

Fixed resistor

Variable resistor

A25 An insulator is any element that contains more than four electrons in the outer ring of its atom; insulators are used to prevent short circuits and loss of current through wires coming into contact with another conductor.

A26 An insulator.

A27 Voltage.

A28 Increase the resistance.

A29 Resistance

A30 I = E/R where I = amperes, E = voltage, R = resistance (ohms)

A31 1) amperes = voltage/resistance, or I = E/R; 2) voltage = (amperes) x (ohms) or E = I x R; 3) ohms = voltage/amperes or R = E/I

A32 1) The series circuit; 2) The parallel circuit; 3) The series/parallel circuit

A33 A series circuit is where the current leaves one battery terminal and returns to the other battery terminal by means of one direct path through the circuit.

A34 A parallel circuit provides more than one path for the current to flow; therefore a break in one path or branch of a parallel circuit will not prevent current from flowing to and through other parts of the circuit. For this reason, each accessory or component in a parallel circuit can be turned on or off independently of the other accessories. This is the type of circuit most used in both automotive and heavy-duty equipment applications, as well as in house wiring.

A35 A series/parallel circuit is a combination of both a series and a parallel circuit. Of the three types of circuits, the series/parallel circuit offers medium resistance, the series circuit offers higher resistance, and the parallel circuit offers the lowest resistance of all.

A36

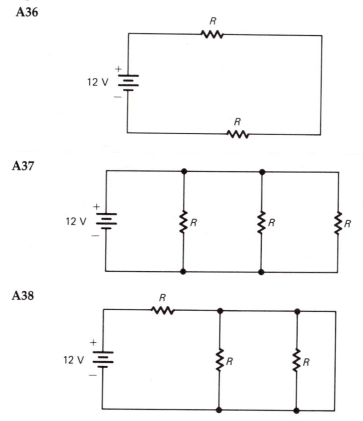

A37

A38

A39 You add all of the resistances.

A40 Voltage drop is the loss in voltage that occurs as the current flows through a resistor, accessory or load.

A41 The total amount of voltage drop that can occur in a circuit is the same as the source voltage.

A42 To establish the total resistance in a parallel circuit, you would use the formula

$$R = \frac{R_1 \times R_2}{R_1 + R_2}$$

A43 The total resistance in a parallel circuit is less than that of any individual resistor.

A44 Like poles repel, unlike poles attract.

A45 Magnetic lines of force radiate from both ends of a bar magnet; however, in a horseshoe magnet arrangement, flow is from the north to south pole.

A46 In a d.c. generator, the conductors (wires of the armature) are rotated across a stationary magnetic field to produce both voltage and current; in the a.c. alternator/generator, the magnetic field is rotated, and made to cut across stationary conductors (wires known as the stator) in order to produce voltage and current.

A47 By applying voltage to the wire, or by moving the wire through a magnetic field.

A48 An electromagnet is produced by passing a current through a wire wound coil with an iron core.

A49 You can determine the direction of the lines of force around a wire by applying the right-hand rule; grasp the wire with the thumb extended in the direction of conventional current flow (positive to negative), and the fingers will then point in the direction in which the lines of force surround the conductor.

A50 An iron core is used with a coil to increase the field strength.

Chapter

2

Introduction to Electronics

WHAT IS A SEMICONDUCTOR?

No discussion of alternators would be complete without a study of semiconductors, since the success of the alternator today has been largely due to the introduction and on-going improvement of these truly wonderful little devices.

The word electronics is now used in all languages, and it immediately conjures up visions of hundreds of items that owe their success to this field, from computers to hand-held calculators as well as the expanded use of electronics in both automotive and heavy-duty equipment electrical systems.

The fundamental operating principle of the semiconductor was first discovered in 1948 and from this basic discovery sprang the modern world of electronics. The term solid-state devices is synonomous with the field of electronics. It refers to devices that have no moving mechanical parts; however, electricity can flow through them.

Ignition systems and sensing devices of all shapes and sizes are now in wide use

on cars and trucks and on heavy-duty equipment, improving their everyday operation in a wide variety of ways. Our intention here is to look at those components of electronics that apply to the vehicle charging system, since many of these same general components are used in other parts of cars and trucks to improve function and operation of vehicle electric systems.

We shall start our basic study of electronics by looking at the function and purpose of semiconductors. The electrical conductivity of semiconductors lies between that of conductors and insulators. Semiconductors can be manufactured to allow conduction or to insulate the flow of electricity.

You may remember from our discussion in Chapter 1 that all matter is composed of atoms. The atom is the smallest particle into which an element can be decomposed. Any element that has less than four electrons (negative charge of electricity) contained within its outer valence (ring) is a good conductor of electricity, while any element that contains more than four electrons in its outer ring is a poor conductor of electricity. In any element, the number of electrons in the valence ring is never greater than eight.

Two elements that have four valence ring electrons which are widely used in semiconductors are silicon and germanium. The electrons in the valence ring of one silicon atom join with the outer ring electrons of other silicon atoms when they are combined in crystalline form, so that the atoms will share electrons in the valence ring. With this combination, we have each atom effectively sharing eight electrons which causes the material to be an excellent insulator since any element that contains more than four electrons in its outer ring is a poor conductor of electricity.

By adding a mixture of other materials to the silicon crystal, the end result is that the new material comes to possess different electrical properties. In fact, the material is no longer a good insulator, and is commonly said to have been doped. The elements that are used most widely to dope the silicon crystal are phosphorous and antimony which both contain five electrons in their valence ring.

Combining the phosphorous element with silicon creates a condition known as covalent bonding, with one electron left over which is commonly referred to as a free-electron which can be triggered into moving through the material quite easily. (NOTE: Any material that contains a free-electron or excess of electrons, is referred to as a NEGATIVE type or N type material.) In addition to the use of phosphorous and antimony to dope the silicon crystal, boron and indium can also be used, since these two additional elements contain only three electrons in their valence ring.

The addition of these various new materials to the silicon crystal in extremely small quantities can produce a wide variety of results in the finished product. Adding the material boron to the silicon will produce covalent bonding which simply means that the final material will possess properties that neither one of the original materials possessed alone. This is similar to alloying metals to produce stainless steel, high carbon steel, etc.

The boron additive to the silicon results in a deficiency of one electron (negative charge) which creates a hole which can be considered to be a positive charge of electricity or a P type of material.

Doping material that is added to either the silicon or germanium semiconductor can be as little as one part doped material to ten million parts of silicon crystal. Another interesting feature is that the silicon or germanium crystal is refined to a state of purity that contains only a few parts of impure material to over one billion parts of pure crystal.

Electricity can be made to flow through semiconductors in the same basic way as electricity is made to flow through a copper wire. This action was described in Chapter 1 under the subheading Electron Flow in a Copper Wire.

In summary, a semiconductor such as germanium or silicon falls between that of a good conductor or good insulator. The two most widely used materials from which semiconductors are manufactured are either germanium or silicon to which has been added such other materials as phosphorous, antimony, boron and indium. When phosphorous is added, the doped material is commonly called an N type substance; if doped with boron, it is called a P type substance, with N denoting negative and P denoting positive. Both the N and P type substances have lower resistance than the associated pure substances.

DIODES

A diode is similar to a one-way check valve in that it is a device that passes electric current in one direction, but blocks or restricts current flow in the other direction. The diode is used extensively in many fields of electronics; however, in automobiles, trucks, and heavy-duty equipment, it is used specifically to change alternating current to direct current. The classic example of the use of the diode is in the battery charging alternator where six diodes (three positive and three negative) are used to handle the alternating current that is developed in the three-phase stator windings, so that current can only flow to the battery in the direction to charge it. Any reversal of battery current is blocked or prevented by the diodes.

The diode allows electrons to flow from its cathode to its anode terminal such as is shown in Fig. 2-1.

Flow through a diode is always indicated by the arrow-head symbol. The diode is actually made up of two sections of material, with one of the semiconductor materials formed into an N (negative) material, while the other part represents the P (positive) material. These two sections of material form a junction of P and N type substance that are structurally integral with one another as shown in Fig. 2-1.

Diode Operation

If we consider the basic principle, that unlike charges attract, while like charges repel, then the structural components of the diode consisting of both N (negative) and P (positive) materials would be attracted to one another. Figure 2-2 shows what actually happens within the diode.

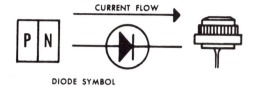

Fig. 2-1. Typical semiconductor diode symbol.

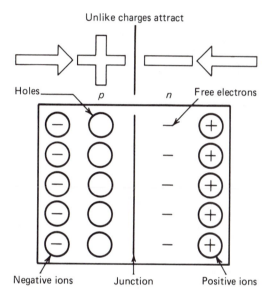

Fig. 2-2. Electrons within a diode. (Courtesy of Delco-Remy Div. of GMC)

In Fig. 2-2, an attraction exists between the free-electrons (negatively charged) and the holes (positively charged); however, as the electrons drift toward the junction area at the center of the diode, they leave behind charged particles called positive ions, which are atoms having a deficiency of electrons. Similarly the holes (positive) leave behind negative ions which exert an attractive force on the remaining holes to prevent them from crossing the junction, because the positive ions exert an attractive force on the remaining free-electrons to prevent additional electrons from crossing the junction. The end result is that a stabilized condition with a deficiency of both electrons and holes occurs at the junction area.

The condition that would exist in the diode if a battery were connected to it is shown in Figs. 2-3 and 2-4.

In Fig. 2-3, the negative battery voltage tends to repel the electrons in the N material, while the positive battery voltage will repel the holes in the P material. This condition will therefore produce current flow from the negative to the positive battery terminal, and is known as a forward bias connection.

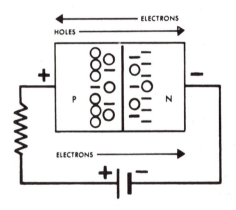

Fig. 2-3. Diode condition when forward biased. (Courtesy of Delco-Remy Div. of GMC)

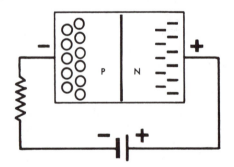

Fig. 2-4. Diode condition when reverse biased. (Courtesy of Delco-Remy Div. of GMC)

In Fig. 2-4, if the battery connections were reversed, the positive battery terminal will attract the electrons away from the junction area in the N type material, while the negative battery terminal will attract the holes away from the junction area of the P material. This arrangement would produce no current flow, with a very high resistance created at the junction area. The diode is therefore blocking current flow, and this would commonly be called a reverse bias connection.

To clarify this arrangement, let's look at Fig. 2-5. When a battery is connected across the diode in forward polarity, a large amount of current will flow. Reversing the battery leads to the diode allows a very small or nearly zero amount of current flow.

If an ohmmeter were placed across a diode, the measured forward resistance value will be very much smaller than the reverse value. Should this not be the case, then the diode is defective. Silicon diodes have a higher forward resistance value than germanium diodes.

Diode Designs

Typical diodes which are used in automotive applications are shown in Fig. 2-6.

Some diodes are designed for higher voltages and currents than are others. Therefore, when replacing a faulty diode,

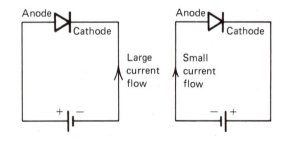

Fig. 2-5. Battery connected to a diode junction.

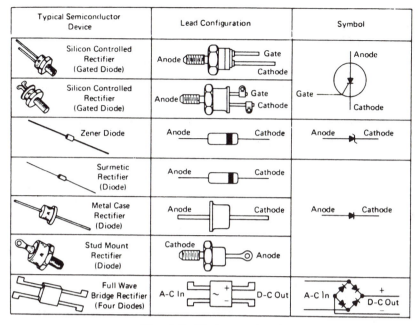

Typical Semiconductor Device	Lead Configuration	Symbol
Silicon Controlled Rectifier (Gated Diode)	Anode — Gate / Cathode	Anode / Cathode
Silicon Controlled Rectifier (Gated Diode)	Anode — Gate / Cathode	Gate — Anode / Cathode
Zener Diode	Anode — Cathode	Anode — Cathode
Surmetic Rectifier (Diode)	Anode — Cathode	
Metal Case Rectifier (Diode)	Anode — Cathode	Anode — Cathode
Stud Mount Rectifier (Diode)	Cathode — Anode	
Full Wave Bridge Rectifier (Four Diodes)	A-C In ~ — D-C Out	A-C In — D-C Out

Fig. 2-6. Diode construction.

use the correct type. Excessive heat or mechanical stress can damage a diode.

An example of a diode's placement would be the ones pressed into the metal end-frame of the alternator housing in order to allow dissipation of heat from the diode. This area is called a heat-sink. (See Chapter 4.)

In any electrical conductor, moisture can create serious problems. Therefore, a dessicant material is used inside the diode housing to absorb any moisture. The glass seal around the diode stem prevents the entry of any moisture.

Diodes can be damaged if reverse polarity connections are made to them. This is discussed in detail in the section on alternator maintenance.

A typical example of the placement of a diode in an oversimplified alternator charging system is shown in Fig. 2-7.

In Fig. 2-7, should the battery polarity be reversed, a small current can flow through the diode. However, this reverse current, if high enough, will break down the covalent bond structure of the diode and a sharp increase in the reverse current will occur which overheats the diode and

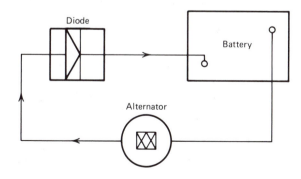

Fig. 2-7. Diode placement to prevent a reversal of current flow.

burns it out. Normally, the diodes selected for operation in any given situation are capable of handling an adequate reverse voltage so that normally this condition will not occur during operation. Attempting to polarize an alternator or reversing the battery leads usually succeeds in burning out the diodes within the alternator.

ZENER DIODE

Another type of special diode that is widely used in electronic ignition systems as well as in many other areas of vehicle electric systems is the zener diode.

The main function of this type of diode is to provide protection for standard diodes in a circuit when reverse current and voltage exist. Although the zener diode can conduct current in a reverse direction, it will only do so when a predetermined reverse bias voltage is obtained. For example, the zener diode used in a particular electronic circuit may have a threshold as high as 100 volts in an electronic ignition system before it will actually allow this reverse bias voltage to conduct. When the contact breaker points open, the zener diode provides an escape route for the kickback energy that occurs so that the collector junction of the transistor used in the ignition system is not damaged. At any voltage below a given value for the particular zener diode being used, no current can flow when the reverse bias voltage occurs.

Another common use for the zener diode is in the control of the electronic voltage regulator in most heavy-duty alternators. The zener diode activates transistors that shut off current to the field winding of the rotor to effectively reduce the alternator voltage output. As soon as the output voltage falls below the trigger value of the zener diode, it will no longer

conduct the reverse current. This allows deactivation of alternator transistors which will again let battery current flow through a brush to the slip-ring and field-winding of the rotor, and alternator output again rises.

Figure 2-8 shows the symbol and action of a typical zener diode.

Figure 2-8 illustrates that the diode will remain in the off position when the applied voltage is less than the conduction voltage of the diode, in this instance less than 10 volts. As the voltage increases, at 10 volts a very high resistance builds up until a critical voltage known as the zener, or operating, voltage is reached. When 10 volts is present in this particular example, the diode will conduct and act like a very low resistance or closed switch. At approximately 10.2 volts the diode is in full conduction or turned on.

TRANSISTORS

The transistor is probably the most important semiconductor device in the electronic circuit because current can be amplified and switched on and off through the transistor. The word transistor basically is a combination of two words, transfer and resist. It is used to control current flow in a circuit. It can be used to control a predetermined flow of current in the circuit and can also be used to resist this flow; in so doing, circuit current is controlled.

Transistors are used at junction points in the electrical system and therefore are often referred to as junction transistors. The transistor can be made from either germanium or silicon material with N and P substances sandwiched together as shown in Fig. 2-9.

In the transistor symbol shown in Fig.

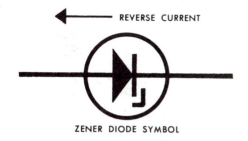

ZENER DIODE SYMBOL

Fig. 2-8. Zener diode symbol and operation.

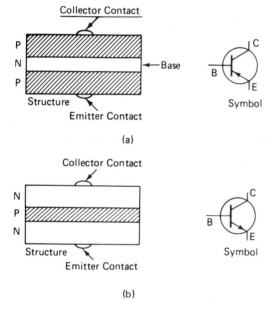

(a)

(b)

Fig. 2-9. (a) PNP transistor structure, (b) NPN transistor structure.

2-9, the B represents the base, which is normally identified by a thick or heavy solid line; the E is the emitter which is the line with the arrow; and the C is the collector, which is always shown as simply a straight line. The arrow (emitter) is shown as pointing in the direction of conventional current flow which is accepted as being from positive (+) to negative (-) in the external circuitry.

Current flow in a PNP transistor is generally considered to be the movement of holes (positive charge), while in the NPN transistor, the current flow is considered to be a movement of electrons (negative charge). Based on this theory, the electrons move against the emitter arrow in the NPN transistor since it is easier to picture the flow of electrons as being emitted by the emitter into the transistor base and collector. This is explained below under Transistor Operation.

Figure 2-9 shows that two types of transistors are readily available for use in electronic systems, namely the PNP or NPN type. In automotive electronics, the PNP type is more commonly used than the NPN type. It is important that you remember this fact, because a PNP transistor cannot be replaced with an NPN transistor in, e.g., an electronic ignition system.

As shown in Fig. 2-9, the transition regions between N-type and P-type substances are called the collector base junction, and the emitter base junction. When these two transistors are connected into a circuit, either an N-type or a P-type will operate as an amplifier, or as an electronic switch.

Transistors used in automotive electrical systems are generally either classified as a signal-type or a power-type. The major difference is that the signal-type operates with an input voltage up to 10 millivolts, whereas the power transistor functions with an input voltage greater than 10 millivolts.

Transistor Operation

As mentioned earlier in this chapter, the transistor can be operated as either an amplifier, or as a switch. The actual construction of the transistor accounts for this

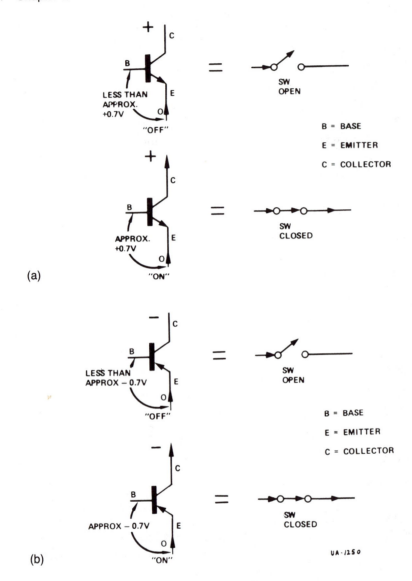

Fig. 2-10. (a) NPN transistor action, (b) PNP transistor action.

unusual operating characteristic. By controlling the base current, a much greater collector current can also be controlled.

The easiest way to follow what actually occurs within the transistor, is to refer to Fig. 2-10.

In an NPN transistor, the emitter (E) conducts current flow to the collector (C) only when the base (B) and collector (C) are positive with respect to the emitter. The transistor, however, cannot conduct until the base voltage exceeds the emitter voltage by approximately 0.4 volt for germanium type transistors, and approximately 0.7 volts for silicon types.

In the PNP type transistor, the emitter (E) current will flow to the collector (C) only when the base (B) and collector are negative with respect to the emitter.

For example, when the transistor is used in a voltage regulator, it functions as a switching device when the collector (C) current is allowed to flow. The transistor will then become saturated and its emitter-collector voltage drops to a very low value. In this condition, the transistor is operating similar to a closed switch (transistor is on) or in a low resistance state.

When collector current is cut off, the transistor appears as an open switch (transistor is off) due to the high resistance within it. See Fig. 2-10 (b).

In Fig. 2-11, we have oversimplified a circuit with a transistor placed into it. With battery power connected to a PNP transistor, current will flow through the emitter-base of the transistor because the switch connected to the transistor base is closed. Current will also flow through the collector circuit where it will meet or join with the current flow leaving the base circuit switch, where the current then returns to the battery to complete the path of flow or circuit path.

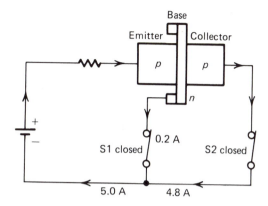

Fig. 2-11. Simplified transistor circuit flow. (Courtesy of Delco-Remy Div. of GMC)

For simplicity, let's assume that the transistor in the example has an emitter-base current of 3 amperes. With both switches closed, you might assume, and rightly so that the current flow through both switches would be the same. It is not!

The reason for unequal current flow through both switches is due to the physical arrangement of the component parts of the transistor, which includes the emitter, the base-ring, and the collector. The emitter and the collector are closer together than the emitter and the base-ring. Because of this placement, the holes (positive charge), injected into the transistor base from the emitter will travel on into the collector because of their velocity (speed and direction).

This is further assisted by the negative potential at the right-hand side of the collector which will attract the positive holes from the transistor base into the collector. The resultant action might produce a current flow of 2.8 amperes through the collector switch, with the remaining 0.2 amperes passing through the base switch. The exact values that will flow through any transistor will vary based upon the specific type and size of transistor used, as well as the circuit design. The collector current in this example would be 14 times that of the base current. This is one of the unusual operating characteristics of a transistor.

Another condition possible in this same circuit would be caused by opening the switch connected to the collector while leaving the switch to the base closed. The result would be that we would have a current of 3 amperes through this circuit only. One other phenomenon of the transistor would be to open the switch connected to the base, while closing the switch to the collector. Again, you would anticipate that the current flow through the closed switch should be that of the circuit, namely 3 amperes.

However, no appreciable current will flow under this condition because with the base circuit switch open, there are no holes (positive charged) being injected into the base from the emitter. Subsequently, the negative battery potential cannot attract nonexistent holes in the base into the collector. In addition, the junction at the base-collector undergoes a very high resistance condition due to the negative battery potential at the collector attracting the holes (positive charged) in the collector away from the base-collector junction, further preventing current flow.

The operation of an NPN transistor is the same as that for a PNP; however, the current flow consists of electron (negative charge) movement from the emitter to the base and collector. The examples given in Fig. 2-11 showed that the transistor can be operated in the amplifier condition such as when both switches were closed. We were able to increase the bias current flow in the base-emitter circuit by stepping it up in the collector emitter circuit. Our example

showed a base current of 0.2 amperes stepped up to 2.8 amperes in the collector circuit for a current gain or amplification of 14 times. When the collector switch was closed, and the base switch was opened, no flow was apparent in the circuit. The transistor acted as a switch to prevent a flow of current through the circuit.

Application of the Transistor

Let's see if we can put into practice the examples just discussed in Fig. 2-11 by applying the same transistor principle to a voltage regulator used with a generator or alternator arrangement in Fig. 2-12.

The purpose of any voltage regulator is exactly what the name implies—to regulate the maximum voltage output of the charging system. It accomplishes this by automatically opening and closing the current flow to the generator field windings so that the output decreases or stops, until the battery or accessories require additional charging or electrical energy.

See Chapter 4 for specific wiring diagrams.

When the generator voltage reaches a pre-set level (adjustable), magnetism de-

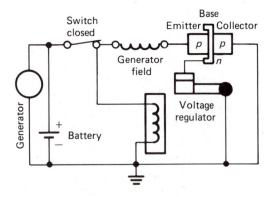

Fig. 2-12. Basic transistor regulator action. (Courtesy of Delco-Remy Div. of GMC)

veloped in the core of the voltage regulator shunt winding will pull the regulator points directly above it apart against light spring pressure. When the contact points separate (see Fig. 2-11) there will be no current at the transistor base, therefore no collector current can flow either. This action will cause the transistor to cut off or stop any current flow to the generator field windings, and automatically reduces the generator output.

Immediately after this occurs, the magnetic field of the shunt winding decreases, and spring pressure pulls the contact points together again. This action is similar to closing a switch, and field current will again flow to the generator field windings allowing the generator to again produce its maximum value. This action of the points opening and closing can occur ten times a second or several thousand times a second depending on actual conditions. With this type of transistorized regulator, minimal current exists at the contact points which ensures much longer point life.

There are other voltage regulators that do not use vibrating contact points at all to control the generator output. This second type of regulator is similar in action to the one shown in Fig. 2-11. If the switch to the base circuit is opened, although we keep the switch to the collector closed, no current flows in the circuit because of the design of the transistor.

Figure 2-13 shows this type of voltage regulator arrangement.

In Fig. 2-13, other diodes can be used to alternately impress both a forward or reverse bias across the emitter-base of the transistor shown (a PNP type). Anytime that a forward-bias is present, the transistor will conduct current through the collector to the generator field windings to allow generation of voltage and current flow to the accessories and battery circuit.

When a reverse-bias is impressed across the emitter-base of the transistor (similar to opening the switch at the base circuit as was explained in Fig. 2-11), no current flows in the collector to the generator field winding, therefore the output of the generator drops off. When a minimum value is reached, the transistor is triggered to a forward-bias condition again, which allows the restoration of field current, and the generator produces current once more.

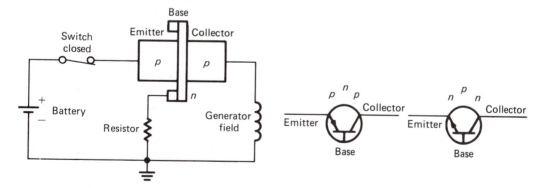

Fig. 2-13. Noncontact point transistorized regulator arrangement. (Courtesy of Delco-Remy Div. of GMC)

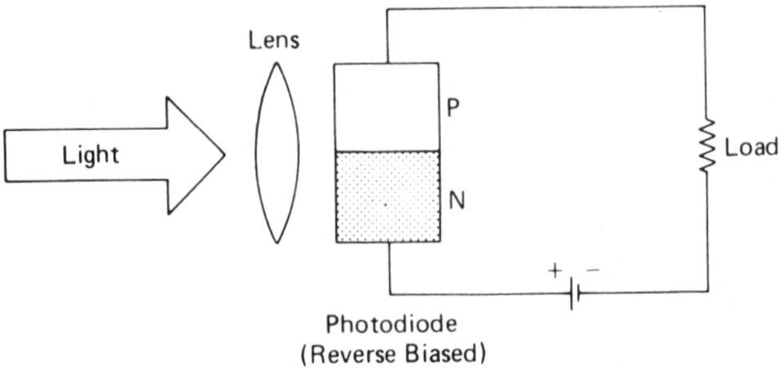

Fig. 2-14. Photodiode concept.

PHOTODIODE

A typical junction type photodiode is shown in Fig. 2-14.

A photodiode functions as a switch when actuated by a light beam. The photodiode does not conduct electric current in the reverse direction while the diode is in the dark; it no longer blocks current flow when it is exposed to light, therefore the light triggers the diode and it operates as a switch. These types of diodes are used as basic elements in breakerless solid-state ignition systems.

LIGHT-EMITTING DIODE (LED)

The light-emitting diode is used extensively in vehicle electric systems for a variety of functions. The LED has a junction that radiates both light and heat rays when it is subjected to an electric current. These diodes have been used, for example, along with a photodiode to time the high-tension spark in a solid-state ignition system.

INTEGRATED CIRCUIT

An integrated circuit is an electronic circuit that consists of several or even thousands of semiconductors grouped together in a very small space. The circuit is a solid-state grouping since there are no moving parts in the diodes and transistors used in the circuit.

Recent advances in the field of electronics have produced the silicon chip, which can be smaller than a pin head. This chip can literally store hundreds of thousands of pieces of information. The integrated circuit consisting of these chips is used in automobiles, trucks and heavy-duty equipment for such things as control and sensing of air and hydraulic brake anti-skid control devices, electronic ignition systems, electronic fuel injection and carburation, and are now being used in heavy truck and off-highway equipment power-shift transmissions.

These chips are capable of receiving, storing and sending out corrected signals to the system, and are commonly known as microprocessors.

USING AN OHMMETER

Ohmmeters are used in electrical circuits to check resistance values between two points and also to check for continuity between two points. For example, by placing one end of the ohmmeter on a wire with the other lead on the opposite end of the wire we can measure the resistance of the wire.

If, however, a break exists in the wire, then no reading will be registered on the ohmmeter face plate signifying a problem.

Caution: An ohmmeter should only be used to test circuit continuity (no breaks in the wiring) and resistance with no power applied to the circuit from the battery. Therefore, disconnect the battery, or if the wire or component has been removed from the circuit, then the ohmmeter can be used. Failure to disconnect the circuit from the battery can result in damage to the ohmmeter unit.

The selector switch used on the ohmmeter can normally be placed at position R1, R10, R100, R1000, R10,000 which controls the top range of resistance that can be measured accurately on the ohmmeter. For example, if the ohmmeter reads 8 on the scale with the selector at position R1, then 8 ohms is the resistance; similarly, if the scale selector switch were at position R10, then 80 ohms would be the measured resistance; at R100 it would be 800 ohms and so on depending on the selector switch position.

Prior to using the ohmmeter, zero-in the scale by plugging in both the red and black contact probes to the meter; touch them together with the range selector switch at the desired position for the test, and with the two contact probes held together at their contact ends, turn the adjustment knob on the meter until the scale needle indicates ZERO.

When using an ohmmeter, the following conditions may exist:

1. **Infinity** With the test probes placed across a circuit, should the needle on the scale swing across and hit the stop peg, then you should switch to the next highest scale; however, if you are already on the highest scale, then the reading that you have obtained obviously has a much higher resistance than you can measure. Therefore, it is described as infinity and the sign for infinity resembles a figure 8 lying on its side (∞).

2. **Open** When checking a wire with an ohmmeter, a deflection of the meter needle is an indication that the wire is good. Failure of the needle to register is an indication that the wire is defective or open.

3. **Grounded** When using an ohmmeter on an insulated circuit no reading should exist between the insulated terminal and ground, otherwise it indicates that there is a short-circuit somewhere connecting both the insulated terminal and grounded connection to the same common location such as the vehicle frame or body. Therefore, a short circuit is generally indicated by a low or zero ohms reading.

Diode Resistances

Obviously the resistance through various diodes and transistors varies depending on its particular location/circuit. However a general consideration in a typical situation would indicate a forward resistance through a diode of 3,000 ohms and a reverse resistance value of possibly 4 million ohms. This is known as the front to back ratio; in this instance it is somewhat greater than 1,000:1. If a diode measures open circuited (infinite ohms) then it is defective, while a zero ohms reading indicates that it is short circuited. Acceptable industry standards or a rule of thumb figure for an operational diode would be a front-to-back ratio of at least 100:1.

TESTING DIODES AND TRANSISTORS

If it is necessary to check the operation of either a diode or a transistor, select an ohmmeter having a 1.5 volt cell across the diode or transistor. To check the diode, refer to Fig. 2-15, and select the lowest scale on the selector switch of the ohmmeter to start with. If the reading is too low, switch the selector to the next higher scale.

When checking the diode, both the forward and the reverse resistance values must be checked. If a reading of zero is obtained with the ohmmeter leads placed both ways across the diode, then the diode is shorted out, and should be replaced. If both readings are high, then the diode is open and should also be replaced. It is important when checking a diode, that the measured forward resistance value is much smaller than the reverse-resistance value, otherwise the diode is defective. A good diode will give one very low and one very high reading.

To check out the condition of a diode when no ohmmeter is readily available, select a 12 volt d.c. test light. When the leads of the light are connected across the diode both ways, failure to light in both checks indicates that the diode is open. If the light glows in both checks, the diode is shorted.

Figure 2-16 shows the check required on the transistor to indicate its condition.

Several steps in using the ohmmeter to check the condition of the transistor are shown in Fig. 2-16.

1. With the ohmmeter connected as shown, note the reading then reverse the leads; the transistor is shorted if both readings register zero.

2. Connect the ohmmeter as shown, and

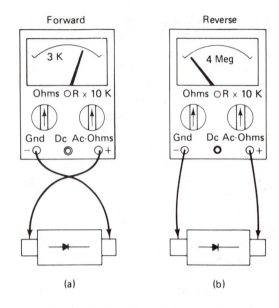

Fig. 2-15. Checking diode condition.

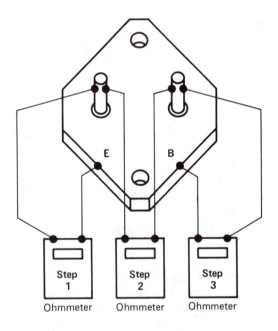

Fig. 2-16. Transistor check. (Courtesy of Delco-Remy Div. of GMC)

if the reading is zero in both directions when the leads are reversed, the transistor is shorted. If both readings are high, the transistor is open.

3. Step 3 is basically the same procedure as for Step 2.

Different ohmmeters can show different readings when checking diodes or transistors, due to battery condition, internal ohmmeter condition (resistance), etc. Therefore, always use the same ohmmeter when checking the condition of diodes and transistors.

CAUTION: Many shops and service personnel today use a digital type of ohmmeter to check diodes and transistors. This can present a problem because some of these digital ohmmeters have an output current limitation of 0.001 amperes, while others may only have an output current of as little as 0.000001 micro-amperes. This low current is inadequate to turn a PN junction on, even though it is forward-biased. The problem is that when the ohmmeter is connected to a forward-bias condition, a very high resistance will be registered that leads you to believe that the diode or transistor is defective, when in fact it may be perfectly OK. Therefore these types of digital ohmmeters should not be used for this purpose.

NOTE: Certain models and makes of digital ohmmeters may be used for checking both diodes and transistors however. Such ohmmeters are designed to produce sufficient current flow, and will therefore provide an accurate test of the diode's or transistor's condition. Always check the particular ohmmeter to be used to be sure that it does use at least one or two 1.5 volt cells.

REVIEW QUESTIONS

Q1 What is a semiconductor?

Q2 What is a diode?

Q3 What is a zener diode?

Q4 What is a transistor?

Q5 What is a photo-diode?

Q6 What is a light-emitting diode?

A7 What is an integrated circuit?

Q8 How does an NPN transistor differ from a PNP transistor?

Q9 What would you use to check the condition of a diode?

Q10 What precaution must be exercised when using digital type ohmmeters on a diode check?

ANSWERS

A1 A semiconductor is the term used to indicate that the electrical conductivity of these units lies between that of conductors and insulators. The two most commonly used materials that semiconductors are manufactured from are either germanium or silicon to which has been added such other materials as phosphorous, antimony, boron and indium.

The material is known as an N type substance when phosphorus is added to the substance, and it is a negative conducting unit, while it is a positive conducting unit when doped with boron and is therefore known as a P unit.

A2 A diode is similar to a one-way check valve in that it is designed to pass electric current in only one direction, while blocking or restricting flow in the other direction. It is used, for example, in an alternator to change alternating current to direct current.

A3 The zener diode is designed to protect standard diodes when reverse current and voltage exist. It can conduct current in one direction (reverse only) and will only do so when a predetermined reverse bias voltage is reached. At any voltage below a given value, no current can flow when the reverse bias voltage occurs.

A4 A transistor is designed to amplify and switch current on and off. It can therefore be used to control a predetermined flow of current in the circuit, and can also be used to resist this flow. The transistor can be made from either germanium or silicon material with N and P substances sandwiched together as necessary.

A5 A photo-diode functions as a switch[...]
beam.

A6 The LED (light emitting diode) has a juncti[...]
light and heat rays when it is subjected to an electric[...]

A7 An integrated circuit is an electronic circuit that co[...]
or even thousands of semiconductors grouped together. Th[...]
solid-state grouping consisting of diodes, transistors, etc.

A8 An NPN transistor differs from a PNP transistor in that in th[...]
unit, the emitter (E) conducts current flow to the collector (C) only w[...]
the base (B) and collector (C) are positive with respect to the emitter. Th[...]
transistor, however, cannot conduct until the base voltage exceeds the
emitter voltage by approximately 0.4 volt for germanium-type transistors, and approximately 0.7 volt for silicon-type transistors. In the PNP
transistor, the emitter (E) current will flow to the collector (C) only when
the base (B) and collector are negative with respect to the emitter.

A9 Select an ohmmeter having a 1.5 volt cell across the diode or
transistor and select the lowest scale on the selector switch to start with.
A good diode should give one high and one low reading when the leads
are reversed on the ohmmeter. If no ohmmeter is available, then select a
12 volt d.c. test light, and if the diode causes the test light to glow both
ways then it is defective.

A10 Some digital type ohmmeters have an output current limitation of
0.001 ampere, while others may only have an output current of as little as
0.000001 ampere which is too low a current to turn on a PN junction and
a false reading can be interpreted. Always check the particular ohmmeter to make sure that it does use at least one or two 1.5 volt cells.

Introduction to Electronics / 55

pter

3

eries

when actuated by a light

on that radiates both
current.

sists of several
e circuit is a

NPN
hen

STORAGE BATTERIES

Few people today, whether involved in the maintenance of cars, trucks or heavy-duty equipment have not at some time or another used some item that requires battery power to make it operate. In this age of electronic wizardry, almost everything from handheld calculators to toys and portable radios, cassette tape decks and portable televisions employ batteries in a wide variety of shapes, sizes, and capacities.

Since this chapter will be concerned with the storage battery as it applies to cars, trucks, and heavy-duty equipment, we will study several types of batteries, their function, design, ratings, testing, and maintenance.

Every car and truck must have a source of electrical energy which is available at all times in order to supply power to the electrical accessories on the vehicle or equipment. When the engine is running, the battery is kept fully charged by the use of a generator or alternator. When the engine is stopped, and electrical accessories are in use, then the battery must supply the necessary power.

When the engine is started, the battery must supply high current to the starter motor as well as provide sufficient energy to the ignition coil to create the high-tension energy required to fire the spark plugs. In diesel engines, the battery is also required to preheat the glow-plugs for cold weather starting.

The amount of electrical energy that is contained in the battery is known as its capacity, which in turn is established by the volume of chemicals within the battery casing.

TYPES OF BATTERIES

Batteries used in cars, trucks, industrial, marine, and heavy-duty equipment are commonly known as being either conventional or maintenance-free batteries.

The conventional type of battery is available in either of two forms: wet or dry. The conventional battery must be checked regularly to ensure that the electrolyte level is maintained by the addition of distilled water. When a conventional battery is ordered new from a supplier, they can supply the battery in either wet or dry form. The wet battery already has the (acid) electrolyte added to it to activate the chemical reaction within the battery so that it is ready for service.

On the other hand, the dry battery is a battery with no electrolyte in it. In this way, the battery can be stored for much longer periods of time without the possibility of the battery becoming discharged. Storage time is therefore increased. When desired, the battery is then activated by the addition of electrolyte.

The maintenance-free battery is a sealed top unit that does not require the addition of make-up water over its normal life, therefore no regular maintenance is required. General maintenance required is discussed later in this chapter.

In addition to these types of batteries, Delco-Remy Division of General Motors Corporation produces a battery under the trade name of the Energizer. It is called an energizer because it stores electrical energy in chemical form.

BATTERY CONSTRUCTION

Minor variations exist between types and styles of batteries manufactured by different companies; however, in the final analysis, they are very similar in general construction.

Figure 3-1 shows two typical batteries manufactured by Delco-Remy (General Motors) and the Robert Bosch Corp.

The battery is made up of individual components which together comprise the battery. Let's look at each of these components and how they function within the overall picture of the battery's operation.

Battery Case

The case is normally constructed of an acid-resistant material which can be either hard rubber, plastic, or polypropylene which has the advantage of lighter weight and improved cold weather durability as compared to hard rubber cases.

The polypropylene case also withstands road shock and vibration better than the hard rubber style.

Moulded externally to the battery case at the bottom are lugs or mounting ridges to allow the battery holddown clamps to secure it into position. This is visible in Fig. 3-1 (b).

Running along the inside of the battery base are moulded element rests which support the individual positive and negative plate assemblies. This is necessary because during the life of any battery, chemical discharge causes particles of material to drop from the plates which can accumulate in a sediment chamber between the element rests and below the bottom of the plates.

Without these sediment chambers at the bottom of the battery case, short-circuits would occur, because the particles of material which drop off from the plates of the battery contain lead which is electrically conductive. Without the sediment chamber, these particles could lodge between both the positive and negative plates creating the short-circuit mentioned above.

Each battery case is subdivided into what are known as cells. These cells consist of a number of positive and negative plates insulated from one another by separators. The number of cells used depends on the battery voltage, with the commonly used 12 volt battery containing six of these cells, while the 6 volt battery would only contain three cells. The stack-up of positive and negative plates is commonly called a cell-pack.

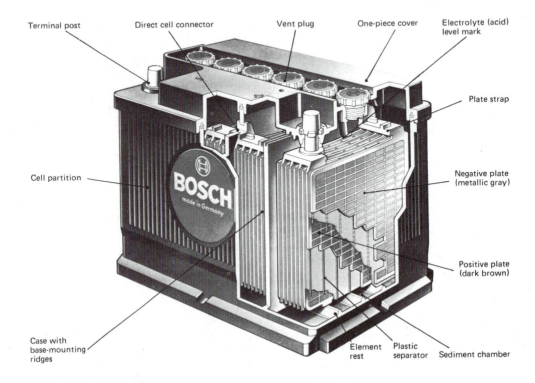

Fig. 3-1. Battery component nomenclature (courtesy of Robert Bosch Corp.)

Battery Cover

The battery cover is a one-piece unit which has individual openings for each cell to allow filling of the cell with electrolyte on conventional type batteries, or the addition of water for maintenance purposes.

Battery or cell plugs are then screwed or pushed into place, with each plug having a small hole in it to serve as a vent. On the newer style batteries, a porous top allows venting of each cell to the atmosphere due to the chemical reaction within the battery. On maintenance-free batteries a special liquid-gas separator is heat-sealed to the top of the battery case, and a cover is heat-sealed to the top of the liquid-gas separator. The liquid-gas separator on the maintenance-free battery is functionally designed to collect very small particles of electrolyte liquid, and to then return the liquid to the main reservoir of the battery.

Elements

The elements or cell-packs contain a number of both positive and negative plates back-to-back, but insulated from one another by the use of separators between each pair of plates. The capacity or battery rating in ampere-hours is established by the physical size of these positive and negative plates, and also by how many plates are used per cell.

The plates within the battery are made up of a grid network as shown in Fig. 3-2.

Currently, two types of grids are in use for the conventional and maintenance-free batteries. In the conventional battery, the grid is made of lead-antimony, while the grid of the maintenance-free battery is made of a lead-calcium alloy. The elimination of the antimony from the maintenance-free battery results in less water usage and gassing throughout the life of the battery. In addition, the lead-calcium grid is very resistant to oxidation or grid corrosion.

As can be seen from reference to Fig. 3-2, the grid looks simply like a flat, rectangular, lattice-style casting surrounded

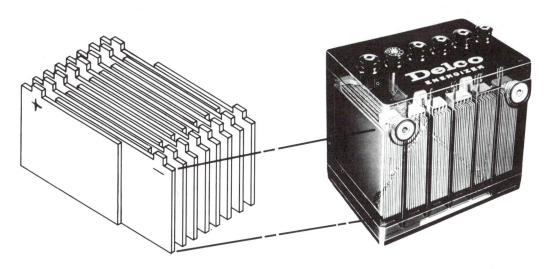

Fig. 3-2. Battery grid network. (Courtesy of Delco-Remy Div. of GMC)

with a heavy border. The shape of the mesh can be either of horizontal and vertical wire, or in some batteries may be diamond-shaped. Lead peroxide (PbO_2) is pasted or coated onto the grid to the positively charged plates. This is dark brown in color, while the material pasted or coated to the negative grid plate contains pure lead in the form of sponge-lead (Pb), which is metallic gray in color. This material is porous, and provides a large effective surface area.

Figure 3-3 shows how each group of positive and negative plates are held together by the use of a plate strap. A plate group is made by lead-burning or welding each stack-up of similar plates together to the plate strap. Each element or plate group usually has one more negative plate than positive plate, so that the outside plates are negative at the exposed positions on both sides of the interlaced group.

Separators

In order to pack as much electrical energy as possible into the smallest space, batteries are now designed to be as small and lightweight as desired.

Because of this design, the positive and negative plates must be kept very close together within the battery case. In order to prevent a short-circuit between these dissimilar plates, an insulating material called a separator must be installed between the individual plates when an element is assembled.

These separators must present no notable resistance to the flow or movement of ions in the electrolyte (dilute sulphuric acid), and must also be able to withstand the chemical reaction of the acid, as well as being microporous and permeable so that the electrolyte can pass through the sepa-

Fig. 3-3. Plate strap location. (Courtesy of Delco-Remy Div. of GMC)

rator. Without the microporous structure of the separator, it is possible that very fine lead fibers could pass through the separator resulting in a short-circuit between the positive and negative grid plates.

Cell Connectors

Figure 3-1 (b) shows how the individual cells of the battery are connected by the use of cell connectors. The plate straps of the cells are connected by the shortest and most direct path through the cell partition.

Battery Terminal Posts

Figure 3-4 shows how the plate strap of each cell is connected back to both the positive and negative battery terminal posts.

Although Fig. 3-4 shows top mounted battery posts, many current batteries employ what are known as side-mount posts. This is strictly a design feature, which lowers the overall height of the battery

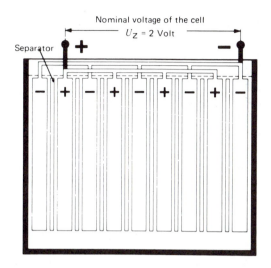

Fig. 3-4. Connection to positive and negative posts and plate straps. (Courtesy of Robert Bosch Corp.)

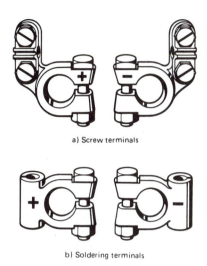

Fig. 3-5. Battery cable terminals. (Courtesy of Robert Bosch Corp.)

assembly, and also makes it more convenient to connect up the battery cable terminals on many applications. Side-mounted battery connections generally provide less self-discharge and less resistance in addition to the design features mentioned.

Battery Cable Terminals

There are several styles of battery cable terminals readily available and used in the industry. Figure 3-5 shows two of the commonly used types.

To avoid damage to the electrical accessories when connecting up the battery cables, the battery terminal posts are identified by either the letters POS or NEG cast or etched into the battery cover immediately adjacent to each post. In addition to this feature, the POS (positive) or NEG (negative) battery posts are manufactured so that the diameter of the positive post is larger than that of the negative post.

Some battery terminals (clamps) are marked with either a + (positive), or - (negative) sign to match that on the battery cover, or the letters POS or NEG.

BATTERY OPERATION—HOW DOES IT WORK?

So far we have looked at the main components of the battery, and how they basically go together. Let's now study the battery in detail to establish just how it is capable of producing the electrical energy used to operate all of the accessories in an electrical system.

Current within the battery is produced by a chemical reaction between the positive and negative coated plates which are submerged in the electrolyte (dilute sulphuric acid). This chemical reaction that occurs within the battery causes the battery to self-discharge. If the battery is not constantly charged by the use of a generator or alternator such as on a car or truck, then eventually the battery becomes completely discharged or flat, and must be recharged before it will produce any more electrical energy.

To recharge a battery, it must be supplied with a flow of direct current in a direction opposite the normal flow of current from the battery during discharge.

The electrolyte weight or specific gravity in a fully charged battery is made up of a solution of dilute sulphuric acid in water.

This specific gravity is approximately 1.270 at 80°F (26.6°C), which means that it is heavier than water which has a specific gravity of 1.000 or 10 lbs/gallon (4.536 kg/3.78 liters). In other words, the electrolyte of the battery is 1.270 times heavier than an equivalent volume of water.

The percentage breakdown of the electrolyte consists of approximately 64 percent water and 36 percent acid, with the acid having a specific gravity of 1.835. These two percentages combine to give us this 1.270 at 80°F (26.6°C) of a fully charged battery.

The voltage produced in each battery cell is dependent upon the chemical difference between the active materials (positive and negative plates) and also on the strength concentration of the electrolyte.

TEMPERATURE CORRECTION OF ELECTROLYTE SPECIFIC GRAVITY

Specific gravity readings of battery electrolyte is directly affected by changes in temperature either above or below 80°F (26.6°C). To correct for specific gravity readings above this figure, simply add 4 points (0.004) to the reading for every 10 degrees above 80°F, or subtract 4 points (0.004) from 80°F for every 10°F (3.7°C) below this figure.

For example, if the electrolyte showed a temperature of 0°F when a thermometer was placed into it, and it read 1.232 with a hydrometer sample, then the corrected specific gravity to 80°F (26.6°C) would be 1.200.

One precaution that must be exercised with respect to electrolyte is that of low ambient temperatures, because the electrolyte can freeze. Typical temperatures at which the electrolyte would freeze are shown in Table 3-1.

Table 3-1
Electrolyte Freezing Temperatures

Specific Gravity	Freezing Temperature
1.270	−83°F
1.160	0°F (−18°C)
1.100	18°F (−8.2°C)

CHEMICAL REACTION WITHIN THE BATTERY

To understand thoroughly the chemical reaction that exists in a battery during discharge (battery supplying electrical energy to a system), consider the following conditions:

1. The positive grid or plate within the battery consists of lead peroxide with chemical formula PbO_2, and its color is dark or chocolate brown, while the negative material in the negative grid consists of pure lead with chemical symbol Pb, and its color is metallic gray.

2. Two classes of conductors are used in electrical systems; the first class includes copper wiring or any metallic substance whereby current flow takes place by

means of electron conduction as was explained in Chapter 1 of this book.

The second class of conductor includes chemical compounds dissolved in water which decompose or dissociate into positive and negative components (ions). Current flow in this second class of conductor takes place by means of larger charged particles (ion conduction). Such a second class conductor is the electrolyte used in the lead-storage battery, which is dilute sulphuric acid whose chemical formula is H_2SO_4; this means that every molecule of sulphuric acid has two atoms of hydrogen, one atom of sulphur, and four atoms of oxygen.

In its normal state, sulphuric acid molecules will tend to split into positively-charged hydrogen (H+) ions, and negatively-charged sulphate (SO_4) ions, whereby the charges will match one another on an overall basis.

The electrolyte solution in the battery when in its usual concentration has almost all the sulphuric acid molecules in a disassociated state. However, if an electrode of metallic lead is immersed into dilute sulphuric acid such as a battery contains, electrically charged particles or ions are forced from the electrode into the electrolyte due to the pressure of the solution.

In other words, positively charged lead ions (or lead atoms which have given up two electrons) pass into the electrolyte (dilute sulphuric acid) leaving negative charges (electrons) remaining on the lead electrode with respect to the electrolyte.

If another electrode of different material is immersed in the electrolyte, different potentials develop at the two electrodes with respect to the electrolyte. This action, creates what is commonly called potential or voltage between the two dissimilar electrodes. In the lead-acid battery, this potential or voltage is equal to 2 volts per cell.

BATTERY DISCHARGE

When the terminals of the battery are connected to each other through an electric load (accessories), electrons will flow from the negative electrode through the load, and back to the positive electrode because of the difference of potential or cell voltage existing between the terminals. The chemical reaction or changes within the battery during discharge (loss of electrical energy), is shown in Fig. 3-6.

During discharge of the battery, oxygen in the positive active material combines with the hydrogen in the electrolyte to form plain water (H_2O). While this is occurring, the lead in the positive active material combines with the sulfate radical, thereby forming lead sulfate ($PbSO_4$).

A similar reaction occurs at the negative plate, where lead (Pb) of the negative active material combines with the sulphate radical to form lead sulphate ($PbSO_4$). We therefore have lead sulphate being formed at both the positive and negative grid plates of the battery during discharge. Both electrodes (positive and negative) have now returned to their initial condition; the chemical energy stored in the cell has been transformed back into electrical energy and has been used up by the electrical load or accessories, and the battery has returned to its discharged state. In a discharged lead-acid battery, the electrolyte is in a diluted state comprising about 17 percent pure sulphuric acid, and about 83 percent water.

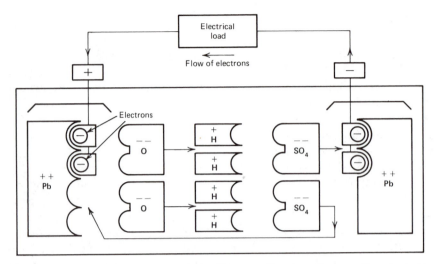

(a) Discharge of battery or current drain. Electrons flow from the negative electrode through the electrical load to the positive electrode. PbSO$_4$ (lead sulphate) forms at both electrodes.

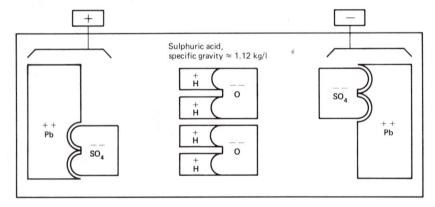

(b) Cell discharged. PbSO$_4$ (lead sulphate) has formed at both electrodes and H$_2$O (water) has formed in the electrolyte.

Fig. 3-6. Chemical reaction during battery discharge.

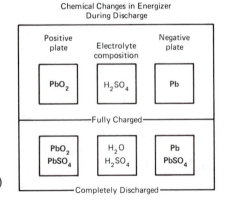

Chemical Changes in Energizer During Discharge

Positive plate	Electrolyte composition	Negative plate
PbO$_2$	H$_2$SO$_4$	Pb

────Fully Charged────

| PbO$_2$ PbSO$_4$ | H$_2$O H$_2$SO$_4$ | Pb PbSO$_4$ |

────Completely Discharged────

(c)

CHEMICAL REACTION WHEN CHARGING A BATTERY

To charge the lead-acid battery, the positive and negative battery posts must be connected to a suitable source of direct current (DC). This can be done by use of a generator, alternator, or battery charger. This charging process does not take place naturally, but must be forced by the introduction of electrical energy into the cell so that it has a higher energy level after the charging process than before. The source of charging current draws electrons from the positive electrode and forces them into the negative electrode.

The chemical reactions which take place in the battery cells during charging are the reverse of those occurring during the discharge cycle. Figures 3-6 and 3-7 show a schematic of the chemical reaction within the battery cells during both the charge and discharge cycles.

During charging, the lead sulphate on both the positive and negative plates is separated into lead (Pb) and sulphate (SO_4). This sulphate leaving both plates combines with hydrogen in the electrolyte to form or recreate sulphuric acid (H_2SO_4). While this is going on, the oxygen (0) in the electrolyte combines with the lead (Pb) at the positive plate to form lead dioxide (PbO_2), and the negative plate returns to the original form of lead (Pb).

GASSING OF THE LEAD-ACID BATTERY

Due to the chemical reaction within the cells of the battery, after a certain period of time under charge, a saturation limit will be reached. If the battery is continually charged after this point has been reached, damage to the battery can occur. This gassing starts at a charging voltage of about 2.4 volts, and will result in a continuing loss of water. The sulphuric acid concentration (specific gravity of the electrolyte) will rise above the value specified for a fully-charged battery. Continued overcharging will damage the battery beyond acceptable usage, and in certain cases the battery could explode.

When a battery is being charged, gassing, together with the increase in sulphuric acid specific gravity and the terminal voltage, indicates that the battery cells are fully charged. A fully charged battery will continue to gas freely for a fairly long time after the battery charger has been disconnected. This gas mixture, which has been developed during charging, consists of a mixture of both hydrogen and oxygen and is therefore highly explosive. For this reason, battery charging rooms must be well-ventilated at all times.

Maintenance of the water level in each battery cell is very important. If this level drops below the tops of the plates, the exposed active material will dry and harden, leading to battery failure. If maintenance-free batteries are overcharged, they can be permanently damaged just as nonmaintenance-free batteries can.

Overcharging in old-style (nonmaintenance-free) batteries forms hydrogen and oxygen gases which cause oxidation of the positive plate grids. This oxidation causes the grids to crumble and therefore leads to early failure. However, in the maintenance-free battery, the plate grid contains lead-calcium alloy, and has no antimony such as is used in the older type battery. This wrought-lead calcium used in maintenance-free batteries is very resistant to oxidation of the grid and also to overcharge or thermal runaway because of the

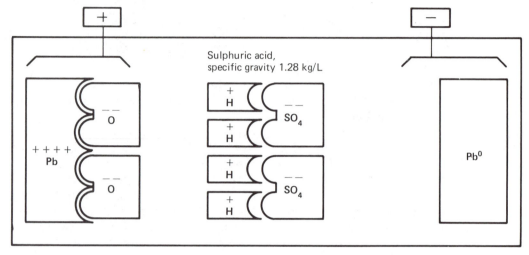

(a) Cell charged. Positive electrode: PbO_2 (lead peroxide). Negative electrode: Pb (metallic lead).

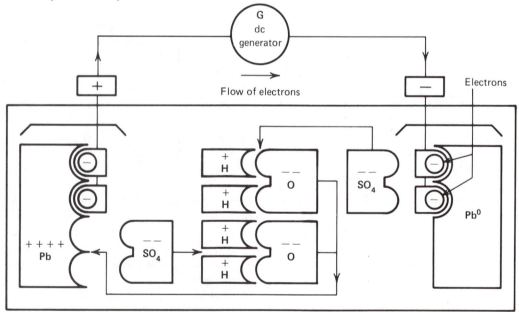

(b) Charging the cell. During charging, the flow of electrons (forced around by a DC generator) is from the positive electrode to the negative electrode, i.e., in the direction opposite to the flow during discharge (current drain).

PbO_2 (lead peroxide) forms at the positive electrode, and Pb (metallic lead) forms at the negative electrode.

Fig. 3-7. Chemical reaction during battery charging.

removal of antimony from the grid.

An older type lead-antimony battery can accept up to ten times as much overcharge current as a fully charged maintenance-free type battery. The maintenance-free battery offers high resistance to the following undesirable characteristics:

- Water usage
- Corrosion of the grid
- Gassing of the cells
- Self-discharge
- Overcharging or thermal runaway

VENTING OF MAINTENANCE-FREE BATTERIES

The maintenance-free battery, or freedom battery as it is called, never requires the addition of water. There are no filler caps in the battery cover, and it is sealed with the exception of small vent holes in the cover which allow small amounts of gases to escape. Because of these vents, the battery should always be kept in an upright position, otherwise electrolyte leakage can occur.

Do not exceed a 45-degree angle when carrying or installing a maintenance-free type of battery.

CHECKING CONDITION OF MAINTENANCE-FREE BATTERIES

Some companies that manufacture maintenance-free batteries employ a special temperature-compensated hydrometer which is built into the battery cover, while others seal them completely. This device allows the service technician or mechanic to readily identify the state of charge of the battery.

One example of how this type of hydrometer operates is shown in Fig. 3-8. This is

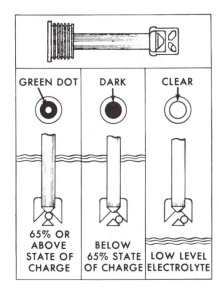

Fig. 3-8. Built-in battery hydrometer operation. (Courtesy of Delco-Remy Div. of GMC)

the method employed on all Delco-Remy Freedom Batteries.

The hydrometer device shown in Fig. 3-8 consists of a small green-colored ball (within a cage fastened to the end of a plastic probe) which can float up or down within one of two small tracks. If the battery electrolyte is at or beyond a specific gravity of 1.220, the ball will float allowing the mechanic or observer to visually see a green dot when he/she looks down on the top of the built-in hydrometer from the top of the battery case.

If the observer sees only a dark surface when viewing the clear top of the hydrometer, it indicates that the specific gravity of the battery is less than 1.220. This is caused by the fact that the ball will sink down one of the two tracks in the cage.

If a dark surface appears within the hydrometer, the battery must be charged until the green ball floats.

In the maintenance-free battery, only one indicator or hydrometer is used in one cell, because since the battery is of sealed construction, the specific gravity per cell will be almost identical. If the hydrometer becomes clear or light yellow in color, this is an indication of low electrolyte caused by possible overcharging, tipping the battery beyond 45 degrees which would allow the electrolyte to spill out, a cracked case, or a worn-out battery.

ADVANTAGES OF MAINTENANCE-FREE BATTERIES

These types of batteries have the following major advantages:

1. Requires no addition of water
2. No spewing or gassing of cells
3. Lower rate of self-discharge
4. Higher resistance to possible overcharging
5. Greater resistance to grid corrosion
6. Service free
7. No terminal oxidation or corrosion (sealed surfaces)

The disadvantages of a maintenance-free battery are that they should not be used in applications where the current draw cannot be replaced by a steady charge from a generator or alternator. An example would be as boost-start batteries because, should the state of charge be allowed to fall too low, then recharging can be impossible. However, various manufacturers do state that an attempt can be made to recharge a maintenance-free battery at a slow rate if the voltage falls within a minimum level. These levels will vary among battery manufacturers, therefore a close check should be made with the supplier prior to attempting to charge a maintenance-free battery.

Delco-Remy Division of General Motors offers the following basic rules regarding charging of any of their Freedom Batteries:

1. Do not charge a battery if the hydrometer is clear or light yellow; replace the battery.

2. Charge rates between 3 and 50 amperes are generally satisfactory for any freedom battery as long as spewing of electrolyte does not occur, or the battery does not feel excessively hot (over 125°F, 52°C); if spewing occurs or temperature exceeds 125°F, the charging rate must be reduced or temporarily halted to permit cooling. Touch the battery case to establish temperature.

3. On rare occasions, the indicator (hydrometer) may turn light yellow. Although the battery is capable of further service, if a cranking complaint has been reported, replace the battery. *Do not charge, test, or jump-start.*

DISADVANTAGES OF A CONVENTIONAL LEAD-ACID BATTERY

1. Requires regular addition of make-up water
2. Spewing or gassing of cells is not unusual (check charging rate)
3. Higher self-discharge rate than maintenance-free battery
4. Lower resistance to overcharging than maintenance-free battery

5. Lower resistance to grid corrosion than maintenance-free battery

6. Requires regular maintenance

The main advantage however of the conventional lead-acid battery is that it can be recharged at any time. Therefore, in situations where it is being used as a booster battery, it can be placed back on charge and brought back to a service condition.

SPECIFIC GRAVITY VERSUS VOLTAGE

There is a direct correlation between the actual specific gravity of the battery electrolyte and that of an equivalent voltage that would be registered on a voltmeter. Table 3-2 illustrates this relationship.

As a battery ages, shedding or loss of active material from the plates will cause the fully charged specific gravity reading to drop. This is further compounded by the normal loss of electrolyte due to gassing of the cells. Operating temperature and rate of charge, plus maintenance practices will determine the battery's life expectancy.

BATTERY CELL AND POST ARRANGEMENT

The arrangement of battery cells and the position of the positive and negative posts will vary between types and styles of batteries. Some common arrangements are shown in Fig. 3-9.

Table 3-2. Specific Gravity and Voltage

Open Circuit Voltage Reading	Corresponding Spec. Gravity	State of Charge	
1.95	1.100	1.100 to 1.130	discharged
1.96	1.110		
1.97	1.120		
1.98	1.130		
1.99	1.140		
2.00	1.150		
2.01	1.160		
2.02	1.170	1.170 to 1.190	25% charged
2.03	1.180		
2.04	1.190		
2.05	1.200	1.200 to 1.220	50% charged
2.06	1.210		
2.07	1.220		
2.08	1.230	1.230 to 1.250	75% charged
2.09	1.240		
2.10	1.250		
2.11	1.260	1.260 to 1.280	100% charged
2.12	1.270		
2.13	1.280		
2.14	1.290		
2.15	1.300		

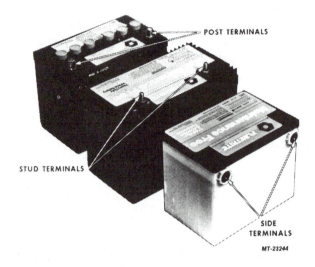

Fig. 3-9. Typical battery styles. (Courtesy of International-Harvester)

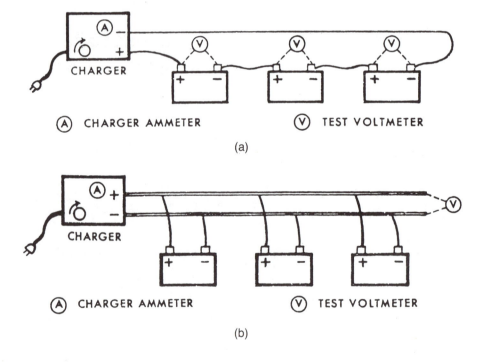

Fig. 3-10. (a) Battery series hookup, (b) battery parallel hookup.

SERIES AND PARALLEL HOOKUP OF BATTERIES

The most commonly used batteries today are either the multiple 6 or 12 volt arrangement. Examples of these arrangements are shown in Fig. 3-10.

When batteries are connected in series such as three 12-volt models of 120 amp capacity each, the net result is that we obtain a voltage of 36 volts, but the amperage remains the same. Similarly, if four 6-volt batteries are connected in series, then we can obtain 24 volts of power, although the amperage would still be the same as that for one battery.

When batteries are connected in a parallel arrangement as shown in Fig. 3-11 (b), then the result is an increase in amperage; the voltage, however, will remain the same as that for one battery. For example, four 6 volt batteries connected in parallel would still only produce 6 volts, however if the amperage rating of each battery were 55 amps, then we would have a total of 220 amps.

BATTERY RATINGS

Earlier in this chapter, we made mention of the fact that the battery capacity is dictated by the number of plates per cell, and also by the total surface area of the active plate material.

In addition to these two controlling factors, strength and volume of electrolyte will also have a bearing on the battery output.

The method used to rate batteries is common in most countries of the world. The Society of Automotive Engineers (SAE) provides information which defines a battery's ability to deliver a given amount of useable cranking power.

Old Ratings

Ampere-Hours (20-hour rate)

This rating is determined by laboratory testing the battery under controlled conditions. It indicates how much energy a battery can store, and in general it shows the amount of active material in the battery.

With the battery fully charged and maintained at a temperature of 80°F (26.6°C), it is subsequently discharged at a constant rate for 20 hours, after which time the average cell voltage must be 1.75 volts or above. This amounts to a steady 5.25 volts on a 6 volt battery, and 10.5 volts on a 12 volt battery.

A battery capable of supplying 4 amperes under such a test would qualify for a rating of 80 ampere-hours (4 amperes x 20 hours).

Zero-Degree Cranking Ability

Sometimes referred to as a Cold Rating, this test is conducted by discharging a fully charged battery at 0°F (-18°C) at a constant rate of either 150 or 300 amperes depending on the voltage and ampere-hour rating of the specific battery. This rating is then considered from two points of view.

One, is the voltage obtained after 5 or 10 seconds of high discharge, and the other is the time in minutes required for the battery to reach the end voltage of the test.

For example, if a 12 volt battery has a 10 second voltage rating of 7.8 volts at 300 amperes draw, will it still maintain this voltage or higher for 10 seconds?

Also the same battery having a time rating of 2 minutes will operate under the same conditions above for 2 minutes before the terminal voltage falls to the end voltage which may be 6 volts for this particular battery. Therefore, the higher the 10 second voltage rating, and the higher the time rating, the greater will be the cranking capacity of the battery.

New Ratings (1971 SAE and BCI)

Although the old ratings were reasonably effective, SAE now uses two tests to rate batteries, the reserve capacity and the cold cranking test.

Reserve Capacity

A reserve capacity rating represents the approximate time in minutes that it is possible to travel at night with a minimum electrical load and no generator/alternator output to the battery.

The time in minutes is based on a current draw of 25 amperes while maintaining a minimum battery terminal voltage of 10.2 volts at 80°F (26.6°C) or equivalent cell voltage of 1.75 volts. This rating replaces the previous 20-hour capacity (ampere-hour) rating, and more accurately represents the electrical load which must be supplied by the battery in the event of a charging system failure. The ampere-hour rating will eventually be dropped.

Cold Cranking Test

This rating specifies the minimum amperes available at 0°F (-18°C) and at -20°F (-28°C). This rating replaces the old method of relating voltage and time as measures of cranking and starting ability. It is much more accurate because it allows cranking capacity to be related to such significant variables as engine displacement, compression ratio, temperature, cranking time, condition of the engine and electrical system, and lowest practical voltage for cranking and ignition. The old tests did not take these factors into account.

This new test relates a discharge rating in amperes that a fully charged battery will maintain for 30 seconds without the terminal voltage falling below 7.2 volts for a 12 volt battery, or 3.6 volts for a 6 volt battery (1.2 volts per cell or greater).

To provide enough starting power under severe conditions, a 12 volt system normally requires at least one ampere for each cubic-inch of engine displacement. For example a 450 cubic inch (7.37 liters) engine would require a battery with a cold cranking rating of at least 450 amperes. Most manufacturers of batteries will provide the ampere-hour ratings. If however, the ampere-hour rating is not available and cannot be determined, then divide the cold cranking rating at 0°F (-18°C) by two. The resultant figure obtained equals the load that should be applied when making a battery capacity test, and is about equal to the value of three times the ampere-hour rating of batteries which used the old rating system.

ESTIMATING BATTERY CAPACITY

The capacity of the battery is generally shown on a decal stuck onto the side or the top of the battery, while others have the rating molded onto the battery case. However, if the battery capacity can not be determined, it can be approximated by multiplying the total area of the positive plates in square inches in each cell by two-thirds.

For example, if a battery has six positive plates, each measuring 4 x 3 inches (10.16 x 7.62 cm) the total area is 72 sq. in. (464.51 sq.cm). Two thirds of this is 48 (309.64); therefore the ampere-hour capacity at a 20 hour rate of discharge is 48 amps.

Most batteries today are capable of at least a capacity of 1 ampere-hour for each

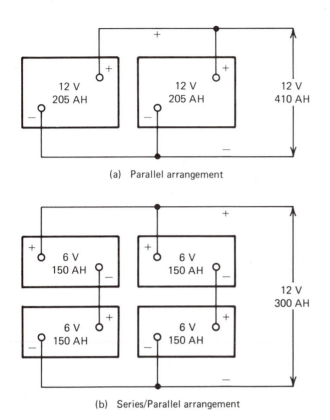

(a) Parallel arrangement

Fig. 3-11. (a) Two 12-volt batteries in parallel arrangement. (b) Four 6-volt batteries in a series/parallel arrangement.

(b) Series/Parallel arrangement

three square inches of plate surface. Suppose the total area of each plate (both sides) was 24 sq.in; multiply this area by the number of positive plates which we will assume to be six, then we have the product 6 x 24 = 144 sq. in.

Using the basic standard, that 3 sq. in. provides 1 ampere-hour capacity, then for 144 sq. in., it would be 144/3 = 48 amp-hours.

ADVANTAGES OF SERIES AND PARALLEL BATTERY HOOKUP

We briefly described earlier the basic arrangement of both series and parallel battery arrangements. Let's look at a specific comparison between the batteries used on a typical diesel highway truck of 325-350 bhp.

Manufacturers of diesel engines in this power range recommend that two 8DR205 or equivalent batteries connected in parallel be used, utilizing the 12 volt high output type starting motor.

However, some truck manufacturers use four 4HR150T or equivalent batteries connected in series/parallel which connects all of the batteries together for starting.

An example of the two systems is shown in Fig. 3-11.

The two 12 volt batteries connected in parallel give a system voltage of 12 volts, but a capacity of 410 amp hour. The system terminal voltage of this arrangement as per the cold cranking test after a 30-second discharge at 300 amperes and 0°F (26.7°C) equals 9.8 volts.

However, with the two 12-volt battery arrangement, fewer terminals are required to make the connections, and consequently, there is less potential of voltage drops due to loose or corroded terminals. This is particularly important to ensure adequate voltage to the starter motor solenoid.

Figure 3-11(b) shows four batteries connected in a series/parallel arrangement. The system voltage is equal to 12 volts, with a capacity of 300 amp hour, since each 6-volt battery is rated at 150 amp hour each. These four 6-volt batteries are classified as an automotive rated battery hookup, therefore unlike the two 12-volt 8DR205 diesel rated batteries, the 30-second diesel rating is not applicable. The system terminal voltage of the four 6-volt batteries after a 5-second discharge at 300 amperes and 0°F (26.7°C) is equal to 9.4 volts.

With the 6-volt arrangement, there are more potential voltage drops which can hamper cranking motor operation, due to the number of connections which are required in this type of system. One major advantage that the parallel system offers is economy, since it is more economical to replace the smaller batteries than the larger 12-volt 205 amp hour units. However, the smaller batteries are of lower capacity and will require more frequent replacement due to cycling (discharging and charging). Therefore, while the series/parallel system is adequate for moderate cold weather operation, the recommended system will provide better sustained cranking motor operation in colder climates. In summation, we have the following:

Series Connection The system capacity is equal to that of one battery (amperage),

while the voltage is equal to that of all the batteries.

Parallel Connection The system capacity (amperes), is equal to the sum of all the batteries, while the voltage is equal to that of only one battery.

BATTERY TERMINAL POST DIMENSIONS

The dimension of the battery posts for all batteries is established by the Society of Automotive Engineers (SAE). The dimensions for these posts, both the positive and negative, are shown in Fig. 3-12.

When battery posts wear through continual removal of the terminal clamps, eventually the connection between the post and clamp can no longer be kept tight. When this situation occurs, the battery post can be repaired by using a small mold placed around the worn or damaged post, and pouring melted lead into the mold and allowing it to harden. Fig. 3-12 shows how to maintain the repaired battery post to the correct specification.

THREADED BATTERY TERMINAL POSTS

Many heavy duty batteries employ threaded terminal posts rather than the clamp type arrangement. When threaded posts are used, they must meet the specifications shown in Fig. 3-13.

SIDE MOUNT BATTERY TERMINALS

Many current automotive type batteries are designed with side-mount terminals, rather than with the long used top-mounted terminals. These side-mount terminals are used because they allow a lower overall battery height. Many of the newer

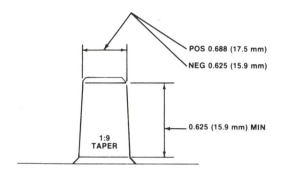

Fig. 3-12. Battery post dimensions. (Courtesy of Society of Automotive Engineers)

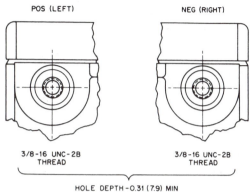

Fig. 3-14. Side-mounted battery terminal specifications. (Courtesy of Society of Automotive Engineers)

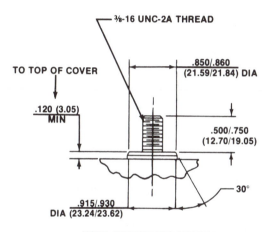

NOTE: DIMENSIONS ARE IN (mm)

CAUTION: Stud length, cable eyelet thickness and terminal nut must be compatible to insure reliable connections. Consult battery supplier for specific stud length.

Fig. 3-13. Threaded battery terminal specifications. (Courtesy of Society of Automotive Engineers)

maintenance-free batteries employ this type of design. Specifications for these side-mount terminals are shown in Fig. 3-14, and battery classification, ratings, and dimensions are listed in Table 3-3.

BATTERY CABLES

Battery cables are classified as low tension cable, since they are seldom required to conduct voltage in excess of 12 through 32 volts. Anything under 50 volts is accepted as being low tension.

SAE specifies three types of general cable for this purpose:

- Type SGT - Starter or ground. Thermoplastic insulated.
- Type SGR - Starter or ground. Synthetic rubber insulated.
- Type SGX - Starter or ground. Cross linked polyethylene insulated.

The wire used is either bunched, concentric or rope stranded, and is manufactured of annealed copper wire. The cross-sectional area of these stranded wires should not be less than the values specified in Table 3-4.

Table 3-3
Battery Classifications, Ratings, and Dimensions

TABLE 1—BATTERY CLASSIFICATIONS, RATINGS AND DIMENSIONS

6 Volt		Ref. No.	Electrical Values Cold Cranking Test		Reserve Capacity Min	Maximum Overall Dimensions						Over Charge Life Units
SAE No.	Assembly Fig. No.		at 0°F (-17.8°C) A	at -20°F (-28.9°C) A		Length		Width		Height		
						mm	in	mm	in	mm	in	
6 Volt Batteries												
1-475	2	1M1	475	380	159	231	9.13	181	7.13	231	9.13	4
1-545	2	1M1A	545	460	185	231	9.13	181	7.13	231	9.13	4
2-520	2	1M2	520	410	192	263	10.38	181	7.13	231	9.13	4
2-560	2	1H2	560	480	220	263	10.38	181	7.13	238	9.38	7
2-650	2	1H2A	650	545	245	263	10.38	181	7.13	238	9.38	7
2-775	2	1H2B	775	610	295	263	10.38	181	7.13	238	9.38	7
2E-595	5	8H2A	595	510	210	492	19.38	104	4.13	238	9.38	5
3EH-830	5	8T2	830	675	340	492	19.38	110	4.34	248	9.77	10
4EH-880	5	ST3	880	700	420	492	19.38	127	5.00	248	9.77	13
2N-495	1	4M2	495	420	170	254	10.00	141	5.57	228	9.00	4
4-700	2	1H4	700	570	275	333	13.13	181	7.13	238	9.35	9
4-720	2	1H4A	720	590	280	333	13.13	181	7.13	238	9.38	9
4-860	2	1T4	860	750	380	330	13.03	178	7.04	241	9.52	18
5D-800	2	2H5	800	675	340	349	13.75	181	7.13	238	9.39	10
7D-900	2	6T3A	900	650	430	428	16.88	193	7.63	276	10.88	13
7DS-900	2		900	650	430	405	15.94	193	7.63	276	10.88	13

12 Volt		Ref. No.	Electrical Values Cold Cranking Test		Reserve Capacity Min	Maximum Overall Dimensions						Over Charge Life Units
SAE No.	Assembly Fig. No.		at 0°F (-17.8°C) A	at -20°F (-28.9°C) A		Length		Width		Height		
						mm	in	mm	in	mm	in	
12 Volt Batteries												
3EE-290	9	13M2	290	230	85	490	19.32	110	4.35	225	8.88	7
3ET-425	9-C	13TC2	425	340	120	490	19.32	110	4.35	249	9.82	9
20H-235	10-C	9HCO	235	170	45	198	7.82	173	6.82	238	9.38	4
21-325	10-J		325	250	68	208	8.19	173	6.81	222	8.77	7
22R-290	11	10MO	290	215	72	228	8.99	173	6.84	227	8.97	5
22R-290/1	11-L-J		290	210	65	227	8.96ᵃ	174	6.86	214	8.44	8
22R-350	11-L-J		350	270	88	227	8.96ᵃ	174	6.86	214	8.44	10
24R-440	11-L-J		440	320	120	260	10.35ᵃ	174	6.86	227	8.94	14
24R-455	11-J		455	340	135	261	10.27	173	6.81	228	8.97	15
22NF-245	11-F	18M1	245	185	52	239	9.44	139	5.50	226	8.91	5
22F-260	11-F-J	17MJ1D	260	190	50	241	9.50	173	6.82	214	8.46	5
22F-305	11-F-J	17MJ1C	305	210	75	241	9.50	172	6.79	207	8.17	5
24-255	10	9M3A	255	190	60	260	10.25	173	6.82	225	8.88	5
24-285	10-J-C	9MJ3C	285	220	75	260	10.25	173	6.82	225	8.88	5
24-305	10	9M3B	305	210	75	260	10.25	173	6.82	225	8.88	5
24-305/1	10	9M3F	305	230	68	260	10.25	171	6.75	225	8.88	5
24H-365	10	9H3A	365	280	98	260	10.25	173	6.82	238	9.38	7
24-375	10-C	9MC3A	375	300	86	260	10.25	173	6.82	247	9.75	9
24T-380	10-J	9TJ3	380	290	113	260	10.25	172	6.79	220	8.67	7
24-385/1	10-J	9MJ3D	385	280	95	260	10.25	172	6.79	222	8.76	8
24-385/2	10-J	9MJ3K	385	305	110	260	10.25	173	6.82	226	8.90	8
24-410	10-J	9MJ3G	410	310	110	260	10.25	173	6.84	227	8.97	6
24R-350	11	10M3	350	280	99	261	10.30	173	6.82	225	8.88	9
27-360	10-J	9MJ6A	360	280	110	306	12.04	173	6.82	225	8.88	9
27-440	10-C	9MC6	440	350	102	304	12.00	171	6.75	222	8.75	9

ᵃAdd 0.5 in for Lifting Ledges.

Many trucks today employ Delco batteries that are identified by the model numbers 1110, 1150, or 1200. These model numbers refer to the type of operation they should be used in. For example, the 1110 model is a high power battery with 625 amps of cold cranking power, the 1150 model is recommended where long periods of idling are encountered, and the 1200 model is recommended for line-haul operation.

BATTERY CLASSIFICATIONS, RATINGS AND DIMENSIONS

SAE No.	Assembly Fig. No.	Ref. No.	Electrical Values Cold Cranking Test at 0°F (-17.8°C) A	at -20°F (-28.9°C) A	Reserve Capacity Min	Length mm	Length in	Width mm	Width in	Height mm	Height in	Over Charge Life Units
27H-435	10	9H5	435	340	125	297	11.72	173	6.82	238	9.38	9
27-500	10		500	400	140	306	12.06	173	6.81	222	8.75	10
27-620	10		620	496	162	305	12.00	173	6.81	223	8.75	—
27R-430	11	10M7	430	320	125	305	12.01	173	6.81	227	8.95	9
27R-455	11	10H7	455	355	136	305	12.01	173	6.81	232	9.15	14
27HF-425	11-F	17H3A	425	320	136	317	12.50	173	6.82	232	9.15	15
27HF-435	11-F	17H3	435	340	125	317	12.50	173	6.82	232	9.15	9
29NF-290	11-F	18M3	290	235	80	330	13.00	141	5.56	228	9.00	4
30H-460	10	9H9	460	330	158	342	13.50	173	6.82	238	9.38	13
30H-580	10	9H9A	580	480	175	342	13.50	172	6.81	233	9.21	13
31-475	18		475	375	130	333	13.13	173	6.80	239	9.41	—
32N-350	11	11M6	350	280	115	361	14.25	139	5.50	226	8.91	9
53-210	14	14M2A	210	155	40	331	13.07	121	4.79	211	8.32	4
60-360	12	15M4A	360	280	110	331	13.07	159	6.27	225	8.88	9
71-275	17-J		275	210	60	208	8.19	179	7.05	216	8.51	—
71-350	17-J		350	270	80	208	8.19	179	7.05	216	8.51	—
72-275/1	17-J	22MJ1A	275	210	60	231	9.10	184	7.27	222	8.77	5
73-430	17-J		430	330	100	231	9.10	179	7.05	216	8.51	—
74-335	17-J	22MJ2A	335	270	98	260	10.25	184	7.27	222	8.77	8
74-410	17-J	22MJ2B	410	310	110	260	10.25	184	7.27	222	8.77	8
74-455	17-J	22MJ2C	455	360	140	260	10.25	184	7.27	222	8.77	9
74-465	17-J		465	375	125	261	10.28	179	7.05	216	8.51	—
U1-160	10	23LO	160	110	23	198	7.80	133	5.25	187	7.38	3
U1-200	10	23LOA	200	150	32	198	7.80	133	5.25	187	7.38	3

SAE No.	Assembly Fig. No.	Ref. No.	Electrical Values Cold Cranking Test at 0°F (-17.8°C) A	at -20°F (-28.9°C) A	Reserve Capacity Min	Length mm	Length in	Width mm	Width in	Height mm	Height in	Over Charge Life Units
4D-640	8	20T4A	640	450	285	539[b]	21.25[b]	222	8.75	276	10.88	9
4D-800	8	20T4B	800	640	310	539[b]	21.25[b]	222	8.75	276	10.88	9
8D-900[a]	8	20T8A	900	650	430	539[b]	21.25[b]	282	11.13	276	10.88	13
		21T1 21T2 1H2C 1H4B 9H9B	See SAE J930a									

[a] Ratings for batteries recommended for motorcoach and bus service are for double insulation. When double insulation is used in other types, deduct 15% from the rating values for cold cranking.
[b] Dimensions over handles.

BATTERY CLASSIFICATIONS, RATINGS AND DIMENSIONS FOR NEW BATTERIES

Temporary SAE No.	Volts	Assembly Fig. No.	Ref. Application	Recommended Electrical Values Cold Cranking Test at 0°F (-17.8°C) A	at -20°F (-28.9°C) A	Reserve Capacity Min	Length mm	Length in	Width mm	Width in	Height mm	Height in	O.C. Unit
T54-310	12	19-K	Ford	310	220	60	186	7.34	154	6.04	212	8.36	—
T55-380	12	19-K	Ford	380	275	75	218	8.60	154	6.04	212	8.36	—
T56-450	12	19-K	Ford	450	330	90	254	10.02	154	6.04	212	8.36	—
TFG10-600	12	10	Prestolite	600	455	170	333	13.10	180	7.12	248	9.75	—
TFG18-600	12	18	Prestolite	600	455	170	333	13.10	180	7.12	249	9.79	—
TFG10-625	12	10	Prestolite	625	470	170	333	13.10	180	7.12	248	9.75	—
TFG18-625	12	18	Prestolite	625	470	170	333	13.10	180	7.12	249	9.79	—
T25-430	12	10-J	Chrysler	430	270	100	222	8.77	170	6.67	224	8.82	—
T24-440	12	10-J	Chrysler	440	350	102	260	10.25	173	6.81	222	8.77	—
T61-310	12	20-K	Ford	310	220	60	192	7.57	160	6.30	225	8.86	—
T62-380	12	20-K	Ford	380	275	75	225	8.87	160	6.30	225	8.86	—
T63-450	12	20-K	Ford	450	330	90	258	10.14	160	6.30	225	8.86	—
T64-475	12	20-K	Ford	475	355	120	296	11.64	160	6.30	225	8.86	—

(Courtesy of Society of Automotive Engineers)

Table 3-4. Stranded Wire Conductor for Batteries

SAE Wire Size	Metric Wire Size, mm²	SGT				SGR				SGX			
		Nom. Wall		Max. Dia.		Nom. Wall		Max. Dia.		Nom. Wall		Max. Dia.	
		in	mm	in	mm	in	mm	in	mm	in	mm	in	mm
6ᵃ	13.0	.060	1.52	.340	7.36	.047	1.19	.340	7.36	.043	1.09	.300	6.49
4ᵃ	19.0	.065	1.65	.420	8.86	.047	1.19	.420	8.86	.065	1.65	.420	8.86
2	32.0	.065	1.65	.505	12.74	.065	1.65	.505	12.74	.065	1.65	.505	12.74
1	40.0	.065	1.65	.557	13.86	.065	1.65	.557	13.86	.065	1.65	.557	13.86
0	50.0	.065	1.65	.600	14.95	.065	1.65	.600	14.95	.065	1.65	.600	14.95
2/0	62.0	.065	1.65	.655	16.15	.065	1.65	.655	16.15	.065	1.65	.655	16.15
3/0	81.0	.078	1.98	.750	18.67	.078	1.98	.750	18.67	—	—	—	—
4/0	103.0	.078	1.98	.810	19.73	.078	1.98	.810	19.73	—	—	—	—

ᵃThe 6 and 4 gage wall thickness can be the same as for GPT.
ᵇMetric dimensions are not direct conversion from inches.

(Courtesy of Society of Automotive Engineers)

BATTERY SELECTION

The actual life of a battery is based upon certain standard practices that must be followed for long life with a minimum of trouble.

Selection of the proper battery is one of the most important criteria in establishing long trouble-free life from the battery. The total electrical load of the electrical system must first be calculated, and then the type of vehicle or equipment operation and application must be analyzed carefully prior to selecting the best battery for the job. Buying a large heavy-duty battery that has a high amperage rating may seem like a good idea; however, if the operating conditions are such that high electrical loads are constantly placed upon the battery during periods of low state of charge conditions from the alternator or generator, then the battery will continually suffer from a low state of charge condition.

If the engine operates constantly at low rpm, then the alternator/generator used must be capable of producing a high charge rate at this slow speed to maintain the battery in a fully charged state, especially if high electrical loads are constantly in use at these low speeds. In addition, increasing the electrical load on the circuit by introducing a variety of add-on accessories may exceed the reserve power capability of the battery as well as the charging system. The system must be designed to ensure that the total load placed upon it can in fact be handled by both the battery and charging system adequately.

Most electrical systems in use on cars, trucks and other forms of equipment are designed to handle all types of conditions; however, special situations may require a reevaluation of the design and load-carrying capacity of the existing circuit.

The introduction of the maintenance-free type of batteries has done much to reduce the minor service checks required on the battery; however, there are other regular service checks, inspections, and tests that are required. Generally, the battery can be serviced and checked on the vehicle or equipment, but if continued problems are encountered that indicate a possible battery problem, then the battery should be removed for further testing and analysis.

SAFETY PRECAUTIONS PRIOR TO SERVICING

Anytime that maintenance or service is to be carried out on the battery or batteries, it is extremely important that you appreciate the possible dangers that can occur through neglect and failure to follow certain safety precautions.

Batteries can explode; therefore, do not develop poor work habits around batteries. The sulphuric acid within the battery is poisonous and can also cause severe burns. Explosive gases are also generated from batteries while in normal use and also while on charge.

Therefore keep sparks, open flames, burning cigarettes or cigars, and other ignition sources well clear of the battery at all times. To protect yourself, wear safety glasses when working around the battery. Avoid leaning directly over the battery when it is on charge since gassing at each cell will emanate a high concentration of poisonous sulphuric acid fumes. The same precaution should be exercised while testing or jump starting the battery. Do not lay wrenches, screwdrivers or other tools on the top of the battery at any time, since they can act as perfect conductors between cell connectors on the exposed-type batteries, or can short out the battery between the positive and negative posts.

Do not break live circuits at the battery terminals, since a spark will normally occur at any point in the circuit when a live circuit is broken.

If the battery is to be charged, be sure that the charger cable clamps or booster cable leads are clean and have a solid connection. Poor electrical connections between clamps and the battery terminal posts can easily create an electrical arc which may cause ignition of the gas mixture from the battery causing an explosion.

When a battery is on charge, avoid using a voltmeter across either the exposed-type cell connectors or the positive and negative posts, since any scratching movement by the end of the voltmeter leads to obtain a good connection can also create a spark causing the battery to explode. Always use a hydrometer to sample the electrolyte and read the specific gravity. This can be converted to a voltage reading if desired according to Table 3-2.

Handling Battery Acid

Battery acid should never be added to a battery that is or has been in service. The only time that sulphuric acid is added to the battery is when it is new and requires activation prior to placing it into service. Most manufacturers supply the correct quantity of acid for each new battery in plastic containers.

However, bulk containers are available and are often used by large fleets where battery turnover is frequent. The acid used in the battery is dilute sulphuric acid which can burn the skin, and can eat its way through clothing very quickly. For this reason, protective clothing should be used, including the use of safety glasses or goggles when using acid. If electrolyte (battery acid) is ever spashed into the eyes, quickly force the eye open and flood it with cool clean water for about five minutes, then immediately see a physician.

If for some reason you were to drink out of a container that had contained some battery acid, drink large quantities of water or milk, and follow this up with milk of magnesia, or a beaten egg or vegetable oil, and contact a doctor.

Electrolyte spilled on clothing or painted surfaces can be neutralized with a solution of baking soda and water, then rinsed with clean water. Should it be necessary for you to prepare a given volume of electrolyte, always pour the concentrated acid into water slowly; and never add the water to the acid, since spattering of the liquid would result because of the high heat generated through the chemical reaction. It is advisable to gently stir the liquid while the acid is being added to the water.

Carrying Batteries

When moving batteries from one spot to another, use a battery cart, or if only one battery is to be moved a short distance, a battery carrier such as shown in Fig. 3-20 should be used.

USING A HYDROMETER

Hydrometers are used in industry for a variety of reasons, but more specifically to check the specific gravity of a liquid. Hydrometers can be used, for example, on automotive applications to check the condition of the coolant in the cooling system, or the electrolyte within the battery. The same hydrometer, however, is not used for both purposes. Another place that the hydrometer is used is in wine or beer processing, where the brewmaster monitors the specific gravity of the liquid to determine when it is ready for bottling.

The specific gravity of the battery electrolyte is a unit of measurement that allows us to quickly determine the condition of the battery by analyzing the sulphuric acid content of the individual cells.

The recommended and accepted specific gravity for 12-volt or 6-volt batteries is 1.265 corrected to a temperature of 80°F (26.6°C).

If the cell electrolyte reads 1.265, it signifies that the battery is fully charged, with the electrolyte containing approximately 36 percent sulphuric acid by weight or 25 percent by volume. The remaining 64 percent (75 percent by volume) is made up of pure water.

Sulphuric acid in its pure concentrated form has a specific gravity of 1.835 while water has a specific gravity of 1.000. The concentration of the cell electrolyte within the battery is therefore 1.265 times heavier than pure water.

Although these specific gravity readings are shown as 1.265 for example, the accepted industry jargon for this reading would be twelve sixty-five; similarly a reading of 1.230, would be called twelve-thirty.

Types of Hydrometers

Several types and styles of hydrometers are readily available and used in the industry for checking the specific gravity of the battery electrolyte.

These various types are shown in the following figures.

Bulb-type Hydrometer

This is the most commonly used type of hydrometer, and is available in several basic styles.

The hydrometer in Fig. 3-15 contains a built-in thermometer encased in the rubber shock-proof mount at its base. This is extremely handy, since you may recollect from earlier discussion that the specific gravity of the electrolyte must be corrected for variations in temperature by adding or subtracting points from the scale when the temperature is above or below 80°F (26.7°C). This correction factor is 0.004 specific gravity points for each 10°F (5.5°C) above or below 80°F (26.7°C). You add 0.004 points to the specific gravity scale for each 10°F increase beyond 80°F, and you subtract 0.004 points for every 10°F below 80°F.

When using the hydrometer care should be exercised when placing the tube end into the battery cell. Don't jam this into the cell, because damage to the tops of the

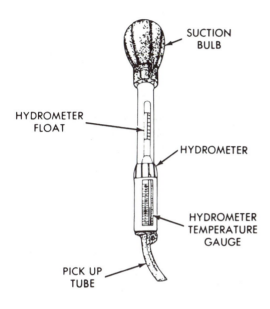

Fig. 3-15. Bulb-type hydrometer.

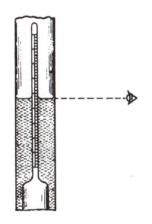

Fig. 3-16. Reading the battery electrolyte hydrometer. (Courtesy of International-Harvester)

separators can result. Gently squeeze the bulb end prior to inserting the hydrometer into the cell electrolyte, then release the bulb gently. This allows a sample of electrolyte to be drawn up into the glass tube. The float within the glass tube will rise and

stay suspended at a given position depending on the specific gravity of the liquid.

To properly read the hydrometer, wear a pair of safety glasses to prevent any possible eye damage from electrolyte splash, then hold the hydrometer steady, and straight up and down as shown in Fig. 3-16; place your eye level with the electrolyte within the hydrometer glass and read the specific gravity on the float. Remember to correct for temperature to 80°F (26.7°C)

Some hydrometers use a series of little balls within the glass tube rather than a float. When a sample of electrolyte is taken, the number of balls that float establishes the percentage state of charge of each cell. Earlier in this chapter a specific gravity versus voltage chart (Table 3-2) was given which can be referred to in order to establish the state of charge of the battery from the sample readings taken by the hydrometer.

CAUTION: Avoid the possibility of allowing sample electrolyte to drip onto your skin, clothing, the vehicle, or painted surfaces.

REFRACTOMETER TEST

A relatively new device that can also be used to check the specific gravity of each cell is a refractometer that employs the basic principle of light refraction or the bending of light rays through a sample of the electrolyte to establish its specific gravity. Fig. 3-17 shows this test instrument.

The device shown in Fig. 3-17 is manufactured by American Optical, Scientific Instrument Division, and it can be used for testing the coolant and battery specific gravity readings. For this reason, the in-

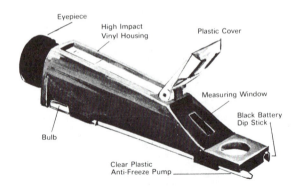

Eyepiece

High Impact
Vinyl Housing

Plastic Cover

Measuring Window

Black Battery
Dip Stick

Bulb

Clear Plastic
Anti-Freeze Pump

Fig. 3-17. Refractometer battery electrolyte tester. (Courtesy of AO Scientific Instruments)

strument is called a Duo-Chek tester by the manufacturer.

The tester is designed specifically for rapid and accurate checking of permanent antifreeze protection, and for checking the condition of the battery state of charge by sampling the electrolyte. It requires only several drops of either coolant or battery acid, depending on which specific gravity you wish to test. The Duo-Chek tester automatically compensates for temperature changes.

Prior to using the tester, swing back the plastic cover at the slanted end as shown in Fig. 3-18. Wipe clean and dry both the measuring window and the bottom of the plastic cover.

Once the tester has been cleaned with tissue or a clean soft cloth, close the plastic cover. To use the tester, do not remove the clear plastic pump from the tester, but release the tip of the pump from the tester housing if a coolant condition test is required.

To test the specific gravity of the battery electrolyte, use the small black dip-stick from the side of the tester to obtain a sample of battery acid. Place a few drops of acid onto the measuring surface through the opening in the cover plate as shown in Fig. 3-18(b).

Reading the Duo-Chek Tester

Several precautions must be exercised when attempting to read the Duo-Chek tester. Never open the plastic cover of the tester when taking readings, since evaporation of water from the fluid sample being tested can affect the reading. Cautions given above for any time that battery acid is being handled hold true here.

Make sure that the eyepiece is in fact completely free of any battery electrolyte before you attempt to look into the measuring window. Rinse the window with clear fresh water and wipe it dry prior to and after testing the sample. American Optical suggests that both safety glasses and gloves be worn when testing acid or caustic solutions.

Refer to Fig. 3-19, and point the tester towards a bright source of light as you look into the eyepiece.

The specific gravity reading on the tester measuring surface, will be at the point where the dividing line between light and dark (edge of the shadow) crosses the scale as shown in the sample reading of Fig. 3-19(b). Note that the scale shows the battery specific gravity on the left-hand side, while the right-hand side of the scale relates to permanent type antifreeze solution.

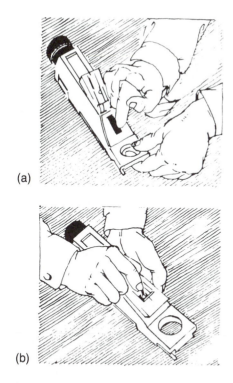

(a)

(b)

Fig. 3-18. (a) Preparing Duo-Chek refractometer battery electrolyte tester for test. (b) Placing drops of battery acid onto Duo-Chek tester. (Courtesy of AO Scientific Instruments)

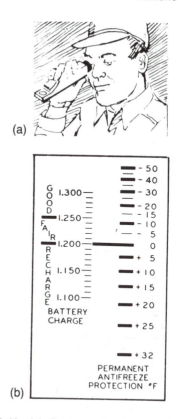

(a)

(b)

Fig. 3-19. (a) Reading the tester, (b) sample reading. (Courtesy of AO Scientific Instruments)

If the reading cannot be properly or accurately read because the edge of the shadow is not sharp enough, the surface of the measuring window probably was not clean enough, therefore wipe the surface clean again, and take another sample. Repeat this procedure for each battery cell.

BATTERY TEMPERATURE VERSUS CRANKING POWER

The battery or surrounding ambient air temperature will cause not only a change in the temperature of the battery electrolyte, but will also increase the frictional drag on rotating engine parts (e.g., while the engine is being cranked) due to oil viscosity changes. Similar cranking can also be encountered in hot weather if the battery's state of charge is low, or if a replacement battery has been installed that is not of the same rating as the replaced unit.

Additional electrical loads placed upon the system can create additional loads on the battery, or if driving conditions are stop-and-go all day long, the battery may not receive a sufficient rate of charge from the generator/alternator.

In summation, battery power, or cranking power, is reduced as the battery temperature is lowered. Table 3-5 shows the typical percentage of output capacity of a fully charged battery at various temperatures.

The base for the 100 percent state of charge is 80°F (26.7°C). Note that a fully charged battery at 0°F (-17.8°C), gives only an equivalent cranking power of 40 percent of what it can produce at 80°F (26.7°C).

If the battery is at less than a fully charged state, it will provide even less of its output capacity as the temperature drops. Therefore, always ensure that the battery can be maintained in a fully charged state in cold weather operation.

BATTERY MAINTENANCE IN VEHICLE

Regular battery maintenance is a normal part of any fleet maintenance program. Obviously, the degree of maintenance will vary slightly between the normal lead-acid and low maintenance or maintenance-free batteries; however, the following checks are typical of what is required.

1. Carefully inspect the battery and its mounting pad, hold down brackets and cables for signs of any loose connections, cracked or broken components, damaged terminal posts or studs, post clamp condition, possible clogged vents or damage to the battery cover, excess dirt build-up, moisture, and corrosion. Any damaged parts should be replaced or repaired immediately.

Figure 3-21 shows these typical checks.

2. If it is necessary to remove the terminal post clamps for cleaning due to corrosion, always remove the ground cable first. If the terminal clamp is tight, do not beat

K-D 2279   Combination Battery Strap

Two-in-one strap designed to carry both top-mounted or side-mounted terminal batteries. Strap made of high strength, acid-resistant plastic. Knurled screws enable it to be used as a charging adapter for side-mounted terminal batteries.

VIP 300 Location 3CH
POP 200 Location DL
K-D 2279

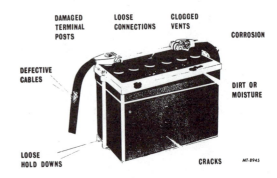

Fig. 3-20. Typical battery strap carrier. (Courtesy of International-Harvester)

Fig. 3-21. Battery inspection. (Courtesy of International Harvester)

Table 3-5
Temperature and Battery Power

Ambient Temperature	Percentage of Battery Capacity (Fully Charged)
80°F (26.7°C)	100 percent
32°F (0°C)	65 percent
0°F (−17.8°C)	40 percent
−20°F (−28.8°C)	20 percent

on it with a hammer, or stretch it beyond use with the use of a large screwdriver. Also avoid prying directly against the top or side of the battery case with a large screwdriver or pry bar in order to remove a tight cable clamp. If the cable clamp is tight, use a battery clamp puller similar to that shown in Fig. 3-22.

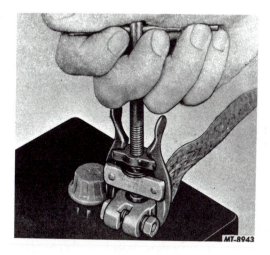

Fig. 3-22. Pulling off a tight battery cable clamp.

Once the terminal clamps have been removed, they can be cleaned in several ways. If excessive corrosion is evident, hot water can be poured over the terminal clamp to remove the major build-up, followed by wire brushing and emery cloth. Special terminal cleaning brushes are available as shown in Fig. 3-23, which can be effectively used for both the battery post and cable clamps.

Battery cable terminal clamps and the top of the battery should be cleaned with a solution of baking soda and water. If excess amounts of corrosion or battery acid exist on the cover of the battery, place all cell caps into place securely, sprinkle baking soda onto the cover which will neutralize the acid, then flush or wash off with clean water. Don't pile the baking soda up on the

cover, since some may enter the individual battery cells and damage the battery.

If the battery cover only has a dusting of acid or corrosion, a wet cloth, baking soda and water can be used.

The top of the battery can be dryed with a low pressure air hose and lint free rag. The battery tray should always be cleaned of corrosion by removal of the battery in order to properly facilitate the job. Wire brush the tray, and paint it with an acid-resistant paint.

Ensure that no nuts, bolts or foreign debris at the base of the battery tray can possibly puncture the battery case. Small hard rocks can also create a problem in this manner by being pounded into the case; therefore, remove any dirt or mud which may contain such dangerous objects.

After the battery and tray have been cleaned and serviced, replace the tray. Take care that the battery hold-down strap is not overtightened since this can lead to case cracking, especially the type of hold-

Fig. 3-23. Cleaning brushes for battery terminals and clamps.

down that runs around the perimeter of the case top. Coat the battery posts and cable terminal clamps with a commercially available terminal grease, and connect the cables to the battery posts. Always connect the grounded cable last; otherwise, severe arcing can occur.

3. On low maintenance type batteries or conventional lead-acid units, the electrolyte level must be checked regularly. The low maintenance batteries require less attention than the conventional type; however, they do require periodic checking.

There is less antimony used in the low maintenance battery than in the conventional, whereas the maintenance-free models contain no antimony at all in the lead of the grid plate.

Odorless drinking water should be added to those batteries that require topping up of the electrolyte. If no level indicator is used on the battery, bring the electrolyte level to 1/2 inch (12.7 mm) above the tops of the separators. On those batteries with a split-guide ring inside the cell filler opening, the electrolyte should be brought to the bottom of this split-guide ring.

Overfilling of the cell will cause the electrolyte to spew from the vent cap when gassing of the battery occurs. Danger of an explosion is increased when this happens, and it causes excessive corrosion to occur on the top of the battery cover and surrounding parts. In addition, short circuits can occur due to this situation.

Maintenance free batteries do not require the addition of water during their lifetime unless the battery has been mounted or carried at an angle in excess of 45 degrees, which allows the electrolyte to spill from the vent holes under the cover. Check the electrolyte level for the specific maintenance free battery as per the manufacturer's instructions.

BATTERY TROUBLESHOOTING

Battery troubles are generally a result of poor maintenance practices and neglect. Hard starting can be a direct result of high-circuit resistance caused by corrosion of battery terminals or associated wiring, loose wires, etc. Do not declare the battery to be faulty until you have checked these other causes first.

The purpose of a battery test is to determine the following:

1. If the battery is satisfactorily charged and can therefore remain in service.

2. If the battery has a low state of charge, and therefore requires recharging prior to placing it back into service.

3. If the battery has failed, is not serviceable, and must therefore be replaced.

Proper testing of the battery should include the following:

1. Visual inspection for physical damage

2. Specific gravity check of each cell with the use of a battery hydrometer

3. Battery capacity check, or what is commonly referred to as a load test

Visual Inspection

This involves a close check of all areas of the battery case, cover, terminals, hold down areas, and cell covers (nonmaintenance-free type) for possible damage. A check of the electrolyte level must also be done. On maintenance-free type batteries, if there has been a loss of electrolyte due to the battery being tipped beyond 45 degrees, electrolyte can spill from the cover vent holes. To gain access to the battery cells on the maintenance-free models, the cover can be removed or the top plaque center section can be cut with a sharp knife blade as shown in Fig. 3-24.

In Fig. 3-24, the battery decal is imprinted with dotted lines; carefully cut along these dotted lines with a sharp knife blade, then carefully pry up the ends of the vent manifold with a small screwdriver. Manually pull the vent manifold straight up in order to expose the cells. After checking the electrolyte level and specific gravity, reinsert the manifold into position, and firmly push it into place until it snaps tightly closed. Acid-resistant tape can be placed over the vent manifold to effect a good seal.

On certain models of maintenance-free batteries (top terminal), after removal of the vent manifold, individual caps are exposed that cover each cell. If a maintenance-free battery requires the addition of water to its cells, add water to just above the tops of the separators, then charge the battery for about 15 minutes at 15 to 25 amperes in order to mix the water with the electrolyte.

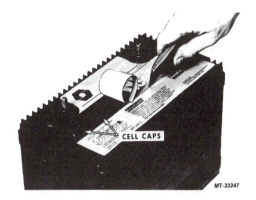

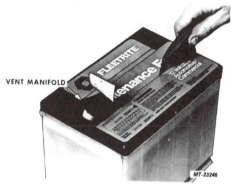

Fig. 3-24. Cutting the top plaque on the battery cover of IHC maintenance-free type batteries. (Courtesy of International-Harvester)

SPECIFIC GRAVITY TEST

If the specific gravity test of the battery after charging, or prior to charging (no additional water added), is 1.225 or higher when corrected to 80°F (26.7°C), this indicates that the battery is at least in a 75 percent charged state, and the load test can now be performed as described under Battery Capacity or Load Test.

If, however, the specific gravity readings are lower than 1.225 but are within 0.050 points between the highest and lowest cells, recharge the battery as recommended in Table 3-10. If the battery state of charge is low, it usually indicates that some problem exists in the vehicle or equipment charging circuit.

Should the specific gravity readings show a variation in excess of 0.050 points between the individual cells, the battery should be replaced because the weak cells will eventually pull the good cells down to their level, as the good cells have to compensate for the weak ones.

Some manufacturers specify that a fully charged battery should have a specific gravity of 1.265, while others state 1.270 corrected in both cases to 80°F (26.7°C), therefore any reading between 1.265 to 1.270 can be considered acceptable for a fully charged battery. In special environments such as subzero or tropical climates, a fully charged battery may read as high as 1.290 or as low as 1.225 respectively. These readings of course are adjusted to suit the particular climate in which the battery will operate.

BATTERY TESTING AND EVALUATION

When any battery is suspected of being faulty, it is important that you follow the manufacturer's recommended procedures in order to positively determine whether or not the battery in question can be:

1. Recharged and placed back into service
2. Boost charged and placed back into service
3. Replaced due to being unserviceable
4. Is perfectly satisfactory, and requires no service

There are a variety of tests that can be done on the battery; not all of these tests are required since each manufacturer lists what they consider acceptable test procedures for their particular brand of battery. However, many of these tests are considered common to all batteries, and each one is listed and explained in the following pages.

Two basic tests are in fact undertaken which will cover all types of batteries in use both in cars and heavy-duty service such as diesel trucks and equipment. These two basic tests are:

1. The hydrometer (specific gravity) test.

2. The voltage test which can only be used on batteries with exposed cell connectors, or removable vent (filler) caps, because it is important that each cell can be individually monitored. Table 3-2 allows you to correlate specific gravity and voltage readings.

NOTE: Maintenance-free batteries cannot be checked for specific gravity with a hydrometer, since they have a sealed cover; however, they do include their own built-in hydrometer for evaluating the condition of the battery. A voltmeter can be used across the battery terminals to monitor the actual overall voltage of the battery at any time with a battery voltage tester as shown in Fig. 3-25.

Several battery manufacturers state that prior to testing the battery, the specific gravity of the electrolyte should be at a minimum of 1.225 to 1.230 (2.075 to 2.08 volts per cell). However, this is necessary only prior to conducting a high-rate discharge test or a full-load battery test.

One test that can be undertaken on batteries with exposed cell connectors is the monitoring of each cell with a voltmeter. Hard cover type batteries require the use of a hydrometer in order to evaluate cell condition by removing each cell vent plug or filler cap, and the maintenance-free type requires monitoring of the built-in hydrometer, plus the use of a voltmeter.

Several types of battery load-testing equipment are available commercially, and the equipment shown here for illustration may not necessarily be common to your shop or service dealership. However, regardless of the particular brand of testing equipment used, the end results obtained are the same. When special test equipment is unavailable, many service personnel use a simple carbon-pile and a bank of head-

New State of the Art Battery Tester K-D 2692 Battery Voltage Tester

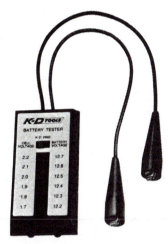

Accuracy is assured with this battery voltage tester which measures both total battery output and individual cell voltage. More accurate than specific gravity.

Quick, direct LED readings let you determine battery condition before recharging. Tests conventional & maintenance free batteries.

Readings within .1 volt indicate battery voltage; if voltage is low check each cell with the same .1 volt accuracy. Fluctuation of .2 volts or more indicates a bad cell.

These two simple tests are illustrated below.

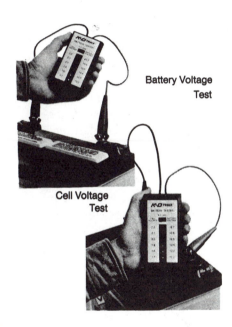

Battery Voltage Test

Cell Voltage Test

Fig. 3-25. Battery and cell voltage test with model KD2692 LED tester. (Courtesy of KD Manufacturing Co., Lancaster, PA.)

lights along with a resistor arrangement in order to apply the necessary load to a battery for testing purposes.

When a battery is suspected of being faulty or in a low state of charge, a quick check that is often used is known as the light load voltage test which is explained below.

Light Load Voltage Test (Use on New Batteries)

This test is a simple and quick check which allows you to evaluate each individual cell voltage prior to charging the battery. If the battery is charged before the light load test, it is possible for any defective cell to give a false reading and therefore pass the test. Batteries with one-piece covers should be tested by the specific gravity test, and not by the voltage method! For the light-load test, use an expanded scale voltmeter with 0.01 scale divisions on its face.

Conduct the light load test as follows:

1. Check and adjust (top up) the electrolyte in each cell by the addition of distilled water if necessary.

2. In order to remove the surface charge from the battery, two methods can be used.

(a) By energizing the starter motor for three seconds; to prevent the engine from starting, pull the high-tension lead from the coil on a gasoline engine; or on a diesel engine, place the fuel stop lever in the off position.

(b) If the battery is not in the equipment, place a 150 ampere load across the battery.

3. For a period of one minute, place a light load on the battery such as turning on the headlights, or place a 10 ampere load across the battery terminals when the battery is not installed in the equipment.

4. Check the voltage of each cell after this one minute time period by placing the prods of the voltmeter across the individual (+) and (-) cell connectors. It is only necessary at this time to note the highest and the lowest cell voltage readings.

5. Once all cell voltages have been monitored, the battery condition can be evaluated as follows:

(a) The battery is in satisfactory condition if all of the cell voltages read 1.95 volts (1.100 specific gravity) or higher, with the difference between cells being less than 0.05 volts.

(b) The battery requires charging if the cell voltages are both above and below 1.95 volts (1.100 specific gravity), but the maximum variation between cell readings is less than 0.05 volts.

(c) Replace the battery if any individual cell reads 1.95 volts or more, and there is a difference of 0.05 volts or greater between cells.

(d) Boost charge the battery if all of the cells read less than 1.95 volts (1.100 SG), and repeat the test.

NOTE: After boost charging should the battery cells still fail to read 1.95 volts (1.100 SG), boost charge it once more, and if any cell fails to read a minimum of 1.95 volts (1.100 SG), replace the battery. If, however, the battery does come up to at least 1.95 volts (1.100 SG) per cell after boost charging, then place it on slow charge prior to returning it to service.

Remember that a fully charged battery should read between 1.265 and 1.270 corrected to 80°F (26.7°C) prior to returning it to service. A reading of 1.230 SG is equivalent to a 75% charge, while a specific gravity reading of 1.200 is only 50% charged.

OTHER BATTERY TESTS

The use of the light-load test is usually confined to brand new batteries after activation, although it can be used as simply a quick check once the battery is in service. However, a high-rate discharge test or battery load test is more often used to check the ability of the battery to deliver current under load. The instrument used for this purpose is basically a high-capacity or variable resistor. Cell or terminal voltage is used to evaluate the condition of the battery after discharging.

IN-SERVICE BATTERY CAPACITY OR LOAD TEST

Satisfactory load testing of the battery can only be accomplished if the specific gravity of the electrolyte is 1.225 or higher when corrected to a temperature of 80°F (26.7°C). Follow the procedure outlined below to conduct a battery load test.

1. If the test is to be done with the battery in the vehicle or equipment, disconnect both battery cables at the terminal posts, and be sure to always disconnect the grounded cable first.

2. Connect the battery load tester leads (Fig. 3-26) to the respective battery terminals. If the tester leads are red and black, which is usual, the red lead would be connected to the positive battery terminal, while the black lead would be connected to the negative battery terminal.

3. Follow closely the manufacturer's instructions and precautions prior to connecting any leads or undertaking any tests.

4. Each manufacturer will list in their test specifications booklet, what load (amperage draw) should be applied to a particular model of battery, and for what time period. This load should not be exceeded. Similarly, if insufficient load is placed upon the battery, then it may appear serviceable, when in fact it is not.

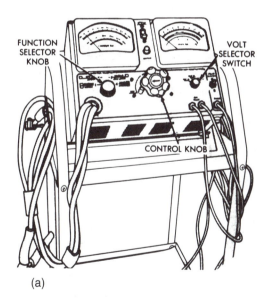

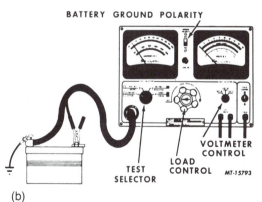

(a) (b)

Fig. 3-26 (a) Load tester mounted on portable dolly; (b) battery load tester connected for test. (Courtesy of Sun Electric Corp.)

IN-SERVICE LOAD TEST OF BATTERIES WITH FILLER CAPS

Prior to load-testing, ensure that the electrolyte level is at the proper level, and that the specific gravity is at a minimum of 1.225, although it is advisable to place the battery on charge to bring it to at least 1.260 at 80°F (26.7°C). Attempting to load test the battery with a low specific gravity will give false readings. Therefore either the battery or the charging system may be at fault, when low specific gravity readings are obtained prior to load testing.

1. Fully charge the battery.

2. Place a 150 amp load on the battery for 3 seconds to remove the surface charge.

3. Place a 10 amp load on the battery and read the voltage from each cell. On vehicles, the headlights can be turned on. Place a resistor across the battery terminals of industrial or marine units such as a 1.2 ohm, 120 watt resistor on 12 volt systems, or a 2.4 ohm resistor, 240 watts on a 24 volt system.

4. If any cell reads 1.95 volts or more, and the difference is less than .05 volts between cells, the battery is in good condition.

5. On some batteries such as Delco conventional batteries used in cars (nonmaintenance-free type), remove the vent caps, and connect a 300 ampere load across the battery terminals for 15 seconds. If a blue haze or smoke is seen in one or more cells, replace the battery.

6. If the battery appears serviceable, connect the specified load as per the Delco test specifications (available from a local dealer), which is generally about three times the ampere-hour rating for 12-volt batteries and about two times the ampere-hour rating for 6-volt batteries.

7. Read the terminal voltage at the end of 15 seconds and compare the readings with those shown in Table 3-6.

PRECAUTIONS ON TESTING MAINTENANCE-FREE TYPE BATTERIES

When testing or charging a maintenance-free type of battery out of the vehicle, special adapter tools are necessary for the side-mount and top screw threaded type of battery terminals. Such an adapter kit is shown in Figure 3-27, which is avail-

Table 3-6. Ambient Temperature

	21°C (70°F and above)	16°C (60°F)	10°C (50°F)	4°C (40°F)	−1°C (30°F)	−7°C (20°F)	−12°C (10°F)	−18°C (0°F)
12-Volt Battery	9.6	9.5	9.4	9.3	9.1	8.9	8.7	8.5
6-Volt Battery	4.8	4.75	4.7	4.6	4.5	4.4	4.3	4.2

ADAPTER CHARGING AND
TESTING TOOL ATTACHED
TO TERMINALS

HEX NUT   ALLIGATOR CLAMPS
LEAD PAD

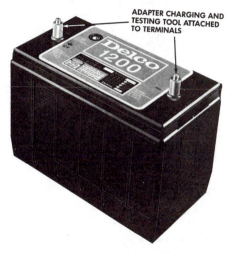

ADAPTER CHARGING AND
TESTING TOOL ATTACHED
TO TERMINALS

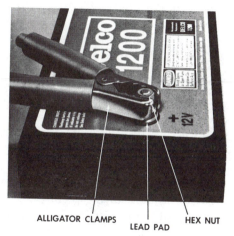

ALLIGATOR CLAMPS   HEX NUT
LEAD PAD

Fig. 3-27. AC Delco battery adapter testing tool ST-1201 for testing and charging freedom batteries. (Courtesy of AC Delco Div. of GMC)

Fig. 3-28. Load clamps securely attached to battery terminals. (Courtesy of AC Delco Div. of GMC)

able from AC-Delco, Part No. ST-1201; this kit is recommended when charging sealed-terminal batteries.

When load testing side-mounted or top-threaded post type Delco maintenance-free batteries, if adapters ST-1201 are not available, it is very important that the leads from the load-tester machine clamps come into contact with the battery terminal lead pads. Tighten down the hex nuts on the threaded battery terminals to hold the load clamps securely as shown in Fig. 3-28.

Note: If the load clamps cannot be securely clamped to the battery lead pads, the suggested load current MUST BE DECREASED as per the manufacturers recommendations in the published test specifications.

LOAD TEST FOR MAINTENANCE-FREE BATTERIES

Prior to load testing the maintenance-free battery, look at the cell test-indicator which should appear green in color. If so, then the battery is in a sufficient state of charge to be tested. A dark color is a positive indication that the battery is in need of charging prior to testing. A light or yellow color, means that the electrolyte level is low and the battery should be replaced. However, certain low maintenance, and some maintenance-free, type batteries can have the vent manifold or battery cover removed as discussed earlier to allow access to the cells for purposes of refilling (if, e.g., the electrolyte has been lost through the battery having been tipped over or mounted at an angle in excess of 45 degrees. Either condition you may recall, allows the electrolyte to spew from the vents of the cover).

However, if the battery does not contain a removable vent manifold, do not attempt charging or testing, but replace the battery. If the maintenance-free battery requires charging, you may have to gently tip the battery slightly from side to side in order to disperse any gas bubbles from the test indicator.

With the battery fully charged, proceed as follows:

1. Connect a 300 ampere load across the battery terminals for 15 seconds in order to remove the surface charge from the battery. With the load turned off, wait at least 15 seconds to allow the battery to recover before proceeding.

2. Complete the load test by connecting a voltmeter and a 235 ampere load across the battery terminals. Read the voltage after 15 seconds, then disconnect the load.

The battery voltage should read as shown in Table 3-6.

CHARGING SYSTEM

A battery may pass the load test, but have an inadequate charge rate for the particular application that it is installed in. Therefore, check and adjust the voltage regulator setting as per the manufacturer's specifications.

An alternator that charges the battery while the engine is idling may be necessary in applications where low idle speeds are a major part of the engine's operating cycle.

LOAD TEST CHARTS

Variations exist in the recommended load test amperes for different makes of batteries. Tables 3-7 and 3-8 show the typical loads required to effectively conduct a load test.

OPEN CIRCUIT VOLTAGE TEST

With the use of an expanded scale voltmeter, the actual voltage across the battery terminals can be determined, or on batteries with exposed cell connectors, individual cell voltages can be established.

A serviceable battery with a low specific gravity will have a voltage reading across the positive and negative battery terminals of less than 12 volts, whereas a battery in good condition would reflect a reading usually in excess of 12.40 volts.

These voltmeter readings are always taken with the battery leads disconnected to ensure an accurate reading.

Tests for maintenance-free heavy-duty

Table 3-7

SPECIFICATIONS

BATTERY MODEL	VOLTS	AMPS FOR LOAD TEST	RESERVE CAPACITY (MINUTES)	COLD CRANKING CURRENT (AMPS)		MAXIMUM DIMENSIONS			APPROX. WEIGHT
				At -18°C (0°F)	At -29°C (-20°F)	LENGTH	WIDTH	HEIGHT (INCL. POSTS)	
1110	12	310*	160	625	490	330 mm (13 in.)	172 mm (6-3/4 in.)	239 mm (9-7/16 in.)	26.8 Kg. (59.2 lbs.)
1150	12	290*	175	580		330 mm (13 in.)	172 mm (6-3/4 in.)	239 mm (9-7/16 in.)	26.9 Kg. (59.3 lbs.)
1200	12	235*	130	475	375	330 mm (13 in.)	172 mm (6-3/4 in.)	239 mm (9-7/16 in.)	24.2 Kg. (53.2 lbs.)

* Battery tester cable clamps should be between terminal nuts and lead pads of terminals. If not possible, load value should be 275 amperes for Model 1110, 260 amperes for Model 1150, and 210 amperes for Model 1200.

(Courtesy of A C Delco Div. of GMC)

Table 3-8

MAINTENANCE FREE BATTERY TEST SPECIFICATIONS

Repl Cat No.	DIMENSIONAL GROUP SIZE		Volts	Amps for Load Test	SAE — BCI Reserve Capacity (Min-utes)	COLD CRANKING CURRENT S.A.E. SPEC J537h		MAXIMUM DIMENSIONS (MM)			APPROX WEIGHT (KG)
	B.C.I.	DELCO — S.A.E.				0 F (-17 c) (in Amps)	-20 F (-29 c) (in Amps)	Length (incl Flanges)	Width	Height (incl Top Post)	
49-5	24F		12	210	100	430	330	270	172	222	17.7
59-5	24		12	210	100	430	330	260	172	222	17.7
55-5	22F		12	180	90	370	300	240	172	210	15.9
71-5	27		12	230	125	500	375	305	172	222	20.9
81-5	27F		12	230	125	500	375	316	172	222	20.9
85-4	71		12	130	60	275	210	207	172	215	12.1
85-5	71		12	170	80	360	270	207	172	215	14.5
87-5	73		12	210	100	430	330	229	172	215	17.0
89-5	74		12	230	125	500	375	260	172	215	19.5
1200	31	31-475	12	235*	130	475	375	330	172	239	24.0

*Battery tester cable clamps should be between terminal nuts and lead pads of terminals. If not possible, load value should be 210 amperes.

(Courtesy of A C Delco Div. of GMC)

batteries have already been given in this chapter. Another example of a maintenance-free battery test specific to Ford products is to first of all give the battery a capacity or load test followed by an open circuit voltage reading if the battery successfully passes the load test.

Should the voltage read less than 12.40 volts, it should be recharged as shown in Table 3-9.

If, however, the battery failed the load test, it should be boost-charged for 15 to 20 minutes, and the load test performed again. If the battery still fails the load test, replace it. If the battery passes the load test after boost-charging, place a voltmeter across the battery terminals, note the voltage, and compare with the minimum acceptable voltages given in Table 3-6.

CHRYSLER THREE-MINUTE CHARGE TEST

If a battery fails the capacity or load test, connect the battery up to a boost charger (portable type), and place a voltmeter across the positive and negative battery posts. (If the battery is in the vehicle, disconnect all leads to it.) Switch on the battery charger timer to the 3 minute level, and with the charger on, adjust the rate of charge to read 40 amperes.

Once the timer cuts off, turn the switch to the fast charge position and carefully note the reading on the voltmeter which you had previously connected across the battery terminals. If the voltmeter reads above 15.5 volts, the battery is most likely sulphated. However, don't discard it until you have placed it on slow charge at a rate recommended for the specific battery under question. Failure of the battery to attain a full charge would signify internal faults, and it should be replaced.

THE FOUR-TWENTY-ONE (421) TEST

This is a test that is done by an automatic charger that is programmed to discharge, then charge the battery. When connected to the battery and switched on, the test machine will apply a load to the battery, after which time the open-circuit voltage is read. The test machine then charges the battery for a given period after which the open-circuit voltage is again noted. The actual difference in voltages is then carefully recorded in order to determine condition of the battery.

Do not charge the battery prior to testing. Check for any damage, and if the battery is in the vehicle, ensure that all electrical accessories are turned off. Ensure that tester leads are properly connected.

Starting the tester allows it to discharge the battery for 15 seconds at 50 amperes. It will then switch off automatically, delay for 5 seconds, then show the open-circuit voltage on the dial face.

NOTE: Current types of 421 testers are equipped with time indicator lights to let you know when they have finished discharging or charging, as the case may be.

The battery is then placed into a charging mode for about 45 seconds to 1 minute, after which the indicator light will signal the completion of charging. Again, note the voltage reading. Comparison of the voltages to the tester manufacturer's recommendations, or to those of the battery manufacturer, will indicate the condition of the battery.

COLD WEATHER ELECTRICAL SERVICE

Preventive maintenance of vehicles and equipment usually improves as the winter months roll around; however, quite often service personnel ignore the necessity for additional maintenance on the electrical system.

In cold weather, starting is difficult if the engine cranking speed is too low. For example, on diesel engines used in trucks, heavy equipment and marine applications, the engine can become hard to start when the cranking speed drops below 150 rpm. Should it drop below 100 rpm, starting may be impossible even with the use of cold weather starting aids.

As far as the electrical system is concerned, where possible use a 24-volt system or the 12-volt high output system to start the engine. Install slave terminals on the batteries to provide for extra power when required. A good electrical system will have a low resistance cranking motor circuit and will recharge the batteries fully before the engine is stopped at the end of each operating shift.

FREEZING OF BATTERIES

Battery electrolyte will freeze at various temperatures depending on its specific gravity. However, the chances of a battery freezing can be minimized by keeping it in a full state of charge at all times in cold weather operation. Table 3-1 shows the temperatures at which the electrolyte within the battery case will freeze.

CAUTION: Under no circumstances add antifreeze to a battery to prevent freezing of the electrolyte. This will damage the battery and render it unfit for use in a short time.

The lower the ambient temperature, the slower will be the chemical reaction within the battery. The effect of low temperature reduces the battery power considerably compared to that which it can produce at 80°F (26.7°C). The effect of this reduction in

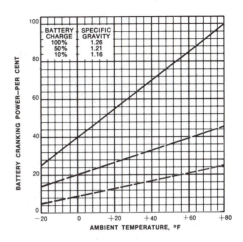

Fig. 3-29. Effect of ambient temperature on battery cranking power.

cranking power is shown in the graph of Fig. 3-29.

BATTERY HEATERS

One method that is used by fleet truck operations is that of a battery box with a heater, especially among diesel engine users during cold weather operation. The types of battery heaters used can be classified as follows:

1. Electric strip heater
2. Forced hot air circulated through the battery box
3. Warm coolant circulated through passages in the battery box

With the electric strip type of heater, the energy source can be an electrical wall socket, readily available at service depots or truck stops. Some electric strip type heaters can be operated directly from the vehicle's own battery power; however, this tends to lower the reserve power needed to start the engine in cold weather. Some trucks do carry a separate battery for this purpose, which is then recharged once the engine is running.

When a battery heater is desired, the actual battery box or compartment must be larger than normal to allow between 5/8 to 3/4 inch (15.87 to 19 mm) thick styrofoam insulation to be placed around all sides of the battery box area. General recommendations are that a 3 inch (7.62 cm) space be designed into the battery box compartment to ensure heating of this area in order to warm the battery.

Figure 3-30 shows the typical arrangement of the electric strip heater which is itself controlled by a temperature sensing device to maintain a temperature of approximately 80°F (26.7°C) inside the battery box compartment.

With the electric strip heater, care must be exercised that the hottest spot at any point in the battery does not exceed 125°F (51.6°C) since battery damgage, plus loss of electrolyte, will occur.

Should the electric strip heater not be considered suitable, and if the engine is in an over-the-road tractor which has occasion to stop at nights, then since the engine would be running at a fast idle for cab heat, some of this heat can be directed to the battery box compartment. However, with the engine running all the time, battery freezing would not occur, although it could drop sufficiently in extreme cold ambients to slow the charging process due to the slower chemical reaction.

Many fleets use in-cab and coolant heaters as well as oil pan heaters where legal. Coolant heat or in-cab heat can be directed through circulation passages in the battery box in order to keep it warm. These heaters would be used only at the service depots where the vehicles are parked at night.

During warm weather operation, any

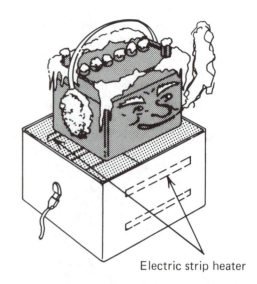

Electric strip heater

Fig. 3-30. Battery box with electric strip heater. (Courtesy of Detroit Diesel Allison, Div. of GMC)

battery box compartment that has been designed for a battery heater should be opened, or the styrofoam and heater removed or disconnected to ensure that the battery receives adequate ventilation. Improper ventilation of the battery area can cause excess gassing and spewing of electrolyte leading to premature battery failure.

WINTER PREVENTIVE MAINTENANCE

To ensure that the battery or batteries will deliver peak power and therefore quick starting in cold weather, the charging rate must be adjusted for the typical ambient temperatures that the vehicle is expected to operate in. Adjust the rate of charge as recommended by the manufacturer.

In addition to the charging rate, regularly check the following areas:

1. Keep the battery and its connections clean and tight by washing off any acid deposits from the top of the battery with a baking soda and water solution, and rinse with clear water. Take care not to allow any of the solution to enter the cell caps.

Loose or badly corroded connections or terminals will cause high resistance in both the charging and starting circuits, with low charging rates and poor starting the end result. Use a battery post cleaning wire brush for this purpose, and also for the cable clamp ends.

As a regular part of the service routine, check the tightness of all connections.

2. Maintain the electrolyte level at all times by the addition of distilled water. Never add acid to the battery since the addition of pure acid to the battery will cause a violent chemical reaction leading to spatter of the acid. This can cause serious personal injury plus battery damage. If, for example, a maintenance free battery with a removable cover, or a regular serviceable type battery had been tipped over producing a loss of electrolyte, then a mixture of acid and water could be prepared in the shop for addition to the battery. However, do not attempt to add acid at any time to an old worn-out battery.

3. Batteries should always be properly mounted in order to avoid damage from road dirt, water, or flying objects.

Vibration can loosen the internal battery plates, wear holes in separator plates,

break the seal between the case and cover, and crack the case in several places. The effects of vibration can be minimized on heavy-duty highway trucks by mounting the batteries between the frame members so that the battery plates are mounted at right angles to the direction of normal forward vehicle movement. Although many companies mount the batteries on the outside of the vehicle frame members (outrigger fashion), this should be avoided at all costs, since vibration is greatest in these areas, plus the possibility of physical damage from road objects is greatest.

If the batteries are used on a stationary application such as a diesel generator set, irrigation pump, etc., mount the batteries as close to the unit as possible, but not directly to it.

Mount all batteries securely in their hold-down trays. However, avoid over-tighening of hold-down brackets since this action can cause cracking of the battery case. Check the degree of resiliency of any cushioning or isolating material, and replace any cushions or shock absorbers that have become hard, brittle, or worn.

4. Damage to a battery is often the direct result of removal or installation procedures. Never attempt to lift a battery by its positive or negative terminal posts, as this can loosen the post and crack the battery case cover. In extreme cases, the post could come right out. Don't pry or hammer at terminal post clamps in order to remove them; loosen all nuts and use a battery cable clamp to remove tight ones such as shown in Fig. 3-22.

Placing a large screwdriver or pry bar under the clamp to force it off of the post can puncture the battery cover or crack it, as well as loosening the post.

Don't hammer on the clamp in order to drive it back onto the battery post when reinstalling it. Use a clamp spreader as shown in Fig. 3-31. Ensure that the clamp ends have not been pulled together through overtightening on previous occasions, and that you have the correct type of clamp, POS or NEG for the corresponding battery terminal.

Remember that the POS battery post is larger than the NEG one, therefore do not attempt to use a NEG clamp on a POS post. Similarly, the use of a POS clamp on a NEG post will result in a loose connection. Ensure that when the cable clamp is placed onto its mating battery post, it is installed all the way down, or is flush with the top of the post as shown in Fig. 3-22.

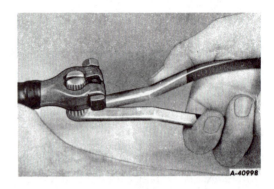

Fig. 3-31. Spreading the battery cable clamp. (Courtesy of International-Harvester)

COLD WEATHER BOOST STARTING PRECAUTIONS

In extreme low temperatures, it is often the practice, albeit not a good one, for service personnel to use booster batteries and/or special generators that develop up to 24 volts and apply this voltage to a 12-volt system of cars and trucks to provide additional power to crank stalled engines.

Severe damage to the electrical system components can be caused by applying cranking voltages that exceed the voltage for which the equipment is designed. Although excessive voltage is specifically damaging to the electronic components, it can also be detrimental to the battery, ignition system, charging circuit, cranking circuit, lights, and other electrical accessories. Therefore, applying voltages higher than those for which the system was designed should *never* be practiced.

The following damage will result from applying excessive voltage during cranking:

1. **Battery** When discharged, the battery will accept a high charging current from the slave setup or booster arrangement. This will usually cause the electrolyte to spew out of the vent plugs resulting in a loss of electrolyte, which lowers the capacity of the battery for future use. Also from a safety standpoint, spewing electrolyte in the presence of a spark may result in an explosion and serious personal injury.

2. **Charging Circuit** Regulator contacts may weld together or diodes and transistors can be burned out, requiring regulator replacement.

3. **Cranking Circuit** The solenoid contacts have a tendency to weld together, which makes it impossible to break the cranking circuit leading to motor winding

damage through burning; or the windings may be thrown out of the armature.

4. **Ignition System** Extremely high currents will pass through either the distributor contact points or semiconductor components in high energy ignition systems causing severe point damage or immediate system failure.

Caution: Do not under any circumstances attempt to boost start any vehicle or piece of equipment rated at 12 volts with a 24-volt arrangement.

ACTIVATING DRY CHARGED BATTERIES

We briefly discussed wet versus dry type batteries earlier in this chapter, with the major difference being that the wet battery contains electrolyte at its time of manufacture, whereas the dry battery contains no electrolyte at manufacture.

When the dry charged battery is required for service, it can be activated by the addition of electrolyte (dilute sulphuric acid) which is readily available from the battery supplier either in bulk form, or in quart or liter containers.

The dry charged battery therefore has longer shelf life than a wet battery which of course will self discharge over a period of time due to the internal chemical reaction within the battery cells.

To activate a dry charged battery, follow the manufacturer's instructions supplied with the battery; however, the following sequence is typical of the procedure that can be followed when activating a dry charged battery.

1. Prior to opening the acid container or containers, remember that acid can burn the skin and clothing, and damage painted surfaces. Wear a protective apron, gloves, and eye protection.

2. Use a small funnel to assist you in pouring the electrolyte into each battery cell. Fill each cell to the top of the separators, which will allow for expansion of the electrolyte as the battery chemically reacts and also in case it requires boost charging.

3. Very gently rock the battery from side to side in order to force out any trapped air. This will also assist in saturating the cell plates with electrolyte.

NOTE: Many dry batteries have protective cell cover seals that must be punctured once the vent plugs or screw-in cell caps are removed. These seals hermetically seal each cell to prevent any moisture from entering the battery during storage. Before adding electrolyte to the battery, break these cell seals by pushing a blunt instrument down into them taking care not to damage the tops of the separator plates.

On batteries with built-in hydrometers such as Delco's Energizer, push the Delco Eye or vent plug down into each cell. Do not attempt to fish out these seals as damage to the separator plates may occur causing a short circuit. The seals will normally drop into the cells and stay there with no damage to the battery.

4. Boost charge automotive 12-volt batteries at about 15 amperes and 6- or 12-volt heavy-duty diesel type batteries at 30 amperes until the specific gravity of the electrolyte is at 1.250 or higher corrected to 80°F (26.7°C); the battery should be at a minimum temperature of 60°F (15.5°C) prior to activating it.

During charging, if smoke appears from any cell, or a blue haze, switch off the charger since the battery is faulty. If the electrolyte bubbles excessively or spews out, then reduce the rate of charge and gradually allow the specific gravity to climb to at least 1.265 at 80°F (26.7°C) or 1.250 at 60°F (15.5°C).

5. Once the battery has reached the recommended specific gravity, allow it to sit for 15 or 20 minutes, then recheck the level of the electrolyte in each cell. If necessary, add additional electrolyte, but do not add water at this time.

6. The open circuit voltage of the battery can also be checked now with a voltmeter placed across the positive and negative battery posts; should the voltmeter read less than 10 volts on a 12-volt battery, or less than 5 volts on a 6-volt battery, a reverse cell or an open circuit exists within the battery, and it should be replaced.

BATTERY STORAGE

Storage of batteries is often considered an unimportant item, when in fact it can cause serious problems if not done properly. Although it is possible to stack batteries one on top of another while they are in cartons such as with dry charged units, do not stack them more than four high. If possible, place them on shelving which removes the weight from each battery.

An example of a battery storage rack is shown in Fig. 3-32.

Wet type batteries while in storage will of course self-discharge; the rate of self-discharge depends upon the ambient temperature in which they are stored. Wet type lead-acid batteries will self-discharge at .001 specific gravity per day over a

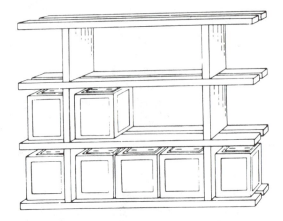

Fig. 3-32. Typical battery storage rack. (Courtesy of International-Harvester)

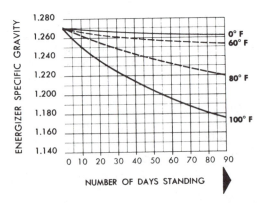

Fig. 3-33. Self-discharge rate of wet type storage batteries. (Courtesy of Delco-Remy Div. of GMC)

typical 30 day period. In order to reduce the degree of self-discharge, store wet batteries in a cool dry place away from heat ducts, and shielded from direct sunlight in the summer.

A typical example of how storage temperatures will affect the specific gravity of the battery is shown in Fig. 3-33.

When storing wet or dry batteries, rotate them on the basis of first-in, first-out so that no battery is stored longer than another prior to using. Check the state of charge of wet batteries once a month, and recharge them at the rate of approximately one ampere per each positive plate.

Dry charged batteries can be stored for up to a year without any problems, or even longer. Maintenance-free batteries have already been filled with electrolyte at the time of manufacture; however, since they contain no antimony in their plate structure, they will self-discharge at a lower rate than a conventional lead-acid type. The maintenance-free battery can be stored for up to one year.

CHARGING OF BATTERIES

A routine maintenance procedure with batteries, is the occasional need to either slow charge or fast charge a battery that has lost some of its potential.

The correct charging rate will depend upon the type and actual rated capacity of the battery. Battery manufacturers publish charts showing the rate of charge recommended for both slow and fast charging.

Automotive (car) batteries usually have a slow charging rate of between 4 to 5 amps, with as much as 7 to 8 amps on the heavy-duty type. Commercial or heavy-duty diesel type batteries usually average a slow charging rate of between 8 to 10 amperes, but in the larger sizes, initial charging currents up to 20 amperes are recommended. Generally speaking, normal recharging rates are about 50 to 70 percent greater than the initial charging rates for new batteries.

Given in this chapter are charts and tables showing the recommended rate of charge, both slow and fast for maintenance type, and maintenance-free batteries. However, if the charging rate of a battery is not known, it may be calculated by dividing the actual capacity by 12; therefore the charging rate (slow charge) for an 80 ampere-hour battery would be 6.6 amperes.

CAUTION: Prior to attempting to recharge any battery, you should remember that the battery while under charge, will emanate explosive fumes. Exercise the necessary safety precautions such as adequate ventilation, safety glasses, etc., while charging batteries.

METHOD OF BATTERY CHARGING

A battery or batteries can be recharged by two widely used methods.

1. Slow charging
2. Fast, or boost, charging

The decision as to whether to use the slow or fast charge method will depend on the time available in which to charge the battery, the actual existing state of charge of the battery in question, and whether or not the battery has just been activated from storage, or is new. Generally boost or fast charging will provide only a surface charge condition, while the slow charge method allows a complete recharge of the battery plates.

The degree of charge that a battery receives is equal to the charging rate in amperes multiplied by the time in hours. Therefore applying a 6 ampere rate to a battery for 6 hours would be equal to a 36 ampere-hour charge to the battery.

In order to fully charge the battery, you must replace the ampere-hours or ampere-minutes that have actually been removed from it. Also when recharging a battery, because of breakdown of the plates (shedding), an extra 20 percent charge rate is usually required in order to ensure complete charging.

The state of charge of the battery can be ascertained in three general ways.

1. **By plate color** Batteries that use clear transparent cases allow you to monitor the color of both the positive and negative plates. When discharged, the positive plates are darker than the negative ones. When fully charged, the positive plate is a rich chocolate brown, and the negative one a grey color.

2. **By the density of the acid** (a widely used method) When the battery is fully charged, and corrected for specific gravity to 80°F (26.7°C), the density of the battery electrolyte should be 1.265 to 1.270. However, some batteries may show specific gravity readings of as high as 1.280 when corrected to 80°F (26.7°C).

Any battery that exhibits the 1.265 to 1.270 reading, is fully charged and can be placed into service without any problem. Some batteries for special ambient operating conditions can exhibit specific gravity readings of from 1.280 to 1.300.

When a battery has been on charge for some time, readings taken a half-hour after the charger has been shut-off, or the battery disconnected, will show minor variations from those taken while the battery is on charge.

3. **By measuring the voltage** When a battery is fully charged, and allowed to stand for more than half an hour, the voltage value per cell will be approximately 2.6; this value however will fall to about 2.1 volts per cell within a few hours.

For example, the voltage of a typical 12 volt battery, is equal to the number of cells multiplied by 2.6 (when just charged), to give us six cells x 2.6 = 15.6 volts, which

will drop to six cells x 2.1 = 12.6 volts in a few hours.

NOTE: When a battery is being charged by either the slow or fast (boost) method, the temperature of the electrolyte should be monitored to ensure that it does not exceed 51.6°C (125°F). If violent gassing or spewing of electrolyte occurs, the charger should be switched off, or its rate reduced, otherwise severe damage to the internal plates will occur, and the battery will have to be replaced. On maintenance-free type batteries, overcharging can cause a loss of water from the electrolyte through the battery cover vents.

SLOW CHARGING

Charging of batteries requires a source of direct current. Slow charging is generally done in a shop environment in which one or more batteries can be charged at the same time. Maintenance shops or service outlets today employ slow chargers that are adjustable by a variable rheostat on the control panel, so that the rate of charge is easily and quickly established to suit batteries of various ratings.

Whether one or more batteries are to be charged, it is very important that the charger's positive and negative leads are readily identifiable. Most chargers will clearly indicate leads by the letters POS (+) or NEG (-) at the respective terminals. Some may simply be color coded, with a red lead for the positive, and black or blue for the negative lead. If for some reason these leads are not readily identifiable, use a voltmeter since its leads are always clearly marked. Unless the voltmeter leads are properly connected, it will not read at all, and will actually cause the needle on the face dial to kick in the wrong direction if improper polarity is attempted. Batteries are usually charged in series as is shown in Fig. 3-34.

Table 3-9 shows the recommended charge rates for both slow and fast charging of batteries. However, a typical charging rate for slow charging would be one ampere per positive plate/cell. With nine plates per cell in the average battery, four of the nine will be positive plates; therefore, the slow charge rate would be four amperes. While the battery is on-charge, check the specific gravity once per hour unless the battery is in a very low state of charge, which means that it can be left on charge for several hours before checking the specific gravity.

Once it has been on charge for several hours, check each cell's specific gravity once per hour; maximum specific gravity is reached when no change occurs in the specific gravity over a three hour period, or when the charging current stabilizes on a constant voltage type of charger.

If a maintenance-free battery is to be charged for a period of time that requires overnight charging, a timer or voltage controlled charger is definitely recommended, since overcharging of the maintenance-free type battery can cause a loss of water from the battery electrolyte. If the battery charger is not equipped with these special safety controls, then ensure that a 3 ampere rate is not exceeded for batteries rated at 80 minutes or less capacity. On batteries that are rated between 80 and 125 minutes, a maximum of 5 amperes should be used. Heavy-duty diesel type batteries rated in excess of 125 minutes should be charged at

Table 3-9
BATTERY CHARGING GUIDE
(6-Volt and 12-Volt Batteries)
Recommended Rate* and Time for Fully Discharged Condition

Reserve Capacity Rating	Twenty Hour Rating	5 Amperes	10 Amperes	20 Amperes	30 Amperes	40 Amperes
75 Minutes or less	50 Ampere-Hours or less	10 Hours	5 Hours	2½ Hours	2 Hours	
Above 75 To 115 Minutes	Above 50 To 75 Ampere-Hours	15 Hours	7½ Hours	3¾ Hours	2½ Hours	2 Hours
Above 115 To 160 Minutes	Above 75 To 100 Ampere-Hours	20 Hours	10 Hours	5 Hours	3 Hours	2½ Hours
Above 160 To 245 Minutes	Above 100 To 150 Ampere-Hours	30 Hours	15 Hours	7½ Hours	5 Hours	3½ Hours
Above 245 Minutes	Above 150 Ampere-Hours		20 Hours	10 Hours	6½ Hours	5 Hours

(Courtesy of Delco)

*Initial rate for constant voltage taper rate charger
To avoid damage charging rate must be reduced or temporarily halted if:
    1. Electrolyte temperature exceeds 125°F.
    2. Violent gassing or spewing of electrolyte occurs.
Battery is fully charged when over a two hour period at a low charging rate in amperes all cells are gassing freely and no change in specific gravity occurs. For the most satisfactory charging, the lower charging rates in amperes are recommended.
Full charge specific gravity is 1.260-1.280 corrected for temperature with electrolyte level at split ring.

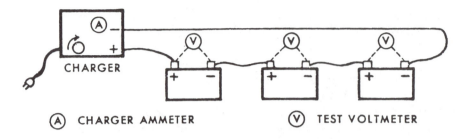

(A) CHARGER AMMETER   (V) TEST VOLTMETER

Fig. 3-34. Batteries connected in series for charging.

the rate recommended as shown in Table 3-9.

Although slow charging will bring most batteries back to a full state of charge, batteries that have been in storage for extended periods, or that have operated with low electrolyte levels, can become sulphated. This condition is caused by rapidly discharging the battery, by allowing the electrolyte level to fall below the tops of the plates, by the use of impure or dirty water, or by allowing the battery to discharge too far, and then to remain discharged. A defective generator/alternator which only partially charges the battery, will eventually cause sulphation of the plates. The sulphation is the chemical effect resulting in the formation of white lead sulphate on the surfaces of the plates, which is a normal result of completely discharging a battery. Such an example is shown in Fig. 3-35.

(a) Plate swelling due to overcharging.

Fig. 3-35. Examples of battery failures. (Courtesy of Delco-Remy Div. of GMC)

(b) Overcharging caused positive plate to swell and short out against negative plate strap.

(c) Short between positive and negative plates at upper left corner.

(d) (3) Lower growth has shorted out negative and positive plates.

(d) (1) Blistered and washed out negative plate.

(d) (4) Growth on top of negative plate caused shorting to positive plate strap.

(d) (2) Washed out positive plate.

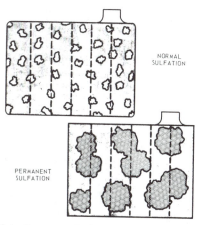

(e) Sulphation growth, both normal and permanent on battery plates.

TYPES OF BATTERY CHARGERS

The two basic types of battery chargers which are widely used for charging a group of batteries are:

1. The current-limiting type which is also called a constant current or Series Charger
2. The voltage-limiting type, sometimes referred to as a constant voltage or Parallel Charger.

When the series charger is used, such as shown in Fig. 3-10(a), all batteries on charge receive the same amount of charging current. When a parallel charger is used, the batteries are connected so that the charging current is divided and each individual battery receives only the charging current that it can accept at the charger's voltage. Because of these differences, the charging procedures also differ. The following recommendations should be closely followed in order to ensure correct charging of batteries for both series and parallel hook-up arrangements.

SERIES HOOKUP CHARGING

The batteries can be connected as shown earlier in Fig. 3-34; however, prior to connecting up all batteries to be charged, conduct the necessary safety and visual checks.

1. If any battery cases or covers are cracked, broken or otherwise damaged, do not attempt to charge them prior to repairing this damage. If nonrepairable, replace them.

2. On batteries with screw or push-in filler caps, remove them and check them with a hydrometer for specific gravity. If the reading is higher than 1.230, the battery is serviceable and does not require charging, unless a fault was found in the vehicle charging system that had allowed a low charge rate to exist for some time; then the battery could be recharged to 1.265 to 1.270 corrected to 80°F (26.7°C).

3. If the battery electrolyte level is low, add distilled water to bring the cell level above the level of the separators, or just to below the level of the split-guide ring prior to charging. After charging, add water to the bottom of the split guide ring.

4. On maintenance-free or Delco-Remy type freedom batteries, always check the color of the magic-eye or built-in hydrometer; if the color is clear or yellow, then the battery must be replaced, unless it has the removable vent manifold that is found on some maintenance-free units to allow topping-up of the water as was described earlier in this chapter. If the hydrometer shows a green color, the battery does not require charging. If the hydrometer is dark, then the battery requires charging.

5. With the individual battery terminals clean, connect up the necessary leads as shown in Fig. 3-34. Keep in mind that the battery charger only has a certain load carrying capability; therefore, make sure that you do not connect up more batteries than the charger is capable of handling. Prior to switching on the battery charger, double check that all leads and connections are tight, since loose connections can result in blowing the fuse of the charger, causing a spark to occur at the loose connection.

6. On the face of the charger is a variable resistor or similar arrangement that allows you to set the charging rate. For most slow charge conditions, this can be set to within 5-10 amperes, or to whatever is recommended by the particular battery manufacturer.

.7. Allow the batteries to remain in this steady state of charge for at least three hours prior to checking their condition. On filler-cap batteries, check the specific gravity of each cell with a hydrometer and correct the readings to 80°F (26.7°C). If no change in the specific gravity reading is observed in three consecutive hourly readings, then remove the battery from charge, as it will not take any more charge.

Also, as mentioned previously, do not allow the temperature of the electrolyte to exceed 125°F (52°C). If any cell gasses or spews electrolyte, reduce the charging rate or remove the battery from test.

8. On maintenance-free or freedom batteries, when the green dot is clearly visible, gently shake or tilt the battery to ensure that the green dot stays visible. With the use of a voltmeter, check the terminal voltage across the positive and negative battery terminals. Take care when using the voltmeter leads that you do not create a spark by scratching the terminals to make good contact, since you could create an explosion. Switch off the charger while voltage testing.

If a voltage of 16 volts or more is noted, remove the battery from charge, then test as per the manufacturer's instructions.

PARALLEL HOOKUP CHARGING

Connect the batteries as shown in Fig. 3-36 for group charging with voltage-limited or parallel battery chargers. Conduct the same basic checks as you would when series charging, namely Steps 1 through 5 above. Then, at Step 6:

6. With the batteries connected as shown in Fig. 3-36, switch on the battery charger with the voltage setting adjusted to a maximum of 16 volts. On initial switch-on, the charger voltmeter may not show 16 volts; however, as the batteries accept the charge, less current is required which will cause the voltage to rise.

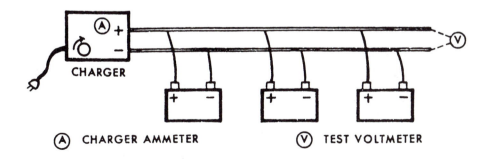

Fig. 3-36. Parallel battery charging arrangement.

The charger's ammeter registers the actual total current flow to the batteries which divides to each individual battery; however, this current flow showing on the face of the ammeter does not individually measure the current flow to each battery, but simply shows the total current flowing to the batteries from the charger.

Steps 7 and 8 are the same as that given for the series hookup.

NOTE: When monitoring the specific gravity of each individual battery cell, a difference of more than 0.050 (50) specific gravity points between cells usually is an indication that one or more cells are defective. Conduct a load test on the battery.

FAST OR BOOST CHARGING

Fast charging, or what is commonly referred to as boost charging in the industry, is only used when time prevents the slow charging of the battery or batteries.

The boost charge method provides a high charging rate for a very short period of time compared to that of slow charging. Charging rates up to 60 amperes for 12-volt batteries are not uncommon, with double the ampere value for 6-volt batteries above the 180 reserve capacity rating.

Typical examples of boost charging rates are given in Table 3-9.

Boost charging of a completely discharged battery will not bring it to a 100 percent state of charge, but will only surface charge it for practical service. In order to completely charge the battery, it must be placed on slow charge for the recommended period as shown in the charging tables.

CAUTION: Do not boost charge any battery with a specific gravity of 1.225 or higher, since severe damage due to overcharge can occur, with the possibility of violent gassing, spewing, and electrolyte temperature increase beyond 125°F (51.6°C). Under these conditions, the battery might explode.

A typical fast charger is shown in Fig. 3-37.

When boost charging a battery in place in the vehicle or equipment, always connect the positive (+) charger lead to the (+) battery terminal, and the negative (-) lead to the (-) battery terminal. Remember that battery terminals are marked with either the letters POS or (+) beside the battery post, and the letters NEG or (-) beside the negative terminal. If no markings are visible, the positive terminal is always physically larger than the negative one.

Charger leads are normally color coded, with red being positive and either black or blue for negative. If you are in doubt regarding battery terminal polarity, use a voltmeter with its probes connected to one terminal post each. If the leads are connected backwards, the voltmeter will not read. The voltmeter leads are color coded also, with red for (+) and black for (-).

Boost charging the battery while still in the vehicle allows you to connect the grounded lead to the engine block for a better connection. Note whether the NEG or POS lead is grounded from the battery to the frame or engine block prior to placing the same charger lead to the block.

Make sure all connections are clean and tight, then switch on the fast charger at the low charge rate. Slowly increase the rate of charge until the recommended ampere value is attained. Any sign of smoke or haze from any battery cell would indicate a shorted battery; switch-off the charger immediately and replace the battery.

If severe gassing or spewing of electrolyte occurs, double check that your rate

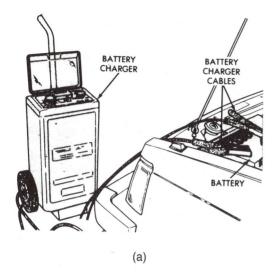

(a)

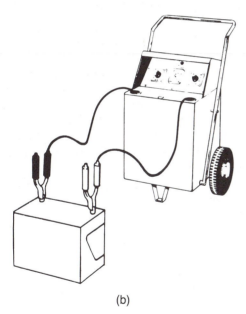

(b)

Fig. 3-37. (a) Boost charger connected to battery while in vehicle. (b) Boost charger connected to battery out of vehicle.

of charge is not in excess of that recommended. Reduce or halt the rate of charge until the condition has been corrected.

EMERGENCY JUMP STARTING

It is very common for people to jump start one vehicle from another vehicle especially in cold weather when a boost charger is not readily available. This practice can lead to serious charging system problems if the jump start procedure is not followed very closely.

Connecting cables improperly can lead to not only charging system problems, but can also damage both the starting system and battery.

Prior to the sequence of events for jump starting, pay special attention to the safety precautions listed below:

Safety Precautions

1. Wear safety glasses or shield your eyes.

2. Cover the vent caps after ensuring that they are tight on the batteries of both vehicles; place a damp cloth over the vents of both batteries to minimize gassing or spewing of electrolyte during jump starting.

3. Clean the tops of both batteries of any sulphation, dirt grease etc.

4. Ensure that both the discharged battery and the booster battery are of the same voltage.

5. Ensure that vehicles are of the same ground polarity.

6. Do not allow the vehicles to touch one another at any time.

7. Ensure that all vehicle electrical loads or accessories are switched off.

8. Make certain that the parking brakes of both vehicles are securely set; place the transmission in neutral or park, as the case may be.

9. Do not lean over the battery when jump starting.

10. On maintenance-free batteries, do not attempt to jump- start a battery if the built-in hydrometer is light yellow in color; replace the battery.

11. Do not allow the clamps from one booster cable to touch the clamps on the other cable.

12. Make certain that no one is standing in front of or behind the vehicles.

13. When connecting booster cables, ensure that you avoid hot or electrical hazards on the vehicle such as moving fans, exhaust manifolds, etc. Avoid causing sparks!

Although the foregoing list may seem lengthy, it is precisely these types of safety precautions that most people forget, leading to either vehicle or personal injury during jump starting.

CAUTION: Do not attempt to jump start vehicles having opposite grounds; otherwise serious charging system damage can result.

After these precautions, proceed as follows:

1. Inspect the vehicle with the discharged battery to establish whether it has a NEG (-) or POS (+) ground. The grounded cable is always the one that is bolted to either the engine block or vehicle frame. The battery cable that is connected to the starter body, relay or solenoid is the non-grounded connection.

2. On negative ground systems, connect one end of a jumper or booster cable to the (+) terminal of the battery in the operating vehicle or booster battery, and the other end of the same cable to the positive (+) terminal of the discharged vehicle's battery.

If both units are positively grounded, connect the negative terminals first from the charged battery to the discharged battery.

3. Connect one end of the second booster cable to the negative terminal of the battery in the operating vehicle, and attach the other end to the negative terminal of the battery in the non-operating vehicle.

If the units are positively grounded, then connect the second booster cable to the positive terminal of the charged battery (operating vehicle), and the other end to the positive terminal of the non-operating vehicle.

NOTE: As a safety precaution, if the vehicle receiving the boost has a dead battery, do not directly connect the ground booster cable from the operating vehicle to the battery terminal of the dead battery. Instead, connect the ground booster cable from the operating vehicle to a ground connection on either the dead vehicle's engine block or frame in order to provide good electrical conductivity and current carrying capacity. Failure to do this can result in excessive resistance through the dead battery and failure to crank the engine of the stalled vehicle fast enough for starting.

4. Avoid jump-starting vehicles by bringing bumpers into contact because by this procedure direct electrical connection is made, and serious short circuiting can occur.

Figure 3-38 shows the typical connections for jump-starting both negative and positive ground systems.

5. Start and idle the engine of the operating vehicle and wait for a few minutes,

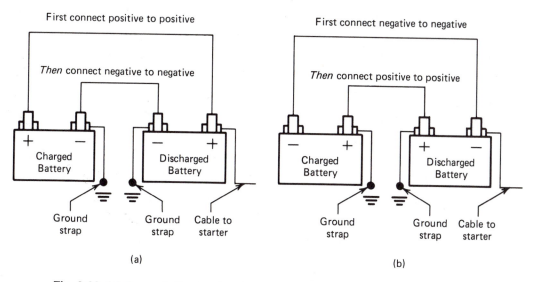

Fig. 3-38. (a) Jump starting hookup for negative ground systems. (b) Jump starting hookup for positive ground systems.

then attempt to start the engine of the stalled vehicle. If the stalled engine does not start within 15 to 20 seconds, pause and wait for 30 seconds to one minute to allow the starter motor to cool. Failure to follow this precaution can lead to serious starter motor damage.

If repeated attempts to start the stalled engine fail, check further for the reasons of failure to start. Don't continue to crank and pull down the battery of the operating vehicle.

6. Once the stalled vehicle has started, idle the engine of the other vehicle, and remove the ground cable connection from the vehicle with the discharged or low battery condition; remove the other end of the same cable from the booster battery vehicle.

7. Failure to follow the reverse sequence of disconnecting battery booster cables can also result in battery damage.

8. Remove the other cable by disconnecting it from the boosted or discharged battery first, then from the booster battery.

9. Remove and discard the damp cloths from the battery vent covers.

BOOSTING 12-24 VOLT ELECTRICAL SYSTEMS

Some heavy-duty diesel starting systems operate on the series/parallel principle, where the starting motor operates on 24 volts, but the charging system is only 12 volts. This is accomplished through the use of a series/parallel switch in the electrical circuit.

Proper precautions must be taken when jump starting vehicles with 24 volt cranking/12 volt operational electrical systems.

Prior to starting, check to make sure that both electrical systems of the stalled vehicle and the operating vehicle are the same.

A vehicle with a 24-volt cranking and 12-volt operational system should be started only with a vehicle containing the same system.

Use two sets of jumper cables heavy enough to carry the current.

To jump start the 12/24 volt system proceed as follows.

1. Ensure that the electrical accessories of both vehicles are off.

2. Start the engine of the operating vehicle.

3. Take one pair of the jumper cables, and connect the vehicle load (A) battery of the running engine to the vehicle load battery of the stalled vehicle. Follow the same procedure when attaching cables as given above for jump-starting of straight 12 volt systems.

4. Take the second set of jumper cables, and connect the cranking (B) battery of the operating vehicle to the cranking battery of the stalled engine. Again ensure that correct polarity is observed when connecting up this set of cables.

5. Attempt to crank and start the stalled engine.

6. When the stalled engine is started, disconnect the jumper cables in the exact reverse order of attachment.

REVIEW QUESTIONS

Q1 What are the two types of batteries in general use for cars, trucks, and heavy-duty equipment?

Q2 How does a wet battery differ from a dry battery?

Q3 What are battery cases manufactured from?

Q4 What is a battery cell-pack?

Q5 What is the average cell voltage produced in a good battery?

Q6 How does a maintenance-free battery differ from a conventional lead-acid battery?

Q7 How can you distinguish the positive battery post from the negative battery post?

Q8 What is the advantage of a side mount battery terminal over a top mounted battery post arrangement?

Q9 What is the electrolyte liquid derived from in a battery?

Q10 What is the normal specific gravity of a fully charged battery?

Q11 How would you correct the specific gravity reading with a change to the ambient temperature?

Q12 Can a specific gravity reading be converted to a voltage reading?

Q13 Can antifreeze be added to the electrolyte to prevent freezing in cold weather?

Q14 What material is the positive battery plates made from and what is the chemical symbol that denotes this material?

Q15 What is the negative battery plate made from, and what is its chemical symbol?

Q16 When a battery is in a discharged state, what is the percentage of the liquid that makes up the electrolyte?

Q17 When a battery gasses, what is the mixture that emanates from the cells?

Q18 What problems would occur due to overfilling of the battery with electrolyte when new, or with water during normal service?

Q19 What prevents a maintenance-free type battery from being overcharged as readily as a lead-acid type?

Q20 What danger exists if a maintenance-free battery is mounted at an angle in excess of 45 degrees?

Q21 What happens to the electrolyte within the maintenance-free type battery during normal charging?

Q22 On maintenance-free batteries, how can its state of charge be readily determined?

Q23 What are the two common battery hookup arrangements used with batteries?

Q24 How is a battery presently rated?

Q25 What does SAE and BCI mean?

Q26 What safety precautions must be exercised when working around batteries?

Q27 How should a battery or batteries be carried?

Q28 How would you remove a tight battery cable clamp?

Q29 What types of battery heaters can be utilized in cold weather?

Q30 What would smoke from a battery cell during charging indicate?

Q31 What is a hydrometer?

Q32 What is a refractometer?

Q33 When would you use a light-load voltage test?

Q34 When would you use a high-capacity discharge, or load test on a battery?

Q35 When testing or charging maintenance-free type batteries, what precaution should be exercised?

Q36 What load should be applied to a battery when conducting a high-discharge or load test?

Q37 What is an open-circuit voltage test?

Q38 What is a 421 test?

Q39 In the absence of a slow charging battery capacity chart, how would you determine what amperage to set the charger at?

Q40 A boost charge will do exactly the same to the battery state of charge as slow charging will. True or False?

Q41 What three ways can you establish the condition of charge of all types of batteries?

Q42 What are the two basic methods (hookups) for charging batteries?

Q43 A battery can be boost charged at any time, and at any rate of charge. True or False?

Q44 What is meant by emergency jump starting?

Q45 Describe how you would jump start a stalled vehicle engine?

ANSWERS

A1 The two types of batteries in general use for cars, trucks, and heavy equipment today are the conventional lead-acid maintenance type, and the antimony-free sealed maintenance-free battery.

A2 A wet battery is a battery that contains electrolyte or has been activated; a dry battery is a battery that contains no electrolyte, and until it has been activated by the addition of electrolyte cannot produce any electrical energy. Once a dry battery has been activated, it then becomes a wet battery.

A3 Battery cases are commonly manufactured from either hard rubber, plastic or polypropylene which has the advantage of light weight and improved cold weather durability compared to hard rubber cases.

A4 A battery cell-pack is the term used to describe the stack-up of the positive and negative plates and their separators for each individual cell.

A5 Average cell voltage of a good battery ranges from 2 to 2.08 volts although some batteries may read slightly higher when new.

A6 The maintenance-free battery differs specifically from the conventional lead-acid battery in that there is no antimony contained in the plates of the maintenance-free type. The grid of the battery in the maintenance-free type is made from a lead-calcium alloy while the conventional type uses lead-antimony.

A7 The positive battery post is always physically larger in diameter than the negative one. Also the battery is usually marked POS (+) and NEG (-) beside each respective terminal.

A8 The major difference is that it provides a lower overall installed battery height, but it also allows a good connection for the cable clamps which can be bolted or held to the threaded post connection by a nut.

A9 The electrolyte that is initially poured into the battery consists of dilute sulphuric acid, approximately 64% water and 36% acid.

A10 Normal specific gravity of the electrolyte in a fully charged battery is 1.270 at 80°F (26.7°C), which means that it is heavier than water which has a specific gravity of 1.000.

A11 For every 10°F (3.7°C) increase beyond 80°F (26.7°C), you must add 4 points (.004) to the hydrometer reading, or subtract .004 points from the hydrometer reading for every 10°F (3.7°C) below 80°F (26.7°C).

A12 Yes it can. Refer to the conversion table in the battery chapter.

A13 No, under no circumstances add antifreeze to batteries, since this will damage the battery with resultant failure in a short period of time.

A14 The positive plates of the battery are composed of lead peroxide whose chemical formula is PbO_2, and which is dark or chocolate brown in color.

A15 The negative plates are composed of pure lead whose chemical symbol is Pb, and which is metallic gray in color.

A16 In a discharged state, the lead-acid battery electrolyte consists of 17 percent pure sulphuric acid, and 83 percent water.

A17 Gassing of a battery produces a mixture of hydrogen and oxygen.

A18 Overfilling of the battery will cause spewing and loss of electrolyte with eventual battery damage.

A19 The maintenance-free type of battery is not as susceptible to overcharging as a conventional lead-acid battery due to the fact that the plate grid contains lead-calcium alloy, and has no antimony in it, therefore the grid is very resistant to oxidation from overcharge.

A20 Mounting any battery at a steep operating angle can result in a loss of electrolyte, and uncovers part of the plates which can lead to sulphation.

A21 Within the cover of the maintenance-free battery is a liquid-gas separator which is designed to collect very small particles of electrolyte and then return the liquid to the main reservoir of the battery. Vents within the cover allow release of any excess fumes should a danger level be reached.

A22 The state of charge of maintenance-free batteries can be quickly determined by viewing the built-in hydrometer within the cover. When the battery is sufficiently charged the clear plastic hydrometer tube will appear green in color; if it is dark, then the battery requires charging, and if it is clear or light yellow this indicates that the electrolyte level is low.

A23 The two common battery hookups are either series or parallel; series hookup provides increased voltage for starting purposes, while parallel hookup provides increased amperage or capacity.

A24 Batteries are presently rated by either the reserve capacity method, or by the cold cranking test.

A25 SAE stands for the Society of Automotive Engineers, while BCI stands for the Battery Council International.

A26. Wear eye protection, protective clothing and gloves, and don't smoke, use open flames, create sparks, or inhale the fumes.

A27 Carry batteries one at a time with the use of a special strap carrier, or use a battery cart for larger or multiple units.

A28 Use a battery clamp puller.

A29 Electric strip heaters, forced hot air to the battery compartment, or warm coolant circulated through passages in the battery box.

A30 Smoke from a battery cell during charging usually indicates a damaged or faulty cell.

A31 A hydrometer is a device for determining the specific gravity of the battery electrolyte.

A32 The refractometer also determines specific gravity of the battery electrolyte.

A33 A light-load voltage test can be done on a recently activated battery to determine its condition.

A34 A high-capacity or load-test should be applied to any battery that is suspected of being faulty for any reason.

A35 When testing maintenance-free batteries, ensure that they are sufficiently charged first by looking at the built-in hydrometer in the cover (green); also the open circuit voltage should correspond to at least a reading of 1.230. Do not attempt to boost charge any battery if the specific gravity is at or higher than 1.230.

A36 The load applied to the battery when load testing will vary between batteries depending on its rating, therefore always check the manufacturer's specifications first.

A37 This is simply a test of the battery voltage with the cables disconnected and a voltmeter placed across the positive and negative battery terminals.

A38 A 421 test is a timed test with an automatic discharge/charge battery machine to simulate typical cycling of the battery.

A39 If the charging rate of the battery is unknown, it can be calculated by dividing the actual capacity of the battery by 12 for the approximate rate of charge.

A40 This is false; the boost charge will only supply a surface charge to the battery.

A41 Condition of charge can be established by the specific gravity cell test, a voltmeter reading, or by the color of the plates on battery cases that are clear plastic.

A42 The two basic battery hookups for charging purposes are the series arrangement where all batteries receive the same amount of charging current, and the parallel charger arrangement, where the charging current is divided to each individual battery, which receives only the charging current that it can accept at the charger's voltage setting.

A43 No. A battery should never be boost-charged if its specific gravity is 1.230 or higher. Also the rate of boost charging must be adjusted to suit each battery depending on its reserve capacity rating.

A44 Emergency jump starting is the process whereby one vehicle can be used to boost start the vehicle with a low battery by the use of jumper cables.

A45 Compare your answer to the detailed explanation given in the battery chapter.

Chapter

4A

Alternators

The introduction of the vehicle electric system charging alternator has done much to reduce the electrical problems originally associated with the variety of add-on devices desired by the general public on their automobiles, such as radios, heaters, four and eight track stereo systems, heaters, air conditioners, plug-in portable accessory devices, and so on. The alternator produces electrical energy from a mechanical drive such as a belt or gear driven arrangement from the engine. Alternators have almost universally replaced the generators used for many years as the standard method of supplying electricity to the charging system.

Alternators are smaller and lighter for the same output capacity than are generators. In addition, the alternator is reasonably simple in construction, has far fewer wearing parts, is much easier to service and maintain, uses solid state devices that are quickly replaceable, and generally is easier to troubleshoot and adjust. Current state-of-the-art alternators include built-in voltage regulators that are nonadjustable in some models, and heavy-duty types that include usually three or four alternate

settings with one screw adjustment, or by relocating a voltage adjustment cap. In addition many heavy-duty type alternators include an option whereby a transformer-rectifier combination may be connected to the alternator for conversion to 110 volts d.c. which is a highly desirable option in many remote locations. The wiring system with many current alternators has been simplified to the point, that only one wire is needed to connect the integral charging system to the battery, along with an adequate ground return.

The increase in traffic congestion in every major city of the world creates an operating situation in which long periods of time are spent with engines at idle speed. Use of d.c. generators for the purpose of charging the battery and handling vehicle electric loads was unsatisfactory, because the d.c. generator was incapable of producing power at these prolonged idling speeds.

With increased vehicle electrical loads presented by the use of accessories such as air conditioning systems in summer, heaters and defrosters in winter, and radios and tape decks in constant operation, it became impractical to continue to use d.c. generators. The main reason for not continuing the use of the d.c. generator was that by broadening the speed range in which it could produce power (especially at idle), it became more difficult to control the commutation or conversion of the induced alternating current into the direct current required for charging the battery.

The elimination of the commutator in the design of the alternator allowed power to be produced from the alternator even at continuous engine idle.

In comparison with the d.c. generator, the a.c. alternator has the following major advantages:

1. Lighter and more compact
2. Fewer moving parts
3. Produces power even at idle speeds
4. Less maintenance
5. Newer models include built-in solid-state regulators
6. Less wear and therefore longer life
7. Reduction in battery size due to the rapid recharging characteristic of the alternator
8. Longer brush life, since only low current passes through them compared to full generator output on a d.c. system
9. Alternators can be rotated in any direction (unless a pulley fan with inclined blades is used)
10. Capable of high maximum speeds
11. Easier to troubleshoot and adjust

BASIC ELECTRICAL SYSTEM LOADS

Typical loads that are placed on the battery and charging system of a vehicle are shown in Fig. 4-1. Items depicted in the figure by solid lines are continuous type

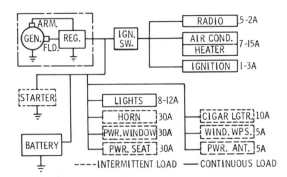

Fig. 4-1. Typical loads on an electrical system. (Courtesy of Motorola Inc., Automotive Products Div.)

loads, while those shown by a dotted line are intermittent type additional loads.

When both the heater and vehicle lights are on, approximately 20 amperes of current demand is in use. With the d.c. type generator system, especially at idle speeds, the battery only was supplying this load demand, thereby slowly discharging the battery. The a.c. alternator, however, is capable of producing this type of output even at continuous idle speeds, therefore the battery will not be in a continuous discharge situation.

BASIC OPERATION

Prior to studying several types of widely used alternators, it may be helpful to first of all explain the simple construction and basic operation of an alternator. This will give you a base from which to work as you progress into the more detailed models.

Basically, there are two types of alternators in use today. These are the automotive type which is widely used on cars and light pickup trucks and vans, and the heavy-duty type of alternator which is used in trucks both on- and off-highway, marine applications, heavy-duty equipment, and in special applications such as police cruisers, ambulances, emergency vehicles, fire-fighting vechicles etc.

All of these alternators work on the same general principle. The components of the a.c., or alternating current, generator (which is another term sometimes used to describe the alternator) function to produce both voltage and current. From earlier discussions on electrical fundamentals you will recall that the flow of electricity (the flow of electrons) is called current. This is a measure of the quantity of electron flow similar to water flow when used in a water system, although it is measured in gallons per minute or liters per minute. The electrical unit that is used for measuring current is the ampere or amp for short. Remember, however, that current cannot flow without pressure being present in the system.

The electrical pressure is known as voltage which is the effort needed to force the current through the wire carrying conductors and electrical accessories. The unit of electrical pressure is the volt. You will also recollect from basic electrical fundamentals, that both electricity and magnetism are involved in the electrical system. If we pass current through a wire, a magnetic field is created around the wire, and an electromagnet is produced. The strength of this magnetic field is proportional to the amount of current flowing in the wire; the greater the current, the stronger the magnetic field.

Under basic fundamentals, we also pointed out that if a piece of straight copper wire is bent into the shape of a coil, we are able to produce a much stronger magnetic field with the same amount of current flowing in the wire due to the fact that we concentrate the magnetic field in a given area. By placing a soft iron core within the coil windings as shown in Fig. 4-2, the strength of the magnetic field around the coil is further increased due to the fact that the iron core will conduct these magnetic lines of force much better than air will. This concentration of the magnetic field, allows the magnetic lines of force to actually become stronger.

Using iron in a magnetic path can increase the magnetic strength as much as 2500 times over a coil that simply has air in the center.

All magnets of course contain a north and a south pole such as is shown in Fig. 4-2.

Within the alternator or a.c. generator, these same basic principles are applied. Fig. 4-3 shows a basic alternator rotor assembly which is the only moving component of the alternator (driven by a belt and pulley, or gear driven). A field winding consisting of many turns of insulated wire wound around an iron spool is contained within the rotor assembly, therefore when current is passed through this field winding, we produce an electromagnet and also a magnetic field just as we did with the simple coiled wire and iron core shown in Fig. 4-2.

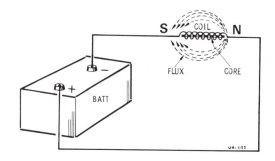

Fig. 4-2. Basic field strength increase. (Courtesy of Motorola Inc., Automotive Products Div.)

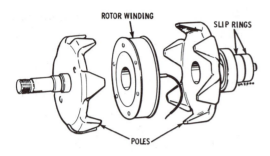

ROTOR WINDING

SLIP RINGS

POLES

Fig. 4-3. Alternator rotor assembly. (Courtesy of Motorola Inc., Automotive Products Div.)

The structure of the rotor assembly consists of the field winding, two iron segments that contain individual poles or interlacing fingers whose number can vary between makes, a support shaft (which is rotated) and two slip rings upon which brushes ride on one end of the rotor shaft and are attached to the leads from the field coil. See Fig. 4-3.

The rotor field winding current flow has a direct bearing upon the strength of the pole pieces (north and south) of the rotor assembly. A certain residual magnetism is retained at all times in these pole pieces. However, by controlling the strength of the rotor field winding, we can control the output voltage of the alternator. In this respect, the alternator is said to be externally excited because the field current is supplied from the battery and ignition switch through resistors, diodes and transistors at a voltage of between 1.5 and 2.5 volts, on the average. Fig. 4-4 shows the circuit for a typical slip-ring and brush type alternator.

The direction of current flow in the rotor field winding will produce a north magnetic pole in each finger of one half of the rotor segment, and a south magnetic pole in each finger of the other half of the rotor segment.

In order to effectively use the force of this rotating magnetic field produced by the rotor, we need to mount a series of copper wires within the magnetic field that will absorb the electrical energy from the lines of force, therefore we commonly use what is known as a stator. The basic stator is a simple loop or loops of wire arranged in such a fashion as to allow these magnetic lines of force from the spinning rotor to cut across this wire.

As this action occurs, electrical pressure or voltage is produced in the loop or loops of wire (the stator, which is stationary); the greater the speed of rotor rotation, the greater will be the voltage induced within the stator windings. Stators currently used in all alternators generally consist of a laminated iron frame and three stator or output windings which are wound into the frame slots. The stator laminations are insulated with an epoxy coating prior to installation of the windings. The assembly is then varnish-coated for added insulation and also to prevent movement of the windings.

The stator assembly is then sandwiched between the opposite ends of the alternator frame.

Battery current that flows through one slip ring into the field winding of the rotor leaves the field coil through the other slipring and brush, and returns to the battery through the ground return path. See Fig. 4-4.

When all components are assembled to produce the alternator, the rotor turns freely within the inner diameter of the stator. However, a very small air-gap does exist between the rotor poles and the stator laminations to prevent contact between the rotor and stator; otherwise, physical damage could occur.

Movement of the rotor will alternately

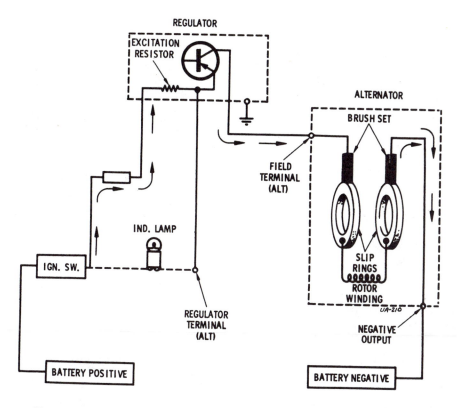

Fig. 4-4. Excitation circuit, slip rings, and brushes. (Courtesy of Motorola Inc., Automotive Products Div.)

allow each pole finger (north and south poles) to pass each loop in the stator windings thereby inducing a voltage and subsequent current flow in the stator windings. The voltage induced within the stator windings will therefore be constantly alternating between these north and south poles. This oscillating, or back and forth voltage, will likewise cause the current (amperes) within the stator windings to flow in one direction, then the other. This type of current is known as alternating current (or a.c.) which is explained in more detail later in this chapter. Since all of the electrical accessories in use today in cars, trucks, etc. are designed for direct current

which flows in only one direction, then we have to change the a.c. to d.c.

The simplest method available for this purpose is to use a diode which only allows current to pass through it in one direction, but not the other; it operates in a manner similar to a one-way check valve. Within the end frame of the alternator, six of these rectifying diodes are located in a heat sink at the end closest to the slip-rings as shown in Fig. 4-6. These six diodes are required because commonly employed stators contain three windings; three diodes are positive in design, while the other three are negative in design in order to handle the alternating current produced

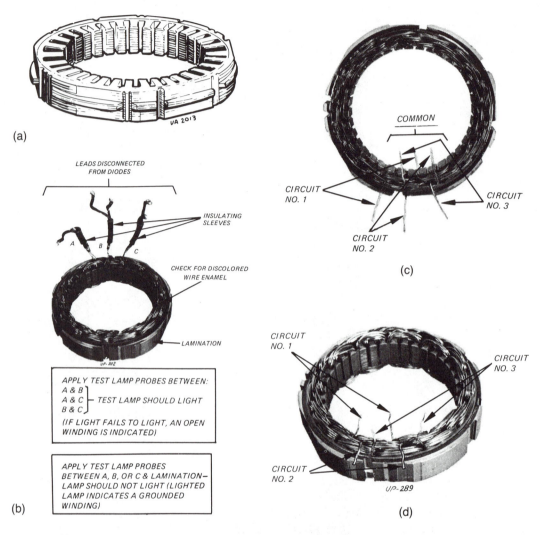

(a)

(b)

(c)

(d)

LEADS DISCONNECTED
FROM DIODES

INSULATING
SLEEVES

A   B   C

CHECK FOR DISCOLORED
WIRE ENAMEL

LAMINATION

APPLY TEST LAMP PROBES BETWEEN:
A & B ⎫
A & C ⎬ TEST LAMP SHOULD LIGHT
B & C ⎭
(IF LIGHT FAILS TO LIGHT, AN OPEN
WINDING IS INDICATED)

APPLY TEST LAMP PROBES
BETWEEN A, B, OR C & LAMINATION—
LAMP SHOULD NOT LIGHT (LIGHTED
LAMP INDICATES A GROUNDED
WINDING)

COMMON

CIRCUIT
NO. 1

CIRCUIT
NO. 3

CIRCUIT
NO. 2

CIRCUIT
NO. 1

CIRCUIT
NO. 3

CIRCUIT
NO. 2

Fig. 4-5. (a) Laminated stator construction; (b) three-phase wye-wound stator; (c) laminated three-phase stator with leads disconnected from rectifying diode; (d) three-phase delta-wound stator. (Courtesy of Motorola Inc., Automotive Products Div.)

within each stator winding. The alternating current is therefore changed into direct current through the diodes.

Finally, we require a voltage regulator to control the a.c. output of the alternator. The a.c. output is dependent upon the quantity of current flow through the rotor field coil windings; therefore, in order to ensure and maintain a constant voltage output, alternators commonly employ a solid-state voltage regulator built into the alternator housing itself. This voltage reg-

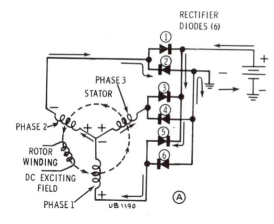

Fig. 4-6. Alternator basic rectification circuit. (Courtesy of Motorola Inc., Automotive Products Div.)

ulator measures the output voltage and automatically adjusts the field current to keep the output voltage constant as the load changes in the vehicle electrical system demand.

Very briefly then, we can summarize the operation of the alternator by saying that the rotor and stator act as a unit to provide alternating current flow, which is then converted to direct current by the diodes for charging the battery, and to supply power for the electrical accessories.

WHAT IS ALTERNATING CURRENT?

Electrical accessories in use on cars and trucks today require d.c., or direct current, flow in order to operate. This simply means that the current flowing through the conducting wires follows the same path at all times.

The electrical flow (electron flow) within the windings of both a d.c. generator and an a.c. alternator is induced by the strength of the magnetic field. In both cases, this induced voltage produces alter-

nating current flow, which is then converted to direct current flow by the use of a commutator in the d.c. generator, and by the use of positive and negative diodes in the alternator.

Figure 4-6 shows the basic rectification of the internally generated a.c. voltage in an alternator to useable d.c. voltage output.

Figure 4-7 shows the two main components of both a generator and an alternator.

The basic difference between the generator and alternator is simply that the magnetic field is stationary in the d.c. generator, while in the a.c. alternator, the magnetic field is rotating. In the d.c. generator, the magnets are bolted to the fixed generator housing with a wire wound armature rotated by a belt driven pulley. In the a.c. alternator, the magnets or pole pieces are part of the rotor which is driven by a belt and pulley or gear driven in heavy-duty applications, while the stator which is made up of loops of wire is stationary. In both cases, electrical energy is produced by the fact that voltage is induced into copper wires cutting magnetic lines of force.

From our earlier discussion on the basic operation of the alternator, you will recollect that the rotor is made up of a series of interlacing fingers, some of which are identified as being magnetic north (north

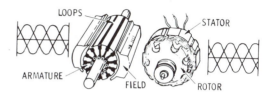

Fig. 4-7. Main components of a D.C. generator and an A.C. alternator. (Courtesy of Motorola Inc., Automotive Products Div.)

poles), while the others were magnetic south (south poles) as shown in Fig. 4-3.

SINGLE PHASE ALTERNATING CURRENT

The simplest form of alternating current is the single-phase type. If we consider Fig. 4-8, we see one pole of the rotor assembly as it relates to one single stator winding.

The strength of the magnetic lines of force shown in Fig. 4-8, are controlled by the small flow of electricity that leaves the battery when the ignition switch is turned on. This electrical flow then passes through one of the small brushes riding on the slip-ring, and into the field-winding wound internally within the rotor which is surrounded by the rotor poles (interlacing fingers) as shown in Fig. 4-4. This type of rotor with the interlacing fingers is often referred to as a claw pole rotor.

As the rotor turns within the inside diameter of the stator assembly, a voltage is induced in the winding of the stator. This induced electromotive force changes with the field strength and with the speed at which the magnetic lines of force are cut.

Since the magnetic lines of force always flow from north to south, the voltage induced in the stator winding will flow one way and then the other. If a voltmeter were placed across the stator winding as shown in Fig. 4-8, the needle of the gauge would swing first one way and then the other indicating that an alternating current is being produced within the stator winding. Fig. 4-10 shows a typical example of what is commonly referred to as a sine wave, or curve of alternating current induced during one complete revolution of the rotor having one north and one south pole. Notice that the greatest amount of induced voltage in the stator winding will occur when the magnet is at 90 degrees and 270 degrees. At these two positions, the relation of the magnet to the stator windings

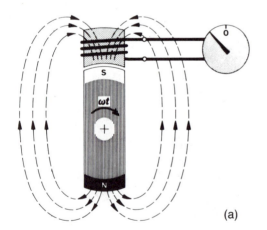
(a)

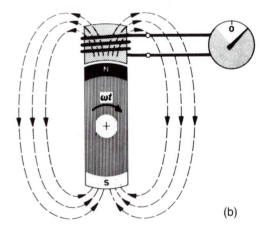
(b)

Fig. 4-8. (a) Magnetic flux (magnetic field) in the stator winding. The lines of force flow from the north to the south pole. (b) When the magnetic field is reversed, the polarity of the induced voltage changes. (Courtesy of Robert Bosch Corp.)

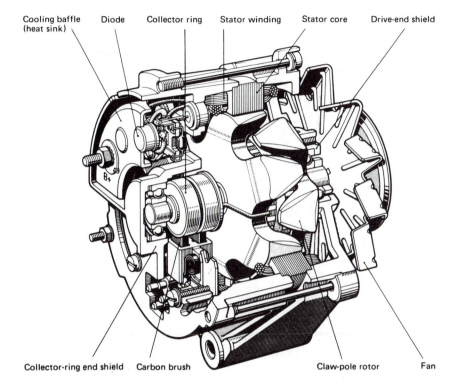

Fig. 4-9. Sectional view of a claw pole alternator. (Courtesy of Robert Bosch Corp.)

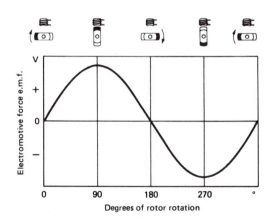

Fig. 4-10. Sine wave of induced alternating current during one turn of the rotor. (Courtesy of Robert Bosch Corp.)

causes the greatest number of magnetic lines of force to be cut.

If we study Fig. 4-10 a little closer, at 0° no voltage is induced in the stator wire (winding) because there are no magnetic lines of force cutting across the conductor. As the rotor turns from 0° towards 90°, the magnetic field at the leading edge of the rotor starts to cut through the wires of the conductor (stator), thereby steadily increasing the induced voltage into the wire until it reaches its maximum at 90°. Continued rotation from 90° to 180° will reduce the magnetic field cutting the wires of the conductor or stator, thereby reducing the induced voltage.

The current flow from 0° to 180° will be in one direction, namely the positive, which is shown as that area above the center line of Fig. 4-10. Rotor rotation from 180° towards 270° will cause the magnetic lines of force which are leaving the north pole to continue to enter the south pole. This action means that these magnetic lines of force are now cutting the stator wires from top to bottom rather than from bottom to top as was shown earlier when the rotor poles were at the 90° position. This action will cause a reversal of induced voltage in the stator windings (wires), so that we now have a negative current flow from 180° back to 360° with the peak voltage being induced at 270°, because of the position of the pole allowing the magnetic field to cut the windings. The voltage will again be zero when the pole piece sits at a horizontal position because once again no magnetic lines of force are cutting the stator windings (wires).

The sine wave shown in Fig. 4-10 represents one complete turn of the rotor with one north and one south pole. This action is more commonly referred to as one cycle. If this one pole rotor were driven at a speed of 3600 rpm, then in one second, it would complete 60 turns or cycles. The number of cycles per second is known as the frequency of the alternator. Since engine speed, and hence alternator drive speed, will vary when a vehicle is being driven, the frequency will not remain constant, but will fluctuate.

The induced voltage, and therefore the current flow, that could be taken from the stator winding employing only one coiled wire would not be very steady, and its output (amperage) would be low. To improve both of these conditions, all alternators in use today employ what is known as a three-phase stator winding.

THREE-PHASE STATOR WINDING

In the three-phase alternator, two additional wire windings are added to the single winding that we just discussed. This results in a stator consisting of three individual windings which are independent of one another as shown in Fig. 4-11.

Closer inspection of Fig. 4-11 will show that these windings are arranged in such a fashion that they are 120 degrees apart; therefore, induced voltage in each individual winding will occur at 120 degree intervals if we continue to use a single pole rotor. In reality, we do not use a single pole rotor, but one having more than that as shown in Fig. 4-9, which can have as many as 12 poles or interlacing fingers. With three individual windings in the stator, plus a rotor with six pole pieces (six positive and six negative fingers), we can there-

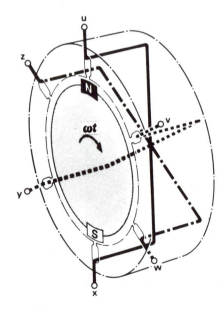

Fig. 4-11. Three-phase stator winding. (Courtesy of Robert Bosch Corp.)

fore produce a greater output at a steadier frequency.

Figure 4-12 shows an example of the sine wave produced per cycle by each winding in the three-phase alternator illustrated in Fig. 4-11.

With a multi-pole (finger) rotor, the generated voltage within the stator windings would now appear as shown in Fig. 4-13.

In Fig. 4-13 the magnetic field produced between the north to south poles jumps the air gap that exists between the rotor and the stator. Magnetic conduction will travel through the iron laminations to the opposite rotor pole piece. Continued rotation of the spinning rotor causes alternate north and south poles to cross each loop in the stator windings, thereby inducing a voltage into these same windings. The speed of the rotor (belt or gear driven, remember) will determine the amount of induced voltage; faster speed, greater voltage. An alternating current is produced in the stator windings as the direction of the rotating magnetic field changes from north

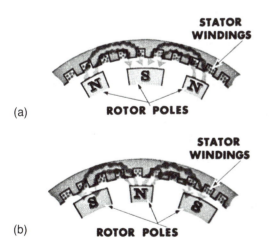

(a)

(b)

Fig. 4-13. Generated voltage in a multi-pole rotor. (Courtesy of Delco-Remy Div. of GMC)

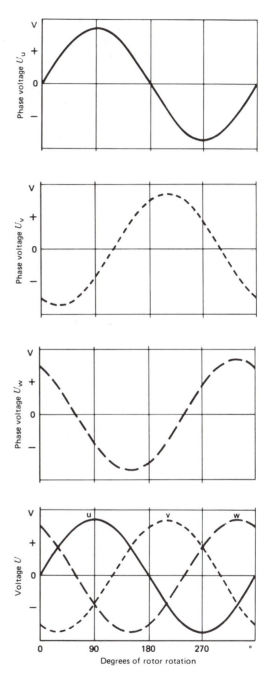

Fig. 4-12. Three-phase sine wave. (Courtesy of Robert Bosch Corp.)

to south and back again to north, as was discussed under single phase induced voltage earlier in this chapter.

Electrons always flow from the negative to the positive terminal; in practice, however, the conventional theory as discussed in the chapter on basic electricity, is normally used. This conventional theory states that the direction of current flow is always away from the positive terminal, and in circuit diagrams this is occasionally indicated by the use of arrows. For this reason, alternating current flow in a stator winding of an alternator may be shown as reaching its maximum positive value when the south pole of the rotor is at a position corresponding to 90° of its rotation, while other books on electricity may show this maximum value at 90° occurring when the north pole of the rotor is in this position.

For purposes of general explanation of alternating current flow, it matters little which pole piece is referred to. Delco-Remy, for example, places the south pole at the 90° position, while the Robert Bosch Corporation places the north pole in this same position when explaining alternating current flow within the typical alternator. Fig. 4-14 shows the sine wave form produced by a single-coil, two-coil and three-coil stator arrangement.

STATOR WIRING DESIGNS

The three-phase windings used in the alternator can be one of two designs.

1. The delta connected stator
2. The wye or Y connected stator

When the ends of the loops of wires are connected as shown in Fig. 4-15 we have both a delta and Y connected stator winding.

Three a.c. voltages are therefore available from the delta connected stator, which is like having three individual single-phase

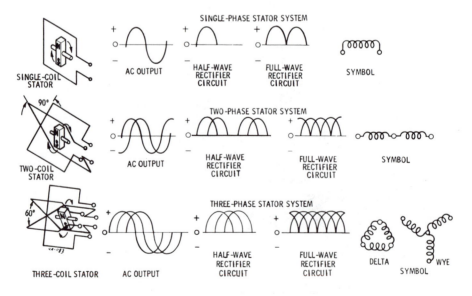

Fig. 4-14. Stator phase systems. (Courtesy of Motorola Inc., Automotive Products Div.)

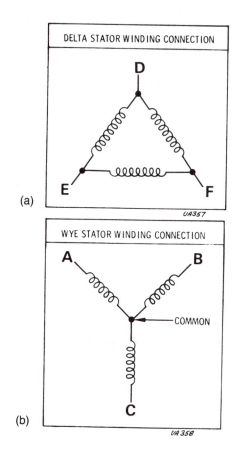

DELTA STATOR WINDING CONNECTION

D

E   F

UA357

(a)

WYE STATOR WINDING CONNECTION

A   B

COMMON

C

UA358

(b)

Fig. 4-15. (a) Delta wound stator winding, (b) wye (Y) wound stator winding. (Courtesy of Motorola Inc., Automotive Products Div.)

The difference in output obtainable from an alternator with the same stator, but with a delta versus a wye winding, is that the delta stator will produce a higher output at the top end of the speed range, while the wye winding will produce current equal to a delta winding at the low speeds at a lower rpm.

RECTIFICATION OF A.C. VOLTAGE

To convert a.c. voltage to d.c. voltage in an alternator, six silicon diodes are used. These diodes function as one-way check valves to allow current flow in only one direction. Three of these diodes are positive (+), while the other three are negative (-), in order to rectify the alternating voltage produced in each of the windings (three-phase).

Figure 4-16 shows a simple layout of a typical diode, both positive and negative. The positive diodes (cathode to heat sink), are mounted in a common insulated heat sink so that they cannot contact the alternator body end frame. The three negative diodes (anode to heat sink) are mounted in another heat sink called the negative diode assembly which is physically and electrically connected to the alternator body which is the negative or ground output terminal. The positive rectifier is insulated from the alternator body in a negative ground system, and connected to the positive output stud of the machine.

The three-phase stator windings are mounted to the stator assembly shown in Fig. 4-17.

As seen in Fig. 4-17, phase one forms the inner winding row, phase two the middle winding row, and phase three the outer winding row. Each winding set has a coil per rotor pole, or two coils per pole pair (360°) connected in series opposing. All

units wired together. However, in the Y connected stator, the voltages produced consist of the voltages in two loops of wire added together which will be approximately 1.7 times as large in magnitude as any one individual loop voltage. Three a.c. voltages, however, are available from the Y connected stator spaced 120° apart. The delta connected stator is common to cars and trucks, with the Y connected stator being optional, for example, on standby diesel electric generating sets.

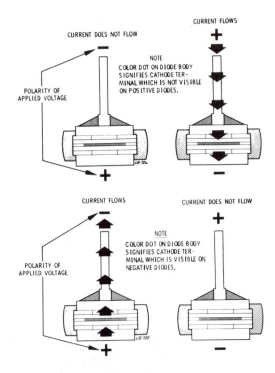

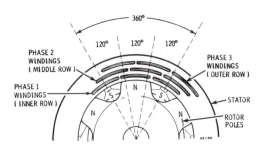

Fig. 4-17. Stator winding assembly. (Courtesy of Motorola Inc., Automotive Products Div.)

Fig. 4-16. Positive and negative type diodes. (Courtesy of Motorola Inc., Automotive Products Div.)

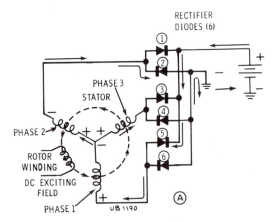

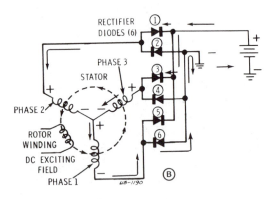

Fig. 4-18. (a) Half-wave rectification of the positive alternation; (b) reversal of phase one voltage (rotor has turned 180°) current reversal. (Courtesy of Motorola Inc., Automotive Products Div.)

windings are spaced 120 electrical degrees (not mechanical) apart with respect to the rotor poles and are terminated in a delta or wye (Y) arrangement.

A typical 12 pole rotor (6 pairs of north and south poles) will produce six output cycles for every revolution of the rotor in each stator winding set. When the rotor is in position to produce maximum positive output from phase one, the other two phases have opposing outputs. At this point, therefore, the instantaneous voltage polarities and direction of current flow will be as shown in Fig. 4-18 (a). This will be known as half-wave rectification of the positive alternation.

As the rotor continues to turn within the

stator windings, the voltage in phase one will be reversed (180°) along with the current flow, so that the battery receives this charge rate through a different set of diodes as shown in Fig. 4-18(b).

Figure 4-18(a) shows half-wave rectification of phase one, while Fig. 4-18(b) shows the full-wave rectification of phase one since both positive and negative alternations of one cycle were rectified from a.c. to d.c. through the positive and negative diodes. With six diodes, and the rotor turning at varying speeds as the engine is operating, this rectification action occurs for a very small period of time (wave-form peak), with all phases being the same.

ALTERNATOR CHARGING SYSTEMS

In the earlier part of this chapter, we discussed the purpose and basic function of the alternator assembly in order to give us a base from which to work from, prior to studying the various types and makes of alternators that are now in use on cars, trucks, heavy-duty off-highway equipment, industrial and marine applications.

To keep this as simple as we possibly can, let's break the types down by manufacturer because specific designs and minor operating changes between different makes can tend to confuse you during an explanation. Your train of thought will be less confused with one type and style, than with five or six different ones being discussed at once. In addition, if each manufacturer's alternator is discussed individually, the chapter section becomes a very handy reference for you at any future date. At the end of the chapter dealing with alternators, a wide variety of questions appears that deals with all of the different makes. Your ability to answer these questions will provide a quick method of review for you at any time that you feel the need to refresh your memory on specific points or topics.

No amount of theoretical training, however, can provide you with the dexterity obtained only by putting into practice what you read. Therefore, once you feel confident about the operation of each alternator, have your instructor or a shop mechanic guide you through all of the maintenance, overhaul, testing and troubleshooting steps required for each model, style, and type of alternator assembly. Supplement this hands-on training with a review of the theory as you progress from step to step, and by all means use the manufacturers' service information manuals when output specs or troubleshooting tips are required. With the wide variety of alternators in use today, along with the product improvement and updates, it is incumbent upon the auto electrician, mechanic, and apprentice to be totally familiar with all current information relating to each and every model that you are dealing with. In this way, your job of maintaining, testing, and troubleshooting the alternator charging system will become a pleasant and rewarding one.

Above all, don't second-guess yourself when dealing with electrical charging systems, because serious damage or expensive downtime can be the result. When in doubt, check it out properly and to your complete satisfaction.

Although there are many manufacturers of alternators world-wide, without a doubt the market is dominated by five or six major producers.

1. Delco Remy Division of General Motors
2. Leece-Neville of the Sheller-Globe Corporation

3. Motorola Incorporated
4. Robert Bosch Corporation
5. Lucas CAV Limited
6. Prestolite Company

The above companies are not listed in any special order of priority.

Many other manufacturers are not listed, because a large number of these build under licence for one of the six already listed.

The current state of the art in alternator design is such that there is not a wide variation in either the design or the components used between different makes, although there are peculiarities specific to particular models and manufacture.

Alternators are not unlike engines today, in that there are literally hundreds of manufacturers of engines world-wide, but in the final analysis all engines contain pistons, crankshafts, valves, cylinder heads, etc. Alternators are no different from engines from this respect; they all contain a rotor, stator, diodes, capacitor, etc. in order to operate efficiently.

Therefore, do not feel threatened if faced with troubleshooting an alternator that you are unfamiliar with. Take a few minutes to familiarize yourself with the minor changes incorporated in the alternator in question, the recommended method of testing, troubleshooting and adjusting, and you will very quickly be capable of correcting the problem at hand.

DELCO-REMY ALTERNATORS

As a major producer of electrical equipment for cars, trucks and heavy-duty equipment, the AC-Delco Division of General Motors Corporation can be credited with many firsts in the design and development of components for vehicle electric systems. Without a doubt, this division of General Motors is one of the world's leaders in the manufacture and development of both electrical and electronic equipment in a wide variety of applications of motive and stationary power.

BASIC ALTERNATOR MODELS (DELCO)

At the present time Delco-Remy manufactures a complete line of alternators for almost any application and rating. Many of these alternators follow the same general design and maintenance procedures, therefore we will concern ourselves with the range of alternators that are most widely used on cars, trucks, buses, and heavy-duty equipment.

Basically, two main types of alternators are used in these applications:

- The slip-ring and brush type
- The brushless type

The slip-ring and brush type models are identified by a plate rivited to the alternator housing, similar to the brushless type. The models that we will deal with are the brush-type 10 SI, 15 SI, 27 SI, and 40 SI, and the brushless type 25 SI, 30 SI, and 30 SI/TR, with the latest addition, the 32 SI oil cooled unit.

The letters SI stand for system-integral to indicate that the regulator is located inside the alternator. In addition, many of these alternators only require one wire between them and the battery, plus an adequate ground return circuit to operate, which simplifies the wiring system, and minimizes possible problem areas.

Some of these alternators use a Y connected stator winding, while others employ the delta wound winding. This will be discussed in more detail later in the chapter, as we look more closely at each model.

RATED OUTPUT

The output capacity of the alternator models that we will look at will vary for different applications. Accessory load, battery capacity rating, alternator field current flow, circuit wiring, and minor internal changes to each model alternator within the same series can vary its rated output. Therefore, when the rated output of any alternator is desired, always refer to the latest Delco-Remy Service Test Specifications Bulletin which is available direct from Delco, or your local Delco-Remy dealer.

As a general discussion point, the alternator models that we listed earlier have the following base ratings which can change within the model range to suit conditions.

- The 10 SI is available at 37, 42, 61, and 63 amperes at 5000 rpm and 14 volts.
- The 15 SI is available at 70, 80, and 105 amperes at 5000 rpm and 14 volts.
- The 27 SI is available at 65 or 80 amperes at 5000 rpm and 14 volts.
- The 40 SI is available at 145 amperes at 5000 rpm and 14 volts.
- The 25 SI is commonly used at 75 amperes at 5000 rpm and 14 volts.
- The 30 SI is commonly used at 90 amperes at 5000 rpm and 14 volts, while the 30 SI/TR is commonly used on a 12/24 volt system at 90 amperes at 6500 rpm.

Remember that the ratings listed above are common ratings which, although widely used with these alternators, can vary within a model series to suit other applications. Each model alternator is designed to provide a specified maximum current output. The output rating is generally stamped on the end frame of the alternator.

OPERATION OF BRUSH TYPE ALTERNATORS

Several years ago when d.c. generators and a.c. alternators were both readily available and used on cars, trucks, buses, etc., the word alternator versus generator indicated to the mechanic what was used to produce electrical energy to the charging system. However today, where load demands are high, alternators are used almost exclusively.

Although the alternator produces a.c. current, this is rectified to d.c. current for charging purposes. Therefore, the main purpose of the alternator is to generate electricity and for this reason, the alternator is now commonly called an a.c. generator. If you read the term a.c. generator in the following pages, this refers to an a.c. alternator.

The various brush-type generators produced by Delco-Remy regardless of their rated output and model designation, all operate on the same basic principle. Therefore in our discussion of the 10 SI, 15 SI, 27 SI, and 40 SI, the actual wiring circuit for one can be considered common to all. Where minor variations exist, these will be pointed out.

With the exception of the 10 SI series, 116 type one-wire system, all other models in this series use a voltage regulator that never requires adjusting, and in fact no provision for actual adjustment is provided. On the 10 SI series, 116 type one-wire system, a voltage adjustment cap in the slip-ring end frame can be repositioned externally to alter the voltage setting.

In addition, some 10 SI series generators are equipped with an R terminal on the

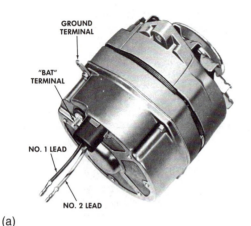

GROUND TERMINAL

"BAT" TERMINAL

NO. 1 LEAD

NO. 2 LEAD

(a)

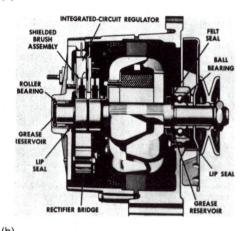

INTEGRATED-CIRCUIT REGULATOR

SHIELDED BRUSH ASSEMBLY

FELT SEAL

BALL BEARING

ROLLER BEARING

GREASE RESERVOIR

LIP SEAL

LIP SEAL

GREASE RESERVOIR

RECTIFIER BRIDGE

(b)

Fig. 4-19. Delco model 10SI Delcotron generator type 116: (a) wire location, (b) cross section view. (Courtesy of AC Delco Div. of GMC)

generator body in order that auxiliary equipment can be operated from this terminal in some circuits. This 'R' terminal usually provides half-system voltage only. All of these brush-type alternators are provided with an integrated circuit regulator mounted inside the slip-ring end-frame. The rotor shaft support bearings are of the pre-lubricated sealed type and require no periodic maintenance. The two

brushes that ride on the rotor shaft slip-rings carry battery current through one of them to supply the field winding, while the other brush acts as a return circuit to the battery. Under normal condition, these brushes will require no service until a major overhaul of the generator assembly.

In all of the brush type generators, the stator windings are assembled to the inside of a laminated core as was shown earlier under the basic alternator explanation. A rectifier bridge which is connected to the actual three-phase stator windings is constructed to hold six diodes. These six diodes, two for each stator lead, change the a.c. voltage to d.c. voltage.

On negative ground systems, three of these diodes are positive (+) and are mounted into a heat-sink which is insulated from the generator end-frame. The other three diodes are negative (-) diodes which are also mounted into a heat sink; however, this heat-sink is mounted directly to the end frame of the generator. Also connected to the stator windings is a diode-trio which controls the field current to the generator. To protect the rectifier bridge diodes and diode-trio from high voltage surges, and also to suppress radio noise, a capacitor or condensor is mounted in the end frame of the generator. The diode-trio works with the three negative diodes in the rectifier bridge to give us a d.c. voltage of the same magnitude as at the generator output terminal.

One other interesting feature of these brush-type generators is that the stator winding in the 10 SI series models is of the wye-wound configuration, while in the 15 SI, 27 SI, and 40 SI, the stator is a delta-wound configuration.

In a wye-wound (Y) stator, the stator windings operate in pairs so that the output voltage is the total voltage between one

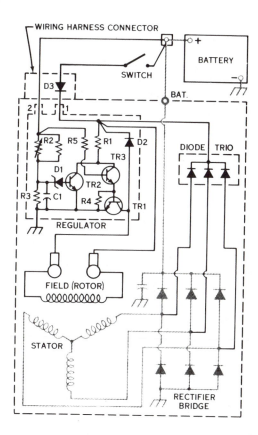

Fig. 4-20. Typical 10SI generator wiring circuit of 110 type, three-wire system. (Courtesy of Delco-Remy Div. of GMC)

stator winding lead and another. With a delta-wound stator the windings are not connected in pairs, but act independently, although they are producing voltage and current flow at 120 degree intervals as was explained earlier under three-phase operation.

With these differences noted, we can study the actual operation of these generators with the aid of a wiring diagram such as shown in Fig. 4-20 and also illustrated in Figs. 4-19(a) and (b).

NOTE: If you have not already done so, it would be to your advantage to first of all read over the section dealing with electronics, specifically the operation of both a diode and a transistor. Failure to understand how these two items function, will make it unclear to you just how the alternator circuit in Fig. 4-20 operates.

FLOW PATH OF FIG. 4-20

Initial a.c. voltages are generated in the stator windings by residual magnetism in the rotor. The two brushes and slip-rings are shown as a small rectangle and circle immediately above the field (rotor) area of the wiring diagram. As we mentioned in earlier discussions on the basic operation of the generator, field current is supplied through one of these brushes and slip-rings, while the other brush and its slip-ring provide a return circuit back to the battery from the field winding of the rotor. Each brush is connected into the solid-state circuit through diodes and transistors that control the current flow to the rotor field windings.

This particular circuit employs a wiring harness that plugs into the back of the generator as shown in Fig. 4-19(a), plus a battery terminal lead, and a ground terminal. These terminals are numbered in Fig. 4-19(a), and duplicated by number on the wiring diagram of Figs. 4-20 and 4-21.

The number 2 terminal is connected to the positive battery terminal which has a very low discharge current into terminal 2 due to the combined resistances of R2, R3, R5, TR1 and TR3.

The base-emitter of transistors TR3 and TR1 is connected to this battery current through resistor R5 and therefore both of these transistors are said to be turned on. When the ignition switch is closed (turned on), current from the battery will flow through the D3 diode which prevents charge current attempting to return to the battery from the diode-trio.

From diode D3, current flows to the number 1 generator terminal where it splits to both resistor R1 and transistors TR3 and TR1 to ground (battery negative), and also to one brush (right-hand one in diagram) and slip-ring, through the generator field winding inside the rotor, out the other brush and slip-ring (left-hand side of diagram) through TR1 and back to the battery ground.

When the engine starts and runs, the amount of generator output will vary with the rotative speed of the rotor. In either case, a.c. voltage is produced within the stator windings as the poles of the rotor and the magnetic field cut the stator windings, thereby inducing current flow in all three windings of the stator.

This stator a.c. voltage is converted to d.c. by the action of the six diodes in the rectifier bridge. This d.c. voltage appears between the battery ground and the generator battery or BAT terminal. In addition, this d.c. generated field current leaving the stator through the diode-trio which works with the three negative diodes in the rectifier bridge to give us a d.c. voltage of the same magnitude as at the generator output terminal, also flows to the field (through brush and slip-ring), TR1, and as mentioned already, through the grounded (negative) diodes in the rectifier bridge back to the stator. This combined action will therefore produce voltage and current flow to the battery and system accessories.

With the generator producing voltage, this voltage will of course increase with an increase in speed so that this increase is applied through resistors R2 and R3. When the voltage between R2 and R3 is high enough, zener diode D1 is triggered,

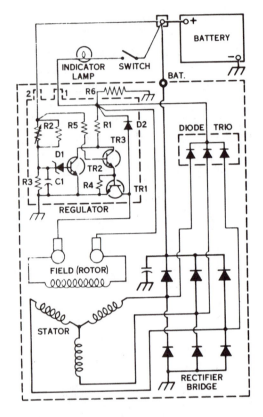

Fig. 4-21. Wiring circuit for a 10SI alternator with an indicator lamp. 15SI and 27SI series are identical except the stator is delta-wound.) (Courtesy of Delco-Remy Div. of GMC)

which conducts voltage to transistor TR2, and it turns on. Placement of transistor TR2 in the circuit will now turn off TR3 and TR1.

Turning off current flow to TR1 automatically reduces both the rotor field current and system voltage; D1 then blocks current flow allowing both TR3 and TR1 to turn back on. Both field current and system voltage increase and the cycle is repeated from ten times per second, to seven thousand times a second to limit the generator voltage to a preset value. The purpose of

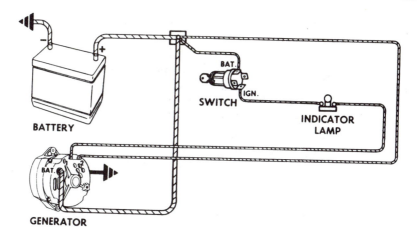

Fig. 4-22. Delcotron generator external wiring circuitry. (Courtesy of Delco-Remy Div. of GMC)

the capacitor C1 is to smooth out voltage surges across resistor R3 to protect the rectifier bridge and diode trio plus suppress radio noise. Some models of generators may contain two capacitors in the end frame.

Resistor R4 prevents excessive current leakage through TR1 at high temperatures, and diode D2 prevents high induced voltages in the field windings when TR1 turns off. To further provide the ideal or optimum rate of voltage charge to the battery, a thermister (resistor R2) causes the regulated voltage to vary with any change in temperature.

If for any reason, an open circuit should occur in the number 2 generator terminal circuit, transistors TR3 and TR1 will automatically turn off which isolates any current flow from the field thereby preventing an overcharge condition.

Minor variations can exist within a series/model wiring circuit such as the 10 SI, 15 SI, and 27 SI 100 type. This minor change can be seen in wiring circuit Fig.

4-21, which differs from that in Fig. 4-20 by the elimination of diode D3, the addition of an indicator lamp in the ignition switch circuit, and the inclusion of an additional resistor R6 which carries some of the indicator lamp current.

As you can see from Fig. 4-20 and Fig. 4-21, very little difference exists between these two circuits. The external circuit that would be used with these internal wiring arrangements would be the same for both with the only exception being that no indicator lamp would be required or used on Fig. 4-20, since it does not use this lamp and resistor R6, but uses instead diode D3. Except for this difference, the circuits are the same.

Figure 4-22 shows the typical external circuit used with these types of generators. Figure 4-22 shows the circuit with an indicator lamp, which would be used with the wiring diagram shown in Fig. 4-21; if the circuit did not use this warning lamp, it simply would not exist. Some systems may use an ammeter instead.

27 SI WIRING CIRCUIT

The wiring circuit commonly used on the 10 SI series generators has also been used on some 15 SI and 27 SI/100 types. However, minor differences exist between this circuit and the one used on the 27 SI series/200 type which has a three-terminal regulator and an external voltage adjustment cap.

This difference is shown in Fig. 4-23.

The basic difference in the flow path of the 27 SI 200 type from that of Fig. 4-21 is that resistors R2 and R3 are connected to the battery through the external voltage adjustment. Also, if the voltage adjustment cube (so called because it can be lifted out and replaced in alternate positions) should become open-circuited, TR3 and TR1 will turn off preventing high system voltage. There is also no D3 diode between the ignition switch and the number 1 terminal, as is shown in the earlier circuit. Also note that this circuit for the 27 SI 200 type has a delta wound stator rather than a Y type.

40 SI WIRING CIRCUIT

The 40 SI Delcotron generator is used on heavy-duty gas and diesel engines with a commonly used output rating of 145 amperes at 5000 rpm and 14 volts. It also can be equipped with a transformer rectifier combination for conversion to 110 volts d.c. with three a.c. terminals connected to the TR combination.

It also uses an external voltage adjustment cap similar to that used with other generator models. Only one wire is needed to connect the generator to the battery circuit along with an adequate ground return, and an R terminal is provided to operate auxiliary equipment in some circuits.

These alternator/generators should not be operated with an open circuit, or without a battery, as damage to the unit could result.

These generators are available with a two-terminal/two-rectifier bridge type, two-terminal/three-rectifier bridge type, three-terminal regulator/two-rectifier bridge type, or a three-terminal/three-rectifier bridge type.

The stator is of the delta wound style in all wiring arrangements.

The three-rectifier bridge type can be used on either a two-terminal or three-terminal regulator wiring arrangement, but is only common to the transformer rectifier combination for conversion to 110 volts d.c.

The 40 SI wiring circuit in Fig. 4-24(b) differs from previous illustrations in that it only contains two transistors, namely TR1 and TR2, whereas the 10 SI, 15 SI, 27 SI and 40 SI model in Fig. 4-24(a) uses three transistors identified as TR1, TR2, and TR3. These circuits are similar to some others discussed so far in that there is an external voltage cube adjustment. The other major exception on the 40 SI circuit in Fig. 4-24(b) is that it does not contain resistor R5 as the others did between R2 and TR2 which is clearly shown in Figs. 4-20, 4-21, 4-23, and 4-24(a).

When the generator is charging, current flows through the diode trio, R1, and R4 which turn on TR1. This action allows the stator to supply d.c. field current through the diode-trio, the field, TR1, and through the grounded diodes (negative) in the rectifier bridges back to the stator. Rectifier bridge diodes convert a.c. voltage to d.c. voltage as in other generators.

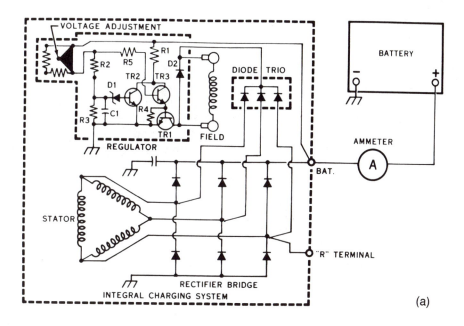

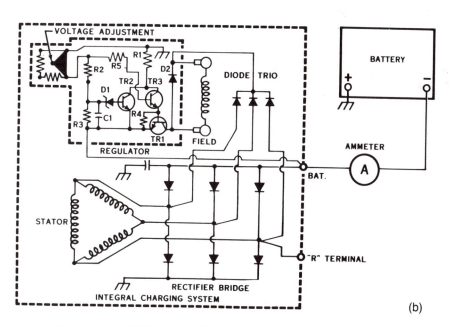

Fig. 4-23. (a) Model 27SI Series 200 negative ground wiring diagram. (b) Model 27SI Series 200 positive ground wiring diagram. (Courtesy of Delco-Remy Div. of GMC)

With an increase in speed and voltage, R2 and R3 are subjected to a higher voltage until the zener diode D1 conducts. In other systems with three transistors (TR1, TR2, and TR3) this action of the D1 zener diode turns transistor TR2 on, which also occurs in the 40 SI, but the reaction in the 40 SI wiring circuit in Fig. 4-24(b) is that only TR1 turns off, rather than TR1 and TR3 as

in the other systems using three transistors.

With TR1 now off, field current system voltage will automatically start to decrease and D1 zener diode then blocks current flow allowing TR1 to again turn on. In systems using three transistors both TR1 and TR3 would turn on.

This action allows field current to flow

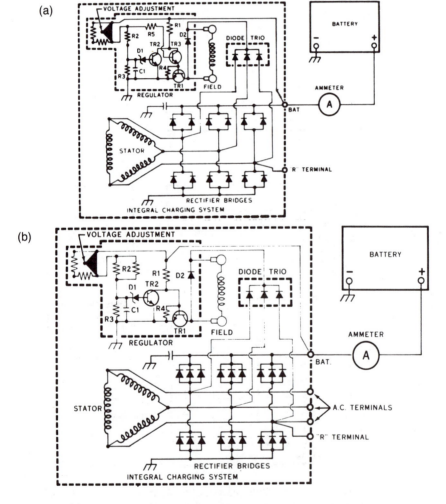

Fig. 4-24. Delcotron 40SI series, 150 type. (a) Two-rectifier bridge type. (b) Three-rectifier bridge type. (Courtesy of Delco-Remy Div. of GMC)

and a subsequent voltage increase in the system, and as mentioned earlier, this cycle of switching can occur at a rate as low as ten times per second, or as high as 7000 times per second.

WIRING DIAGRAMS FOR DELCO BRUSHLESS GENERATORS

Now that we have studied the wiring circuits commonly used on all Delco slip-ring and brush type Delcotron generators, this would be an ideal time to look at the circuits used on the Delcotron brushless generators. The brushless generator derives its name from the fact that it contains no brushes to carry electricity to and from the rotor slip-rings as in the conventional alternator. The brushless type employs a rotor with permanent magnetism; therefore, when it is rotated it induces a voltage in the stator windings. This current then flows through diodes and resistors back to the stator winding. A detailed explanation of the operation of the brushless generator is found herein.

These brushless generators feature a built-in voltage regulator; some models employ an external voltage adjustment cap that can be repositioned to change the voltage setting. Others require end cover removal to expose a voltage adjustment potentiometer, while yet others cannot be adjusted for voltage.

Commonly used models in the brushless series are the 20 and 29 SI/300 type for highway fleet general use, with the 20 SI rated at 35, 45 and 60 amperes at 6500 rpm, while the 29 SI is rated at 90 amperes at 6500 rpm.

The 25 SI series, 400 and 450 types are also used in highway fleet general use with

output ratings starting as low as 35 amperes on the 450 type, to 50 or 75 at 5000 rpm; other ratings such as 50 amperes at 6500 rpm or 75 amperes at 8000 rpm are also available. The type 400/25 SI is commonly rated at 75 amperes at 5000 rpm.

In the heavy-duty line, there is the 30 SI and 30 SI/TR (transformer rectifier) type which provides a separate voltage to charge a cranking battery. These models are used on series/parallel hookups and are commonly rated at 60 or 90 amperes anywhere from 5000 to 8000 rpm. A 31 and 32 SI are also available which are oil cooled high output generators rated between 50 to 85 amperes at 6500 rpm.

BRUSHLESS GENERATOR FLOW PATHS

20 and 29 SI Series

Figure 4-25 shows that the wiring circuit for the 20 and 29 SI is very similar to that used with the brush-type generators, namely the 10, 15, and 27 SI which was shown earlier in Fig. 4-21 along with a detailed explanation of the flow path.

The only difference between this circuit and that shown in Fig. 4-21 is that resistors R2 and R3 in the brushless circuit are connected to the battery through the voltage adjustment rather than the number 2 terminal on the brush type.

In addition the d.c. voltage from the rectifier bridge in the 20/29 SI series appears between ground and the POS generator terminal rather than at the generator BAT terminal as on the 10/15/27 SI series. If the connection between POS and R2 on the 20/29 SI should become open-circuit, transistors TR3 and TR1 will turn off preventing high system voltage.

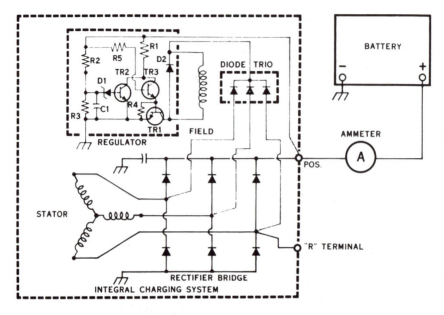

Fig. 4-25. Model 20SI alternator wiring diagram. 29SI is the same, but the stator is delta wound rather than wye wound. (Courtesy of Delco-Remy Div. of GMC)

25 SI Series Wiring Circuit

With the 25 SI Delcotron generator, only one wire is needed to connect the battery and Integral Charging System along with an adequate ground return to complete the circuit. The one output terminal on the generator body is specially designed so that it is electrically insulated from the housing, therefore no voltage reading can be registered with a voltmeter prod placed against this hex head bolt.

NOTE: On negative (-) ground models, a RED output terminal is used which should only be connected to the battery positive (+) circuit or terminal.

On positive (+) ground models, a BLACK output terminal is used which should only be connected to the battery negative (-) circuit or terminal.

This generator is equipped with an R terminal on some models to provide a feed to operate auxiliary equipment.

A plug beside the R terminal can be removed to allow access to a voltage adjustment screw inside the regulator of the generator.

The flow path for the 25 SI series generator shown in Fig. 4-26, is slightly different than that for the 29/29 SI.

Rotor movement through its permanent magnetism induces voltage flow in the stator windings which causes current flow through diodes D1, D2, D3, R1, R3, and the generator diodes back to the stator winding which is Y wound. Y wound means that the output voltage is the total voltage between one stator winding lead and another.

Transistors TR1 and TR2 are turned on, and the battery can supply current through R5, the field coil and TR1, and R2

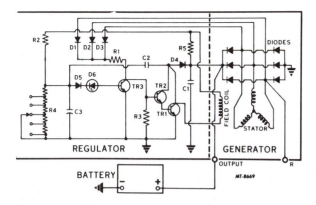

Fig. 4-26. Model 25SI brushless generator, negative ground. (Courtesy of Delco-Remy Div. of GMC)

and R4. With a speed increase and therefore voltage increase, the generated voltage across R4 is likewise impressed through diodes D5 and D6 due to the current flow through R5, R2, and R4.

When the pre-set (adjustable) voltage is reached, both D5 and D6 conduct and TR3 turns on which turns off TR1 and TR2, subsequently decreasing generator voltage because of a reduction in current flowing to the rotor field coil windings. This reduction of generated voltage causes D5, D6, and TR3 to again turn off and TR1 and TR2 to turn back on. This switching from off to on can occur as little as 10 times per second or as high as 7000 times per second to limit the generator's pre-set voltage.

Capacitor C1 functions as it did in other circuits, protecting the generator diodes from high transient voltages with this rapid switching, and also suppressing radio interference.

On 24 volt systems, an additional capacitor C2 causes TR1 and TR2 to quickly turn on and off. Diode D4 works along with TR1 and TR2 to prevent high field-coil induced voltages when these two transistors turn off. To smooth out voltage across R4, capacitor C3 is used. To compensate for line voltage drop, R5 raises the generator volt-

age slightly to maintain a more constant voltage across the battery as the generator output increases.

The wiring circuit used with the 25 SI series 400 and 450 types varies slightly so that an alternate circuit may be found on some of these models. This alternate circuit is shown in Fig. 4-27.

The circuit shown in Fig. 4-27 can be either positive or negative ground.

Flow in Fig. 4-26 is similar to that in Fig. 4-27, with the difference being that current from the stator flows through the three diodes to R6 to turn on TR1 and TR2. Current also can flow from the stator windings through the diode trio D1, D2, and D3, to the rotor field coil windings and TR1, returning to the stator windings through the other three diodes. When current flows through R1, R2, and R3, a voltage high enough will conduct through zener diode D4 and the base-emitter of TR3 to turn it on, which turns off TR1 and TR2. This action reduces flow to the rotor field winding reducing system voltage and both D4 and TR3 turn off; TR1 and TR2 turn back on to provide current flow to the rotor field winding once more, and generator output again increases. This switching from off to on occurs rapidly as explained

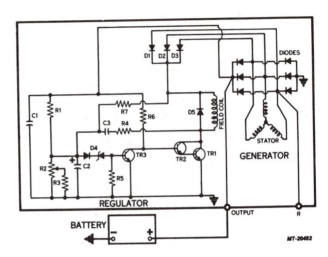

Fig. 4-27. Alternate wiring diagram for a model 25SI alternator unit. (Courtesy of Delco-Remy Div. of GMC)

for other generators. Potentiometer (adjustable) R2 and R3 controls the generator's output voltage limit.

Capacitor C1 functions the same as in the other circuit; D5 prevents high transient voltages in the rotor field coil windings when the field current is decreasing, while R5 prevents current leakage through TR3 at elevated temperatures.

R7, C3, and R4 operate together to rapidly turn TR1 and TR2 on and off.

30 SI AND 30 SI/TR SERIES WIRING CIRCUIT

The wiring diagram and circuit used with the 30 SI models uses a delta wound stator rather than a wye (Y) as has been shown in the last several circuits. The stator windings of a delta unit are not connected in pairs.

The basic flow path for the 30 SI series is very similar to that shown earlier for the 10 and 27 SI that used the voltage adjustment cap. The 30 SI uses the same numbered resistors, diodes and transistors on its wiring diagram as that used in both the 10 and

27 SI voltage adjustable type. The 10 and 27 SI units however are slip-ring and brush type, whereas the 30 SI units are brushless.

The flow path through the 30 SI circuit is therefore identical to that already explained previously for both the 10 and 27 SI units with the external voltage adjustment cap which was shown in Fig. 4-23.

To avoid showing a wiring circuit for both the 30 SI and the 30 SI/TR models, we will show only the circuit for the 30 SI/TR because the integrated circuit is the same for both with the exception that the upper half of the wiring diagram shown in Fig. 4-28 includes the transformer rectifer circuit with two delta wound stators, a TR bridge with six more diodes, and a C or cranking battery, plus the regular system battery. The 30 SI does not have the additional battery for cranking, or the two delta stators and transformer wiring.

The flow path for the lower portion of the 30 SI/TR and 30 SI generators is the same as that for both the 10 and 27 SI external voltage cap adjustment types explained earlier in this chapter, and shown in Fig. 4-23.

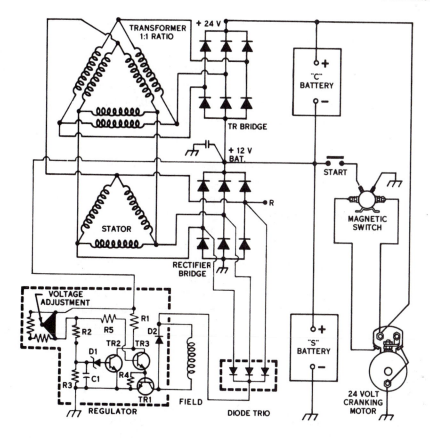

Fig. 4-28. Model 30SI/TR negative ground circuit. (Courtesy of Delco-Remy Div. of GMC)

In Fig. 4-28, a TR (transformer-rectifier) unit is mounted to the rectifier end frame, and is connected to the C or cranking battery as shown in the diagram. Both batteries are automatically connected into a series hookup arrangement to provide 24 volts for cranking or starting purposes only.

Within the transformer windings, we have a dual delta wound stator. The inner stator is wired to the delta stator in the lower half of the diagram, therefore induced a.c. voltages in the stator while the generator is operating will also be sensed at the upper stator (inner) windings.

An a.c. current will therefore flow in the primary (inner) delta stator in the upper half of the diagram. Basic electricity taught us that if we pass a current through a wire, then we create a magnetic field. This changing a.c. current, creating a magnetic field, will induce voltages in the transformer secondary winding similar to the action in an ignition coil or transformer. The difference here is that we do not require an increase in voltage such as we obtain in a coil with fewer windings in the primary than in the secondary. Here, the windings in the secondary are similar to those in the primary. The induced current and voltage flow in the secondary winding is rectified through the rectifier bridge to charge the C or charging battery.

This transformer rectified circuit eliminates the need for a series/parallel switch and the associated wiring which is shown under the chapter dealing with starter motors.

NOTE: The basic difference in the wiring circuit when a positive rather than a negative system is used is simply that everything shown in Fig. 4-28 that has a positive sign should be changed to a negative sign; also, the diodes in both rectifier bridges would conduct current flow in the opposite direction, and resistor R1 would be grounded rather than running up to the +12 V BAT terminal. The negative battery posts in the wiring circuit would also become positive (+).

With the 30 SI/TR circuit, the cranking battery is charged at a low rate to maintain its full state of charge while the engine is running. The vehicle electrical system with the exception of the cranking motor is 12 volts.

This completes the wiring circuits for both the slip-ring and brush type generators as well as for the brushless type. You will have noticed quite a similarity between many of the wiring circuits discussed within this chapter. This similarity makes it a relatively easy task to assimilate fairly quickly the flow paths and differences between all of the generator models produced by AC Delco. This should help you to remember many of these flow paths with a short review of each circuit anytime that you contemplate testing or troubleshooting one of these systems.

MOTOROLA ALTERNATORS

Alternators produced by Motorola are of conventional design, with both slip-ring and brush type and solid-state regulator models available in a wide variety of rated outputs to meet a variety of conditions and applications.

The field for the alternator is wound around the core of the rotor which generally contains the standard design twelve poles (six sets of pole pairs, north and south). The rotor is then supported in the alternator end frames by a pair of sealed ball bearings.

The alternator is externally excited by a field current of approximately 2.5 amperes supplied to the field by a set of electrographite brushes through conventional copper slip-rings on one end of the rotor shaft.

The brush-holder is easily removed after removal of the voltage regulator for either inspection or replacement which does not require the disassembly of the alternator.

A typical Motorola alternator is shown in Figs. 4-29 and 4-31.

The stator is connected to a three-phase, full-wave bridge rectifier package containing six diodes (three positive and three negative) which convert the a.c. current/voltage flow to d.c. Power to the regulator and alternator field is provided by the field diode which is commonly referred to as a diode trio package contained within the alternator. This is a low current version of the positive half of the rectifier package which gives us a d.c. voltage of the same magnitude as at the regulator output terminal. The system permits the use of an indicator or alternator warning lamp, and also isolates the regulator and field from the battery to prevent battery drain when the alternator is not operating.

Fig. 4-29. Rear view of a typical Motorola alternator assembly. (Courtesy of Motorola Inc., Automotive Products Div.)

Rated alternator outputs are achieved at 6000 rpm alternator speed at an ambient temperature of 75°F (23.8°C). The alternator itself is designed to operate in ambients of −40°F to +212°F (−40°C to 100°C). A cooling fan mounted behind the drive pulley ensures adequate cooling of the rectifier bridge and internal components of the alternator. These alternators, as with other makes, can be driven (rotated) in either direction since a.c. is produced internally, which can then be rectified. However, operation of any alternator with the wrong directional air flow fan can lead to overheating and serious alternator damage.

TYPES OF ALTERNATOR TERMINATIONS

Motorola uses a variety of alternator designs and therefore several types of alternator terminations. These are discussed in the following paragraphs.

Grounded Output Alternators

These alternators can be either positive or negative ground depending on which half of the rectifier bridge is grounded, with their operation being the same.

The basic difference between the positive and negative grounded systems is that the rectifier and field diode or isolation diodes polarities are reversed, and the brush assembly of the positive ground alternator is insulated (two floating terminals) from the housing.

Figure 4-33 shows typical Motorola alternator circuit diagrams where the isolation and field diodes are clearly shown for both a wye and delta wound stator.

Grounded Brush Alternator

This system is used in negative ground systems with solid-state regulators that employ PNP type output transistors.

The alternator has one brush terminal internally connected to the housing (ground).

Floating (Insulated) Brush Alternator

In this alternator assembly, both brushes are insulated from the alternator housing (ground). This feature is used on positive ground applications with regulators that contain PNP type output transistors or in negative ground applications with regulators containing NPN output transistors.

Floating (Insulated) Output Alternators

This alternator assembly has both the positive and negative diode sets insulated from the housing (ground), therefore these units can be used in positive or negative ground systems simply by connecting the appropriate output terminal to ground.

ALTERNATORS WITH AN ISOLATION DIODE

The isolation diode electronically operates a charge indicator lamp (see Fig. 4-33) by being located in series with the alternator output so that the lamp is electrically connected across the diode. The auxiliary or regulator terminal of the alternator is a sense point for the voltage regulator in the charging system, therefore it is important that the correct regulator be used with the isolation diode alternators for proper system operation.

Figure 4-30 shows both a single and dual isolation diode assembly which physically contains one or more silicon diodes installed in a separate heat sink.

The output current capability of the alternator establishes the number of diodes used because the entire alternator output must flow through the isolation diode. A further example of how both the single and dual isolation diode would appear on the end frame of the alternator assembly is shown in Fig. 4-31.

ALTERNATORS WITH FIELD DIODE

The field diode is actually three diodes, and is commonly called the diode trio. Its function is to supply power to the rotor field winding when the alternator is charging. A charge indicator lamp can also be used with this design. The diode trio

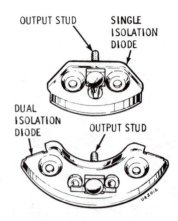

Fig. 4-30. Isolation diode assemblies. (Courtesy of Motorola Inc., Automotive Products Div.)

works with either the three negative or three positive diodes of the rectifier bridge in various makes of alternators to give us d.c. voltage of the same magnitude as at the generator or regulator output terminal. The diode trio is quite small because they only have to handle the small field current.

Figure 4-32 shows several types of field diodes currently used in various Motorola alternators.

MOTOROLA SC SERIES ELECTRONIC ALTERNATOR

This series of electronic alternator is available in either 12, 24 or 32 volt models, and was designed for use on heavy-duty truck, bus, industrial, and marine applications. They employ the standard slip-ring and brush design, and include an integral regulator which can be easily removed if necessary.

The alternator features an insulated (floating) output system for use in both positive and negative ground applications. High outputs are provided at comparatively low cut-in speeds with total

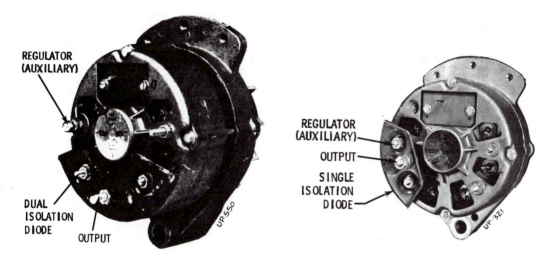

Fig. 4-31. Location of isolation diodes. (Courtesy of Motorola Inc., Automotive Products Div.)

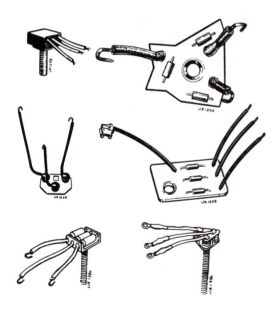

Fig. 4-32. Types of field diodes. (Courtesy of Motorla Inc., Automotive Products Div.)

weight of the unit being only 25 pounds (11.43 kg).

The integral regulators incorporate all silicon devices, an adjustable output voltage control and protection circuitry against load dump and transients.

The 12-volt model can produce either 88 or 160 amperes, the 24-volt model either 100 or 120 amperes, and the 32-volt unit 100 amperes, with an alternator speed of approximately 6000 rpm. The rotor used with this heavy-duty unit is a 16 pole assembly with a field current draw of approximately 2.4 amperes. Twelve rectifier diodes (6 positive and 6 negative) are connected to the stator in three-phase full-wave rectification. The field diode assembly (diode trio) is connected to the stator terminals to supply regulator power and field current after initial excitation.

Figure 4-34 shows a cutaway view of the

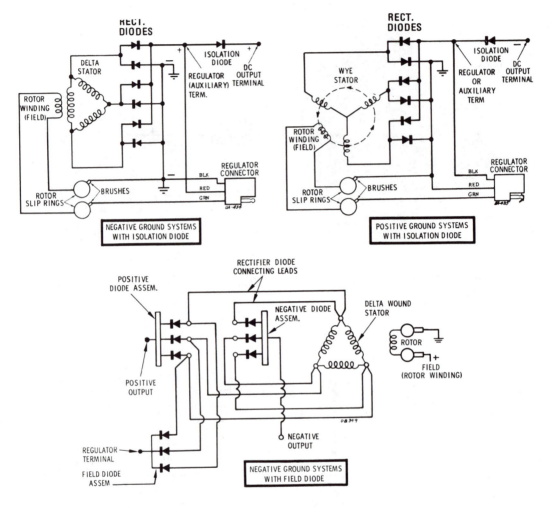

Fig. 4-33. Typical Motorola alternator circuit diagrams. (Courtesy of Motorola Inc., Automotive Products Div.)

major components of the heavy-duty SC series alternator assembly.

Figure 4-35 shows the alternator wiring schematic for a current 12-volt production unit.

The voltage regulator used with this alternator has an external voltage adjusting switch with five voltage select positions to tailor the charging rate between 13.2 to 14.4

volts on the 12-volt systems, between 26.8 to 29.2 on the 24-volt systems, and from 36.6 to 40.2 volts on the 32 volt systems. This voltage select control screw is located on the top right of the regulator housing at the rear of the alternator as can be readily seen in Fig. 4-34.

The field diodes (diode trio) supply field current to the rotor when the engine is

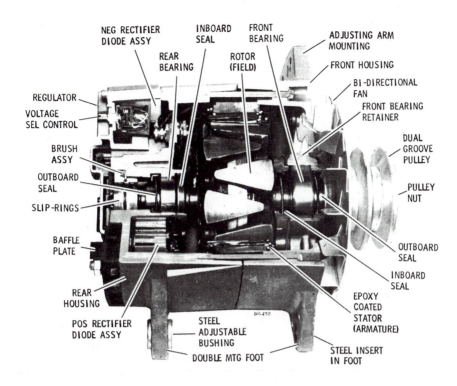

Fig. 4-34. Model SC alternator cutaway. (Courtesy of Motorola Inc., Automotive Products Div.)

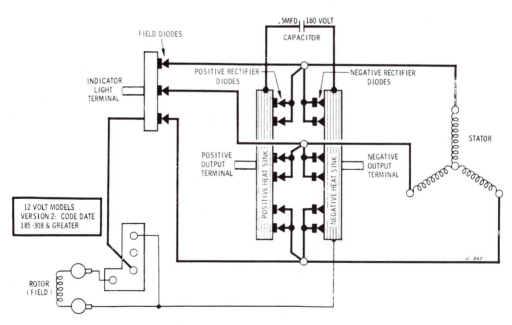

Fig. 4-35. Model SC alternator wiring diagram. (Courtesy of Motorola Inc., Automotive Products Div.)

running via the electronic regulator assembly. Within the voltage regulator is a zener diode and a driver switching-type transistor to monitor alternator output.

As with all types of electronic regulator assemblies, the rotor field current flow is switched on and off rapidly by the action of a transistor in series with the rotor field winding. When the pre-set voltage range is reached, the zener diode will conduct causing the driver transistor to turn off the field switching current which will immediately reduce alternator output.

When the system voltage drops below the zener diode firing or conducting voltage, the driver transistor turns on the current flow to the rotor field winding to increase the output of the alternator.

This switching action from on to off occurs at a rate as low as ten times per second to as high as 7000 times a second and maintains a more or less constant voltage in the system to the battery.

The positive and negative diodes function to convert the stator induced a.c. voltage to d.c. voltage. The diode trio or field diodes work with the six negative or positive diodes (depending on the type of ground, + or −) to give us a d.c. voltage of the same magnitude as at the generator output terminal. However, the diode trio handles only a small amount of field current.

EXTERNAL ALTERNATOR FIELD EXCITATION SC SERIES

From previous discussions on the basic operation of all alternators we know that the rotor field windings require a supply of current to initiate a magnetic field in the rotor pole fingers in order for the alternator to produce its rated output capacity. This, of course, is done by supplying a small amount of current flow from the battery positive terminal usually in the range of 1.5 to 2.5 amperes. This excitation current can be controlled in several ways such as illustrated in Fig. 4-36 and Fig. 4-37.

In negative ground systems, any two-way switch can be used to supply power to the excitation terminal; however, on positive ground installations, a positive potential is necessary for rotor field excitation such as is shown in Fig. 4-37. If an indicator lamp is used, it should be wired into the circuit as shown in Fig. 4-38.

MOTOROLA 9DA SERIES ALTERNATORS

This series of alternators is widely used on passenger car applications that require normal or special charging requirements, with models available in 55 or 62 amp, 12-volt negative ground systems with or without an integral, solid-state voltage regulator.

The alternator can be obtained with a solid-state regulator to form a complete charging system, or is available with a two-pin plug for connection to a remote mounted regulator assembly. Both models are of three-phase design with diode rectification and weigh about 10 pounds (4.536 kg) minus the drive pulley.

The rotor is a 12 pole (six sets of pole pairs, north and south), with rotor field current being approximately 2.5 amperes supplied through slip-rings and brushes made of electrographite. Figure 4-39 shows a typical 9DA alternator assembly.

The wiring circuit for the 9DA follows the same flow path as that for the heavy-duty SC series described within this chapter. The wiring circuit for the 9DA remote and integral regulator models is shown in Fig. 4-40.

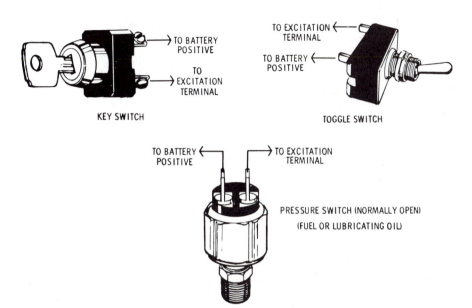

Fig. 4-36. Excitation switches, negative ground systems. (Courtesy of Motorola Inc., Automotive Products Div.)

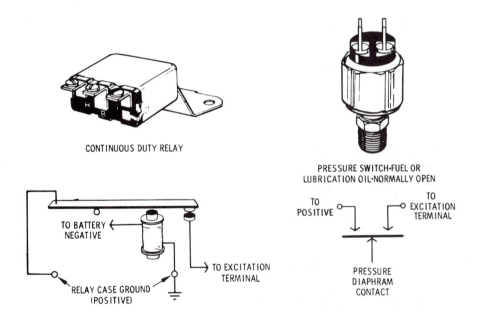

Fig. 4-37. Excitation switches, positive ground systems. (Courtesy of Motorola Inc., Automotive Products Div.)

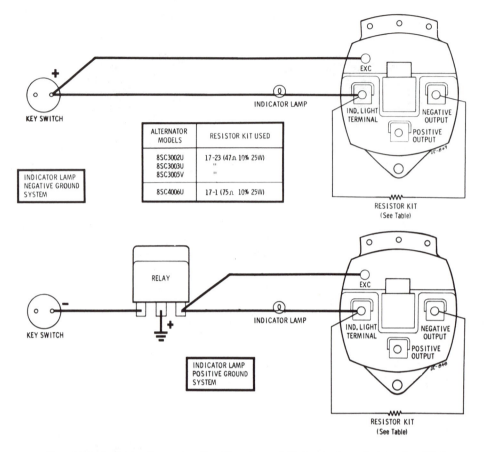

ALTERNATOR MODELS	RESISTOR KIT USED
8SC3002U	17-23 (47Ω 10% 25W)
8SC3003U	"
8SC3005V	"
8SC4006U	17-1 (75Ω 10% 25W)

INDICATOR LAMP NEGATIVE GROUND SYSTEM

INDICATOR LAMP POSITIVE GROUND SYSTEM

Fig. 4-38. Indicator lamp circuits. (Courtesy of Motorola Inc., Automotive Div.)

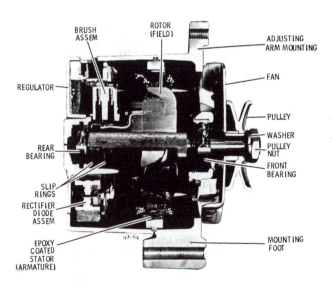

Fig. 4-39 Model 9DA alternator assembly: (a) cutaway view.

INTEGRAL & REMOTE REG MODELS

Starting with carbon pile off, slowly increase load while observing ammeter and maintaining 5000 RPM. Increase load until a minimum output voltage of approximately 13.7 volts is obtained. Record the output current at this point and refer to the chart for minimum acceptable ratings

MINIMUM ACCEPTABLE OUTPUT VALUES (72° F)

ALT MODEL	VOLTAGE (VOLTS)	OUTPUT CURRENT (AMPS)
55 AMP	13.7	51
62 AMP	13.7	58

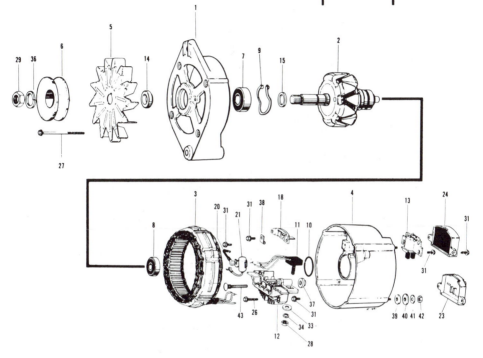

REF NO.	DESCRIPTION	REF. NO.	DESCRIPTION
1	HSNG, FRNT	23	COVER ASSY (REM REG.)
2	ROTOR	24	VOLT REG. (INTEG REG.)
3	STATOR	26	SCREW, TAPPING, HEX 8-32x1''
4	HSNG, REAR	27	BOLT, THROUGH, 10-32x3''
5	FAN	28	NUT, NO. 10-24
6	PULLEY	29	NUT, 5/8-18x15/16
7	BRNG, FRONT	31	SCREW, TAPPING, HEX 8-32x1/2''
8	BRNG, REAR	33	INSULATOR, WASHER NO. 10
9	RET, FRNT BRNG	34	WASHER, SPLIT-LOCK NO. 10
10	RET, REAR BRNG	35	WASHER, SPLIT-LOCK NO. 8
11	DIODE, TRIO (INTEG REG.)	36	WASHER, SPLIT-LOCK 5/8
12	RECT BRIDGE ASSY	37	INSULATOR, BRIDGE MTG
13	BRUSH ASSEM	38	MISC. CLAMP, HOLD-DOWN
14	SPACER, FAN & PUL	39	WASHER, NO. 12
15	SPACER, ROTOR	40	WASHER, NO. 12
18	TERMINAL	41	WASHER, .228x.562
20	CABLE	42	NUT, 12-24
21	CAPACITOR	43	BOLT, CARRIAGE 12-24x1.80''

Fig. 4-39 continued: (b) exploded view. (Courtesy of Motorola Inc., Automotive Products Div.)

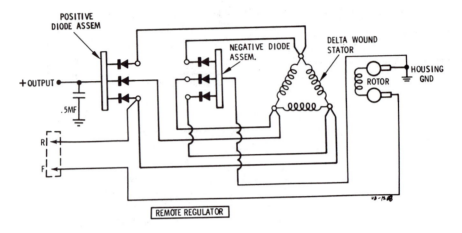

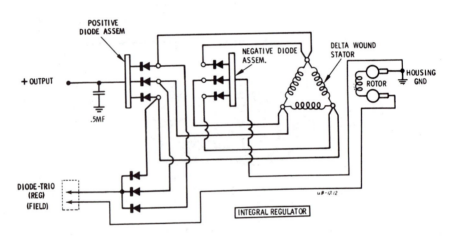

Fig. 4-40. Model 9DA alternator schematic wiring diagram. (Courtesy of Motorola Inc., Automotive Products Div.)

A design feature of this alternator assembly is that it can have its rear housing rotated to one of four positions spaced 90° apart for special installation requirements, simply by removing the regulator and brushes from the rear cover area, then removing the four through-bolts. The housing can then be rotated either clockwise or counter-clockwise to the desired position, then the through-bolts, brushes,

and regulator can be replaced into position.

The integral regulator for voltage control on these models of alternators is shown in Fig. 4-41.

The regulator shown in Fig. 4-41 utilizes all silicon semiconductors and thick-film assembly techniques. Once the voltage has been adjusted to the proper regulating value, the complete circuit is encapsulated

Fig. 4-41. Integral voltage regulator. (Courtesy of Motorola Inc., Automotive Products Div.)

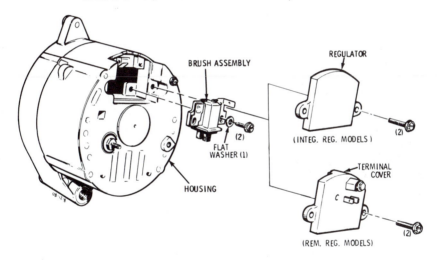

Fig. 4-42. Location and removal of voltage regulator/terminal cover. (Courtesy of Motorola Inc., Automotive Products Div.)

in epoxy to protect the circuit and the components from possible damage due to handling or vibration and moisture encountered in typical vehicle applications.

The voltage regulator is also temperature compensated to provide a slightly higher voltage at low temperatures, and a lower voltage at higher temperatures which is necessary in order to maintain a proper

state of charge to the vehicle battery.

Removal of the voltage regulator and terminal cover plus the brush holder assembly is shown in Fig. 4-42, which also indicates that a terminal cover is used on the rear of the alternator when a remote mounted voltage regulator is used. The integral regulator assembly is bolted directly to the rear of the alternator.

Chapter
4B

Alternator/Regulator Troubleshooting

Problems with the vehicle charging system can be minimized with proper periodic maintenance procedures. When problems occur in the electrical charging system, they can usually be traced fairly quickly. This is possible because of the use of solid-state devices by most manufacturers of charging system components, and because of the introduction of sophisticated electronic testing equipment.

Although much of this test equipment can be expensive, it will more than pay for itself in the time that is saved in analyzing a charging system problem, pinpointing very quickly the component actually at fault. Thus, there is no need for substituting components one at a time to try to solve the problem. In addition, the use of solid state devices and test equipment does much to safeguard against possible damage while troubleshooting and testing the system.

Although particular makes and styles of charging systems will exhibit unique problems, in general problems of battery undercharge or overcharge can be considered common to almost every alternator/regulator system in use today.

Minor design and style changes may make it appear that one system is totally different from another. However, on closer inspection, the systems are found to be quite similar. A review of typical wiring circuits used by Delco-Remy, Motorola and Leece-Neville alternator/regulators will quickly convince you of their basic similarities.

In general, the voltage regulators used with today's alternators are either built-in to the rear of the alternator assembly, or they are solid-state devices which can be remotely mounted from the alternator assembly.

Prior to successfully troubleshooting an alternator/regulator charging system, the battery must be in at least a 75% state of charge condition. This is necessary because not only does the battery supply initial external field excitation to the alternator rotor field circuit, but also represents a continuous although variable electrical load to the alternator.

There are a variety of "do not" testing precautions that must be exercised when testing alternator/regulator charging circuits, and these are discussed in this chapter. However, the six most important ones are listed below.

1. Make certain when installing a battery that its ground polarity and the ground polarity of the alternator are the same. Connecting a battery with reverse polarity to that of the alternator will result in destruction of the rectifier diodes in the alternator.

2. Never operate an alternator with the system battery disconnected and the engine running, since the loss of the battery will result in the charging voltage rising to unsafe levels.

3. Never disconnect any wires from the charging system while the engine is running. This also applies to battery cables, otherwise alternator diodes may be damaged or the voltage regulator destroyed.

4. Never ground any system connections or make test connections while the engine is running or the ignition switch is on. This may damage internal circuitry in the transistorized regulator or alternator.

5. Never make jumper wire connections while the engine is running or that would apply full battery voltage to the field connections of the regulators or alternator, since this will also cause component damage.

6. Do not connect the ignition terminal of the regulator directly to the ignition coil or the ignition terminal of a relay, since this may fail the regulator due to the improper flow of high voltage ignition currents.

Additional precautions are given in Table 4-1.

CHARGE INDICATOR LAMP

Figure 4-43 shows one example of how a charge indicator lamp is tied into the circuit. The circuit is not complete in the illustration; only the indicator lamp part is shown.

In Fig. 4-43 when the ignition switch is turned on, the contacts are closed; prior to starting the engine, current will flow from the battery and through the indicator lamp

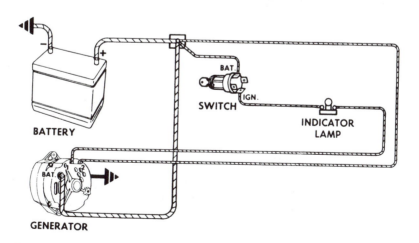

Fig. 4-43. Typical alternator charging lamp indicator circuit.

Table 4-1. Alternator Precautions

Some of the more important "Do's" and "Don'ts" that should be observed during charging system operations and test procedures are listed below.

Do Not Short Field terminal of alternator to ground while charging system is in operation. Indiscriminate grounding of alternator or regulator terminals can result in damage to the charging or electrical system of the vehicle.

Do Not Disconnect voltage regulator while alternator is in operation. Also, don't remove regulator ground lead while system is functioning or regulator damage may occur.

Do Not Disconnect load (alternator output lead) while alternator is operating.

Do Not Disconnect battery while charging system is in operation.

Do Not Remove alternator from vehicle without first disconnecting the ground cable (the negative (−) battery cable in most cases).

Do Not Remove battery from vehicle without disconnecting the ground cable first (negative (−) side of battery is most cases), then disconnect the insulated cable (positive (+) side of battery in most cases).

Do Not Allow charging system voltage to exceed approximately 16 volts during in-vehicle tests, or system damage may result.

Do Not Attempt to polarize an alternator.

Do Make sure all charging system connections are clean and tight (especially regulator ground lead output terminal and battery connections).

Do Observe proper system ground polarity when installing battery or alternator.

Do Make sure battery is in good condition and fully charged before performing in-vehicle and troubleshooting tests.

Do Use accurate test equipment since system malfunction can sometimes be indicated by very small differences in voltage and current.

Do Disconnect battery ground cable to avoid possible system damage when charging battery or welding on the vehicle.

Do Check harness wire size to prevent excessive loss, especially when replacing the alternator with a higher capacity unit.

Do Check alternator drive belt for proper tension and condition before proceeding with system tests.

(Courtesy of Motorola Inc., Automotive Products Div.)

circuit relay contact points to ground, which completes the circuit and a lighted indicator lamp signifies that the alternator is not charging. When the engine is running, and the alternator is charging, the voltage at the relay terminal of the unit will flow to the indicator lamp relay winding, thereby causing the relay contacts to separate and the light will go out.

ALTERNATOR/REGULATOR TEST EQUIPMENT

Particular manufacturers provide special tools and test equipment designed exclusively for use with their own products, which make overhaul, repair, and testing of these products much faster and professional. However, some of these special tools are also commonly used with other makes of alternator/regulators.

Typical equipment required for general electrical in-vehicle testing of the alternator/regulator should include the following locally available meters and gauges.

1. A carbon-pile capable of variable adjustment from 0 to 600 ampere load capacity. Typical models available are:

(a) Sun Electric Model Y-20 (See Fig. 4-45 or equivalent.

(b) Snap-on model

(c) Allen model

2. 12 volt test lamp which can be home-made with a 3 to 15 candle-power lamp in a socket, with two 3 foot (0.9 m) test leads fitted with alligator clips on the wire ends, preferably with an insulated cover over them to prevent short-circuiting in tight spots.

3. Ohmmeter used for checking continuity of a circuit, as well as resistance anywhere in the circuit.

There are many types and styles of ohmmeters available, from the widely used Simpson 260 shown in Fig. 4-44(a) to the newer digital readout types shown in Fig. 4-44(b).

CAUTION: Some models of digital ohmmeters in use by many shops and service personnel have an output current limitation of 0.001 amperes, while others may only have an output current of as little as 0.000001 micro-amperes. This low current is inadequate to turn a PN junction on. Therefore when using this type of ohmmeter to test diodes in the charging system, a very high resistance will be registered that leads you to believe that the diode is defective when it may be o.k.

Therefore, these types of digital ohmmeters should not be used for this purpose. Use an ohmmeter with a 1.5 volt test cell.

4. VAT (volts-amperes tester) which can be used to monitor both voltage and amperes in the circuit with the use of a switch.

The unit should have a range of approximately −10 to +100 or higher d.c. amperes depending on the particular maximum range necessary for typical requirements.

(a)

(b)

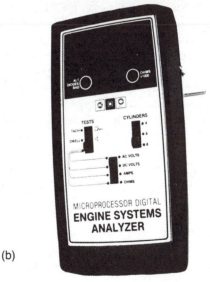

Fig. 4-44. (a) Simpson model 260 volt/ohm/milliammeter, (b) digital type milliammeter.

A typical example of a VAT tester is the Sun Electric Model 24 or equivalent shown in Fig. 4-45.

5. Battery Hydrometer or equivalent such as an American Optical refractometer

for checking the specific gravity of the battery electrolyte. Typical battery hydrometers and a refractometer can be seen under the battery section in chapter 3.

6. Assortment of jumper wire leads equipped with alligator clips at each end, made from No. 10 good quality copper wire, in various lengths from 2 to 10 feet (.6 to 3 meters) in two-foot increments.

Prior to testing a charging circuit, ensure that the battery is at least 75% charged (1.240 specific gravity), although some manufacturers require that the state of charge be at least 1.245 prior to effectively testing the circuit condition.

When viewing the cell condition tester on maintenance-free batteries, the green color can signify as little as a 65% battery state of charge. Therefore, it is imperative that the condition of the battery be established first with either a hydrometer reading on a nonmaintenance-free type, or by a voltmeter or light-load test of the battery on the maintenance-free type.

Further check that the fan belts are properly adjusted and in serviceable condition.

Wires, cables and plug-in harnesses should be free of corrosion and tight.

Alternator Fails to Charge

Typical causes of charging system complaints are listed below, with either battery overcharge or undercharge being the two most common complaints.

1. Faulty alternator

2. High circuit resistance caused by poor battery connections, or wiring resistance caused by corrosion or loose connections or opens.

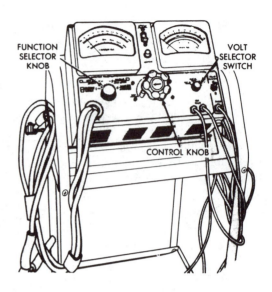

Fig. 4-45. VAT (volt/amp tester). (Courtesy of Sun Electric Corp.)

3. Open excitation resistor between the battery and alternator rotor field.

4. Poor regulator ground connection

5. Inoperative regulator

6. Broken wiring to regulator or faulty leads.

Low or Unsteady Charging Rate

1. Drive belt loose or damaged

2. Faulty alternator

3. High circuit resistance in the charging or ground return, or battery connections

4. Regulator lead connections faulty

5. Regulator faulty

Excessive Charging Rate

This condition can usually be pinpointed by the fact that frequent burning out of fuses and lights exists, plus the battery requires frequent refilling on the nonmaintenance-free types.

1. Ensure that all of the connections on both the regulator and alternator are tight.

2. Voltage regulator is shorted

3. Poor or broken regulator ground connection

MOTOROLA ALTERNATOR/ REGULATOR TEST PROCEDURE

The test procedure used on different models of Motorola alternators/regulators will vary somewhat; however, these variations are minor, and can be specially noted in the particular Motorola service manual or test bulletin for the unit to be tested. The following procedure is general in nature to the actual test requirements required to effectively troubleshoot one of these alternator/regulators. Always refer to the latest Motorola service literature to be certain that you are aware of latest product improvements and test procedures, specific voltage and alternator output ratings, etc.

Although it is often necessary to remove the alternator/regulator from the vehicle or equipment that it is fitted to, in order to repair or bench test the unit, it is highly desirable and often time-saving to first conduct a test of the charging system in the vehicle or equipment. The main reasons for this are that you can monitor the system condition under actual working conditions using the vehicle wiring harness and electrical loads that are a permanent part of the system.

PRELIMINARY CHECKS AND TESTS

When problems occur in the charging system, it is more often a condition of battery undercharge rather than overcharge that initiates the test. The reason for this condition is that there are more conditions that can cause an undercharge condition. Such conditions would include:

1. Alternator drive belt tension, worn or glazed belts. Adjust the drive belt if necessary, or replace worn ones.

2. Check all wiring terminals, especially plug-in type harnesses for signs of corrosion or looseness. This condition creates high circuit resistance and can cause undercharging, overcharging and damage to the charging system.

3. Badly corroded battery cables or terminals also create high resistance in the circuit, resulting in poor starting and a possible low charging rate to the battery. Clean all corroded terminals and replace faulty or damaged battery cables.

4. It is imperative in any alternator system to ensure that the battery itself is in a sufficient state of charge prior to conducting any tests on the charging system, since a low or discharged battery can cause low readings while performing charging system tests. Remember that the rotor field windings receive initial excitation from the battery in order to produce a strong enough magnetic field in the alternator rotor pole pieces.

TEST EQUIPMENT REQUIREMENTS

Standard test equipment found in garages and service shops is adequate for testing these charging systems, since the tests herein deal with voltage only. Specifically, a d.c. voltmeter with a 0–20 volt scale is required, plus any commercial type battery hydrometer with a temperature correction scale, or better yet use Motorola's own electronic battery tester No. 7BT1181W (6/12 model).

CAUTION: While an alternator is producing voltage such as during a vehicle charging condition test, never open or break the positive or negative circuit, since the loss of battery voltage will result in the charging voltage rising to unsafe levels. This high voltage can damage the alternator and regulator, electrical accessories, and instruments.

BATTERY CONDITION

As already indicated, the battery must be in a suitable state of charge prior to attempting to monitor and analyze the condition of the charging system. On maintenance-free type batteries, the cell test indicator should appear green in color which would indicate that the battery is at least 75% charged and that the charging system test can be carried out. If, however, the cell test indicator is dark in color, this is a positive indication that the battery is in need of charging prior to charging system testing. A light or yellow color in the cell test indicator of a maintenance-free battery means that the electrolyte level is low and the battery has lost fluid. In this case, replace the battery for a new one, or one that is in a sufficient state of charge to

allow testing of the charging system. If the vehicle is required right away, don't waste time charging the existing vehicle battery, but replace it with a spare battery that is known to be good for the test period. This battery can be left in the vehicle while required, and the original battery can be replaced at some future service interval while the vehicle is in the shop.

Table 4-2 shows the typical state of charge of a battery based on the specific gravity of the electrolyte.

ALTERNATOR TERMINAL IDENTIFICATION

Different models of Motorola alternators have their terminals in various locations; therefore, for reasons of clarity Fig. 4-46 shows typical terminal locations and identification of several widely used Motorola alternators.

PROBLEM AREA DETERMINATION SECTION

From the troubleshooting chart (Table 4-3), the problem area can be isolated to one of either an overcharged or undercharged battery condition; therefore, the necessary tests required to isolate and cor-

Table 4-2. Battery Charge Condition

1.260 Specific Gravity Battery	1.280 Specific Gravity Battery	State of Charge
1.260	1.280	100% charged
1.230	1.250	75% charged
1.200	1.220	50% charged
1.170	1.190	25% charged
1.140	1.160	Very Low Capacity
1.110	1.130	Discharged

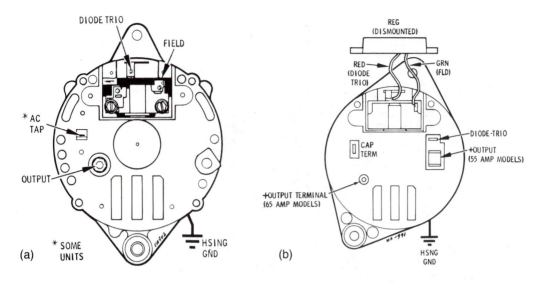

Fig. 4-46. (a) Model 9Da alternator, 55-62 ampere passenger car 12 volt. (b) Model 9BB and FB alternators, 55-65 amperes, 12-volt units used on VW Rabbit, Scirocco, etc. (Courtesy of Motorola Inc., Automotive Products Div.)

rect this condition are shown in step form under these two main headings, namely battery undercharged or battery overcharged. Follow the suggested procedure for your particular problem condition.

NOTE: The vehicle engine should be running at an idle speed for all of the tests listed under battery undercharged or battery overcharged condition unless otherwise specified.

Condition A: Battery Undercharged

1. Charging indicator lamp remains on.

   (a) Perform an open-diode-trio test as per the test arrangement shown in Fig. 4-47, test number (1).

2. Charging indicator lamp remains off with the ignition switch on, but the engine stopped (not running).

   (a) Perform a voltage regulator test as

described under test number two (2), Fig. 4-48.

   (b) Should the regulator test satisfactorily, the problem is most likely an open field circuit, therefore the alternator assembly should be removed for bench repair.

3. Further investigation requires alternator removal and diode replacement.

Condition B: Battery Overcharged

1. Conduct a wiring harness voltage test
2. Voltage regulator is shorted, therefore replace the unit

Test No. 1: Open Diode-Trio Test

Conduct this test when the battery is undercharged and the charging system indicator lamp is on.

Connect test jumper wires (insulated

Table 4-3. Troubleshooting Guide

PROBLEM	PROBABLE CAUSES	CORRECTIVE ACTION
A. Battery undercharged -ammeter(if used)indicates constant discharge. -indicator lamp remains on.	1. Defective cables, dirty battery posts, corroded terminals, etc. 2. Loose or broken belt. 3. Worn or broken brushes. 4. Defective alternator system.	1. Check, clean, repair or replace as needed. 2. Check belt. 3. Replace brush assy. 4. Refer to Problem Area Determination Section.
B. Battery undercharged -indicator lamp off with key on & engine stopped.(Normal condition is lamp on.)	1. Indicator lamp burned out or defective wire harness. 2. Plug at rear of alt. 3. Broken brush. 4. Defective alternator system.	1. Check bulb & harness. 2. Check plug to insure it is fully seated. 3. Replace brush assy. 4. Refer to "Problem Area Determination Section"
C. Battery overcharges -excessive use of water. -ammeter (if used) shows constant excessive charge. -voltmeter indicates greater than 14.5 volts (connected across battery with no load)with engine idling.	1. Plug at rear of alt. or wire harness. 2. Defective alt. system.	1. Refer to "Problem Area Determination Section" 2. Refer to "Problem Area Determination Section"
D. Battery charges at idle, but discharges under load conditions.	1. Slipping belts. 2. Alternator defective.	1. Check belts and adjust tension or replace as necessary. 2. Disassemble, check diodes.
E. Indicator lamp glows slightly under moderate load;battery appears charged.	1. Defective diode-trio	1. Remove & replace.

Courtesy of Motorola Inc.

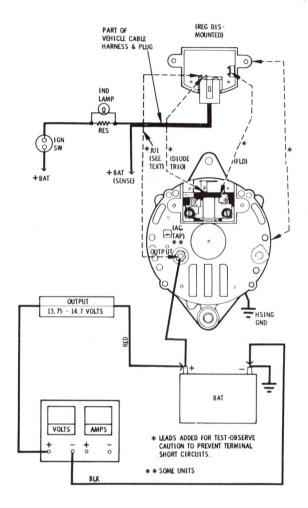

Fig. 4-47. Open diode trio test number one. (Courtesy of Motorola Inc., Automotive Products Div.)

alligator clip ends) and voltmeter leads to the battery and alternator as shown in Fig. 4-47. Ensure that the integral regulator is removed from the rear of the alternator housing and placed in a position that will prevent any possibility of terminal short circuits. As shown in Fig. 4-47, the vehicle cable harness plug to voltage regulator must remain connected during the test.

With all wiring hookups connected as shown in Fig. 4-47, make certain that no vehicle accessories (loads) are turned on, then start and idle the engine. Should the

reading on the voltmeter be between 13.75 to 14.7 volts, this is an indication that the diode-trio is open and the alternator should be removed for repair or replacement. If however, the voltage reading is less than 13.75 volts, remove test wire jumper JU1 and proceed directly to Test No. 2 item B, which is the regulator test.

Test No. 2: Regulator Test

This test would be conducted when the battery remains undercharged, and the

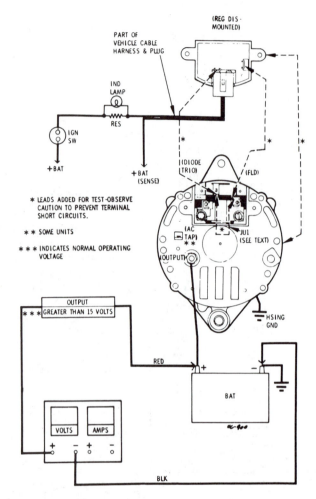

Fig. 4-48. Regulator test number two. (Courtesy of Motorola Inc., Automotive Products Div.)

charge indicator lamp remains in the off condition. The test hookup for the regulator condition is as shown in Fig. 4-48. Note that the voltage regulator is removed as it was in Test No. 1, and that jumper wire JU1 has been repositioned from the vehicle wiring harness probe and alternator output as was shown in Fig. 4-47, and is now placed across the diode-trio and the alternator field terminals.

Test No. 2: Step A

Step A is undertaken to establish if the voltage regulator is in an open condition. With the test wires connected as in Fig. 4-48, turn the vehicle ignition switch on. However, do not attempt to start the engine at this time. Disconnect one end of the test jumper wire JU1 which should cause the charging circuit indicator lamp to go out or off because of the break or open circuit condition at the regulator.

Reconnecting the jumper wire JU1, should cause the charging circuit condition lamp to come on (light up) with an open regulator condition. If, however, the charging lamp does not come on when the JU1 jumper wire is reconnected, check first that the bulb is not burnt out, and then check the condition of the vehicle wiring harness and plug.

Should the lamp still fail to come on after these two checks and necessary repairs, then the alternator field circuit is open. This condition will require the removal and repair of the alternator assembly.

If, however, the charge indicator lamp now comes on after checking the lamp and wiring harness condition, proceed to test step B.

Test No. 2: Step B

Step B is used to check out the condition of the voltage regulator. The same wiring hookup is used as for Step A.

With the charge indicator lamp on, start and run the engine at a fast idle of about 1000 rpm with the vehicle headlights turned on. The voltmeter should show at least 15 volts or more, otherwise the alternator is faulty. If 15 volts or more are achieved, remove test jumper wire JU1 and conduct Test No. 4 given below which is an alternator output test to establish the proper voltage regulation.

Test No. 3: Wiring Harness Voltage Test

This test quickly establishes the condition of the plug-in terminal of the vehicle wiring harness. Figure 4-49 shows the required test hookup arrangement.

With the harness plug removed from the voltage regulator, connect the voltmeter leads as in Fig. 4-49; the voltmeter should register a battery voltage which is normally around 12.6 volts for a fully charged battery with the ignition key switch off.

If the voltmeter reading is zero, then the wiring harness sense lead is open. Repair or replace the plug-in assembly.

Test No. 4: Alternator Output Check

This test is conducted after successfully completing Tests 1, 2, and 3. Figure 4-50 shows that the test hookup arrangement is similar to that used in the other three tests to date. However, jumper wire JU1 is not required.

With the test leads connected as in Fig. 4-50, start the vehicle engine and adjust the throttle to establish a test speed of 1500 rpm. Apply an accessory load to the circuit by turning on both the vehicle headlights and the heater/defroster fan switch to its low position. The voltmeter should indicate somewhere between 13 to 14.7 volts, otherwise the regulator is defective and should be replaced. This completes a typical test of the Motorola charging circuit, which differs when testing other Motorola alternator/regulators. However, the test sequences are similar to that just described.

DELCO-REMY ALTERNATOR/ REGULATOR TEST PROCEDURE

The design of the Delco alternators is similar throughout the total range of rated output capacities. The main difference is that some models are of the slip-ring and brush type, while others are of the solid-state brushless design. The test procedure for both is very similar; however, some models are designed with a voltage regulator that is non-adjustable, while others use

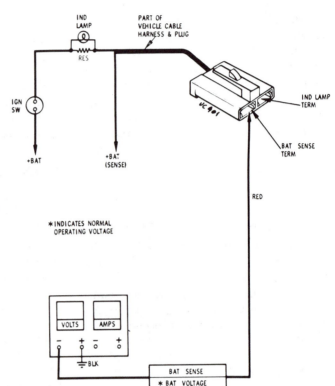

Fig. 4-49. Vehicle wiring harness voltage test. (Courtesy of Motorola, Inc., Automotive Products Div.)

an external voltage adjustment cap in the slip-ring end frame, or on the brushless design units. This voltage adjustment cap is located in the rectifier end frame. Since there are minor test variations between the brush type and brushless type alternators, we shall look at the basic test procedure for each one, after which we can compare the actual differences for review purposes.

Prior to conducting a test of the charging system on either one of these types of alternators, refer to the general alternator/ regulator troubleshooting section at the start of this chapter with reference to battery state of charge, wiring condition, plug in harness connections, etc. Since the most widely used automotive passenger car type of Delco alternator is the 10 SI, 15 SI

and 27 SI types, the following test procedure will be common to these models.

Within this range of models, the 100, 110, 116 and 136 type units have no external or internal voltage regulator adjustment, while the 10 SI 116 type (one-wire system) and 27 SI 200 type three terminal regulator type are equipped with an external voltage adjustment cap in the slip ring end frame.

DELCOTRON GENERATOR TROUBLESHOOTING

This troubleshooting sequence covers the 10 SI, 15 SI and 27 SI series, 100 type non-regulator adjustment units. The charging circuit test procedure is broken

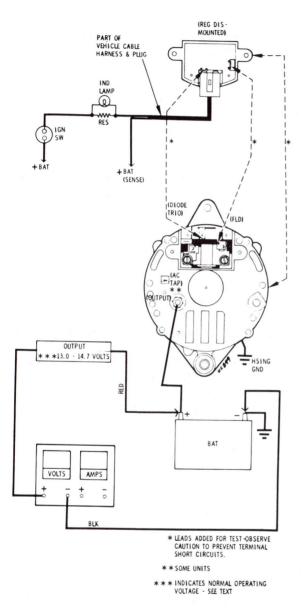

Fig. 4-50. Alternator output check. (Courtesy of Motorola Inc., Automotive Products Div.)

into two components which we will identify as Test No. 1 and Test No. 2. Test No. 1 deals with abnormal indicator charging lamp operation, while Test No. 2 deals with abnormal charging system operation. If the particular charging circuit that you are checking does not use a charge indicator lamp, or if it is equipped with an ammeter rather than the charging lamp, then disregard the step-by-step process of Test No. 1, because it does not apply to the circuit.

Test No. 1: Abnormal Indicator Lamp Operation

The condition of the charging circuit indicator lamp would normally be as shown in Table 4-4.

If the charge indicator lamp operates as shown in the table, then no problem exists in this circuit, and you can proceed to Test No. 2. If, however, the conditions shown above are not evident, then proceed as follows to correct the situation.

1. Switch off, Lamp on. Disconnect the wires from the alternator number 1 and 2 terminals. If the lamp stays on, then a short circuit exists between the two wire leads. If, however, the lamp goes out, then the rectifier bridge inside the alternator requires replacement or an undercharged battery condition will exist.

2. Switch on, lamp off, engine stopped. The conditions in 1 above or an open circuit can cause this condition which can be checked as follows:

    (a) Check the fuse for continuity, a burned out or faulty bulb socket, or a possible open in the number one lead circuit between the generator and ignition switch.

    (b) If no problems are found, proceed to Test No. 2, abnormal charging system condition.

3. Ignition switch on, lamp off, and engine running. If a fuse is used between the ignition switch and charging system indicator lamp, check that it is not blown. Other causes of this condition are listed under Test No. 2

NOTE: The charging circuit lamp may stay on at idle and slightly above idle; however the lamp should go out when the

Table 4-4
Indicator Lamp Operation

Switch	Lamp	*Engine Condition
Off	Off	Stopped
On	On	Stopped
On	Off	Running

engine is operated throughout its normal speed range, otherwise an abnormal condition exists.

Test No. 2: Abnormal Charging System Operation

Prior to proceeding with this test, check all of the conditions listed at the start of the alternator/regulator troubleshooting section, such as state of battery charge, belt adjustment, corroded terminals, loose connections, etc. Refer to Fig. 4-51, which shows a typical wiring diagram for these series of alternators. Note also the BAT and 1 and 2 terminals on the rear cover of the alternator assembly.

1. Turn ignition switch on and connect a voltmeter from:

    (a) Generator BAT terminal and ground

    (b) Generator No. 1 terminal and ground

    (c) Generator No. 2 terminal and ground

A zero voltmeter condition would indicate that an open circuit exists between the voltmeter connection and the battery.

2. Connect a voltmeter across the battery positive and negative terminals with all accessory loads turned off. Start and run the engine at a fast idle speed. If the

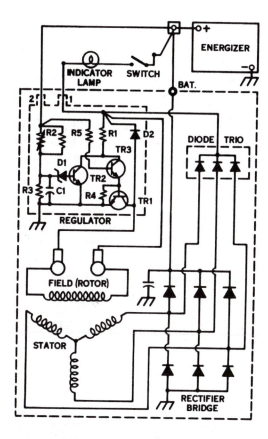

Fig. 4-51. Typical wiring diagram, series 10SI, 15SI, and 27SI, 100 type Delcotron generators. (Courtesy of Delco-Remy Div. of GMC)

battery voltage reads 15.5 volts or more on a 12-volt system, or 31 volts or higher on a 24-volt system, then the alternator should be removed, disassembled, and repaired.

3. If previous steps are satisfactory, proceed as follows:

(a) Disconnect the battery ground cable.

(b) Connect an ammeter in the circuit at the alternator BAT terminal.

(c) Reconnect the battery ground cable.

(d) Connect a carbon pile across the battery as shown in Fig. 4-52, but ensure that the carbon pile is turned off. Increase the load to the circuit by turning on the vehicle radio, windshield wipers, headlights (high beam), and the heater/defroster fan blower motor to maximum.

(e) Start and run the engine at a moderate speed with all accessories as listed in Step (d). Adjust the carbon pile across the battery as necessary in order to obtain the maximum current output.

(f) Stamped on the generator frame is the rated output of the unit, or this can be found in the test specifications bulletins. If the ampere output is within 10 amperes of that listed, then the generator is probably not defective. However, recheck the previous steps of Test No. 2 to be certain. If the generator output is OK, but the charge indicator lamp remains on, then check the

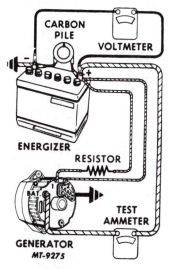

Fig. 4-52. Connections required for a bench check of a Delcotron generator and placement of carbon pile to obtain maximum current output. (Courtesy of Delco-Remy Div. of GMC)

diode-trio and rectifier bridge, which requires disassembly of the alternator assembly.

(g) If the alternator ampere output is not within 10 amperes of the rated output as stamped on the frame, then inspect the rear of the end frame for access to a test hole such as shown in Fig. 4-53. If this test hole is accessible, proceed to Step (h). If the test hole is not accessible, then proceed directly to Step (i).

(h) Carefully place a screwdriver into the test hole taking care not to insert it any deeper than one inch (25.4 mm) into the end frame; otherwise damage can result. The object of placing the screwdriver into the test hole is to allow it to contact the small tab shown in Fig. 4-53 and ground it to the alternator end frame. In this way, the alternator field winding can be grounded.

(i) Run the engine at a moderate speed, and adjust the battery carbon pile until maximum current output is achieved as per specifications.

(j) If the generator output is now within 10 amperes of its rated output, check the field winding by removing and disassembling the alternator assembly.

(k) If the output is not within 10 amperes of its rated output, check the field winding, diode trio, rectifier bridge and stator as discussed in the overhaul section.

(l) Should no test hole be accessible on the end plate of the alternator, then disassemble the alternator and make whatever tests and checks are required to correct the condition.

This completes the test procedure for this type of alternator assembly.

27 SI DELCOTRON 200 TYPE THREE TERMINAL REGULATOR TEST

The 27 SI series, 200 type three terminal alternator consists of an integral charging system featuring a solid state voltage regulator that is mounted inside the slip-ring end frame. This model regulator can however have its voltage adjusted by repositioning a voltage adjustment cap in the slip ring end frame.

Troubleshooting procedures for this series generator and the 10 SI series, 116 type with a one wire system is similar, since the 10 SI unit also has the external voltage regulator adjustment feature.

Figure 4-54 shows the basic wiring circuit used with these units, while Fig. 4-55 shows the location and adjustment of the external voltage adjustment cap. Prior to troubleshooting these series generators, check the state of charge of the battery, belt adjustment, wiring connections, etc. Then, proceed as follows:

Fig. 4-53. Location of test hole in alternator end frame. (Courtesy of AC Delco Div. of GMC)

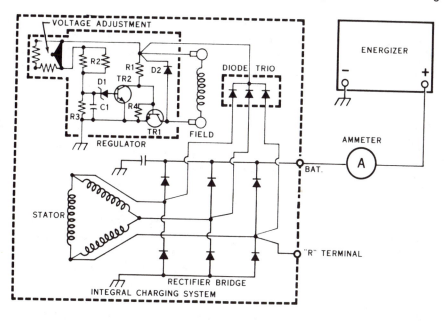

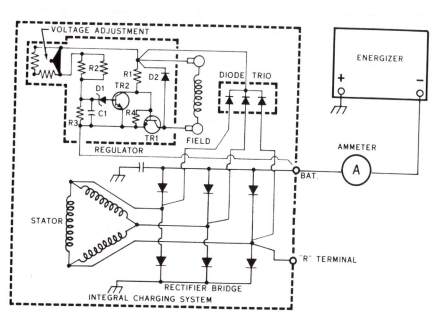

Fig. 4-54. Typical external voltage adjustment for a 27SI generator wiring diagram. (Courtesy of Delco-Remy Div. of GMC)

1. Place a voltmeter lead to the generator BAT terminal and the other lead to ground. An open circuit exists between the voltmeter connection and battery if the reading on the gauge of the voltmeter is zero.

2. Connect both ends of the voltmeter (red to positive, and black lead to negative) across the battery terminals. Start and run the engine at a moderate speed while noting the reading on the face of the voltmeter. This reading, if in excess of 15.5 volts on a 12 volt system, and 31 volts on a 24 volt system, indicates that there is damage internally within the alternator assembly, therefore remove it for disassembly and repair.

3. Repeat the same procedure as was outlined in Test 2 (Abnormal Charging System Operation), Step (3) as was given earlier for the 10, 15 and 27 SI non-voltage adjustable type 100 generators. This step dealt with the following:

(a) Disconnect the battery ground cable

(b) Connect an ammeter in the circuit at the alternator BAT terminal

(c) Reconnect the battery ground cable

4. Connect a carbon pile across the battery as shown in Fig. 4-52, but ensure that the control is set at zero or off. Turn on all vehicle accessories.

5. Start and run the engine at a speed equivalent to about 4000 generator rpm (about 1500 to 2000 rpm engine speed; this depends on generator to pulley size ratio) and adjust the carbon pile across the battery to obtain maximum generator current output. It may be necessary to increase engine speed to obtain maximum current output.

6. The generator is OK if the rated output is within 10 amperes of that listed on the frame or in the applicable service test specs. The voltage setting can be changed on these series alternators in order to correct the condition by simply removing the voltage adjustment cap from the top rear of the alternator assembly as shown in Fig. 4-55 and rotating the cap in increments of 90° as desired to alter the voltage setting, then placing the cap back into the connector body.

7. In Fig. 4-55, the voltage cap is shown set for the medium-high voltage position. The cap has a LO, 2, 3 and HI position, with 2 being aligned with the arrow of the connector body, the setting is medium-low, 3 is medium-high, and LO and HI are exactly what they so indicate.

8. When amperes are not within 10 amperes of rated output, proceed as follows for both negative and positive ground systems:

(a) On negative ground systems, insert a screwdriver into the generator end frame hole as was done earlier on the test procedure for the non-adjustable type alternators in Fig. 4-53 in order to ground the tab to the end frame, then proceed to Step 9.

(b) On positive ground systems, insert a screwdriver into the test hole of the end frame to touch the tab. Now connect a voltmeter to the metal screwdriver with the other lead to the alternator BAT terminal. If the voltmeter reads battery voltage, replace the rotor and regulator. If, however, the voltmeter does not read battery voltage, disconnect the voltmeter and connect a jumper wire clip from the screwdriver blade to the alternator BAT terminal.

9. Start and run the engine at moderate

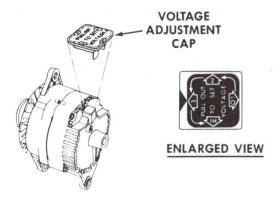

VOLTAGE ADJUSTMENT CAP

ENLARGED VIEW

Fig. 4-55. Location and positioning of voltage adjustment cap, shown here in medium high (3) position. (Courtesy of Delco-Remy Div. of GMC)

speed, then adjust the carbon pile across the battery to obtain maximum current output from the generator.

10. If the output is now within 10 amperes of rated output, replace the regulator and check the field winding.

11. If the output is not within 10 amperes of rated output, check the field winding, diode trio, rectifier bridge and stator as described in the generator overhaul section.

12. Remove the ammeter from the generator and be sure to turn off both the accessories and the carbon pile.

DELCOTRON DIAGNOSTIC TESTER

In order to simplify the testing and troubleshooting of their own alternators with built-in voltage regulators, Delco-Remy has introduced several special test tools to aid the mechanic in quickly diagnosing a charging system problem. This tester is available through any General Motors dealer or local electric automotive

accessory rebuild shop or supplier. It is manufactured by the Kent Moore Tool Division, and is available under Part No. J-26290. This unit is shown in Fig. 4-56.

Fig. 4-56. Diagnostic tester J-26290. (Courtesy of Kent-Moore Tool Div.)

The tester is simply plugged into any Delcotron SI generator and its ground lead clip connected to a good clean ground in order for it to operate. A typical wiring arrangement of the diagnostic tester is shown in Fig. 4-57, which is self-explanatory. The tester is designed as a quick check to determine if the Delcotron SI generator should be removed from the vehicle. Figure 4-57(b) illustrates a similar type of charging system and battery tester.

The tester will indicate about 98% of all charging system faults. The test sequence is printed on a label attached to the rear of the tester body, and can be followed in a step-by-step procedure. Should you not have one of these diagnostic testers readily available, or the label of instructions has been damaged so that you can not read the test procedure, the following is a step-by-step procedure for its use.

NOTE: Be certain that the engine is at a fast idle speed when using the diagnostic tester in Part 2 of the test procedure.

Engine Off, Lights and Accessories Off

1. Light on tester flashes. Skip steps 2 and 3 and proceed to Part 2 of the test.

2. Light stays on in tester. Indicates a fault in the diagnostic tester which should be replaced.

3. Light stays off on tester. Pull plug from Delcotron generator:

(a) Flashing light. Indicates that the

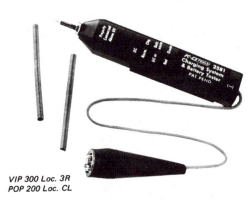

VIP 300 Loc. 3R
POP 200 Loc. CL

Tester connects to the battery in seconds and shows you instantly the condition of your charging system and battery.

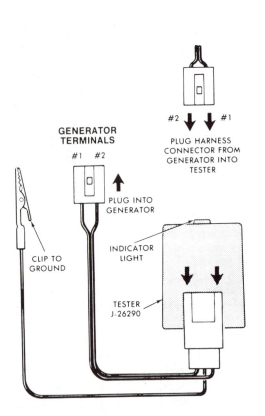

GENERATOR TERMINALS
#1   #2

PLUG HARNESS CONNECTOR FROM GENERATOR INTO TESTER
#2   #1

PLUG INTO GENERATOR

CLIP TO GROUND

INDICATOR LIGHT

TESTER J-26290

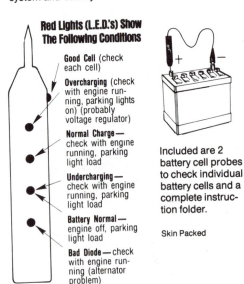

Red Lights (L.E.D.'s) Show The Following Conditions

Good Cell (check each cell)

Overcharging (check with engine running, parking lights on) (probably voltage regulator)

Normal Charge — check with engine running, parking light load

Undercharging — check with engine running, parking light load

Battery Normal — engine off, parking light load

Bad Diode — check with engine running (alternator problem)

Included are 2 battery cell probes to check individual battery cells and a complete instruction folder.

Skin Packed

Fig. 4-57. (a) J-26290 diagnostic tester connections to alternator, (courtesy of AC Delco Div. of GMC). (b) KD-2581 charging system and battery tester, (courtesy of K-D Manufacturing Co., Lancaster, PA).

generator should be removed and the rectifier bridge replaced.

(b) Light on tester stays off. Indicates a faulty tester, or no voltage to the tester. Check for 12 volts at the No. 2 terminal of the harness connector. Repair wiring or terminals if 12 volts is not available. Replace the diagnostic tester if 12 volts is available.

Engine at a Fast Idle, Lights and Accessories Off

4. Light on tester off. Charging system good, do not remove the generator (Delcotron).

5. Light remains on in tester. Indicates a component failure within the Delcotron generator. Remove the generator and check the diode-trio, rectifier bridge and stator.

6. Tester light flashing. Indicates a problem within the Delcotron. Remove generator and check regulator, rotor field coil, brushes and slip rings.

Wiring Arrangement for Using Delcotron Diagnostic Tester/J-26290 (Kent-Moore Tool Number)

Use with any Delco-Remy 3 wire 10-SI or 27-SI 12 volt, negative-ground Delcotron SI generator. The lead assembly may be replaced if damaged (part number 1892721).

GMC/DELCO TRANSISTORIZED REGULATOR DIAGNOSIS

The procedure for diagnosis of charging systems is shown on pages 184 and 185. These charts are provided through the Courtesy of the Oldsmobile Division of General Motors Corporation.

TROUBLESHOOTING DELCO BRUSHLESS TYPE GENERATORS

The brushless type alternator/generator is a very popular series used on heavy-duty trucks and equipment. Typical models were covered earlier under Delco-Remy alternator operation. In review, these models are the 20 and 29 SI series, 300 type, the 25 SI series, 400 and 450 types, and the 30 SI and 30 SI/TR series units. The latest addition to the Delco-Remy line of heavy-duty alternators is the 32 SI/600 which is direct-mounted to the engine where it is gear driven and lubricated by engine oil. It is rated at 85 amps at 12 volts, or 50 amps with 24 volts. The troubleshooting and charging system output checks on these models of alternators is the same as that given earlier for other series of Delco alternators. The 27 SI test sequence can be used for all of these models. Although the sequence for troubleshooting is the same as for the 27 SI unit, there are some topics concerning these series units that merit some additional comments.

ENERGIZING SPEED

No output can be obtained from the brushless type generator until the voltage regulator assembly turns on which was discussed in considerable detail earlier in the Operating Principles section. This turn-on speed is higher than some speeds at which generator output can be obtained. Because of this situation, it is imperative that, when you are checking generator output at low rpm's, you increase the speed enough to turn the regulator on, then reduce the rpm in order to check the output. Once the regulator has been turned on, it will remain on until the engine is stopped.

CHARGING SYSTEM DIAGNOSIS - TRANSISTORIZED REGULATOR

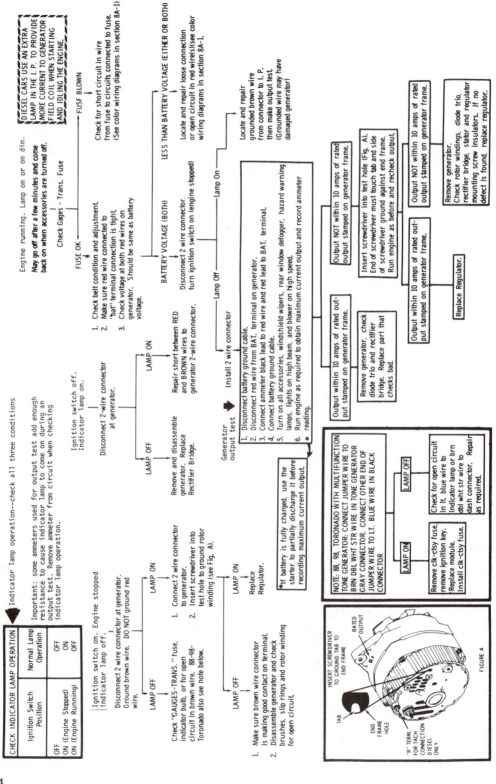

▼ Indicator lamp operation--check all three conditions

CHECK INDICATOR LAMP OPERATION	
Ignition Switch Position	Normal Lamp Operation
OFF	OFF
ON (Engine Stopped)	ON
ON (Engine Running)	OFF

Important: some ammeters used for output test add enough resistance to cause indicator lamp to come on during an output test. Remove ammeter from circuit when checking indicator lamp operation.

Ignition switch on. Engine stopped indicator lamp off.

Disconnect 2 wire connector at generator. Ground brown wire. DO NOT ground red wire.

LAMP OFF

Check "GAUGES-TRANS." fuse, indicator bulb, or for open circuit in brown wire. 88-98-Toronado also see note below.

LAMP ON

1. Make sure brown wire connector is making good contact on terminal.
2. Disassemble generator and check brushes, slip rings and rotor winding for open circuit.

Ignition switch on. Indicator lamp on.

Disconnect 2-wire connector at generator.

LAMP OFF

Remove and disassemble generator. Replace Rectifier Bridge.

LAMP ON

1. Connect 2 wire connector to generator.
2. Insert screwdriver into test hole to ground rotor winding (see Fig. A).

LAMP OFF

Replace Regulator.

LAMP ON

Repair short between RED and BROWN wires to generator 2-wire connector.

Install 2 wire connector

▶ Generator output test

1. Disconnect battery ground cable.
2. Disconnect red wire from BAT. terminal on generator.
3. Connect ammeter black lead to red wire and red lead to BAT. terminal.
4. Connect battery ground cable.
5. Turn on all accessories, windshield wipers, rear window defogger, hazard warning lamps, lights on high beam, and blower on high speed.
6. Run engine as required to obtain maximum current output and record ammeter
* reading.

*If battery is fully charged, use the starter to partially discharge it before recording maximum current output.

NOTE: 88, 98, TORONADO WITH MULTIFUNCTION TONE GENERATOR: CONNECT JUMPER WIRE TO BRN DBL WHT STR WIRE IN TONE GENERATOR GRAY CONNECTOR. CONNECT OTHER END OF JUMPER WIRE TO LT. BLUE WIRE IN BLACK CONNECTOR

LAMP ON

Remove clk-ctsy fuse, remove ignition key. Replace module. Install clk-ctsy fuse.

LAMP OFF

Check for open circuit in lt. blue wire to indicator lamp or brn dbl wht str wire to dash connector. Repair as required.

Output within 10 amps of rated output stamped on generator frame.

Remove generator, check diode trio and rectifier bridge. Replace part that checks bad.

Output NOT within 10 amps of rated output stamped on generator frame.

Insert screwdriver into test hole (Fig. A). End of screwdriver must touch tab and side of screwdriver ground against end frame. Run engine as before and recheck output.

Output within 10 amps of rated output stamped on generator frame.

Output NOT within 10 amps of rated output stamped on generator frame.

Remove generator. Check rotor windings, diode trio, rectifier bridge, stator and regulator mounting screw insulators. If no defect is found, replace regulator.

Replace Regulator.

Engine running. Lamp on or on dim.

May go off after a few minutes and come back on when accessories are turned off.

Check Gages - Trans. Fuse

FUSE OK → FUSE BLOWN

1. Check belt condition and adjustment
2. Make sure red wire connected to 'bat' terminal connection is tight.
3. Check voltage at both red wires on generator. Should be same as battery voltage.

Check for short circuit in wire from fuse to circuits connected to fuse. (See color wiring diagrams in section 8A-1)

BATTERY VOLTAGE (BOTH) — LESS THAN BATTERY VOLTAGE (EITHER OR BOTH)

Disconnect 2 wire connector. turn ignition switch on (engine stopped)

Locate and repair loose connection or open circuit in red wire(s)(see color wiring diagrams in section 8A-1.

Lamp Off — Lamp On

Locate and repair grounded brown wire from connector to I.P. then make output test. (Grounded wire may have damaged generator)

┌─────────────────────────────────────┐
│ DIESEL CARS USE AN EXTRA   │
│ LAMP IN THE I.P. TO PROVIDE   │
│ MORE CURRENT TO GENERATOR   │
│ FIELD COIL WHEN STARTING   │
│ AND IDLING THE ENGINE   │
└─────────────────────────────────────┘

INSERT SCREWDRIVER TO GROUND TAB TO END FRAME

RATED OUTPUT

TAB

END FRAME HOLE

"R" TERM. FOR TACH CONNECTION DIESEL ONLY

FIGURE A

CHARGING SYSTEM DIAGNOSIS - TRANSISTORIZED REGULATOR (CONTINUED)

Battery runs down

Check Indicator Lamp Operation

- **NOT NORMAL**
  - Use diagnosis chart on previous page.

- **NORMAL**
  - **Check belt adjustment.**
    - **BELT WORN OR LOOSE**
      - Replace or adjust as required.
    - **BELT GOOD AND PROPERLY ADJUSTED**
      - Check generator wiring connections (2-wire terminal and BAT terminal on back), and battery wiring connections.
        - **WIRING CONNECTIONS BAD**
          - Repair as required.
        - **WIRING CONNECTIONS OK**
          - Check for drain on battery with everything turned off by connecting an AMMETER positive lead to the positive battery terminal, and the negative lead to the positive battery cable.
            - **BATTERY DOES NOT HAVE DRAIN**
              - Connect voltmeter to battery. Note voltage then start engine and note voltage.
                - **VOLTAGE DID NOT INCREASE**
                  - Insert screwdriver into hole in end frame. End of screwdriver must touch tab and side of screwdriver ground against end frame. Note voltage.
                    - **VOLTAGE DID NOT INCREASE**
                      - Remove and disassemble generator. Check rotor field, stator, diode trio, rectifier bridge, and regulator mounting screws. Replace part that checks bad.
                    - **VOLTAGE INCREASED**
                      - Replace the Regulator.
                - **VOLTAGE INCREASED**
                  - Perform output test Procedure is on previous page.
            - **BATTERY HAS DRAIN**
              - Refer to car electrical schematic. Remove fuses from fuse panel one at a time until problem circuit is found. Repair as required.

NOTE: Prolonged use of rear window defogger may cause run down condition to exist Unit should be used only when required.

DIESEL CARS (2 BATTERIES) DISCONNECT AND TEST ONE AT A TIME

Battery overcharged (Excessive water usage)

→ Indicated by clear or light test indicator.

Test battery using battery test procedure chart in this manual.

BATTERY TESTED GOOD

Connect negative lead of voltmeter to ground, probe RED wire at 2-wire generator connector with positive lead, note voltage with all accessories off and engine above idle. Probe RED wire at "BAT" terminal of the generator and note voltage. Voltage should be the same at both points.

- **VOLTAGE HIGHER AT "BAT" TERMINAL THAN AT 2-WIRE CONNECTOR**
  - Check for good clean connections at "BAT" terminal on generator, at 2-wire generator connector and between RED wires at junction block. If connections are OK check for resistance in RED wires between generator and junction block. Repair as required.

- **VOLTAGE THE SAME AT "BAT" TERMINAL AND 2-WIRE CONNECTOR**
  - **VOLTAGE LESS THAN 15 VOLTS**
    - 15 volts or less will not boil water out.
  - **VOLTAGE MORE THAN 15 VOLTS**
    - Remove generator then remove end frame. Disconnect ground end of resistor. Connect ohmmeter to end frame and probe the brush holder at screw B (by the test hole tab). Reading should be infinite or close to infinite using RX1 scale.
      - **OHMMETER READING LOW**
        - Check washers and insulators on attaching screw B (by brush holder). If no trouble found, replace regulator.
      - **OHMMETER READING INFINITE OR HIGH**
        - Replace Regulator.

GENERATOR SCHEMATIC

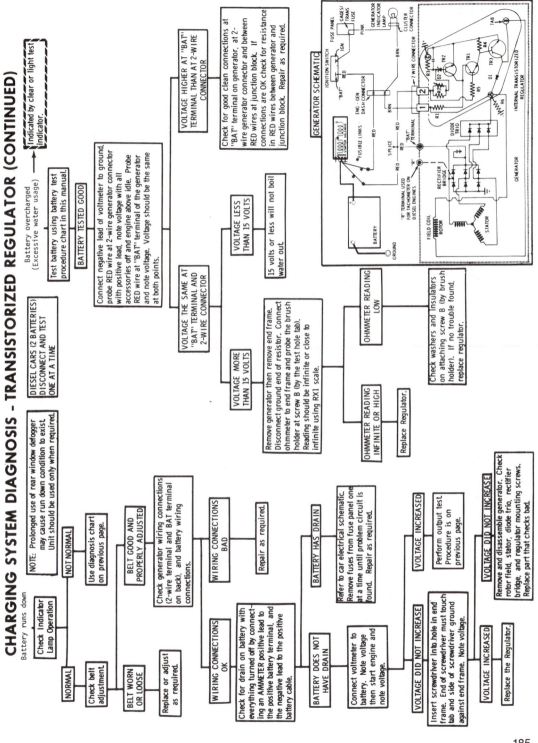

185

RATED VOLTAGE

The output of these generators should be checked at the rated voltage shown in Table 4-5.

It is permissible to also check generator output in amperes at any voltage within the operating range shown in Table 4-5 since the current output will be fairly close to the value that would be obtained at rated voltage.

Table 4-5
Rated Voltage Table

System Voltage	Rated Voltage	Operating Range
12	14.0	13.0 - 15.0
24	28.0	26.0 - 30.0
32	37.5	33.0 - 39.0

MAGNETIZING THE ROTOR

On slip-ring and brush type alternators, it is not necessary to polarize the alternator in order to ensure that current will flow to the battery. In fact, any attempt to polarize these types of alternators will damage the diodes which would then require replacement.

On the brushless type Delco alternators, however, after disassembly or servicing, it may be necessary to re-establish the proper magnetism with respect to current flow direction. To magnetize the rotor of the brushless type alternators, connect the system to the battery circuit in the normal manner, then momentarily connect a jumper wire lead from the battery positive (+) post, to the Integral Charging System relay terminal. This procedure applies to both negative and positive ground systems

and is necessary to restore the normal residual magnetism in the rotor.

CAUTION: On the 30 SI/TR series alternator, be sure to connect the jumper lead from the system battery and not the cranking battery (remember that the 30 SI/TR system takes the place of a series/parallel switch for 24 volt starting), so that 12 volts only will be applied to the relay terminal.

On those series alternators without a relay terminal, remove the end plate from the alternator and place a jumper wire lead from the battery positive post to one of the stator lead terminals on the rectifier bridge.

VOLTAGE REGULATOR ADJUSTMENT

Voltage regulator adjustment is possible on some series of brushless generators, however not on others. Specifically, there is no adjustment possible on the 20 SI and 29 SI series, 300 type units. The 25 SI series, 400 and 450 types can be adjusted by one of two methods depending on the particular system wiring arrangement. These two different arrangements are shown in Figs. 4-58 and 4-59.

The type of voltage regulator adjustment shown in Fig. 4-58 would be found on a 400 type, 25 SI unit. The wiring circuit for this unit is explained in Fig. 4-26 under operating principles.

To adjust the voltage regulator on the 25 SI, 400 type, proceed as follows:

1. Remove the pipe plug from the left side at the rear of the alternator (integral charging system) immediately above the relay terminal as shown in Fig. 4-58.

2. Turn the internal adjusting screw either clockwise or counter-clockwise to raise or lower the voltage output respectively. The output voltage change can be

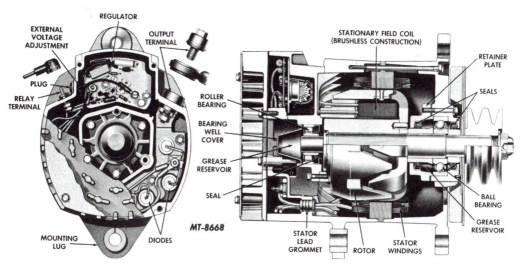

Fig. 4-58. Location of voltage regulator adjustment screw. (Courtesy of AC Delco Div. of GMC)

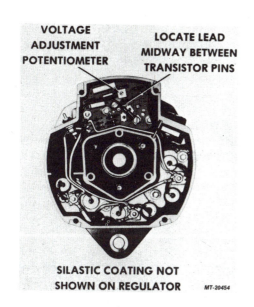

Fig. 4-59. Location of voltage regulator adjusting screw, 25SI-450 type. (Courtesy of Delco-Remy Div. of GMC)

monitored by the use of a voltmeter placed across the battery positive and negative posts while running the engine with all of the vehicle electrical accessories turned on, and a carbon pile across the battery as shown and discussed under the 27 SI test sequence in Fig. 4-52.

Double check the voltage setting on the vehicle over a reasonable service period. If however no change occurs in the charging rate, the generator would require removal, disassembly, and repair.

CAUTION: On any alternator charging system, the battery supplies a small amount of current to the field circuit to create magnetism. If the state of charge of the vehicle battery is low, it is possible that the voltage regulator will not limit the produced generator voltage. This can be misleading, because you may adjust the regulator adjusting screw clockwise to increase the rate of charge, with no change occurring on the voltmeter scale. An increase in the voltage regulator setting has actually been accomplished. However, this increase will not show up on the voltmeter until the state of charge of the battery increases. This is why it is imperative that prior to checking and adjusting the voltage regulator assembly, the state of charge of the battery is first of all checked to ensure that it is at least 75% charged, otherwise false interpretations can result.

3. Be sure to replace the pipe plug after the regulator is adjusted.

The same procedure as outlined for adjustment of the 25 SI 400 type applies to the 450 type. However, the voltage is adjusted by removing the generator end cover which will expose the potentiometer adjusting screw as shown in Fig. 4-59. Turning the screw clockwise increases voltage output, and turning counter-clockwise decreases voltage output.

Adjustment of the voltage output on the 30-SI, 30-SI/TR and 32-SI units is achieved by removal of a voltage adjustment cap and placing it in one of four positions similar to that discussed earlier under the troubleshooting procedure for the 27-SI, 200 type alternator. (See Fig. 4-55.)

NOTE: On many series of Delco generators, a relay or R terminal is provided to operate auxiliary equipment. Depending on how the relay terminal connector is actually wired, the auxiliary equipment will receive either system voltage, or half system voltage. An example of this variation in output voltage to the R terminal is found in the 20-SI and 29-SI, 300 type brushless alternator whereby a flexible lead is connected to the relay terminal and to the voltage regulator insulated screw at the diode-trio single connector within the integral charging system. The R terminal

on this arrangement will operate at system voltage, and it is usually connected externally to a charge indicator light. However, on the same models of generator, the relay terminal can also be connected to the rectifier bridge which will allow the R terminal to operate at half-system voltage.

Therefore, should you monitor the voltage at the R terminal anytime and find that it is only reading half-system voltage, there is nothing wrong with the generator assembly.

TROUBLESHOOTING THE 30-SI/TR SERIES DELCOTRON INTEGRAL CHARGING SYSTEM

We have discussed the general procedures required to troubleshoot both the slip-ring and brush type Delco alternators, as well as the brushless type.

The sequence for both types follows the same general pattern; however, the procedure for the 30-SI/TR unit does present some changes to the normal routine given so far. The reasons for these changes you may recollect from our earlier discussions of the operating principles of Delco alternators, namely that the 30-SI/TR unit is a standard 30-SI alternator assembly with the addition of a transformer rectifier unit, or TR unit mounted on the end frame. The purpose of the TR unit is to provide a separate voltage to charge a cranking battery which is connected in series with a 12-volt system battery to provide 24-volt cranking power.

When the engine is running, the cranking battery receives a low rate of charge. Since it does not supply any power to the vehicle accessories at any time, it does not require as high a state of charge as does the S or system battery. The accessories in the vehicle electrical system all operate on 12 volts, other than the starter motor which is of course 24 volts. The main purpose, then, of the 30-SI/TR unit is to eliminate the use of the older style series/parallel switch.

Under the section that dealt with operating principles for Delco generators (alternators) earlier, a typical wiring circuit for both the 30-SI and 30-SI/TR units was discussed. Figure 4-60 shows the typical external wiring circuit that would be used with the 30-SI/TR series unit.

The layout of the external wiring circuit in Fig. 4-60 shows both the C and S batteries, with the C battery being used only during cranking along with the S or system battery to provide 24 volt starting. The transformer rectifier (TR) is simply an add-on item to the basic 30-SI unit in order to charge the cranking battery at a low state of charge when the engine is running.

When a problem exists in the 30-SI/TR charging system such as either the cranking or system battery being under or overcharged, check out the system as follows:

1. Take care not to allow any leads or terminals to touch ground.

2. Disconnect the batteries to isolate the generator and TR unit.

3. Completely remove the TR unit from the generator by removing the necessary screws and wires, which will now leave us with a 30-SI 12-volt charging system connected to only the S or system battery once the battery leads are reconnected.

4. Check out the operation of the 30-SI generator in the same manner as that discussed earlier for the 27-SI unit. If the 30-SI unit checks out OK, then proceed to check the rectifier bridge of the TR unit as follows.

5. Disconnect the transformer leads

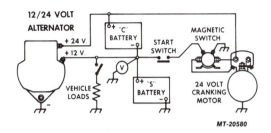

Fig. 4-60. Model 30SI/TR external wiring circuit. (Courtesy of Delco-Remy Div. of GMC)

from the rectifier bridge as shown in Fig. 4-61 and connect an ohmmeter with a 1.5 volt test cell to the heat sink, with the other lead to one of the three terminals. This is actually Step A in Fig. 4-61. From earlier discussions of solid state devices, you may remember that when checking a diode, the ohmmeter should register one high and one low reading when the ohmmeter leads are connected one way, and then reversed, which would indicate a good diode. If both readings are the same, then the diode is faulty. The ohmmeter check should be done between the same heat sink and the other two terminals, and then between the other heat sink and each of the three terminals for a total of six checks with two readings taken for each check.

To ensure an accurate reading on the ohmmeter, it is necessary to press the ohmmeter lead very firmly against the flat metal clips of the rectifier bridge studs if so equipped. If this is not done, and the ohmmeter lead is connected to the threaded stud of the rectifier bridge only, then a poor or false reading may be obtained.

CAUTION: The rectifier bridge assembly can be used on both positive and negative ground systems. Therefore, when installing a new rectifier bridge on negative ground systems, the bridge is

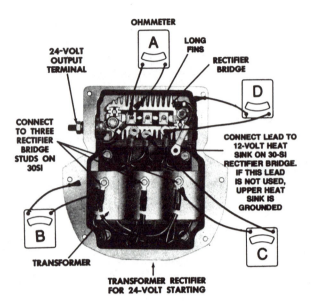

Fig. 4-61. Model 30SI/TR transformer and rectifier bridge diodes check with an ohmmeter. (Courtesy of Delco-Remy Div. of GMC)

assembled with the long cooling fins next to the generator end frame, and the short fins next to the transformer as is presently shown in Fig. 4-61.

On positive ground systems, the rectifier bridge is turned 180 degrees, so that the short fins are next to the end frame, and the long fins are now next to the transformer.

6. Refer to Fig. 4-61, and connect the ohmmeter three ways as indicated, in positions B, C and D. Each ohmmeter reading should be infinite (very high), otherwise replace the transformer.

7. Install the TR unit back onto the generator and when it is wired into place and secured by the holding screws, remove the 24-volt lead from the generator (do not allow it to touch ground).

8. Connect an ammeter between the 24 volt TR terminal and the previously disconnected lead.

9. Place a load across the 12 volt cranking battery such as one or two 12 volt head-

lamps, or the equivalent of 5 to 20 amperes.

10. Start and run the vehicle engine at a high enough rpm to produce maximum rated generator output.

11. The registered amperes flowing to the cranking (C) battery must be at least 5 amperes or more, otherwise the TR unit is faulty and should be replaced. If current flow to the TR unit is 5 amperes or greater, then the TR unit is operational.

LEECE-NEVILLE ALTERNATORS

Leece-Neville has been a major producer of heavy-duty generators and alternators for many years, and their products can be found on all major makes of heavy-duty trucks and equipment. Their range of current alternators is wide and they are manufactured in the two most widely used voltages of 12 and 24 volt. Rated outputs of their most widely used truck type alternators range from 65 to 145 amperes, therefore they are capable of covering a broad spectrum of demand. Although many models are available, we will look at two typical heavy-duty truck models used by a variety of truck manufacturers. These models are numerous but also operate on the same basic prinicple due to a common design arrangement.

The 2300JB through 2805JB series units are one widely used model of alternator, while the JA series units are the other which are available in several ratings and voltages. Leece-Neville commonly rate their 12 volt alternators as 14 volt units, while their 24 volt units are rated at 28 volts. This rating is typical of the voltages that are produced by the alternator assembly at its rated amperage.

These Leece-Neville alternators are self-load limiting, which feature a fully adjustable, built-in solid-state voltage regulator. The rotor shaft may be rotated in either direction without affecting the output or cooling of the unit, due to its bi-directional pulley fan arrangement. Six silicon diodes mounted in heat sinks convert alternating current from the delta wound stator into direct current. A capacitor connected between the heat sinks assists in suppressing transient voltage spikes which could possibly burn out or damage the diodes. The brushes and voltage regulator are located in a waterproof housing and may be removed for replacement or inspection without disassembling the alternator unit. An external relay terminal can be used for power supply to electrical accessories, or for chargelight relays.

A common feature of these alternators is that the unit has ungrounded output terminals so that it can be adapted to either a positive or negative ground system. The only wiring hookup required is the vehicle wiring to the correct output terminals

which eliminates the need for field relays or ignition switch connections.

The regulators used with these alternators are equipped with transient voltage protection, therefore they can withstand instantaneous opening of the charging circuit under full load conditions.

Troubleshooting Leece-Neville Alternators

The sequence for troubleshooting and testing the operation of the series JA and JB alternators follows the same basic pattern of checks and tests, therefore the following procedure can be considered common to both types. Prior to troubleshooting any alternator system, check the recommendations suggested at the start of the section dealing with general alternator troubleshooting.

The most important checks are that the battery be in at least a 75% state of full charge, terminals and connections must be clean and tight, the belts should be correctly adjusted, and the alternator assembly should be secure on its mounting brackets. As indicated at the start of the general troubleshooting section on alternators and charging systems, trouble in the system usually results from the state of charge of the battery being either continually low or overcharged (excess use of water on non-maintenance-free batteries).

To assist you in determining if the problem is in the alternator or the voltage regulator, connect an accurate voltmeter across the positive and negative posts of the battery with the engine stopped. Note the specific reading on the voltmeter. Start the vehicle engine and raise its speed to about 1000 rpm, at which time the voltmeter reading should increase over what was noted earlier when the engine was stopped. If the voltmeter reading rises excessively, the charging system may be defective or in need of adjustment. If the voltmeter reading does not increase, proceed to the full field test.

FULL FIELD TEST

This test will allow you to determine whether the problem is in the voltage regulator or in the alternator assembly. Obtain a short stiff piece of wire such as a paper clip or 1/16 inch (1.58 mm) gas welding rod, and jumper wire with alligator clips. Refer to Fig. 4-62 and connect the jumper wire at one end to the alternator negative output terminal; insert the short stiff piece of wire into the small hole at the rear of the brush and voltage regulator housing.

NOTE: The small hole in the rear of the alternator is not located in the same location on all Leece-Neville alternators; however, it is in the general area shown in Fig. 4-62.

The connections shown are used on both positive and negative ground electrical systems. With the jumper wire and small wire connected as shown in Fig. 4-62, firmly push the wire into the hole so that it contacts the outer brush terminal.

One of two things should occur during this test with the wire.

1. With the engine running at a fast idle, the voltmeter shows an increased reading over that obtained with the voltmeter previously placed across the battery terminals, and the engine running. A rise in the voltmeter reading is an indication that either the voltage regulator or diode-trio is at fault, which would require disassembly of the alternator assembly for inspection and repair.

Fig. 4-62. Inserting short stiff wire approximately 1.5 inches (38 mm) long into small hole at rear of alternator assembly. (Courtesy of Leece-Neville, Sheller-Globe Corp.)

2. No rise is indicated on the voltmeter face. Remove the voltage regulator assembly by taking out the small screws on its cover as shown in Fig. 4-63. Remove the diode-trio after disconnecting the necessary wires and noting their respective locations as shown in Fig. 4-63 (b).

Inspect the printed circuit of the voltage regulator unit for possible signs of burning which will create an open. Common location of such a burn area is in the tract or path from the positive regulator terminal to a brush terminal. Of course, any burnt area of the printed circuit in the voltage regulator will render it unusable, and it should be replaced. While inspecting the voltage regulator, always check the brush spring caps and their contact screws for dirt or corrosion and clean them if required. Failure of the alternator to produce power flow after regulator replacement would necessitate disassembly and repair of the alternator unit.

(a)

(b)

Fig. 4-63. (a) Voltage regulator cover removed; (b) lifting diode-trio from A.C. terminal studs. (Courtesy of Leece-Neville, Sheller-Globe Corp.)

An alternate method of checking the alternator output is to individually check each phase (3 phase) by the use of a two filament sealed beam headlight connected in parallel across the alternator as shown in Fig. 4-64.

With the engine running at a steady rpm, the headlight lamp should glow with the same brilliance on each phase as shown in Fig. 4-64. Dimness of the headlight lamp on one or two phases would indicate either a defective diode-trio, power diode or alternator stator. If, however, the diode-trio tests out as serviceable, then the alternator requires disassembly and repair.

VOLTAGE REGULATOR ADJUSTMENT

Prior to adjusting the voltage regulator, make certain that all wires and connections are tight and clean, that the battery connections are also in a similar state, and that the charge condition of the batteries is at least at full charge. If necessary, charge the batteries to obtain a full-charge condition.

Connect an accurate voltmeter with graduated scale (not a dash mounted unit from the vehicle) across the battery or batteries. Ensure that all vehicle accesso-

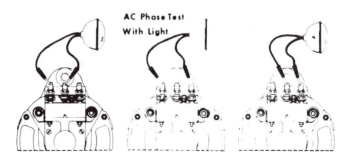

AC Phase Test
With Light

Fig. 4-64. Checking alternator output. (Courtesy of Leece-Neville, Sheller-Globe Corp.)

ries are turned off anytime that the voltage regulator is to be adjusted.

Remove the small plastic protective cap from the top of the voltage regulator and insert a small screwdriver into the hole until it engages the adjusting screw, as shown in Fig. 4-65.

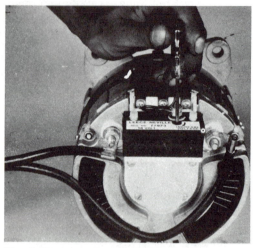

Fig. 4-65. Adjusting voltage screw. (Courtesy of Leece-Neville, Sheller-Globe Corp.)

Run the engine at about 1000 rpm, and turn the adjusting screw clockwise to increase the voltage output, and counter clockwise to decrease the voltage as indicated on the voltmeter until the desired and corrected voltage is attained.

The voltage adjustment screw should be turned carefully, since if it is turned past its stop at either end, damage can result.

Typical recommended voltages for 12, 24 and 32 volt systems as per Leece-Neville specifications are as follows.

1. All 12-volt systems ... 13.5-13.7 volts for on-highway trucks such as tractor/trailers and 13.8-14.2 volts for vehicles that require high power demands such as ambulances, school buses, etc.

2. All 24-volt systems ... 27.4-28.0 volts, tailor to suit operation

3. All 32-volt systems ... 36.8-37.5 volts, tailor to operation

Application, ambient temperatures, geographical locations, and barometric pressure will all affect what the particular voltage setting should be. However, the ideal setting can be established over a reasonable service period, where the battery is kept in a fully charged condition without excess use of water.

Replace the plastic or nylon screw back into the regulator adjustment hole when finished.

PRE-REGULATOR ADJUSTMENT CHECK

If repairs have been done to the voltage regulator, or it has been disassembled for brush replacement of the alternator, a loss of residual magnetism can occur. In order to restore the residual magnetism of the alternator rotor, and prior to testing the voltage regulator setting, momentarily flash the field by connecting a jumper between the diode trio terminal, and alternator positive output terminal as shown in Fig. 4-66.

Leece-Neville Transformer Rectifiers

These units operate in the same general manner as those used by Delco-Remy on their 30-SI/TR models, Delcotron Integral Charging System, discussed in this chapter. The main function of the 5114T and 5116T transformer rectifiers used by Leece-Neville is to replace the conventional Series/Parallel switch. As with any system that employs a transformer rectifier unit, they are used to provide a source of power for charging the cranking battery on 12 volt vehicles equipped with a 24 volt starter motor assembly. Figure 4-67 shows the arrangement and wiring circuit for both a negative and positive ground system that employs the transformer rectifier unit.

The alternator used with the TR system is of conventional 12 volt output capacity. All vehicle accessories, therefore, are powered from a 12-volt system battery, while the system utilizes two sets of 12-volt batteries in series to provide 24 volts for cranking.

The sequence for charging the batteries with this system is rather unique in that the cranking battery is charged by the

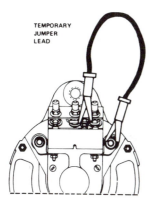

Fig. 4-66. Restoring alternator residual magnetism. (Courtesy of Leece-Neville, Sheller-Globe Corp.)

NEGATIVE GROUND

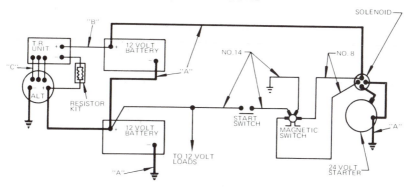

POSITIVE GROUND

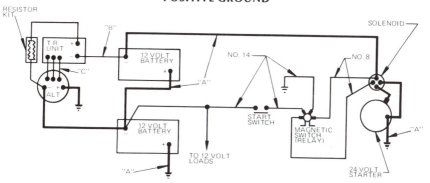

Fig. 4-67. Transformer rectifier circuit. (Courtesy of Leece-Neville, Sheller-Globe Corp.)

transformer rectifier unit at a rate conducive to its state of charge. For example, the maximum rate of output from the TR unit is 20 amps which is sufficiently high to charge the cranking battery, since with the engine running, no load is placed on the cranking battery. If the cranking battery is in a good state of charge, or as it rises to its full charge state, the output current from the TR unit will gradually drop to about one amp when the terminal voltage of the battery reaches 13.8 volts.

It should be noted, that if an 85 ampere alternator is used on a vehicle, for example, and if the TR unit is supplying its maximum current of 20 amperes to the charging battery, then the available alternator output to the vehicle system would be reduced to 65 amperes. Once the cranking battery has reached its full-state of charge, then the full 85 amperes would be available to the vehicle accessories system. On an average vehicle application, the cranking battery will reach a full-state of charge within approximately 15 minutes. The adoption of one of these transformer rectifier units allows conversion of any existing 12 volt system into a 12/24 volt unit.

Troubleshooting the Leece-Neville TR Unit

The TR (transformer rectifier) unit is sealed at manufacture, therefore only several tests can be carried out on it to determine its condition. Its output can be checked while on the vehicle while it is coupled to its alternator assembly, which is considered the best method of checking for any problem. However, the use of an ohmmeter will assist you in determining possible problem areas on the TR unit after it has been removed from the alternator assembly.

Transformer Primary Continutiy Check

Use the ohmmeter, as shown in Fig. 4-68, to establish that continuity exists between each of the three phases of the TR unit. Due to the extremely low resistance that exists between the transformer windings, the exact level of resistance of each phase cannot be determined. If the resistance readings at each phase are high, or vary somewhat, then the winding is open, and the TR unit should be replaced.

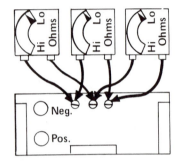

Fig. 4-68. Checking resistance of each phase, transformer primary circuit. (Courtesy of Leece-Neville, Sheller-Globe Corp.)

Ground Test

Using an ohmmeter as shown in Fig. 4-69, an infinity reading should be obtained between any of the five terminals of the TR unit and the housing (ground). An internal ground would be indicated if any other reading but infinity (high) is obtained. Replace the TR unit if any other such reading is obtained.

Rectifier Test

Figure 4-70 shows the hook-up of the ohmmeter required to test the rectifier of the TR unit. An infinity reading should be obtained when the ohmmeter leads are connected as shown at A in the figure; when the ohmmeter leads are reversed as in B, a low reading should be obtained. If no reading is obtained in either connection A or B, the rectifiers are open, while a similar reading in both directions indicates shorted rectifiers.

Should either one of these conditions be noticed, then replace the TR unit.

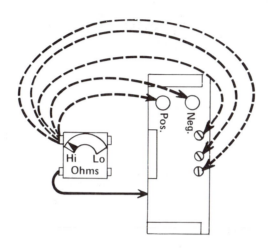

Fig. 4-69. Ground test of the TR unit. (Courtesy of Leece-Neville, Sheller-Globe Corp.)

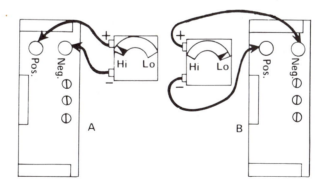

Fig. 4-70. Rectifier test. (Courtesy of Leece-Neville, Sheller, Globe Corp.)

Chapter
4C

Alternator Disassembly and Repair

Although there are many makes, styles and designs of alternators used on cars, trucks, buses, industrial, and marine applications, the general design and disassembly procedures are basically the same. The following procedures, checks, and tests are not meant to be all inclusive, but do deal with typical and widely used different makes of alternators. The test procedures required to establish the condition of the diodes, regulators, rectifiers, stators, rotors, etc. are common to all units with the use of an ohmmeter being mandatory for most of the checks.

PULLEY REMOVAL

The first thing you do after you remove a belt-driven alternator from the unit is to remove the drive pulley. Pulley removal involves either the use of a puller, or the removal of a retaining nut first, then the puller. An example of pulley removal can be seen in Fig. 4-71.

Figure 4-71(a) shows the use of a special socket (Snap-On No. S-8183) which is a cut-away socket that can accept an Allen wrench. This arrangement can be used to remove and also to re-tighten the pulley nut upon reassembly. It may be necessary to place a piece of small pipe over the Allen wrench to give you more leverage when removing or installing the pulley retaining nut.

An alternate method is to use an Allen wrench and a box wrench over the pulley retaining nut. In this instance, clamp the pulley in a vise using an old oversize belt or similar material wrapped around the pulley to protect it from the vise jaws. The alternator shaft can be held stationary with the Allen wrench, while loosening or tightening the retaining nut with the box-end wrench; or an air impact wrench and socket can be used as shown in 4-71(b).

Always exercise care when clamping any pulley in a vise, since any damage to the pulley groove can cause severe and irreparable damage to the pulley. Drive belts will suffer shortened lives if installed into a damaged pulley groove. Remove the woodruff key from the shaft after pulley removal.

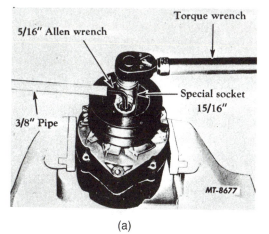

(a)

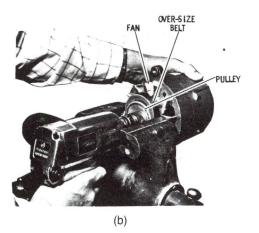

(b)

Fig. 4-71. (a) Use of special socket and Allen wrench to remove alternator pulley. (Courtesy of International Harvester) (b) Air impact wrench and socket to remove alternator pulley nut in a vise. (Courtesy of Motorola Inc., Automotive Products Div.)

SEPARATION OF THE ALTERNATOR HOUSING

Prior to separating the alternator housing, place a small match mark on both halves to ensure reassembly in the same position. Also on some models of alterna-

tors, it is necessary to first of all remove the voltage regulator assembly from the rear end frame on direct mounted units. This is achieved, for example, on Motorola units by simply removing the two regulator/cover mounting screws, then pulling the cover straight back to unplug the unit as shown in Fig. 4-72.

On this type of voltage regulator arrangement used by Motorola, the brush assembly should then be removed by the removal of the two brush assembly mounting screws as shown in Fig. 4-72.

On alternators without the external voltage regulator on the end frame, it may first of all be necessary to remove the end plate screws such as that found on the rear of Delco brushless type alternators. After this, and on most other alternator models, take out the four long through bolts that pass from one half of the alternator assembly, through the stator and into the other half of the alternator unit. Separate the drive end frame and rotor as one assembly, and the stator and rear housing as another. It may be necessary to use two screwdrivers for this purpose.

Typical housing separation is shown in Fig. 4-73, along with through bolt removal.

STATOR AND ROTOR SEPARATION

Separate the stator from the generator end frame by removing the stator wire lead attaching nuts or screws as the case may be. To remove the drive end frame from the rotor, it is necessary on some alternators to place the rotor/housing assembly on an arbor press and push the rotor with its front bearing from the housing.

Other models of alternators such as Delco-Remy automotive models require that the rotor be placed in a soft jaw vise to permit removal of the shaft nut. First re-

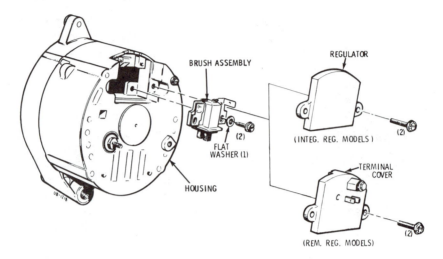

Fig. 4-72. Voltage regulator and brush holder removal. (Courtesy of Motorola Inc., Automotive Products Div.)

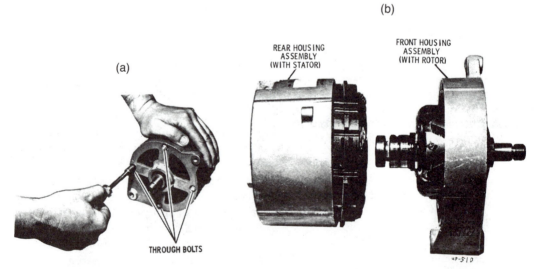

Fig. 4-73. Alternator through bolt removal (a) and housing separation (b). (Courtesy of Motorola Inc., Automotive Products Div.)

move the four through bolts, separate the drive end frame from the stator assembly, remove the nut, washer, pulley, fan and collar, and then separate the drive end frame from the rotor shaft. Remove any other components that require replacement or repair taking care not to damage anything. Note and label all terminals and wires, etc.

STATOR/RECTIFIER BRIDGE DISASSEMBLY

When the stator is connected to the alternator rectifier bridge assembly, it is often necessary to unsolder the stator leads from the bridge assembly terminals on some models of alternators.

On others, simply remove the stator lead terminal nuts. An example of unsoldering the stator leads from the rectifier bridge assembly is shown in Fig. 4-74.

ALTERNATOR REPAIR CHECKS

Once the alternator has been disassembled, the following checks and tests are required to establish its suitability for reuse, and what parts are in need of replacement.

Stator Tests

A check of the stator windings can be done with the aid of a 110 volt test lamp or an ohmmeter as shown in Fig. 4-75.

NOTE: When conducting a stator test on a Leece-Neville type alternator, this company cautions against attempting to measure the resistance of the stator windings with a conventional ohmmeter due to the extremely low resistance of the windings. These stators should be checked and

Fig. 4-74. Disconnecting the stator from the rectifier. (Courtesy of Motorola, Inc., Automotive Products Div.)

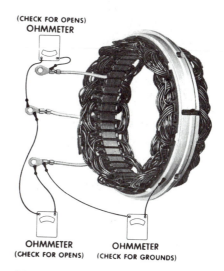

Fig. 4-75. Checking stator windings, (Courtesy of AC Delco Div. of GMC.)

tested for grounds and continuity between phases with a 115-220 volt test light, since the higher voltages applied to the stator increase the chances of detecting a faulty or borderline unit. This check, however, must not be done while the stator is connected to the heat sinks.

In Fig. 4-75, if the test lamp lights, or the ohmmeter reading is low when connected from any stator lead to the stator frame, then the windings are grounded. If the lamp does not light up, or if the ohmmeter reading is high when successively connected between each pair of stator leads, then the stator windings are open (no continuity).

IMPORTANT: Delta wound stators cannot be checked for opens or short circuits without laboratory test equipment; however, if all other electrical checks are normal and the alternator assembly does not supply its rated output, then check the regulator unit. Shorts or opens in the stator windings are difficult to locate because of the low resistance of the windings.

ROTOR FIELD WINDING CHECKS AND TESTS

Several tests are required on the rotor to determine its suitability for reuse. These tests can be broken into four individual checks which are explained as Tests 1, 2, 3 and 4 below.

Test No. 1 (a): Current Draw or Winding Resistance

To complete this test, connect a fully charged battery and ammeter in series with the edges of the rotor slip rings. It is important that the test leads from the battery circuit be connected or placed against the edges of the rotor slip rings in order to avoid creating an arc mark on the brush contact surface of the slip rings.

Figure 4-76 shows the rotor and the typical connections required for Tests No. 1 through No. 4.

When checking the current draw or rotor winding resistance, the ambient and

rotor temperature should be between 70-80°F (21-26.6°C). The current draw to the field windings of the rotor will vary between different makes of alternators, but can also be different even on the same make and basic model of alternator. Several examples of typical field current draw would be:

1. Motorola 9DA Series alternators. Current draw is 2.7 to 3.2 amperes at 12.6 volts battery power.

2. Delco-Remy 10-SI type 116 p/n 1102927. 4.0-5.0 amperes at 80°F (26.6°C) and 12 volts.

3. Delco-Remy 15-SI type 100 p/n 1101448. 4.4-4.9 amperes at 80°F (26.6°C) and 12 volts.

4. Delco-Remy 30-SI type 400 p/n 1117742. 3.5-4.5 amperes at 80°F (26.6°C) and 12 volts.

5. Delco-Remy 32-SI type 600 p/n 1117183. 6.5-7.5 amperes at 12 volts and 80°F (26.6°C).

6. Motorola SC Series alternators. 2.1-2.5 amperes at 10 volts and 70-80°F (21.-2.6°C).

7. Motorola 9BB and 9FB Series alternators. 2.7-3.2 amperes at 12.6 volts and 70-80°F (21-26.6°C).

The above examples are typical of the field current draw for most models of alternators; however, always refer to the manufacturer's latest service literature to locate the specific current draw for your particular model of alternator. Motorola publishes their rotor field current draw amperes in the respective service manual for the particular alternator model. Delco-Remy publishes all of their alternator rotor field current specs in Bulletin 1G-188, while Leece-Neville publishes a reading in ohms

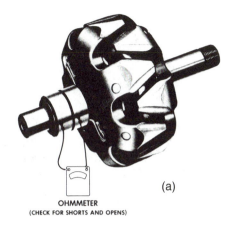

(a)

OHMMETER
(CHECK FOR SHORTS AND OPENS)

Fig. 4-76. (a) Field winding resistance check. (Courtesy of AC Delco Div. of GMC) (b) Rotor inspection and tests. (Courtesy of Motorola Inc., Automotive Products Div.)

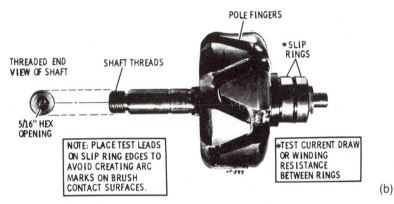

POLE FINGERS

*SLIP RINGS

THREADED END
VIEW OF SHAFT

SHAFT THREADS

5/16" HEX
OPENING

NOTE: PLACE TEST LEADS ON SLIP RING EDGES TO AVOID CREATING ARC MARKS ON BRUSH CONTACT SURFACES.

*TEST CURRENT DRAW OR WINDING RESISTANCE BETWEEN RINGS

(b)

of resistance through the rotor field coil winding within the respective alternator maintenance bulletin. Shorted windings are indicated if the ammeter reads above the specified values. A reading below the specified value would indicate shorted windings.

Test No. 1(b): Rotor Winding Resistance

The resistance of the rotor windings can be checked with an ohmmeter to establish the actual resistance through the windings. To check the resistance, this value can be calculated simply by using Ohm's Law. Divide the voltage by the current that was established in Test No. 1 which gives us $R = E/I$ and the resistance can be found without an ohmmeter.

However, since an ammeter and a fully charged battery may not be available, or the actual field current specifications may not be readily available, then the field resistance can be found with the ohmmeter and compared to published specs.

To check the field winding resistance, place one lead of the ohmmeter against one slip-ring and the other lead to the opposite slip-ring as shown in Fig. 4-76(a).

Typical examples of field resistance are shown below.

1. Motorola 9DA Series alternators. 3.8-4.6 ohms at 70-80°F (21-26.6°C).

2. Motorola 9BB and 9FB alternators are the same as the 9DA models.

3. Motorola SC Series alternators. 4.0-4.6 ohms at 70-80°F (21-26.6°C)

4. Leece-Neville 4000 Type alternators. 3.0-3.3 ohms for all 12 volt units, and 10.0-10.4 ohms for all 24 volt units.

5. Leece-Neville 2000 Type alternators have varying resistances based on the specific release date of the unit; however, an example would be the 2300JB manufactured after D.C. 7613. 4.9 to 5.5 ohms

6. Leece-Neville Type 2700JB, 2800JB and 2805JB. 1.9-2.3 ohms

Delco-Remy units can be figured out as mentioned from the Ohm's Law formula given above.

Test No. 2: Grounded Slip-Ring or Winding

Use a 12 volt d.c. test lamp, ohmmeter, or 110 volt a.c. test lamp. Place one test lead to the rotor body and the other on either slip ring. An open circuit from the slip rings to the rotor body is a correct condition. If the test lamp lights, or if the ohmmeter reading is low, the rotor winding is grounded.

Replace the rotor if the winding is open, shorted or grounded.

Test No. 3: Condition of Slip Rings

Slip-ring brush contact surfaces can be cleaned up and finished with 400 grain or finer crocus cloth by spinning the rotor in a small lathe or suitable drill press to ensure that the slip-rings remain concentric or round. If the slip-rings are rough or out of round, they can be trued in a lathe. Take care that only enough material is removed to true up the slip-rings and finish with crocus cloth. Clean the assembly by blowing away all dust or fine filings.

Test No. 4. Rotor Shaft and Body

Check the condition of the rotor shaft threads. Check the condition of the bearing surface and, if damaged, replace the rotor.

DIODE TRIO CHECK

The physical shape of the diode trio used with alternators will vary between makes; however, the purpose of the check remains the same, to establsih whether or not each diode in the trio is in satisfactory condition. Several ways can be employed to effectively test the diode condition which are by the use of an ohmmeter with a 1.5 volt cell, a commercial diode tester or 12 volt d.c. test lamp.

CAUTION: Do not use a 120 volt a.c. test lamp or diode damage will result.

Diodes are tested to insure that they only pass current in one direction. Diodes which do not pass current in either direction are open, while diodes passing current in both directions are shorted. Figure 4-77 shows the ohmmeter lead connections required to check out the condition of the diode-trio.

POSITIVE/NEGATIVE HEAT SINK TESTS (RECTIFIER BRIDGE)

A total of six checks (two readings per check) must be made on the heat sink or rectifier bridge diodes in order to establish their condition. Various types of heat sinks

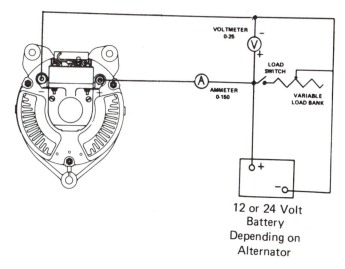

Fig. 4-77. Diode-trio check. (Courtesy of Leece-Neville, Sheller-Globe Corp.)

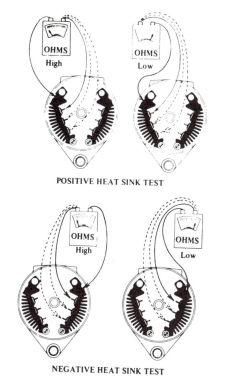

Fig. 4-78. Heat-sink diode checks. (Courtesy of Leece-Neville, Sheller-Globe Corp.)

(style) and rectifier bridges are used. Figure 4-78 shows typical examples of how to check these diodes properly. The diode tests can be made with the use of a 1.5 volt cell ohmmeter, commercial diode tester, or 12 volt test lamp d.c.

CAUTION: Do not use a 120 volt a.c. test lamp or diode damage will result.

On Leece-Neville alternators, the positive heat sink is the one to which the positive output terminal is connected. This is recognizable by the fact that the square hole in the terminal end of the positive heat sink is larger than the terminal hole of the negative heat sink. Fig. 4-78 shows that, whether the positive or negative heat sink diodes are being checked, one high reading and one low reading should be obtained when the leads are connected, otherwise the diode is defective.

On Leece-Neville alternators, a capacitor connected across the heat sinks can also be tested by the use of a capacitor tester or ohmmeter connected across the terminals as shown in Fig. 4-79. If a capacitor tester is

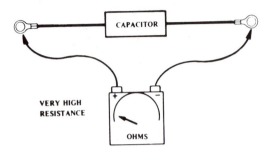

Fig. 4-79. Capacitor test. (Courtesy of Leece-Neville, Sheller-Globe Corp.)

used, its value is 0.158 MFD (micro-farads), and 100 working volts d.c. If an ohmmeter is used, a low resistance reading indicates a shorted or leaking capacitor, therefore it should be replaced.

MOTOROLA RECTIFIER BRIDGE DIODE TESTS

Figure 4-80(a) shows a typical rectifier bridge and diode-trio suppressor capacitor arrangement from a 9DA series alternator. The other charts show the lead placement for the ohmmeter as well as the typical readings obtained using a Simpson 260 VOM-The readings are approximate and may vary between ranges and also with the use of a different make of ohmmeter.

DELCO REMY RECTIFIER BRIDGE CHECK (DIODES)

Figure 4-81 shows the ohmmeter lead connections for testing the diode condition of the rectifier bridge on a typical Delco-Remy Delcotron Generator assembly. Connect the ohmmeter leads first to the grounded heat sink or frame and each of the three terminals in succession, then reverse the lead connections to the grounded heat sink and same terminal.

The same test is conducted between the grounded heat sink and the other two terminals, and also between the insulated heat sink and each of its three terminals for a total of six checks similar to that done on both Leece-Neville and Motorola units.

A good diode should show one high and one low reading; otherwise the diode is defective.

ALTERNATOR BRUSH TERMINAL TEST

The brushes used in most electronic alternators today are assembled into a brush holder which is then held into position by the use of two small screws. To check the brushes for continuity, an ohmmeter with a 1.5 volt test cell or a 12 volt d.c. test lamp can be used. An example of testing both a single and dual terminal brush arrangement is shown in Fig. 4-82.

An original brush set can be reused if it passes the tests shown in Fig. 4-82, and if the brushes are not worn beyond mid-way, are not oil soaked, cracked, or otherwise damaged.

ALTERNATOR REASSEMBLY

The reassembly of the alternator is basically the reverse of disassembly; however, caution must be exercised when pressing on any bearings. Examples of bearing and rotor to front housing installation can be seen in Figures 4-83 and 4-84.

ALTERNATOR OUTPUT TEST: AFTER REPAIR

To determine if the output of the repaired alternator is within the manufacturer's specifications, the alternator

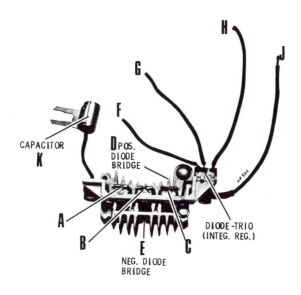

(a)

OHMMETER/LAMP LEAD PLACEMENT		*OHMMETER RANGE READING		LAMP ON OFF	
RED (+)	BLK (−)		(OHMS)		
A,B,C,	D	RX1	5-20	X	
D	A,B,C,	RX1	∞		X
A,B,C,	E	RX1	∞		X
E	A,B,C	RX1	5-20	X	

(b)

DIODE—TRIO TEST CHART

OHMMETER/LAMP LEAD PLACEMENT		*OHMMETER RANGE READING		LAMP ON OFF	
RED (+)	BLK (−)		(OHMS)		
F,G,H	J	RX1	5-20	X	
J	F,G,H	RX1	∞		X

(c)

*Typical values taken with Simpson 260 VOM. Readings are approximate and may vary between ranges and with different VOM's.

OHMMETER/LAMP LEAD PLACEMENT		*OHMMETER RANGE READING		LAMP ON OFF	
RED (+)	BLK (−)				
D	K	RX10,000	∞		X

(d)

*Typical values taken with a Simpson 260 VOM.

Fig. 4-80. (a) Motorola rectifier assembly, (b) rectifier diode test chart, (c) diode-trio test chart, (d) suppressor capacitor test chart. (Courtesy of Motorola Inc., Automotive Products Div.)

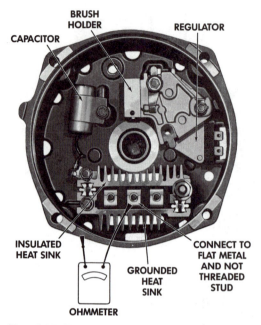

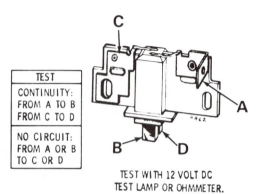

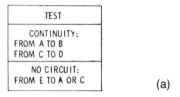

TEST
CONTINUITY: FROM A TO B FROM C TO D
NO CIRCUIT: FROM A OR B TO C OR D

TEST WITH 12 VOLT DC TEST LAMP OR OHMMETER.

A AND C ARE INSULATED BRUSHES.

TEST
CONTINUITY: FROM A TO B FROM C TO D
NO CIRCUIT: FROM E TO A OR C

(a)

Fig. 4-81. Testing Delco-Remy rectifier bridge. (Courtesy of Delco-Remy Div. of GMC)

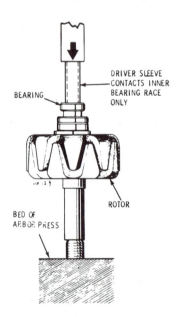

Fig. 4-83. Rotor rear bearing installation. (Courtesy of Motorola Inc., Automotive Products Div.)

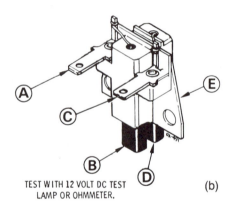

TEST WITH 12 VOLT DC TEST LAMP OR OHMMETER.

(b)

Fig. 4-82. (a) Single terminal brush holder test; (b) dual terminal brush holder test. (Courtesy of Motorola Inc., Automotive Products Div.)

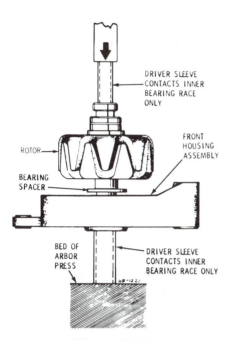

Fig. 4-84 Rotor/front housing assembly. (Courtesy of Motorola Inc., Automotive Products Div.)

(a)

(b)

Fig. 4-85. (a) Generator/alternator test stand (Courtesy of Sun Electric Corp.). (b) Typical alternator test stand (courtesy of Robert Bosch Corp.).

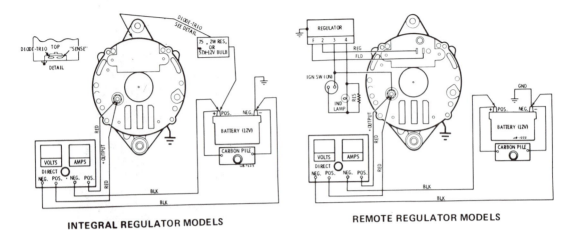

INTEGRAL REGULATOR MODELS   **REMOTE REGULATOR MODELS**

Fig. 4-86. Motorola 9DA series alternator output test. (Courtesy of Motorola Inc., Automotive Products Div.)

assembly must be mounted in a test stand or fixture whereby the alternator can be driven and its output monitored with the necessary test instruments. Several major companies produce test stands for this purpose. Figure 4-85 shows examples of these machines with alternators mounted ready for testing.

Typical test hookup for several major types of alternators is shown in Figs. 4-85, 4-86, and 4-87.

With the alternator mounted in the test stand, select the voltage and circuit polarity from the dials on the face of the test machine. With the alternator hooked up as shown in Fig. 4-86, turn the test machine drive motor on and adjust the drive speed to obtain 5000 rpm (alternator speed). Slowly increase the load on the alternator charging circuit through the use of the variable carbon pile until a minimum voltage of 13.7 is obtained with the alternator at 5000 rpm. Note and record the output current and compare it to the manufacturer's specifications.

On Leece-Neville alternators that use an integral regulator, a test machine can be used, or the alternator can be connected as shown in Fig. 4-87.

Prior to checking the output of the alternator, immediately after the battery has been connected, it is necessary to restore the residual magnetism in the rotor which may have been weakened or lost through the repair and handling procedures. To restore this magnetism, connect a jumper wire with alligator terminals at each end to the diode trio terminal and the alternator output positive terminal as shown in Fig. 4-88. **CAUTION:** This connection should only be done momentarily. Simply flash the field with the end of the jumper wire.

The output test must be conducted as per the manufacturer's specificatons regarding rated output and voltage at a particular speed for the alternator under test. Refer to Leece-Neville test specificatons for the unit under test. Output testing of Delco Remy alternators was given in detail earlier under the troubleshooting section.

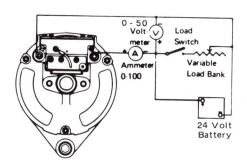

Fig. 4-87. Leece-Neville alternator output test. (Courtesy of Leece-Neville, Sheller-Globe Corp.)

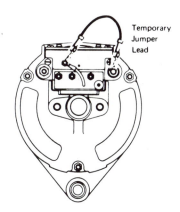

Fig. 4-88. Flashing the field to restore rotor magnetism. (Courtesy of Leece-Neville, Sheller-Globe Corp.)

REVIEW QUESTIONS

Q1 What is the basic difference between a d.c. generator and an alternator?

Q2 What is the major advantage of using an alternator over a generator on passenger cars, etc.?

Q3 Can an alternator be rotated in either direction?

Q4 Where is the field winding of the alternator located?

Q5 What are the functions of the alternator slip rings?

Q6 What is meant by the terms externally excited and internally excited?

Q7 Is the stator winding a single phase or a three phase winding?

Q8 How is the a.c. voltage converted to d.c. voltage at the alternator output?

Q9 How is a.c. current flow in a d.c. generator converted to d.c. at its output?

Q10 Do all alternators use a voltage regulator?

Q11 Do magnetic lines of force flow from north to south or vice-versa?

Q12 Are voltage regulators used with alternators adjustable?

Q13 Does electron flow originate at the positive or negative side of the battery terminal?

Q14 What are the two types of three-phase windings commonly used in alternators, and what is the difference between these?

Q15 What problems can occur if the battery leads are connected up backwards to the alternator?

Q16 Where are the rectification diodes (six) actually located in the alternator assembly?

Q17 What are the two basic types of alternators now in use?

Q18 What do the letters SI stand for in reference to an alternator assembly?

Q19 How is the voltage regulator adjusted on an AC Delco alternator that is designed for voltage adjustment?

Q20 What is the purpose of an R designated terminal used with some alternators?

Q21 What is the purpose of the alternator diode trio arrangement?

Q22 What type of stator winding employs a pair of its windings to produce output voltage?

Q23 What is the purpose of the capacitor or capacitors (two in some) used inside the alternator assembly?

Q24 On heavy-duty alternators a transformer rectifier is often used. What is the purpose of this TR unit?

Q25 On AC Delco alternators such as the 25SI model, how would you know if the system was positively or negatively grounded?

Q26 How would you adjust the voltage regulator on the AC Delco model 25 SI brushless type alternator?

Q27 What is the average current flow that is supplied through the alternator slip rings from the battery system to excite the field windings?

Q28 How would you remove the brush-holder on a Motorola type alternator?

Q29 What is an SC model Motorola alternator?

Q30 Where is the voltage adjustment located on the Motorola SC model alternator?

Q31 In solid state alternator systems, how often do the switching action (voltage control) devices operate?

Q32 What are the two most important precautions that must be adhered to when attempting to test an alternator?

Q33 What state of charge should the battery be at prior to testing the alternator charging circuit?

Q34 How can you determine the rated output of an alternator?

Q35 What is the purpose of inserting a screwdriver blade into the small test hole at the rear of the alternator assembly during an output test?

Q36 On AC Delco alternators fitted with a voltage adjustment cap or cube, how many positions of adjustment are there? List them.

Q37 What special test tool can be used on all AC Delco SI generators to determine a possible problem area in the system?

Q38 What is meant by energizing speed in reference to an alternator test?

Q39 How would you polarize an alternator assembly after installing it on the engine, and why is polarizing necessary?

Q40 From the information under the section dealing with AC Delco alternators, how can the R terminal system voltage be set to half-charge or full charge conditions? (Refer to the information on the 20SI and 29SI models!)

Q41 When using an ohmmeter on a diode, what readings would signify that the diode was operational?

Q42 On an AC Delco model alternator employing a TR unit for a series/parallel system, what test would indicate that the TR unit is serviceable?

Q43 When adjusting a voltage regulator adjustment screw, what happens when the screw is turned CW (clockwise) and CCW (counter-clockwise)?

Q44 To polarize the voltage regulator on a Leece-Neville alternator system, what is required?

Q45 Does the cranking battery on a Leece-Neville series/parallel system receive a constant rate of charge at all times?

Q46 List the three tests that can be conducted on the Leece-Neville TR (transformer rectifier) unit?

Q47 What should be done to the alternator prior to taking it apart, but having established that it does require disassembly?

Q48 What holds the two halves of the alternator together as well as the stator assembly?

Q49 How are the stator leads connected to the rectifier bridge assembly?

Q50 What should not be used to check the condition of the alternator diode-trio? Why?

ANSWERS

A1 The basic difference between a d.c. generator and an alternator lies in the fact that the generator employs a stationary magnetic field with a rotating armature, while the alternator employs a rotating magnetic field (rotor) and a stationary set of windings known as a stator.

A2 The major advantage of the alternator over the older d.c. generator is that it is lighter, but more important, it can produce a steadier and higher output at lower speeds.

A3 Yes. The only condition to this is that a bidirectional fan must be used which will direct cooling air into the alternator regardless of its rotative direction. Otherwise the fan should be fitted to ensure one direction of rotation only.

A4 The field winding is contained within the rotor assembly and connected to the slip rings.

A5 The alternator slip rings are connected to the field coil located within the rotor assembly; battery current flows through one slip ring into the field winding of the rotor (externally excited), and back out through the other slip ring and brush to the battery ground return.

A6 Externally excited refers to a generator/alternator that receives current from an external source such as through a brush and slip ring; internally excited is a generator that receives a supply of current from the armature brush to vary the magnetic field strength of the poles.

A7 The stator winding is wound to produce three separate windings, therefore the term three phase versus single phase.

A8 A.C. voltage in the alternator is converted to d.c. at the alternator's output by six rectifying diodes; three diodes are positive in design, while three are negative in design, to handle the alternating current that is produced in the stator.

A9 In a d.c. generator a.c. current is produced within the armature as it rotates; this current flow is then converted to d.c. current through the commutator.

A10 Yes; all alternators employ a voltage regulator; some are externally mounted while the newer units often have the voltage regulator assembly mounted into the actual alternator housing for compactness.

A11 Magnetic lines of force flow from north to south.

A12 Most voltage regulators are adjustable; however some of the newer integral regulator types are not.

A13 Electron flow is actually from the negative to positive terminal; however, the conventional theory is most often used and referred to by most manufacturers, which considers the flow to be from positive to negative. Therefore, you should always consider this fact unless the particular service information states differently.

A14 The two types of stator windings used are the delta and wye connected units. The delta stator will produce a higher output at the top end of the speed range, while the wye connected stator will produce equal current at the low speed end, but at a lower rpm than the delta wound unit.

A15 Damage to the diodes can result.

A16 The diodes are arranged so that the three positive ones are located in a common insulated heat sink so that they cannot contact the alternator body end frame, while the negative diodes are mounted in another heat sink which is physically and electrically grounded to the alternator body which is the negative or ground output terminal in a negative ground system; in a negative ground system, the positive rectifier is insulated from the alternator body and connected to the positive output stud of the machine.

A17 The two basic types of alternators now in use are: (a) the slip-ring and brush type, and (b) the brushless type.

A18 The letters SI stand for system integral to indicate that the regulator is located inside the alternator.

A19 A voltage adjustment cap in the slip-ring end frame can be re-positioned externally to alter the voltage setting on these units (brush type or brushless use the same basic arrangement).

A20 An R designated terminal is used for wiring auxiliary equipment power supply from the generator; this R terminal usually provides half-system voltage only.

A21 The diode-trio controls the field current to the alternator assembly.

A22 A wye wound stator; the stator windings operate in pairs so that the output voltage is the total voltage between one stator winding lead and another.

A23 The capacitor inside the alternator is to smooth out voltage surges across the resistor to protect the rectifier bridge and diode trio, and to suppress radio noise.

A24 A transformer rectifier unit is used on some heavy duty alterna-tors for conversion to 110 volts d.c.; however, the TR units are used specifically to provide a separate voltage to charge the cranking battery on series/parallel circuits, namely 24-volt cranking, but 12-volt power supply to the accessories, since the alternator is itself a 12 volt unit. This feature does away with the need for an SP (series/parallel) switch.

A25 The 25SI AC Delco model alternator is a brushless type unit with one output terminal only; this terminal is electrically insulated from the housing, therefore no voltage reading can be obtained by touching a voltmeter prod to its hex head bolt. On negative ground models, a RED output terminal is used which must be connected to the battery positive circuit or terminal, while a BLACK output terminal is used on positive ground systems and should be connected to the battery negative circuit or terminal.

A26 The voltage adjustment screw is located beside the R terminal on the alternator. Remove the plug and insert a screwdriver into the voltage adjustment screw.

A27 The average current flow to excite the alternator field windings is usually in the region of 2.5 amperes, although values slightly less or slightly higher can be found in different makes and models of alternators.

A28 The brush-holder can be removed from a Motorola type alternator after removal of the voltage regulator assembly which is mounted to the alternator assembly.

A29 An SC model Motorola alternator is a heavy duty 12, 24 or 32-volt assembly which features an insulated or floating output system for either positive or negative ground systems. It also incorporates an adjustable output voltage control and protection circuitry against load dump and transients.

A30 The voltage select control screw is located on the top right of the regulator housing at the rear of the alternator.

A31 The switching action within the solid state alternator regulator system can be as low as 10 times per second to as high as 7000 times per second depending on conditions.

A32 The two most important precautions are:

(a) Correct battery polarity; reversed polarity can destroy the rectifier diodes.

(b) Never operate the alternator with the battery disconnected and the engine running since the charging voltage can rise to unsafe levels.

A33 The battery should be at as high a state of charge as possible. On some alternators a figure of 75% state of charge is required; however, on some of the current SI alternators, a much higher state of charge is necessary, even though the battery hydrometer eye appears green (minimum 65% state of charge condition).

If the battery is in a low state of charge it should be placed on charge or a good battery substituted for the duration of the test period.

A34 Many alternators have their rated output stamped on the generator frame, or it can be found in the manufacturer's test specifications bulletins.

A35 The reason for inserting a small screwdriver blade into the test hole at the rear of the alternator is to allow it to contact the small tab shown in Fig. 4-53, to ground it to the alternator end frame so that the alternator field winding can be grounded. If the alternator output is now within 10 amperes of specifications, then the field winding is probably at fault.

A36 There are four voltage adjustment positions; Lo, 2 (Medium-low), 3 (Medium-high), and Hi.

A37 Kent-Moore tool J-26290 can be plugged into any Delcotron SI generator with its ground lead connected to a good clean ground; the tester will indicate about 98% of all charging system faults. The test sequence is printed on a label attached to the rear of the tester body.

A38 The energizing speed is that rpm at which the generator will turn on. No output can be obtained from many brushless type generators until the voltage regulator assembly turns on. This speed is higher than some speeds at which generator output can be obtained; therefore, it is necessary when testing to increase the speed of the alternator/engine enough to turn on the regulator, then to reduce the rpm in order to check the output, since once the regulator has turned on, it will remain on until the engine is stopped.

A39 Polarizing is not necessary and should never be attempted on slip-ring and brush type alternators since any attempt to do so will result in damage to the diodes which would then require replacement.

NOTE: Newer brushless type alternators may require polarizing to establish the correct flow of current to the battery from the alternator assembly; this can be done by connecting the system to the battery circuit in the normal manner, then momentarily connecting a jumper wire lead from the battery positive post to the integral charging system relay terminal whether the system is positively or negatively grounded. in order to restore the residual magnetism in the rotor.

A40 The output available at the R terminal of the alternator is dependent upon how the relay terminal connector is actually wired. When the relay terminal and voltage regulator insulated screw at the diode-trio single connector within the integral charging system is wired together, the R terminal will operate at system voltage. However, if the relay terminal is connected to the rectifier bridge, it will allow the R terminal to operate at half-system voltage, which can be used to supply power for those instruments that require a CV or constant voltage condition.

A41 When one high and one low reading is obtained by placing the prods of the ohmmeter across the diode terminals, then reversing them to note if in fact one high and one low reading is obtained.

A42 The registered amps flowing to the cranking battery must be at least 5 amperes or more with the engine running, otherwise the TR unit is faulty and should be replaced.

A43 Turning the voltage adjustment screw CW increases the output, while CCW rotation decreases the output.

A44 Momentarily flash the field by connecting a jumper wire between the diode trio terminal and alternator positive output terminal as shown in Fig. 4-66.

A45 No; the cranking battery is charged at a rate conducive to its state of charge; in other words, the maximum rate of output from the TR unit is 20 amperes which is sufficiently high to charge the cranking battery. As the cranking battery approaches its full-state of charge, the current output will gradually drop to about one amp when the terminal voltage of the battery reaches 13.8 volts. Therefore on an 85 ampere alternator, the rate of charge to the system battery would only be 65 amperes when the cranking battery is receiving 20 amperes, but the system battery would receive a greater rate of charge as the cranking battery approaches its full state of charge.

A46 The three tests that can be conducted on the Leece-Neville TR unit are:
    (a) Transformer Primary Continuity Check
    (b) Ground Test
    (c) Rectifier Test

A47 Match mark the halves of the housing assembly to ensure reassembly in the same position.

A48 Generally four or more long through bolts.

A49 On some models of alternators, the stator leads are connected to the rectifier bridge by leads and nuts; however, it is necessary on some models to unsolder these leads.

A50 Do not use a 120 volt a.c. test lamp or diode damage will result; use an ohmmeter with a 1.5 volt cell, a commercial diode tester or 12 volt d.c. test lamp.

Chapter
5

D.C. Generators and Voltage Regulators

D.C. GENERATORS

This chapter will deal very briefly with the d.c. generator. The reason for this is that the d.c. generator has been totally replaced by the a.c. generator or alternator with its solid state devices. The alternator is capable of producing a higher output than the d.c. generator at a lower engine speed. In addition, the solid-state devices in use today in automotive, heavy equipment and marine installations make the a.c. generator much more reliable and lighter, and it requires less overall maintenance.

However, some older vehicles and equipment still are in use equipped with d.c. generators. The mechanic and auto electrician should be familiar with the operation of this unit anyway.

Figure 5-1 shows both an external and cutaway view of a typical d.c. generator; while Fig. 5-10 shows a wiring circuit for the d.c. generator system.

The main difference between the operation of the d.c. generator and the a.c. generator (alternator), shown in Fig. 4-7, is that in the d.c. unit, the field poles (magnets) are stationary, while in the a.c. alternator, the magnets (rotor poles) rotate. The stator of the a.c. unit (as we know from discussions above) contains three windings of copper wire insulated from the alternator housing to produce a three-phase arrangement. The stator is held or is a stationary member, while the rotor spins inside these windings.

The d.c. generator consists of an armature assembly which is a soft iron core wound with many turns of copper wire. This armature is placed within the generator housing or stator frame which contains the pole shoes or magnets, and the armature is rotated by either a belt driven pulley or can be gear driven. The ends of the copper wires which are wound around the core of the armature are connected to what is commonly called a commutator. As the armature rotates, current is produced in the windings (a.c.), which is converted to d.c. at the commutator. Spring-loaded brushes riding on the commutator pick up this current flow and send it to an external voltage regulator assembly which monitors both voltage and current, and thereby controls the output of the generator assembly.

Residual magnetism contained in the pole shoes (magnets) generates the necessary magnetic lines of force that are cut by the rotating armature windings. The strength of the field (magnets) is controlled by passing the generated current through wires that are wound around the individual pole shoes (magnets). These windings are insulated from the generator housing; however, when changing current passes through them due to either a change in engine speed, or the voltage regulator ac-

tion, then the magnetic field strength is also altered.

BASIC GENERATOR ACTION

As discussed above, electro-magnetic induction produces both a voltage and current flow. In its simplest form this basically involves moving a conductor through a magnetic field at right angles. In this way, voltage is produced which causes current to flow within the conducting element.

The d.c. generator employs a mechanically driven armature (as shown in Fig. 5-1) which is made from a series of thin

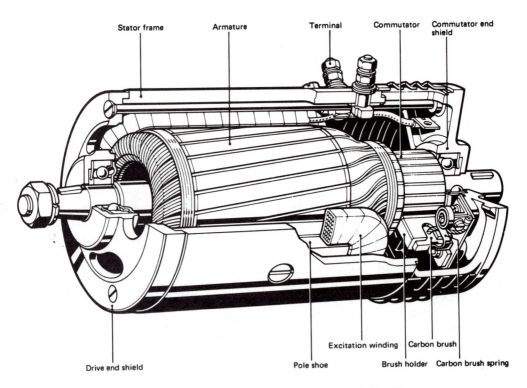

Fig. 5-1. D.C. generator assembly. (Courtesy of Robert Bosch Corp.)

stamped metal plates or laminations insulated from one another. The armature core is manufactured in this fashion in order to reduce eddy currents which would exist if the armature core was made from one solid piece of metal. Figure 5-2 illustrates these armature laminations. If eddy currents were allowed to develop, they would tend to overheat the armature metal thereby causing unnecessary losses in generated power, plus possible damage to the generator windings. You will notice from Fig. 5-2 that the iron laminations are designed with slots in them. The reason for these slots is to allow the insertion of insulated copper wires which will act as conductors for the generated electricity as the armature is rotated within the stationary pole shoes or magnets.

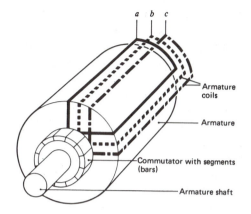

Fig. 5-3. Basic arrangement of the armature coils which are connected in a series hookup. (Courtesy of Robert Bosch Corp.)

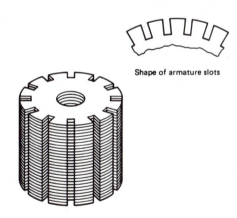

Fig. 5-2. Armature laminations of a D.C. generator. (Courtesy of Robert Bosch Corp.)

Figure 5-3 shows the basic arrangement of the armature coils which are connected in a series set up. On one end of the armature shaft assembly is what is known as a commutator. This is a series of copper bars or segments which are connected to a like number of armature coils. The end of

each coil is soldered into one of these commutator segments together with the end of the next coil so that all armature coils are in effect conductively or electrically connected to produce a closed armature winding circuit. It is important to note, however, that the commutator segments are insulated both from the armature shaft and the other segments. Since spring-loaded carbon brushes ride on the surface of these commutator bars, the insulation between the segments is lower (undercut) than the commutator surface itself.

The carbon brushes themselves are contained in spring loaded guides or holders as shown in Fig. 5-5, so that they will be in positive contact at all times with the rotating armature/commutator assembly during generator operation.

On the actual generator frame (housing), a wrap around cover band is installed so that it is possible at any time to gain access to the brushes for replacement, or to inspect the condition of the commutator itself.

D.C. generators are available with several sets of poles or magnets; however, for simplicity we will concentrate on the operation of a two-pole unit consisting of one north and one south pole.

There are two basic circuits within the d.c. generator, and these are illustrated in Fig. 5-4 as the field circuit and the actual load circuit. For explanation purposes, Fig. 5-4 shows only one loop of wire within the armature. Rotation of the armature assembly causes the loop of wire to cut through the magnetic lines of force emanating between the north to south pole which will induce a voltage within the rotating loop of wire. With a closed circuit, a generated voltage will produce a flow of current which will be collected at the carbon brushes riding on the commutator assembly. This current will then flow through attached wiring and the voltage regulator unit to the battery and other electrical equipment. This type of d.c. generator is commonly referred to as a shunt-wound assembly, since the armature winding and the excitation winding are connected in parallel.

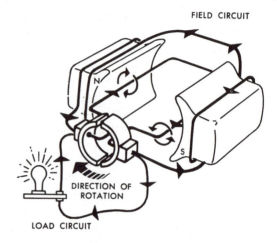

Fig. 5-4. Basic field and load circuit of a DC generator. (Courtesy of Delco-Remy Div. of GMC)

Residual magnetism contained within the pole shoes initiates the induced voltage within the rotating wire or armature winding. However, once the engine starts, the current flow produced in the armature windings will vary the field strength (magnetically) of the pole shoes, since both the field circuit and the load circuit are joined

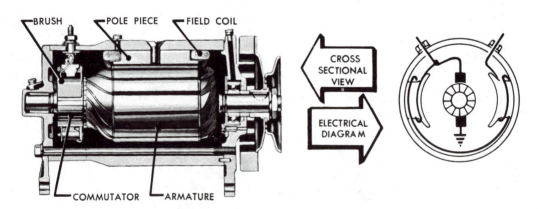

Fig. 5-5. Arrangement of both the field and load wiring within a typical two-pole DC generator. (Courtesy of Delco-Remy Div. of GMC)

together through the conductor (wiring and brushes).

This arrangement can be easily seen in Fig. 5-10 which illustrates that the field windings are connected to the insulated generator brush or load circuit. Therefore, an increase in the generator output will likewise increase the current flowing through the field windings. The greater the current flow through the field windings, the greater will be the strength of the magnetic field between the magnets.

The field poles or magnets therefore become electromagnets. This increased field strength increases the induced voltage in the armature windings thereby forcing more current through the field coils to create an even stronger magnetic field which will produce more voltage in the armature windings. The addition of conductors or armature windings to the generator allows an almost constant value of d.c. voltage to be produced at a given load and speed, since all armature windings are connected together at the commutator. Any voltage produced in one loop is therefore added to the voltage that is developed in the other loops or armature windings, since they are all connected in series.

The maximum induced voltage created in a typical two-pole generator will occur only when each loop of wire, or armature winding, is at right-angles to the magnetic field.

Figure 5-6 illustrates that the maximum induced voltage will only occur when each individual loop or armature winding is at 90 degrees and 270 degrees of rotation: (a) armature loop or winding in a vertical position, no voltage induced; (b) maximum induced voltage shown when the loop or winding is at right angles to the magnetic lines of force.

In Fig. 5-6, no voltage is induced into the

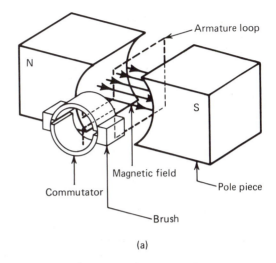

(a)

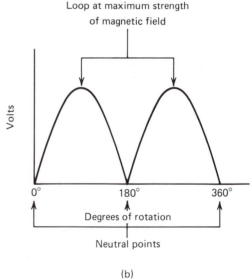

(b)

Fig. 5-6. (a) Armature loop or winding in a vertical position, no voltage induced. (b) Maximum induced voltage shown when the loop or winding is at right angles to the magnetic lines of force. (Courtesy of Delco-Remy Div. of GMC)

armature winding or loop when it is vertical to the magnetic lines of force. This situation exists when the split (undercut between the commutator segments) in the commutator ring is directly under the brushes, therefore no arc or spark will occur as one commutator segment moves from under the brush and is replaced by another one. This halfway point is commonly known as the neutral point.

GENERATOR POLARITY

All d.c. generators must be polarized prior to being placed into operation after having been electrically disconnected from the circuit. Failure to polarize the generator will result in damage to the regulator, and failure of the generator to produce current flow to the battery. Polarizing ensures that the positive side of the battery will be connected to the positive side of the generator, as well as the negative battery connection being connected to the negative side of the generator. The direction of current flow within the conductors of the generator depends upon the polarity of the poles. The method used to polarize the generator circuit is dependent upon whether the circuit is connected in what is commonly known as either an A or a B circuit form. These two types of circuits are discussed below.

A and B GENERATOR CIRCUITS

A generator's output is controlled by one of three ways:

- Speed of armature rotation
- Number of armature conductors
- Magnetic field strength

Although all of the foregoing items can control the output of the generator, the easiest and most widely used method involves control of the magnetic field to limit both the voltage and current produced.

This is obtained by employing a three-post voltage and current regulator assembly that includes a cut-out relay. Figure 5-7 shows both an A and B circuit regulator assembly.

POLARIZATION OF THE A CIRCUIT GENERATORS

Figure 5-8 shows that in an A circuit generator, the generator field curcuit is connected to ground through the contact points of both the current and voltage regulator assembly. Note also that the field circuit is connected to the insulated brush of the generator assembly. To polarize the A circuit type generator, simply connect a jumper wire from the insulated or hot side of the battery, to the armature or A terminal of the generator. All wiring must be connected. In Fig. 5-8, the jumper wire is placed directly on the B or BAT terminal of the regulator assembly, and momentarily touched against the G or GEN terminal of the regulator assembly. This sets up the proper polarity and current flow from the insulated brush of the generator. Note that when you momentarily touch the jumper wire from the BAT to GEN terminals of the regulator, a small spark or flash will occur, which is normal.

It is strongly recommended for all 24 and 32 volt generator circuits that the brushes be temporarily insulated while polarizing; otherwise, due to the low resistance of the generator armature, an extremely high discharge current will flow through the armature resulting in burning of the armature assembly.

To temporarily insulate the brushes, remove the generator inspection clamp ring at the commutator end of the assembly, and place a strip of light matchbook type

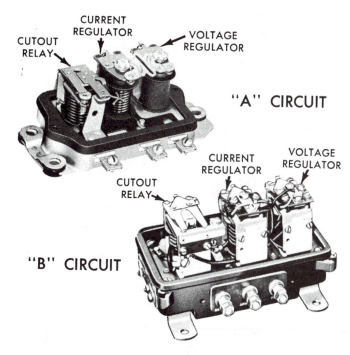

CUTOUT RELAY
CURRENT REGULATOR
VOLTAGE REGULATOR

"A" CIRCUIT

CURRENT REGULATOR
VOLTAGE REGULATOR

CUTOUT RELAY

"B" CIRCUIT

Fig. 5-7. Voltage and current regulator of an A circuit unit and of a B circuit unit. (Courtesy of Delco-Remy Div. of GMC)

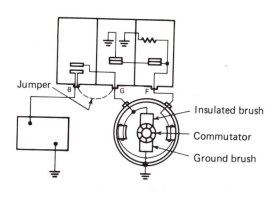

Jumper

Insulated brush
Commutator
Ground brush

Fig. 5-8. Polarization of an A circuit generator. (Courtesy of Delco-Remy Div. of GMC)

cardboard under each brush while you polarize.

POLARIZATION OF B CIRCUIT GENERATORS

Figure 5-9 shows the arrangement of the B circuit generator assembly. Note that it differs from the A circuit by the fact that the field circuit is connected to the grounded brush of the generator rather than to the insulated brush as is the case with the A circuit generator. In addition, the B circuit is internally grounded within the generator assembly rather than through the contact points of the regulator as is the case with the A circuit assembly.

Prior to attempting to polarize a B circuit

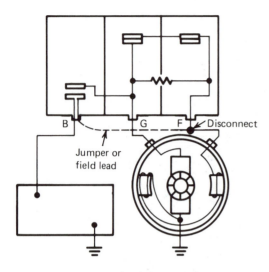

Fig. 5-9. Polarization of a B circuit generator. (Courtesy of Delco-Remy Div. of GMC)

generator, you must remove the field lead from the voltage regulator assembly. With this lead disconnected, but all other leads connected, momentarily flash the disconnected field lead to the battery (B or BAT) terminal of the regulator. Failure to disconnect the field lead, then attempting to use a jumper wire to polarize between the regulator battery and field terminals would allow a high current to flow from the battery through the regulator points, to and through the armature assembly with possible serious damage.

There is no specific advantage to employing either an A circuit or a B circuit since both operate in the same basic fashion.

Remember that if the generator field coil lead is connected to the insulated brush inside the generator, this will be an A type of circuit, whereas if the field coil lead is connected to the grounded brush inside the generator, or to the generator frame, then the generator is a B type circuit. If a

wire is used as the return circuit in place of the vehicle frame directly, then this is an insulated circuit and can either be of A or B configuration, therefore check closely before making any connections to establish the type of circuit.

Many types and styles of d.c. generators have been built, and we will not delve into these here. However, let's study Fig. 5-10 which discusses the operation of a typical d.c. generator system.

The three post regulator assembly depicted in Fig. 5-10 consists of a separate voltage and current regulator, along with a cut-out relay. The voltage regulator component of the assembly protects the system from exceeding a specified maximum, while the current regulator limits the maximum generator output. The function of the cut-out relay is to open or close the generator to battery circuit when necessary. When the generator output voltage is high enough to charge the battery, the cut-out relay closes the circuit. When the generator output is reduced, the cut-out relay opens the circuit to prevent a reversal of current and to prevent damage to the circuit. The cut-out relay consists of an iron core around which is wrapped two types of wire, namely a shunt and a series winding, with the shunt wiring being made up of fine wire, while the series winding consists of heavy guage wire. Generator voltage is always impressed through the shunt winding, while generator output or current passes through the series winding.

A set of contact points is assembled above the iron core of the cut-out relay. When the generator is not in operation, these points are held apart by the action of a flat spring riveted to the side of the cut-out relay armature assembly. When the generator voltage is high enough to actually charge the battery, the induced magnetism within the cut-out relay windings is sufficient to pull the armature which supports the moveable contact point towards the fixed contact point. When the points come into contact, current flowing through the series winding assists the magnetism created in the shunt winding to hold the points closed and allow a completed circuit to the battery so that it will receive a charge.

Should the generator output decrease through a speed reduction, current in the battery would exceed that being produced in the generator with the result that a reverse flow of current back through the cut-out relay series winding will similarly reverse the magnetic field that previously existed in the series winding. No reversal, however, will take place in the shunt winding (voltage flow) with the net result that the shunt and series windings of the cut-out relay now oppose one another. This reaction results in the magnetic field not being strong enough to hold the contact points together, and the flat spring will separate the points which effectively opens the circuit between the battery and the generator assembly.

Within the voltage regulator assembly of the regulator, a shunt winding (fine wire) is connected across the generator. Some generators may contain an accelerator winding (series wound) which speeds up the action of the vibrating contacts. The winding and core are assembled into a core similar to that of the cut-out relay just described.

Above the end of the core is a contact point attached to a flat steel armature connected to the frame by a flexible hinge. Immediately above this armature is a fixed contact point which is held in contact with the moveable point by the action of a small spiral spring when the voltage regulator is not in operation. With the voltage regulator points in contact, the generator field circuit is completed to ground.

The voltage at which the contact points will separate is controlled by the tension of the small spiral spring which can be ad-

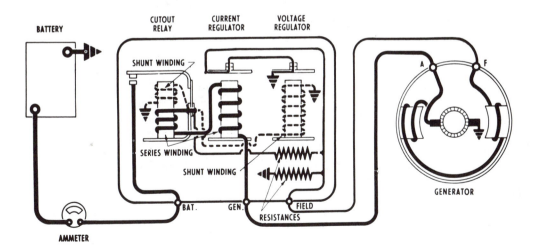

Fig. 5-10. DC generator system schematic. (Courtesy of Delco-Remy Div. of GMC)

justed. With the generator in operation, this predetermined voltage can be reached by the voltage flowing through the windings of the regulator. When this occurs, the magnetic field produced in the winding will pull the armature containing the moveable contact point down thereby opening the circuit at the contact points.

This action induces a resistance back into the generator field circuit which immediately reduces the field current and voltage being produced by the generator. This output reduction from the generator automatically reduces the strength of the magnetic field of the regulator shunt winding (fine wire). This allows the force of the spiral spring to again pull the voltage regulator contact points together to directly ground the generator field circuit and allow both current and voltage to increase.

This opening and closing of the voltage regulator points will occur continuously (many times per second), so that the points can actually attain a vibrating condition, hence the term "vibrating contact point regulator". This continuous action automatically makes and breaks the circuit between the generator and voltage regulator and therefore controls or regulates the voltage produced to a predetermined maximum.

The action of the current regulator portion of the regulator assembly parallels that of the voltage assembly in that its points will also open and close during its operation. Remember however, that the current regulator has generator output impressed through a few turns of heavy wire (series winding). A set of points above its core is arranged in the same fashion as that for the voltage regulator. The current regulator points will also be in contact with one another when the generator output is less than that needed to overcome the tension of the spiral spring holding the points together. Generator field circuit is completed to ground through the contact points in series with those of the voltage regulator.

When the generator output is high enough, the magnetic field created in the winding pulls the contact points apart, thereby inserting a resistance into the generator field circuit which reduces both the generator and field current output. When the generator output is thus reduced, the existing magnetic field of the current regulator is reduced, and the force of the spiral spring will pull the contact points together once again so that the generator output can again increase. As with the action of the voltage regulator points, those of the current regulator will also open and close many times per second so that the generator output is held within a safe maximum value.

Contained within the regulator assembly are two resistances, which are designed to partially dissipate any voltage surges that might damage the regulator assembly. One resistance is placed in the field circuit when either the current or voltage regulator unit operates, while the second resistance or resistor is connected between the regulator field terminal and the cut-out relay frame, which effectively places it in parallel electrically with the field coils of the generator assembly.

Anytime that the voltage or current regulator points open, a surge of induced voltage will occur in the field coils due to the changing magnetic field. Excessive arcing at the contact points is avoided by the resistors absorbing and dissipating these potential harmful surges.

Temperature compensation of voltage regulation is achieved by means of a bimetal thermostatic hinge on the armature which is designed to allow the regulator to operate at a higher voltage when ambient temperatures are low, which is required in order to charge the battery. A similar type of temperature compensation can be found on the current regulator.

VOLTAGE REGULATORS

Although many production vehicles now employ solid state rectification devices along with integral voltage regulators, there are many vehicles still on the road that employ the older models of alternators which utilized an external voltage regulator to control the output of the alternator.

A typical voltage regulator used with these earlier alternators, known as a double-contact regulator assembly, is shown in Fig. 5-11.

The regulator functioned to limit the alternator's generated voltage to a pre-set voltage by controlling the generator field current. Within the double contact regulator is a field relay unit which allowed the instrument panel light (telltale) to illuminate with the ignition key on, but the engine not running. As soon as the engine started and the generator was charging, the light goes out.

The double contact voltage regulator unit uses two sets of contact points to obtain desired field excitation under variable conditions. Figure 5-12 shows a wiring diagram for the charging system with a double contact regulator assembly.

ADJUSTMENT—DOUBLE CONTACT REGULATORS

The various adjustments required on the double contact voltage regulators are

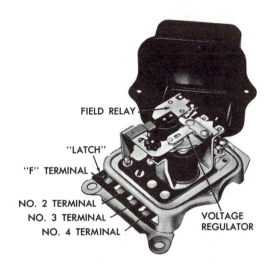

Fig. 5-11. Double contact regulator. (Courtesy of Delco-Remy Div. of GMC)

shown in Figs. 5-13, 5-14, 5-15, and 5-16. When adjusting the voltage as per Fig. 5-13, the screw can be rotated either CW or CCW. A voltage increase will occur if the adjusting screw is turned CW because it increases the tension of the voltage regulator coil spring, thereby necessitating a higher magnetic field strength to separate the contact points.

To adjust the voltage regulator field relay closing voltage, the heel iron must be bent gently as shown in Fig. 5-13.

In addition to the voltage adjustments shown in Figs. 5-13 and 5-14, the field relay point opening dimension and the field relay air gap setting must also be correctly adjusted. The air gap is set by turning the nylon self-locking adjusting nut as shown in Fig. 5-13, while the points are adjusted by bending the support bracket of the points. All of these adjustments should only be done with the battery disconnected to prevent current flow and damage to the system.

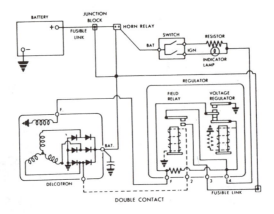

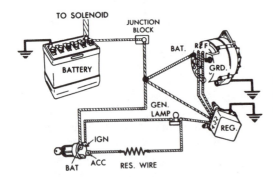

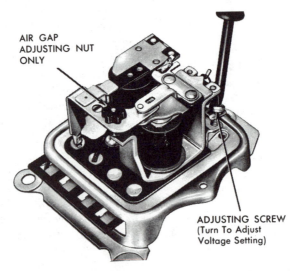

Fig. 5-12. (a) Voltage regulator circuitry. (b) Typical voltage regulator external wiring diagram. (Courtesy of GMC)

Fig. 5-13. Adjusting voltage regulator setting. (Courtesy of GMC)

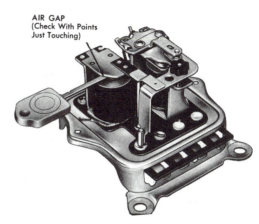

Fig. 5-16. Checking field relay air gap. (Courtesy of GMC)

Fig. 5-14. Adjusting field relay closing voltage. (Courtesy of GMC)

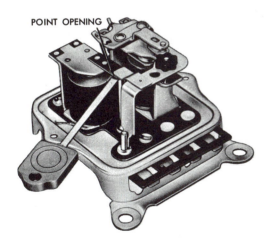

Fig. 5-15. Checking field relay point opening. (Courtesy of GMC)

SYSTEM CONDITION CHECK

In order to check the overall charging system condition, Fig. 5-17 (a) shows the test hookup arrangement for the voltage check, while Fig. 5-17 (b) shows the arrangement for an ammeter test.

Charging system checks are necessary when the alternator indicator lamp stays on while the engine is running, or if the ammeter on those systems so equipped indicates a discharged or continually low rate of charge. When the ignition switch is turned on, the telltale lamp should be on with the engine stopped; similarly if equipped with an ammeter, it should show a discharge when the ignition switch is turned to the ACC position.

Proceed as follows:

1. Run the engine at approximately 1500 rpm or higher.

2. Turn on the headlights (high-beam), plus the heater blower switch to the hi

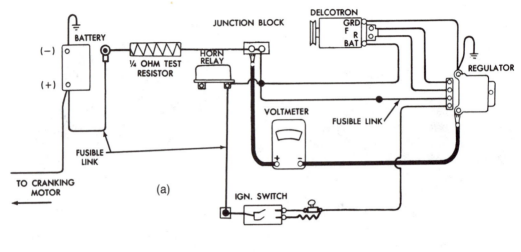

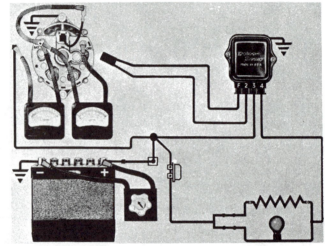

Fig. 5-17. (a) Voltage setting test connections. (b) Alternator output test, ammeter method. (Courtesy of GMC)

position, and after several minutes time, note the reading on the voltmeter.

3. If the voltage is at 12.5 volts or more, turn off the accessories and stop the engine.

4. Connect a ¼ ohm resistor (25 watt fixed) into the circuit as shown in Fig. 5-17 (a).

5. Start and run the engine at or higher than 1500 rpm for 15 minutes, then disconnect and reconnect the regulator connector in order to cycle the regulator voltage.

6. If the voltage is between 13.5 and 15.2, then the regulator is functioning properly; however, if it is less than this, voltage regulator adjustment is required. A voltage

reading of less than 12.5 volts indicates that the alternator is at fault and should be removed for repair; however, if the voltage is above 12.5 volts, but less than the 13.5 proceed to the next step.

7. Leave the engine running at 1500 rpm or higher and disconnect (unplug) the four-terminal connector harness, remove the regulator cover, and plug the connector back into the regulator.

8. Adjust the voltage as shown in Fig. 5-13, until it is set to the manufacturer's specifications.

Prior to replacing the regulator cover, or removing it, unplug the connector to prevent any short circuits.

ALTERNATOR OUTPUT TEST— AMMETER METHOD

With the arrangement shown in Fig. 5-17 (b), start and slowly accelerate the engine to 1500 rpm and adjust the carbon pile (variable load bank), to hold the voltage at 14 volts.

Note the amperage on the ammeter and compare to specs. Failure of the alternator to meet the test specs requires that it be removed and checked out.

OPERATION OF VOLTAGE REGULATOR

An example of the regulator operation can be understood by referring to Figs. 5-10 and 5-12 (a).

Turning the ignition switch on allows current to flow to ground to complete the circuit by passing to the Number 2 regulator terminal, through the field relay shunt winding and back to the battery.

This current flow creates a magnetic pull above the winding that closes the relay contact points, and current from the battery flows to the Number 3 regulator terminal through the field relay contacts and lower contacts of the voltage regulator to ground via the F terminal.

The output of the generator (current) flows to the Number 3 regulator terminal and through the field relay contacts and the voltage regulator shunt windings where the magnetism created in this winding will cause the lower contact points to separate. With the points apart, the generator field current is routed through a resistor which will therefore reduce the field coil current; this reduction in current flow reduces the magnetic field that was holding the lower points apart, and spring tension now pulls them together to allow the generator output to again increase. This action is repeated many times per second to limit the maximum voltage produced.

At higher generator speed, a slightly higher voltage is routed through the voltage regulator shunt winding which will cause the upper contacts to close. When this action occurs, both ends of the field coil are grounded and no current can flow through the coil, therefore the voltage decreases rapidly and the upper points will open again because of the reduced magnetic field. Field current can again flow through the regulator resistor and field coil to allow the voltage to increase, and the upper contacts will close once more.

The action just described will therefore occur many times per second to automatically limit the generator voltage to a preset value established through adjustment. Should a capacitor be found at the number 4 terminal, its purpose is strictly for radio noise suppression.

EXTERNAL TRANSISTOR REGULATORS

Earlier generators and some existing alternators use a transistorized regulator that functions as any other regulator, and that of course is to limit the maximum voltage output of the charging system.

An example of this type of regulator can be seen in Fig. 5-18.

Adjustment of the transistorized regulator shown in Fig. 5-18 is done by removing the Allen head plug, inserting a slotted head screwdriver into the screw and turning it either clockwise to raise the voltage setting, or counter-clockwise to reduce the voltage setting. Generally, two adjustments either way from center are possible.

THREE-POST VOLTAGE REGULATOR

The three post regulator assembly is actually a voltage regulator, current regulator and cut-out relay all assembled into one unit as shown in Fig. 5-19.

In Fig. 5-19, the cutout relay closes the generator to battery circuit when the generator voltage is high enough to charge the battery. The cutout relay points open to prevent a reversal of flow from the battery anytime that the generator output is less than that of the battery. The generator field circuit is grounded through the contact points of the voltage regulator. This ground circuit is opened anytime that the current or voltage flowing through their respective windings generates sufficient magnetic force to pull the points apart.

When the points separate, generator output will decrease rapidly reducing the magnetic field in the windings. The points will again close, grounding the generator circuit and allowing the output to again increase. The cutout relay points are held open by spring force and closed by the pull on the armature which is created by the magnetic field in both its shunt and series windings. The opening and closing of the points in the three unit regulator can occur many times per second. This opening and closing of the points thereby controls the generator output so that both the current and voltage levels are not exceeded. The points in the voltage and current regulator are normally held closed by spring force.

All springs are adjustable through a screw located on the spring bracket. Point setting, air gap, etc. are done in a similar fashion as that shown for the two-post regulator shown in Figs. 5-13 through 5-16. The three-post regulator is only used on a d.c. generator assembly found on older vehicles.

GENERATOR OUTPUT CHECKS

To check the output of the generator assembly, the following test instruments are required:

- Ammeter
- Voltmeter
- Variable resistance such as a carbon pile
- Accurate tachometer to monitor generator rpm
- Several jumper wires fitted with small alligator clips

Output tests of the A circuit and B circuit vary slightly, with the necessary connections shown in Figs. 5-20 and 5-21.

On A circuit generators, connect a jumper lead to the generator field terminal and ground prior to running the unit at its recommended test speed. Drive or operate the generator on the vehicle to the point that battery voltage is obtained, close the circuit switch, then increase the drive speed of the generator to that recom-

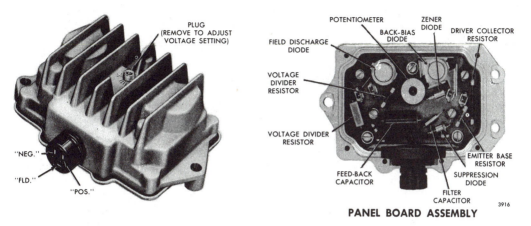

Fig. 5-18. Externally mounted transistorized regulator assembly. (Courtesy of Delco-Remy Div. of GMC)

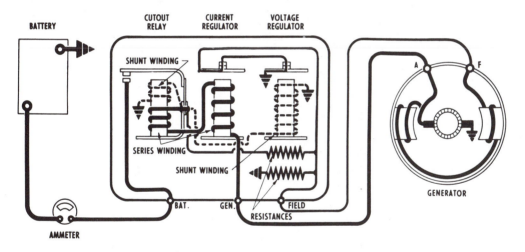

Fig. 5-19. Wiring circuit of a standard three-unit regulator assembly. (Courtesy of Delco-Remy Div. of GMC)

mended by the manufacturer in their test specification sheets, and adjust the carbon pile load bank to obtain the specified voltage. With the voltage as per specs, carefully note the current on the ammeter and compare to specifications.

On B circuit generators, connect a jumper wire between the field and armature terminals prior to testing the generator output.

GENERATOR OVERHAUL

When the generator requires repair, it should be disassembled and visually inspected for such possible defects as:

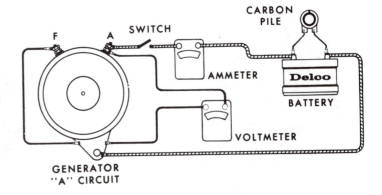

Fig. 5-20. An A circuit generator output test hookup. (Courtesy of Delco-Remy Div. of GMC)

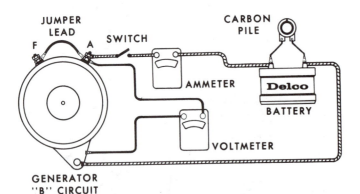

Fig. 5-21. A B circuit generator output test hookup. (Courtesy of Delco-Remy Div. of GMC)

- Worn or cracked and broken brushes
- Damaged brush holders
- Brush springs for signs of overheating and loss of tension
- Worn bearings
- Scored or dirty commutator (copper oxide film accumulation)
- Burned commutator bars or segments
- Signs of melted solder
- Oil saturated wiring
- Armature damage
- Metal or copper filings internally within generator body
- Broken insulation on wiring or between armature windings
- Spring tension check with a spring scale
- Security of pole shoe screws
- Pulley condition and fan condition
- State and condition of external wiring

Additional checks to the generator assembly would include such items as checking the armature assembly on a growler for an open circuit, short circuit, or grounded circuit; possible machining of the commutator segments to make it serviceable; and undercutting between the commutator segments to prevent brush damage and shorting.

Testing of the generator armature follows the same sequence used when checking the armature of a starting motor, which is shown in detail in chapter 6. Figures 5-22 through 5-24 show these basic checks.

VISUAL INDICATION OF
OPEN CIRCUIT IN ARMATURE

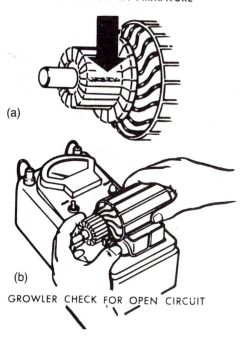

(a)

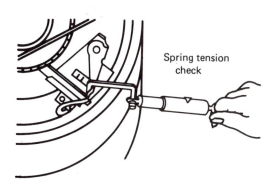

(b)

GROWLER CHECK FOR OPEN CIRCUIT

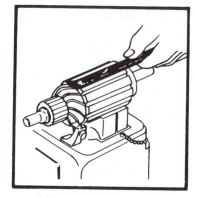

(c) GROWLER CHECK
FOR SHORT CIRCUIT

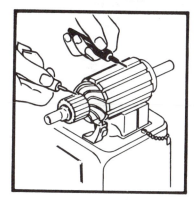

(d) TEST LAMP CHECK
FOR GROUND CIRCUIT

Fig. 5-22. (a) Visual check of armature commutator. (b) Growler check of armature for an open circuit and short circuit. (c) Short circuit check. (d) Test lamp check of armature for a grounded circuit. (Courtesy of Delco-Remy Div. of GMC)

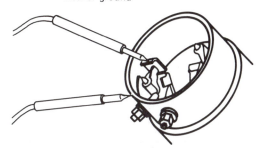

Spring tension check

Insulated brush holder test for ground

Fig. 5-23. Checking brush spring tension. (Courtesy of Delco-Remy Div. of GMC)

Fig. 5-24. Checking insulated brush holder for possible grounds. (Courtesy of Delco-Remy Div. of GMC)

GENERATOR FIELD COILS

Grounded field coils in an A circuit generator would reflect itself by the fact that both current and voltage control cannot be obtained over the generator. Grounded field coils on the other hand in a B circuit generator will still allow current and voltage to be controlled; however, the increased current flow in the field circuit will cause burning and oxidation of the regulator points, eventually creating an open circuit condition through the high resistance created. A test lamp connected to either end of the field coils will reveal a break or possible open in the circuit.

BRUSH TENSION CHECK

To check the tension of the generator brush holder, obtain a small spring scale and connect it as shown in Fig. 5-23. Obtain the test information from the manufacturers service test literature.

INSULATED BRUSH HOLDER CHECK

Check the insulated brush holder for possible grounds as shown in Fig. 5-24.

REVIEW QUESTIONS

Q 1 Why are d.c. generators seldom used any more on passenger cars?

Q 2 What are the main components of a d.c. generator, and how does it differ from an alternator?

Q 3 Why are the armatures used with generators and alternators manufactured from a series of thin stamped steel plates or laminations rather than a solid unit?

Q 4 How is the current produced in the d.c. generator converted to d.c. and led out of the generator to the battery system?

Q 5 Is a d.c. generator internally or externally excited?

Q 6 What is the difference between an A and B circuit generator?

Q 7 How would you polarize both an A and B circuit generator?

Q 8 Why is it necessary to polarize a d.c. generator?

Q 9 What is the basic purpose of the three post regulator used with the d.c. generator?

Q10 What happens at the cut-out relay when the battery is fully charged, or the generator slows down (reduced output)?

Q11 What is the visual difference between a shunt and series winding; how are they shown in a wiring diagram?

Q12 How are the current and voltage regulator outputs adjusted?

Q13 What is the purpose of the resistors used in the voltage regulator?

Q14 How would you know whether a three-post regulator or two-post regulator assembly was designed for use with a positive or negative ground system?

ANSWERS

A 1 D.C. generators are seldom used anymore because they are heavier than alternators, provide less output at low speeds, have more moving parts, and are less reliable.

A 2 The main components of the d.c. generator are the armature/commutator and field magnets or pole shoes; the a.c. alternator has a rotor which is the magnetic portion that is driven whereas the magnets in the d.c. generator are stationary. Also, the alternator employs a three-phase stator which doesn't move, whereas the armature in the d.c. generator which is similar does move.

A 3 They are manufactured from a number of thin stamped metal plates or laminations insulated from one another to reduce eddy currents, which would tend to overheat the armature or stator metal thereby causing unnecessary losses in generated power, plus possible damage to generator windings.

A 4 Current produced in the d.c. generator's armature is induced into individual windings inserted into the segments of the armature core and connected to bars on the commutator. From the commutator, carbon or copper alloy brushes riding on the commutator transfer this power to the regulator assembly, and then to the battery.

A 5 A d.c. generator is internally excited when it is running; residual magnetism creates the initial power output followed by current flow around the field magnet windings which will vary the magnetic strength and therefore the generator's output.

A 6 In an A circuit generator, the field circuit is connected to ground through the contact points of both the current and voltage regulator which are in series, although it is actually the voltage regulator points that are grounded. The field circuit is also connected to the insulated brush of the generator assembly. In a B circuit generator, the field circuit is connected to the grounded brush of the generator rather than to the insulated brush as is the case with the A unit. In addition, the B circuit is internally grounded within the generator assembly rather than through the contact points of the regulator as is the case with the A circuit generator.

A 7 To polarize an A circuit generator simply connect a jumper lead from the insulated or hot side of the battery to the armature or A terminal of the generator or regulator with all wires connected properly. On a B circuit generator, the jumper wire is placed directly on the B or BAT terminal of the regulator assembly, and momentarily touched against the G or GEN terminal of the regulator assembly.

A 8 Polarizing is necessary in order to set up the correct polarity and current flow from the generator to the battery.

A 9 The three-post regulator used with the d.c. generator consists of a current and voltage regulator post, plus a cut-out relay to connect the generator output to the battery.

A10 The cut-out relay contact points will be pulled apart to prevent a reversal of flow. This occurs because the magnetic field previously created in the shunt and series windings now oppose each other and spring pressure pulls the points apart.

A11 The shunt winding consists of many turns of fine wire, while the series winding consists of a heavier gauge wire. The shunt wire is always shown as a dotted line and the series as a solid line in any wiring diagram.

A12 Both the current and voltage regulator outputs are controlled by adjustment of the small spiral spring at the backside of the post. Normally these springs hold the current and voltage contact points together; therefore, the greater the spring force, the greater the generator output must be in order to increase the magnetic field around the cores to pull the points apart.

A13 The purpose of the resistors in the voltage regulator unit is to absorb and dissipate any voltage surges especially when the voltage/current points separate. The other resistor is connected between the regulator field terminal and the cut-out relay frame to absorb any additional surges in the system when the cut-out relay points separate.

A14 Generally it is stamped on the base plate of the regulator assembly; however, the nylon/plastic nuts on top of the voltage and current regulator posts signify this; red plastic nuts indicate a positive ground system, while black is a negative ground system.

Chapter
6

Electric Starting Motors

Major producers of both automotive and heavy-duty electric starting motors include such companies as Delco-Remy, Prestolite, Leece-Neville, Robert Bosch, Lucas C.A.V. Common voltages of electric starter motors are 12, 24, and 32 volt, with the 24 and 32 volt units being used on heavy-duty diesel engines. All electric starting motors operate on the same basic principle, although they will differ in physical size as you move from say a small gasoline engine starter on up to the large heavy-duty diesel engine models. In addition, some starters use a number of gears to transmit the drive from the armature shaft of the starter to the starter motor drive pinion. Various types of motor pinion drives are also used, and these will be explained as we progress into this section. The main purpose of any starting motor is, of course, to supply enough cranking power to effectively rotate the engine fast enough under all types of conditions to start it.

The starting motor must develop a high cranking torque (twisting or turning force) for a limited period of time when the starting switch is closed. It must include a means of engaging its pinion with the flywheel ring gear on the engine with which it is used, and of disengaging the pinion as soon as the engine starts in order to prevent overspeeding of the starter and possible damage.

Prior to discussing the actual operation of starter motors, refer to Figs. 6-1 and 6-2 which show both a typical starter used with automotive gasoline engines, and two heavy-duty types that are used with diesel engines. Familiarize yourself with the location of the major components and their nomenclature. This will assist you as we continue to discuss both the operation and design features of the most widely used starter motor models.

The nose housing on most modern starter motors can be located in several positions by removing the retaining bolts, rotating the nose housing to the desired position, and re-installing the bolts. This feature allows for variations in mounting to suit all engines.

MAIN COMPONENTS

The main components of a starter motor assembly are:

- Frame and field assembly
- Armature
- Commutator end head
- Pinion housing
- Drive pinion (different types available and used)
- The intermediate housing assembly

Each of the main components listed above can be described as follows:

1. The frame or starter motor body physically supports the other component parts of the motor, the field coils, the brush holders and brushes, and the pole shoes (magnets). The field coils are wrapped around the pole shoes to provide the strong magnetic field necessary to produce torque, while the pole shoes (magnets) and frame provide the path for the magnetic field.

2. The motor armature consists of a laminated soft iron core mounted on an armature shaft, a commutator and the windings which are wound in slots in the core and connected to the commutator. The commutator itself consists of a number of copper segments insulated from one another, and also from the armature shaft which extends through the pinion housing and supports the pinion drive assembly.

3. The commutator end head supports a bearing in which the armature shaft rotates.

4. The pinion housing encloses the actual pinion drive mechanism, and also supports the other end bearing that the armature shaft rotates in.

5. The drive pinion is shifted by an electric solenoid to engage the starter with the engine flywheel ring gear. The type of drive mechanism used with the pinion (small gear) on the end of the armature shaft, protects the pinion assembly from damage due to overspeed once the engine starts. However, the types of drive are discussed in more detail later.

6. The intermediate housing is that part of the starter motor assembly located between the main frame and the pinion housing.

It is found on heavy-duty starter motors such as shown in Fig. 6-2. This intermediate housing contains a bronze bearing which supports the center of the armature shaft, as well as containing the mechanism of the shift lever. Some intermediate housings are equipped with a solenoid access hole, providing a means for solenoid and drive timing adjustment, and solenoid removal for servicing. In addition, some units contain an oil reservoir to provide lubrication for the bronze center bearing, plus an oil seal to prevent any oil, water, or dirt from entering the motor.

BASIC MOTOR OPERATION

Now that we are familiar with the major components of a starter motor assembly, let's look at the principles of its operation.

This will involve some of the material from the earlier chapter dealing with basic electricity, which is reviewed in the following paragraphs.

The starter motor in its simplest form is shown in Fig. 6-3. In addition to the components shown in Fig. 6-3, we also require a starting switch, which can be ignition key combined, or it may be a separate switch that can only be energized once the ignition key is turned on. Usually one or more switch relays are also used which are required to carry the heavy current to the motor or solenoid.

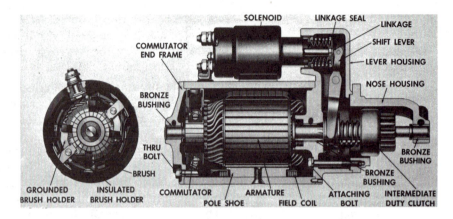

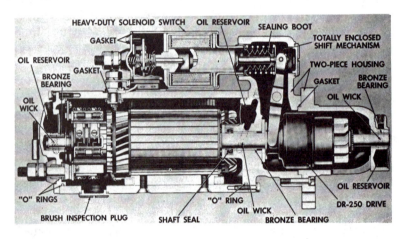

Fig. 6-1. Typical automotive enclosed shift starter motor. (Courtesy of AC Delco Div. of GMC)

(a)

(b)

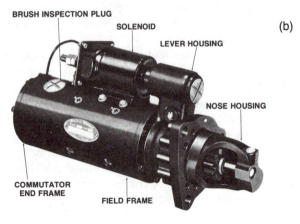

Fig. 6-2.

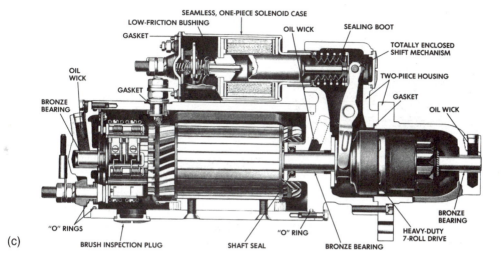

(c)

Fig. 6-2. (a) Sectional view of DR-250 heavy-duty starter motor. (b) Typical 40-MT/400 starter motor for diesel engine applications. (c) Sectional view of 40-MT/400 starter motor. (Courtesy of AC Delco Div. of GMC)

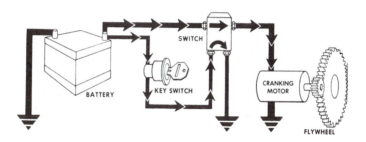

Fig. 6-3. Simplified starter motor cranking circuit. (Courtesy of Chevrolet Motor Division of GMC)

From an earlier study of Fig. 6-1, you will have noticed that every starter motor contains pole shoes (magnets) bolted to the starter motor frame.

The armature consists of a series of copper wires wound around a soft iron core. This assembly is then placed within the motor field frame so that it is surrounded by these field poles, or magnets. The number of magnets will vary in the various starter motor sizes and models. In addition, the physical diameter of starters becomes larger as the cranking requirements increase in order to produce more torque.

To simplify the operation of what actually causes rotation of the starter motor armature and pinion, let's use a simple two pole or two magnet unit consisting of one north pole and one south pole as shown in Fig. 6-4.

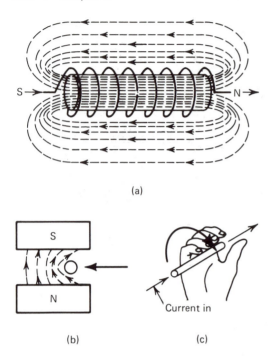

(a)

(b)   (c)

Current in

Fig. 6-4. Basic theory of starter motor operation: (a) magnetic field with current flowing through a wire coil; (b) weak and strong magnetic field; (c) right-hand rule theory.

From our earlier discussion on basic electrical fundamentals, you will recall that when current flows through a wire a magnetic field is created around that wire proportional to the current flowing in the wire as shown in Fig. 6-4 (a).

Similarly, if we pass a wire through a magnetic field, then current is induced in the wire. The stronger the magnetic field, the greater the current induced in the wire. Also the faster that the wire cuts these magnetic lines of force, then the greater the inducement. If we bend a length of copper wire into a coil and wrap it around a soft iron core, then the magnetic field becomes more concentrated due to the fact that iron is a better conductor of

magnetism or electricity than the surrounding air is.

The iron frame and pole shoes (magnets) of the starter motor plus the iron laminations and copper windings of the armature represent an area in which the strength of the magnetic field can be concentrated.

Figure 6-4 (a) shows that the magnetic lines of force always emanate from the north to the south pole. Figure 6-4 (b) shows that the path of current flow through the wire is established by the flow path of the magnetic lines of force, plus the direction of movement of the conductor (wire) in relation to the magnetic field. The wire in Fig. 6-4 (b) is moving to its left to effectively cut the magnetic lines of force. This left side therefore becomes the leading side of the wire. Figure 6-4 (c) shows the method used to establish the direction of current flow by grasping the wire as shown with the right hand.

When we place a conductor (wire) or series of wires around a soft iron core and pass current through these wires (armature), a magnetic field is created around the wires. At the same time as this is happening, we have the armature surrounded by pole shoes (magnets) which are also creating a magnetic field. We therefore have not one, but two magnetic fields within the assembly. This is shown in simplified form in Fig. 6-5.

From earlier discussions, we know that magnetic lines of force emanate from the north to the south pole, and that from the right-hand rule that current flowing through the wire will produce a magnetic field which encircles the wire in a clockwise direction. See Fig. 6-5 (a).

This arrangement produces a magnetic field around the wire or wires (armature assembly), whereby the field strength is

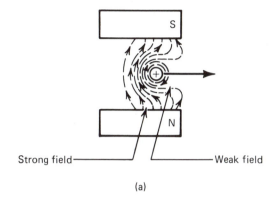

Strong field ———— ———— Weak field

(a)

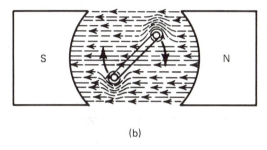

(b)

Fig. 6-5. (a) Field strength stronger on the left-hand side than on the right-hand side; (b) strong and weak magnetic field reaction on armature wires.

stronger on the left hand side of the wires than on the right hand side.

This condition, shown in Fig. 6-5 (b), will tend to make the conductor (wires) want to move from the strong (left-hand side), field to the (right-hand side) weak magnetic field. This is the basic principle of a starter motor and the means by which it causes starter motor armature rotation.

Now that we have set forth the basic theory behind the motor's rotation, let's take it a stage further and look at how the battery is connected into the basic circuit as shown in Fig. 6-6. For simplicity, we have shown only one loop of wire and one set of pole shoes (one north and one south).

In Fig. 6-6, battery current can flow to and through both the loop of wire (armature winding) and around the wire wrapped over each pole piece (N and S). This current is carried through two carbon or bronze type brushes to a commutator bar after passing through both pole pieces first. The current therefore flows from the battery, around the north pole piece, through the wire to the south pole piece, into the brush and commutator segment, through the loop of wire to the other commutator segment, out the other brush, and back to the battery to complete the circuit.

The magnetic fields created in both the magnets or pole pieces, plus that in the wire loop, result in the condition described earlier in Fig. 6-5. Both strong and weak magnetic fields are created which cause the loop of wire to rotate towards the weak side of the magnetic field resulting in the rotation of the starter motor armature.

The use of one wire loop as shown in these illustrations would, in theory, produce a turning force; however, there would never be enough torque produced in this one wire loop to effectively rotate any engine. To produce a starter motor with

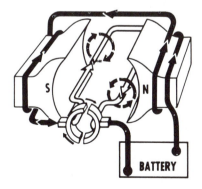

Fig. 6-6. Battery flow through a basic starter motor. (Courtesy of Delco-Remy Div. of GMC)

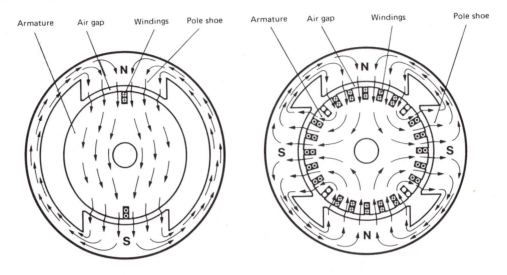

Fig. 6-7 (a) Two-pole motor with only one set of wires. (b) Four-pole motor with twelve pairs of conductors. (Courtesy of Robert Bosch Corp.)

enough power to rotate an engine, we must add a large number of these wire loops individually wrapped around a soft iron core such as an armature. Also starter motors today employ more than one set of pole shoes or magnets, with four and six magnets being commonly used in order to increase the magnetic field and increase the torque produced by the motor.

An example of a two pole motor with only one set of wires or conductors is shown in Fig. 6-7(a), while Fig. 6-7(b) shows a typically used motor that employs four poles with twelve pairs of conductors.

The individual loops of wire are assembled into the armature in individual slots. In addition, the armature is made up of a series of individual sheet steel laminations which are insulated from one another, then pressed together on the armature shaft to form the completed armature core. Once the commutator is mounted to the armature shaft, we have a completed unit.

Figure 6-8 shows the armature laminations, the actual armature core made from the laminations, and the complete armature assembly.

STARTER MOTOR COUNTER-ELECTROMOTIVE FORCE (CEMF)

Maximum torque produced by a starter motor must occur at initial engagement in order to effectively cause engine rotation. In other words, the breakaway torque has to be high enough to initiate rotation to overcome the resistance of friction, engine compression, oil drag, etc. Without delving into a detailed explanation of torque, the slower the rotation, the greater the torque. As speed increases, torque decreases, and vice-versa. Once the armature starts rotating, the initial breakaway torque will decrease. However, the starter motor must still have adequate torque to rotate the engine until it starts. This brings us to a point that requires further explanation.

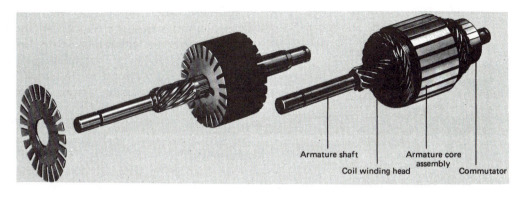

Armature lamination   Armature core   Assembled armature

Fig. 6-8 Typical armature assembly of starter motor. (Courtesy of Robert Bosch Corp.)

As the current and voltage flow through the wire loops of the armature and the pole pieces, the net effect of the induced voltage, called the counter-electromotive force or CEMF, will oppose the battery voltage and therefore reduce the current supplied by the battery. This action occurs because the voltage induced in the wires is directly proportional to the speed at which the wire or conductor cuts across the magnetic lines of force. Similarly, the value of the CEMF is also proportional to the speed at which the wire is rotating. Therefore, as the speed of the armature increases, the CEMF will increase, and the battery current flowing through the motor windings will likewise decrease. This CEMF, however, will never reach the battery voltage level, but there is a decrease in starter motor torque with an increase in speed.

STARTER MOTOR PINION ENGAGEMENT

There are many sizes and types of starter motors in use around the world

today. The type of pinion drive used will vary between manufacturers and will depend, to some degree, on the type of engine that the starter motor is fitted to.

Several types of drives have been used over the years for starter motor pinion engagement. These drives are as follows:

- Roll type clutch drive
- Bendix type drive
- Sprag type clutch drive
- Dyer type drive

The drives mentioned can be found on many types of different starter motors.

Roll Type Clutch

Fig. 6-9 shows the concept employed with a roll type clutch drive.

As noted in Fig. 6-9, a shell and sleeve assembly is splined internally to match either a straight or spiral splined armature shaft. The pinion (gear) sits inside the shell where it is held by the action of spring loaded rollers bearing against the round area immediately behind the pinion. These spring-loaded rollers are wedged against

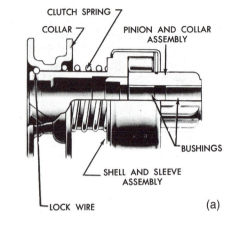

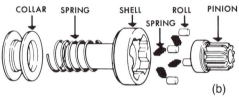

Fig. 6-9. Roller type starter motor clutch drive: (a) cutaway view, (b) exploded view. (Courtesy of Delco-Remy Div. of GMC)

the pinion and a taper cut inside of the shell.

The number of rollers used can vary between makes; however, four is fairly common. Also, variations in the types of roller springs exist, with some manufacturers employing either helical or accordion style. To complete this arrangement, a collar connected to a shift lever, along with a spring located over the sleeve, provides the necessary components. When the starter switch is energized, the collar is moved horizontally along the shaft to compress the coil spring on the sleeve.

The action of the compressed spring will force the pinion into mesh with the flywheel ring gear. However, if the pinion does not engage properly with the ring gear (tooth abutment), then the spring continues to be compressed as the shift lever continues to move which will allow closure of the solenoid or relay switch used with the starter. This completes battery power to the starter armature and it begins to rotate. This causes the pinion to snap into engagement with the flywheel ring gear due to the compressive force on the coil spring between the shift collar and the pinion.

Rotation of the armature cranks the engine, with the drive torque being carried through the shell to the pinion by the rollers which are tightly wedged between the taper of the shell and the pinion area.

Once the engine fires and runs, the pinion is now turning at engine speed, which is faster than that of the armature. This action causes the rollers to move away from the taper of the shell, thereby freeing up the contact that existed previously between the shell and pinion, so that the pinion is free to overrun or turn faster than the shell. This action minimizes the possibility of the engine driving the armature of the starter motor. However, when the engine starts, immediately release the starting switch to avoid prolonged overrun.

Once the solenoid or switch is de-energized, the solenoid return spring (or in some units, manual action) causes the shift lever and collar to move the pinion out of mesh which in effect terminates the cranking cycle.

Sprag Type Clutch Drive

The operation of the sprag clutch is similar to that of the roller clutch described above. However, the sprag unit employs a series of sprags rather than rollers between the shell and sleeve assembly. The number of sprags can vary between manufacturers,

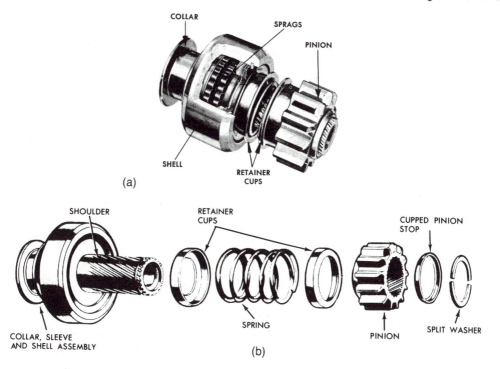

Fig. 6-10. (a) Sprag clutch assembly. (b) Disassembled view of late type heavy duty sprag clutch drive assembly. (Courtesy of Delco-Remy Div. of GMC)

but 30 is a usual number. Figure 6-10(a) shows a cutaway view of this drive and the action of the sprags which are similar in operation to those found in certain automatic car transmissions.

The sprags are held in position against the shell and sleeve surfaces by a garter spring, with the shell and collar being splined to the starter motor armature shaft. The pinion is in turn splined to the sleeve which is cut with a spiral spline and a stop collar.

Solenoid engagement causes the complete clutch assembly to move along the splined shaft, and the pinion attempts to engage with the ring gear of the flywheel. If tooth contact exists, continued movement of the shell and spiral splined sleeve

causes rotation of the pinion. It will snap into engagement with the ring gear via the action of the compressed meshing spring.

The operator, however, may have to attempt starter engagement again, if insufficient rotational movement is not obtained, since this may prevent pinion engagement with the ring gear. This safety feature is controlled by two retainer cups which will stop shift collar and lever movement to prevent closure of the switch contacts; otherwise, with the pinion not engaged, chewing up of the pinion and ring gear could result.

Once the pinion does engage through normal means, the motor switch contacts will close, allowing full battery power to the windings, and cranking will take place.

Rotational torque is carried through the shell, sleeve, and pinion by the sprags which tilt and wedge tightly between the shell and sleeve.

Once the engine fires and runs, the ring gear begins turning faster than the motor pinion and sleeve, which can result in overspeeding of the starter armature. To prevent this condition, the motion transfer to the pinion and sleeve will cause the sprags to tilt in the opposite direction, thereby freeing the pinion and sleeve from the shell and armature. This results in an overrun condition (freewheeling) of the pinion; however, to prevent prolonged overrun, (as with the roll type clutch drive) the operator should disengage the power flow to the motor switch or solenoid just as soon as the engine starts.

Bendix Type Drive

The Bendix drive, used for many years, is not used too much anymore due to the introduction of the roll and sprag overrunning clutch drives. Several improvements were made to the Bendix drive over the years; however, the basic concept remained the same. Figure 6-11 shows the bendix drive arrangement.

The Bendix principle of engagement is one of inertia to cause the pinion to engage with the flywheel ring gear. From the views shown in Fig. 6-11, the operation of the Bendix drive is as follows:

Type A

This system incorporates a pinion and sleeve assembly, a drive spring, and a drive head. The pinion and sleeve assembly fits loosely over the armature shaft, but is connected through the drive spring to the drive head which is keyed to the shaft. Closing the starter switch causes the arma-

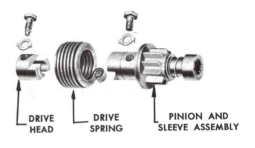

(a)

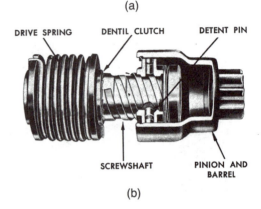

(b)

Fig. 6-11. Bendix type starter motor drive gear: (a) typical inertia drive, (b) Folo-Thru drive. (Courtesy of Delco-Remy Div. of GMC)

ture to rotate, as well as the drive head and drive spring to the sleeve. The drive pinion is usually unbalanced by a counter-weight on one side, and it has screw threads or spiral splines cut on its inner bore to match those on the outer surface of the Bendix sleeve. Type A is shown in Fig. 6-11(a).

When the armature rotates, the spiral splined sleeve rotates within the pinion which moves along the shaft to engage the flywheel ring gear. Cranking occurs when the pinion reaches its stop on the sleeve, with the spring taking up any shock loading. Once the engine fires and runs, the faster turning ring gear will drive the pinion back out of mesh. The operator should, however, immediately release the starter switch in order to de-energize the starter motor armature.

Should tooth abutment occur during the cranking period, the spring will compress to allow the sleeve to move until the pinion engages.

Type B

This is known as a follow through (or Folo-Thru) Bendix drive. This drive has two extra features, namely a spring-loaded detent pin and a "folo-thru" drive arrangement. The spring-loaded detent pin moves into a notch cut in the spiral spline to lock the pinion in the cranking position to prevent pinion disengagement during false starts. This action is accomplished by using a spring loaded pin which rides on one of the pinion screw threads and drops into a hole when the pinion is in the fully engaged position. When the engine starts, the flywheel ring gear drives the starter pinion, and a clutch mechanism built into the pinion protects the starter from excessive RPM. When the engine reaches 400 to 500 rpm, the pinion spins fast enough to create the needed centrifugal force to throw the spring loaded pin out of the hole in the shaft and allow the pinion to disengage. A second pin rides on the spiral spline and acts as an anti-drift device during engine operation. Type B is shown in Fig. 6-11(b).

The second feature, namely the Folo-Thru drive, is actually a sleeve or screw-shaft (two-piece) connected by a dentil clutch arrangement which consists of ratcheting type teeth to prevent armature overspeed, yet allows the pinion and its sleeve to overrun the ratchet teeth until the detent pin has disengaged the notch.

Type C

This system includes a small rubber

cushion located inside the cup to take up the shock of initial cranking. It also includes a small spring located over the screwshaft inside the pinion barrel to stop the pinion from drifting into the ring gear during engine operation.

Type D

This system includes a friction-clutch used on some of the larger diesel cranking motors. Instead of the drive spring or rubber cushion arrangement, a series of flat spring-loaded clutch plates inside the housing allow slippage during initial engagement to relieve any shock loading. It also includes a meshing spring to allow the pinion to clear a tooth abutment condition, plus an anti-drift spring located over the spiral splined sleeve.

Dyer Drive

The dyer drive is no longer used on current production starters; however, many can still be found on older pieces of equipment. See Fig. 6-12.

The arrangement of the dyer drive is such that positive pinion engagement must occur with the flywheel ring gear before the switch contacts will close and allow battery power to the armature. The pinion guide is a close fit on the spiral splines of the armature shaft, while the pinion is splined loosely to the same shaft.

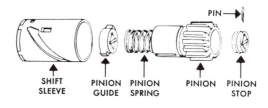

Fig. 6-12. Dyer drive starter gear arrangement. (Courtesy of AC Delco Div. of GMC)

The spring between the guide and pinion holds the internal teeth of the pinion and guide against the armature shaft splines.

Movement of the shift lever will cause the shift sleeve and pinion assembly to be moved along the armature shaft to engage the flywheel ring gear. As they move along the spiral splines of the armature shaft, these parts will rotate, therefore if tooth abutment does occur, the pinion spring which is under compression will force the pinion guide to continue to move and rotate the pinion until the pinion engages the ring gear. Once this occurs, full battery power can flow to the starter.

Rotation of the armature creates friction between the pinion guide and shift sleeve so that the sleeve moves back to its original position on the shaft. Once the engine fires and runs, the ring gear will drive the pinion back down the shaft out of engagement.

SWITCHES AND SOLENOIDS

Switches and solenoids used with starter motors can be direct or remote mounted from the starter. Several arrange-ments can be used. Some applications use a key switch to carry the small current required to activate a switch or solenoid; however, the high current draw to the armature of the starter motor would burn out key type switches, therefore a heavy-duty switch or solenoid is necessary to avoid this condition. Several styles of switches are shown in Figure 6-13.

The switches used in starting circuits are electromagnetic in that they are energized electrically (contacts closed) and released (contacts opened) by spring pressure when the electrical circuit is broken. Since starter motor current can range from several hundred amperes up to over a thousand amperes on large diesel starting motors, these switches and solenoids play an important part in the activation of the starter motor.

The basic difference between a straight magnetic switch and a solenoid is that the magnetic switch simply opens and closes the circuit from the battery to the starter motor, while the solenoid not only opens and closes the circuit between the battery and starter, but also has a plunger that shifts the motor drive mechanism into mesh with the flywheel ring gear.

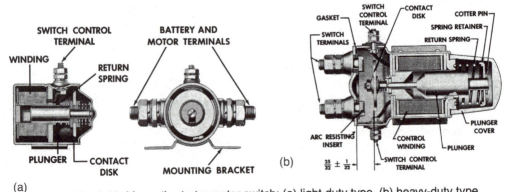

Fig. 6-13. Magnetic starter motor switch: (a) light-duty type, (b) heavy-duty type. (Courtesy of AC Delco Div. of GMC)

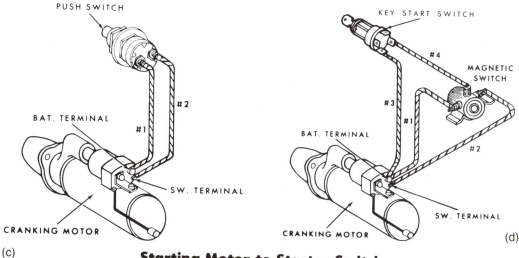

Starting Motor to Starter Switch or Starter Relay Circuit Chart

Wire Size	TOTAL LENGTH OF A + B—FEET*	
	12 Volt	24 & 32 Volt
12	8	16
10	11	22
8	17	34
6	27	54
4	42	84
2	64	132

(e)

*Resistance of Starter Switch Circuit should not exceed .0114 ohm total.

Fig. 6-13 continued: (c) a typical circuit employing a push-type switch; (d) wiring circuit employing a key and magnetic switch; (e) starting motor to starter switch or starter relay circuit chart.

Figure 6-13 shows a simple magnetic switch which basically contains a winding mounted around a hollow cylinder, within which is a moveable hollow core or plunger. Connected to one end of the plunger is a contact disc. When electricity is passed through the switch winding, a magnetic field draws the plunger and its contact disc tightly against two main switch terminals which are connected to the main battery power flow. In this manner, the starter motor can be energized. The switch itself is energized by a small current fed through a key switch hook-up, or similar arrangement.

Once the engine starts, and the starter button or key switch is returned to the normal off or run position, the magnetic switch is de-energized. An internal return spring forces the plunger back to its released position thereby effectively breaking the contact disc from the starter motor switch terminals.

The solenoid is usually mounted directly to the top of the starter motor so that it can not only complete the circuit to the starter, but also control the shift linkage as shown in Fig. 6-14 (a). Figure 6-14 (b) shows the actual terminal arrangement of the solenoid.

The solenoid contains two sets of windings known as the pull-in winding and the hold-in winding. The pull-in winding contains the same number of turns as the hold-in winding, but the pull-in unit contains a larger diameter wire. The hold-in winding contains many turns of fine wire.

From an earlier chapter in this book, you may recollect that magnetism is created when current is passed through a wire. When the operator turns the key switch to the start position, current will flow from the battery to the S or switch terminal of the solenoid, through the hold-in winding to ground, and back to the battery to complete the circuit. Current will also flow through the pull-in winding to the M terminal of the solenoid and through the starter motor windings to ground. The magnetism created in both sets of wind-

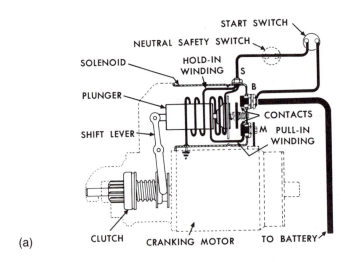

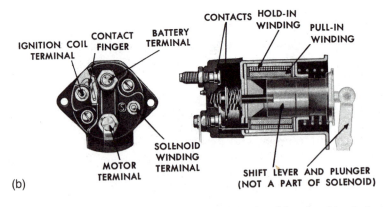

Fig. 6-14. (a) Solenoid's relationship to starter motor, (b) solenoid construction and terminal identification. (Courtesy of AC Delco Div. of GMC)

ings is strong enough to pull the plunger of the solenoid into the core which shifts the drive pinion into mesh with the flywheel ring gear, as well as moving the contact disc to close the circuit between the solenoid B (battery) terminal and the starter motor (M) terminal. This completed circuit allows the armature of the starter motor to rotate.

Once the plunger of the solenoid has been pulled in to the engagement position, less magnetism is required to hold it there, so once the contact disc comes into actual contact with the solenoid B and M terminals, the pull-in winding is shorted and no current flows through it anymore. This is an important feature because this action will not only reduce battery current draw, but does much to reduce heat build-up within the solenoid assembly.

Once the engine starts, and the operator releases the switch for the starter, current flow will pass through the contact disc to the solenoid M terminal, through the pull-in winding in a reverse direction to the solenoid or S terminal, through the hold-in winding and back to the battery. This action, as brief as it is, causes an opposing magnetic field in both the pull-in and hold-in windings to cancel each other out. The internal return spring will positively return the shift mechanism to the non-engaged position.

HEAVY-DUTY STARTER MOTOR SWITCH WIRING

Current diesel-engine powered class 8 trucks generally employ a 12-volt high-output torque starter motor in which the current draw is considerably higher than in a similar series/parallel (24-volt starting/12-volt charging) system. In order to carry the higher current safely, one of two types of switches must be used:

1. A push-type switch of adequate current-carrying capacity, or
2. A key-type switch, or any other with low current-carrying capacity in conjunction with a magnetic switch.

A typical circuit employing a push-type switch is shown in Fig. 6-13(c). To determine what size stranded wire should be used between the push-switch and starter motor terminals, measure the total length of wires no. 1 and no. 2 shown in Fig. 6-13(c), and select the proper size from the table in Fig. 6-13(e).

In Fig. 6-13(c), wire no. 1 may be connected from the push-switch to an ammeter instead of to the BAT terminal on the starter motor solenoid. In this case, measure the length of wire no. 1 from the switch to the ammeter. For example, a no. 10 wire should be used for both wires no. 1 and no. 2 if wire no. 1 is 45 inches long and wire no. 2 is 50 inches long for a total length of 95 inches or 7.9 feet.

Figure 6-13(d) illustrates a wiring circuit employing a key type switch and magnetic switch. To determine the size stranded wire to be used in this system, measure the length of wires no. 1 and no. 2 and select the proper size from Fig. 6-13(e). For example, the length of wire no. 1 is 25 inches and the length of wire no. 2 is 30 inches, for a total length of 55 inches or 4.6 feet. Therefore, from Fig. 6-13(e), a no. 12 stranded wire should be employed for wires no. 1 and no. 2. The stranded wire size for wires no. 3 and no. 4 should be no. 16 minimum; or a larger wire can be used.

TYPICAL STARTING MOTOR CIRCUITS

Although all starter motors are designed to crank the engine, all starters are not of the same design or arrangement.

Basically these starters can be classified as:

1. Inertia drive motors; low power applications

2. Pre-engaged motors; low to medium power applications

3. Sliding armature motors; medium power

4. Sliding gear motors; medium to high power applications

5. Sliding pole shoe motors; also medium power applications

Inertia Drive Starting Motors

These starters are used without any shift mechanism to control the pinion movement; instead, the rotation of the armature assembly throws the pinion forward on spiral splines which are externally cut on the armature shaft, and internally cut on the sleeve of the pinion. This action is not unlike that of a Bendix drive arrangement.

These starters are used on very light motor applications. Figures 6-15 and 6-16 show two of these inertia type starting motors produced by Robert Bosch Corporation. Figure 6-15 shows a Model CB motor rated at only 0.15 horsepower or 0.11 kW, while Fig. 6-16 shows a DG model which is fitted with an over-running clutch and is available in 0.3 horsepower or 0.22 kW ratings and higher.

Pre-Engaged Starting Motors

These types of starters are controlled by a solenoid switch mounted directly to the top of the starting motor assembly. See Fig. 6-17. The engagement action of these types of starter motors is shown in Fig. 6-18.

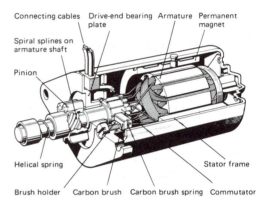

Fig. 6-15. CB model inertia starter motor assembly. (Courtesy of Robert Bosch Corp.)

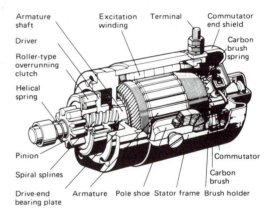

Fig. 6-16. DG model starter motor (inertia drive). (Courtesy of Robert Bosch Corp.)

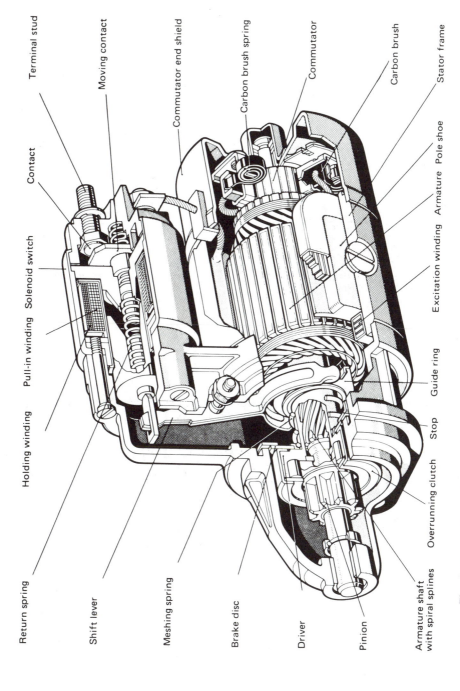

Return spring

Shift lever

Meshing spring

Brake disc

Driver

Pinion

Armature shaft
with spiral splines

Holding winding

Pull-in winding   Solenoid switch

Contact

Terminal stud

Moving contact

Commutator end shield

Carbon brush spring

Commutator

Carbon brush

Stator frame

Excitation winding   Armature   Pole shoe

Overrunning clutch

Stop

Guide ring

Fig. 6-17. Cutaway view of a preengaged starter motor model EF. (Courtesy of Robert Bosch Corp.)

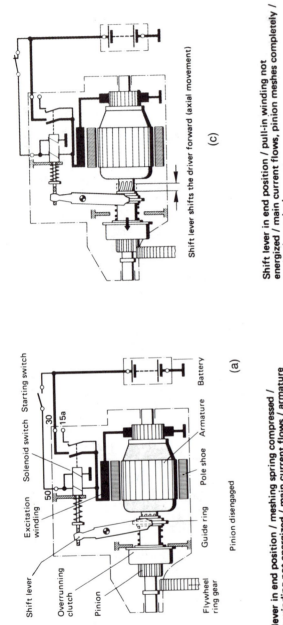

Shift lever — Solenoid switch — Starting switch

Excitation winding

50 — 30 — 15a

Overrunning clutch

Pinion

Flywheel ring gear — Guide ring — Pole shoe — Armature

Pinion disengaged

Battery

(a)

Shift lever in end position / meshing spring compressed / pull-in winding not energized / main current flows / armature turns / pinion teeth wait for spaces between ring gear teeth and then mesh completely / vehicle engine is cranked.

(b)

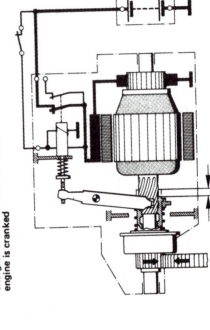

Shift lever shifts the driver forward (axial movement)

(c)

Shift lever in end position / pull-in winding not energized / main current flows, pinion meshes completely / engine is cranked

Driver shifted forward by armature rotation (helical movement)

(d)

Fig. 6-18. Preengaged starter motor action.

Sliding Armature Starting Motors

These types of starter motors are common to many European engines. Figure 6-19 shows a cross-sectional view of such a starter, while Fig. 6-20 shows the sequence of events when engaging and disengaging the starter motor with the engine.

Sliding Gear Motors

These motors are rather unique in that they operate in two stages so that the pinion and ring gear are protected. Figures 6-21 and 6-22 show two typical sliding gear type starter motors produced by the Robert Bosch Corporation.

The armature shaft used with the sliding gear starter motor is supported at both ends on bearings, while the shaft is hollow and serves as the housing for a multi-disc clutch at its drive end. The solenoid switch on these motors is mounted in behind the commutator rather than on the top of the motor housing as is conventional policy with many manufacturers. This solenoid arrangement is necessary in order to move the engagement rod forward to cause the sliding pinion to engage with the flywheel ring gear. When the solenoid is energized, as shown in Fig. 6-23, it butts up against the engagement rod which is located within the hollow armature shaft.

Sliding Pole Shoe Motor

This type of starter motor is common to passenger car engines rather than heavy trucks and equipment. It has been used in North America by both Ford and American Motors. Such a unit is shown in Fig. 6-24.

These types of starters use no solenoid, but instead employ one of the field coils and a sliding pole shoe to do the job normally undertaken by the solenoid unit. When the switch to the starter is closed, current flows to a magnetic switch which is energized and pulls in a contact disc to connect battery power to the starter.

A pull-in and a hold-in winding is wrapped around one of the field coils of the motor. Therefore, the magnetic field produced by the action of current passing through these two windings forces the sliding pole shoe to move which, in turn, shifts the drive pinion assembly into mesh with the engine flywheel ring gear. While this action is occurring, the armature begins to rotate and crank the engine. When the pole shoe moves, it opens a set of contacts connected to the pull-in winding, and the hold-in winding magnetic field is strong enough to keep the pole shoe and drive pinion in engagement with the flywheel ring gear.

OPTIONAL STARTING MOTORS

In addition to the conventional types of starting motors discussed so far, there are special applications that employ nonconventional types of starters. Such an example is shown in Fig. 6-25, where an intermediate transmission is fitted to the starter assembly so that the net effect is that the pinion output is not in line with the armature assembly. This is similar to a drop-box arrangement found on many off-highway powershift transmissions.

GEAR REDUCTION STARTERS

In order to provide increased torque for starting purposes, some starters employ a gear reduction arrangement as shown in Fig. 6-26, where a small gear attached to the armature shaft meshes with and drives a reduction gear at a speed reduction of approximately two to one. The starter is equipped with a conventional over-running clutch drive-shaft.

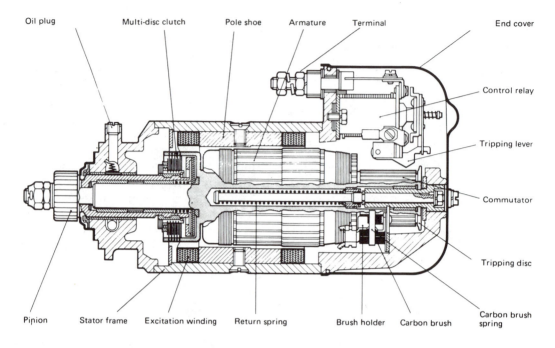

Oil plug Multi-disc clutch Pole shoe Armature Terminal End cover Control relay Tripping lever Commutator Tripping disc Carbon brush spring

Pinion Stator frame Excitation winding Return spring Brush holder Carbon brush

Fig. 6-19. Cross-sectional view of a sliding armature starter motor. (Courtesy of Robert Bosch Corp.)

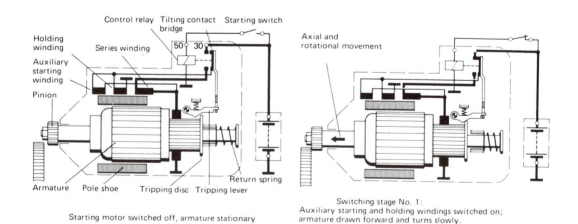

Control relay Tilting contact bridge Starting switch Holding winding Series winding Auxiliary starting winding Pinion 50 30 Axial and rotational movement Armature Pole shoe Tripping disc Tripping lever Return spring

Starting motor switched off, armature stationary

Switching stage No. 1:
Auxiliary starting and holding windings switched on; armature drawn forward and turns slowly.

Fig. 6-20. Sliding armature starter motor engagement sequence.

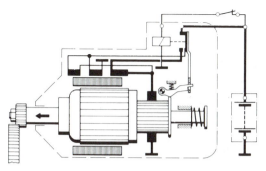

Current flows in auxiliary starting and holding winding; pinion meshes with ring gear.

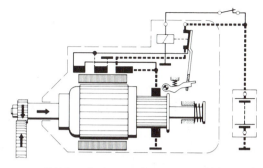

Vehicle engine has started, armature speed is increased, current in the series winding decreases, only the holding winding holds the armature engaged

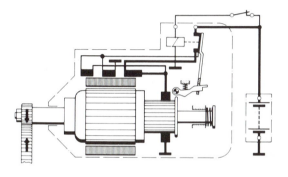

Switching stage No. 2:
Series winding switched on, complete mechanical connection; vehicle engine is cranked.

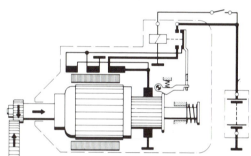

Switch-off process:
Current through starting motor windings is cut off, pinion demeshes, return spring draws armature back to its rest position (= Fig. 39)

Fig. 6-20. continued.

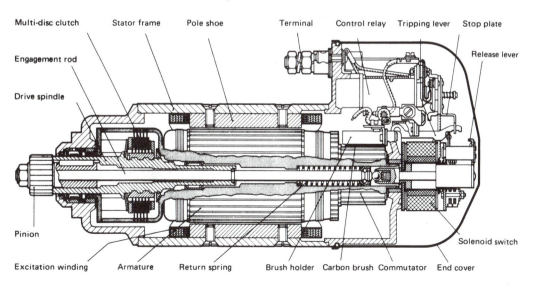

Multi-disc clutch   Stator frame   Pole shoe   Terminal   Control relay   Tripping lever   Stop plate

Engagement rod

Drive spindle

Release lever

Pinion

Excitation winding   Armature   Return spring   Brush holder   Carbon brush   Commutator   End cover

Solenoid switch

Fig. 6-21. Model KB sliding gear starter motor. (Courtesy of Robert Bosch Corp.)

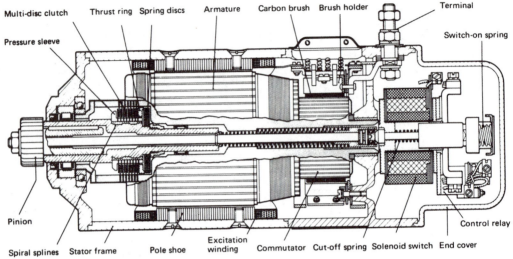

Fig. 6-22. Model TB sliding gear starter motor. (Courtesy of Robert Bosch Corp.)

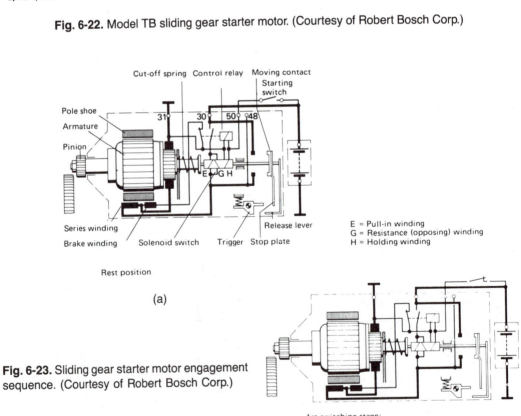

E = Pull-in winding
G = Resistance (opposing) winding
H = Holding winding

Rest position

(a)

Fig. 6-23. Sliding gear starter motor engagement sequence. (Courtesy of Robert Bosch Corp.)

1st switching stage:
Control relay winding and holding winding on solenoid switch are energized

(b)

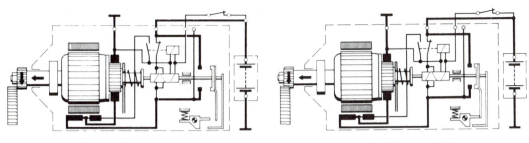

Pull-in winding on solenoid switch is energized, pinion
is forced forward, armature turns slowly

(c)

Pinion meshes with torque still low

(d)

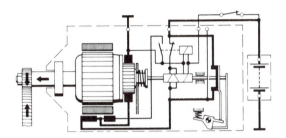

2nd switching stage:
Trigger is released, series winding is switched in by moving contact, starting motor has full torque, engine is cranked

(e)

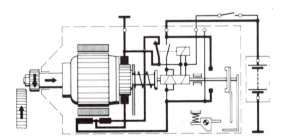

Starting motor switched off, pinion demeshes, armature is braked

(f)

Fig. 6-23 continued: Sliding gear starter motor
engagement sequence. (Courtesy of Robert
Bosch Corp.)

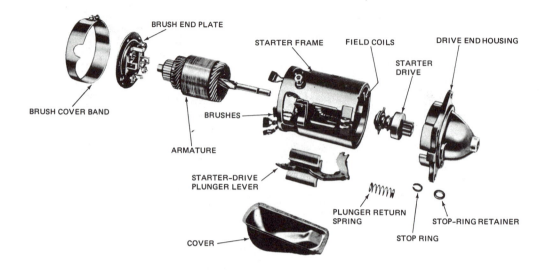

BRUSH END PLATE

STARTER FRAME   FIELD COILS   DRIVE END HOUSING

STARTER DRIVE

BRUSH COVER BAND

BRUSHES

ARMATURE

STARTER-DRIVE PLUNGER LEVER

PLUNGER RETURN SPRING   STOP-RING RETAINER

STOP RING

COVER

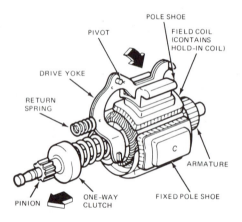

POLE SHOE

PIVOT   FIELD COIL (CONTAINS HOLD-IN COIL)

DRIVE YOKE

RETURN SPRING

ARMATURE

PINION   ONE-WAY CLUTCH   FIXED POLE SHOE

Fig. 6-24. Sliding pole shoe starter motor. (Courtesy of Ford Motor Company)

COAXIAL STARTING MOTORS

These types of starter motors include a solenoid winding installed within the pinion housing to eliminate the piggy-back mounting of the solenoid and the shifting linkage. Less room is required for the installation of the unit on the engine. This enclosed design prevents dirt, mud, slush, or snow from entering the unit. This also offers the advantages of positive shift en-

gagement, compactness, and extremely flexible terminal mounting positions.

Figure 6-27 shows the arrangement of this type of starter.

In the coaxial starter, the solenoid winding, the contacts, and the solenoid core are assembled in the pinion housing. The solenoid core has a spring-loaded sleeve which provides a quick and positive release of the solenoid core when the starting switch is released which in turn provides a fast

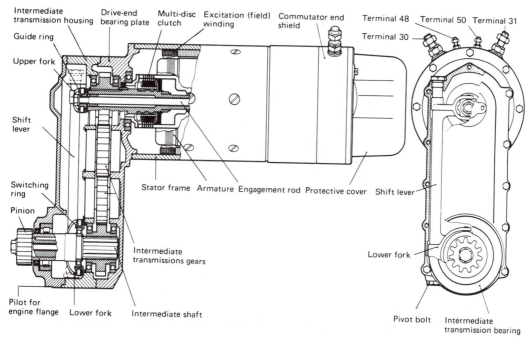

Fig. 6-25. Model TF 24-volt starter with an intermediate transmission. (Courtesy of Robert Bosch Corp.)

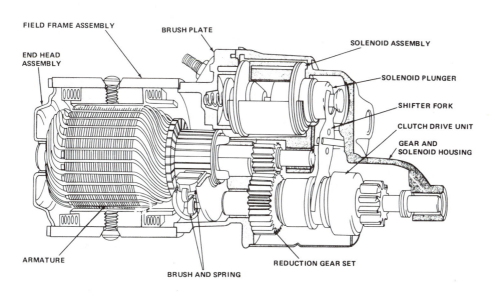

Fig. 6-26. Gear reduction type starter motor. (Courtesy of Chrysler Corporation)

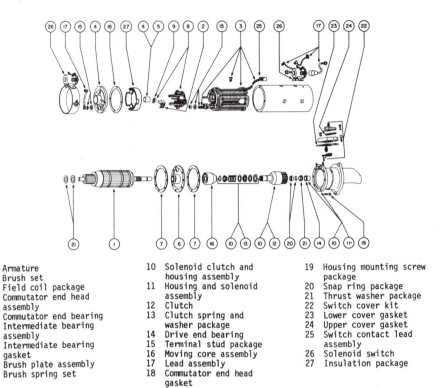

1 Armature
2 Brush set
3 Field coil package
4 Commutator end head
   assembly
5 Commutator end bearing
6 Intermediate bearing
   assembly
7 Intermediate bearing
   gasket
8 Brush plate assembly
9 Brush spring set

10 Solenoid clutch and
    housing assembly
11 Housing and solenoid
    assembly
12 Clutch
13 Clutch spring and
    washer package
14 Drive end bearing
15 Terminal stud package
16 Moving core assembly
17 Lead assembly
18 Commutator end head
    gasket

19 Housing mounting screw
    package
20 Snap ring package
21 Thrust washer package
22 Switch cover kit
23 Lower cover gasket
24 Upper cover gasket
25 Switch contact lead
    assembly
26 Solenoid switch
27 Insulation package

Fig. 6-27. Coaxial starter motor. (Courtesy of Prestolite Co.)

break of the solenoid contacts. The second purpose of the core spring is to allow the solenoid core to move forward when the pinion butts against the flywheel ring gear. The core is allowed to continue forward which further compresses the spring, closes the switch contacts, and completes the starting circuit. As the armature rotates it spins the pinion and the compressed spring in the solenoid core snaps the pinion into the flywheel ring gear. An overrunning clutch is commonly used with these starter motors.

Coaxial starting motors incorporate a ballast resistor shorting terminal when used on vehicles. This terminal is energized when the ignition key is in the start position, which activates the contact disc within the solenoid to make contact with the starter terminal, field lead and ballast resistor shorting terminal. Energizing the ballast resistor shorting terminal allows full battery voltage to the ignition coil side of the ballast resistor which bypasses the circuit through the ignition switch and ballast resistor. This circuit is shown in Fig. 6-28.

TESTING

To check the operation of the resistor shorting circuit, connect a jumper wire from the ignition coil negative terminal to ground as shown in Fig. 6-28. This will prevent the engine from starting and also bypass the contact breaker points of the

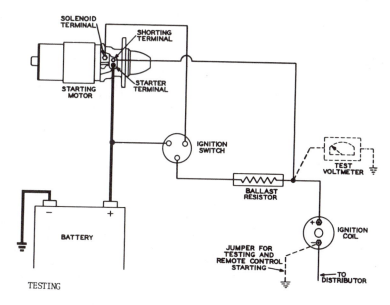

Fig. 6-28. Coaxial starter motor circuit with a ballast resistor used on a contact breaker type distributor. (Courtesy of Prestolite Co.)

distributor if used. Connect a voltmeter to the ignition coil side of the ballast resistor and turn the key to the on position, but do not crank the engine. The voltmeter should read 6 to 9 volts.

When the engine is cranked, the voltmeter should indicate full battery voltage. If the voltmeter readings are not as indicated, remove the switch cover and check for mechanical interference between the contact disc assembly and the ballast shorting terminal. If the voltmeter shows no reading while the contact disc and shorting terminal are making contact, the wire between the starter and ballast resistor is open.

If a remote starter switch is to be used on this type of application, always connect a jumper wire from the ignition coil negative terminal to ground or disconnect the lead from the ballast resistor shorting terminal on the starting motor.

PRESTOLITE HEAVY-DUTY STARTER MOTOR

This starter assembly is a heavy-duty solenoid actuated unit, with an armature shaft center bearing and a Positork drive assembly which is an indexing type of drive to assure complete drive pinion engagement before the motor begins to rotate, thus reducing drive pinion and flywheel ring gear wear. An example of this starter is shown in the exploded view in Fig. 6-29.

SERIES/PARALLEL STARTER CIRCUITS

Many diesel engines in trucks and heavy-duty equipment employ a 24-volt starter motor with a 12-volt charging and accessory system. Two types of series/parallel circuits are readily available and used in the industry.

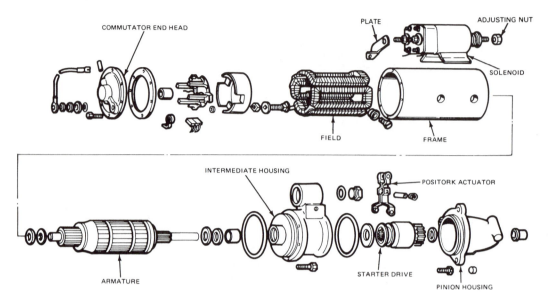

Fig. 6-29. Prestolite Positork starter assembly. (Courtesy of Prestolite Co.)

1. A series/parallel switch arrangement
2. A transformer rectifier assembly built-in to the charging system alternator assembly.

We will not deal here with the second type, since it was discussed in some depth earlier under the chapter dealing with alternators wherein both the Delco-Remy and Leece-Neville units were shown.

The transformer rectifier type is now the more commonly used of the two types; however, many pieces of equipment still employ the former type that uses a separate series/parallel switch. The reason for using the series/parallel circuit whether it is the older or newer type is, of course, to allow the use of a 24-volt starter motor which is often necessary and desirable on diesel powered equipment.

Either four heavy-duty 6-volt batteries can be used, or two heavy-duty 12-volt units. For starting purposes, the batteries

are connected in series through the series/parallel switch arrangement to provide 24 volts for cranking. Once the engine starts, the charging system automatically is switched back to a 12-volt set-up so that all accessories can be operated on the conventional 12 volt circuitry. However, some diesel powered equipment can and does operate on both 24-volt starting, and 24-volt charging systems. An example of a typical series/parallel switch wiring circuit is shown in Fig. 6-30.

The two most commonly used series/parallel circuit arrangements are those manufactured by both Delco-Remy and the Leece-Neville companies. Therefore, we shall concentrate on these two types.

The current model of Leece-Neville series/parallel switch arrangement uses a solenoid that operates eight sets of contacts as shown in Fig. 6-30.

As can be readily seen in Fig. 6-30, two batteries are connected into the circuit

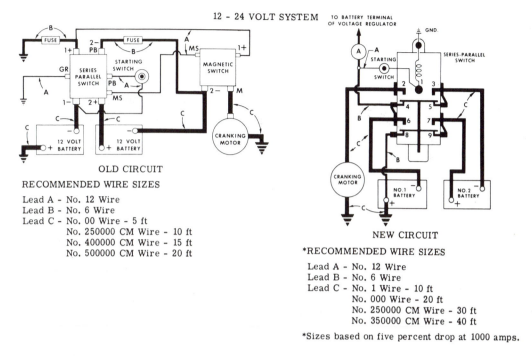

Fig. 6-30. Series-parallel system wiring diagram. (Courtesy of Leece-Neville, Sheller-Globe Corp.)

12 - 24 VOLT SYSTEM

OLD CIRCUIT

RECOMMENDED WIRE SIZES

Lead A - No. 12 Wire
Lead B - No. 6 Wire
Lead C - No. 00 Wire - 5 ft
        No. 250000 CM Wire - 10 ft
        No. 400000 CM Wire - 15 ft
        No. 500000 CM Wire - 20 ft

NEW CIRCUIT

*RECOMMENDED WIRE SIZES

Lead A - No. 12 Wire
Lead B - No. 6 Wire
Lead C - No. 1 Wire - 10 ft
        No. 000 Wire - 20 ft
        No. 250000 CM Wire - 30 ft
        No. 350000 CM Wire - 40 ft

*Sizes based on five percent drop at 1000 amps.

along with a starting switch, series/parallel or (SP switch), an alternator, plus the necessary wiring to the starter motor.

Contact sets 2, 3, 6, and 7 when closed, connect the batteries in series for cranking. Contact sets 4, 5, 8 and 9 which are smaller, connect the batteries in parallel for charging purposes. The solenoid is activated when the starter switch is closed, therefore the action is as follows:

1. When the solenoid is energized it will:

   (a) Open the charging contacts.

   (b) Close the cranking contacts 2, 3, 6 and 7 which connect the two 12-volt batteries in series.

2. Once the engine starts, the series/parallel switch will:

   (a) Open the cranking contacts 2, 3, 6 and 7.

   (b) Reconnect the batteries in parallel by closing the charging contacts 4, 5, 8 and 9, and connect the generator/alternator to both batteries.

TROUBLESHOOTING THE LEECE-NEVILLE S/P CIRCUIT

If the S/P switch should fail to operate correctly, remove it from the vehicle circuit and proceed as follows:

1. With a test lamp, check terminals 2 through 9 for possible short circuits (grounds) to the switch base. Ensure that a circuit does exist, however, between terminals 4-5 and 8-9. There should be no circuit

between terminals 2-3 and 6-7 which are the cranking terminals.

2. To establish if the solenoid plunger is actually moving when it is energized, apply rated battery voltage to the operating coil terminal number one (1) and to the switch base.

3. If the two tests indicate that the switch is operational, then proceed to check out the other areas of the cranking and charging circuit, prior to attempting to condemn or disassemble the S/P switch.

NOTE: When it becomes necessary to check the S/P switch assembly, avoid using jumper cables to bridge the cranking circuit contacts 2, 3, 6, or 7 because burning of the contacts can occur. Using a jumper switch across terminals 2 and 3, for example, will result in the starter motor attempting to crank the engine on only one battery. The contacts will weld or burn out. The same condition will result at terminals 6 and 7 if a jumper wire is used.

DELCO-REMY SERIES/PARALLEL CIRCUITS

Delco supplies S/P switches to a variety of heavy-duty truck manufacturers, who wire the circuit in one of three acceptable ways:

1. An A circuit as shown in Fig. 6-31. The A or vehicle accessory battery is connected to the number 1 switch terminal. If more than one wire lead is connected to this number 1 terminal, an A circuit is confirmed.

2. Figure 6-32 shows a B circuit wherein the number 2 terminal contains more than one lead.

3. A combined series/parallel and magnetic switch is identified by four large terminals as shown in Fig. 6-33.

In all types of circuits, it makes no difference whether the leads at terminals 6 and 7 are reversed. The circuit will still operate.

CIRCUIT OPERATION

"A" Circuit: Charging and Combined S/P and Magnetic Switch Models

Current flows from the alternator to terminal 1 of the S/P switch when the S/P switch is in the charging or disengaged position and the engine is running. Current divides to both circuit batteries via half passing through the A or accessory battery to ground, while the other half passes through contact points between terminals 1 and 3, the B battery (cranking only), and the contact points between terminals 2 and 5 to ground.
See Fig. 6-31(a).

"A" Circuit: Cranking

Closing the switch to coil terminal 7, energizes the S/P switch assembly allowing the plunger to be pulled into the core by the magnetic field produced in the coil winding. See Fig. 6-31(b). This action happens very quickly, and in fact takes three distinct forms:

1. Step one involves the opening of the normally closed (NC) points between terminals 1, 3, 2, and 5 by the plunger as it moves.

2. The plunger, as it continues to move, causes the large contact disc to close terminals 1 and 2.

"A" CIRCUIT CHARGING

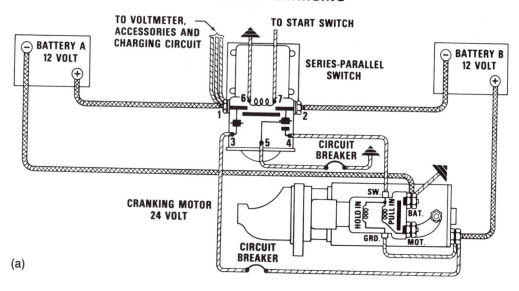

"A" CIRCUIT CRANKING

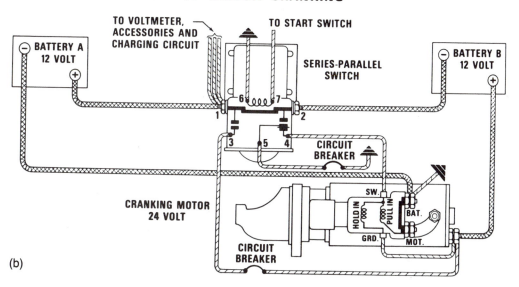

Fig. 6-31. (a) "A" circuit charging, (b) "A" circuit cranking. (Courtesy of Delco-Remy Div. of GMC)

"B" CIRCUIT CHARGING

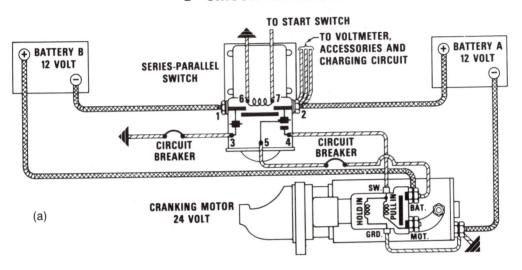

(a)

"B" CIRCUIT CRANKING

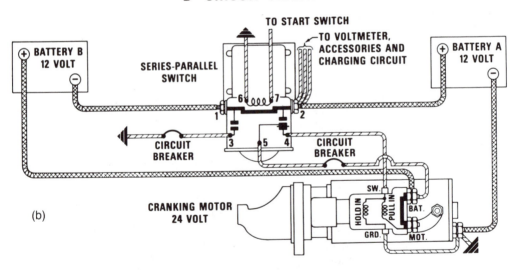

(b)

Fig. 6-32. (a) "B" circuit charging, (b) "B" circuit cranking. (Courtesy of Delco-Remy Div. of GMC)

COMBINED SERIES-PARALLEL & MAGNETIC SWITCH CHARGING

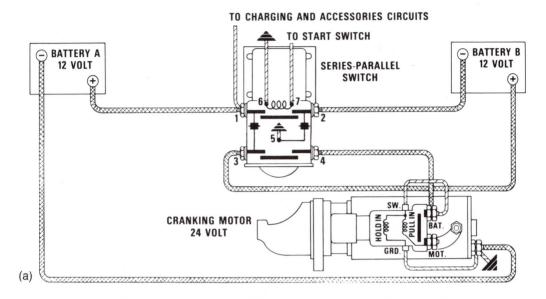

COMBINED SERIES-PARALLEL & MAGNETIC SWITCH CRANKING

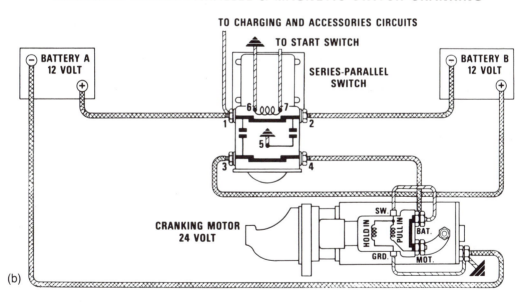

Fig. 6-33. (a) Combined series-parallel and magnetic switch charging. (b) Combined series-parallel and magnetic switch cranking. (Courtesy of Delco-Remy Div. of GMC)

3. The normally open points between terminals 4 and 5 are also closed by the movement of the plunger.

Movement of the large contact disc ties terminals 1 and 2 together which effectively places both the A (system battery), and B (cranking battery) in series for 24 volt starting or cranking. Both batteries supply current to the starter end terminal, frame area and MOT terminal of the solenoid, pull-in coil and over to the SW terminal of the solenoid. The rest of the circuit allows the remaining current flow to travel from the end terminal of the starter motor to the GRD terminal of the solenoid, through the hold-in coil and to the SW terminal of the solenoid. Total circuit current flows through terminals 4 and 5 to ground. The starter drive pinion is pulled into mesh with the engine flywheel ring gear to close the terminals between the BAT and MOT of the solenoid, which allows full battery voltage in series (24 volts) to the cranking motor. Once the engine starts, the S/P switch returns by spring force to its disengaged position.

Cranking: Combined S/P and Magnetic Switch Circuit

Closing the circuit to the switch coil 7 pulls the solenoid plunger into the core. Normally, closed terminals at 1, 3, 2, and 5 are opened by plunger movement, plus the two large contact discs between 1, 2, 3, and 4 come into contact with these terminals to tie both batteries into series for 24 volt starting. Current flows to the BAT terminal of the solenoid and to the SW terminal where part of the current passes through the pull-in winding to the MOT solenoid terminal, and cranking motor circuit to the motor end terminal and back to

the A or system battery. The rest of the circuit current flows through the hold-in winding, out the GRD terminal to the motor end terminal and back to the A or system battery. Engagement of the pinion with the flywheel ring gear closes the circuit from the BAT and MOT solenoid terminals to give full battery voltage to the starter. When the engine starts, and the switch is opened the S/P switch is opened by internal spring pressure as the solenoid is de-energized. See Fig. 6-33(b).

B Circuit: Charging

Current flows to the number 2 S/P switch terminal when the engine is running. This current splits with half going to the A or system battery to ground, while the other half passes through the points of terminals 2 and 5 through the B or cranking battery to the contacts between terminals 1 and 3 to ground. See Fig. 6-32(a).

B Circuit: Cranking

Initial solenoid action is the same as that described for the A circuit cranking above. With terminals 1 and 2 bridged by the large contact disc of the solenoid, current flows to the BAT terminal of the solenoid where it travels through contact points at terminals 4 and 5 to the SW terminal. See Fig. 6-32(b).

Current flows through the hold-in and pull-in coils and to the GRD terminal and the frame terminal of the motor and on to both the A and B batteries. The pinion engages the flywheel ring gear and the circuit between the BAT and MOT terminals of the solenoid to provide full voltage to the starter motor (24 volts). When the engine starts, the switch contacts are opened by the operator and the S/P switch returns to its charging position. Typical problems encountered with S/P switches are given in Table 6-1.

OVERCRANK PROTECTION DEVICES

Although the use of the sprag overrunning clutch and roller type clutch drives has done much to improve the life of starter motors, damage can still result as a consequence of not releasing the switch quickly enough after the engine starts, or attempting to start an engine before it has actually stalled out. Shortened life can also be caused by accidental starter motor engagement while the engine is running.

One of the principal factors in shortened starter motor life is continued attempts to start a faulty engine, or long periods of starter motor engagement during either cold or hot weather in an attempt to start the engine. Few people ever allow the starter to cool for several minutes after continued cranking for several minutes, even when they know that continued cranking is damaging to the starter motor and windings. Starter motor manufacturers recommend that no starter motor should ever be cranked longer than 30 seconds without allowing it to cool down.

Several optional devices are available to prevent both accidental starter motor engagement while the engine is running, rapid de-energizing of the motor upon start-up, and protection against cranking

Table 6-1. Series-Parallel (S/P) Switch Troubleshooting Chart

Problem Symptom	Problem Cause	Remedy
Corrosion in switch	Water	Check switch gaskets
Blown fuse or circuit breaker	(a) Under capacity fuse or breaker	Install correct breaker
	(b) Pinion and ring gear abutment	Replace pinion or ring gear
	(c) Grounded motor	Repair motor
	(d) Faulty wiring	Repair wiring
Oscillating solenoids and burned contacts	Low batteries	Check batteries
	Wiring resistance	Check for cause
	Defective solenoid	Replace solenoid
Both A and B batteries undercharged	Low regulator setting	Adjust regulator
	Faulty alternator	Repair alternator
	Faulty wiring	Repair wiring
	Faulty regulator	Repair regulator
	Undercapacity Alternator	Replace with larger output alternator
Battery B Undercharged	High circuit resistance through B	Remove resistance
Burned or melted circuits in switch	No circuit breakers in #3 or #5 circuit	Install breakers
	Circuit breaker rating too high	Install proper units
	Improperly wired circuit breakers	Rewire circuit breakers to proper circuit

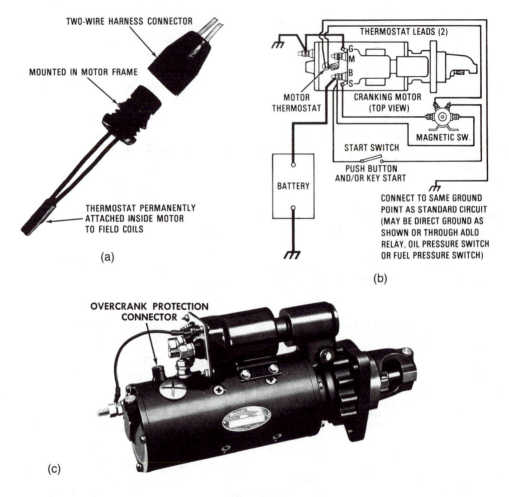

Fig. 6-34. (a) Typical thermostatic wiring circuit, (b) typical thermostat, (c) typical motor showing thermostat connector. (Courtesy of Delco-Remy Div. of GMC)

beyond the 30 second time period. An example of such a device to prevent cranking the engine beyond the 30 second time period is shown in Fig. 6-34(a).

In the starter motor circuit shown in Fig. 6-34(b), the built-in thermostat located inside the motor and permanently attached to the field coils ensures that the starter motor cannot be continually cranked beyond the 30 second time interval or at least against continued cranking for excessively long periods of time.

With the circuit shown in Fig. 6-34(b), battery current can flow to the magnetic switch winding and the thermostatic control to ground when the switch is closed by the operator, an action which connects the motor solenoid to the battery via the S terminal. The pinion will engage the flywheel ring gear once the solenoid plunger is activated through the shift lever movement.

Once the pinion is engaged with the flywheel ring gear the main contacts of the solenoid close, and full battery power can crank the armature assembly of the motor. The action of the pinion drive mechanism will allow pinion overrun once the engine starts as was explained earlier under types of drive mechanisms to protect the armature from excessive overspeed until the starter switch is opened by the operator. If the switch is not opened by the operator quickly, armature damage can result.

If cranking time is ever allowed to continue for excessive periods of time, the temperature rise within the armature and field windings will cause the thermostatically controlled switch to open the circuit, and the engine cannot be cranked again for anywhere from 1 to 6 minutes depending on the surrounding ambient temperature and the rate of cooling.

Figure 6-34(c) shows the location of the overcrank protection connector.

ADLO CIRCUITS

Another type of protective circuit is the ADLO or automatic disengagement and lockout action, which can be used on starter motors with solenoid electrical systems, and which is also fitted with Delcotron type Delco-Remy alternators, although other companies also offer similar features. Figure 6-35 shows the wiring circuit that would be used with the ADLO feature.

The circuit shown in Fig. 6-35 (a) is known as a frequency sensing relay. When the operator pushes the starter button or moves the key switch to the start position, battery current can flow through the magnetic circuit to ground through the normally closed (NC) frequency sensing relay contacts. The solenoid on the starter is energized from the closed contacts of the magnetic switch. As soon as the engine starts, voltage from the alternator R or AC terminal energizes the frequency sensing relay winding through the capacitor C1 which causes the relay contacts to open.

This action will automatically break the circuit through the magnetic switch, and the battery current can no longer flow to the starter. Opening of the relay switch contacts causes an induced voltage within the magnetic switch winding, thereby causing current flow through resistor R1, diode D2 and the relay winding to cause rapid opening of the contacts which will reduce contact arcing. These induced voltages in the relay winding flow through ground and diode D1 back to the winding. Regardless of the operator keeping the starter switch closed (engaged) the motor would be disconnected the instant that the engine starts.

In Fig. 6-35 (b) the relay winding is connected directly to the generator R or the AC terminal. To ensure that the proper amount of R or AC terminal voltage with the start switch closed is maintained, resistor R1 connected between the switch and field winding of the generator assures rapid opening of the relay contacts immediately as the engine starts.

AUTOMATIC STARTER DISENGAGEMENT

On diesel trucks and heavy equipment, de-energizing the motor after the engine starts can do much to increase the life of the starting motor. Continued rotation of the cranking motor armature after the engine is running results in high armature and drive speeds which increases the wear

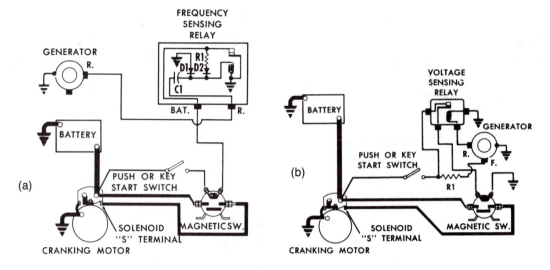

Fig. 6-35. (a) ADLO circuit with frequency sensing relay. (b) ADLO circuit with voltage sensing relay. (Courtesy of Delco-Remy Div. of GMC)

rate of the brushes, bearings, and drive components.

Figure 6-36 shows the sequence of events that occurs when an engine is started conventionally by the operator. The individual sequences shown in Fig. 6-36 (a) are as follows:

1. From .0 to .04 seconds. The starter solenoid is energized. The clutch shifts into mesh with the flywheel ring gear (clutch, meaning the overrunning clutch used with the pinion drive assembly). Solenoid contacts close.

2. .04 to .54 seconds. The engine is cranked by the motor. Motor current is high and the battery voltage is low. The pinion and armature are locked solidly together by the clutch sprags.

3. From .54 to 1.04 seconds. The engine fires and accelerates to its governed speed on units equipped with a constant speed or hydraulic governor, such as a generator

set. Let's assume that this speed is 2100 rpm. The pinion to engine speed ratio is usually about 10.5 to 1. Therefore, the starter pinion will be turning at 10.5 times 2100, or 22,000 rpm, while the armature reaches about 6000 rpm.

4. From 1.04 to 1.84 seconds, the pinion clutch is in full overrun, with the pinion spinning at approximately 21,500 rpm and the armature turning at approximately 6500 rpm.

5. From 1.84 to 6.0 seconds, the solenoid is de-energized with its contacts open. The clutch shifts out of mesh with the flywheel ring gear. The pinion slows down to armature speed within one second and the armature is braked to a stop in approximately four seconds.

On engine applications such as standby or regular generator sets which are started automatically when a power failure results to the normal electricial utility network, it

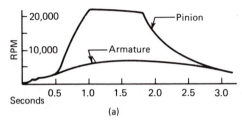

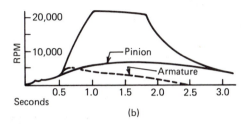

Fig. 6-36. (a) Conventional starter motor action. (b) Automatic starter motor disengagement. (Courtesy of Detroit Diesel Allison Div. of GMC)

is desirable to employ an automatic disconnect device to the starting system. Many engines in these types of applications use a fuel pressure switch located on the diesel engine secondary fuel filter to interrupt the cranking circuit immediately after the engine has started. The opening pressure of the fuel switch can be adjusted to match the fuel pressure developed by the engine at 350 rpm, which is generally the speed range at which the engine fires during cranking.

Figure 6-36 (b), shows the sequence of operation when a starter motor disengagement is obtained automatically through the use of a fuel pressure switch in the circuit. Figure 6-37 indicates the wiring arrangement used in an automatic starter disengagement system. The dotted line in Fig. 6-36 (b) shows the sequence of operation when disengagement is obtained automatically by the use of the fuel pressure switch in the circuit.

Automatic starter disengagement is accomplished in approximately 0.2 seconds after the engine starts, which reduces the number of pinion revolutions from 420 to 90, and reduces the armature speed from 270 to 70 which is a speed reduction in the order of 4 to 1. Proportionately reduced wear on all components is the result. The wiring circuit is arranged so that while the engine is running, the fuel pressure switch

contacts are open. It is therefore impossible for the operator to inadvertently attempt engagement of the starter motor circuit.

The fuel pressure switch is normally a 6 $\pm$ 1 psi (41 $\pm$ 7 kPa) breaking type unit. A magnetic switch should also be used as shown in Fig. 6-37. The fuel pressure switch only handles the small coil current of the magnetic switch, while the contactors of the magnetic switch handle the heavy current of the starter solenoid pull-in windings and hold-in windings.

ON VEHICLE TROUBLESHOOTING: STARTER MOTORS

Starter motor troubles are often a direct result of poor maintenance practices caused by such simple items as low battery charge condition, corroded terminals, and loose or corroded battery cables or connections at either the starter or solenoid. Many times a starter has been diagnosed as being the culprit, when in fact a simple connection or low battery condition was the remedy required to correct the fault. Problems associated with batteries can be found in Chapter 3 which discusses conventional and maintenance-free batteries. Next to low batteries, more cranking problems are caused by defective cables and connections than any other reason. When

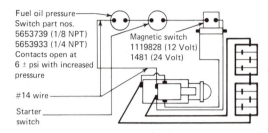

Fuel oil pressure—
Switch part nos.
5653739 (1/8 NPT)
5653933 (1/4 NPT)
Contacts open at
6 ± psi with increased
pressure

Magnetic switch
1119828 (12 Volt)
1481 (24 Volt)

#14 wire——

Starter——
switch

Fig. 6-37. Automatic starter disengagement wiring circuit. (Courtesy of Detroit Diesel Allison Div. of GMC)

cables are bolted to the vehicle frame to complete the ground circuit, it is suggested that the area around the bolt hole be cleaned of dirt, paint undercoating, etc. and the area thoroughly tinned with solder to insure a low resistance connection.

If the cranking motor solenoid or magnetic switch does not operate properly, check control circuit elements such as the key switch, starter button, and relay. If voltage is low at the solenoid due to high circuit resistance for example, it can prevent proper indexing of the drive if tooth abutment occurs. A common condition and symptom caused by this condition is chattering which will destroy the cranking contacts quickly. Shift solenoids can draw from 45-90 amperes; therefore, it is imperative that switches, push buttons, relays, and wiring be of sufficient capacity to carry the solenoid current.

CRANKING POWER VERSUS AMPERE-HOURS

Many people are confused about the difference between cranking power and the battery ampere-hour rating. Simply stated, the ampere-hour rating is a measure of the battery's ability to supply a light load for a long period of time. It is not a measure of cranking power, which is itself rated at a 0°F temperature indicated in watts; therefore, the higher the rating, the

greater the cranking power available.

The battery capacity is very important on vehicles that have switched from an existing 24-volt system to the now widely used 12-volt, high-performance starter motor. This is why it is important to have battery and starter cables that are capable of carrying the proper current with minimal voltage drop. This can be done by taking a voltage drop test, which is explained herein in detail. The voltage drop should not exceed the following on heavy-duty vehicle cranking systems:

1. 24-volt system: 1.2 volts per 1000 amps.
2. 12-volt high-performance system: 0.75 volts per 1000 amperes.

Stranded copper cable is recommended for battery starter cable with the following recommendations suggested:

24 and 32 Volt Systems

Total Length of Cranking Circuit	Size of Cable
Up to 188 inches	No. 0
188–237	No. 00
237–300	No. 000
300–380	No. 0000

Cranking Voltage Test

One of the quickest methods to use to establish if a problem exists in the starter

Following is an **example for a typical 12V** high performance circuit using separate cables to and from the cranking motor for each set of batteries.

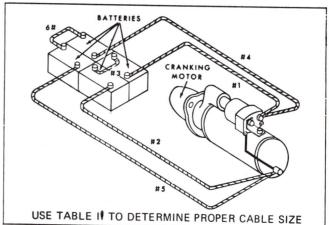

EXAMPLE:

Stranded Cable No.	Length		Stranded Cable No.	Length
1	55		4	70
2	60		5	80
3	10		6	10
Total 125 inches			Total 160 Inches	

In the EXAMPLE above, use #00 cable for cables 1, 2 and 3, and #000 cable for cables 4, 5 and 6.

USE TABLE II TO DETERMINE PROPER CABLE SIZE

Figure 1

TABLE II

12 VOLT HIGH PERFORMANCE SYSTEM

Total Length of Cranking Circuit	Size of Cable
Up to 144"	#00
144" — 180"	#000
180" — 230"	#0000

Following is an **example** for a typical **12 Volt** high performance circuit using one cable to the cranking motor and one for return.

The lengths for cables 1 and 2 are measured from the motor to the first battery post, and that cables A, B and C must not be included in the summation. The table for this type circuit follows:

TABLE III

Total Length of Cables 1, 2 & 3	Use Cable Size For All Cables
To 70 inches	# 00
71 to 90 inches	000
91 to 115 inches	0000

Cables A, B, C, and #3 should never be smaller than #00.
If the circuit length of 1, 2, and 3 exceeds 115 inches, the wiring hook-up should be as shown in Figure 1 and Table II should be referred to for proper cable size.

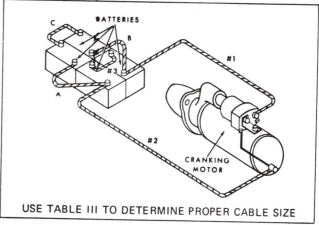

USE TABLE III TO DETERMINE PROPER CABLE SIZE

Figure 2

motor to battery circuit is what is commonly known as a voltage drop test. This test allows you to establish just how much voltage is being lost through the circuit. Insufficient voltage can lead to chattering of the solenoid, and failure of the starter motor to crank.

The control circuit can be checked as follows:

1. Check the key switch, starter button, and relay switch if used.

2. Ensure that all connections in Step 1 are clean and tight.

3. Refer to Fig. 6-38(a), and connect up a voltmeter as shown. Ensure that the correct polarity is observed between the voltmeter and starter connections. Wrong polarity will be indicated by the voltmeter needle kicking to the left instead of the right.

4. To complete the cranking voltage test as shown in Fig. 6-38, prevent the engine from starting. If a gasoline engine, disconnect the ignition coil secondary lead, and if a diesel engine, either tie the stop lever in the stop position, or de-energize the fuel solenoid. Proceed to crank the engine while carefully noting the voltmeter reading. This reading will vary with different systems; An accepted standard is 10 volts for a 12-volt system and 20 volts for a 24-volt system; however, some vehicle manufacturers specify that as little as 9.6 volts or better is acceptable. Obviously, the higher the reading, then the better condition the cranking circuit is in. Therefore, any resistance in switches, wiring, etc. should be eliminated to provide as high a reading as possible.

5. Perform a battery capacity test as described in Chapter 3 dealing with battery

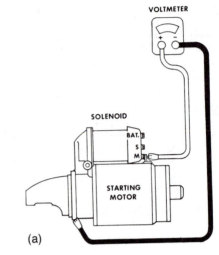

(a)

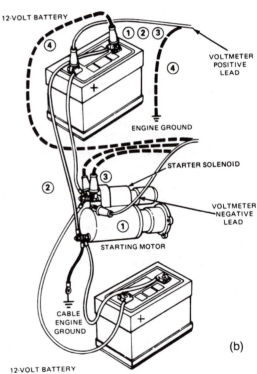

(b)

Fig. 6-38. (a) Cranking voltage test. (Courtesy of International Harvester) (b) Starter circuit resistance test. (Courtesy of AC Delco Div. of GMC)

maintenance, if the reading in Step 4 is low.

Starter Circuit Resistance Test

With a voltmeter connected as shown in Fig. 6-38(b), check the resistance between the starter motor and each set of batteries. Crank the engine with the ignition off, and use a remote starter switch connected to the starter relay or solenoid. On a gasoline engine equipped with an electric fuel pump, or diesel engine with a fuel solenoid, disconnect these items before starting the test.

Maximum voltage drop for each set of batteries should be as follows:

1. Connection 1, 0.5 volts with the voltmeter negative lead connected to the starter terminal and the positive lead to the battery positive terminal.

2. Connection 2, 0.1 volts with the voltmeter negative lead connected to the battery terminal of the starter relay and the positive lead to the battery positive terminal.

3. Connection 3, 0.3 volts with the voltmeter negative lead connected to the starter terminal of the starter relay and the positive voltmeter lead connected to the positive terminal of the battery.

4. Connection 4, 0.1 volts with the voltmeter negative lead connected to the battery negative terminal and the positive lead connected to the battery positive terminal.

5. The maximum allowable voltage drop for a 24-volt starter is half that allowed for a 12-volt starter system in steps 1 through 4.

Voltage Drop Reading

Perform a voltage drop test throughout the cranking circuit with the use of a voltmeter. This test involves three basic steps:

(a) The cranking circuit voltage drop

(b) The control circuit voltage drop

(c) The grounded side voltage drop

The voltage drops are established by connecting a voltmeter across the complete circuit or sections of a circuit in parallel, then reading the voltmeter while the circuit is being cranked.

Figure 6-39 shows the basic hookup for establishing the voltage drop from the battery to the starter. To obtain an accurate reading, ensure that the voltmeter is connected to the battery post and not the clamp area. Prevent the engine from starting as was explained in Step 4 earlier. Crank the engine and note the reading on the face of the voltmeter.

While checking the voltage reading in Fig. 6-39, the maximum voltage drops for a

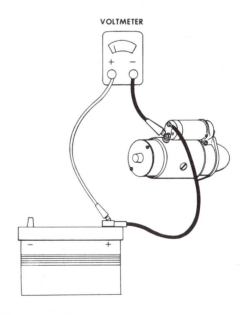

Fig. 6-39. Cranking circuit test. (Courtesy of International Harvester)

standard 12-volt circuit would be in the following areas:

1. Starter motor to battery cable length under 3 feet (0.914 m) a maximum of 0.1 volts

2. Same as (a), but cable length of 3-6 feet (0.914-1.82 m), a maximum of 0.2 volts

3. A mechanical switch, a maximum of 0.1 volts

4. A starter solenoid switch, a maximum of 0.2 volts

5. A starter magnetic switch, a maximum of 0.3 volts

6. Each connection, zero voltage drop

When voltage drop tests are performed correctly, poor connections or corroded or undersized cables can be detected. When connecting the voltmeter to a switch terminal or motor terminal, connect the voltmeter lead to the terminal stud rather than to the terminal, so that the drop across the connection will be measured.

Also, when performing these tests, connect one voltmeter lead only, then crank over the engine. As soon as the engine is turning, connect the second voltmeter lead to the necessary terminal and read the voltage.

Disconnect the voltmeter lead while the engine is being cranked; otherwise, it is possible in some parts of the circuit to impose a heavy current through the voltmeter which can cause serious damage.

Figure 6-40 shows the location of the various voltmeter lead connections in order to accurately monitor the voltage drop throughout typical starting systems. Systems that are different from those shown simply require that you bridge each cable connection and add the various read-ings together to obtain the total system voltage drop.

Control circuit voltage drop

The control circuit is that area from the battery post to the solenoid switch terminals. Generally if the voltmeter shows less than 0.5 volt during this part of the test, then the circuit is in good condition. If however, there is more than a 0.5 volt drop, then excessive resistance is evident in the system, and it should be corrected.

Grounded side voltage drop test

Both hard starting and charging system problems can occur if poor connections or high circuit resistance is encountered on the battery ground circuit.

With the voltmeter leads connected across the starter motor and battery ground post, the allowable voltage drop is usually in the region of 0.2 volt. More than 0.2 volt indicates a poor ground, a loose motor mounting bolt, or bad battery ground to the engine or frame.

No load test hookup

This test should be performed if the previous tests reveal no particular problem area, but the starter motor still fails to operate. Remove the starter motor from the engine (see below) and proceed as follows:

If a bench tester machine is available, then the starter can be clamped into a drive fixture as shown in Fig. 6-41, with the necessary test batteries and gauges readily visible. However, if no test bench is available, then clamp the starter motor into a heavy-duty vise in the shop, connect up the necessary leads, ammeter, voltmeter, carbon pile load bank, and an accurate tachometer as shown in Fig. 6-42.

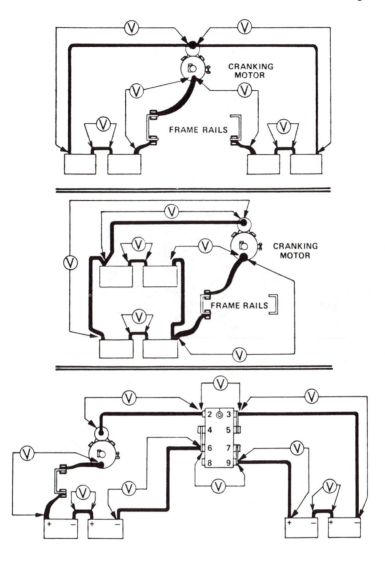

Fig. 6-40. Typical voltmeter connections for measurement of voltage drop on three different systems. (Courtesy of Leece-Neville, Sheller-Globe Corp.)

The no-load test should be preceded by a visual inspection of the starter motor assembly for any signs of physical damage. Check such items as the pinion for freedom of movement on the armature screw shaft. Take a screwdriver and pry the pinion to see if the armature is free to rotate. Are the pole shoe screws tight? If not, the armature will come into contact with the pole shoe and will be unable to turn. If the armature is tight, or cannot be rotated, then disassemble the starter and

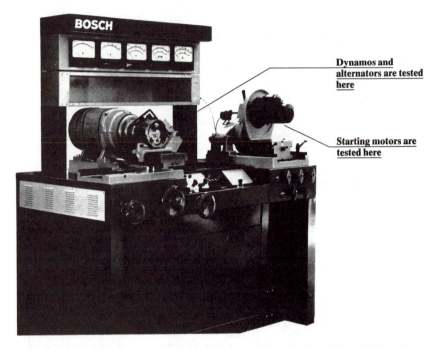

Fig. 6-41. Starter motor test stand. (Courtesy of Robert Bosch Corp.)

bypass the no load test for now.

If however, the armature is free to rotate, conduct the no load test as follows:

1. Connect the starter motor as shown in Fig. 6-42, and ensure that the ammeter used is capable of reading the amperage range for the particular starter motor to be tested.

2. Ensure that the tachometer is set for the scale that the motor will rotate at.

3. Obtain the specified voltage from the manufacturer's test specification bulletin, and vary the carbon pile resistance unit to establish this voltage, then read the current draw in amperes along with the armature speed on the tachometer.

Typical examples of voltage, minimum and maximum amperage draw, and mini-

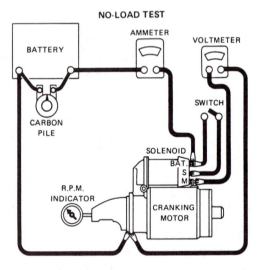

Fig. 6-42. Test connections for no-load bench test of starter. (Courtesy of International Harvester)

mum and maximum armature speed for several Leece-Neville and Delco-Remy heavy-duty starters are given in Table 6-2.

Removal of Starter Motor from Vehicle

The removal of the starter motor from the vehicle engine is similar to all automative procedures in that it simply necessitates disconnecting wires, and then removing the retaining bolts from the starter to the engine assembly. However, the following sequence lists the necessary steps required to ensure satisfactory removal.

1. Always disconnect the battery cables prior to attempting to remove the starter motor to prevent possible shorting out of wiring, and also to prevent personal injury should the starter switch be energized accidentally.

2. Disconnect the necessary wires from the starter that would otherwise prevent starter removal. Tag all wires to ensure that they will be installed back in the same position. You may be the one doing the reinstallation, or it might be someone else.

3. Remove the starter mounting bolts, but do not completely remove the last bolt until you are certain that you can support the starter assembly with one hand. On some heavy-duty trucks and equipment, two people are often required to effectively remove the starter. If this is not possible, sling the starter or support it to allow you to remove all of the retaining bolts without it falling on top of you.

Starter Motor Installation

Installation of the starter motor is basically the reverse of removal. However, note the following sequence.

1. Is the starter to be installed the same unit that came off? If so, are the nose cone

Table 6-2. Heavy-Duty Starter Specifications

Leece-Neville

Starter Model	Voltage Rating	Rotation at Drive End	Starter Test Voltage	Amperage Draw	Minimum RPM	Maximum RPM
7200 Series	12	CW or CCW	6	100-105		3100
7314-MA	12	CW	5.5	95-105		4000
Hi-Output Thick Frame 7200/7400/7500	12	CW or CCW	5.5	95-105		4000
Series	24	CW	12	85-90		3800

Delco-Remy

1109099 (10MT)	12	CW	9	60-85	6800	10300
1109197 (20MT)	12	CW	9	40-140	8000	13000
1114835 (40MT)	12	CW	9	140-215	4000	7000
1109793 (50MT)	24	CW	20	95-120	5500	7500

and solenoid mounted in the correct positions? If it is a replacement starter, does it conform to the same mounting location, bolt hole alignment, solenoid and nose cone position, drive gear to flywheel ring gear tooth number and type, etc?

2. Are the battery cables still disconnected?

3. Are all wires and cables free of corrosion, insulation breaks, etc.?

4. Do you have the correct length retaining bolts readily available, with lockwashers?

5. Position the starter on the engine, and install one or more bolts finger-tight to retain it in position. On some starters it may be necessary to first connect up the solenoid wires; otherwise, this may be extremely difficult to do once the starter is bolted up tight.

6. Once the starter is bolted up and the bolts torqued to specs, connect any remaining wiring. Ensure that all wires and connections are tight.

7. Connect up the battery cables and tighten them securely.

8. Check the operation of the starter for satisfactory engagement, and proper cranking speed. Ensure that no unusual noises such as clunking, whining, etc. are evident. Stop and start the engine several times. Feel the starter frame, and ensure that no overheating is occurring.

9. If the battery or batteries are located in a box, secure the lid.

STARTER OVERHAUL

Disassembly and inspection of all types and sizes of starting motors can be considered similar in most respects with minor changes being found in the design. The necessary checks and tests however can be considered common to all whether or not the unit is an automotive or heavy-duty type. It is advisable to match mark the starting motor on the field frame, lever housing, and nose housing so that all parts can be assembled in their previous locations later.

Minor variations will exist between starters, therefore the disassembly given is simply by way of example, and should not be considered all inclusive. Figure 6-43 shows a disassembled starter.

1. Remove the solenoid switch assembly by disconnecting the necessary terminal nuts, jumper strap if used, stud connections, wires and solenoid cover screws, etc.

2. On some starters, remove the brush opening cover band, and remove the brushes from their holders after pulling back on the brush spring with a hooked piece of wire, then slip the brushes out of their holders.

3. Remove the socket head screws from the nose housing and slide the housing from the armature shaft.

4. Remove the bolts from the brush support end housing and separate it from the field frame.

5. Disconnect any linkage from the shift lever assembly to pinion.

6. Withdraw the armature from the field frame.

7. If necessary, remove the pole shoe retaining screws and remove these units one at a time. See Fig. 6-44. Once the starter motor assembly has been completely disassembled, carefully inspect all parts for signs of overheating, wear patterns, and any physical damage.

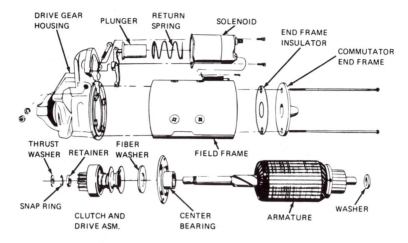

Fig. 6-43. Disassembled starter motor. (Courtesy of Chevrolet Motor Div. of GMC)

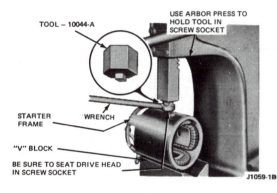

Fig. 6-44. Starter motor pole shoe retaining screws. (Courtesy of Ford Motor Company)

The checks required on the starter are given below.

1. Do not submerge starter parts in solvent or degreasing tanks, instead use mineral sprits and a stiff brush to degrease all parts. If the drive mechanism appears to be serviceable, simply use a cloth to remove any dirt.

2. Brushes and brush holders should be inspected for signs of discoloration due to overheating, especially the brush springs which might have lost their tension. The brushes should be at least 60 to 70 percent of the length of a new brush, otherwise replace them. See Fig. 6-45 for brush and holder replacement.

Whether or not new brushes are being used, ensure that they are a free-fit in the brush holder guides. Inspect the brushes to make certain that they do in fact ride on the full surface area of the commutator along their length.

Brush spring tension can be checked with a small spring pull-type scale attached to the end of the spring as shown in Fig. 5-23 and compared to manufacturer's specifications for the particular starter being rebuilt. Replace any weak or faulty springs.

3. The armature should be placed on a growler and checked for short-circuits, opens or grounds in the same manner as that used to check the armature assembly on a d.c. type generator. Such a check is

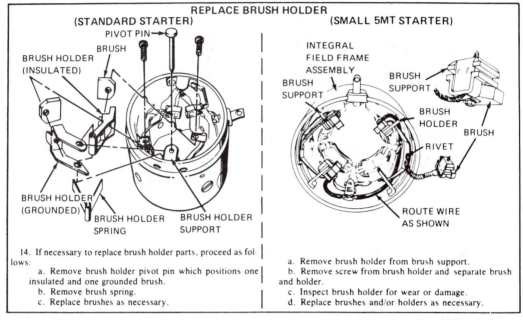

Fig. 6-45. Brush and holder replacement. (Courtesy of Chevrolet Motor Div. of GMC)

shown in Fig. 6-46 (a), which shows the placement of the armature between the growler poles or magnets. To check for grounds, short-circuits, and opens, proceed as follows:

1. Grounds in the armature are found, as shown in Fig. 6-46(b), by placing each prod of the growler test lamp so that one test prod is in contact with the armature core, and the other is in contact with the commutator segment. Should the growler test lamp light, then the armature is grounded.

2. Short circuits are established as shown in Fig. 6-46 (a). The flat steel strip attached to the growler assembly by a small chain is placed lengthwise along the armature, which is then turned slowly. Should the steel strip vibrate at any time, this is an indication that there is a short circuit at that point.

3. Opens within the armature assembly can be located visually by inspecting the condition of the commutator bars. Loose or bad connections will cause arcing and burning of the commutator. If the commutator is considered serviceable, the commutator can be turned down in a lathe to provide a clean new surface for the brushes to ride on. Once this has been done, the insulation between the commutator bars should be undercut approximately 1/32 inch (0.793 mm) deep, and also 1/32 inch (0.793 mm) wide. This can be done with a special machine such as that shown in Fig. 6-47. If this is not available, then a used hand hacksaw blade can be used. Break it in half, and lightly sharpen one end to permit light undercutting as suggested.

4. The starter field frame coils should be inspected for signs of overheating, arcing, and breaks in the insulation. In order to

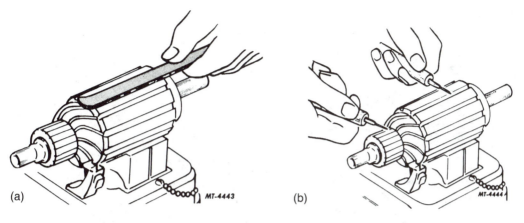

Fig. 6-46. (a) Armature in growler, (b) checking for armature grounds. (Courtesy of International Harvester)

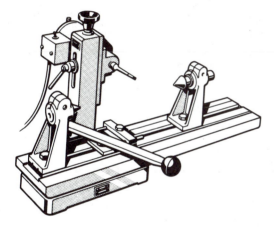

Fig. 6-47. Starter motor commutator undercutting machine. (Courtesy of Robert Bosch Corp.)

check the field coils for possible grounds or opens, a conventional test lamp can be used.

With the ground wire to the field coil disconnected, touch one end of the test lamp prods to the starter motor field frame and the other to the field connector. The lamp should not light! If however the test lamp does light up, the field coils are grounded, and must therefore be repaired or replaced.

If the test lamp does not light when the test lamp prods are connected to the ends of the field coil leads, then the field coils are open. Fig. 6-48 shows tests for opens and grounds. Should it become necessary to remove the starter motor field frame pole shoes, the locating screws must be removed. These screws are extremely difficult to remove without the use of special tools. An impact screwdriver, or socket screwdriver attachment is generally required for this purpose, along with a pole shoe spreader. See Fig. 6-44.

Take note when reinstalling the pole shoes that they are replaced in the same position. Some pole shoes have a long lip on one side that makes it imperative that the long lip be installed in the direction of rotation of the armature assembly. Ensure that the pole shoes screws are torqued to specifications upon reassembly.

5. The starter clutch drive should be carefully inspected for possible signs of damage. If necessary, disassemble it and

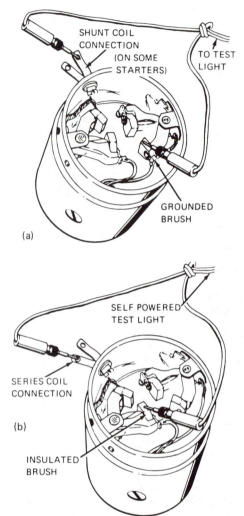

(a)

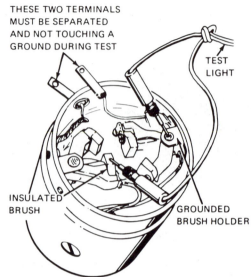

On starters with shunt coil, separatate series and shunt coil strap terminals during this test. Do not let strap terminals touch case or other ground. Using a test lamp place one lead on the grounded brush holder and the other lead on either insulated brush. If the lamp lights, a grounded series coil is indicated and must be repaired or replaced.

(c)

Using a test lamp, place one lead on the series coil terminal and the other lead on the insulated brush. If the lamp fails to light, the series coil is open and will require repair or replacement. This test should be made from each insulated brush to check brush and lead continuity.

Fig. 6-48. (a) Testing shunt coil for open, (b) testing series coil for an open, (c) testing series coil for ground. (Courtesy of Chevrolet Motor Div. of GMC)

repair or replace the damaged parts. Depending on the type of drive pinion and clutch assembly used, the procedure will vary slightly. Systematically disassemble the unit, and reassemble in the opposite direction. Some units require lubrication upon reassembly, expecially the overrunning sprags in the intermediate type of sprag clutches. However, do not lubricate the sprags on heavy duty type sprag clutches. If in doubt as to whether or not to lubricate your starter, consult the manufacturer's service literature.

6. If any bearings in the starter end frame are worn, be sure to replace them,

otherwise the armature may rub against the pole shoes when the motor is in operation. Also ensure that the armature shaft is smooth and concentric at the bearing ends, otherwise excessive runout could occur which could again lead to the armature rubbing against the pole shoes.

7. Inspect and repair the starter motor solenoid as necessary.

8. When reassembling the armature assembly into the field frame, gently pull the assembly out of the frame a short distance to allow the brushes to be properly located over the commutator, then gently slide the armature into its correct position in the field frame and end cover so that the bearing is supporting the armature assembly.

CHECKS AFTER STARTER REASSEMBLY

Several checks are required to ensure that no starter motor damage will occur as a result of improper assembly, or that it will fail to function when installed on an engine. It is imperative that the pinion clearance to nose cone be checked as follows:

1. Disconnect the starter motor field coil connector at the solenoid switch and make certain that you insulate it after it is disconnected.

2. Connect up a battery of the proper voltage to the starter motor and solenoid as shown in Fig. 6-49 (a), with one battery lead to the switch terminal of the solenoid and the other to a good ground return such as the field frame, or to a vise if the starter motor is being tested there.

3. To activate the starter and to allow the pinion assembly to move along the arma-ture shaft so that it butts up against the nose cone, connect a jumper wire from the M or motor terminal of the solenoid with the other end to the motor frame.

4. Quickly check the pinion clearance for the particular starter under test as shown in the three examples in Fig. 6-49. Leaving the jumper wire connected so that the pinion stays in its engaged position can result in possible overheating of the solenoid.

5. While checking the pinion clearance, manually push the pinion towards the starter motor in order to eliminate any overtravel.

No adjustment is necessary on those units that meet the recommendations shown in Fig. 6-49; however, starter motors with intermediate duty clutches have no provision for pinion clearance adjustment. Most heavy duty type motors do however provide an adjustment for the pinion as shown in Fig. 6-49(c) and (d).

STARTER MOTOR TROUBLESHOOTING

The function of the starter motor is to crank the engine at a high enough speed to initiate combustion within the engine cylinders. In order that the starter motor can do this effectively, heavy cables, connectors, and switches are necessary because of the large current required at the starter motor during cranking. For this reason, resistance in the starter motor electrical system must be kept at an absolute minimum, otherwise slow cranking or inability to crank can result.

Loose connections, relay contacts, or corroded or faulty cables can result in slower than normal cranking, or failure to crank at all. Batteries in a low state of

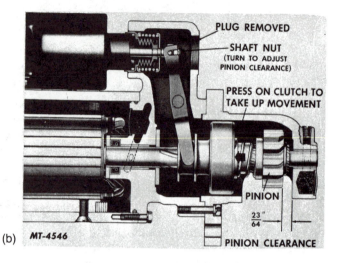

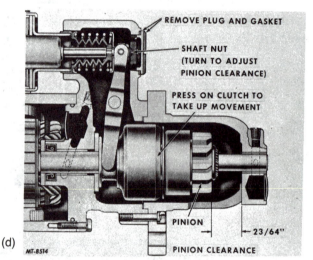

Fig. 6-49. (a) Pinion drive check with wiring hookup. (b) Pinion clearance check —intermediate duty clutch. (c) Pinion clearance check—heavy-duty sprag clutch. (d) Pinion clearance check—DR 250 heavy-duty drive. (Courtesy of Delco-Remy Div. of GMC)

charge are also typical problems associated with the starter motors failure to crank the engine fast enough especially in cold weather operation.

Starter complaints will usually fall into the categories shown in Table 6-3.

The starter may start the engine, but in the process loud whining, growling, or a loud whoop can be further indications of problems in the starter motor circuit. Examples of these problems are listed in Table 6-4.

Starter motor noises such as those listed in Table 6-4 (1,2) can be corrected by plac-

Table 6-3. Starter Problems

Condition	Possible Causes	Correction
Engine fails to rotate, but the starter spins.	Starter motor	Remove starter and inspect for worn or damaged components.
	Worn flywheel ring gear teeth	Inspect and repair
Engine fails to rotate	Loose or corroded battery cables	Clean and tighten.
	Low battery charge	Check battery and charge or replace.
Engine fails to rotate.	Starter solenoid	Repair or replace.
	Loose or broken cable to starter	Tighten or replace cable.
	Motor problem	Repair or replace starter.
Engine cranks slowly.	Loose or corroded battery cables	Clean and tighten cables.
	Low battery charge	Charge or replace battery.
	High circuit resistance	Test cables and connections, and repair or replace.
	Starter problem	Check and repair starter.

ing shims between the starter motor and engine block mounting pad. This is not possible on all starter motor types; however, it is often employed on passenger car and light truck applications. Figure 6-50 shows the location of these shims with an example shown in the figure as to how the clearance can be altered. The reason for the insertion of the screwdriver through the bottom of the starter motor is to allow you to move the starter pinion and clutch assembly into mesh with the flywheel ring gear.

Figure 6-51 shows the actual engagement of the starter pinion with the flywheel ring gear so that it is centered as shown.

Removal of the lower engine flywheel housing cover is required for this check so you can visually establish that centering of the pinion to ring gear is actually obtained.

This clearance between the ring gear and pinion will vary between engines and types of starter motors. For example, General Motors Corporation specifies that this clearance on their light duty truck starter motors should be a minimum of 0.200 inch (5.08mm) otherwise the starter must be shimmed away from the flywheel. If however, the clearance is 0.260 inch or more, then shimming of the starter motor outboard mounting pad only is required.

Fig. 6-50. Starter motor shim placement. (Courtesy of Chevrolet Motor Division of GMC)

Table 6-4. Starter Motor Noise Diagnosis

PROBLEM	CAUSE
1. High pitched whine during cranking (before engine fires) but engine cranks and fires okay.	Distance too great between starter pinion and flywheel.
2. High pitched whine after engine fires. As key is being released engine cranks and fires okay; this intermittent complaint is often diagnosed as "starter hang in" or "solenoid weak."	Distance too small between starter pinion and flywheel. Flywheel runout contributes to the intermittent nature.
3. Loud "whoop" after the engine fires but while the starter is still held engaged. Sounds like a siren if the engine is revved while starter is engaged.	Most probable cause is a defective clutch. A new clutch will often correct this problem.
4. "Rumble", "growl" or (in severe cases) a "knock" as the starter is coasting down to a stop after starting the engine.	Most probable cause is a bent or unbalanced starter armature. A new armature will often correct this problem.

The problems shown in Table 6-4 (3,4) usually require starter motor removal and repair or replacement.

STARTER PINION WEAR

Wear on the starter motor pinion and flywheel ring gear can be caused by attempting to start the engine after it fires and is still rotating, or by inadvertently engaging the starter while the engine is running. Misalignment of the starter caused by improper installation (failure to shim correctly, a typical automotive problem), wear of the armature bushings, etc. can lead to premature pinion/ring gear tooth wear.

Examples of tooth wear are shown in Fig. 6-52.

FLYWHEEL RING-GEAR TYPES

It is often necessary to remove a starter motor in the field or shop and replace it with a starter possibly of a different make, or of the same manufacture, but with a different part number. Many people as-

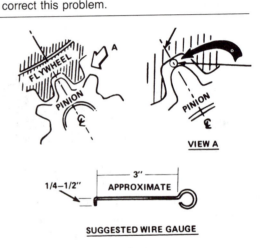

Fig. 6-51. Starter pinion and ring gear engagement. (Courtesy of Chevrolet Motor Div. of GMC)

sume that since the voltage of the replacement starter is the same as that of the failed starter, it can be installed without any problem. Unfortunately, this is not always the case.

Factors that must be considered are:

1. Is the replacement starter of the same physical size?

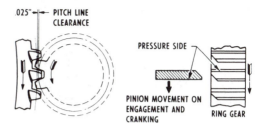

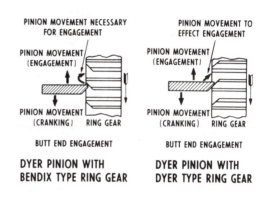

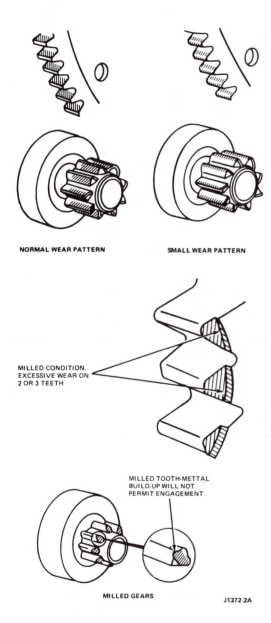

Fig. 6-52. Typical starter pinion ring gear tooth wear. (Courtesy of Ford Motor Company)

2. Will it fit the existing mounting location?

3. Is it of the same voltage?

Fig. 6-53. Types of flywheel ring gears and pinion mating. (Courtesy of Detroit Diesel Allison Div. of GMC)

4. Does it rotate in the same direction?

5. Does it have the same number and pitch of teeth as the one that it is replacing?

6. Can its nose cone be repositioned if necessary to allow proper mounting?

These are typical questions that must be asked prior to fitting an exchange or replacement starter as well as checking the flywheel ring-gear to see that it is not damaged from past misengagements and abuse.

Figure 6-53 shows the types of flywheel ring gears that are used with the over-

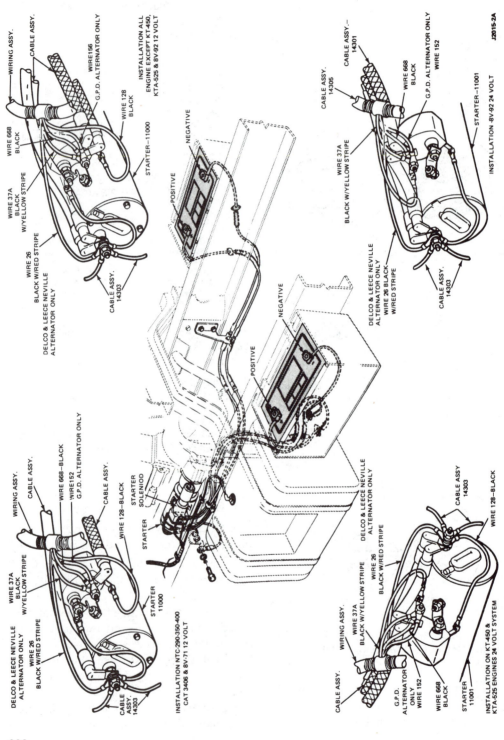

Fig. 6-54. Starter wiring circuit, typical heavy duty truck. (Courtesy of Ford Motor Company)

300

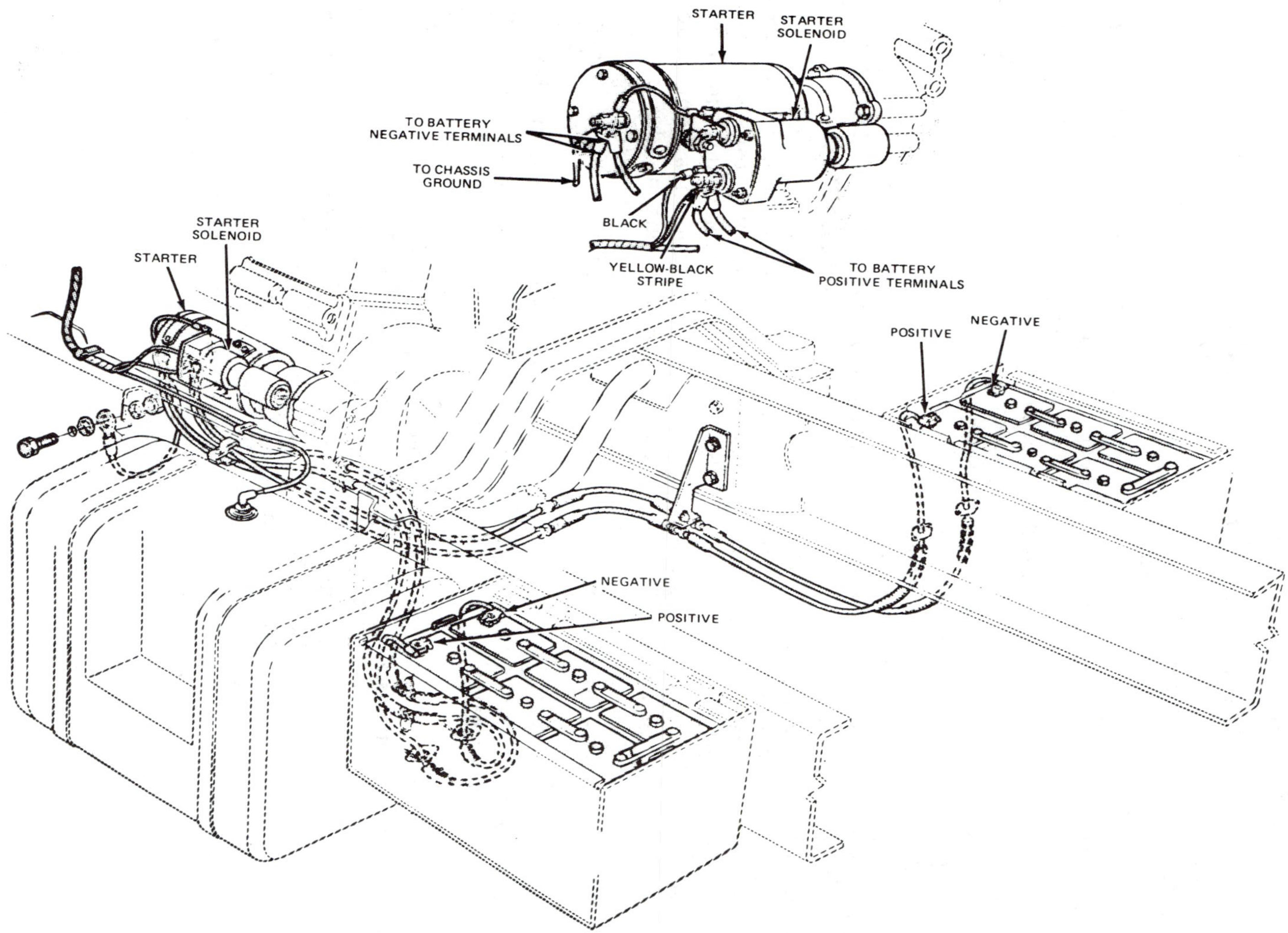

STARTER

STARTER
SOLENOID

TO BATTERY
POSITIVE TERMINALS

BLACK

YELLOW-BLACK
STRIPE

TO BATTERY
NEGATIVE TERMINALS

TO CHASSIS
GROUND

NEGATIVE

POSITIVE

NEGATIVE

POSITIVE

STARTER
SOLENOID

STARTER

Fig. 6-55. 12-volt Delco starter motor cable connections. (Courtesy of Ford Motor Company)

301

running clutch, Bendix pinion and Dyer drive starter motor pinion systems. These ring-gears will only operate satisfactorily when matched to a starter drive gear as shown.

The Bendix chamfered ring gear is used with starting motors having a Bendix drive or the widely used over-running clutch type drive on the starter motor. The non-chamfered ring gear can be used with either a Dyer drive starting motor or an overrunning clutch type starting motor. Dyer chamfer type ring gears are recognized by the chamfer being on the loaded side of the ring-gear tooth.

Using a Dyer drive ring gear with an over-running clutch type starting motor can cause starter drive to ring gear abutments, while the use of a Bendix chamfer ring gear with the over-running clutch starter will aid its engagement.

An over-running clutch type starter motor drive can also be used on nonchamfered ring gears.

STARTER WIRING CIRCUITS: HEAVY DUTY TRUCKS

The wiring arrangement for starter motors on heavy-duty trucks is very similar regardless of the make of truck and the actual type of starter used. Figure 6-54 shows the wiring circuit and connections commonly employed by Ford Motor Company on their series of CL9000 and LTL diesel powered Class 8 vehicles employing either Caterpillar, Cummins or Detroit Diesel Allison engines.

STARTER CABLE WIRING CONNECTIONS: HEAVY DUTY TRUCKS

Starter motor wiring hookup will vary depending on the particular unit being used. An example of a typical heavy-duty truck starter motor is shown in Fig. 6-55, which in this instance is a 12 volt Delco starter motor.

MAKING AND INSTALLING STARTER MOTOR CABLES

Due to the high current flow to the starter motor assembly especially on heavy-duty diesel type starters, for maximum protection cables should be shrouded with sleeving in order to avoid abrasion damage from vibration. The cables should also be supported at intervals to prevent sagging.

Although there is a variety of cable terminal styles readily available and used throughout the industry, it is recommended that the ends of starter motor cables be tinned and soldered to their respective terminal fittings in order to reduce the possibility of voltage drop and to insure a good electrical connection under all operating conditions.

When grounding any wires or cables to the vehicle frame, wire-brush the area to remove any rust and paint so that bare metal is exposed to insure a good connection.

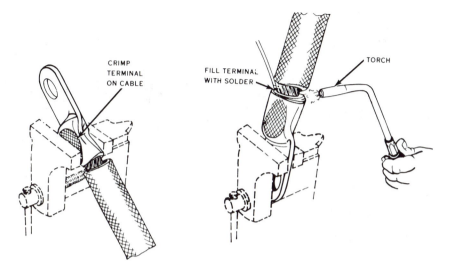

Fig. 6-56.

Figure 6-56 illustrates the method for attaching a new starter cable terminal and filling it with solder.

The following wiring diagrams (pages 304-308) are typical of those used with the various types of starter motors and drives found on heavy-duty diesel truck and industrial engines. The table below recommends what size cable to use with each one of these types of wiring circuits.

Starting Motor to Battery Cable Size Chart

Cable Size B & S Gage	TOTAL LENGTH—FEET	
	12 Volt	24 & 32 Volt
0	10	20
00	12	24
000	16	32
0000	20	40
2 Parallel Cables		
00 + 00	24	—
000 + 000	32	—
0000 + 0000	40	—

*This chart does not apply to high output starting motors. See 12 Volt High Output Starting Motor to Battery Cable Size Chart

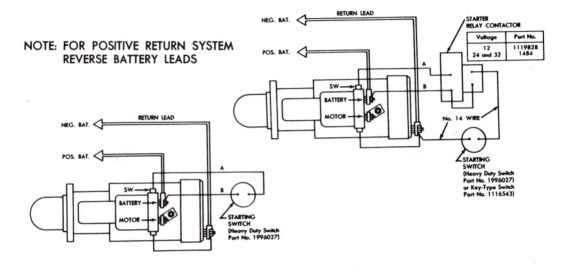

NOTE: FOR POSITIVE RETURN SYSTEM
REVERSE BATTERY LEADS

SPRAG HEAVY DUTY CLUTCH WIRING DIAGRAMS
INSULATED STARTING MOTOR—INSULATED SYSTEM

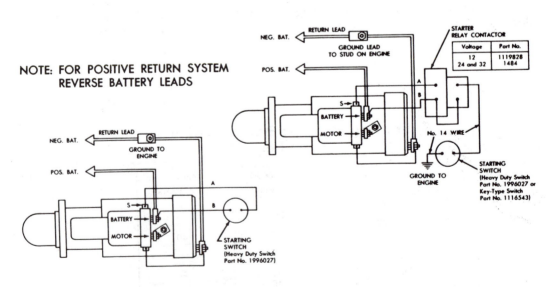

NOTE: FOR POSITIVE RETURN SYSTEM
REVERSE BATTERY LEADS

SPRAG HEAVY DUTY CLUTCH WIRING DIAGRAMS
INSULATED STARTING MOTOR—GROUNDED SYSTEM

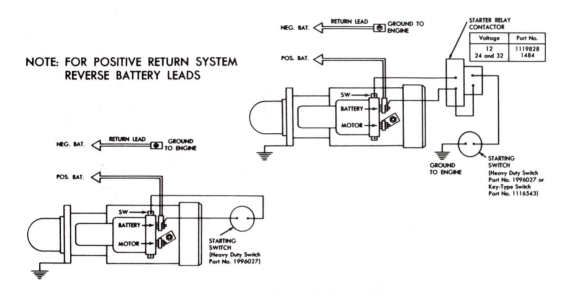

NOTE: FOR POSITIVE RETURN SYSTEM
REVERSE BATTERY LEADS

**SPRAG HEAVY DUTY CLUTCH WIRING DIAGRAMS
GROUNDED STARTING MOTOR**

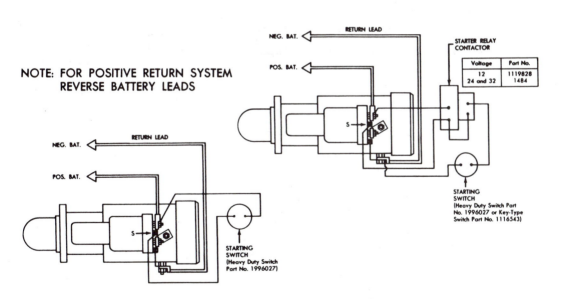

NOTE: FOR POSITIVE RETURN SYSTEM
REVERSE BATTERY LEADS

**SPRAG INTERMEDIATE DUTY CLUTCH WIRING DIAGRAMS
INSULATED STARTING MOTOR—INSULATED SYSTEM**

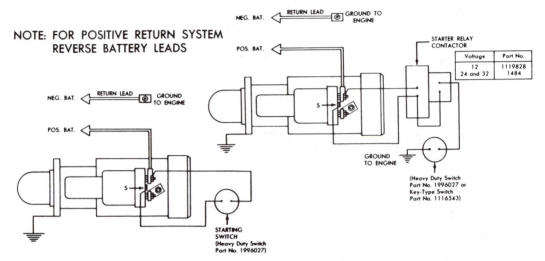

NOTE: FOR POSITIVE RETURN SYSTEM
REVERSE BATTERY LEADS

Voltage	Part No.
12	1119828
24 and 32	1484

SPRAG INTERMEDIATE DUTY CLUTCH WIRING DIAGRAMS
GROUNDED STARTING MOTOR

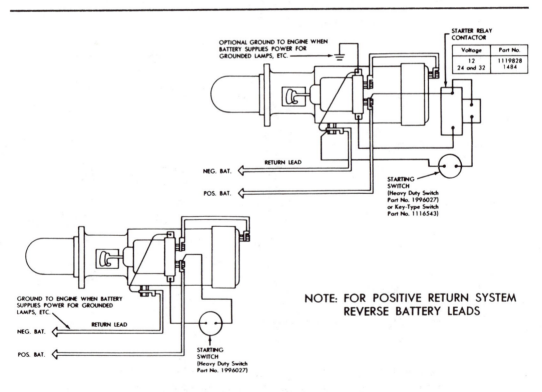

Voltage	Part No.
12	1119828
24 and 32	1484

NOTE: FOR POSITIVE RETURN SYSTEM
REVERSE BATTERY LEADS

DYER DRIVE INSULATED STARTING MOTOR WIRING DIAGRAM

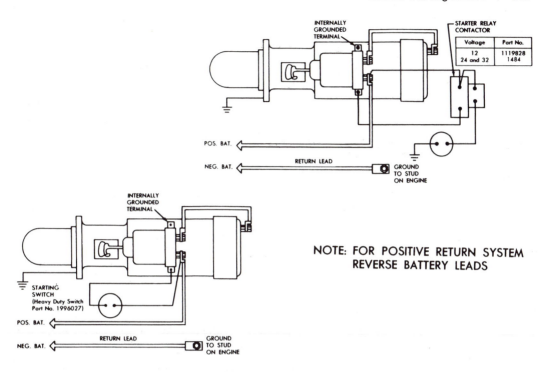

Voltage	Part No.
12	1119828
24 and 32	1484

NOTE: FOR POSITIVE RETURN SYSTEM
REVERSE BATTERY LEADS

DYER DRIVE GROUNDED STARTING MOTOR WIRING DIAGRAM

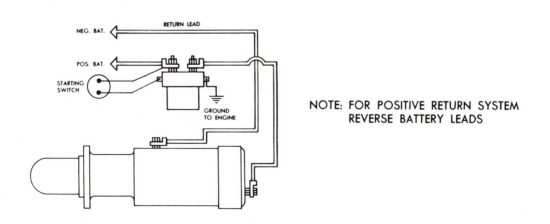

NOTE: FOR POSITIVE RETURN SYSTEM
REVERSE BATTERY LEADS

INSULATED BENDIX DRIVE STARTING MOTOR WIRING DIAGRAM

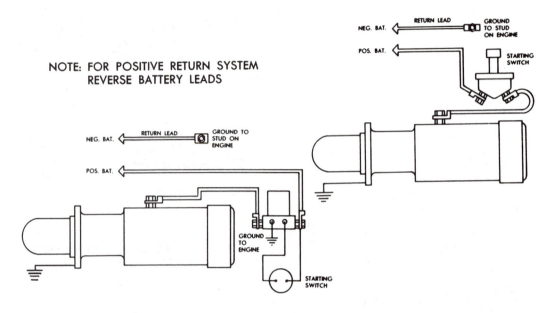

NOTE: FOR POSITIVE RETURN SYSTEM
REVERSE BATTERY LEADS

GROUNDED BENDIX DRIVE STARTING MOTOR WIRING DIAGRAM

REVIEW QUESTIONS

Q1 What are the common voltages of electric starting motors?

Q2 Do all starter motors rotate in a CW (clockwise) direction?

Q3 Name the four types of starter motor pinion drives.

Q4 Are all starter motor pinion drives direct or at a 1:1 ratio?

Q5 Do all starting motors employ solenoids mounted onto the top of the starter body?

Q6 Can you change the location of the nose cone on the starter motor for ease of installation?

Q7 How is the starter motor generally wound and why?

Q8 What are the main components of the starter motor?

Q9 How does battery current flow into the starter motor?

Q10 What is the main difference between a magnetic switch and a solenoid assembly?

Q11 How many sets of windings are contained within the starter motor solenoid?

Q12 What is a Series/Parallel circuit?

Q13 What is the recommended maximum cranking time for an electric starter motor?

Q14 What devices are available to ensure that excessive or prolonged starter motor cranking periods are not encountered?

Q15 What is an ADLO starter motor circuit?

Q16 Describe how an automatic starter disengagement system other than that described in Question 15 might work?

Q17 What is a starter motor voltage drop test?

Q18 When would you conduct a no-load test on the starter motor?

Q19 What checks are required on a starter motor at overhaul?

ANSWERS

A1 Common electric starter motor operating voltages are 12, 24 and 32-volt.

A2 No; the starter is mated to the engine; many industrial and marine engines employ engines that run in either a CW or CCW rotation, therefore the starter is fitted to its mating engine.

A3 The four types of starter motor pinion drives are:

(a) Dyer drive

(b) Sprag over-running clutch

(c) Bendix drive

(d) Roller type clutch drive

A4 No; some heavy duty starter motors run through a gear reducing drive to increase the torque.

A5 No; some heavy-duty starter motors employ a remote mounted magnetic switch assembly rather than a direct mounted solenoid.

A6 Most modern starter motors, especially heavy-duty truck and equipment starters, can have the position of the nose cone relocated to one of several positions by removing the retaining bolts and rotating the nose cone to the desired position.

A7 The starter motor is generally series wound to provide maximum breakaway torque when starting.

A8 The main components of the starter motor are the field coils and magnets, the armature and commutator, brushes, pinion drive, and solenoid shift mechanism.

A9 Battery current flows from the ignition switch to the solenoid; on to the north pole shoe (magnet) and through the field winding to the south pole, into the brush and commutator segment, through the armature windings and out the other brush back to the battery to complete the circuit.

A10 A magnetic switch simply opens and closes the circuit from the battery to the starter motor. The solenoid, in addition to this function, also shifts the starter motor drive pinion into engagement with the engine flywheel ring gear.

A11 There are two sets of solenoid windings, namely the pull-in set and the hold-in set.

A12 A series/parallel circuit is a system that employs a 24 volt starter motor but a 12-volt charging system; one battery supplies power to the vehicle lights and accessories so that they all operate on 12 volts; both batteries are coupled in series for 24-volt starting either through a series/parallel switch arrangement or through a system that employs a TR (transformer rectified) alternator system.

A13 Maximum cranking time of an electric starter should not exceed 30 seconds with 1.5 to 2 minutes allowed for cooling purposes in between.

A14 A built-in thermostat inside the motor and permanently attached to the field coils ensures that the starter motor cannot be continually cranked beyond 30 seconds at a time.

A15 An ADLO circuit is an automatic disengagement and lockout action feature that can be used with the starter circuit; it includes a system that sends voltage from the alternator R or ACC terminal as soon as the engine starts to energize a frequency sensing relay winding to automatically break the circuit through the starter magnetic switch and battery current can no longer flow to the starter motor.

A16 An automatic starter disengagement system employs a switch controlled by fuel pressure (generally diesel engines) to break the circuit to the starter motor the instant that the engine fires to prevent damage to the starter armature through possible overspeeding.

A17 This test is to establish if a problem exists in the starter motor to battery circuit through a high voltage loss; a voltmeter can be used along the circuit to establish this condition.

A18 When a voltage drop test indicates that no problem exists in the starter motor circuit, a no load test can be conducted with the starter motor in a test machine or vise where at a given voltage an amperage draw and starter rpm can be compared to the manufacturer's specifications.

A19 Starter overhaul checks involve:

(a) signs of overheating

(b) melted windings or signs of solder

(c) insulation breaks

(d) continuity checks

(e) brush wear and spring tension

(f) armature and commutator wear or damage

(g) brushing or bearing wear

(h) pole shoe security

(i) short circuits and opens (armature)

(j) drive mechanism

(k) solenoid assembly checks

Chapter

7

Conventional Ignition Systems

IGNITION SYSTEMS

Ignition systems are used today on both gasoline and LP-Gas engines to supply a high-tension electrical spark at the electrode of the spark plug which initiates combustion within the engine cylinder. Two general types of ignition systems are now in wide use all over the world:

1. The contact-breaker point ignition system which has been in use for many years, commonly known as a conventional system.

2. The electronic, or capacitor-discharge, type of ignition system which requires no contact-breaker points.

We will look at both types of ignition systems within this chapter, and discuss their operation, maintenance, and general troubleshooting.

BASIC IGNITION COMPONENTS

Prior to studying the ignition system in detail, let's first of all establish what com-

ponents are necessary in order for the system to function properly.

The basic ignition system requires the following components (See Fig. 7-1):

1. An ignition coil
2. A distributor assembly
3. Spark plugs and wiring
4. Storage battery
5. Ignition switch

The basic function of these components is as follows:

The ignition coil contains both a primary and secondary winding that is designed to act as a step-up transformer. Battery voltage, namely 12 volts, flows through the primary coil winding and to ground through the closed contact breaker (distributor) points. When the points are separated by the rotating distributor cam coming into contact with the breaker block of the points, a voltage surge occurs in the primary winding to about 250 volts.

Since the secondary winding contains approximately one-hundred times as many turns of wire as does the primary, the voltage is stepped up by this ratio of

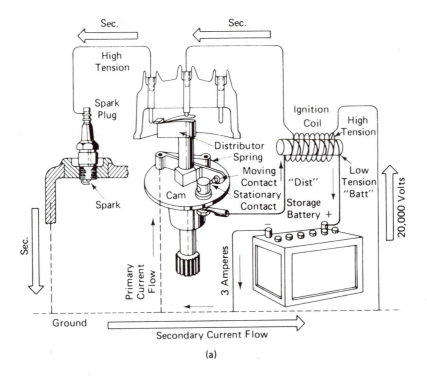

(a)

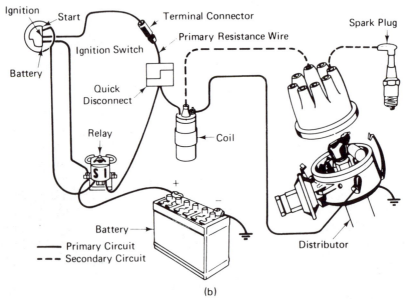

(b)

Fig. 7-1. Basic conventional ignition system: (a) functional schematic, (b) actual operational vehicle schematic.

turns between the primary and secondary windings; therefore, if the voltage produced in the primary winding reaches approximately 250 volts, the secondary winding voltage will attain about 25,000 volts. This high tension voltage is sent from the coil to the center of the distributor cap where it passes through the carbon brush that is in contact with the spinning rotor arm. Since the rotor arm is turning with the distributor shaft, the high tension voltage passes from the center electrode or carbon brush of the distributor cap and along the rotor arm to its end.

Voltage is then distributed from the rotor arm to side inserts located evenly around the distributor cap and then to a high tension cable (wire) to the respective spark plug. The number of side inserts in the distributor cap is equal to the number of engine cylinders or spark plugs. Therefore, an 8-cylinder engine would contain 8 inserts spaced 45° apart around the inside of the distributor cap. A 4-cylinder engine would have 4 side inserts 90° apart, while a 6-cylinder engine would naturally have 6 inserts spaced 60° apart.

Each distributor cap has individual towers for each spark plug wire to fit into.

The function of the ignition switch is to control or open and close the ignition circuit between the ignition system and the vehicle battery. Within the distributor assembly, which is engine-driven, is an advance mechanism to change the ignition timing with an increase in engine speed.

These component parts are shown in Fig. 7-7.

The ignition coil acts as a transformer to boost the battery voltage (12 volts) to approximately 25,000 volts at the spark plug on conventional ignition systems, and to 35,000 to 40,000 volts on high energy or electronic type ignition systems. The ignition coil functions as shown in Fig. 7-2. Contained within the ignition coil, or step-up transformer, is a circular core composed of insulated iron wires or laminated strips. Use of individual wires (open core) allows the changing magnetic field of the coil primary winding to change its strength faster than if a solid (closed core) arrangement were used. Assembled around the coil core is both a primary and secondary winding with the number of turns in the primary winding being in the region of 200, while those in the secondary winding amount to as many as 20,000 in the average coil unit.

The secondary winding although wrapped around the coil core is insulated from this core. The wire used for both windings is copper. The primary winding consisting of larger diameter copper wire is wound around the secondary winding and is also insulated from the secondary winding. Some coils may contain less, some more; however, on the average, 15,000 to 30,000 turns of very thin copper wire are found in the secondary coil winding, with a ratio of secondary to primary turns being between 60 and 150 to one.

The reason for the iron core of the coil is to increase the strength of the magnetic field created when electricity is fed through the windings from the battery. You may remember from the discussion of basic electricity that when a current is passed through a wire, a magnetic field is created. If this wire is wrapped around a metal core, the magnetic field is more concentrated than it would be if no iron core was present.

The coil windings are enclosed by either a soft iron shell, or by a jacket of metal plates that reduces stray magnetic fields. The assembly is then placed into a one-piece steel or diecast aluminum case which

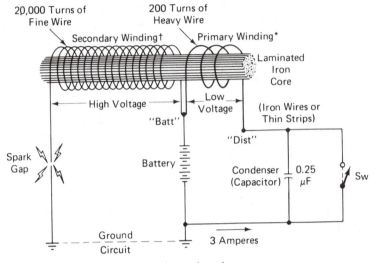

20,000 Turns of Fine Wire

200 Turns of Heavy Wire

Secondary Winding†

Primary Winding*

Laminated Iron Core

High Voltage

Low Voltage

(Iron Wires or Thin Strips)

"Batt"

"Dist"

Spark Gap

Battery

Condenser (Capacitor) 0.25 μF

Sw

Ground Circuit

3 Amperes

* Resistance = 1.5 Ohms, Approximately
† Resistance = 12,000 Ohms, Approximately

(a)

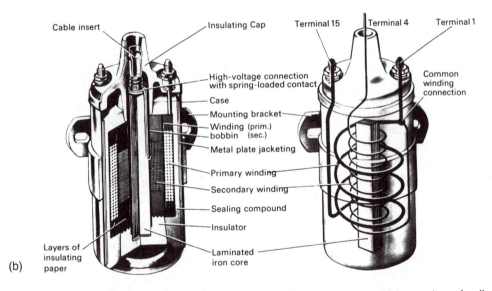

Cable insert

Insulating Cap

Terminal 15

Terminal 4

Terminal 1

High-voltage connection with spring-loaded contact

Common winding connection

Case

Mounting bracket

Winding (prim.) bobbin (sec.)

Metal plate jacketing

Primary winding

Secondary winding

Sealing compound

Insulator

Layers of insulating paper

Laminated iron core

(b)

Fig. 7-2. Basic ignition coil construction: (a) circuit arrangement, (b) inner view of coil.

can be hermetically sealed by a coil cap after having been filled with oil inside the casing, or by sealing compounds and insulators which bind the ignition coil into a compact vibration-proof assembly. The coil cap is constructed to contain both the primary and secondary high voltage terminals.

Note in Fig. 7-2 (a) that the primary and secondary windings are connected. In order for the coil to effectively increase the 12 volts from the battery circuit to fire the spark plug, we must introduce a switch that can automatically be turned on and off. This is achieved through the contact breaker points in the conventional ignition system. In addition, a condensor or capacitor is used to prevent burning of the contact breaker points when they separate. This function is discussed in more detail later. A typical ignition/coil circuit is shown in Figs. 7-1 and 7-3.

Electrical flow in Figs. 7-1 and 7-3 is as follows. When the ignition switch is closed, battery power will flow to and through the coil primary winding from the positive or negative battery terminal. Current will flow and complete the circuit only if the contact breaker points are in contact (closed circuit).

The opening and closing of the contact breaker points in the distributor is automatically achieved during cranking, or when the engine is running, by the cam of the distributor shaft which is engine-driven. The flow of current through the primary winding of the coil does not occur immediately due to the basic circuit resistance and the battery voltage. Peak current value in the coil is attained within 10 to 15 milliseconds and reaches an average value of about 4 amperes.

Within the primary coil winding, a magnetic field develops as the current flows and builds to its peak value. This magnetic field induces a voltage which opposes that of the battery, therefore during the build-up of this magnetic field the primary current is less than its full value. This induced opposition voltage disappears, however, when the full magnetic field has been generated. Full battery voltage and peak

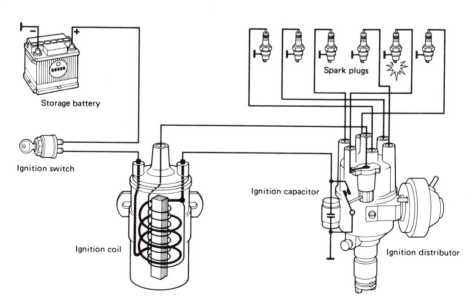

Fig. 7-3. Typical flow in the ignition coil circuit. (Courtesy of Robert Bosch Corp.)

coil current is then reached and maintained as long as the contact breaker points are closed.

The ignition coil action relies on the storage of electromagnetic energy and the process of inductive kickback or what is sometimes called counter-electromotive force (emf). When the contact points are closed, the coil stores electrical energy in the form of a magnetic field as mentioned. If we now open the distributor contact breaker points, this stored energy due to current flow will decrease very rapidly in the primary winding of the coil, and a high voltage is induced in the coil's secondary winding due to the stored electromagnetic energy being returned to the circuit. This inductive kickback voltage or counter emf causes the previously existing magnetic field to instantly collapse which induces a voltage in the primary winding and the secondary winding.

The voltage produced within the primary winding because of this self-induction process will approach 250 volts in the conventional coil. This voltage will be transformed or stepped-up in direct relation to the ratio of the turns of copper wire between the primary and secondary windings. The average ratio is usually a mean figure of 100, which will boost this 250 volts in the primary winding to approximately 25,000 volts at the secondary winding. This high tension voltage is carried from the center of the coil to the distributor where it is distributed in firing order sequence to the spark plug and cylinder which will initiate ignition.

The high tension voltage sent to the distributor flows into the center of the cap, through a carbon brush which is in contact with the spinning rotor contact, across the rotor gap to the pickup probe connected to the spark plug wire, and on up to the spark plug itself where it flows across the plug electrode and back to the secondary winding through ground, the battery and switch.

The purpose of the ignition condensor or capacitor at the distributor is to prevent burning of the contact breaker points as they separate, due to the induced voltage within the coil. If a spark was allowed to occur at the separating points, three undesirable characteristics would result.

1. Consumption of energy by the contact point spark at the sacrifice of ignition energy

2. Short contact point life through burning and pitting

3. High transfer resistance at the points resulting from high temperature, and a poorly conducting charred coating on the points, all of which reduce the secondary available voltage and the ignition power.

Figure 7-4 shows the basic construction of a typical ignition distributor capacitor. The capacitor consists of a roll of two layers of thin metal or aluminum foil and several layers of special insulating capacitor paper. Contacts are attached to the two metal strips, and the entire roll is impregnated in an oily or wax type material to insulate it, then the roll is inserted into a metal shell or can and sealed. As the contact points separate, the capacitor absorbs the initial surge of inductive current and therefore forms a shunt path in parallel with the opening contact points.

If a capacitor were not connected in this fashion, a large spark would jump between the contacts and the stored energy in the coil would in fact be wasted. The capacitor therefore minimizes the spark discharge, because it is uncharged at the split instant that the points separate. The

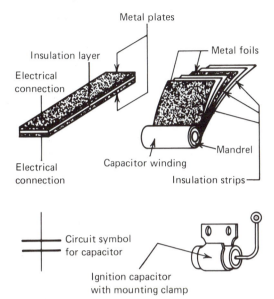

Metal plates

Insulation layer

Electrical connection

Metal foils

Electrical connection

Capacitor winding

Mandrel

Insulation strips

Circuit symbol for capacitor

Ignition capacitor with mounting clamp

Fig. 7-4. Typical ignition capacitor. (Courtesy of Robert Bosch Corp.)

capacitor will charge to the same value as that of the primary coil winding, namely about 250 volts, although this can reach as much as 300 to 400 volts in some systems. There is a small time delay in the capacitor reaching its full state of charge which is about 0.1 milliseconds. Therefore, by the time that it has been charged, the contact points have been forced so far apart that a spark cannot now discharge across the points.

Therefore, the energy that would otherwise be wasted in a spark discharge proceeds to charge the capacitor instead.

The remainder of the stored magnetic-field energy in the coil is transformed in a rising surge of secondary voltage as the capacitor is being charged, and this surge voltage is relayed to the spark plug. In essence then, the capacitor not only minimizes sparking and burning of the contact

points, but also returns energy to the secondary circuit, which results in an increased secondary output voltage.

Before the capacitor can discharge, the magnetic field in the coil has collapsed, and the high voltage surge in the secondary circuit has already triggered the ignition spark at the spark plug.

Although the capacitor is designed to protect the points from pitting in the conventional system, at sparking rates under 3000 per minute, contact point opening is considered slow and slight arcing will in fact occur at the separating distributor points because the induced primary voltage will rise more rapidly than the voltage required for discharge across the gap between the points, and this induced voltage develops a spark. Vehicles driven constantly in city traffic will, therefore, require more frequent changing of contact breaker points than those operating over long distances and highway driving cycles.

THE DISTRIBUTOR ASSEMBLY

The major function of the ignition distributor assembly, shown in Fig. 7-5, is to distribute the high tension spark generated in the coil to the correct cylinder in firing order sequence so that the engine will run smoothly. Within the conventional and some high energy ignition distributors is a built-in mechanical and vacuum advance mechanism to vary the ignition timing automatically as a result of engine throttle position and load characteristics.

The distributor operates in unison with the ignition coil, in that it makes and breaks the electrical circuit from the primary winding of the coil to ground return. It therefore controls the magnetic buildup time within the coil based on how quickly the contact points separate in the conventional distributor. In the high-energy or electronic type of distributor, the primary flow in the ignition coil is controlled by a rotating timer core which is discussed in Chapter 8. The condensor or capacitor is also contained within the distributor. Its function was already discussed in detail during our study of the coil action earlier.

Other ignition distributors now in use contain no mechanical or vacuum advance mechanisms. Such a unit is found on many General Motors products and is known as EST or Electronic Spark Timing. Because of the various types of distributors in use, we will look at and discuss the operation and maintenance of each of them. Each distributor is engine driven through a gear drive usually from the engine camshaft, and is timed to the engine upon initial installation.

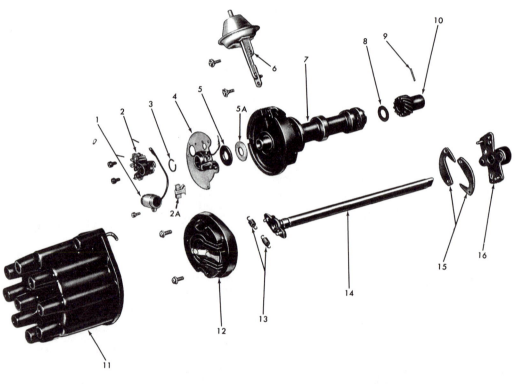

1.	Condenser	5.	Felt Washer	8.	Shim Washer	13.	Weight Springs
2.	Contact Point Assembly	5a.	Plastic Seal	9.	Drive Gear Pin	14.	Mainshaft
2a.	Cam Lubricator	6.	Vacuum Advance	10.	Drive Gear	15.	Advance Weights
3.	Retaining Ring		Unit	11.	Cap	16.	Cam Weight
4.	Breaker Plate	7.	Housing	12.	Rotor		Base Assembly

Fig. 7-5. Component parts of a conventional ignition distributor. (Courtesy of General Motors Corporation)

CONVENTIONAL CONTACT BREAKER POINT DISTRIBUTOR

Figure 7-5 shows the major component parts of the conventional type of distributor and their arrangement.

Operation of the conventional distributor shown in Fig. 7-5 is as follows. Gear 10 is attached to the driveshaft 14, therefore when gear 10 is driven (usually from the engine camshaft), the shaft will also rotate. On four-cycle engines, the distributor will rotate at half engine speed, while on two-cycle engines, the distributor rotates at engine speed.

At the upper end of shaft 14 is a cam known as a breaker cam because as it rotates, it allows the points to make and break contact. It achieves this by the cam

lobes coming into contact with a rubbing block on the moveable arm of the contact breaker points shown in Figs. 7-1 and 7-6.

The number of cam lobe projections is determined by the number of engine cylinders. For example, a 4-cylinder engine would have 4 cam lobes, a 6-cylinder engine has 6, etc. Each time that the contact points are opened, the current flow through the primary winding of the ignition coil is interrupted as explained under coil operation, and a spark is sent to a specific spark plug.

The contact breaker points are attached to a stationary breaker plate shown as item 4 in Fig. 7-5.

Immediately above the breaker plate, and attached to the distributor shaft, is a centrifugal advance mechanism that con-

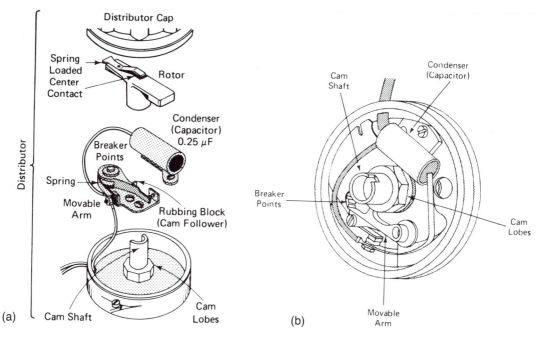

Fig. 7-6. (a) Disassembled view of upper components of the conventional ignition distributor. (b) Assembled view of upper components of the conventional ignition distributor.

tains a set of steel weights held together by light springs (item 15 in Fig. 7-5.)

Attached to the top of this centrifugal advance mechanism by two screws is a rotor that, as it turns with the driveshaft, will distribute the high tension spark received from the coil to the correct spark plug in proper firing order sequence. One example of the type of rotor found on most vee-type engines and its relation to the advance mechanism is shown in Fig. 7-7.

Take careful note that the rotor shown in Fig. 7-7 must be installed to the advance mechanism by aligning the round tip extension and the square tip extension as shown. Any attempt to install the rotor without these tip locators being in the proper position usually results in breakage of the rotor unit when the retaining screws are installed. Should you be successful in installing the retaining screws without the rotor breaking, then distributor cap damage normally follows. In addition, the engine to distributor timing will also be one half-turn out.

Other types of distributors employ a rotor that is a push fit onto the top of the distributor drive shaft, and which employs the centrifugal advance mechanism underneath the breaker plate rather than on the top end. Such a unit is shown in Fig. 7-8(a).

The outward movement of the centrifugal advance weights will increase as the engine speed increases, so that their action will advance the distributor cam assembly in relation to the shaft thereby providing an earlier spark to the spark plug. This action of advance will vary slightly between different types and styles of distributors; however, for all intents and purposes, its action is the same.

Figures 7-9 and 7-10 show the rolling contact and sliding contact type of centrifugal advance weight mechanisms.

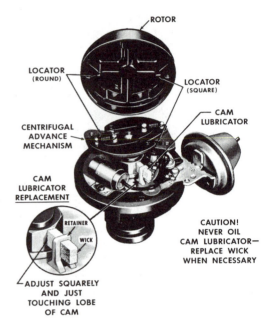

Fig. 7-7. Top view of conventional ignition distributor. (Courtesy of GMC)

The cam of the distributor is mounted to the shaft so that it can be moved or rotated ahead of the shaft as the engine is running. The weight force would force the cam to move in the direction of shaft rotation so that the contact breaker points would be opened earlier than normal, with the result that the spark would be delivered to the plug earlier resulting in an automatic advance to the ignition timing with an increase in engine speed.

The degree of centrifugal advance will not be the same for all engines, but is designed to obtain the maximum performance and efficiency from the engine throughout the speed range. With this advance mechanism, no advance will occur at idle, while full advance will occur at high engine speed. Centrifugal advance can range from 12 or 15 degrees to as high as 35 to 40 degrees at full engine speed.

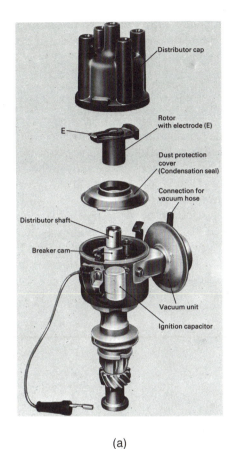

(a)

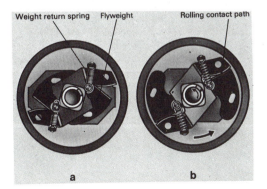

Fig. 7-9. Rolling contact type centrifugal advance mechanism: (a) distributor/engine stopped, (b) engine running.

Fig. 7-8. (a) Rotor location. (b) Sectional view of assembled conventional distributor. (Courtesy of Robert Bosch Corp.)

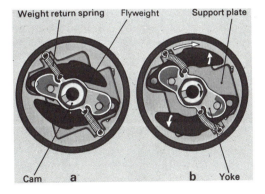

Fig. 7-10. Sliding contact type centrifugal advance mechanism: (a) engine stopped, (b) engine running.

Ignition advance is necessary so that at higher speeds, the increased fuel/air charge has ample time to burn to obtain full power from combustion.

For example, at an engine idle speed the spark at the plug may occur 4 degrees BTDC (before top dead center), at 1200 rpm the spark might be delivered to the plug at 10 degrees BTDC, while at 3000 rpm, the spark may be delivered to the plug at 28 degrees BTDC. In each case, however, the maximum power would be developed with the piston at the same position, which might be designed for 5 degrees ATDC (after top dead center).

In addition to the centrifugal advance mechanism, a vacuum advance mecha-nism is also employed which will provide additional advance to that provided by the former mechanism.

Vacuum Advance Mechanism

This mechanism is designed to advance the ignition timing under part-load opera-tion only. Figure 7-11(a) shows the basic arrangement of the vacuum advance mechanism.

The vacuum advance mechanism is de-signed to provide maximum advance at part throttle, dropping off as the throttle is opened and intake manifold depression or vacuum decreases.

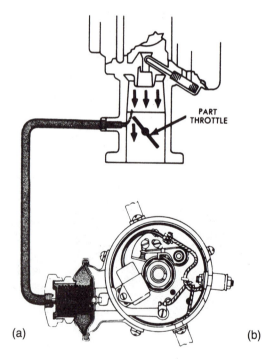

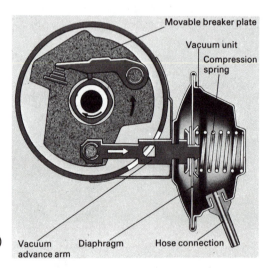

(a)

(b)

Fig. 7-11. (a) Connection between the vacuum advance unit and the engine carburetor or intake manifold (courtesy of Delco-Remy Div. of GMC). (b) Advance unit in the advanced position (courtesy of Robert Bosch Corp.)

Within the vacuum unit as shown in Fig. 7-11 (b) is a diaphragm and spring assembly along with a vacuum advance arm which is connected to the breaker plate of the distributor.

With the throttle butterfly valve in the venturi passage of the carburetor at its normal idle position, the tube between the vacuum unit and carburetor is subjected to atmospheric pressure; therefore, no vacuum exists in the connecting line. As the throttle valve is partially opened, the connecting tube is subjected to intake manifold vacuum which will draw air from the airtight vacuum unit. This action will pull the vacuum advance arm and rotate the breaker plate to an advanced position. This is achieved by rotating the breaker plate opposite the distributor shaft's rotation in order to allow the breaker cam to contact the rubbing block earlier and thereby open the points earlier.

The advance provided by both the vacuum and centrifugal advance mechanisms together contribute to the smooth operation and increased economy of the engine under varying throttle and load conditions. As long as some vacuum exists in the intake manifold, a combination vacuum and centrifugal advance will occur; however, at wide open throttle conditions, ignition advance is a result of centrifugal advance only.

GENERAL IGNITION SYSTEM SERVICE—CONVENTIONAL TYPE

The most common service procedure with the conventional type of contact breaker-point ignition is the regular replacement of the points and the condensor. The points will develop irregularities such as pitting after having been in service for a number of miles or hours if on stationary units. Point replacement is not a difficult task, and can be accomplished without the need for a lot of special service tools.

The removal of the points requires that you first of all remove the distributor cap. Two general types of distributor cap retainers are used, and these are shown in Fig. 7-12, with two spring clamps being used on one, and two spring loaded screws used on the other.

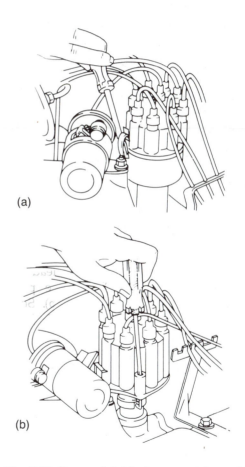

(a)

(b)

Fig. 7-12. Types of distributor cap retainers: (a) spring clamp type, (b) spring loaded screw type. (Courtesy of AC Delco Div. of GMC)

Once the distributor cap has been removed, it may or may not be necessary to remove the rotor. Some engines employ small rotors, while others use a large round rotor that is attached to the centrifugal advance weight plate by two retaining screws. It is usually easier to get at the points on this type by removing the screws and lifting the rotor off. Figure 7-7 shows that the large round rotor has one round and one square locating tang on its underside; therefore, ensure that when the rotor is replaced these tangs mate with their corresponding holes on the weight carrier.

CONTACT BREAKER POINT REMOVAL

The points are attached to a mounting plate which is firmly held in position to the distributor base plate by one or two small screws. To remove the points, simply loosen and remove the screws and lift the point set out of the distributor after removing the necessary wires.

Figure 7-13 shows a typical view and location of the contact point set attaching screw.

To remove the points, it is necessary to lift off the distributor primary lead and condensor wire lead from the point bracket as shown in Fig. 7-13 (b). Some vehicles may use a spring-loaded clip to hold these wires in place, while others may use a small retaining nut.

With the points removed, clean the distributor breaker plate with a lint-free rag.

BREAKER POINT INSTALLATION

When installing the points, carefully wipe any protective film from their contact surfaces before actually placing them into position. Most contact point sets have a

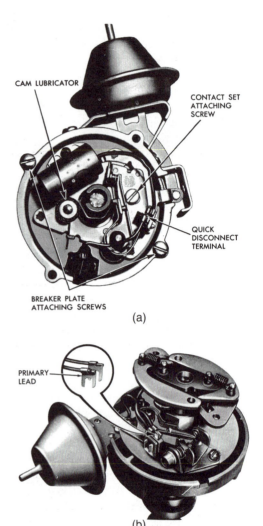

Fig. 7-13. (a) Contact breaker point plate and attaching screws. (b) Distributor lead arrangement. (Courtesy of GMC)

small pin or peg on the underside of the mounting bracket plate. This must be aligned with a matching hole in the distributor breaker plate in order for the point set to sit properly. With the contact point set in position, install the locating screw or screws, and snug them up lightly.

In order to adjust the point gap, the breaker rubbing block must be under the distributor shaft cam lobe as shown in Fig. 7-14. This is necessary because, as the engine rotates, the cam lobes of the shaft will lift the rubbing block, thereby opening the points to cause a break in the primary ignition coil circuit. This will induce a high tension voltage buildup in the coil secondary winding.

Prior to attempting to adjust the point gap, connect the primary distributor lead and condensor leads that were removed earlier and shown in Fig. 7-13 (b). It is also extremely important that the stationary and moveable contact points are actually in alignment, and perfectly square to one another. An example of what is meant by this can be seen in Fig. 7-15. Note that both points must be level with one another when viewed from the side; they also must be square to one another.

Failure to align the contact breaker points properly will result in very short point life and poor engine performance. Should it be necessary to align the points, a small tool with a tee handle on it is available from most tool suppliers for this purpose. Figure 7-16 shows this tool and its use.

When you are satisfied that the points are in alignment, proceed to check the point gap with a feeler gauge. Some tune-up kits supply a small plastic gauge for this purpose. Ensure that the rubbing block is in alignment with the distributor cam as shown in Fig. 7-14. Refer to the manufacturer's service information for the correct point gap, or the tune-up kit may have this stamped on the box or packet.

Should the point gap require adjustment, insert a screwdriver as shown in Fig. 7-17, and move the breaker point plate in the required direction to increase or de-

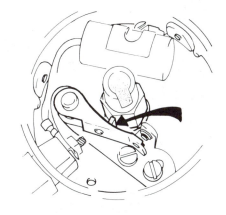

Fig. 7-14. Location of contact breaker point assembly rubbing block to distributor cam to properly adjust point gap.

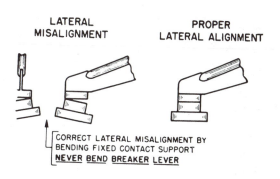

Fig. 7-15. Correct versus incorrect point alignment. (Courtesy of GMC)

crease the point gap, then retighten the locating screws. Some distributors employ a small eccentric adjusting screw that can simply be rotated to adjust the point gap. The locating screw is then tightened to lock the adjustment.

If used points are to be installed back into the distributor after cleaning, the same basic procedure can be followed. Generally, new points are adjusted to a wider gap than used points, because as

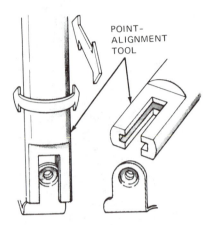

Fig. 7-16. Point alignment tool. (Courtesy of Ford Motor Company)

accumulations build up on the contact surfaces of the points, the gap is reduced. On used points (because of the irregular surfaces that exist even after cleaning) a slightly smaller gap is set. In either case, once the points have been adjusted, a dwell meter should be used to accurately set the points. However, prior to doing this, it is advisable to check the spring tension of the points as shown in Fig. 7-18 with the use of a special spring scale and wire hook gauge. This procedure is only necessary on those contact point sets that come in two individual pieces. On the preassembled factory sets, this tension has already been set. Insufficient spring tension can lead to point bounce, while too much tension can lead to rapid point wear.

CONDENSOR REPLACEMENT

When the contact breaker points are replaced, the condensor should also be replaced, since a faulty condensor can lead to burning of the points. The condensor can be located inside the distributor

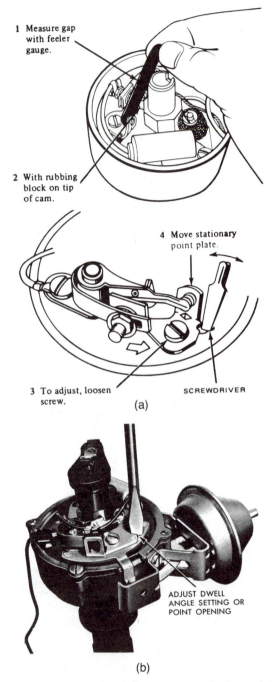

Fig. 7-17. (a) Point gap check. (b) Setting point opening. (Courtesy of GMC).

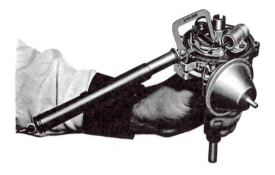

Fig. 7-18. Checking contact breaker point spring tension. (Courtesy of GMC)

alongside the points, or in some cases it is placed externally on the distributor housing. In either case, it is mounted on a small bracket and held in position with one small screw with one lead (wire) attached to the lead of the coil primary circuit such as is shown in Fig. 7-8. Many newer condensors are actually mounted to the point set, so that both the points and condensor are actually one kit sometimes referred to as a uniset. If however, the condensor is mounted on a separate bracket, ensure that it is in fact the correct one for the system. This can be checked by obtaining the condensor part number and looking at the appropriate service literature or checking with the local partsman.

Installation of the wrong condensor can affect point life considerably. Continual short point life is usually an indication of the wrong condensor.

Dwell Check

Dwell is discussed under (HEI) High Energy Ignition systems in this book. Basically dwell is the period of time during which the contact breaker points actually remain closed, or to be specific, it is the number of degrees of distributor cam rota-

tion that the contact breaker points remain closed. Since many types of different dwell meters are available, we will not discuss them in detail here.

When the dwell meter is properly connected to the engine ignition system, it registers in degrees the duration of contact point closure or dwell. This is a much more accurate way of setting the contact point gap than with a feeler gauge. Many engines today have a sliding gate type window in the distributor which allows the contact point gap and therefore the dwell to be set while the engine is running. A small Allen (hex) wrench is used to alter the point gap. Figure 7-19 shows a typical example of this arrangement.

If a dwell meter is unavailable, the adjustment shown in Fig. 7-19 for GMC vehicles should be turned clockwise until the engine starts to misfire. Then turn the adjustment screw back out one half turn (CCW) which will set the dwell within the acceptable limits. Some distributors use either a slotted-hole and locking screw arrangement for dwell adjustment which is located under the distributor cap at the point bracket.

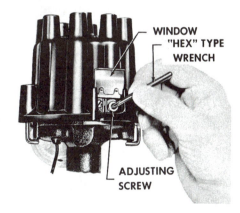

Fig. 7-19. Adjusting distributor dwell angle. (Courtesy of GMC)

The dwell reading is normally taken with the engine at an idle rpm, although some manufacturers recommend a reading at a higher rpm also. The dwell meter is connected across the contact breaker points in a conventional ignition system with the other meter lead to ground. In this way, as the points open and close, the circuit to the meter is subjected to a make/break energy pulse which is analyzed in the meter and this signal is reflected on the scale as degrees of dwell or point closure.

It is extremely important that the point dwell be set correctly. If for example the dwell called for was 30° and it was set/adjusted to 35°, the net result is that the battery current/voltage flow through the closed points becomes longer than normal with possible point damage.

On the other hand, if the point dwell was set at a lower level than the recommended 30° stated in this example, then this lower dwell (points remain closed for a shorter duration of distributor cam rotation in degrees) can create a situation whereby the ignition coil will not be able to build to its peak voltage at higher speeds due to short saturation time, leading to a lower firing voltage at the spark plugs and possible engine misfire.

Electronic and high energy ignition systems require specially adapted dwell meters.

DISTRIBUTOR CAP INSPECTION

The distributor cap must be maintained in a clean condition, must be free of hairline cracks, must have clean spark plug and coil wire towers, and must have burn-free and non-eroded internal insert terminals in order to perform properly.

Distributor caps are held onto the top of the distributor assembly by spring clips that are attached to the distributor housing, or by screws. (See Fig. 7-12.) Some of these screws are held permanently into the distributor cap and are also spring loaded; therefore, they must be pushed down and turned into position, or pushed down and rotated one-half turn until they locate on a recess cast into the distributor body or housing.

Distributor caps are located on the top of the distributor by a locating tab formed or molded on the cap which mates with a like tab recess on the actual distributor body. This ensures that the cap will not move and also that it is placed into the correct position relative to the distributor itself for proper timing distribution of the high tension spark from the coil to the rotor cap, and then out through the side inserts or contacts to the individual spark plugs. Contained within the center of the distributor cap is a carbon insert or brush, as some trade people call it, that functions to transfer the high tension spark from the coil wire onto the spinning rotor arm assembly.

This carbon insert or brush can become worn, and is actually replaceable in some distributor caps by loosening off a retaining screw in the center tower of the cap. Others employ a spring loaded replaceable carbon brush that is inserted into the center tower hole from the inside of the cap.

Should this center insert break, chip off, or wear out, then irregular distribution of the spark to the plugs will result.

Between the spark plug pickup towers and the cap are side ribs or inserts that are individually separated from other spark plug tower electrodes inside the cap by being equally placed around the cap to prevent flashover caused by dirt or other debris.

The inside and outside of the cap should always be kept dry and free of dirt to prevent tracing or flashover problems.

Carbon from center electrode or brush wear should be removed. Burned or eroded spark plug pickup terminals inside the cap should be cleaned up or replaced, or a new cap fitted. Cracks or broken spark plug towers on the distributor cap are reasons for replacing the cap.

Although the distributor rotor should be checked individually, it should be considered in relation to the cap since the center of some rotors have a spring loaded contact arm that comes in contact with the center electrode. Check this for signs of burning, pitting, or damage. Also check the end of the rotor arm for erosion or wear. Clean it up if corroded. Check the slot for wear where it fits over the distributor shaft or distributor weights on some V8 engines.

Figure 7-20 shows the typical checks and services necessary on the distributor cap.

HIGH TENSION POLARITY CHECK

In some instances, especially when servicing an ignition system, it is possible to inadvertently connect the wrong wires to the ignition circuit. This does not happen often, but on vehicles with a lot of miles on them or that operate in extremely dusty or dirty environments, the primary markings often cannot be clearly seen. Or, if the system has been rewired or retrofitted, the markings may not be according to standard accepted color coding. If this has occurred, a much higher voltage is required to fire the spark plug.

A commonly used and relatively simple way to check this is to check the high tension discharge through a piece of carbon, e.g., by the use of a simple lead-pencil.

Figure 7-21 shows the arrangement for this polarity check. Due to the fact that most ignition systems today employ insulated rubber/neoprene type boots over the ends of the spark plug wires, some form of jumper must be used from the plug wire lead to the lead pencil. A simple jumper can be made from a paper clip inserted up into the plug lead. (Make sure that you do not force the paper clip between the lead and wire or puncture the insulation on the spark plug wire in any way.)

Support the spark plug lead as shown in Fig. 7-21 so that it is about ⅛ inch (3 mm) away from the lead of the pencil. This can be done through the use of a pair of insulated spark plug wire pliers such as shown in Fig. 7-21.

With the pencil also held ⅛ inch (3 mm) from the spark plug terminal, start and run the engine. The polarity is correct if the bright arc appears on the spark plug side of the lead pencil. If the bright arc is on the other side (towards the wire and paper clip), then the primary wires of the ignition system are reversed. Gloves can be worn, or the pencil also held with insulated pliers in order to avoid a shock.

DISTRIBUTOR TEST MACHINES

When a distributor is suspected of being faulty, prior to disassembling it for inspection and possible rebuilding, it should be mounted in a test machine as shown in Fig. 7-22, and the distributor speed and rate of centrifugal advance and vacuum advance checked. In addition, distributor shaft concentricity can be checked to establish if the support bearings are worn, or if the shaft is possibly bent. Most of these testers also have built-in dwell meters.

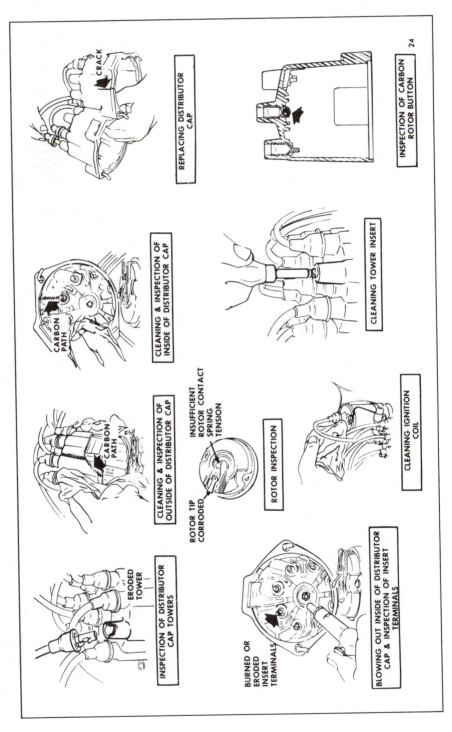

Fig. 7-20. Distributor cap checks and tests. (Courtesy of GMC)

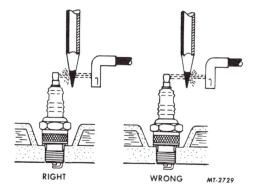

Fig. 7-21. Method of checking for correct ignition polarity. (Courtesy of International Harvester)

RIGHT   WRONG   MT-2729

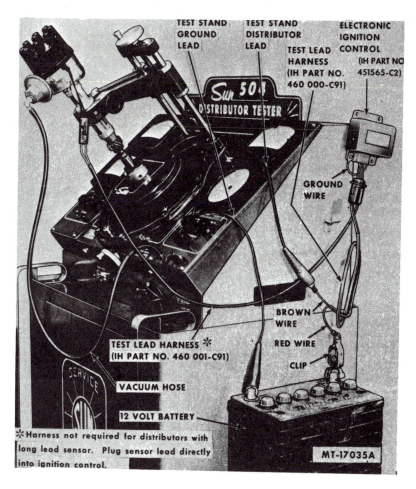

Fig. 7-22. Typical ignition distributor tester. (Courtesy of Sun Electric Corporation)

DISTRIBUTOR TEST SPECIFICATIONS

Each particular type, model and year of distributor has specific test specifications particular to the vehicle to which it is fitted. These specs can be found in the respective engine manufacturer's or vehicle service manual. Distributor Test Stand equipment also provides, in many instances, a master book listing all of these required test specs. As an example of the types of specs that you would require to check out the distributor, Table 7-1 shows one such set of specs for International-Harvester vehicles, employing a conventional contact breaker point distributor. Table 7-2 shows typical specs for a breakerless ignition distributor.

CONVENTIONAL IGNITION TROUBLESHOOTING

Typical causes of problems in the conventional contact breaker point ignition system are listed in Table 7-3.

DISTRIBUTOR TEST SPECIFICATIONS (For Use With Distributor Test Stand)			
Engine Model	V-345 Propane	V-266, V-304, V-345, V-392 Low Compression	
Distributor: Part No. (Manufacturer's No.)	484795C91 (IDN-4102C)	484799C91 (IDN-4102E)	487830C91 (IDN-4102K) 487877C91 (IDN-4103G)
Point Gap: mm (in)	0.35 - 0.45 (.014 - .018)		
Dwell, Degrees	28 - 32		
Contact Point Pressure (oz)	17 - 22		
Condenser Capacity, Mfd.	.25 - .28		
Vacuum Advance: Vacuum Req'd to Start Advance cm of Hg. (In. of Hg.)	13 - 18 (5 - 7)	13 - 19 (5 - 7.5)	13 - 18 (5 - 7)
Advance Check Points: Vacuum, cm of Hg. (In. of Hg.) Degrees	15 (6) 0 - 1.4	18 (7) 0 - 3	20 (8) 2.8 - 8
Vacuum Degrees	23 (9) 3 - 5.8	23 (9) 2.2 - 6.7	24 (9.5) 6 - 8
Vacuum Degrees	38 (15) 6 - 8	38 (15) 6 - 8	48 (19) 6 - 8
Mechanical Advance: Distributor RPM to Start Advance	250 - 375	250 - 350	325 - 475
Advance Check Points: Distributor RPM Degrees	400 0 - 2	300 0 - 1	--- ---
Distributor RPM Degrees	--- ---	--- ---	700 7.1 - 9.1
Distributor RPM Degrees	700 4 - 6	650 5.7 - 7.7	1000 9.1 - 11.1
Distributor RPM Degrees	--- ---	--- ---	1800 14.5 - 16.5
Distributor RPM Degrees	2000 10.5 - 12.5	2000 12.5 - 14.5	--- ---
Total Advance, Degrees Mechanical and Vacuum	16.5 - 20.5	18.5 - 22.5	20.5 - 24.5
Distributor Shaft End Play, mm (in)	0.89 - 1.02 (.035 - .040)		
Distributor Shaft Side Play New, mm (in) Maximum Permissible, mm (in)	0.05 - 0.1 (.002 - .004) 0.15 (.006)		
Distributor Rotation (As Viewed From Top)	Right Hand (Clockwise)		

Table 7-2. Breakerless Ignition Distributor Sample Test Specifications

Engine Model	MV-404	MV-446	V-537
Distributor: Part No. (Manufacturer's No.)	484790C91 (IDN4003)	484792C91 (IDN-4003A)	484794C91 (IDN4006)
Air Gap, mm (in.) Trigger Wheel-to-Sensor (1)	0.2 (.008)		
Dwell, Degrees (2)	26-32		
Vacuum Advance:			
Vacuum Req'd to Start Advance KPa (In. of Hg.)	16.9-23.6 (50-70)	33.8-40.5 (10.0-12.0)	-----
Advance Check Points: Vacuum, KPa (In. of Hg.) Degrees	27.0 (8) 1.5-4.0	43.9 (13) 1.5-4.0	----- -----
Vacuum Degrees	37.1 (12) 2.0-4.0	50.7 (15) 2.0-4.0	----- -----
Mechanical Advance:			
Distributor RPM to Start Advance	300-500	300-500	275-475
Advance Check Points: Distributor RPM Degrees	600 1.0-3.0	600 1.0-3.0	500 0.2-2.5
Distributor RPM Degrees	1000 5.3-7.3	1000 5.3-7.3	800 3.7-5.7
Distributor RPM Degrees	1450 10.0-12.0	1450 10.0-12.0	1000 5.2-7.2
Distributor RPM Degrees	1800 10.8-12.8	1800 10.8-12.8	1400 6.4-8.4
Distributor RPM Degrees			1700 6.9-8.9
Total Advance, Degrees Mechanical and Vacuum	12.8-16.8	12.8-16.8	6.9-8.9 (Mech. Only)
Distributor Shaft End Play, mm (in.)	0.10-0.46 (.004-.018)		0.05-0.25 (.002-.010)
Distributor Shaft Side Play (3) New, mm (in.) Maximum Permissible, mm (in.)	0.05-0.1 (.002-.004) 0.15 (.006)		0.05-0.1 (.002-.004) .15 (.006)
Distributor Rotation (As Viewed From Top)	Left Hand (Counterclockwise)		Right Hand (Clockwise)

(1) Clearance between sensor and end of trigger wheel tooth.

(2) At 300 distributor RPM (with 12-13 volts primary input).

(3) With force of 1/2 pound applied as side load to top of shaft.

Courtesy of International Harvester

Table 7-3. Ignition Troubleshooting (Conventional System).

CONDITION	POSSIBLE CAUSE	REMEDY
Engine fails to start.	No primary voltage to coil.	Check battery, ignition switch, primary feed and ground circuits.
	Moisture in distributor cap or high tension cable boots.	Clean and dry parts. Correct cause for entry of moisture.
	Contact point gap incorrect.	Inspect points. Adjust gap.
	Burned or worn contact points.	Replace point set.
	Broken or open rotor.	Replace rotor.
	Faulty condenser.	Replace condenser.
	Faulty distributor cap.	Replace cap.

CONDITION	POSSIBLE CAUSE	REMEDY
	Coil high tension cable not sealed in coil tower or on distributor cap.	Check cable installation.
	Faulty high tension cables.	Replace cables.
	Open or shorted coil.	Replace coil.
Engine backfires but fails to start.	Incorrect ignition timing.	Check timing. Adjust as needed.
	Moisture in distributor cap.	Dry cap and rotor.
	Distributor cap faulty or carbon tracked.	Replace cap.
	Spark plug cables connected incorrectly.	Check cables for correct position.
Engine does not operate smoothly or engine misfires at high speed.	Incorrect ignition timing.	Check timing. Adjust as needed.
	Spark plugs fouled.	Clean and regap plugs.
	Spark plug electrodes worn (gap too wide).	Regap or replace plugs.
	Faulty distributor cap.	Replace cap.
	Spark plugs cables faulty.	Check cables, replace if needed.
	Contact point gap incorrect.	Inspect points. Adjust gap.
	Burned or worn contact points.	Replace point set.
	Improper breaker spring tension.	Check and adjust spring tension.
	Worn distributor shaft bushings, bent distributor shaft, worn distributor cam, or faulty spark advance system.	Rebuild or replace distributor.
Excessive fuel consumption.	See causes listed under "Engine does not operate smoothly."	
Erratic timing advance.	Vacuum leaks in vacuum advance system.	Check vacuum hoses. Replace as needed.
	Faulty vacuum advance diaphragm assembly.	Check operation of advance diaphragm. Replace if needed.
	Sticking or worn advance plate.	Replace breaker plate assembly.
	Misadjusted, damaged or weak mechanical advance springs.	Readjust spring tension. Replace distributor shaft assembly.
	Mechanical advance flyweight bushings worn.	Replace distributor shaft assembly.
	Distributor cam assembly binding or excessively loose on distributor shaft.	Free-up and lubricate cam assembly. Replace distributor shaft assembly, if needed.

Courtesy of International Harvester

PREVIEW QUESTIONS

Q1 What is the purpose of an ignition coil?

Q2 What is the function of the condensor in the distributor?

Q3 What is the function of the contact breaker points in the distributor?

Q4 How is the high tension voltage developed in the ignition coil distributed to the spark plug?

Q5 How is the ignition timing altered in the distributor as a function of engine speed/load?

Q6 How is the distributor rotor attached to the drive shaft?

Q7 What does the term ignition point dwell mean?

Q8 Can ignition points be set to any gap in any position?

Q9 What problem will occur if the wrong condensor is fitted to the distributor?

Q10 Can the dwell be adjusted with the engine running?

Q11 How would you establish proper polarity in the ignition system?

ANSWERS

A1 The purpose of the ignition coil is actually to act as a step-up transformer. It does this through two sets of windings, namely the primary and secondary. The primary steps up the battery voltage to about 250 volts, while the secondary winding which has many more windings boosts this voltage up to an average of around 25,000 volts in order to fire the spark plug.

A2 The condensor or capacitor in the distributor is used to minimize arcing at the contact-breaker points as they separate.

A3 The contact breaker points open and close the primary coil circuit from the battery to ground; they complete the circuit when they are closed, and open the circuit when they separate.

A4 The high tension voltage leaves the ignition coil secondary winding and is carried through high tension cable to the distributor cap at its center. A brush or carbon contact directs the voltage onto the top of the spinning distributor rotor which sends it out to the respective distributor cap contact in firing order sequence. It then passes through the spark plug lead to the correct spark plug.

A5 Ignition timing is altered automatically in the distributor by both a vacuum and mechanical advance mechanism; one is related to intake manifold depression (vacuum) as a function of throttle position, while the mechanical system employs a set of spinning weights and centrifugal force to move the contact point breaker plate.

A6 The distributor rotor can be placed onto the drive shaft by a slot in the rotor or shaft to align it properly; with this type the rotor is a push-fit to the shaft. Other types employ a rotor that can only be installed in one way due to a square and round hole arrangement that mates with the weight carrier assembly; it is then secured by two small screws.

A7 Ignition point dwell refers to the period of time during which the contact breaker points remain closed.

A8 No; points are gapped for a particular ignition system and have to be adjusted when the moveable point rubbing block is on the nose or high point of the distributor cam so that they are in the normally open position.

A9 Fitting the wrong condensor can result in short point life.

A10 The dwell can be adjusted with the engine running on those engines that employ access to the point adjustment screw. Other engines must be stopped for adjustment, then rechecked.

A11 Proper ignition polarity can be established by the use of a lead pencil at the spark plug lead. The polarity is correct if the bright arc appears on the spark plug side of the lead pencil with the engine running; if the bright arc is on the other side, then the primary ignition system wires are reversed.

Chapter

8

Semiconductor and Electronic Ignition Systems

One of the major drawbacks of a conventional contact breaker point ignition system is that it is limited to about 18,000 sparks per minute and a peak voltage of between 15,000 to 20,000 volts. The peak voltage is limited by both the electrical and mechanical on/off switching capabilities produced as the points make and break.

Advances in engine design, particularly with emphasis on both fuel economy and particulate exhaust emissions, created a need for wider gap spark plugs and, therefore, an ignition system capable of producing a higher spark voltage to fire these plugs. In addition, finer control of ignition quality necessitated the design of a system that could operate without the bounce effect associated with breaker point ignition systems.

Several ignition systems have been developed and many have been designed that are available as aftermarket products which can be installed on a used vehicle. However, most major vehicle manufacturers now use some form of electronic ignition system on their factory-produced vehicles.

The three major types of ignition systems that evolved from the straight conventional breaker point/coil ignition system are as follows:

- Transistorized Coil Ignition System
- Capacitor Discharge Ignition System
- High Energy Ignition System

Of the three types listed above, the high energy ignition system is now the most widely used in passenger cars. Current production factory vehicles employ breakerless ignition systems with electronic spark timing employed on many, in which the distributor assembly has no vacuum or centrifugal advance systems, but is controlled by a solid state on-board computer linked to various engine sensors.

TRANSISTORIZED COIL IGNITION SYSTEM

The main advantage of this system is that primary currents of about 9 amps can be obtained versus the usual average of 4 amps in the conventional ignition system. With this system, electronic switching of the coil primary current through the use of transistors is used rather than the opening of the conventional system's contact breaker points. Figure 8-1 shows the basic circuit used with a breaker triggered inductive semiconductor ignition system.

In Figure 8-1 (a), the primary coil current is controlled by the transistor (T). A breaker switch (S) controls this electronic switching on/off to the coil primary winding. With switch (S) closed, a current of about 8 amperes average can flow through the emitter and collector of the transistor to the coil primary winding. Current flowing through the breaker switch, however, amounts to only 1 amp.

As the ignition point (spark plug firing) is approached, the breaker switch will stop the current flow to the coil primary winding through the transistor (T) which blocks the current flow, because the path from the emitter to the collector has become an insulator. For a complete description of transistor operation, refer to Chapter 2 on transistors in this book. Resistor R1 protects the transistor against voltage overload while in the cutoff mode, and against over-current while in the conducting mode. Resistor R2 limits the transistor emitter-base current, while resistor R3 supplies a positive bias voltage with respect to the collector to the base of the transistor at the instant of switch-off so that the transistor can switch more rapidly.

Figure 8-1 (b) shows the complete circuit diagram for a typical breaker triggered semiconductor ignition system. The series resistor R1 is actually composed of the primary coil series resistor R11 and the resistor R12 which can be shorted out when the engine is being started. Diode (D) protects the transistor emitter-base path from overloads, whereas the zener diode (ZD) and capacitor C2 protects the emitter-collector path of the transistor. The condenser C1 protects the complete igni-

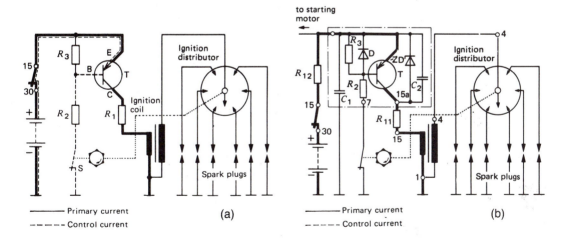

Primary current
Control current
(a)

Primary current
Control current
(b)

Fig. 8-1. Breaker triggered inductive semiconductor ignition system: (a) basic circuit diagram of breaker triggered transistorized coil ignition; (b) complete circuit diagram of breaker triggered transistorized coil ignition. (Courtesy of Robert Bosch Corp.)

tion system electronics from overvoltage in the power supply system.

This system employs the conventional contact breaker points; however, point sparking does not occur, therefore the capacitor is not required as with a conventional circuit. Bounce effect of the points still occurs in this system, but to a smaller degree than in the straight conventional system, therefore it is possible to obtain a frequency of about 21,000 switching operations per minute with this system versus the usual 18,000 per minute with the conventional system. Major advantages of this system over the conventional model are (1) the higher secondary voltage available across the entire engine speed range which results in a lower rate of ignition faults and (2) the ability to supply a slightly higher sparking rate.

CAPACITOR DISCHARGE IGNITION SYSTEM

This system is used on a large variety of internal combustion engines. Examples include smaller gasoline engines such as used in power chain saws, lawn mowers, outboard motors, snowmobiles and motorcycles.

Figure 8-2 illustrates the layout of the circuit used with the (CD) capacitor discharge system.

The storage capacitor in Fig. 8-2 (a) is charged to approximately 400 volts from the electronic charging circuit which is connected to the 12 volt battery power. This higher voltage is obtained by means of voltage pulses which are transformed into DC voltage within the electronic charging circuit.

The energy within the storage capacitor is transferred to the ignition circuit via a solid-state switch device known as a thy-

ristor which conducts currents of up to 100 amperes. The thyristor blocks flow to the ignition circuit until the ignition point is reached, at which time the thyristor receives a current pulse through the control electrode to initiate charging of the capacitor. The thyristor blocks the circuit again when the storage capacitor is almost completely discharged.

The stored energy (400 volts) discharged from the storage capacitor is discharged to the ignition coil where a secondary voltage of as high as 40,000 volts can be sent to the spark plug. Actual triggering of the CD ignition system can be by means of a mechanical switch or a semiconductor device.

The rectifier arrangement of a CD system usually employs a bridge configuration consisting of four diodes as shown in Fig. 8-3, which is known as a full-wave rectifier arrangement.

The diodes in Fig. 8-3 conduct alternately in pairs with CR1 and CR3 operating together while CR2 and CR4 are non-conducting during one half-cycle, while on the other half-cycle, CR2 and CR4 will conduct while CR1 and CR3 are in a non-conducting state.

The actual output from the rectifier shown in Fig. 8-3 is switched as shown in Fig. 8-4.

In Fig. 8-4, an electronic switch or semiconductor remains open until it is time to deliver the spark to the plug, at which time the switch is closed by a trigger pulse. The electric charge stored in the capacitor (C) will then discharge through the primary winding of the ignition coil. As soon as the capacitor is discharged, the electronic switch is automatically opened again by action of the kickback voltage or reverse flow from the coil.

In a CD ignition system that employs

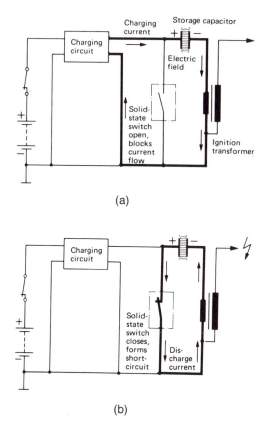

(a)

(b)

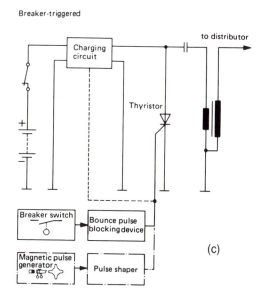

(c)

Fig. 8-2. (a) Energy storage through charging the capacitor, charging current = primary current. (b) Transferring the stored energy to the ignition circuit by discharging the capacitor. (c) Basic circuit diagram of capacitor discharge ignition system-breaker triggered. (Courtesy of Robert Bosch Corp.)

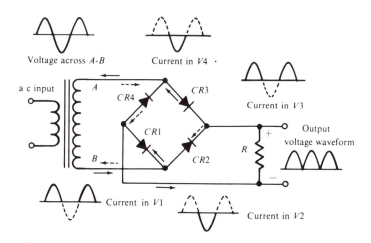

Fig. 8-3. Bridge rectifier.

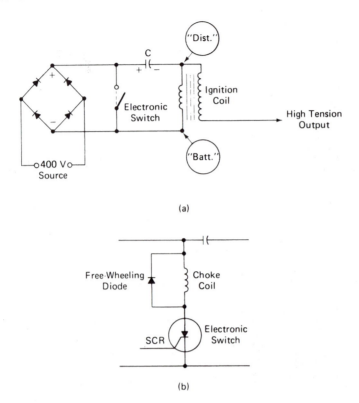

(a)

(b)

Fig. 8-4. (a) CD ignition system switching arrangement. (b) Choke coil and free-wheeling diode function to prevent SCR damage owing to kickback voltage.

breaker-points, bouncing of the points can cause misfiring of the engine. If this condition exists, spurious pulses can be generated which are sufficient to trigger the thyristor. To prevent this from occurring, a bounce pulse blocking device as shown in Fig. 8-2 (c) is used in the CD system. On those CD systems that do not use contact breaker points in the system, but employ a magnetic pulse generator similar to that found in high energy ignition systems discussed herein, a continuous sparking rate of 40,000 sparks per minute can be maintained without difficulty, compared to the normal of 18,000 per minute with a conventional ignition system. The CD sys-

tem discussed is a high-voltage design; however, a low-voltage type is used on aircraft engines wherein the storage capacitor is directly charged from a rectifier to around 3000 volts. The voltage is then fed directly to the distributor to a special low-voltage surface gap spark plug.

HIGH ENERGY AND BREAKERLESS IGNITION SYSTEMS

High energy and breakerless ignition systems are basically one and the same. No contact breaker points are employed, but instead a magnetic pulse generator is used to establish the primary coil circuit.

The coil itself can be located under the top half of the distributor cap.

In addition, some HEI (high energy ignition) systems employ the conventional vacuum and centrifugal advance mechanisms. Others do not have these features, but are controlled by an electronic computer on the vehicle that is connected to a variety of engine mounted sensor units.

Figure 8-5 shows a typical HEI type distributor assembly.

HEI DISTRIBUTOR

The HEI distributor is an extremely compact unit in that it combines all of the necessary ignition components in one single assembly. External electrical connections are generally the ignition switch feed wire, a tachometer pickup, and a number of spark plug leads equal to the number of engine cylinders. When the ignition

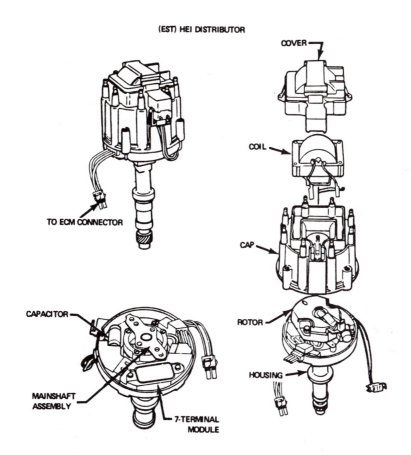

Fig. 8-5. HEI—high energy ignition system distributor assembly. (Courtesy of Chevrolet Motor Div. of GMC)

switch is turned to both the run and start positions, full battery voltage flows to the distributor. In the majority of HEI systems, there is no resistor wire connected from the actual ignition key switch to the distributor.

You will notice in Fig. 8-5 that the ignition coil is contained within the top half of the distributor cap and is connected through a resistance brush to the rotor. The major differences between the HEI distributor and the conventional breaker-point unit is that a module and pick-up coil replaces the contact breaker points. Figure 8-6 shows the location of both the module and pick-up coil on the distributor assembly.

HEI DISTRIBUTOR OPERATION

Figure 8-7 (a) shows a simplified arrangement of the two major components of the HEI system. A toothed wheel known as either a reluctor or armature is driven directly from the distributor shaft. The speed of this reluctor will establish the timing of the spark generated and sent to the plug. Because reluctor speed varies the timing, some manufacturers refer to it as a timer core, as is shown in Fig. 8-7 (b).

In Fig. 8-7 (a) and (b) as the toothed reluctor wheel rotates with the distributor shaft, its teeth will approach a point where they are in direct alignment with the center of the pickup coil which is an electromagnet. When this occurs, a small air-gap exists between the toothed wheel and the pickup coil. Battery power is continuously flowing through the pickup coil to produce a magnetic field in both the coil and the core. As each tooth of the rotating reluctor approaches the pickup coil core or center, the reluctance of the magnetic circuit will rapidly decrease, but the magnetic

ALUMINUM NON-MAGNETIC SHIELD REMOVED

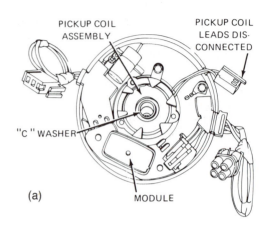

(a)

PICKUP COIL REMOVED AND DISASSEMBLED

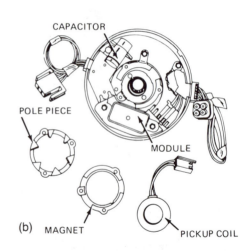

(b)

Fig. 8-6. (a) Assembled view of module and pickup, (b) disassembled view of module and pickup. (Courtesy of Chevrolet Motor Div. of GMC)

field strength will increase. This strong magnetic field is established through the center of the pickup coil and induces a voltage in the pickup coil which is then directed to an electronic module. As the

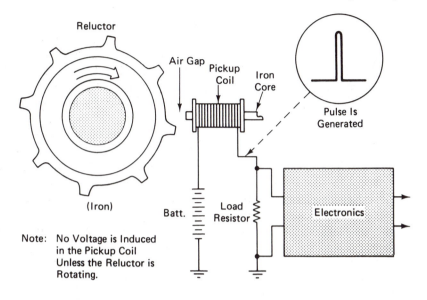

Fig. 8-7a. Basic HEI system arrangement. (Courtesy of Delco-Remy Div. of GMC)

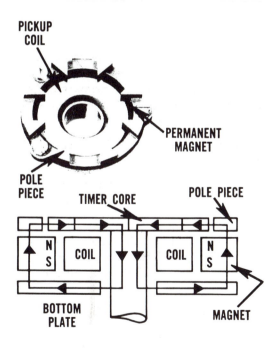

Fig. 8-7b. Side view of basic HEI system. (Courtesy of Delco-Remy Div. of GMC)

tooth moves away from the core, the reluctance of the magnetic circuit will increase rapidly, while the magnetic field strength decreases. Therefore, the induced voltage disappears with no voltage signal going to the electronic module. The net result is that the changing field strength induces a positive voltage followed by a negative voltage in the coil winding. This pulse voltage is sent to the electronic module.

When the module receives the voltage signal from the pickup coil, primary winding coil flow is initiated. When the tooth of the reluctor wheel or timer core moves away from the pole piece teeth (center of pickup coil), the voltage signal is lost and the module turns the coil primary current off which induces the high voltage flow in the secondary winding of the coil to fire the spark plug.

Figures 8-8 and 8-9 show a typical circuit layout for an HEI system along with an actual explanation of its operation.

Since the ignition module located in the distributor assembly contains a micro-miniature electronic circuit with components so small that they cannot be seen even with a magnifying glass, the module is strictly a replacement item and is therefore nonrepairable. Since we are concerned with how the module actually turns the ignition coil primary current on and off only those components related to this action are shown in Fig. 8-8 and 8-9.

In Fig. 8-8, current is flowing through all areas shown by the bolder lines. To avoid any charge that could accumulate on the coil frame, it is grounded. The purpose of the capacitor in this circuit is simply to prevent radio noise interference. Battery power supplies the current when the engine is running.

Anytime that the teeth of the timer core or reluctor wheel are not in alignment with the pickup coil core or pole piece teeth, no ignition coil primary current will flow since the current flow through R5, D1, the pickup coil and resistor R9 to ground reduces the voltage potential between R2 and R3 to such a low value that TR1 will not turn on. The basic flow is therefore from the battery or energizer through the switch, the ignition coil primary, TR1 and R1 to ground.

In Fig. 8-9, spark plug firing is initiated when the reluctor teeth approach alignment since a voltage is induced in the pickup coil as explained in detail earlier. Positive potential at terminal G stops current flow through the pick up coil, and the circuit current flow is as shown by the bolder lines in Fig. 8-8. This action turns transistor TR3 on, which subsequently lowers the voltage potential between R4 and R6 so that TR2 is turned off. This combined action will turn TR1 on which initiates current flow through the ignition coil primary winding.

As mentioned earlier, when the reluctor tooth starts to turn past the pickup core, the pickup coil voltage is reversed and the system returns to the current flow shown in Fig. 8-8, with the spark plug not firing. Prior to this action occurring, however, the primary current must first of all decrease, which induces the voltage in the ignition coil secondary to fire the spark plug.

As a summation of the sequence of events that actually occur in firing the spark plug, Fig. 8-10 shows a simple line type diagram of a typical oscilloscope pattern.

The sequence of events shown in Fig. 8-10 is as follows.

Period A: No current flows through the ignition coil at this time since the timer core teeth are not in alignment with the pickup coil.

Period B: As the teeth of the reluctor wheel or timer core approach alignment with the pickup coil, the primary current increases, which is reflected as a small secondary voltage.

Period C: Primary current reaches its maximum value.

Period D: Spark plug firing occurs as the timer core teeth start to separate with a decrease in primary winding current.

Period E: The induced secondary winding voltage is lower but is sustained throughout period E to maintain the spark.

Period F: Plug firing ceases, and the remaining energy in the ignition coil is dissipated in the form of damped oscillations. The cycle would then repeat again at period A.

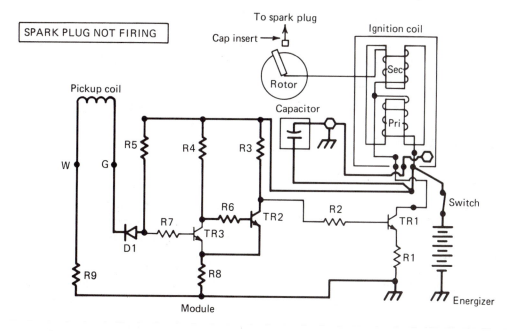

Fig. 8-8. HEI system, spark plug not firing. (Courtesy of Delco-Remy Div. of GMC)

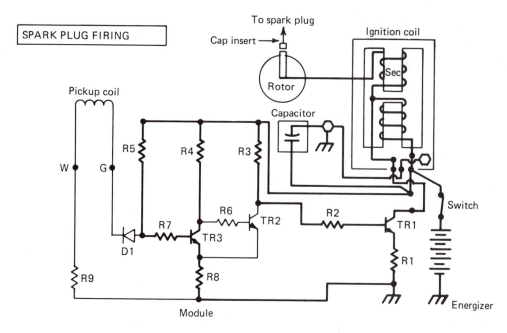

Fig. 8-9. Spark plug firing. (Courtesy of Delco-Remy Div. of GMC)

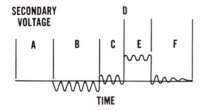

Fig. 8-10. Typical HEI system oscilloscope pattern. (Courtesy of Delco-Remy Div. of GMC)

IGNITION DWELL

This is the term used to express the number of degrees of distributor cam rotation during which the contact breaker points on the conventional system remain closed (spark plug not firing). On electronic type HEI systems, the module within the distributor assembly automatically controls the dwell period, stretching it with increasing engine speed.

When the points are closed in a conventional ignition system, current flows through the primary circuit of the ignition coil. When the points open, this primary current is switched off. In electronic ignition systems this primary current flow in the coil is generally controlled by a transistor.

Every interruption of the primary current triggers an ignition pulse in the coil secondary circuit to produce the necessary high tension voltage to the spark plug. At high engine speed, the conventional contact breaker points can open and close so fast that point bounce can exist. At these high speeds, the actual time that the points remain closed (dwell time) can be so short that the secondary voltage and ignition energy drops off severely to the point that engine misfire can result.

The opening and closing of the points in the distributor forces the dwell angle to be reduced as the number of cylinders in the engine are increased. For example, the dwell angle is about 50 degrees on a 4-cylinder engine, 38 degrees on a 6-cylinder engine, and about 30 to 33 degrees on an 8 cylinder unit. As engine speeds increase, the points are opened and closed much more rapidly, so that the time that the points remain closed becomes shorter. Because of the short time that the points remain closed, the ignition coil primary current does not reach its maximum value as limited by the self-inductance and short contact point closure.

Figure 8-11 shows how the dwell period changes if the contact breaker point gap is improperly adjusted. A large contact

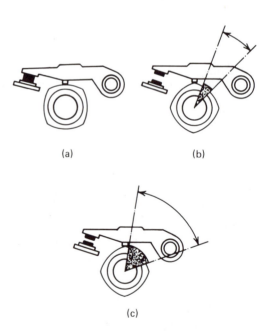

Fig. 8-11. Point gap versus dwell angle: (a) Contact closed, (b) large points gap—small dwell angle, (c) small points gap—large dwell angle. (Courtesy of Robert Bosch Corp.)

breaker point gap will result in a small dwell angle, which although good for ignition performance at low engine speeds would be poor at high engine speeds.

A small contact breaker point gap results in a large dwell angle which would be suitable for high engine speeds. However, at low engine rpm's, arcing across the points would be increased resulting in short point life. The point gap recommended by the engine manufacturer is therefore a compromise between a small and wide point gap.

It is imperative that the dwell angle be correctly set for the particular distributor. This is achieved by using a dwell meter such as can be found in any garage or service station. This adjustment is usually accessible through an inspection window on the distributor cap of conventional ignition systems as shown in Fig. 7-19.

Should a dwe-l meter not be available, the point gap can be adjusted instead. Due to the variation in distributor cam shapes, a strict cross-reference between dwell angle and point gap cannot be made. Where possible always adjust the dwell angle since it is more accurate than the gap setting method.

The dwell angle or point gap should always be set prior to adjusting the engine ignition timing. If the timing is set first, then the dwell or point gap is altered, the timing will be altered. You can, therefore, appreciate why dwell angle must be correctly set in the conventional ignition system if optimum ignition performance is to be realized. In current high energy ignition systems (HEI), the automatic control of the dwell period through the electronic module does much to improve the efficiency of the ignition circuit; as engine speed increases, the dwell period is stretched.

The actual dwell period in the electronic type ignition system is the period during which the electronic module maintains a complete circuit between the battery and the primary winding of the ignition coil.

IGNITION SYSTEM PERFORMANCE CHARACTERISTICS

In order for either a contact-breaker point or electronic ignition system to perform correctly, several areas with respect to general servicing require attention, such as those discussed herein. In addition, the following points should be considered:

1. Engine timing that is advanced too far will cause a pinging noise in the engine due to the spark plug igniting the air/fuel mixture too early during the compression stroke. This can cause serious internal damage to the piston because of the high pressures created which tend to want to force the piston back down in the cylinder as it is being pushed up by the crankshaft and connecting rod.

2. Engine timing that is too far retarded will cause a noticeable lack of power and acceleration because the air/fuel mixture will be late in igniting, resulting in incomplete combustion. The full energy is therefore not received from the fuel charge. Overheating can result from this condition.

3. A defective vacuum advance unit will result in slow acceleration at part-throttle performance with a resultant increase in fuel consumption.

4. A defective centrifugal advance mechanism will result in sluggish engine performance due to the retarded condition that results at higher engine speeds accompanied by the results stated in item 2 above.

5. Incorrect dwell can lead to point damage or failure of the coil to produce its maximum secondary voltage, leading to engine misfire.

VARIATIONS IN HEI SYSTEMS
(General Motors Type)

General Motors Corporation uses two types of HEI distributors. One type employs the conventional style of spark advance with a set of weights to alter the spark advance as a result of increasing engine speed. The other system employs the usual vacuum advance concept described earlier in this chapter. In some applications, additional electronic controls are added to the basic mechanical HEI system to further control spark timing at certain engine operating levels to improve both fuel economy and engine performance characteristics.

The electronic systems employed with some HEI systems on GMC vehicles can take one of three forms.

1. EST or Electronic Spark Timing where no direct mechanical control is used for spark timing. Instead, engine parameters are monitored and these inputs are electronically processed to obtain optimum spark timing. This system is shown in Fig. 8-12.

2. ESC or electronic spark control system is a closed loop system that controls engine detonation by adjusting spark timing in the retarded mode as a function of how much detonation exists in the engine. This detonation is sensed by an engine located sensor as shown in Fig. 8-13.

For example, the electronic spark control on VIN-4 GMC engines modifies (retards) the spark advance when detonation occurs and holds this retard mode for 20 seconds after which the spark control will again return to EST (electronic spark timing). The detonation monitoring process is continuous so that timing is automatically variable. The ESC controller is a hard wired signal processor/amplifier which operates

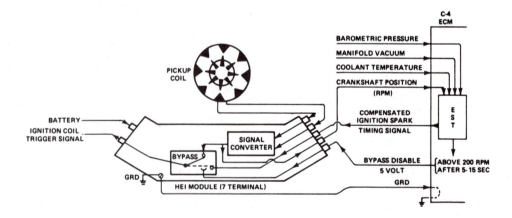

Fig. 8-12. EST—electronic spark timing control circuit. (Courtesy of Chevrolet Motor Div. of GMC)

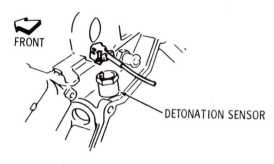

Fig. 8-13. Detonation sensor. (Courtesy of Oldsmobile Div. of GMC)

from 6 to 16 volts. There is no memory capability, however, in the controller.

The ESC sensor is a magnetorestrictive device mounted in the engine block as shown in Fig. 8-13 to detect the presence or absence as well as intensity of the detonation existing in the engine throughout all operating conditions. This output sends an electrical signal to the controller. Should the sensor unit fail, no ignition/spark timing retard would occur.

3. EMR or electronic module retard is a spark control system employed with an HEI system with a timing retard feature. When the timing retard circuit is grounded the firing of the spark plugs is delayed for a calibrated number of crank degrees. Control of the grounding circuit is via a vacuum operated electrical switch. When the retard circuit is open, there is no delay and the distributor fires the spark plugs as controlled by engine speed and vacuum.

Figure 8-14 shows a typical EMR check chart and module connections. Should it become necessary to remove and/or replace the EMR-HEI module, the ignition timing must be rechecked and set to the manufacturer's specification.

HEI SYSTEM— ADJUSTING IGNITION TIMING

The sequence for checking and adjusting the ignition timing on vehicles equipped with HEI systems is similar to that used for conventional ignition systems.

A typical procedure is given below.

Test Equipment

Equipment required to check and adjust ignition timing varies slightly between engines depending on whether the fuel system is carburetted or fuel injected. However, the following tools are required:

1. Timing light or timing advance meter
2. Jumper lead or inductive type pickup (spark plug connection)
3. Tachometer to monitor engine speed

Always follow the manufacturer's recommendations when connecting test equipment. Due to the wide range of test equipment readily available, no attempt can be made here to cover all of the available tools and their hookup. However, the sequence described can be considered general.

1. Ignition Off: When connecting the timing light, proceed as follows. Connect the red lead to the battery positive terminal, and the black lead to the battery negative terminal or a good ground. Connect the other lead to the number (1) one spark plug. Ensure that you connect an adapter between the spark plug and spark plug wire so that the timing light lead will couple to the adapter.

Do not pierce the spark plug wire or attempt to insert a wire between the spark

EMR CHECK 2.8L V6

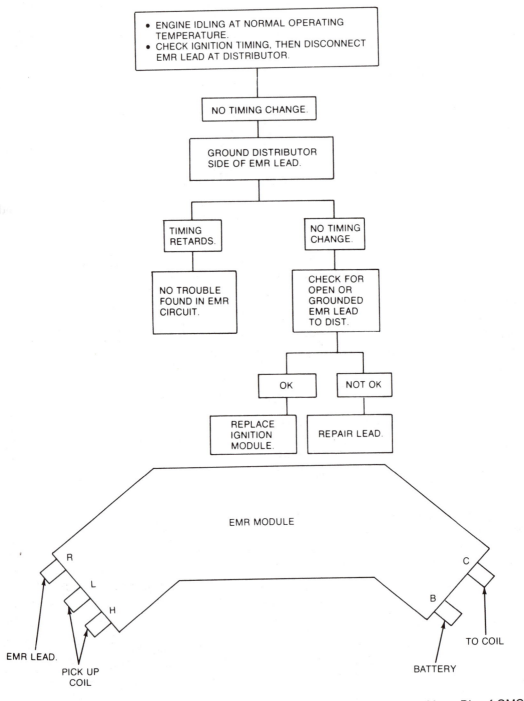

- ENGINE IDLING AT NORMAL OPERATING TEMPERATURE.
- CHECK IGNITION TIMING, THEN DISCONNECT EMR LEAD AT DISTRIBUTOR.

NO TIMING CHANGE.

GROUND DISTRIBUTOR SIDE OF EMR LEAD.

TIMING RETARDS.

NO TIMING CHANGE.

NO TROUBLE FOUND IN EMR CIRCUIT.

CHECK FOR OPEN OR GROUNDED EMR LEAD TO DIST.

OK

NOT OK

REPLACE IGNITION MODULE.

REPAIR LEAD.

EMR MODULE

R

L

H

C

B

EMR LEAD.

PICK UP COIL

BATTERY

TO COIL

Fig. 8-14. EMR—electronic module retard check chart. (Courtesy of Chevrolet Motor Div. of GMC)

plug protective boot and spark plug lead wire. Once the spark plug cable insulation has been punctured, voltage will jump to the nearest ground and the plug will misfire.

2. Locate the ignition timing marks at the front of the engine which are usually located on the engine front cover. See Fig. 8-15 (a) and (b). If covered with road dirt or oil and dust, clean off the timing tab/plate. If it is hard to see the timing marks, chalk the mark that is recommended for proper timing to assist you when using the timing light.

NOTE: Many current engines employ a magnetic timing probe hole as shown in Fig. 8-15(c), where a magnetic pickup can be placed in the receptacle of the timing tab and pressed down firmly so that the pickup is as close to the crankshaft pulley surface as possible without actually making contact.

3. Refer to the vehicle emissions control information which is generally contained on a label in the region of the engine compartment (on the fender well, radiator support, bulkhead, etc.) and note the in-

(a)

(b)

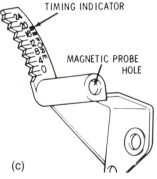

(c)

Fig. 8-15. (a) Pointer mounted timing marks. (b) Pulley mounted timing marks. (Courtesy of Ford Motor Co.) (c) Magnetic timing probe hole. (Courtesy of Oldsmobile Div. of GMC)

structions with respect to timing requirements, procedure, etc.

4. If the engine is fitted with a distributor that has a vacuum advance feature, or
an ignition timing vacuum switch, disconnect and plug the vacuum source hose to
either the distributor or switch assembly. If
this is not done, a false reading will generally result when checking timing. On some
engines, it is necessary to disconnect and
plug the EGR vacuum hose. The emissions
control label on the vehicle will guide you
on these points.

5. Connect a tachometer to the engine
such as the magnetic probe pickup type, or
to the distributor pickup terminal tachometer point. For GMC vehicles, see
Fig. 8-12; for Ford, Fig. 8-16.

6. Ensure that the vehicle parking
brake is on and the transmission selector
lever is in the PARK position on automatic
type transmissions.

7. Prior to timing the engine, if it is not
already at operating temperature, run it
until it is. This is very important.

8. Adjust the engine idle speed until it
conforms with the rpm called for on the
vehicle emissions label.

9. With the engine running at the correct idle speed, aim the timing light at the
crankshaft pulley and timing tab of the
engine front cover and observe the timing
light flashes on the pulley in relation to the
notches on the front cover, and compare to
specifications.

10. If the timing is incorrect, loosen the
distributor retaining bolt/clamp and rotate
the distributor CW or CCW as necessary in
order to alter the timing as per the emissions control label in the engine compartment. Tighten the distributor clamp bolt
and recheck the timing.

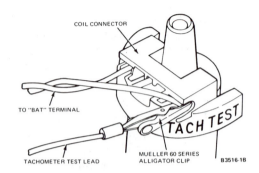

Fig. 8-16. Tachometer connections to ignition coil
on Ford vehicles. (Courtesy of Ford Motor Co.)

11. Disconnect the tachometer and timing light, remove the spark plug adapter,
replace any vacuum or EGR lines that were
disconnected during the timing check, and
see that the spark plug boot is replaced
correctly over the No. 1 spark plug.

12. If a timing advance meter is used
rather than the strobe type timing light,
the sequence is basically the same with the
exception of the hookup of the leads for
the timing advance meter. Follow the particular tool manufacturer's specifications
for this.

IGNITION DISTRIBUTOR REMOVAL AND INSTALLATION (All Engines)

The removal and installation of the distributor assembly can be considered
common for all types of engines.

1. Prior to removing the distributor assembly, disconnect the battery cables to
prevent any possibility of live wires short
circuiting.

2. Disconnect any wires from the distributor to ignition coil on the conventional

ignition type system, and on the electronic or HEI systems, disconnect the ignition switch battery feed wire from the distributor cap.

3. Remove the distributor cap by either releasing the spring type side clips, or by depressing either two or four screws located at the cap to distributor body base and rotating them until they are free. On some HEI distributors, it may be necessary to remove the secondary wiring from the cap by lifting two latch release retaining tabs as shown in Fig. 8-17.

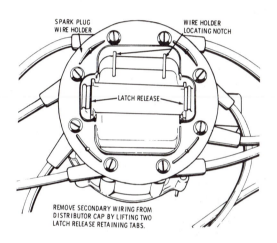

SPARK PLUG WIRE HOLDER

WIRE HOLDER LOCATING NOTCH

LATCH RELEASE

REMOVE SECONDARY WIRING FROM DISTRIBUTOR CAP BY LIFTING TWO LATCH RELEASE RETAINING TABS.

Fig. 8-17. Secondary wire holder release, HEI system. (Courtesy of the Oldsmobile Div. of GMC)

4. Remove the vacuum hose from the vacuum advance unit if so equipped.

5. Take careful note of the position of the rotor prior to removing the distributor to assist you later on installation. It is advisable that you match-mark the rotor to distributor body at this time, or turn the engine over to the ignition timing mark on the pulley to timing tab, and note the rotor

position. Scribe a mark on the distributor body to engine block in line with the rotor.

6. Remove the distributor clamp retaining bolt, and gently pull the distributor up just until the rotor stops turning and again note the rotor position carefully.

7. Pull the distributor up out of its bore for complete removal.

Installation

Installing the distributor is basically the reverse of removal; however, careful attention must be given to ensure that the assembly is in fact installed in the correct position. If careful note was made of the rotor position upon removal, then this will be your guide. However, ensure that the engine has not been turned over in the interim so that timing will be incorrect.

1. If the engine has been rotated after the distributor assembly has been removed, simply rotate it over so as to place the TDC or O mark on the timing tab of the engine front cover in alignment with the saw mark or slot of the crankshaft pulley. See Fig. 8-15.

2. To ensure that the engine piston of the number one cylinder is actually at TDC within the cylinder ready to start the power stroke, you can check that both rocker arms to valve stems have some clearance. If no clearance exists between these, then the engine is actually on the end of its exhaust stroke in the number one cylinder, therefore the engine must be rotated another full turn prior to attempting to install the distributor assembly.

An alternate method to establish TDC in the number one cylinder (power stroke) is to remove the spark plug and place your finger over the hole while slowly cranking the engine until compression is felt, then aligning the pulley to timing mark at TDC.

3. Turn the rotor to the previously noted match-mark on the distributor body, or alternately turn the rotor to a point between No. 1 and the last spark plug tower of the firing order on the distributor cap, and insert it into the engine block mounting hole.

4. Usually the distributor will enter the hole almost all the way, then resistance will be encountered; therefore, gently rotate the rotor while gently pushing down until the distributor gear engages its drive mechanism. On some engines such as Ford vehicles, it may be necessary to crank the engine with the starter after the distributor drive gear is partially engaged in order to engage the oil pump intermediate shaft. Should this action be required, manually turn the crankshaft back to the initial timing alignment (make sure that No. 1 piston is on the start of its power stroke, and not finishing exhaust) which can be noted between the crankshaft pulley and timing pointer.

5. The distributor should be aligned with the previous match mark on the engine block (Step 5, Distributor Removal). At this time the rotor should also be in correct alignment with the match mark. If the rotor and distributor to engine match mark are not in alignment, pull the distributor assembly out of the block part way, align the rotor and distributor to the correct position, and insert it back into the block.

6. On (HEI) High Energy Ignition type systems, the armature teeth must be in perfect alignment with the pickup point of the stator assembly as shown in Fig. 8-18. The rotor should be at the No. 1 cylinder firing position at this time. Many distribu-

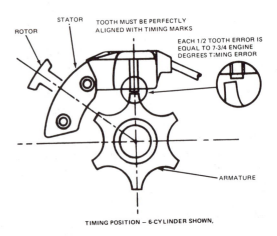

Fig. 8-18. Static distributor armature timing position. (Courtesy of Ford Motor Co.)

tor caps are marked with an embossed No. 1 to indicate the No. 1 terminal.

Note that in Fig. 8-18, even a half-tooth error in the alignment of the armature teeth will cause a severe error in engine timing. It matters not whether the engine is a V-8, in-line six, or otherwise: the degree of error will be the same. The example shown in Fig. 8-18 is for Ford vehicles, with the degree of error being 7¾ degrees per half tooth whether the engine is a six or eight-cylinder unit.

7. Install the distributor retaining clamp and bolt and snug up gently.

8. Connect up all necessary wiring to the distributor and vehicle wiring harness, after installing the distributor cap.

9. Start and warm up the engine and proceed to check the ignition timing with a timing light or meter, and adjust to specifications listed on the engine decal. Connect the vacuum lines and check the advance with the timing light when the engine is accelerated.

NOTE: As previously mentioned under use of timing lights, false triggering can result in apparent multiple sparks and/or an erratic timing indication on some timing lights having capacitive pickups due to the higher coil charging currents used with HEI systems. For this reason, refer to the manufacturer's (Engine Service Manual) to determine what timing lights can be successfully employed. Should one of the recommended timing lights not be readily available, satisfactory use of an existing timing light may be possible by insulating the high tension lead with a piece of split rubber vacuum hose, prior to attaching the timing light pickup.

SERVICE PROCEDURES WITH DISTRIBUTOR ON THE ENGINE

Removal of the distributor assembly is only necessary if major engine work is to be done, or the distributor itself is suspected of being at fault and requires testing. Normally, the following jobs can be done with the distributor in place on the engine.

1. Distributor cap removal or inspection
2. Spark plug cable removal or installation
3. Conventional coil lead removal
4. HEI system coil servicing (in cap)
5. Rotor removal or replacement
6. Contact breaker point servicing (conventional system)
7. Condensor replacement (conventional system)
8. Cable holder servicing (HEI system)
9. Ground terminal or wire connector servicing such as HEI system wire harness and capacitor assembly

10. HEI system module replacement

NOTE: When making compression checks on an engine equipped with an HEI distributor, disconnect the ignition switch feed wire at the distributor.

HEI DISTRIBUTOR DISASSEMBLY, TEST AND REASSEMBLY

All HEI distributors with the coil contained in the distributor cap are presently employed on all gasoline powered General Motors Corporation vehicles.

Figure 8-19 shows the recommended sequence to check out the performance of the assembly. Also see Fig. 8-6. For more complete information on GMC high energy ignition distributors, obtain a copy of Delco Remy Service Bulletins 1D-182 and 1D-183.

GMC ENGINE ELECTRICAL-DIAGNOSTIC CONNECTOR

Some models of GMC vehicles are equipped with an engine electrical diagnostic connector located on the inner fender at the front of the vehicle on the left or (driver) side (see Fig. 8-20(a)). Figure 8-20(b) illustrates the specific terminal numbers and their usage.

To analyze the engine electrical system such as the battery, ignition primary and secondary wires, and the starter motor and generator along with their assorted wiring, special shop testers are available from a variety of sources for this purpose. Should none of this special equipment be available, then a voltmeter can be used in conjunction with the step-by-step procedure given in the manufacturer's service manual which will vary slightly between makes of vehicles. A schematic of the en-

DISTRIBUTOR DISASSEMBLY
TEST AND REASSEMBLY
(COIL IN CAP)

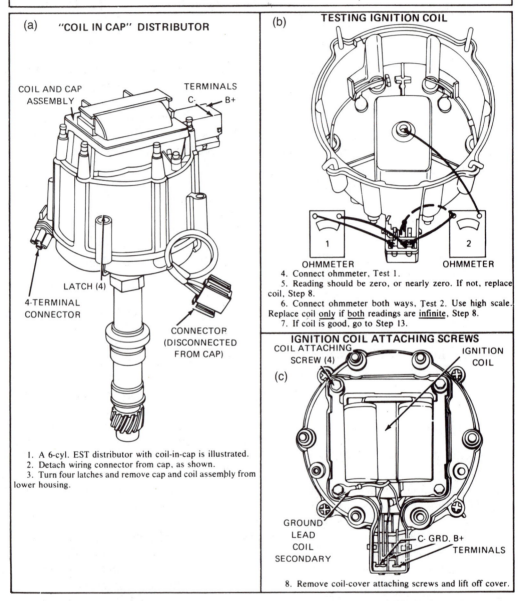

(a)   "COIL IN CAP" DISTRIBUTOR

COIL AND CAP
ASSEMBLY

TERMINALS
C-   B+

LATCH (4)

4-TERMINAL
CONNECTOR

CONNECTOR
(DISCONNECTED
FROM CAP)

1. A 6-cyl. EST distributor with coil-in-cap is illustrated.
2. Detach wiring connector from cap, as shown.
3. Turn four latches and remove cap and coil assembly from lower housing.

(b)   TESTING IGNITION COIL

1   OHMMETER   2   OHMMETER

4. Connect ohmmeter, Test 1.
5. Reading should be zero, or nearly zero. If not, replace coil, Step 8.
6. Connect ohmmeter both ways, Test 2. Use high scale. Replace coil only if both readings are infinite, Step 8.
7. If coil is good, go to Step 13.

IGNITION COIL ATTACHING SCREWS

(c)

COIL ATTACHING
SCREW (4)

IGNITION
COIL

GROUND
LEAD
COIL
SECONDARY

C- GRD. B+
TERMINALS

8. Remove coil-cover attaching screws and lift off cover.

Fig. 8-19. Distributor disassembly test and reassembly: (a) Coil in cap distributor, (b) testing ignition coil, (c) ignition coil attaching screws, (d) ignition coil removed from cap, (e) testing pickup coil. (Courtesy of Cadillac Motor Car Div. of GMC)

(d) IGNITION COIL REMOVED FROM CAP

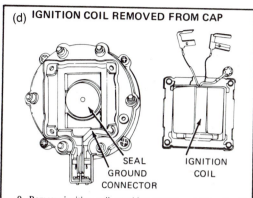

SEAL
GROUND
CONNECTOR

IGNITION
COIL

9. Remove ignition coil attaching screws and lift coil with leads from cap.

10. Remove ignition coil arc seal.

11. Clean with soft cloth and inspect cap for defects. Replace, if needed.

12. Assemble new coil and cover to cap.

(e)   TESTING PICKUP COIL

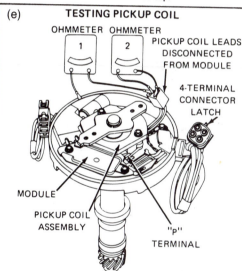

OHMMETER OHMMETER

PICKUP COIL LEADS
DISCONNECTED
FROM MODULE

4-TERMINAL
CONNECTOR
LATCH

MODULE

PICKUP COIL
ASSEMBLY

"P"
TERMINAL

13. On all distributors, remove rotor and pickup coil leads from module.

14. Connect ohmmeter Test 1 and then Test 2.

15. If vacuum unit is used, connect vacuum source to vacuum unit. Replace unit if inoperative. Observe ohmmeter throughout vacuum range; flex leads by hand without vacuum to check for intermittent opens.

16. Test 1 — should read infinite at all times.

Test 2 — should read steady at one value within 500-1500 ohm range.

NOTE: Ohmmeter may deflect if operating vacuum unit causes teeth to align. This is not a defect.

17. If pickup coil is defective, go to Step 18. If okay, go to Step 23.

Fig. 8-19 continued.

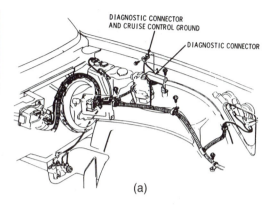

DIAGNOSTIC CONNECTOR
AND CRUISE CONTROL GROUND

DIAGNOSTIC CONNECTOR

(a)

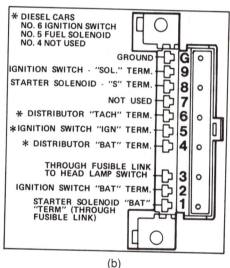

* DIESEL CARS
    NO. 6 IGNITION SWITCH
    NO. 5 FUEL SOLENOID
    NO. 4 NOT USED

GROUND

IGNITION SWITCH - "SOL." TERM.

STARTER SOLENOID - "S" TERM.

NOT USED

* DISTRIBUTOR "TACH" TERM.

* IGNITION SWITCH "IGN" TERM.

* DISTRIBUTOR "BAT" TERM.

THROUGH FUSIBLE LINK
TO HEAD LAMP SWITCH

IGNITION SWITCH "BAT" TERM.

STARTER SOLENOID "BAT"
"TERM" (THROUGH
FUSIBLE LINK)

(b)

Fig. 8-20. (a) Engine diagnostic connector location, (b) engine electrical diagnostic connector terminals. (Courtesy of the Oldsmobile Div. of GMC)

gine electrical diagnostic wiring arrangement is shown in Fig. 8-21.

GENERAL MOTORS HEI
TEST EQUIPMENT

In order to quickly and effectively analyze problems in the HEI (high energy

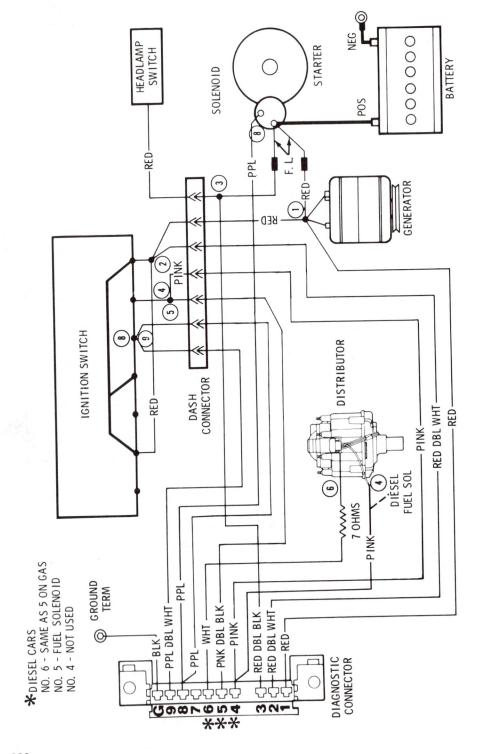

Fig. 8-21. GMC engine electrical diagnostic connector schematic. (Courtesy of the Oldsmobile Div. of GMC)

ignition) systems now employed on all GMC vehicles, the use of a variety of special tools and equipment will not only save time when troubleshooting, but can pinpoint the problem area very quickly. Shown within this section are the various special tools that are available through Kent-Moore Tool Division. In the USA contact: Kent-Moore Tool Division, 29784 Little Mack, Roseville, Mich. 48066. In Canada contact: Kent-Moore of Canada, Ltd; 2465 Cawthra Road, Mississauga, Ontario. L5A 3P2.

The tester shown in Fig. 8-22 provides a means of testing the GMC HEI modules in or out of the vehicle through a go/no-go method of testing the suspected components. It performs a dynamic test on the original four terminal module introduced in 1975, and on the three and five terminal modules introduced in 1978. The test set also includes the J-26792 HEI Spark Check tool, which indicates if the HEI system is generating acceptable voltage. Also in-

cluded is J-24642-100 Test Verification Kit for checking suspected HEI distributor components such as the ignition coil, pick-up coil, and module. Complete operating instructions are provided to perform all component tests in less than 10 minutes.

This device utilizes a totally new method of counting engine rpm's using a magnetic probe positioned in the timing mark tab adjacent to the engine harmonic balancer. See Fig. 8-15(c).

The tach shown in Fig. 8-23 can be used on all current GMC gasoline engines that have the holder for the probe, and also can be used on the Vee type diesel engines produced by both the Oldsmobile and Chevrolet Divisions. This tach can also be used on propane equipped vehicles along with J-26911 Propane Enrichment Device to ensure that the idle adjustment screws are correctly positioned. The digital readout shows the exact engine rpm to the technician so the proper positioning of the idle screws can be obtained.

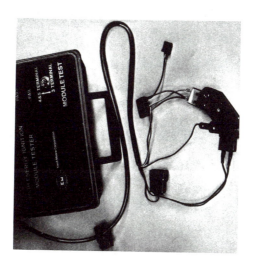

Fig. 8-22. Kent-Moore J-24642-C high energy ignition module tester. (Courtesy of Kent-Moore Tool Div.)

Fig. 8-23. Kent-Moore J-26925 Mag-Tach engine tachometer. (Courtesy of Kent-Moore Tool Div.)

Fig. 8-24. Kent-Moore J-23040 Tac-Cal, tachometer calibrating device. (Courtesy of Kent-Moore Tool Div.)

Present and future automotive emissions standards make it imperative that engines be properly tuned. In order to do this, tachometers that are inaccurate will cause the engine RPM rate during the tune-up operation to deviate from the manufacturer's recommended level.

Tool J-23040 (Fig. 8-24) provides the capability for testing the accuracy of most primary and secondary tachometers by supplying appropriate signals for testing. Necessary connections for hooking the tachometer to the calibrator are provided on the face of the instrument. The accuracy is within ± 2%.

REVIEW QUESTIONS

Q1 What is the major advantage of a transistorized ignition system?

Q2 How does the current draw in the electronic ignition system differ from that of the conventional system?

Q3 What controls the primary coil current flow in an electronic ignition system since no points are used?

Q4 What are typical secondary voltages obtainable from the electronic ignition system?

Q5 Where is the distributor coil located in the HEI systems employed in GMC vehicles?

Q6 What is used to generate the opening and closing of the coil primary circuit in the HEI system employed by GMC, Ford etc.?

Q7 What is the dwell period in an electronic ignition system?

Q8 Do all distributors employ both a vacuum and mechanical advance control systems to alter ignition timing?

ANSWERS

A1 The major advantage of the transistorized or electronic ignition system is the elimination of the contact breaker points in current systems which allows a higher voltage to be generated and also fewer maintenance problems.

A2 Current draw in an electronic ignition system usually is about 9 amperes versus 4 amperes in a conventional ignition system, therefore higher peak voltages can be developed.

A3 Primary coil current flow in the electronic ignition system is controlled by a transistor and breaker switch arrangement.

A4 Typical secondary voltages in the HEI system can reach 40,000 volts.

A5 The distributor coil is located in the distributor cap.

A6 A pulse generator is used rather than contact breaker points in the HEI distributors used by GMC and Ford engines; a toothed wheel known as either a reluctor or armature is driven directly from the distributor shaft to make and break an electromagnetic field.

A7 The dwell period in the electronic ignition system is the period during which the electronic module maintains a complete circuit between the battery and the primary winding of the ignition coil.

A8 No; many electronic ignition distributors employ engine sensors which generate a signal and send it to an electronic control module which then alters the engine timing as necessary.

Chapter
9

Ford Electronic Ignition Systems

Various ignition systems are currently used on Ford vehicles. These are described below. The Duraspark II (2) is a solid state ignition system incorporating high energy secondary components. This system has been available since 1976 and is still in use. The current Escort/Lynx vehicles also use the Duraspark II system; however, the distributor cap is of a different design than that used with larger motors.

The Duraspark II system uses a larger distributor rotor, cap and adapter, ignition secondary wires, and a wide gap spark plug to take full advantage of the higher energy produced. Figures 9-1 and 9-4 show the Duraspark system used on the non-Escort/Lynx vehicles and the Escort/Lynx vehicles.

The basic difference between the Duraspark II and earlier Duraspark II ignition systems is that the Duraspark II systems employ a ballast resistor connected to the primary coil lead. An ignition schematic for both the Duraspark model I and II systems is shown in Fig. 9-2 and 9-3.

In addition to Ford passenger vehicles using the Duraspark II ignition system, 1981 medium and heavy trucks are equipped with the Duraspark II solid state breakerless ignition system (with the exception of Super Duty Vehicles such as the 7.8L (477 CID) V-8 and 8.8L (534 CID) V-8 engines, which are fitted with solid state breakerless systems with a standard distributor cap, and 7 mm secondary wires).

The Duraspark III ignition system is an (EEC) or Electronic Engine Control system that is used on 5.0L (302 CID) and 5.8L (351-W CID) engines on light trucks for California use. This system provides the power switching of the ignition coil with the EEC processor controlling the Duraspark III input signal. The distributor, rotor, and cap are unique to the EEC system. The secondary wires and spark plugs are the same as the Duraspark II system. Both system control modules have the same general exterior appearance as can be noted from a comparison of Figs. 9-4 and 9-5.

DURASPARK II SYSTEM OPERATION

As mentioned previously, this system is a solid state unit incorporating high energy secondary components with the distribu-

366

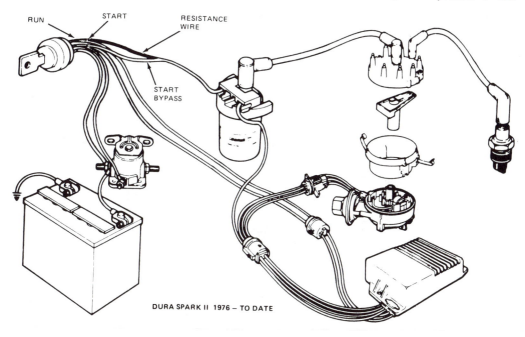

Fig. 9-1. Duraspark II, 1976 and up non-Escort/Lynx vehicles. (Courtesy of Ford Motor Co.)

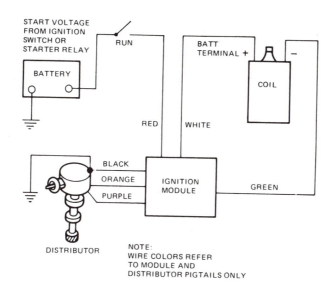

Fig. 9-2. Duraspark I ignition schematic. (Courtesy of Ford Motor Co.)

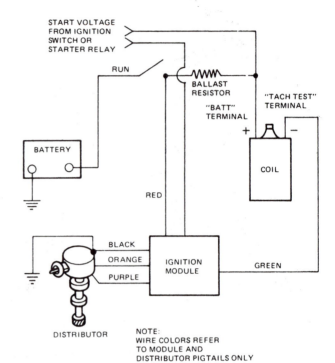

Fig. 9-3. Duraspark II ignition schematic. (Courtesy of Ford Motor Co.)

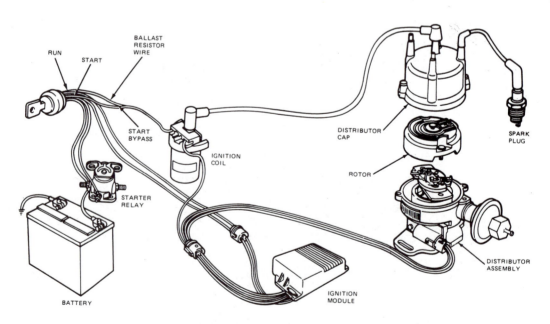

Fig. 9-4. Escort/Lynx Duraspark II ignition system. (Courtesy of Ford Motor Co.)

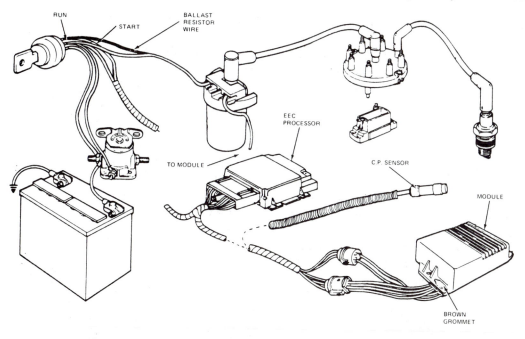

Fig. 9-5. Duraspark III ignition system. (Courtesy of Ford Motor Co.)

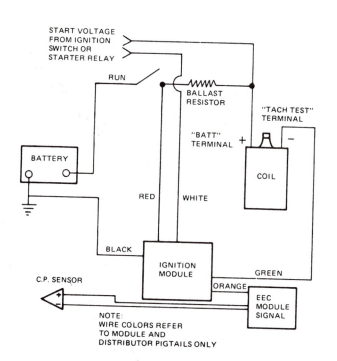

Fig. 9-6. Ignition schematic, Duraspark III EEC vehicles. (Courtesy of Ford Motor Co.)

tor, coil and module being the same as that used on the Ford SSI (Suppressor Spark Ignition) system. The distributor used with this system is shown in Fig. 9-7. Notice that an adapter is required in order to support the physically larger cap used along with a larger rotor, both of which are necessary because of the higher voltage used with this system.

Spark plug type terminal towers are part of the distributor cap, and the secondary wiring is 8 mm with silicone jacketing for improved dielectric and temperature capability. In addition, suppressor spark plugs are used because of the improved internal carbon seal of increased resistance to reduce radio frequency noise.

Overall engine performance and longer spark plug life is attained with this system through a combination of higher system voltage and a wide gap spark plug. Reference to the system wiring schematics in Figs. 9-3 and 9-4 show that a ballast resistor of 1.1 ohm value is inserted into the primary coil wire harness. This resistor functions to allow an increase in energy to the coil with a resultant increase in secondary voltage to the spark plugs. Identification of this system is accomplished by noting that it employs a large blue distributor cap and blue secondary wiring.

As a point of interest, the SSI Ford ignition system also uses a ballast resistor integral with the coil primary wiring; however, the resistor value is higher than that used with the Duraspark II system in that its value is 1.35 ohm versus 1.1 ohm. In addition, the SSI system uses a one-piece distributor cap which is also blue in color; however, it is the same diameter as the distributor housing and does not use an adapter such as the Duraspark II system. In addition, the secondary wires are 7 mm in diameter, are also black in color, and

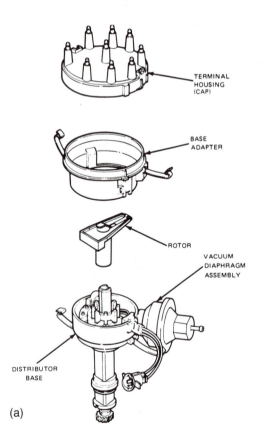

(a)

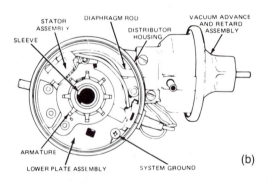

(b)

Fig. 9-7. (a) Components of Duraspark II ignition distributor assembly. (b) Top view of Duraspark II distributor and parts identification. (Courtesy of Ford Motor Co.)

they plug into the distributor cap receptacles as with a conventional ignition system.

Both the SSI and Duraspark systems do, however, employ the same basic distributor and ignition modules.

Distributor Features

The operation of the distributor used with these systems parallels that employed by most engine manufacturers today. Rather than employing contact breaker points, a rotating armature is driven directly from the distributor shaft (similar to the GMC and other ignition systems), causing fluctuations in the magnetic field through the magnetic pick-up assembly. As the pole pieces of the armature align with the pick-up point of the stator assembly, a small air-gap exists between the pole piece (toothed wheel) and the pick-up point of the stator assembly. Battery power is continuously flowing through the stator assembly to produce a magnetic field. As each tooth of the rotating armature approaches the pickup coil of the stator assembly, the reluctance of the magnetic circuit will rapidly decrease, but the magnetic field strength will increase. This strong magnetic field is established through the center of the pick-up coil or stator which is then directed to an electronic module. As the tooth moves away from the core, the reluctance of the magnetic circuit will increase rapidly, while the magnetic field strength decreases; therefore, the induced voltage disappears with no voltage signal going to the electronic module. The net result is that the changing field strength induces a positive voltage followed by a negative voltage in the ignition coil winding. This continual fluctuation or pulse voltage therefore causes a varying voltage to be generated by the pick-up coil. This causes the electronic module to turn the ignition coil current off and on to provide the secondary voltage to the spark plugs.

All distributors used with these systems are equipped with both conventional vacuum and centrifugal weight force spark advance mechanisms, in which the vacuum advance governs ignition timing related to engine load characteristics, while the centrifugal weight advance mechanism governs ignition timing as a direct result of engine speed (rpm). On some distributors, a dual diaphragm vacuum advance is used to provide ignition timing retard when a closed throttle condition exists such as at curb idle, or when the vehicle is coasting with a closed throttle situation. The main reason for this timing retard is to help control exhaust emissions. Figure 9-8 shows a single diaphragm vacuum advance concept, while Fig. 9-9 shows the dual diaphragm vacuum advance concept.

The operation of the vacuum advance mechanism parallels the explanation given earlier and shown in Fig. 7-11.

In Fig. 9-8 (Ford), the spring-loaded di-

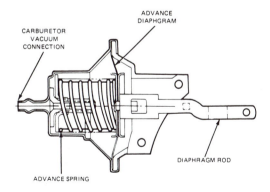

Fig. 9-8. Single diaphragm vacuum advance system. (Courtesy of Ford Motor Co.)

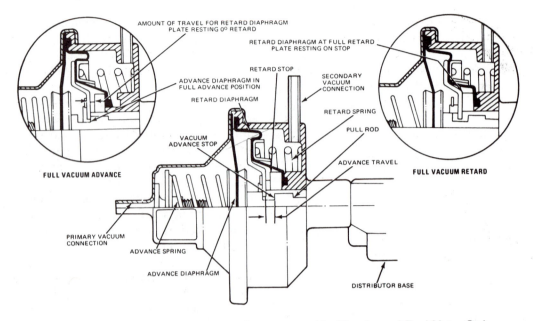

Fig. 9-9. Dual diaphragm vacuum advance assembly. (Courtesy of Ford Motor Co.)

aphragm is connected to the moveable stator assembly by the diaphragm rod. Engine vacuum from the carburetor connection causes the diaphragm to move against the force of the internal spring. Increased vacuum causes the moveable stator assembly to pivot on the distributor lower plate assembly. Note that in the breakerless systems employed by Ford, the stator assembly moves opposite to distributor rotation thereby advancing the spark timing.

DUAL DIAPHRAGM OPERATION

This dual diaphragm feature is designed to provide both vacuum advance and retard to the ignition timing depending on throttle and vehicle load/speed conditions. In order to accomplish this, two sources of vacuum are required.

1. Carburetor venturi vacuum which

acts upon the advance diaphragm to provide timing advance during normal off idle driving conditions (opening throttle situations). The advance diaphragm as shown in Fig. 9-9 is connected to the moveable stator assembly by the diaphragm rod similar to that used in the single diaphragm unit. Ignition timing is advanced during normal road-load operation, but not during an idle condition or an engine acceleration condition. Timing advance is achieved as for the single diaphragm unit.

2. Intake manifold vacuum which acts upon the retard diaphragm to retard ignition timing during a closed throttle condition. This occurs because the intake manifold vacuum at a closed throttle position is stronger than carburetor vacuum (this line connected to the carburetor is subjected to atmospheric pressure at closed throttle). The retard diaphragm is

connected to the diaphragm rod by means of a sliding linkage, therefore when intake manifold vacuum is applied to the retard diaphragm, it moves inward toward the distributor and the advance spring moves the advance diaphragm causing the moveable stator assembly to pivot in the same direction as distributor rotation. This retard occurs during idle or deceleration only except on those engines that are equipped with a distributor modulator in the vacuum supply line.

IGNITION CIRCUIT OPERATION

The basic operation of the ignition system is similar to that used in current production vehicles manufactured by other manufacturers. The system consists of the usual primary or low voltage circuit, as well as a secondary or high voltage circuit. Components that make up the primary circuit and the secondary circuit are shown graphically in Fig. 9-10.

As shown in Fig. 9-10, the primary circuit consists of:

1. Battery
2. Ignition switch
3. Primary circuit resistance wire (integral wire in SSI and Duraspark II)
4. Coil primary windings
5. Input from the EEC system or distributor magnetic pickup coil assembly
6. Ignition module

Components of the secondary system include the following items:

1. Ignition coil secondary windings
2. Distributor rotor
3. Distributor cap (and adapter on Duraspark II systems)

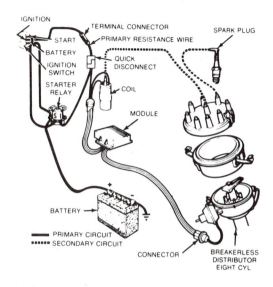

Fig. 9-10. Duraspark II primary and secondary circuits. (Courtesy of Ford Motor Co.)

4. High tension spark plug wiring
5. Spark plugs

Power from the ignition switch energizes the primary circuit creating a magnetic field in the coil primary winding. As mentioned in some detail earlier, the armature spokes are rotating (driven from the distributor shaft), and when they align with the center of the magnetic pickup coil, or stator assembly shown in Fig. 9-7(b), the module turns off the current flowing in the primary winding of the ignition coil (same action as when the contact breaker points separate in the conventional ignition system) which induces a high voltage within the secondary winding of the coil because of the rapidly collapsing magnetic field. The module allows current from the ignition switch to flow through the primary windings of the ignition coil, through the module to ground.

The high voltage produced in the coil secondary windings flows to the distributor cap where the spinning rotor (driven from the distributor shaft) distributes this high tension spark to the plugs through the cap terminals and leads.

Figure 9-11 shows an exploded view of typical distributor assemblies used with the Ford Duraspark system.

FORD DUAL MODE TIMING IGNITION MODULE

Certain applications employ the use of a special Duraspark II ignition module in conjunction with an altitude compensator. The module in conjunction with a barometric pressure switch alters the base engine timing to suit altitude. These modules have three connectors instead of the normal two. The barometric switch provides

an automatic retard signal to the module at different altitudes, thereby providing advanced timing at higher altitudes and retarding timing for spark knock control at lower altitudes.

FORD COLD START SPARK ADVANCE (CSSA)

Some models of Ford engines employ a CSSA system which is added to the distributor spark control system to momentarily trap the spark port vacuum on the

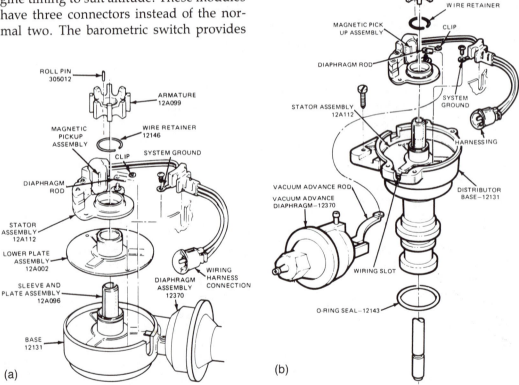

(a) (b)

Fig. 9-11. (a) Duraspark eight cylinder distributor assembly. (b) Six-cylinder breakerless distributor assembly. (Courtesy of Ford Motor Co.)

distributor spark advance diaphragm any-time that the engine coolant temperature is below 53°C (128°F). Figure 9-12 shows the system arrangement.

At the CSSA PVS (ported vacuum switch) temperature or higher, the vacuum from the carburetor spark port reaches the distributor through the SDV (spark delay valve), through the CSSA PVS, through the cooling PVS. At temperatures above 103°C or 225°F, the cooling PVS passes engine manifold vacuum to the distributor in order to increase the engine idle rpm, which assists engine cooling.

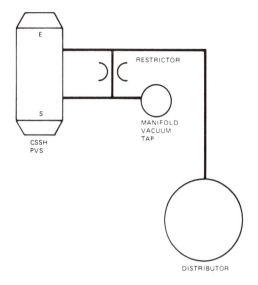

Fig. 9-13. Cold start spark hold system. (Courtesy of Ford Motor Co.)

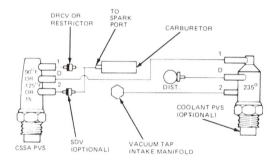

Fig. 9-12. Cold start spark advance (CSSA) system. (Courtesy of Ford Motor Co.)

FORD COLD START SPARK HOLD SYSTEM (CSSH)

This system is not unlike the CSSA system; however, it is designed to allow momentary spark advance hold during acceleration when the engine is cold, when the coolant temperature is lower than 53°C (128°F). The high vacuum already in the distributor diaphragm is slowly bled down through the restrictor as shown in Fig. 9-13, so that vacuum advance will only be held during the early stages of accelera-tion. Once the engine has warmed up, the

CSSH/PVS (ported vacuum switch) is open and the distributor vacuum becomes the same as that in the engine manifold.

FORD BI-LEVEL ROTOR AND DISTRIBUTOR CAP

The Duraspark III ignition system is used with the EEC (electronic engine con-trol) system which was designed to provide up to 50 degrees of distributor advance. This feature allows a greater flex-ibility in choosing engine calibrations re-lated to engine operating conditions. Compared to the conventional distributor's approximate 20 degrees of centrifugal ad-vance, much more flexibility is apparent with the EEC system. In order to allow this 50 degrees of distributor advance, a bi-level rotor and distributor cap is used as shown in Fig. 9-14.

Both the rotor and cap electrodes are

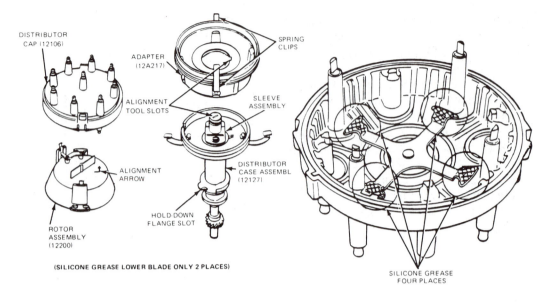

DISTRIBUTOR
CAP (12106)

ADAPTER
(12A217)

SPRING
CLIPS

ALIGNMENT
TOOL SLOTS

SLEEVE
ASSEMBLY

ALIGNMENT
ARROW

DISTRIBUTOR
CASE ASSEMBL
(12127)

HOLD-DOWN
FLANGE SLOT

ROTOR
ASSEMBLY
(12200)

(SILICONE GREASE LOWER BLADE ONLY 2 PLACES)

SILICONE GREASE
FOUR PLACES

Fig. 9-14. Bi-level rotor and distributor cap. (Courtesy of Ford Motor Co.)

designed to handle this additional spark advance capability by using two separate levels of secondary voltage distribution through an upper and lower electrode level. Rotor movement allows one of the high voltage electrode pick-up arms to align with one arm of the distributor cap center electrode plate, allowing high voltage to be transmitted from the plate through the rotor, distributor cap, and high tension wire to the respective spark plug.

NOTE: Numbers in the top of the distributor cap are spark plug wire/cylinder identification numbers only, therefore the engine firing order cannot be read off of the top of the distributor cap.

The design of the bi-level rotor and cap is such that the upper and lower level electrodes fire alternately in a pattern that actually jumps from one side of the cap to the other. It does not follow the sequence

of a conventional distributor wherein the firing order follows the circular path of the rotor.

FORD BREAKERLESS IGNITION TESTER (BIT)

In order to effectively troubleshoot and analyze problems within the Duraspark I, II, or III ignition systems, a special breakerless ignition tester (BIT) is required. Ford recommends that the Rotunda Breakerless Ignition Tester (BIT) be used for ignition system checkout and also when checking out the EEC (electronic engine control) system. Figure 9-15 shows the Rotunda Tester and its accessories.

Operating Features of the BIT

This tester is designed for easy use, as the following features will show.

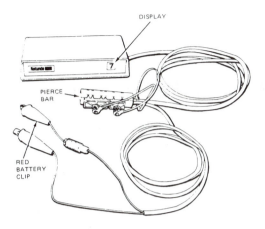

Fig. 9-15. Rotunda breakerless ignition tester (BIT). (Courtesy of Ford Motor Co.)

Display

The LED (light emitting diode) indicates the ignition test result codes and other information. During engine cranking, a displayed code will be stored in a memory bank. For this reason, anytime that a test checkout is to be conducted, you should watch the BIT display during the test crank procedures. These codes will flash onto the right-hand side of the Rotunda BIT unit such as is shown in Fig. 9-16.

Sleep mode

Once the BIT has been used to check out the system, and the ignition key has been turned off, the tester will automatically power itself down several seconds later, therefore no display or decimal will be shown on the BIT face. Should the ignition switch be turned on again with the tester still connected to the battery power supply, the trouble code that was displayed earlier will again show up on the BIT facia, unless the battery power has been disconnected after the first test.

Temperature mode

A built-in safety feature prevents possible damage to the tester from either too high or too low an operating temperature. Should the BIT operating temperature climb above +75°C, or fall below −75°C, the BIT will enter what is known as the sleep mode, and will not return to normal operation until these temperatures return to the limits stated.

Voltage mode

Another safety feature of the BIT is that should the battery voltage be too low, the tester will display an A on the right-hand side of the face panel. It will also enter the sleep mode should the battery voltage be too high.

Tone mode

When the ignition switch is turned to the off position, if no trouble code is displayed, then a tone will sound. Should this tone also sound when the engine is running, then an out-of-limit condition has occurred.

CAUTION: Should a problem arise with the BIT, do not attempt to open the tester case. Since it does not include any batteries, no adjustments are possible, and no fuses are used internally. Service information is readily available by calling 507-455-2626 or return the complete BIT.

1. In the USA, return it to: Owatonna Tool Company, Eisenhower Drive, Owatonna, Minn. 55060

2. In Canada, return it to: Jobborn Ltd; 97 Frid, Hamilton, Ontario. L8P-4M3

Breakerless Ignition Tester Hookup

To use the BIT, it should be hooked-up

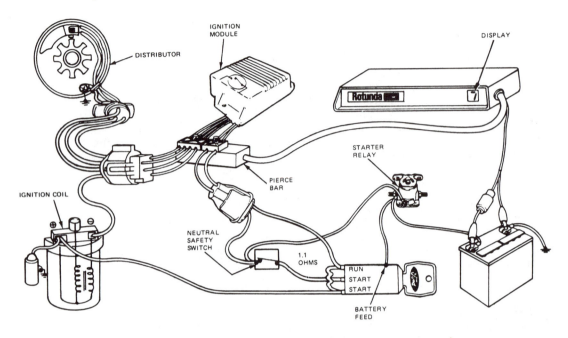

Fig. 9-16. Breakerless ignition tester hookup. (Courtesy of Ford Motor Co.)

as shown in Fig. 9-16, while the ignition switch is turned off.

1. It is important that no other test equipment is connected at this time.

2. The LED display must light sequentially; if it does not, then disconnect the tester, wait for 15 seconds and reconnect it. If it still does not sequence, then check the fuse circuit.

3. Sometimes it is possible for a missing distributor roll pin to cause wrong test results, so check this.

4. With the ignition key turned to the run position, a number 8 should display on the face of the BIT for a few seconds followed by a decimal only or a code number and a decimal. Should the BIT continue sequential lighting, or alternate

between 8 and blank with the key in the run position, test the red wire feed circuit to the ignition module.

5. While watching the display face of the BIT, attempt a normal Start/Run sequence while noting and remembering any codes shown during cranking.

6. Should a code be displayed during this time, and the engine symptom be observed, use the test code information table (Table 9-1) as a general guide and follow the appropriate diagnostic procedure given in this table.

7. Should a code be displayed with no engine symptom observed, disconnect the red tester clip from the battery, pause 15 seconds and reconnect the lead. Repeat the test procedure in order to verify that the code number is in fact repeated. Again refer to Table 9-1 to find the cause. Should

Table 9-1. Test Code Information

TEST CODE INFORMATION TABLE		
Code	**Condition Detected**	**Area To Check**
No Code, Decimal Only	None Found	No Out of Limit Ignition System Condition was Detected.
A	Low Battery Voltage	Battery or Charging System.
0	Low Voltage Feed to Ignition Module While Cranking	White Wire Feed Circuit to Ignition Module from Starter Relay "S" Terminal Circuit.
1	Low Voltage Feed to Ignition Module While Running	Red Wire Feed Circuit to Ignition Module from Ignition Switch.
2	Ground Circuit Open or Has Resistance	Black Wire Circuit from Ignition Module to Distributor Ground Screw Must be Under .3 OHMS.
3	Incorrect Trigger Signal	Check Orange/Purple Wires for Opens/Shorts. Orange/Purple Wires and Pickup Coil Must be over 70,000 OHMS to Ground. If OK, Replace Pickup Coil.
4	Purple Wire Circuit Short to Ground	Purple Wire and Pickup Coil Must be over 70,000 OHMS to Ground. If OK, Replace Ignition Module.
5	Dwell Incorrect	Ignition Module Disconnected. Key in RUN. Green Wire Must be within 1 Volt of Battery. Key OFF. Coil
6	Coil Current Not Switching Properly	Disconnected. Green Wire Must be Over 3,000 OHMS to Ground. Coil Connected Resistance Red to Green Wires Must be Under 1.2 OHMS for
7	Low Primary Current	Dura-I and Under 3 OHMS for Dura-II. Black Wire to Distributor Ground Screw Must be Under .3 OHMS. If OK, Replace Ignition Module.
9	Incorrect Secondary Voltage	Check Ignition Coil and Other High Voltage (Secondary) Parts.
Tone Sounds, Ignition Key in RUN	Loss of Voltage to Breakerless Ignition System	Battery Feed Circuit Through Ignition Switch and Feed Wire Splice.

Courtesy of Ford Motor Co.

the test code not repeat, then the condition is no longer present.

8. If an engine symptom is observed, but no code is displayed then the symptom is most probably not associated with an ignition system complaint. Therefore, proceed to check out other possible engine problem areas.

9. No out-of-limit condition in the ignition system is apparent if no code is displayed on the BIT face, and no engine symptom is observable. If you still suspect an ignition system problem, then test for a longer time period or until the code or symptom appears.

BIT TEST CODE INFORMATION

The use of a pierce bar allows the tester to monitor the breakerless ignition module wires. This pierce bar is shown in Fig. 9-16. Should any out-of-limit condition exist, a code such as that shown in Table 9-1 will be displayed. To find the cause, check the entire circuit indicated, including wires and connectors, etc. such as the distributor coil, ignition switch, and breakerless ignition module. Wire colors are in reference to module wires, which may change as you follow the circuit through the connectors to the ignition module and vehicle wiring harness.

(EEC) ELECTRONIC ENGINE CONTROL TESTING INSTRUCTIONS

The (BIT) breakerless ignition tester (Rotunda Unit) can be used to test the EEC system. However, the BIT may possibly display incorrect codes that are in fact unnecessary for the EEC system.

The following instructions are typical of the sequence used to check the EEC system.

1. Should a code 4 or 8 flash on the face of the BIT when testing an EEC equipped vehicle, disconnect the BIT's red battery clip for 15 seconds in order to clear the tester, then reconnect the lead.

2. The same sequence given in Step 1 should also be employed if a code 3 appears. This may have to be done several times until a code other than 3 appears. It sometimes helps when a code 3 is shown on the BIT face to reconnect the BIT with the ignition key in the run position and the engine running above 750 rpm if possible with the vehicle doors closed since seat belt chimes, solenoids, and buzzers can cause a code 3 to be displayed.

3. Should only a code 3 appear when you repeat this procedure, you will have to perform the ignition system or EEC system diagnostics test in order to isolate the problem. If, however, any other test code appears, then proceed according to the BIT's test code as shown in Table 9-1.

REVIEW QUESTIONS

Q1 What is the purpose of a dual diaphragm vacuum advance system used on the Ford ignition system.

Q2 What is the advantage of the bi-level rotor concept used by Ford Motor Co. on their vehicles?

Q3 Can the firing order of the system be determined from the bi-level distributor cap on the Ford system?

ANSWERS

A1 Ford vehicles employ a dual diaphragm advance system with some of their ignition systems as a means of monitoring both carburetor venturi vacuum, and intake manifold vacuum; the venturi vacuum controls the advance portion of the distributor while the intake manifold acts upon the retard diaphragm.

A2 Ford employs a bi-level rotor on some of their vehicles to allow greater flexibility in choosing engine calibrations; the system allows up to 50 degrees of distributor advance.

A3 The firing order cannot be read directly from the distributor cap of the bi-level rotor since the upper and lower level electrodes fire alternately in a pattern that jumps from one side of the cap to the other.

Chapter
10
Chrysler Ignition Systems

CHRYSLER LEAN-BURN ELECTRONIC IGNITION SYSTEM

Chrysler vehicles manufactured in the U.S.A. since 1973 have employed some form of electronic ignition system. Two main types have been used, namely the reluctor style (toothed wheel) similar to that used by both General Motors and Ford vehicles, and the Hall-Effect unit which is discussed herein in some detail. (See Fig. 10-6.)

Changes have been made along with system improvements to the Chrysler ignition systems since 1973 as with other manufacturers' systems. However, the basic arrangement has not changed drastically.

The reluctor type of distributor is commonly used on Chrysler product V-8 engines, while the Hall-Effect distributor is employed on their 4-cylinder engines. An ECU (Electronic Control Unit) is employed with both types of distributors in conjunction with a variety of engine sensors similar to those used by both Ford and General Motors, such as an oxygen sensor, a coolant temperature sensor, throttle position transducer, vacuum transducer, air

temperature sensor, carburetor-idle-stop-switch sensor, and a spark-control module. Basic location of these components is shown in Fig. 10-1. Figure 10-2 illustrates the ELB wiring system. Note that within the Spark Control Computer, in addition to the vacuum transducer, there is also an air temperature sensor. The lean-burn system uses air/fuel ratios in the region of 17:1 and 18:1 as compared with the normal 14:1 or 15:1 for highway driving.

TESTING: CHRYSLER LEAN BURN SYSTEM

To troubleshoot and analyze the electronic lean-burn ignition system used on Chrysler vehicles, a special analyzer is available and is shown in Fig. 10-3.

Since the analyzer shown in Fig. 10-3 has all of the necessary instructions on how to use the tester on the front face (decal), we will not go into it step-by-step here. Along with the necessary leads and adapters, the analyzer can be connected to the system for rapid troubleshooting.

Should an analyzer not be readily available, effective troubleshooting of the system cannot be readily accomplished, other than those checks that would normally be done on a vehicle with no computer. In many instances, loose or dirty connections or plug-in harnesses can be a reason for improper engine operation. Prior to condemning the electronic ignition system, however, run through the same basic checks that you would normally do on a vehicle with a conventional ignition system.

FAILURE OF ENGINE TO START: ELB SYSTEM

If an ELB equipped vehicle fails to start but the engine will crank, check all pri-

mary and secondary ignition wires for secure connection and cleanliness. Check for a good spark from the coil, distributor, and spark plug. If a good spark is apparent, but the engine still fails to start, then a voltmeter/ohmmeter can be used to check the system as follows:

1. Disconnect the plug-in wiring harness from the coolant switch sensor on the engine.

2. Place a small piece of thin cardboard or insulating paper between the curb-idle screw and carburetor idle-stop switch if they are in contact with one another.

3. Refer to Fig. 10-2, ELB wiring system schematic, and connect a voltmeter lead with the ignition switch on between the

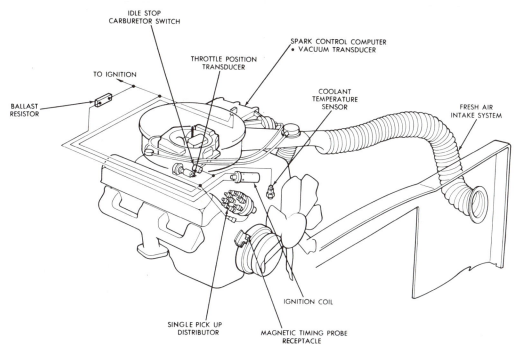

Fig. 10-1. Chrysler ELB (electronic lean burn) component location on engine. (Courtesy of Chrysler Corp.)

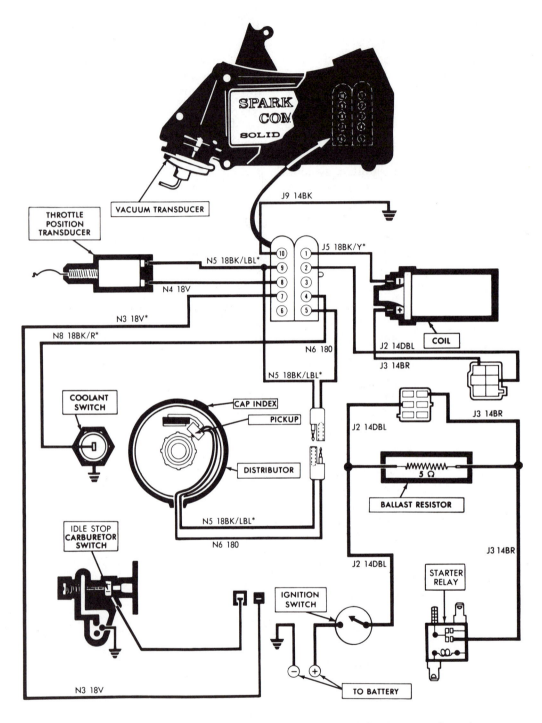

Fig. 10-2. Chrysler ELB ignition system wiring schematic (basic system layout). (Courtesy of Chrysler Corp.)

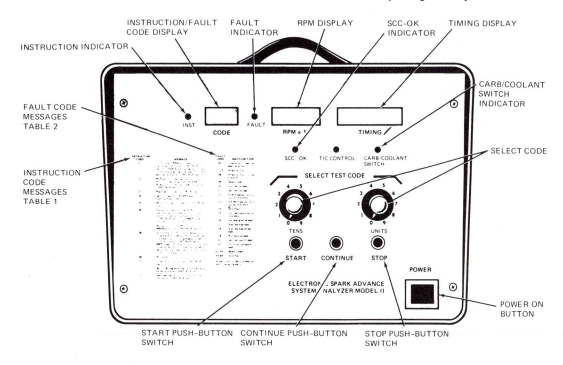

Fig. 10-3. Electronic lean burn ignition analyzer. (Courtesy of Chrysler Corp.)

carburetor idle-stop switch terminal and ground. With a voltage reading between 5 and 10 volts (less than 10), move on to Step 5 of the procedure. If, however, the voltage is higher than 10 volts, carefully check for a good ground at terminal number 10 of the spark control computer.

Should a reading of less than 5 volts be recorded, turn the ignition switch off; disconnect the plug-in connector from the bottom of the spark control computer, then turn the ignition switch back on and check the voltage reading at terminal number 2 of the spark control computer which should be no more than one volt lower than that of the battery. If so, go to Step 4; if not, check for poor connections, etc. between terminal 2 and the ignition switch.

4. Turn ignition off and pull wiring connector loose from the computer. Using the ohmmeter, check for continuity between terminal 7 and the carb-idle-stop switch terminal; then check for additional continuity between terminal 10 of the connector and ground and replace the computer if a reading is noted.

If no reading is noted, check for poor connections, etc. and go to Step 5 if the engine fails to start.

5. With the ignition on, check voltage at terminal 1 which should be within a volt of the battery level, in order to proceed to Step 6. A low reading requires that you check for poor connections, etc. in order to establish the reason for the low reading.

6. Measure the resistance between

numbers 5 and 9 terminal with the ignition switch on which should be between 150 and 900 ohms in order to proceed to the next step. A reading outside of this level requires that you disconnect the pickup coil leads from the distributor to measure the resistance at this lead going into the distributor. If it is between 150 and 900 ohms, then it indicates that between terminals 5 and 9 and the distributor connector, poor connections, opens, or shorts exist. If, however, the resistance reading is still not within these limits, the distributor pick-up coil is faulty and should be replaced.

7. There should not be any continuity shown on the ohmmeter when it is connected between ground and the individual terminal leads feeding into the distributor. If this is the case, reconnect the distributor lead. If there is continuity, then shorts exist.

8. Remove the distributor cap and check the air gap between the reluctor wheel and the distributor pick-up coil as shown in Fig. 10-4, using a non-magnetic feeler gauge. Ensure that the tooth of the reluctor wheel is in the exact position shown. Too wide a gap can result in a low magnetic field strength as the reluctor teeth approach the pickup coil, while too small a gap can result in failure of the magnetic field to decrease quickly enough as the teeth move away from the pickup coil preventing a rapid cut-off to the generated voltage pulse.

9. Install the distributor cap and wiring and attempt to start the engine. If it doesn't start, replace the spark control computer.

10. If the engine still fails to start, obviously the problem is not the computer. Is there another mechanical problem that you

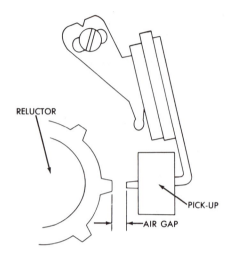

Fig. 10-4. Air gap adjustment location on Chrysler electronic ignition distributor (reluctor type).

failed to check earlier prior to testing the electronic ignition operation? Double check possible mechanical items, then recheck the procedure given for the ignition system.

Once the problem has been found and the engine is running, you should check engine timing, and connect an oscilloscope to determine any weak points in the system, or obtain Chrysler's own special analyzer in order to properly diagnose the system for other possible trouble areas.

INTERNATIONAL-HARVESTER IGNITION SYSTEMS

IHC has used both contact breaker point type and breakerless distributors in their light and medium duty trucks. They have used the Holley Model 1530 breakerless electronic ignition systems on some vehicles, with their later units employing Prestolite IDN-4000 breakerless integral electronic control distributors. The Prestolite unit is a trigger wheel type of unit similar to those described already under breakerless ignition systems in this Chapter. A typical troubleshooting chart for this and similar type ignition systems is shown in Table 10-1.

ALTERNATE IGNITION SYSTEMS

Although the (HEI) High Energy Ignition distributors used by companies such as General Motors Corporation, Ford, etc. are widely used on production vehicles, several other types of after-market products are available as bolt-on kits for use on older vehicles where the advantages of a breakerless ignition system is desired.

Table 10-2 shows the various types of electronic ignition systems that are currently used on passenger car and commercial vehicles.

There are actually three basic arrangements employed in electronic ignition systems in order to eliminate contact breaker point designs.

1. Magnetic impulse (arrangement used in the GMC and Ford distributors shown herein), plus an alternate magnetic impulse design commonly known as a Hall-Effect arrangement.

2. Metal detection arrangement

3. Optical arrangement

Magnetic Impulse Arrangement

Since this arrangement was discussed in considerable detail under the GMC and Ford ignition systems above, we shall look at the Hall-Effect type of magnetic-impulse breakerless electronic ignition arrangement. It should be noted however prior to looking at the Hall-Effect arrangement, that in addition to the HEI (high energy ignition) system employed by GMC and Ford, another design of this type of system utilizes the distributor shaft cam lobes to produce magnetic-impulses rather than the widely used armature spoked wheel set-up in the GMC and Ford system.

An example of this cam-lobe type unit is shown in Fig. 10-5, in which each time that

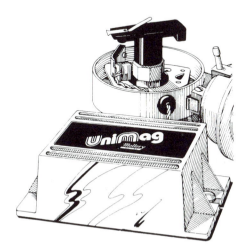

Cam Lobe   Magnetic Pick-up

Fig. 10-5. Cam-lobe type of magnetic impulse breakerless ignition system. (Courtesy of Mallory Electric Co.)

Table 10-1. Electronic Ignition System Troubleshooting.

Listed here are only those causes for the indicated problem
conditions which are chargeable to the ignition system.

CONDITION	POSSIBLE CAUSE	REMEDY
Engine fails to start	No primary voltage to coil.	Check battery, ignition switch, primary feed and ground circuits. (Perform "Primary Voltage Drop Test"). Repair as needed.
(Perform "Ignition System Trouble Shooting Test")	Moisture in distributor cap or high tension cable boots.	Clean and dry parts. Correct cause for entry of moisture.
	Trigger wheel-to-sensor air gap incorrect.	Check air gap. Adjust if needed.
	Open rotor.	Replace rotor.
	Faulty distributor cap.	Replace cap.
	Coil high tension cable not seated in coil tower or or distributor cap.	Check cable installation.
	Faulty high tension cables.	Replace cables.
	Coil open or shorted.	Test coil, replace if faulty.
	Faulty electronic control unit.	Replace control unit.
Engine backfires but fails to start.	Incorrect ignition timing.	Check timing. Adjust as needed.
	Moisture in distributor cap.	Dry cap and rotor.
	Distributor cap faulty or carbon tracked.	Check cap for loose terminals, cracks and dirt. Clean or replace as needed.
	Spark plug cables connected incorrectly.	Check cables for correct position.
Engine does not operate smoothly or engine misfires at high speed	Spark plugs fouled.	Clean and regap plugs.
	Spark plug electrodes worn (gap too wide).	Regap or replace plugs.
	Spark plug cables faulty.	Check cables, replace if needed.
	Spark advance system(s) faulty.	Check operation of advance system(s). Repair as needed.
	Worn distributor shaft bushings.	Check for worn bushings. Rebuild or replace distributor.
Excessive fuel consumption.	See causes listed under "engine does not operate smoothly."	
Erratic timing advance	Vacuum leaks in vacuum advance system.	Check vacuum hoses. Replace as needed.
	Faulty vacuum advance diaphragm assembly.	Check operation of advance diaphragm. Replace if needed.

Table 10-1 (continued). Electronic Ignition System Troubleshooting.

Sticking or worn sensor plate.	Replace electronic control unit.
Misadjusted, damaged or weak mechanical advance springs.	Readjust spring tension. Replace distributor shaft assembly.
Mechanical advance flyweight bushings worn.	Replace distributor shaft assembly.
Trigger wheel assembly binding or excessively loose or distributor shaft.	Free-up and lubricate trigger wheel assembly. Replace distributor shaft assembly, if needed.

Courtesy of International Harvester

Table 10-2
Typical Types of Electronic Ignition Systems.

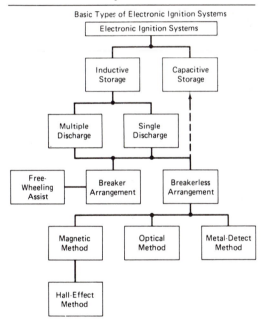

Basic Types of Electronic Ignition Systems

a cam-lobe passes the pickup a voltage is induced in the coil, which is then relayed or conducted to the ignition module where an integrated circuit (IC) amplifier conditions and amplifies the pulse voltage. In addition, a constant dwell action is provided by a dwell computer at all engine speeds, therefore regardless of engine rpm, a constant high output voltage can be maintained.

Still another arrangement of an HEI system of the magnetic-impulse design employs a permanent magnet in the core assembly to establish the magnetic field rather than having battery current flowing through the pickup coil.

In the Hall-Effect unit, a rotating metallic-chopper spins between a magnet and a Hall-Effect chip as shown in Fig. 10-6, which effectively causes the magnetic field to be subjected to a make-and-break effect commonly known as chopping.

The Hall-Effect ignition distributor is widely used in Chrysler Corporation 4-cylinder engine vehicles. Generally, no centrifugal advance mechanism is used with this system, since the frequency of the voltage pulses is so accurate that they are used to provide a spark advance.

Metal Detection Ignition Arrangement

This system is similar to the Hall-Effect system, but it employs a sensor-coil rather than the semiconductor chip. This sensor coil is connected into a high-frequency

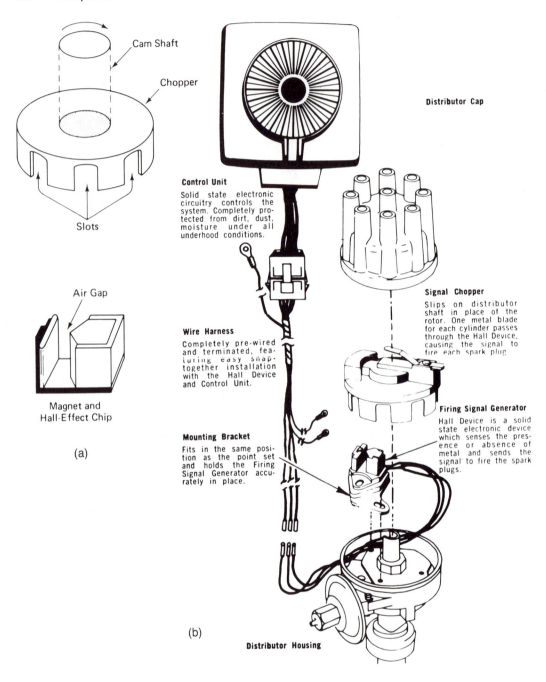

Cam Shaft

Chopper

Slots

Air Gap

Magnet and
Hall-Effect Chip

(a)

Distributor Cap

Control Unit

Solid state electronic
circuitry controls the
system. Completely pro-
tected from dirt, dust,
moisture under all
underhood conditions.

Signal Chopper

Slips on distributor
shaft in place of the
rotor. One metal blade
for each cylinder passes
through the Hall Device,
causing the signal to
fire each spark plug.

Wire Harness

Completely pre-wired
and terminated, fea-
turing easy snap-
together installation
with the Hall Device
and Control Unit.

Firing Signal Generator

Hall Device is a solid
state electronic device
which senses the pres-
ence or absence of
metal and sends the
signal to fire the spark
plugs.

Mounting Bracket

Fits in the same posi-
tion as the point set
and holds the Firing
Signal Generator accu-
rately in place.

(b)

Distributor Housing

Fig. 10-6. (a) Hall effect concentric chopper unit; (b) Hall effect ignition system
distributor.

oscillator circuit, namely Oscillator 1 as shown in Fig. 10-7.

In Fig. 10-7, a trigger wheel similar to the chopper arrangement of the Hall-Effect system rotates past the face of the sensor coil to increase and decrease the oscillator frequency as each individual tooth passes by. The output of Oscillator 2 does not change as the trigger wheel rotates, since it is of a fixed frequency design. The combined outputs of both oscillators are fed into a mixer, in which their individual frequencies combine to produce a beat frequency.

From the mixer, the beat frequency voltage is relayed to and through a frequency selective filter and pulse shaper circuit to the trigger output.

Optical Ignition Arrangement

In this system, there is no armature or trigger wheel used. Instead, a light beam interruptor is rotated by the camshaft and a photoelectric cell acts as an electronic switching device which has the advantage of optimizing the available dwell time. This arrangement is shown in Fig. 10-8.

Current flow in the ignition coil primary winding is received via the output from the phototransistor which is applied to an amplifier where it is stepped up to a suitable level to control the current flow to the coil. Optical ignition systems can be employed with either an inductive discharge or capacitive discharge system. The number of slots in the interruptor disc matches the number of engine cylinders. The high-tension spark can be produced in the system in one of two ways, when the interruptor stops the light beam or by use of the light beam. Some systems have employed an infrared source of radiation, instead of a visible light source.

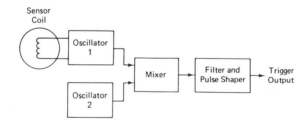

Fig. 10-7. Metal detection ignition arrangement.

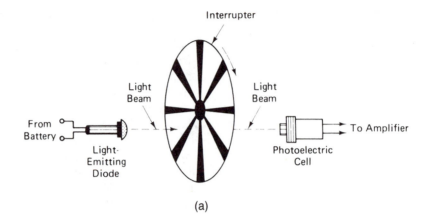

(a)

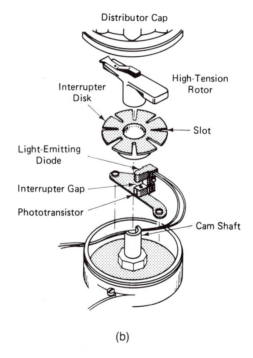

(b)

Fig. 10-8. (a) Basic optical ignition arrangement, (b) component location. (Courtesy of Speedatron)

REVIEW QUESTIONS

Q1 What is a hall-effect ignition distributor?

Q2 What is a metal-detection ignition arrangement?

Q3 What is an optical ignition arrangement?

ANSWERS

A1 A hall-effect ignition distributor employs a rotating metallic-chopper spinning between a magnet and a hall-effect chip which effectively causes the magnetic field to be subjected to a make and break effect commonly known as chopping.

A2 A metal detection ignition system is a unit that employs a sensor coil rather than the semiconductor chip; this sensor coil is connected to a high-frequency oscillator circuit, whereby a trigger wheel similar to the chopper arrangement of the hall-effect system rotates past the face of the sensor coil to produce an increase or decrease of the oscillator frequency as each tooth passes by.

A3 In an optical ignition arrangement there is no armature or trigger wheel, instead a light-beam interruptor is rotated by the camshaft, and a photoelectric cell acts as an electronic switching device which has the advantage of optimizing the available dwell time.

Chapter

11

Magneto Systems

Prior to the introduction of the battery type ignition system, gasoline engines relied on a magneto ignition system to fire the spark plugs. Although magneto ignition is no longer employed on passenger cars and trucks, it is still used in specific applications in which no electrical accessories are required, generally on industrial or farm equipment where a small motor drives a number of attachments in a remote location. Magnetos are also used on engines of the dual fuel variety such as diesel/natural gas engines used on pipelines. These engines can run on diesel fuel alone or can be converted to run on natural or methane/sewer gas. When gas is used, a spark plug must be employed to fire the mixture. A magneto can be used for this purpose, especially if the engine is equipped with an air starter motor rather than an electric starter motor, when battery power is available.

In addition to the magneto used for firing spark plugs, magneto generators or permanent-magnet generators can produce AC voltage for vehicles or other equipment with a lighting system. Probably the most common use today for magnetos is in internal combustion engines found in motorcycles, snowmobiles, lawn mowers, power saws, outboard motors, farm equipment, and stationary industrial units.

Magneto Construction

Both Robert Bosch Corporation and Fairbanks-Morse are well-known producers of magneto systems. The design and operation of magnetos will differ somewhat; however, their function remains basically the same. Two basic components form the magneto:

1. A rotating steel flywheel fitted with a number of permanent magnets attached to the engine crankshaft (keyed to a fixed position and held in place by bolts or a nut); and,

2. A stationary aluminum armature base plate that is mounted concentrically to the flywheel; this base plate serves to hold the ignition armature, the contact breaker points and capacitor. Activation of the contact point breaker lever is generally via a cam track which is ground onto the flywheel hub.

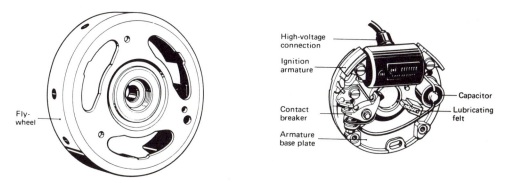

Fig. 11-1. Magneto flywheel and base plate assembly. (Courtesy of Robert Bosch Corp.)

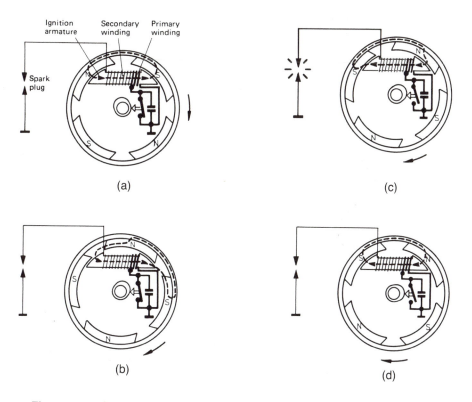

Fig. 11-2. Magneto ignition system: (a) initiation of electron flow in the primary and secondary windings, (b) point opening, (c) delivery of high-tension spark, (d) point closing. (Courtesy of Robert Bosch Corp.)

Figure 11-1 illustrates a typical magneto flywheel and base plate assembly.

Magneto Operation

When the magneto is used for ignition purposes, an ignition coil is installed in the circuit in order to step up the voltage requirements necessary to fire the spark plugs. The sequence of events involved in generating a high tension spark to the plug is shown in Fig. 11-2. The four views illustrate the initiation of the electron flow in the primary and secondary windings of the magneto ignition armature, the opening of the points to cause a voltage increase in the secondary winding, the delivery of the high tension spark to the plug or external coil, and the reclosing of the contact breaker points. The following points should be noted in Fig. 11-2:

1. Initial magnetic flow north to south pole with points closed and flow through the primary winding.

2. Flywheel moving around, note position of magnetic poles and camshaft approaching breaker point lever.

3. Note reversal of magnetic flux due to position of north and south magnets and that points have opened thereby generating voltage in the secondary winding; voltage can go to a spark plug or an external ignition coil.

4. Plug has fired and camshaft is rotating around to reclose points; note magnetic flow through magnets.

The rotation of the flywheel causes a large number of reversals to be induced in the primary winding of the ignition armature with the points closed. When the

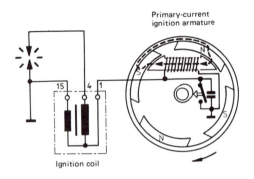

Fig. 11-3. Magneto unit with an external ignition coil. (Courtesy of Robert Bosch Corp.)

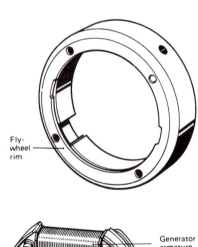

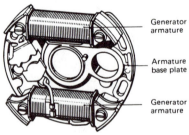

Fig. 11-4. Permanent magnet magneto generator. (Courtesy of Robert Bosch Corp.)

points are opened, the magnetic flux in the armature core reverses direction which induces the high voltage surge in the secondary winding to the spark plugs; however, in ignition systems requiring higher voltage surges, an external ignition coil can be used as shown in Fig. 11-3.

When a magneto armature is used for purposes of generating electricity for storage batteries or lighting purposes, the armature base plate is fitted with two armatures as shown in Fig. 11-4 which produces AC voltage. In order to convert this AC voltage to DC for battery charging a rectifier would have to be fitted to the AC output circuit.

Chapter
12

Ignition Switches

IGNITION SWITCH ASSEMBLIES

For anti-theft reasons, most vehicle manufacturers today have installed the actual ignition switch assembly on the steering rod column so that it is inaccessible unless the steering column is lowered from its normal mounting position. On most GMC vehicles, for example, the actual ignition switch (not the key switch) is located on top of the column jacket near the front of the dash inside the channel section of the brake pedal support. Actuation of the switch is through a rod and rack assembly shown in Fig. 12-1. On Ford vehicles, the ignition switch is also located on the top of the steering column as shown in Fig. 12-1 and is only accessible when the steering column is lowered.

In the arrangement shown in Fig. 12-1, a mechanical block is used rather than a starter safety switch to prevent engine starting in other than P or N (park or neutral). Rotation of the key switch causes a gear sector to rotate a mating rack which is attached to a wedge-shaped finger that is capable of sliding through a hole in the bowl plate anytime the driver places the gear selector in either P or N. If the driver has the gear selector lever in any position other than P or N, then the bowl plate has been rotated to a position whereby turning the key switch will cause the wedge-shaped finger to butt up against the bowl plate. Since the wedge-shaped finger cannot pass through the hole or mating slot in the bowl plate, the actuator rod which is connected to the actual column mounted ignition switch is incapable of completing the electrical circuit to the starter motor.

Ignition Switch Replacement

Replacement of the ignition switch as mentioned previously requires that the steering column be lowered from its normally mounted position first. It is not necessary to remove the steering wheel unless the key lock cylinder is to be replaced also. If, however, the key lock cylinder is to be removed, then the steering wheel should be pulled from its shaft. The following procedure is typical for lock cylinder removal and installation.

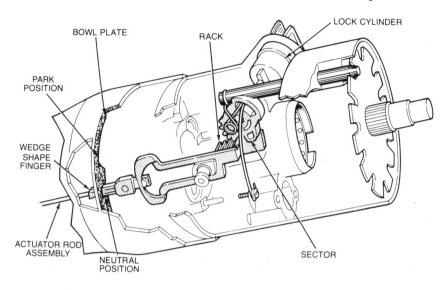

PARK POSITION

BOWL PLATE

RACK

LOCK CYLINDER

WEDGE SHAPE FINGER

ACTUATOR ROD ASSEMBLY

NEUTRAL POSITION

SECTOR

Fig. 12-1. Ignition key connection to ignition switch actuator rod assembly. (Courtesy of Cadillac Motor Car Div. of GMC)

1. Disconnect the battery ground cable to immobilize the circuit.

2. Remove the steering wheel.

3. Lower the steering column by removing the shroud and necessary retaining bolts.

4. Remove the turn signal switch from the column. Usually you can pull the switch rearward enough to slip it over the end of the shaft without pulling the wiring harness out of the steering column.

5. Refer to Fig. 12-2 for removal and assembly procedures.

The lock cylinder should always be checked for proper operation if it is to be reused, or the new one should be checked for freedom of movement prior to installation. Insert the key and check the extension of the actuator tip as shown in Fig. 12-3. For example, Cadillac recommends that this dimension should be a maximum

of 1.27 mm (.050 inch); otherwise, the lock cylinder should be replaced. Figure 12-3 shows the lock cylinder tip retracted. Tip extension and retraction should be free and smooth with no sign of bind or sticking, otherwise replace the lock cylinder.

The ignition key warning switch (buzzer) is located in the steering column housing. To remove it, refer to Fig. 12-4(a). With a short piece of wire (paper clip) bent to a right angle ¼ inch (6.3 mm) from the end, hook the wire into the loop of the clip and pull the switch and clip together. If the lock cylinder is still in position, it should be in the on position at this time to facilitate removal of the buzzer switch assembly.

NOTE: The steering column should be properly supported when it has been lowered to prevent possible damage to the collapsible safety components.

To remove the actual column mounted ignition switch, it should be placed in the

DISASSEMBLE

1. Place lock in "run".

2. Remove lock plate, turn signal switch and buzzer switch (see service manual.)

3. Remove screw & lock cylinder. **CAUTION:** *If screw is dropped on removal, it could fall into the column, requiring complete disassembly to retrieve the screw.*

ASSEMBLE

1. Rotate as shown, align cylinder key with keyway in housing.

2. Push lock all the way in.

3. Install screw. Tighten to 4.5 N·m for regular columns—2.5 N·m for adjustable columns.

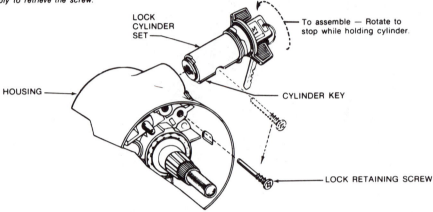

Fig. 12-2. Key lock cylinder removal. (Courtesy of Chevrolet Motor Div. of GMC)

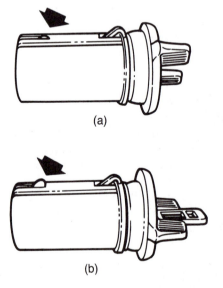

Fig. 12-3. (a) Lock cylinder actuator key removed, (b) lock cylinder actuator key in place. (Courtesy of Cadillac Motor Car Div. of GMC)

off-unlocked position which (if the lock cylinder has already been removed) can be done by pulling up on the actuating rod until it stops, then move it back down two detents as shown in Fig. 12-4(b). On some GMC vehicles it may also be necessary to remove the dimmer switch (headlights) prior to ignition switch removal. Proceed then to remove the ignition switch mounting screw and switch assembly.

Ignition Switch Installation

Rotate the lock cylinder to the off-unlock position and place the gearlever in N (neutral). Refer to Fig. 12-4 (b), and place the actual ignition switch into the off-unlock position by moving the slider two positions to the right from the accessory position. Engage the actuator rod into the slider hole and place the ignition switch

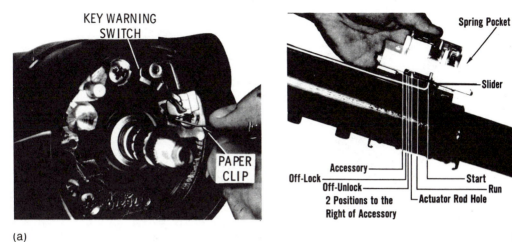

Fig. 12-4. (a) Ignition buzzer switch removal, (b) positioning ignition switch. (Courtesy of Chevrolet Motor Div. of GMC)

assembly into position on the steering column and secure it in place with the correct screws taking care not to move the switch out of the detent position (off-unlock).

FORD IGNITION SWITCH ARRANGEMENT

The ignition switch arrangement used by Ford is similar to that found on General Motors vehicles as can be readily seen in Fig. 12-5.

Ford Ignition Switch Adjustment

On the ignition switch arrangement shown in Fig. 12-5, the switch should be adjusted to ensure that it will operate properly especially after replacement of the key lock cylinder or ignition switch assembly. This can be done as follows:

1. Insert a ⁵⁄₆₄ inch (1.98 mm) drill bit through the lock pin hole located on the right of the switch next to the steering column as far as it will go which is about ³⁄₈

inch (9.5 mm). If trouble is encountered in inserting the drill bit, simply rotate the ignition key back and forth to either side of the lock position.

2. Loosen the ignition switch mounting nuts (shown in Fig. 12-5) low down on the steering column.

3. Turn the key to the lock position indicated by the feel of the detent, then remove the key.

4. Gently oscillate the switch up and down on the steering column until you establish the mid-travel point of the actuator rod free-play, then tighten the retaining nuts to 4.51-7.34 N.m (40-65 inch-lbs).

5. Remove the drill bit from the key switch locking pin hole.

6. Plug in the electrical connector and turn the key switch to its different positions to ensure that it does in fact operate properly.

Replacement of the ignition switch is similar to that explained for GMC vehicles.

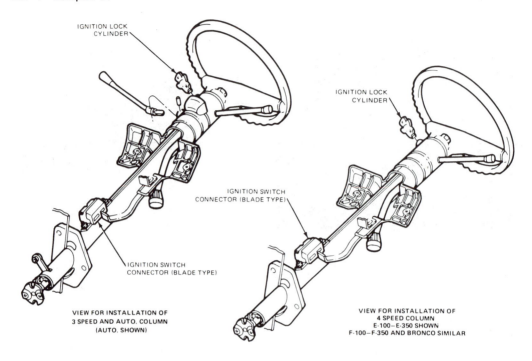

Fig. 12-5. Blade-type connector ignition switch. (Courtesy of Ford Motor Co.)

Should it be suspected that a fault does exist in the actual column mounted ignition switch assembly, then a continuity test can be done with the aid of a self-powered test lamp or ohmmeter between the plug terminals indicated for each switch position, as shown in Fig. 12-6, by disconnecting the multiple connector and spreading apart the locking fingers to allow the snap-in plugs to be pulled apart.

IGNITION SWITCH ON LIGHT-DUTY TRUCKS

The purpose of the ignition switch is to complete the circuit between the battery and the push button start switch on heavy trucks and equipment, or to supply current to the starter solenoid on those com-

bination ignition/start type switches.

Problems associated with the key type switch are not common; however, when the switch is suspected of being at fault, several simple tests can be conducted to establish if in fact the switch assembly is the problem area. Problems that occur with the ignition switch on current production passenger cars and light trucks often require that the steering column be lowered in order to gain access to the lock cylinder assembly. This is necessary due to anti-theft systems, in which the actual ignition switch is part of the lock cylinder set. The switch is located inside the channel section of the brake pedal support, for example, on many current General Motors vehicles. It is therefore completely inaccessible without first lowering the steering column.

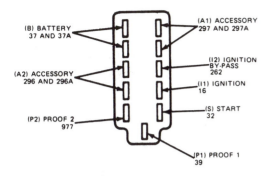

SWITCH POSITION:	CONTINUITY SHOULD EXIST ONLY BETWEEN:
ACCESSORY	37-37A-297-297A; 296-296A
LOCK	37-37A; 297-297A; 296-296A
OFF	37-37A; 297-297A; 296-296A
RUN	16-37-37A-297-297A-296-296A
START	39-977-GROUND; 37-37A-32-262

● CONTINUITY BETWEEN CIRCUIT 16 AND CIRCUITS 37-37A-32-262 IN START POSITION IS ALSO PERMISSIBLE.

● CIRCUIT PAIRS 37 AND 37A, 296 AND 296A, AND 297 AND 297A ARE CONNECTED TOGETHER INTERNALLY IN THE SWITCH.

Fig. 12-6. Blade-type connector ignition switch continuity test. (Courtesy of Ford Motor Co.)

An example of how to replace the lock cylinder assembly on light duty General Motors trucks is shown in Fig. 12-2, along with the necessary procedural steps.

IGNITION SWITCH ON HEAVY-DUTY TRUCKS

The ignition switch used on heavy-duty trucks does not directly energize the starter motor solenoid, but simply carries the small current necessary to energize the fuel solenoid switch on diesel engines when turned to the "ign" position. It can also carry the small current necessary to activate a heavy-duty magnetic switch which when energized carries full battery power to the starter motor for cranking purposes. Other circuits may employ a push button switch located alongside the key switch to energize the starter motor. Prior to removing or replacing the ignition

switch on heavy-duty trucks, the switch assembly should be tested for continuity using a self-powered test light or ohmmeter as shown in Fig. 12-7, once it has been removed from the vehicle.

When testing for continuity of the switch assembly, do not use anything else but the key in order to actuate the switch to its various positions; otherwise, switch damage that did not exist before can be the result. Should the switch assembly fail any of the continuity tests as shown in Fig. 12-7, replace the switch assembly.

IGNITION SWITCH REMOVAL AND INSTALLATION: HEAVY-DUTY TRUCKS

The removal and installation of the ignition switch assembly is fairly simple and is similar for most trucks. The following pro-

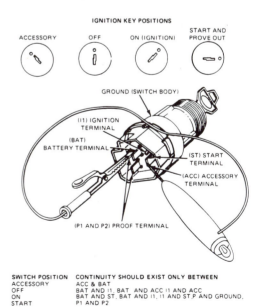

SWITCH POSITION	CONTINUITY SHOULD EXIST ONLY BETWEEN
ACCESSORY	ACC & BAT
OFF	BAT AND I1, BAT AND ACC I1 AND ACC
ON	BAT AND ST, BAT AND I1, I1 AND ST
START	BAT AND ST, BAT AND I1, I1 AND ST,P AND GROUND, P1 AND P2

Fig. 12-7. Ignition switch continuity test, Ford CL9000 truck. (Courtesy of Ford Motor Co.)

cedure is common to heavy-duty Ford vehicles.

1. Pull out the ignition wire harness from the rear of the switch assembly.

2. Refer to Fig. 12-8 (a), and turn the key to the "acc" position. Then depress the release pin in the face of the lock cylinder, and turn the key CCW and pull the key and lock cylinder out of the switch unit. Should it only be necessary and desired to replace the lock cylinder of the assembly at this time, proceed to Step 3 of the "Installation" procedure given below.

3. Refer to Fig. 12-8 (b), and remove the ignition switch retainer screw and retainer under the instrument panel in order to remove the switch assembly.

Ignition Switch Installation

1. Refer to Fig. 12-8 (b), and place the switch and its retainer in the instrument panel and secure it with its screw.

2. Proceed to install the switch bezel and tighten it.

3. If the lock cylinder has been replaced, turn the key to the accessory position. Place both the cylinder and key into the ignition switch, depress lightly and release the pin, then turn the key CW. Push the new lock cylinder into the switch and turn the key to check the lock cylinder operation.

4. Plug the wiring harness back into the rear of the ignition switch assembly, and check the operation of the switch.

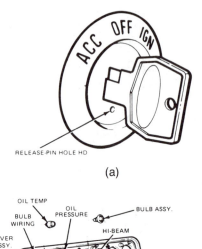

(a)

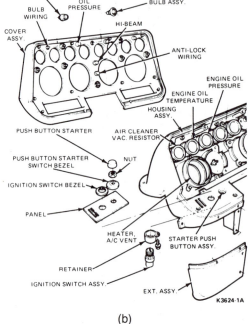

(b)

Fig. 12-8. (a) Ignition switch removal, Ford CL9000, (b) ignition switch disassembled. (Courtesy of Ford Motor Co.)

REVIEW QUESTIONS

Q1 Where is the actual ignition switch (not the key switch) located on many cars today?

Q2 What is used with the ignition switch to prevent starting of the engine in any other range but P or N in an automatic transmission equipped car?

Q3 Can the ignition switch be removed without lowering the steering column?

Q4 What is required in order to remove the key lock cylinder?

Q5 What position should the ignition switch be in when removing and installing it?

ANSWERS

A1 For anti-theft purposes, most ignition switches are attached to the lower column area underneath the vehicle dash, often within the channel section of the brake pedal support.

A2 A mechanical block feature is normally employed with the ignition key/switch arrangement whereby a wedge-shaped finger will not pass through a blocker plate hole when the transmission shift linkage is in any position other than P and N.

A3 For the reasons mentioned in Question 4, it is necessary to lower the steering column in order to repair the ignition switch assembly.

A4 To remove and replace the ignition switch key lock cylinder involves removal of the steering wheel.

A5 When removing or installing the ignition switch, it should be in the unlocked position to allow you enough flexibility to maneuver it in or out of position without undue force being placed on the linkage.

Chapter

13

Spark Plugs

The main function of any spark plug is to receive the high-tension spark from the coil secondary winding or electronic module in order to initiate combustion within the engine cylinder. Many types of spark plugs are employed in order to offer peak performance in different designs of internal combustion engines with various operating environments and speed/load conditions. The spark plug has to withstand very high mechanical, thermal, and electrical loads, therefore correct selection of the proper spark plug is a major prerequisite to a properly performing engine.

In modern gasoline engines, high economy and clean exhaust gases require that the engine be operated on a fuel/air mixture as lean as possible. This condition, however, leads to fairly high combustion chamber temperatures. Regardless of the engine being of standard compression or of high compression design, the spark plug is exposed to the open flame created within the combustion chamber. Therefore, provision must be made for good heat flow from the plug to the engine block by cooling the plug seat. The actual heat range of a spark plug will determine its thermal

characteristics, therefore to prevent the plug from operating either too hot or too cold under continuous operation, the proper heat range plug must be installed in the engine.

Types of fuel used in modern internal combustion engines can vary slightly between oil suppliers with the result that combustion chamber deposits will occur. Because of these deposits within the combustion chamber, electrical conductivity between the insulator nose of the spark plug and these deposits can produce uncontrolled ignition. Additional deposits from the type of engine oil used can also cause misfiring spark plugs.

SPARK PLUG CONSTRUCTION

All spark plugs are constructed in the same general manner. However, variations in design do exist. Regardless of this design variation, most spark plug producers offer plugs that can be interchanged with those of another make without affecting the engine performance. Figure 13-1 shows the construction of a typical spark plug.

In Fig. 13-1, the terminal stud 2 is manufactured from high-quality steel, and the center electrode 8 is made from a special heat resistant alloy. Both the terminal stud and center electrode are sealed within the insulator 3 with special conductive material. The insulator 3 is inserted into the steel plug shell 13 together with an internal seal 12 and a crimping ring 14, whereby it is crimped and shrunk under high pressure. The ground electrode 9 is also manufactured from special alloys and is then welded to the plug shell 13. Since the spark plug is subjected to combustion chamber deposits, the electrodes must be resistant to oxidation and to lead and sulphur deposits depending on whether leaded gasoline or non-leaded gasoline is being used.

Carbon and oil carbon deposits can produce an electrical shunt which will cause a loss of ignition energy which will produce a misfiring condition at idle and in the low part of the load range. However, as the engine load increases, the plug will tend to self-clean when a temperature of about 450°C (840°F) is reached. This tends to reduce the misfire condition, but a further increase in combustion chamber temperature causes the additional fuel and oil additives to create this shunt condition. Therefore, the spark plug position in the combustion chamber and the cooling of the plug seat have much to do with the operating characteristics and service life of the spark plug.

Figure 13-2 shows the basic makeup of an A.C. Slimline and nonresistor type spark plug.

SPARK PLUG HEAT FLOW PATHS

The design of the spark plug is such that the path of heat flow from the plug is as shown in Fig. 13-3.

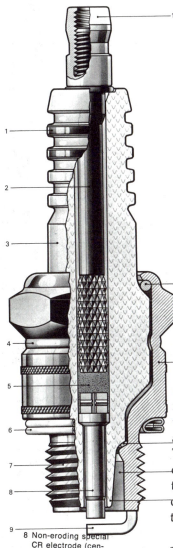

1 Leakage-current barrier
2 Terminal stud
3 Pyranit insulator
4 Swaged and heat-shrunk fitting zone
5 Special conductive seal
6 Captive gasket
7 Precision thread with guide
8 Non-eroding special CR electrode (center electrode)
9 Non-eroding ground electrode
10 Insulator nose
11 Scavenging area
12 Internal seal
13 Spark-plug shell
14 Crimping ring
15 SAE terminal nut (by choice)

Fig. 13-1. Spark plug construction. (Courtesy of Robert Bosch Corp.)

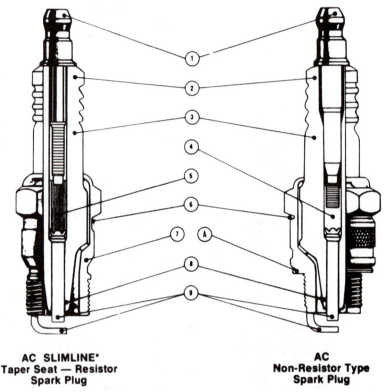

AC SLIMLINE*
Taper Seat — Resistor
Spark Plug

AC
Non-Resistor Type
Spark Plug

(1) **TERMINAL SCREW** — One piece to the seal area . . . helps reduce possibility of impact breakage.

(2) **BUTTRESS TOP INSULATOR** — The long flashover path helps provide fast starts in damp weather.

(3) **SUPER CERAMIC INSULATOR** — Near-diamond hardness ceramic provides added strength, protection against corrosion, increased shock resistance and improved insulation under high temperature operation.

(4) **IRON-GLASS SEAL** — Powdered metal with a glass binder provides a gas-tight bond between the terminal screw and the lower electrode . . . seals against compression leakage through the center of the spark plug.

(5) **IMPROVED ONE-PIECE INTEGRAL SUPPRES-SOR** — Located close to the firing tip . . . reduces radio frequency interference . . . meters spark energy for long electrode life . . . seals against compression leakage.

(6) **"CICO" WELD** — Electrically shrinks the shell to tighten internal gaskets . . . provides a positive seal between the shell and insulator.

(7) **TAPER SEAT** — Eliminates the need for a gasket . . . provides close tolerance installation in cylinder heads designed for this type spark plug.

(A) **GASKET SEAL** — Specially prepared surface accelerates heat transfer . . . provides maximum contact area and perfect sealing.

(8) **HOT TIP INSULATOR** — Heats fast, fires hot . . . helps burn away fouling deposits.

(9) **AC's** electrodes of nickel and chrome alloys resist wear from erosion and corrosion.

*The AC "Slimline" Spark Plug is physically smaller than a regular sized spark plug . . . but the performance characteristics of "Slimline" and a similar regular size spark plug are literally identical. The smaller sized spark plug was developed for specific engine applications . . . it allows engine designers a greater latitude in spark gap location, spark plug accessibility and spark plug cooling.

Fig. 13-2. AC spark plug design. (Courtesy of AC Delco Div. of GMC)

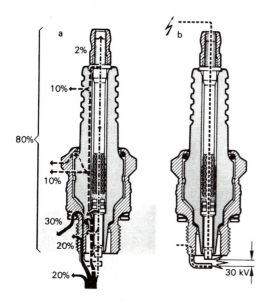

Fig. 13-3. Spark plug heat flow and typical temperatures: (a) heat flow percentages, (b) high tension voltage flow path. (Courtesy of Robert Bosch Corp.)

Figure 13-4 shows the thermal stresses on the insulator at (a) and the ambient temperatures at (b). Temperatures shown are in degrees Celsius (Centigrade). Average temperature on the insulator tip of the plug is between 850° to 900°C (1560° to 1650°F).

Figure 13-5 shows typical temperatures of the ground electrode for different heat range spark plugs.

The spark plug electrodes employ alloys on a nickel base to protect them from corrosive attack which increases the spark plug life. The most widely used materials for spark plug electrodes are:

- nickel-chrome alloy
- nickel alloy
- nickel alloy with copper core
- silver
- platinum

Typical styles of spark plugs are shown in Table 13-1. In this table, you will notice

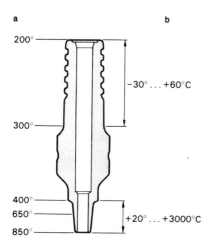

Fig. 13-4. (a) Spark plug thermal stresses on the insulator, (b) ambient temperatures. (Courtesy of Robert Bosch Corp.)

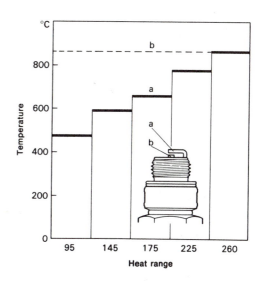

Fig. 13-5. Heat range of the spark plug ground electrode (a) and the center electrode (b).

Table 13-1. Types and Styles of Typical Spark Plugs

Air spark gap	Mixture accessibility	Voltage Requirement	Erosion reserve	Regapping	Ignition properties during idling	Remarks
Center electrode fully covered	normal	relatively low	large	good	not always favorable	standard spark plug
Center electrode semicovered	good	relatively low	normal	good	favorable	standard spark plug, advantageous for 2-stroke engines
Ring electrode and ring twin side electrode	normal	normal	large	none	good	specially suitable for 2-stroke engines
Recessed electrode			very small	none		only for racing engines
			normal	possible		only for racing engines
Platinum side electrode	very good	relatively low	large	difficult	good	completely unaffected by chemical attack from combustion gases
Surface gap	adequate	slightly higher	large	none	not always favorable	advantageous in conjunction with CDI or MCDI in 2-stroke engines
Surface-air gap	good	normal	large	good	good	with modulator electrode (2) (1 = ring electrode)

(Courtesy of Robert Bosch Corp.)

that three basic plug gap types are used, namely the surface gap and surface air gap type, as well as the conventional air gap type.

In the air gap type spark plug the high tension voltage passes from the center electrode to the ground electrode, while in the surface gap plug there is an insulator between these two electrodes. The ring-shaped ground electrode is located directly on the insulator tip so that the ignition spark will glide over the exposed surface of the insulator to burn away any deposits.

In the surface air gap spark plugs, the spark will discharge across both an air gap and a surface gap. The net result is that the spark length is longer than that found with the conventional air gap plug which contributes to ignition reliability. However, the voltage requirement when the spark plug is cold has to be higher. This can be corrected by the use of a modulator electrode, which is a ground electrode. While the engine is warming up the ignition spark discharges across the air gap between the center and modulator electrodes. When the engine has reached operating temperature, the required voltage for the combined surface-air gap decreases to less than that of the pure air gap, therefore the spark discharge transfers across the surface air gap and the insulator surface around the spark can be cleaned of any accumulating deposits.

SPARK PLUG HEAT RANGE IMPORTANCE

Because of the design and operating characteristics of various engines, it is impossible to use one standard spark plug for all engines. If one plug were used, it would get very hot in a particular engine, while only attaining a low temperature in another. With a very hot plug, the air/fuel mixture would ignite early (prior to plug firing) and pre-ignition would be the result, while with a cool running plug, the insulator tip would become fouled with deposits leading to engine misfire.

For the foregoing reasons, spark plugs with different load capacities are used which establishes a given heat range of operation.

This spark plug heat range is established by the manufacturer under controlled testing conditions. The heat range is determined by:

1. Thermal (heat) conductivity of the insulator and the electrodes, both the center and ground.

2. Total area of the insulator surface exposed to the gases of combustion.

3. The actual volume and shape of the space between the insulator and shell (or scavenging area).

4. The type of installation and position of the center electrode in the insulator.

5. The type and shape of the material for the sealing ring between the insulator and plug shell.

Average pre-ignition temperature start at about 900°C (1650°F) and the burn-off or self-cleaning temperature at about 450°C (840°F).

Examples of typical spark plugs that are widely used are shown in Fig. 13-6.

General rule-of-thumb guidelines for the proper selection of a spark plug that will offer the best performance are given below. (See Spark Plug Selection tables (Tables 13-1, 13-2, 13-3 and 13-4.)

1. Select a plug recommended by the

Table 13-2. Robert Bosch Spark Plug Code
Numbers and Letter Chart

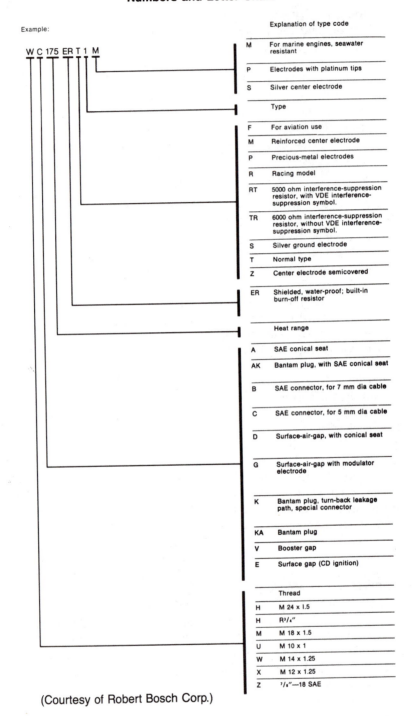

Example:

W C 175 ER T 1 M

Explanation of type code

M	For marine engines, seawater resistant
P	Electrodes with platinum tips
S	Silver center electrode
	Type
F	For aviation use
M	Reinforced center electrode
P	Precious-metal electrodes
R	Racing model
RT	5000 ohm interference-suppression resistor, with VDE interference-suppression symbol.
TR	6000 ohm interference-suppression resistor, without VDE interference-suppression symbol.
S	Silver ground electrode
T	Normal type
Z	Center electrode semicovered
ER	Shielded, water-proof; built-in burn-off resistor
	Heat range
A	SAE conical seat
AK	Bantam plug, with SAE conical seat
B	SAE connector, for 7 mm dia cable
C	SAE connector, for 5 mm dia cable
D	Surface-air-gap, with conical seat
G	Surface-air-gap with modulator electrode
K	Bantam plug, turn-back leakage path, special connector
KA	Bantam plug
V	Booster gap
E	Surface gap (CD ignition)
	Thread
H	M 24 x l.5
H	R³/₄″
M	M 18 x 1.5
U	M 10 x 1
W	M 14 x 1.25
X	M 12 x 1.25
Z	⁷/₈″—18 SAE

(Courtesy of Robert Bosch Corp.)

Table 13-3. Champion Spark Plug Sales Symbols

The sales symbol on a spark plug is composed of a basic "Heat Range" number with prefix letters and suffix letters/numbers to identify major features of the plug design.
The following charts contain a detailed description of the Champion Sales Symbols.

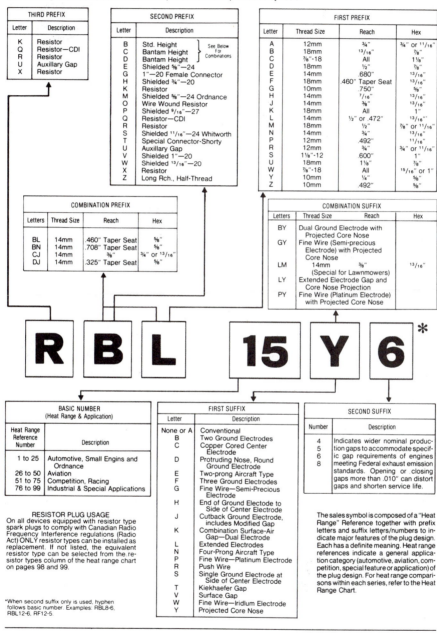

THIRD PREFIX

Letter	Description
K	Resistor
Q	Resistor—CDI
R	Resistor
U	Auxillary Gap
X	Resistor

SECOND PREFIX

Letter	Description
B	Std. Height (See Below For Combinations)
C	Bantam Height (See Below For Combinations)
D	Bantam Height (See Below For Combinations)
E	Shielded 5/8"—24
G	1"—20 Female Connector
H	Shielded 3/4"—20
K	Resistor
M	Shielded 5/8"—24 Ordnance
O	Wire Wound Resistor
P	Shielded 9/16"—27
Q	Resistor—CDI
R	Resistor
S	Shielded 11/16"—24 Whitworth
T	Special Connector-Shorty
U	Auxillary Gap
V	Shielded 1"—20
W	Shielded 13/16"—20
X	Resistor
Z	Long Rch., Half-Thread

FIRST PREFIX

Letter	Thread Size	Reach	Hex
A	12mm	3/4"	3/4" or 11/16"
B	18mm	13/16"	7/8"
C	7/8"-18	All	1 1/8"
D	18mm	1/2"	7/8"
E	14mm	.680"	13/16"
F	18mm	.460" Taper Seat	13/16"
G	10mm	.750"	5/8"
H	14mm	7/16"	13/16"
J	14mm	3/8"	13/16"
K	18mm	All	1"
L	14mm	1/2" or .472"	13/16"
M	18mm	1/2"	7/8" or 11/16"
N	14mm	3/4"	13/16"
P	12mm	.492"	11/16"
R	12mm	3/4"	3/4" or 11/16"
S	1 1/8"-12	.600"	1"
U	18mm	1 1/8"	7/8"
W	7/8"-18	All	15/16" or 1"
Y	10mm	1/4"	5/8"
Z	10mm	.492"	5/8"

COMBINATION PREFIX

Letters	Thread Size	Reach	Hex
BL	14mm	.460" Taper Seat	5/8"
BN	14mm	.708" Taper Seat	5/8"
CJ	14mm	3/8"	3/4" or 13/16"
DJ	14mm	.325" Taper Seat	5/8"

COMBINATION SUFFIX

Letters	Thread Size	Reach	Hex
BY	Dual Ground Electrode with Projected Core Nose		
GY	Fine Wire (Semi-precious Electrode) with Projected Core Nose		
LM	14mm (Special for Lawnmowers)	3/8"	13/16"
LY	Extended Electrode Gap and Core Nose Projection		
PY	Fine Wire (Platinum Electrode) with Projected Core Nose		

R B L 15 Y 6*

BASIC NUMBER (Heat Range & Application)

Heat Range Reference Number	Description
1 to 25	Automotive, Small Engins and Ordnance
26 to 50	Aviation
51 to 75	Competition, Racing
76 to 99	Industrial & Special Applications

FIRST SUFFIX

Letter	Description
None or A	Conventional
B	Two Ground Electrodes
C	Copper Cored Center Electrode
D	Protruding Nose, Round Ground Electrode
E	Two-prong Aircraft Type
F	Three Ground Electrodes
G	Fine Wire—Semi-Precious Electrode
H	End of Ground Electode to Side of Center Electrode
J	Cutback Ground Electrode, includes Modified Gap
K	Combination Surface-Air Gap—Dual Electrode
L	Extended Electrodes
N	Four-Prong Aircraft Type
P	Fine Wire—Platinum Electrode
R	Push Wire
S	Single Ground Electrode at Side of Center Electrode
T	Kiekhaefer Gap
V	Surface Gap
W	Fine Wire—Iridlum Electrode
Y	Projected Core Nose

SECOND SUFFIX

Number	Description
4 5 6 8	Indicates wider nominal production gaps to accommodate specific gap requirements of engines meeting Federal exhaust emission standards. Opening or closing gaps more than .010" can distort gaps and shorten service life.

RESISTOR PLUG USAGE
On all devices equipped with resistor type spark plugs to comply with Canadian Radio Frequency Interference regulations (Radio Act) ONLY resistor types can be installed as replacement. If not listed, the equivalent resistor type can be selected from the resistor types column of the heat range chart on pages 98 and 99.

*When second suffix only is used, hyphen follows basic number. Examples: RBL8-6, RBL12-6, RF12-5.

The sales symbol is composed of a "Heat Range" Reference together with prefix letters and suffix letters/numbers to indicate major features of the plug design. Each has a definite meaning. Heat range references indicate a general application category (automotive, aviation, competition, special feature or application) of the plug design. For heat range comparisons within each series, refer to the Heat Range Chart.

Form 7SC 01999521 68175 Litho in Canada

(Courtesy of Champion Spark Plug Co.)

Table 13-4. AC Spark Plug Identification Chart

PREFIX

B — Series Gap
C — Commercial
CS — Chain Saw
G — Gas Engine
H — High altitude or weather proof (shield connector 3/4-20 thread)
M — Marine
MC — Motorcycle types (are now S)
LM — Lawn mower type
R — Resistor
S — Shielded (5/8-24 thread)
S — Sport Vehicle
SR — Shielded Resistor
SN — Snow Types (are now S)
TC — Tractor-Commercial (now C types)
V — Surface Gap
W — Water proof (shield connector, 5/8-24 thread)
WR — Waterproof - Shielded Resistor

SUFFIX

A — Clip Gap
C — Colder version of old M44 plug
E — Special Design Electrode with extended tip
F — 1/2" Reach (.440 threaded, .060 pilot) for Imported Applications
FF — 1/2" reach, fully threaded (14 mm.)
G — Pin Gap (Cold Running Plug)
I — Iridium center electrode
K — Special Design Electrode
L — Long reach (7/16" for 14 mm., 3/4" for 18 mm.)
XL — Extra long reach (3/4" for 14 mm.)
M — Special Design Electrode
N — Extra long reach (14 mm.) (3/4" reach with 3/8" thread length)
LT — Long Reach (.715"), Tapered Seat

SUFFIX (Cont'd.)

O — Threaded Terminal (no screw-on Nut)
P — Platinum electrodes
R — Resistor (Sport Vehicle Plugs)
S — Extended tip
S — (7/8") Moderate long reach (23/32")
T — Tapered seat shell design
TS — Tapered seat with extended tip
W — Recessed termination
X — Special gap (usually denotes wide gap)
Y — 3 prong cloverleaf electrode
Z — Special gap (usually denotes wide gap)

(Courtesy of AC Delco Div. of GMC)

NOTE: The above suffix's are combined to form such AC suffix designation as: FG, XLS, TS, FFM, TSX, SZ, etc.

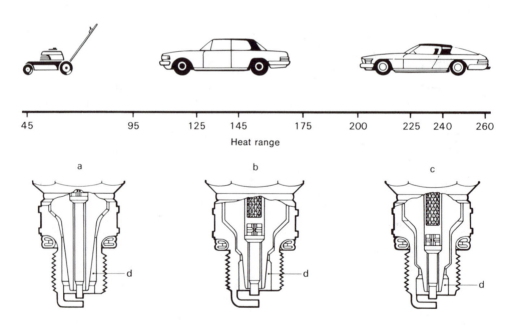

Fig. 13-6. (a) Long insulator nose spark plug, (b) medium-long insulator nose spark plug, (c) short insulator nose spark plug, (d) scavenging area of spark plug. (Courtesy of Robert Bosch Corp.)

engine manufacturer for your engine and application.

2. Should pre-ignition occur with the plug chosen in (1), then go to the next higher heat range (colder plug) to avoid pre-ignition problems.

3. If plug fouling occurs, install the next lower heat range spark plug (hotter).

HEAT RANGE CHART

Figure 13-7 shows the temperatures at which both spark plug fouling and pre-ignition will occur.

Due to the various types of engine operating conditions that spark plugs are subjected to, there are periods of time where a colder spark plug would be desirable, and others where a hotter plug would be desirable. The ideal plug would be one that could operate between the pre-ignition and fouling temperatures shown in Fig. 13-7.

A hot spark plug will transfer heat slowly and will therefore operate at a higher temperature than a cold spark plug which has a much faster rate of heat transfer and will therefore operate at a cooler temperature if installed in the same engine and operated under the same conditions. Basically speaking, then, a cold spark plug is usually more suited for full load or continuous high-speed highway or interstate driving, whereas in stop-and-go city driving, where long periods of idling cannot be avoided, the hot spark plug will prove better. The length of the insulator tip shown in Fig. 13-8 shows that in a hot spark plug, the longer insulator tip provides a longer heat path that will therefore raise the operating range of the plug. However, in a cold plug with a short insulator tip, the heat will flow away from

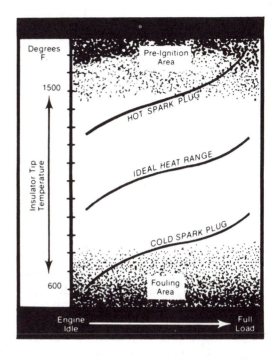

Fig. 13-7. Spark plug heat range chart. (Courtesy of AC Delco Div. of GMC)

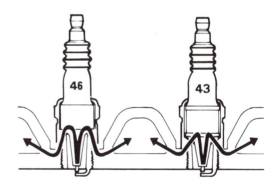

Fig. 13-8. Heat flow path for AC spark plugs. (Courtesy of AC Delco Div. of GMC)

the plug faster, thereby lowering the heat range of the plug. In summation, the shorter the heat path, the faster the plug will dissipate its heat, and will therefore run cooler. An example of the heat flow path is shown in Fig. 13-8 for AC spark plugs. The numbers on the spark plugs shown in Fig. 13-8 indicate that the number 46 plug is a hotter running plug than the number 43. The number 4 in both plugs indicates that the plugs have a 14 mm thread size. This numbering sequence is explained in detail in Fig. 13-11 and Table 13-4.

SPARK PLUGS WITH BOOSTER GAPS

Engine exhaust emissions can be reduced anytime that clean spark plugs are employed for the reasons discussed earlier regarding electrical shunts with dirty plugs. In certain applications, and also depending on the grade of fuel used, the use of a spark plug with a booster gap can do much to ensure that the plug remains clean through the use of an exceedingly fast voltage rise at the plug electrodes. The term self-cleaning plug is often used to characterize the type of spark plug which has the following features shown in Fig. 13-9.

1. No misfiring of the plug through fouling such as is encountered in stop-and-go city driving, or in high performance vehicles with high heat range spark plugs.

2. Fouled spark plugs will self-clean after a short period of continuous driving.

3. Spark plug life up to 100,000 km (60,000 miles) is possible.

The main features of this type of plug are shown in Fig. 13-9. The booster gap is sealed in a small glass tube filled with an inert gas within the plug connector. In addition, the plug is interference-suppressed and insensitive to shock and vibra-

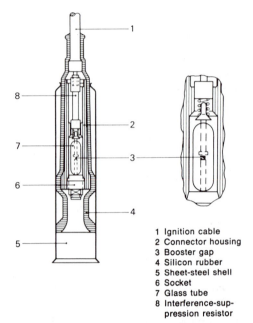

1 Ignition cable
2 Connector housing
3 Booster gap
4 Silicon rubber
5 Sheet-steel shell
6 Socket
7 Glass tube
8 Interference-suppression resistor

Fig. 13-9. Straight plug connector with a booster gap. (Courtesy of Robert Bosch Corp.)

tion problems. The initial cost of these plugs is higher than the conventional spark plug; however, improved performance will result. They are available for use with both the conventional style ignition system and HEI (High Energy Ignition) type systems.

SPARK PLUG DESIGNS

Spark plugs are available for all types of internal combustion engines. Standard thread sizes are:

1. 18 mm which have been used in larger, slow to medium speed, 4-stroke gasoline engines but are preferable for use in 2-stroke engines.

2. 14 mm which is the standard design

plug used in most 4-stroke gasoline engines.

3. 10 mm and 12 mm plugs are available and used in engines where space is limited or where the combustion chamber shape is unusual; plug life is generally shorter than with the larger diameter plugs.

Overall height of spark plugs can also vary as shown in Fig. 13-10.

Note, in Fig. 13-10, that the plug reach or length of the threads that extend into the combustion chamber area can also vary. It is important to note this, because obviously the installation of a long reach plug into a short reach hole would cause catastrophic results. Similarly the installation of a short reach plug into a long reach hole will result in lower compression and poorer engine performance. Also once the plug is removed, the thread bore of the cylinder head will require cleaning with a tap to remove combustion chamber deposits that accumulate in the threads. An example of the code letters and numbers used by Robert Bosch, Champion, and A.C. are given in Tables 13-2, 13-3, and 13-4.

AC-DELCO SPARK PLUG IDENTIFICATION

The following symbols are used by the AC-Delco Division of General Motors Corporation to identify their line of spark plugs.

Examples of AC spark plug thread sizes and plug types are shown in Fig. 13-11. The last digit in an AC spark plug number indicates its heat range; an 8 indicates a hot spark plug, a 6 is medium hot, a 4 is medium cold, and a 2 is cold.

SPARK PLUG SERVICE

Plug Removal

When it becomes necessary to remove one or more spark plugs for reasons of replacement, checking cylinder compression, etc., follow the procedure outlined below.

1. Remove the wire from each spark plug by either grasping the insulated rubber boot, twisting it and pulling it, or on those engines with molded boots, use a spark plug wire removal tool such as shown in Fig. 13-12. Make sure that you twist the boot until it loosens and then pull it from the plug. Pulling on the high tension spark plug wire may damage the connection. On some engines, no spark plug rubber type boot is used. Instead, an insulated hard push-on style protector is

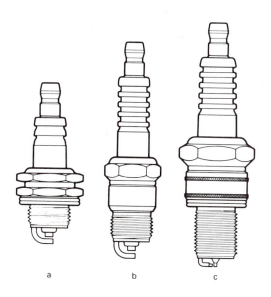

Fig. 13-10. (a) Bantam, (b) conical seat, (c) platinum electrode spark plugs. (Courtesy of Robert Bosch Corp.)

THREAD SIZE = FIRST DIGIT IN TYPE NUMBER
REACH = SUFFIX LETTERS

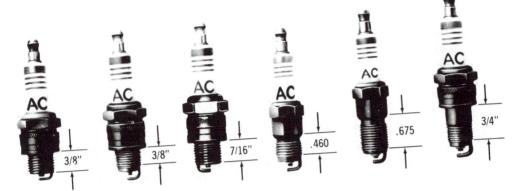

C43
14 MM THREAD
3/8" Reach

R46SZ
14 MM THREAD
3/8" Reach
(Extended Tip
with Skirted
Shell and wide
Firing Gap

45L
14 MM THREAD
7/16" Reach

R45TS
14 MM THREAD
Taper Seat
.460 Reach
(Extended Tip
with Skirted
Shell)

R43LTS
14MM Thread
Taper Seat
.675 Reach
(Extended Tip)

R45NSX
14MM Thread
3/4" Reach
3/8" Threaded
Length
(Extended Tip With
Skirted Shell and
Wide Firing Gap)

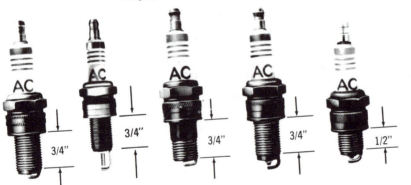

R44XL
14 MM THREAD
3/4" Reach

R44XLSM
14 MM Thread
3/4" Reach

R46N
14MM Thread
3/4" Reach
(3/8" Threaded
Length)

R45XLS
14 MM THREAD
3/4" Reach
(Extended Tip
with Skirted
Shell)

43FS
14 MM THREAD
1/2" Reach
.440" Threaded
(Extended Tip)

7G & 8G
DIESEL GLOW PLUG
Check catalogue for
application as these
glow plugs are not
interchangeable.

Fig. 13-11. Spark plug thread size and identification. (Courtesy of AC Delco Div. of GMC)

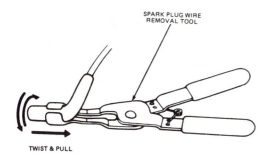

Fig. 13-12. Spark plug wire boot removal tool. (Courtesy of Ford Motor Co.)

used which requires the removal of the protector by a small twist and pull. This type unit is pushed directly onto the threaded stud of the top of the spark plug and does not use the normal SAE terminal nut.

2. Make sure that when removing more than one spark plug lead, if they are not numbered, you number them in order as you take them off. See Fig. 13-13. Should this not be done, then to reconnect to the proper plug, you will have to start at the number one lead on the distributor cap and progressively work your way around the leads in firing order sequence.

NOTE: On some engines such as the

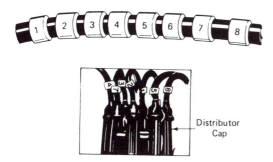

Fig. 13-13. Spark plug lead firing order markers.

Ford Duraspark III system with a bi-level rotor, this process does not follow in firing order sequence around the distributor cap. (See Chapter 9.)

3. Always try to clean the immediate area around the spark plug with compressed air to avoid dirt and impurities from falling into the cylinder.

4. Using a suitable socket or box wrench, carefully insert the tool over the plug until it is securely attached. If using a sliding tee bar tool, ensure that the handle is above the spark plug to allow the tee bar socket to be fully inserted over the plug, otherwise plug damage can occur. If a universal socket attachment is not being used, take care that the tool is not tilted when loosening the plug; otherwise, the insulator of the plug may be broken off or damaged.

5. If, while removing the spark plug, increased resistance is met, the threads are most likely plugged with combustion blowby. Once it has been unscrewed a few turns, drip some light oil or kerosene with a squirt can around the threads, then screw the plug in again to allow the fluid to penetrate, then attempt to remove the plug. You may have to alternately loosen and tighten the plug. If, for example, a short plug was inserted into a long thread hole, in order to remove it without damaging the thread hole in the cylinder head, this procedure might be required. Should you come across this situation, check to make sure that the threads can be cleaned up with the use of a spark plug thread tap. If severely damaged due to cross-threading, then a heli-coil insert will have to be inserted or use the AC spark plug thread repair tool, Fig. 13-20 or KD Rethreader Kit in Fig. 13-19.

GAP BRIDGED	OIL FOULED	CARBON FOULED

IDENTIFIED BY DEPOSIT BUILD-UP CLOSING GAP BETWEEN ELECTRODES. CAUSED BY OIL OR CARBON FOULING. REPLACE PLUG, OR, IF DEPOSITS ARE NOT EXCESSIVE, THE PLUG CAN BE CLEANED.	IDENTIFIED BY WET BLACK DEPOSITS ON THE INSULATOR SHELL BORE ELECTRODES. CAUSED BY EXCESSIVE OIL ENTERING COMBUSTION CHAMBER THROUGH WORN RINGS AND PISTONS, EXCESSIVE CLEARANCE BETWEEN VALVE GUIDES AND STEMS, OR WORN OR LOOSE BEARINGS. REPLACE THE PLUG. IF NOT REPAIRED, USE A HOTTER PLUG.	IDENTIFIED BY BLACK, DRY FLUFFY CARBON DEPOSITS ON INSULATOR TIPS, EXPOSED SHELL SURFACES AND ELECTRODES. CAUSED BY TOO COLD A PLUG, WEAK IGNITION, DIRTY AIR CLEANER, DEFECTIVE FUEL PUMP, TOO RICH A FUEL MIXTURE, IMPROPERLY OPERATING HEAT RISER OR EXCESSIVE IDLING. CAN BE CLEANED.

	NORMAL	

	IDENTIFIED BY LIGHT TAN OR GRAY DEPOSITS ON THE FIRING TIP.	

PRE-IGNITION	OVERHEATING	FUSED SPOT DEPOSIT

IDENTIFIED BY MELTED ELECTRODES AND POSSIBLY BLISTERED INSULATOR. METALLIC DEPOSITS ON INSULATOR INDICATE ENGINE DAMAGE. CAUSED BY WRONG TYPE OF FUEL, INCORRECT IGNITION TIMING OR ADVANCE, TOO HOT A PLUG, BURNT VALVES OR ENGINE OVERHEATING. REPLACE THE PLUG.	IDENTIFIED BY A WHITE OR LIGHT GRAY INSULATOR WITH SMALL BLACK OR GRAY BROWN SPOTS AND WITH BLUISH-BURNT APPEARANCE OF ELECTRODES. CAUSED BY ENGINE OVERHEATING, WRONG TYPE OF FUEL, LOOSE SPARK PLUGS, TOO HOT A PLUG, LOW FUEL PUMP PRESSURE OR INCORRECT IGNITION TIMING. REPLACE THE PLUG.	IDENTIFIED BY MELTED OR SPOTTY DEPOSITS RESEMBLING BUBBLES OR BLISTERS. CAUSED BY SUDDEN ACCELERATION. CAN BE CLEANED IF NOT EXCESSIVE. OTHERWISE REPLACE PLUG.

B3235-2C

Fig. 13-14. Inspection and interpretation of spark plug deposits and condition. (Courtesy of Ford Motor Co.)

Spark Plug Inspection

Note which cylinder each spark plug comes from, as this can help you pinpoint whether one or more cylinders are misfiring due to oil accumulation, etc. Carefully examine the ends of the spark plugs for signs of damage and combustion deposits. Figure 13-14 shows the typical plug deposits encountered under varying operating conditions.

1. If the plugs have a low number of operating miles (kilometers), or hours on stationary units, clean the plugs on a sand blast cleaner (Fig. 13-16) and check their condition visually for signs of broken or cracked insulators, badly pitted electrodes, etc.

2. If the plug appears serviceable, gently file the electrode with a small plug file as shown in Fig. 13-15 (a).

3. Check and set the spark plug gap as shown in Fig. 13-15 (b) and (c).

4. If a used plug is to be installed in the engine after cleaning and setting of the electrode gap, it should also be tested in a suitable spark plug tester to determine if it is in fact satisfactory. Such a tester is shown in Fig. 13-16; this machine allows you to apply pressure to the area of the plug electrode while passing a high-tension spark through the plug. While this is being done, the machine operator can look into an inspection window to check if the plug is firing evenly and strongly. In addition, a meter on the machine indicates the condition of the spark plug during testing.

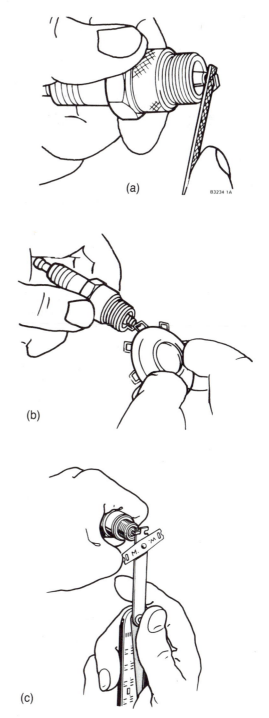

(a)

(b)

(c)

Fig. 13-15. (a) Filing the spark plug electrode. (b) Checking the spark plug gap (Courtesy of Ford Motor Co.). (c) Setting the plug electrode gap with a gapping tool (Courtesy of Robert Bosch Corp.).

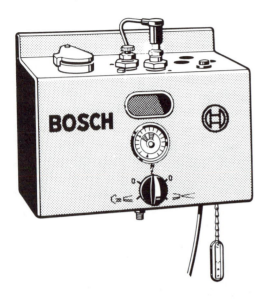

Fig. 13-16. Spark plug test machine. (Courtesy of Robert Bosch Corp.)

5. Ensure that any dirt on the outside of the spark plug is removed with a clean lint-free rag, especially on the insulator area, and that it is also moisture free prior to installation.

6. Spark plug life on the conventional plug is usually in the region of 16090 to 19308 km (10,000 to 12,000 miles), although shorter life is dependent on operating conditions. Self-cleaning plugs are capable of mileages of 80,450 to 100,000 km (50,000 to 60,000 miles).

Spark Plug Installation

When a new or used spark plug is to be installed, follow this procedure:

1. Check the gap of the plug prior to installation.

2. Clean the seating area of the plug in the cylinder head.

3. Does the plug that you are installing: (a) Use a sealing gasket? (b) If not; conical or tapered seat plugs do not require the use of a gasket. If a plug that requires a gasket is installed without the gasket, overheating and pre-ignition of the plug will occur because the heat dissipation will be inadequate and combustion chamber gases will leak past the threads causing them to become plugged which will make plug removal hard. Should a plug be installed with two gaskets, or an insufficient reach plug be used, the lower threads in the head will become clogged with deposits. In addition, unexpelled residual gases collecting around the plug restricts the inflow of a fresh air/fuel mixture to the area immediately around the spark gap, and plug misfiring will occur. This same condition can exist with a conical or tapered seat plug (requires no gasket), if it is installed with a gasket.

Also ensure that you have the correct length spark plug prior to installation. Too long a plug can result in actual physical piston to plug contact; if this doesn't occur, future plug removal will be difficult.

4. Do not coat the spark plug threads with oil or graphite prior to installation, since they are precoated at the factory with an anti-corrosion oil.

5. Screw the plug in to its bore until snug, then obtain a torque wrench to final tighten. Typical values for spark plugs are shown in Table 13-5.

The spark plug tightening torques given in Table 13-5 are for Robert Bosch products. However, due to a recent change issued through the International Standards Organization (ISO) and the Society of Automotive Engineers (SAE), the torque recommendation for 14 mm tapered seat spark plugs has been lowered from the values shown in this chart to 7-15 lb. ft. Recommended tightening torques do vary among spark plug manufacturers as you can see by comparing the AC spark plug chart tightening torque for their plugs versus the specifications given in Table 13-6.

6. Industry practice is not to use a torque wrench when tightening spark plugs, therefore the following suggested guideline should be followed to avoid overtightening the plug.

(a) With a new spark plug, run the plug down until you feel the gasket bite lightly. Turn the plug through an additional 90 degrees.

(b) With a used plug that is to be installed, turn the plug down until it bottoms, then tighten an additional ½th of a turn, or equal to about 5 minutes on a clock face.

(c) On conical or tapered face spark plugs (no gasket), tighten until you feel the plug bottom, then turn an additional equivalent of 2 to 3 minutes on a clock face.

7. Coat the inside of each spark plug

Table 13-5
Torque Values

Plug Thread	Tightening Torque in Newton Meters	
	Cast Iron Heads	Light Alloy
M 10 x 1	10 - 20	8 - 15
M 12 x 1.25	15 - 25	12 - 20
M 14 x 1.25	20 - 35	15 - 30
M 14 x 1.25*	15 - 25	12 - 20
M 18 x 1.5	30 - 45	20 - 35
M 18 x 1.5*	15 - 30	15 - 25

*Conical Seat (no gasket); 1 (Nm) Newton Meter = 1.355 lbf/ft.

rubber boot with a small amount of silicone dielectric compound or equivalent using a small screwdriver blade.

8. Ensure that each spark plug lead is attached to its matching spark plug, and ensure that each wire is fully depressed so that the molded boot is firmly in place.

9. If it is necessary to replace the spark plug boot, proceed as follows:

(a) Cut off the old boot and apply silicone dielectric compound to the area

Table 13-6
AC Spark Plug Tightening Torques

INSTALLATION TORQUE SPECIFICATION CHART

Spark Plug Thread	With Torque Wrench		Without Torque Wrench
	Cast Iron Heads	Aluminum Heads	Cast Iron or Aluminum Heads
10mm	8-12 lb. ft.	8-12 lb. ft.	¼ turn
12mm	10-18 lb. ft.	10-18 lb. ft.	⅜ to ½ turn
14mm Tapered seat	7-15 lb. ft.	7-15 lb. ft.	—
14mm Gasket seat	25-30 lb. ft.	18-22 lb. ft.	½ to ¾ turn
18mm Tapered seat	15-20 lb. ft.	15-20 lb. ft.	—
18mm Gasket seat	32-38 lb. ft.	28-34 lb. ft.	½ to ¾ turn
⅞-18	35-43 lb. ft.	31-39 lb. ft.	½ to ¾ turn

(Courtesy of Robert Bosch Corp.)

of the old wire where it will come into contact with the new boot.

(b) Position the new boot onto the tool or equivalent shown in Fig. 13-17.

(c) Position the tool onto the wire terminal and slide the boot onto the wire. Then remove the tool.

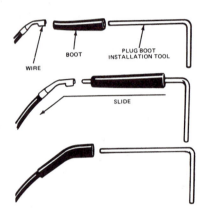

Fig. 13-17. Installation of spark plug wire boot. (Courtesy of Ford Motor Co.)

SPARK PLUG WIRE RESISTANCE CHECKS

Spark plug wires used today will differ with both vehicle models of the same manufacturer and also with vehicles of different manufacture. Most HEI systems use a carbon-impregnated cord conductor encased in a silicone rubber jacket.

Common wire size is usually either 7 or 8 mm; however, the insulation material underneath the jacketing can vary. For example, Ford vehicles can use either an EPDM insulation material, or another layer of silicone separated by glass braid. The EPDM wiring is used where engine temperatures are cooler and are identified by the letters SE. The silicone jacket silicone insulation type is used where high engine temperatures are present and is identified with the letters SS to distinguish it from the other type. Figure 13-18 shows a typical HT wire.

Both types of Ford spark plug wires are blue in color; therefore, the only way to tell them apart is to look at the lettering stamped on the wires.

On any HEI (high energy ignition) system, regardless of the make of vehicle, never puncture the silicone wiring or use adapters that can cause misfiring such as by forcing contacts between the boot and wiring when using an engine timing light.

Any time that an HEI system spark plug wire is removed for any reason from the plug, coil, or distributor cap, silicone dielectric compound must be applied to the boot prior to its reconnection. If spark plug wires are replaced, the replacement wires will generally not have cylinder numbers or manufacturing dates on them; therefore, they will require tagging upon installation.

Resistance Check

To effectively check the resistance of the high tension wiring, turn the ignition off and remove the distributor cap. Again, do not puncture the wiring with a sharp probe to check the resistance, but measure the resistance from the ends of the wire or the wire terminals inside the distributor cap.

The resistance measured in a high tension wire varies depending on the type and length of wire used. Therefore, most manufacturers recommend that the resist-

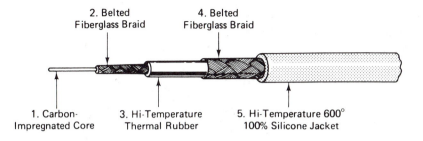

2. Belted
Fiberglass Braid

4. Belted
Fiberglass Braid

1. Carbon-
Impregnated Core

3. Hi-Temperature
Thermal Rubber

5. Hi-Temperature 600°
100% Silicone Jacket

Fig. 13-18. Typical suppressor high tension spark plug wire.

ance of the wire be measured with an ohmmeter and compared with that of a new piece of similar high tension wire. A general rule of thumb used by most mechanics is that 15,000 ohms per foot makes the wire questionable, while 20,000 ohms per foot is reason enough for replacement. However, some mechanics allow up to 30,000 ohms per foot prior to replacement of the wire.

Another interesting situation with high tension wiring is that with the latest type of silicone wiring, the resistance through a length of 6 inches of wire will read approximately the same as the resistance through a 3-foot length. Therefore, the rule of thumb is not of much value to you here. Again, compare a suspected faulty wire with that of a new wire resistance characteristic.

Should a high-tension wire show a resistance check in excess of that specified for a new wire, then remove it from the distributor cap and recheck. If it is still in excess of that for a new piece of wire, replace it.

Ignition spark plug wires used on conventional ignition systems tend to deteriorate when used with the higher voltage of electronic ignition systems.

SPARK PLUG CORONA DISCHARGE

Spark plugs are protected by an insulating nipple or rubber boot which is attached to the end of the spark plug wire and which extends down over the plug insulator. These boots or nipples prevent flashover, or loss of high voltage from the plug terminal, by keeping the insulator of the plug free of oil, dust, dirt, and water accumulations, which would otherwise result in missing in engine firing. Although a dirt film can accumulate on the exposed area of the plug electrode, no flash-over will occur as long as the boot is in position and properly fitted.

Service personnel sometimes mistake corona discharge for flash-over and suspect that a plug boot or insulator is at fault. Corona discharge is a steady blue light that appears around the insulator usually just above the shell crimp. It is positive evidence of a high-tension field, and has no ill effect upon ignition performance. Corona discharge is normally only visible with the engine running in a darkened area and the hood lid up. It is felt that this discharge does tend to repel dust particles, and as such a clear ring develops on the insulator just above the shell. This ring effect is sometimes mistaken for possible combustion blowby between the spark plug shell and insulator, but it usually is not.

CYLINDER HEAD RETHREADER KITS

In addition to the AC spark plug hole clean-up tools shown in Fig. 13-20, it may be necessary in cases of severe damage to actually install another insert. This condition is more commonly encountered in aluminum cylinder heads, which many passenger cars are now fitted with.

Such a tool kit is available from KD Tools of K-D Manufacturing Company in Lancaster, PA 17604, USA, and is shown in Fig. 13-19.

Stripped or damaged threads are repaired by the insertion of a solid steel insert in order to eliminate the possibility of coil windout when the spark plug is removed. Kit K-D 2125 covers 14mm spark plugs; kit K-D 2180 covers 18mm spark plugs; a jobber assortment kit is available under part number K-D 2185 with an assortment of steel insert replacements; kit K-D 2174 is a metric rethreader die set.

SPARK PLUG HOLE SERVICE

In severe cases of cross-threading of the spark plug hole, a heli-coil insert usually must be installed (or a tap-loc-insert). This often requires that the cylinder head be removed. However, in cases where minor spark plug hole thread damage has occurred, or combustion blowby has plugged up the threads, AC Delco Division of General Motors Corporation offers several special tools which can be used to correct these conditions. Fig. 13-20 shows the basic design of a spark plug hole cleanup tool. It is available in seven actual models to suit a variety of spark plug hole sizes.

Fig. 13-19. Spark plug rethreader kit. (Courtesy of KD Tool Co.)

Fig. 13-20. AC Delco spark plug hole cleanup tool. (Courtesy of AC Delco Div. of GMC)

The spark plug hole cleanup tool cleans up the threads and seat in one operation. Note, in Fig. 13-20, that just above the threads of the tool are serrations. These serrations effectively remove any carbon or dirt accumulation from the seat area which is very important prior to installing the spark plug, especially the tapered or bevelled seat type that does not use a gasket. Clean threads and a clean seating area result in elimination of:

1. a loss of compression and power due to improperly seated spark plugs; and

2. spark plug overheating, pre-ignition, and detonation through improper seating.

The lower threaded area of the tool is designed to repair crossed threads without actually removing any thread metal. In addition to allowing the spark plug to seat properly, clean threads result in an accurate torque of the spark plug. These special tools are available in a set to handle all sizes of spark plugs, as indicated below.

1. Type 14N: 14 mm ¾ inch (19 mm) reach special for cars and trucks with engines designed to use N type spark plugs (¾ inch reach with ⅜ inch thread length) or (19mm reach with 9.5 mm thread length).

2. Type 14S: 14 mm (⅜ inch to ½ inch reach/9.5 mm to 12.7 mm reach) will service both GMC and Chrysler engines, in addition to foreign cars, power mowers, and marine engines.

3. Type 14ST: 14 mm (taper seat plugs only); handles Buick, some Chevrolets, some Kaiser Jeeps, McCulloch Chain Saws (some), small engines by Cox Mfg. Co., and Ohlsson and Rice (some).

4. Type 14XL: 14 mm (¾ inch or 19 mm reach full thread) for use on Chrysler Imperial, Dodge, Plymouth, Rambler, foreign cars with long reach plugs. Do not use this type on engines designed to use N type spark plugs (¾ inch reach with ⅜ inch thread length or 19 mm with 9.5 mm thread length).

5. Type 18S: 18 mm taper seat spark plug hole tool for Ford, Lincoln, and Mercury vehicles.

6. Type 18F: 18 mm flat seat tool for trucks, tractors, aircraft, mobile, and stationary industrial engines.

7. Type 875: ⅞ inch (22.2 mm) spark plug hole for use on tractors and other types of off-highway equipment, mobile, and stationary engines.

SPARK PLUG SPECIAL ADAPTERS

Several types of special spark plug adapters are required today in order to connect up dwell meters, etc., to HEI (High Energy Ignition) systems and other breakerless distributor ignition systems. Several of these units are shown and discussed below.

GMC HEI Tester—ST 125

This is the recommended HEI system tester to establish if a fault exists in the ignition system. Figure 13-21 shows the ST 125 tester.

The ST 125 tester is basically a test type spark plug; it looks like a spark plug without any threads on it and is used by simply removing a convenient spark plug lead and attaching it to the tester. The tester is

Fig. 13-21. GMC high energy ignition tester ST-125. (Courtesy of AC Delco Div. of GMC)

then connected to any suitable clean ground, the engine is cranked over, and the spark can be observed at the tip of the tester. If a good clean spark is noted then the HEI system is functioning properly. However, if no spark appears, then there is a problem in the HEI system which would require further checking.

Shielded Spark Plug Connector

In order to connect automotive type ignition cable to spark plugs employing ⅝ inch - 24 (15.8 mm - 24) shielding barrel threads, a type WC 1 connector is used consisting of a brass nut and ceramic sleeve bushing (AV-C-S) along with a rubber grommet as shown in Fig. 13-22.

Fig. 13-22. Shielded spark plug connector. (Courtesy of AC Delco Div. of GMC)

ELECTRONIC ENGINE ANALYZERS

There are many electronic testers available and also various equipment produced by major companies that are necessary and specifically recommended in order to quickly and effectively diagnose ignition system and engine problems. This chapter shows many of these testers and their general function when used on the engine.

K-D 2551 Electronic Ignition Tester

The tester shown in Fig. 13-23(a) connects in seconds and analyzes electronic ignition malfunctions through solid state logic. Go-no-go lights pinpoint the specific problem so there's no need to check meter values. This hand held unit includes these significant features:

1. Works on most domestic and some foreign cars.
2. solves intermittent failure problems.
3. Works even when battery is too low to start the engine.

The unit shown in Fig. 13-23(b) is used for coil and E.C.U. output tests. It is designed

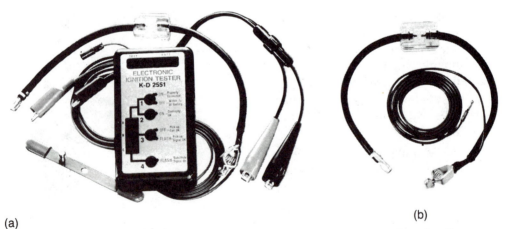

(a)

(b)

Fig. 13-23. K-D 2551 electronic ignition tester. (Courtesy of K-D Manufacturing Co., Lancaster, PA)

for maximum dependability and gives a visual and audio indication of the spark.

K-D 2610 Digital Engine Analyzer

With the compact analyzer, shown in Fig. 13-24, large easy-to-read digital readouts give you instant measurements with accuracy unobtainable in existing meters.

Auto ranging: No range selector buttons or switches; it automatically adjusts.

Tach: Reads to 9999 rpm. Reads direct—no scale selection required.

Dwell angle: Reads direct—no scale selection required.

Voltage: Reads in .10-volt increments to 50 VDC.

Ohms: Checks ballast resistors to ignition wiring, and decimal placement is automatic. Covers all automotive applications.

Amps: Covers charging system and most starter current requirements.

Worn cam: Indicator light shows dwell angle variations greater than ±2° in one distributor shaft revolution.

Bad alternator diode: Indicator light shows shorted or open alternator diodes.

The K-D 2610 works on most four-, six-, or eight-cylinder engines and all ignition systems, conventional or electronic.

K-D 2634 Digital Tach-Dwell Meter

The meter shown in Fig. 13-25 offers these important features of the 2610 Digital Engine Analyzer:

Auto ranging: No range selector buttons or switches; it automatically adjusts.

Tach: Reads to 9999 rpm. Reads direct—no scale selection required.

Dwell angle: Reads direct—no scale selection required.

Worn cam: Indicator light shows dwell angle variations greater than ±2° in one distributor shaft revolution.

Fig. 13-24. K-D 2610 digital engine analyzer. (Courtesy of K-D Manufacturing Co., Lancaster, PA)

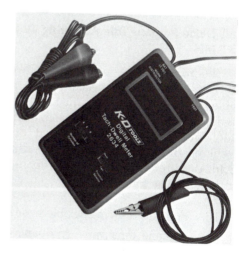

Fig. 13-25. K-D 2634 digital tach-dwell meter. (Courtesy of K-D Manufacturing Co., Lancaster, PA)

The 2634 also works on all four-, six-, or eight-cylinder engines and most ignition systems, conventional or electronic.

AC-Delco Inductive Timing Light ST-127

This timing light is of the usual pistol grip style as shown in Fig. 13-26, but with the following specific features:

1. Inductive hookup, therefore it is not necessary to disconnect any spark plug wires.

2. Operates on solid-state, transistorized, and HEI (High Energy Ignition Systems).

3. Connects directly to all 12 volt batteries for ease of use.

4. Conventional trigger actuation.

5. Grease and oil resistant leads and heavy-duty clips.

AC-Delco Propane Idle Adjusting Tool BT-7816

The increasing use of propane powered vehicles requires that special tools be available in order to correctly adjust such items as idle rpm. Fig. 13-27 shows such a typical tool kit. This tool can be used on all vehicles from 1978 on that are equipped with carburetors, for setting propane enrichment. The kit includes:

1. A 36 inch (91.4 cm) flexible hose

2. A propane tank valve (propane tank is obtained locally)

3. A deadman safety valve

4. A flow meter

5. A stopper and case

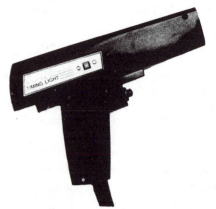

Fig. 13-26. Inductive timing light. (Courtesy of AC Delco Div. of GMC)

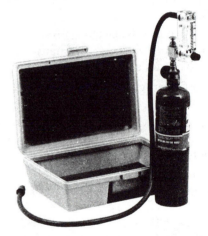

Fig. 13-27. BT-7816 propane kit. (Courtesy of AC Delco Div. of GMC)

ENGINE FIRING ORDERS AND CYLINDER NUMBERING SEQUENCE

Figures 13-28 through 13-39 illustrate the vehicle identification number plate location and also the cylinder numbering sequence and firing order along with the location of the timing marks.

AMERICAN MOTORS (CAR and JEEP)

TIMING MARKS

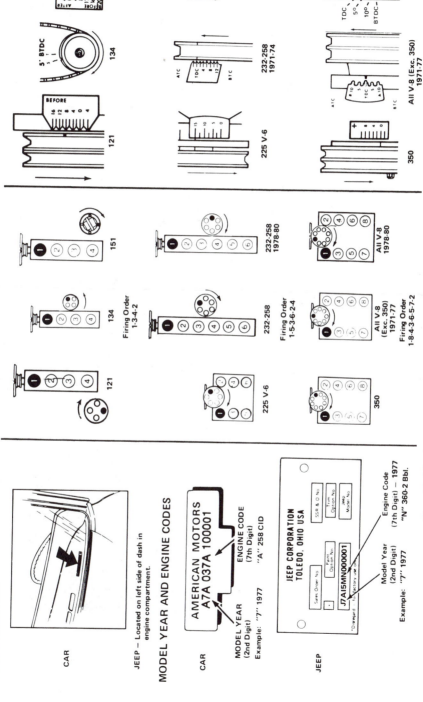

CYLINDER NUMBERING SEQUENCE AND FIRING ORDER

VEHICLE IDENTIFICATION

VEHICLE IDENTIFICATION NUMBER PLATE LOCATION

CAR

JEEP — Located on left side of dash in engine compartment.

MODEL YEAR AND ENGINE CODES

CAR

AMERICAN MOTORS
A7A 037A 100001

MODEL YEAR
(2nd Digit)
Example: "7" 1977

ENGINE CODE
(7th Digit)
"A" 258 CID

JEEP

JEEP CORPORATION
TOLEDO, OHIO USA

J7AI5MN000001

Model Year
(2nd Digit)
Example: "7" 1977

Engine Code
(7th Digit) — 1977
"N" 360-2 Bbl.

Fig. 13-28. American Motors car and jeep firing order and timing marks. (Courtesy of AC Delco Div. of GMC)

431

CHRYSLER CORPORATION (PLYMOUTH, DODGE, CHRYSLER CARS and LT. TRUCKS)

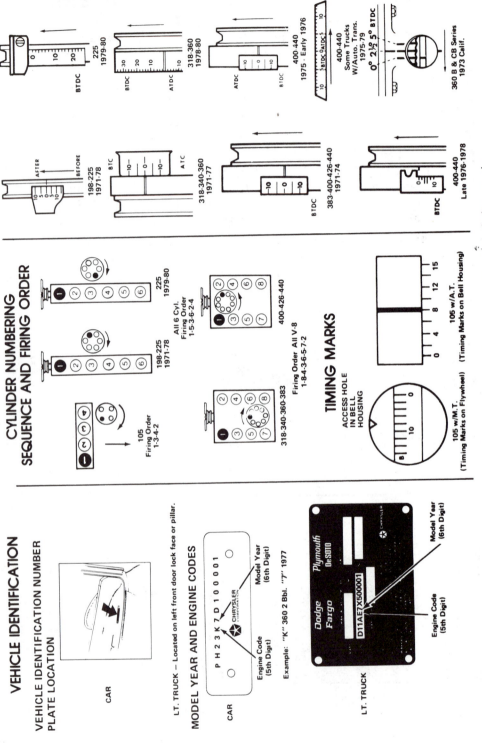

Fig. 13-29. Chrysler Corporation cylinder firing order and timing marks. (Courtesy of AC Delco Div. of GMC)

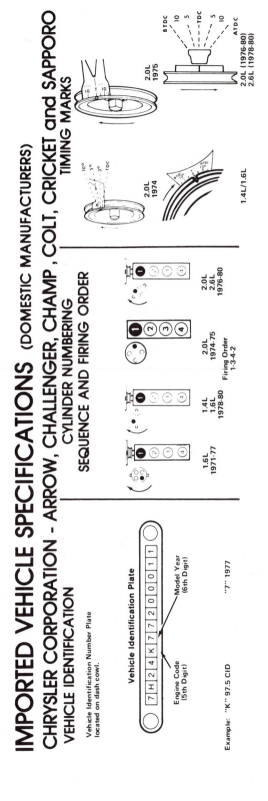

IMPORTED VEHICLE SPECIFICATIONS (DOMESTIC MANUFACTURERS)

CHRYSLER CORPORATION - ARROW, CHALLENGER, CHAMP, COLT, CRICKET and SAPPORO

VEHICLE IDENTIFICATION

Vehicle Identification Number Plate located on dash cowl.

Vehicle Identification Plate

| 7 | H | 2 | 4 | K | 7 | 7 | 2 | 0 | 0 | 0 | 1 | 1 |

Engine Code (5th Digit)

Model Year (6th Digit)

Example: "K" 97.5 CID   "7" 1977

CYLINDER NUMBERING SEQUENCE AND FIRING ORDER

1.6L 1971-77

1.4L 1.6L 1978-80

2.0L 1974-75
Firing Order 1-3-4-2

2.0L 2.6L 1976-80

TIMING MARKS

2.0L 1975

2.0L 1974

1.4L/1.6L

2.0L (1976-80)
2.6L (1978-80)

Fig. 13-30. Chrysler imported vehicle firing order and timing marks. (Courtesy of AC Delco Div. of GMC)

433

FORD MOTOR COMPANY (FORD and LINCOLN-MERCURY CARS and LT. TRUCKS)

VEHICLE IDENTIFICATION

CYLINDER NUMBERING SEQUENCE AND FIRING ORDER

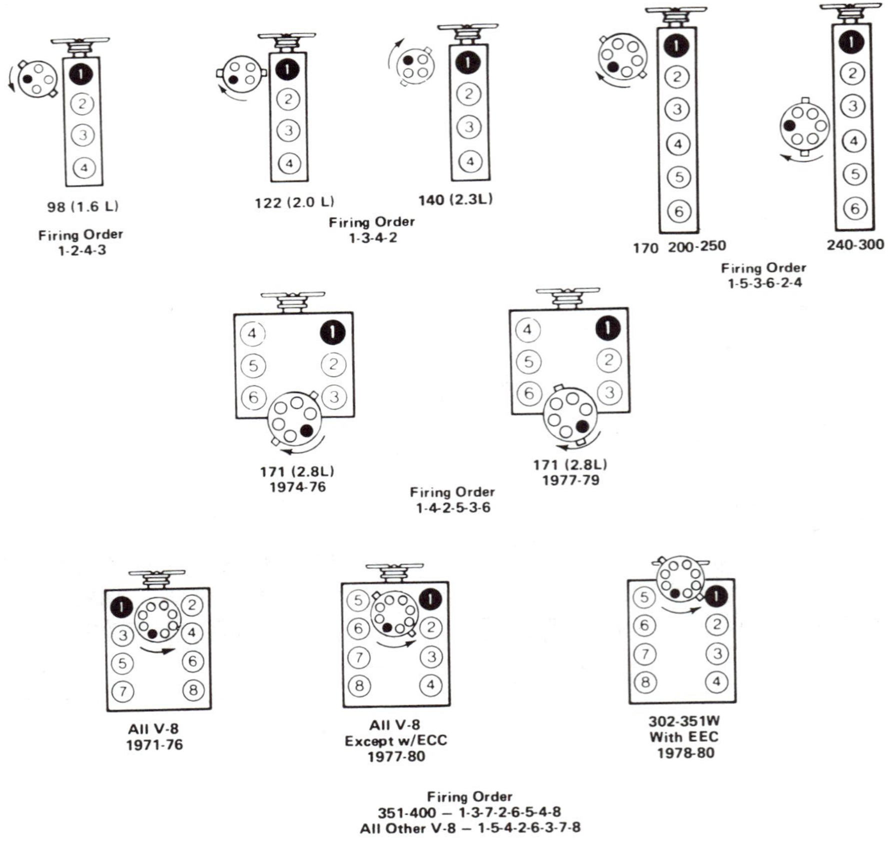

240-300
Firing Order
1-5-3-6-2-4

170 200-250

122 (2.0 L)
Firing Order
1-3-4-2

140 (2.3 L)

98 (1.6 L)
Firing Order
1-2-4-3

171 (2.8L)
1977-79

171 (2.8L)
1974-76

Firing Order
1-4-2-5-3-6

302-351W
With EEC
1978-80

All V-8
Except w/ECC
1977-80

All V-8
1971-76

Firing Order
351-400 — 1-3-7-2-6-5-4-8
All Other V-8 — 1-5-4-2-6-3-7-8

VEHICLE IDENTIFICATION NUMBER

PLATE LOCATION

CAR

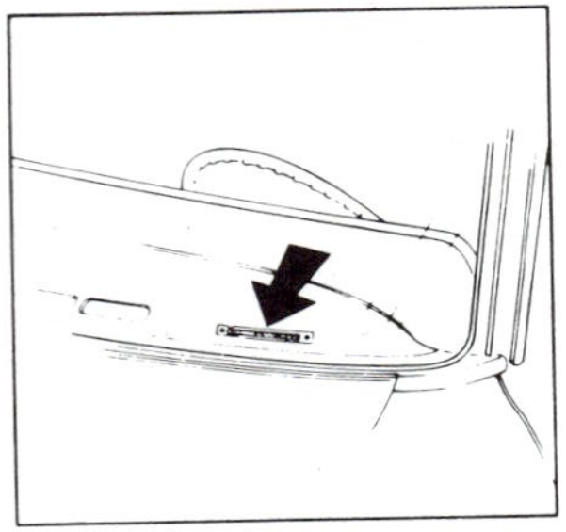

LT. TRUCK – RATING PLATE

Located in one of following places depending on year and model:

. Lock face of left front door
. Inside of glove box door
. Instrument panel on passenger side
. Upper cowl panel in engine compartment on passenger side
. Right hand side of radiator support

MODEL YEAR AND ENGINE CODES

7S63H100001

Model Year
(1st Digit)

Engine Code
(5th Digit)

Example: "7" 1977   "H" 351 CID

CAR

RATING PLATE

LT. TRUCK

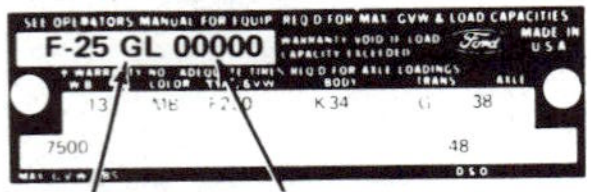

F-25 GL 00000

Engine Code   Serial Number
(Build Code Date)

Example: "G" 302 CID

Fig. 13-31. Ford and Lincoln-Mercury firing order and timing marks. (Courtesy of AC Delco Div. of GMC)

TIMING MARKS

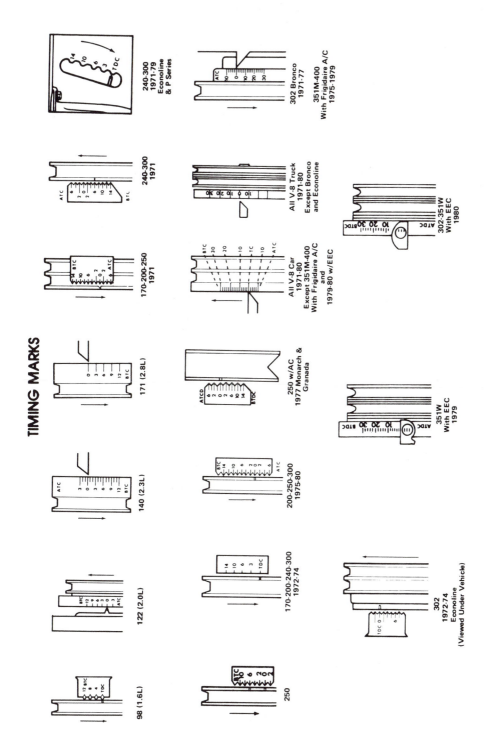

240-300
1971-79
Econoline
& P Series

302 Bronco
1971-77

351M-400
With Frigidaire A/C
1975-1979

240-300
1971

All V-8 Truck
1971-80
Except Bronco
and Econoline

302-351W
With EEC
1980

170-200-250
1971

All V-8 Car
1971-80
Except 351M-400
With Frigidaire A/C
and
1979-80 w/EEC

171 (2.8L)

250 w/AC
1977 Monarch &
Granada

351W
With EEC
1979

140 (2.3L)

200-250-300
1975-80

122 (2.0L)

170-200-240-300
1972-74

302
1972-74
Econoline
(Viewed Under Vehicle)

98 (1.6L)

250

Fig. 13-31. Continued.

435

FORD MOTOR COMPANY - CAPRI, COURIER, and FIESTA

VEHICLE IDENTIFICATION

VEHICLE IDENTIFICATION PLATE LOCATION

Capri — 1971-74 Top right of grille apron
1975-77 Top of right wheelhousing
Courier and Fiesta — Right rear of engine compartment

MODEL YEAR

5th digit of VIN (V = 1979, A = 1980)

ENGINE CODE

Capri and Fiesta — Stamped on I.D. plate
Courier — 4th digit of VIN

CYLINDER NUMBERING SEQUENCE AND FIRING ORDER

TIMING MARKS

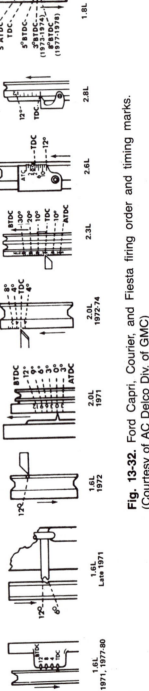

Fig. 13-32. Ford Capri, Courier, and Fiesta firing order and timing marks.
(Courtesy of AC Delco Div. of GMC)

436

GENERAL MOTORS CORPORATION - BUICK OPEL and CHEVROLET LUV

TIMING MARKS

VEHICLE IDENTIFICATION

CYLINDER NUMBERING SEQUENCE AND FIRING ORDER

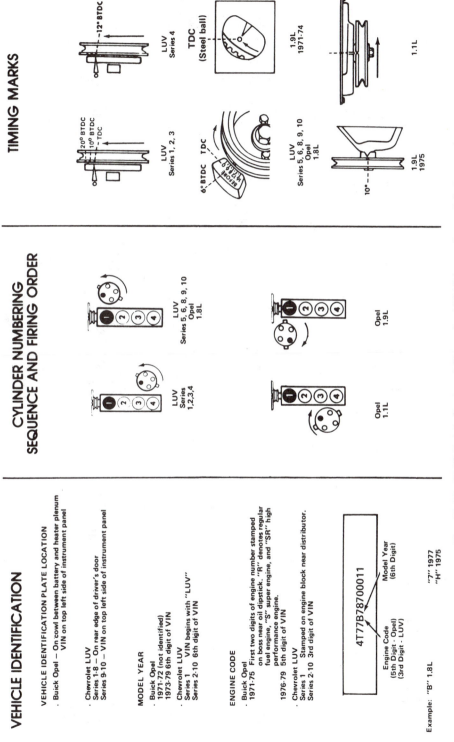

VEHICLE IDENTIFICATION PLATE LOCATION

· Buick Opel — On cowl between battery and heater plenum
  VIN on top left side of instrument panel

· Chevrolet LUV
  Series 1-8 — On rear edge of driver's door
  Series 9-10 — VIN on top left side of instrument panel

MODEL YEAR

· Buick Opel
  1971-72 (not identified)
  1973-79 6th digit of VIN

· Chevrolet LUV
  Series 1   VIN begins with "LUV"
  Series 2-10 6th digit of VIN

ENGINE CODE

· Buick Opel
  1971-75 First two digits of engine number stamped
  on boss near oil dipstick. "R" denotes regular
  fuel engine, "S" super engine, and "SR" high
  performance engine.
  1976-79 5th digit of VIN

· Chevrolet LUV
  Series 1   Stamped on engine block near distributor.
  Series 2-10 3rd digit of VIN

4T77B78700011

Engine Code   Model Year
(5th Digit - Opel)   (6th Digit)
(3rd Digit - LUV)

Example: "B" 1.8L   "7" 1977
                                 "H" 1975

Fig. 13-33. GMC Buick Opel and Chevrolet LUV firing order and timing marks.
(Courtesy of AC Delco Div. of GMC)

437

BUICK

VEHICLE IDENTIFICATION

VEHICLE IDENTIFICATION NUMBER PLATE LOCATION

MODEL YEAR AND ENGINE CODES (1)

4N37C7X 100000

Engine Code — Model Year
(5th Digit) — (6th Digit)

(1) Engine Code Note: Example: "C" 231 — "7" 1977
    1972-80 — Part of VIN
    1971 — Stamped on engine block
    6-cyl. — R.H. Side
    8-cyl. — L.H. Bank

TIMING MARKS

250
1975

250
1971-74

196-231-252
(1978-80)
350 - 4 Bbl.
(Code X)

231 - (1975-77)
350 - 2 Bbl. (Code H)
350 - 4 Bbl. (Code J)

151
(Code 5)

173

305-350 (Code L)
(Late 1977-1980)

305
350 - 4 Bbl. (Code L)
(Early 1977)

301-400

265 - 301
1978-80

260 - 4 Bbl. (Code R)
403

350 - 4 Bbl. (Code R)
403

CYLINDER NUMBERING SEQUENCE AND FIRING ORDER

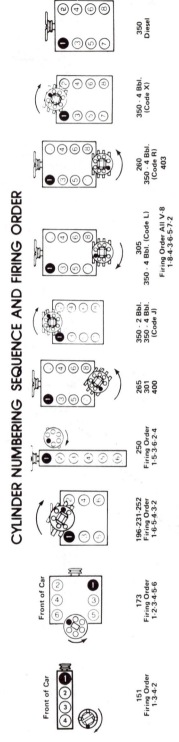

350
Diesel

350 - 4 Bbl.
(Code X)

260
350 - 4 Bbl.
(Code R)
403

305
350 - 4 Bbl. (Code L)
Firing Order All V-8
1-8-4-3-6-5-7-2

350 - 2 Bbl.
350 - 4 Bbl.
(Code J)

265
301
400

250
Firing Order
1-5-3-6-2-4

196-231-252
Firing Order
1-6-5-4-3-2

173
Firing Order
1-2-3-4-5-6

Front of Car

151
Firing Order
1-3-4-2

Front of Car

Fig. 13-34. Buick firing order and timing marks. (Courtesy of AC Delco Div. of GMC)

438

CADILLAC

VEHICLE IDENTIFICATION

VEHICLE IDENTIFICATION NUMBER PLATE LOCATION

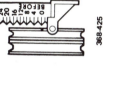

MODEL YEAR AND ENGINE CODES (1)

6B69S7Q 100001

Engine Code   Model Year
(5th Digit - 1972-80)   (6th Digit)
(8th Digit - 1971)
Example: "S" 425-4Bbl.   "7" 1977

TIMING MARKS

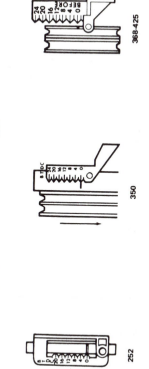

472-500
1971-75

500
1976

350

368-425

252

CYLINDER NUMBERING SEQUENCE AND FIRING ORDER

252

Firing Order
1-6-5-4-3-2

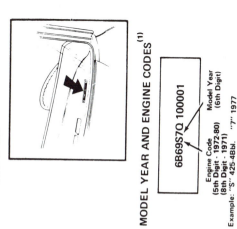

350

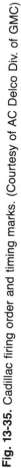

350
Diesel

Firing Order
1-8-4-3-6-5-7-2

500
1974 w/HEI
368-425-500
1975-80

472-500
1971-74 wo/HEI

Firing Order
1-5-6-3-4-2-7-8

Fig. 13-35. Cadillac firing order and timing marks. (Courtesy of AC Delco Div. of GMC)

439

CHEVROLET CAR; CHEVROLET and GMC LIGHT TRUCKS

CYLINDER NUMBERING SEQUENCE AND FIRING ORDER

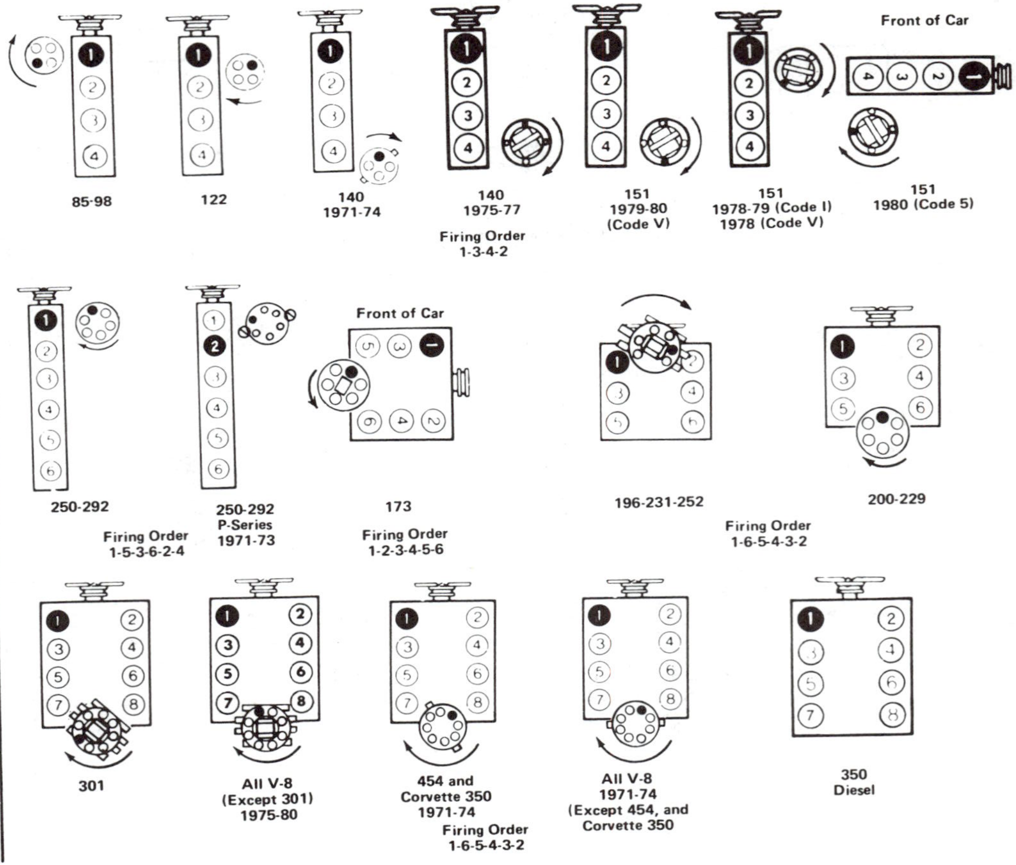

VEHICLE IDENTIFICATION

VEHICLE IDENTIFICATION NUMBER PLATE LOCATION

CAR

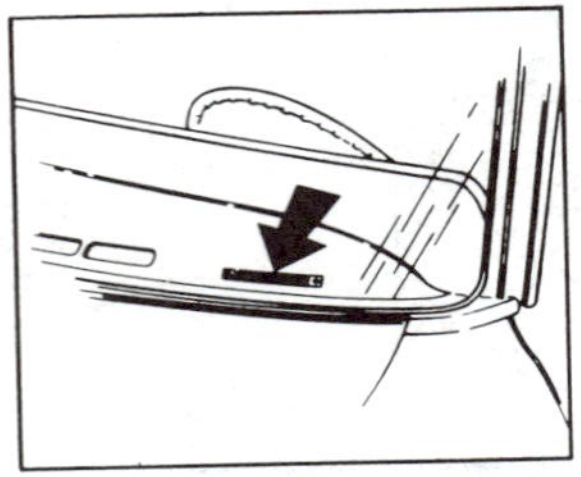

TRUCK

A combination vehicle identification number and rating plate is located as follows:
Left door pillar (except "P" series forward control)
Dash and Toe Panel ("P" series forward control)

MODEL YEAR AND ENGINE CODES

CAR

1H57U7B100025

Engine Code (5th Digit)

Model Year (6th Digit)

Example "U" 305   "7" 1977

TRUCK

CCQ 137F100025

Engine Code (3rd Digit)

Model Year (6th Digit)

Example "Q" 250 CID   "7" 1977

(1) Engine Code Note:
. 1972-78 — Part of VIN
. 1971 (Car), 1971-72 (Truck)
Stamped on Engine Block
4/6 cyl. — R.H. Side
8 cyl. — Front of R.H. Block

Front of Car

85-98

122

140
1971-74

140
1975-77

Firing Order
1-3-4-2

151
1979-80
(Code V)

151
1978-79 (Code I)
1978 (Code V)

151
1980 (Code 5)

250-292

250-292
P-Series
1971-73

Firing Order
1-5-3-6-2-4

Front of Car

173

Firing Order
1-2-3-4-5-6

196-231-252

200-229

Firing Order
1-6-5-4-3-2

301

All V-8
(Except 301)
1975-80

454 and
Corvette 350
1971-74

Firing Order
1-6-5-4-3-2

All V-8
1971-74
(Except 454, and
Corvette 350

350
Diesel

Fig. 13-36. Chevrolet car and Chevrolet and GMC light-truck firing order and timing marks. (Courtesy of AC Delco Div. of GMC)

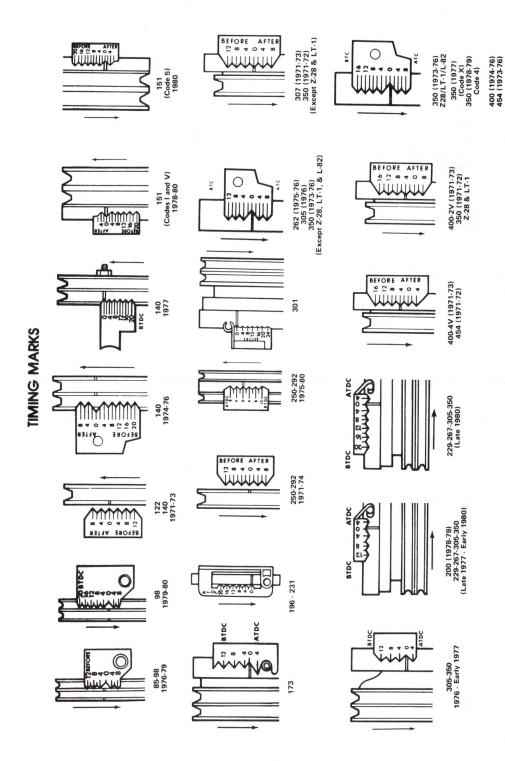

TIMING MARKS

151 (Code 5) 1980

307 (1971-73)
350 (1971-72)
(Except Z-28 & LT-1)

350 (1973-76)
Z28/LT-1/L-82
350 (1977)
(Code X)
350 (1978-79)
(Code 4)

400 (1974-76)
454 (1973-76)

151 (Codes I and V) 1978-80

262 (1975-76)
305 (1976)
350 (1973-76)
(Except Z-28, LT-1, & L-82)

400-2V (1971-73)
350 (1971-72)
Z-28 & LT-1

140 1977

301

400-4V (1971-73)
454 (1971-72)

140 1974-76

250-292 1975-80

229-267-305-350
(Late 1980)

122
140
1971-73

250-292 1971-74

200 (1978-79)
229-267-305-350
(Late 1977 - Early 1980)

98 1979-80

196 - 231

85-98 1976-79

173

305-350
1976 - Early 1977

Fig. 13-36. Continued.

441

OLDSMOBILE

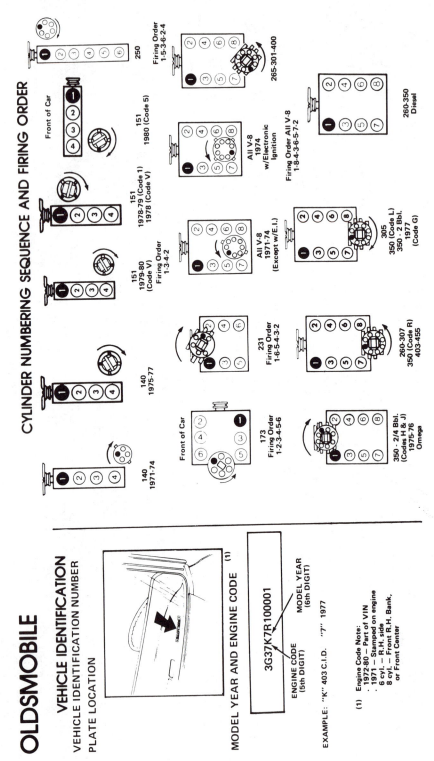

CYLINDER NUMBERING SEQUENCE AND FIRING ORDER

VEHICLE IDENTIFICATION

VEHICLE IDENTIFICATION NUMBER

PLATE LOCATION

MODEL YEAR AND ENGINE CODE (1)

3G37K7R100001

ENGINE CODE
(5th DIGIT)

MODEL YEAR
(6th DIGIT)

EXAMPLE: "K" 403 C.I.D.   "7" 1977

(1) Engine Code Note:
   . 1972-80 — Part of VIN
   . 1971 — Stamped on engine
   6 cyl. — R.H. side
   8 cyl. — Front R.H. Bank,
   or Front Center

250

140
1971-74

140
1975-77

151
1979-80
(Code V)

Firing Order
1-3-4-2

151
1978-79 (Code 1)
1978 (Code V)

151
1980 (Code 5)

Front of Car

173
Firing Order
1-2-3-4-5-6

231
Firing Order
1-6-5-4-3-2

350 - 2/4 Bbl.
(Codes H & J)
1975-76
Omega

305
350 (Code L)
350 - 2 Bbl.
1977
(Code G)

350 - 2/4 Bbl.
1977
(Code R)

260-307
350 (Code R)
403-455

All V-8
1971-74
(Except w/E.I.)

All V-8
1974
w/Electronic
Ignition

Firing Order All V-8
1-8-4-3-6-5-7-2

265-301-400
Firing Order
1-5-3-6-2-4

260-350
Diesel

Fig. 13-37. Oldsmobile firing order and timing marks. (Courtesy of AC Delco Div. of GMC)

OLDSMOBILE

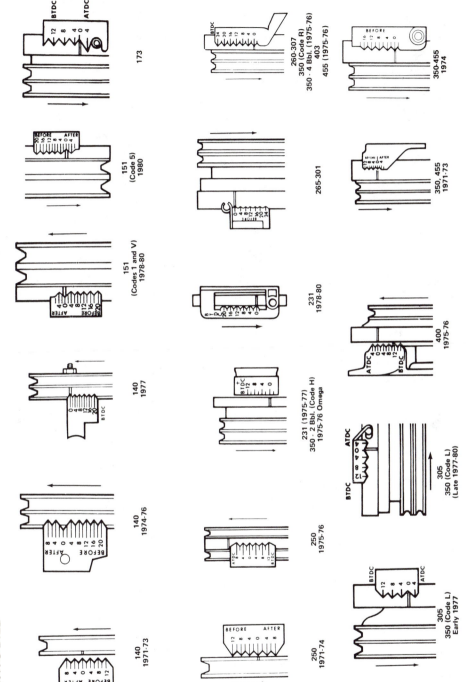

Fig. 13-37. Continued.

443

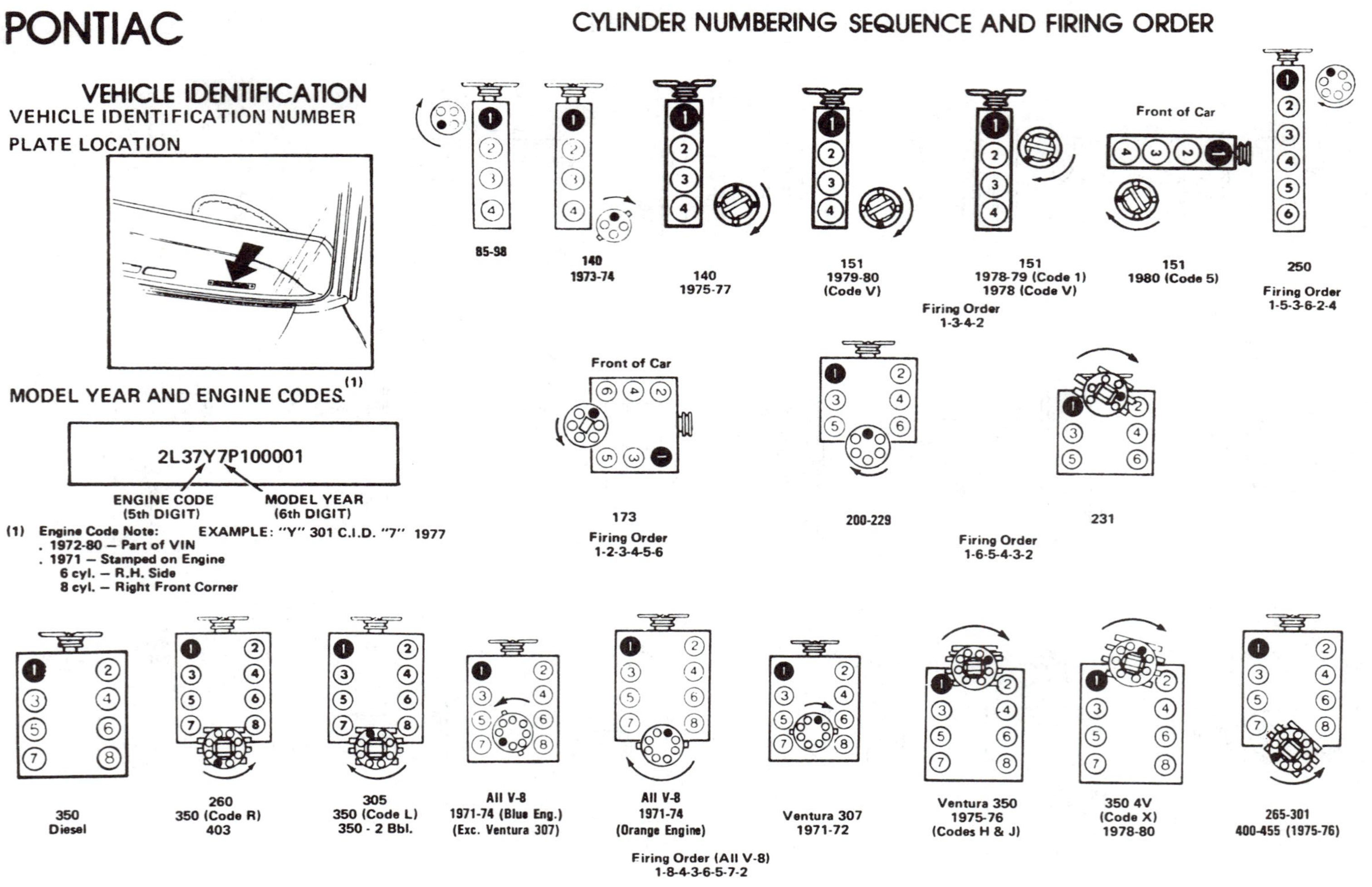

PONTIAC

CYLINDER NUMBERING SEQUENCE AND FIRING ORDER

VEHICLE IDENTIFICATION

VEHICLE IDENTIFICATION NUMBER

PLATE LOCATION

MODEL YEAR AND ENGINE CODES.[1]

2L37Y7P100001

ENGINE CODE
(5th DIGIT)

EXAMPLE: "Y" 301 C.I.D. "7" 1977

MODEL YEAR
(6th DIGIT)

(1) Engine Code Note:
    : 1972-80 – Part of VIN
    : 1971 – Stamped on Engine
      6 cyl. – R.H. Side
      8 cyl. – Right Front Corner

250
Firing Order
1-5-3-6-2-4

Front of Car

1980 (Code 5)
151

151
1978-79 (Code 1)
1978 (Code V)
Firing Order
1-3-4-2

151
1979-80
(Code V)

140
1975-77

140
1973-74

B5-98

231

200-229

173
Firing Order
1-2-3-4-5-6

Front of Car

Firing Order
1-6-5-4-3-2

265-301
400-455 (1975-76)

350 4V
(Code X)
1978-80

Ventura 350
1975-76
(Codes H & J)

Ventura 307
1971-72

All V-8
1971-74
(Orange Engine)

Firing Order (All V-8)
1-8-4-3-6-5-7-2

All V-8
1971-74 (Blue Eng.)
(Exc. Ventura 307)

305
350 (Code L)
350 - 2 Bbl.

260
350 (Code R)
403

350
Diesel

Fig. 13-38. Pontiac firing order and timing marks. (Courtesy of AC Delco Div. of GMC)

444

PONTIAC

TIMING MARKS

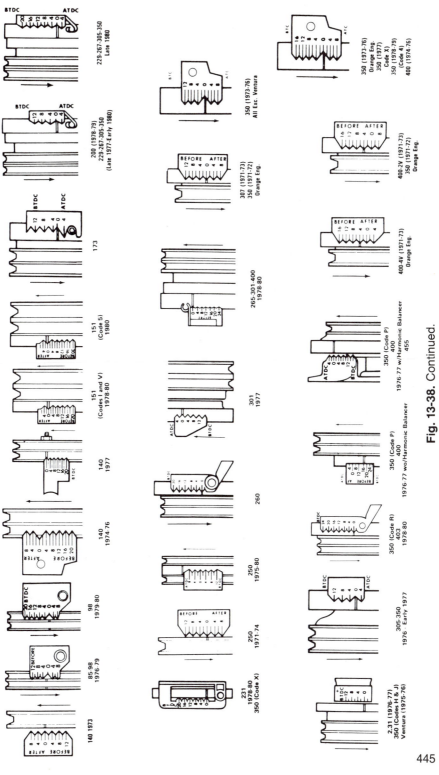

Fig. 13-38. Continued.

445

INTERNATIONAL TRUCKS

VEHICLE IDENTIFICATION

- MODEL YEAR
  1971-72 — Not Part of VIN
  1973-80 — Sixth Digit of VIN

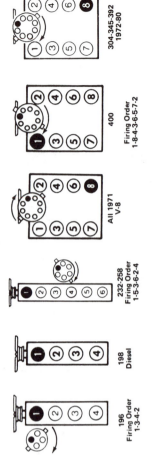

G0062GD100001

YEAR IDENTIFIER

YEAR MODEL LINE STARTED IN PRODUCTION

C = 1973   E = 1975   G = 1977   J = 1979
D = 1974   F = 1976   H = 1978   K = 1980

- Engine Code — Not part of
  Vehicle Identification Number
  C.I.D. indicated on engine tag.

CYLINDER NUMBERING SEQUENCE AND FIRING ORDER

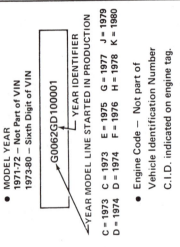

196
Firing Order
1-3-4-2

198
Diesel

232-258
Firing Order
1-5-3-6-2-4

All 1971
V-8

400
Firing Order
1-8-4-3-6-5-7-2

304-345-392
1972-80

TIMING MARKS

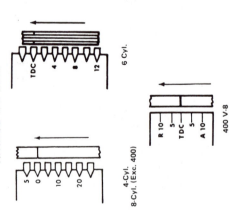

4-Cyl.
8-Cyl. (Exc. 400)

6 Cyl.

400 V-8

Fig. 13-39. International Trucks firing order and timing marks. (Courtesy of AC Delco Div. of GMC)

OSCILLOSCOPE FUNCTION AND PATTERN INTERPRETATION

An oscilloscope is a test instrument that can be used on both conventional and electronic ignition systems. In its simplest form, the oscilloscope is a glorified voltmeter. It graphically illustrates on a screen the highs and lows produced in the ignition system. The waveform produced on the screen can be interpreted by the technician. These waveforms have to be compared to that of a correctly operating waveform after which an analysis of the problem can be made and corrective action taken to correct the fault.

There are a wide variety of oscilloscope test machines on the market today, and each one may include some features particular to that machine. However, in general, all oscilloscopes function in the same manner. Fig. 13-40 shows a typical electronic engine tester equipped with an oscilloscope.

The oscilloscope can be employed to diagnose such problem areas in the ignition system as:

1. Short circuited spark plugs

2. Excessive primary circuit resistance

3. Shorted condensor

4. Uneven distributor cam lobes

5. Worn distributor shaft and bushing

6. Defective wiring

7. Worn engine timing chain or gears

8. Burned or pitted points (conventional system)

9. Bouncing points (low spring tension, conventional ignition system)

10. Reversed coil polarity

11. High external secondary resistance

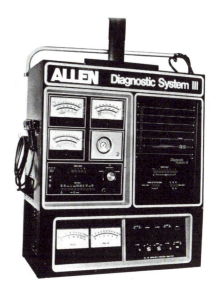

Fig. 13-40. Engine tester fitted with an oscilloscope.

12. Pinpointing of one cylinder with high secondary resistance

13. High internal secondary resistance, such as a wide plug gap, lean air/fuel mixture, carbon buildup in a cylinder (higher compression than normal)

14. Voltage required to jump the gap between the rotor and the distributor cap terminal

15. Ignition coil secondary voltage potential

16. Location of a fouled or shorted plug, or gap that is too small

17. Incorrect dwell angle

Each particular model of oscilloscope or engine analyzer has its own set of operating instructions. Although many of the controls and features are similar, you should ensure that you are familiar with a specific test machine's individual variations prior to using it to analyze an engine ignition problem.

In general, the clamp-around type of inductive pickup used with the oscilloscope can be placed around an individual spark plug cable, and the screen of the scope will depict a waveform pattern for that one cylinder. If, however, the clamp is placed around the high-tension lead from the ignition coil to the distributor cap, a parade-type of waveform pattern will be shown on the scope screen. This shows successive waveforms for each cylinder of the engine in firing order sequence.

OSCILLOSCOPE IGNITION TESTER

Principles of Scope Testing

All scopes have a screen on which a graphic illustration is projected of a voltage versus time pattern to supply information about voltage changes in all phases of an ignition cycle as they actually occur.

Figure 13-41 illustrates this voltage versus time graph as it would normally be viewed on the scope screen. The horizontal line on the screen represents the elapsed time in one engine cycle, while the vertical line or scale is representative of voltage. The higher the voltage in a given circuit being tested, the higher the wave pattern will travel on the vertical portion of the screen.

The scope screen pattern is naturally synchronized with engine speed and will therefore repeat itself on a continuous basis as it receives an electrical signal from the scope trigger pickup, which is shown in Fig. 13-42.

Controls on the scope are similar on all machines with the most common ones being as follows:

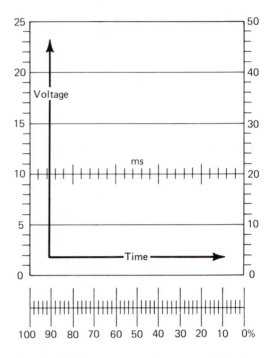

Fig. 13-41. Voltage versus time graph. (Courtesy of Sun Electric Corp., Sun Technical Services)

1. **Pattern selector** is used to change the way in which the pattern is shown on the screen.

2. **Function selector** is used to analyze either the primary or secondary ignition circuit.

3. **Pattern height control** is used to select either the left or right on the vertical scale to obtain a voltage reading (measurement) for both the primary and secondary circuits of the ignition system.

4. **Brightness control** adjusts the intensity of the scope pattern.

5. **Vertical control** raises or lowers the screen pattern.

6. **Horizontal control** adjusts the pattern left to right across the screen.

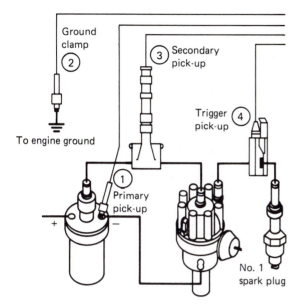

Fig. 13-42. Scope connections to a conventional ignition system. (Courtesy of Sun Electric Corp., Sun Technical Services)

7. **Pattern length control** adjusts the horizontal length of the pattern.

8. **Raster spacing control** adjusts the spacing between the individual cylinder patterns when the pattern selector is in the raster position.

SCOPE CONNECTIONS

Both conventional and electronic ignition systems are tested in a similar manner; however, there is one exception to this which involves General Motors High Energy Ignition (HEI) systems with distributor mounted coils. These coils require the use of a special adapter for both the primary and secondary circuit tests. The scope connections for a conventional contact-breaker point ignition system and a

General Motors HEI system are shown in Fig. 13-42 and 13-43.

Caution: To prevent damage to the ignition components of an electronic ignition system such as the GM HEI, do not open circuit the ignition system during scope testing because of the higher voltage values encountered with these systems.

OSCILLOSCOPE PATTERN INTERPRETATION

In order to completely understand and interpret the patterns that appear on the scope screen, practical exposure to the use of the oscilloscope will train you to recognize abnormal wave forms or patterns within a short time period.

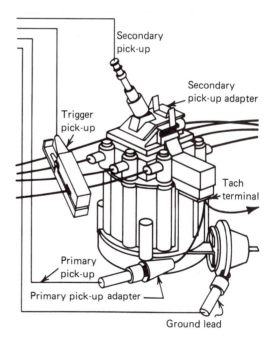

Fig. 13-43. Scope connections to a General Motors HEI system. (Courtesy of Sun Electric Corp., Sun Technical Services)

In order to become proficient at the use of a scope, many hours can be spent in analyzing various patterns of both a conventional and electronic ignition system primary and secondary circuit.

Since a separate book could be written dealing with the various patterns, the author urges you to obtain the following manual: *Understanding Automotive Oscilloscope Patterns,* which is developed and produced by Sun Technical Services of the Sun Electric Corporation, 1 Sun Parkway, Crystal Lake, Illinois 60014, (815-459-7700).

This manual was developed by Sun due to the demands from automotive mechanics for a comprehensive oscilloscope manual. The manual covers 162 pages dealing specifically with scope testing of both conventional and electronic ignition systems and is illustrated in color throughout.

CONVENTIONAL IGNITION SYSTEM—SECONDARY SCOPE PATTERN INTERPRETATION

Figure 13-44 illustrates the pattern that would be viewed on the scope screen during a check of the secondary ignition voltage. This pattern is actually divided into three distinct areas: (1) firing, (2) intermediate, and (3) dwell.

The reason for this test is to indicate the following ignition system conditions:

1. Firing voltage
2. Spark duration
3. Coil and condensor oscillations
4. Contact breaker point condition and action
5. Dwell and cylinder timing accuracy
6. Secondary circuit resistance

Secondary Firing Section

Figure 13-44 (b) illustrates that the actual firing section of the scope pattern has both a firing and a spark line. From our earlier discussion you may recollect that the vertical line is representative of voltage; therefore, in this instance the height of the firing line represents the voltage necessary to overcome both the spark plug and distributor rotor air gaps, while the horizontal line represents the time and voltage required to maintain the high tension spark at the plug gap. Additional information in this figure is as follows:

Point A signifies the exact point at which the breaker points separate or open causing a collapse of the ignition coil's magnetic field with the resultant high voltage being that area from point A to point B. The higher point B is on the vertical scale, the higher the voltage required to jump or bridge the spark plug and rotor air gaps. This is sometimes called the firing or ionization voltage.

Point B to C to D represents the condition whereby once the voltage has bridged the spark plug gap, there is a rapid decrease in this secondary ignition voltage to point C from B. Since the voltage will continue for some period of time across the spark plug gap, this voltage will remain reasonably constant until the spark is eliminated at point D.

Secondary Intermediate Section

During the intermediate section of the secondary voltage impulse, the remaining ignition coil energy beginning at point D as shown in Fig. 13-44 (c), will fade or dissipate as an oscillating current that drops to zero at point E through the combined effects of both the coil and condensor.

Secondary Dwell Section

Figure 13-44 (d) represents the ignition dwell section from point E to point A. This section, or ignition point dwell as it is commonly referred to, represents the period of time during the actual ignition cycle that the contact breaker points re-main closed. This closing of the points is shown in Fig. 13-44 (d) as a short down-ward line at position E followed by a series of small rapidly diminishing oscillations that represent magnetic field buildup within the ignition coil winding. At posi-tion A the points have again opened to fire the next cylinder in the engine's firing order.

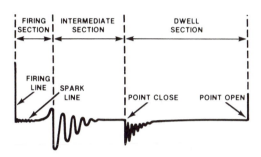

(a) Secondary pattern divided into three sections.

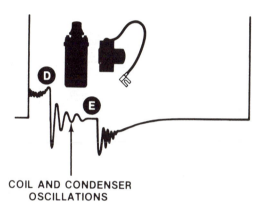

COIL AND CONDENSER
OSCILLATIONS

(c) Secondary intermediate section.

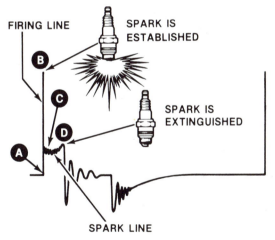

(b) Secondary firing section.

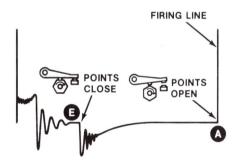

(d) Secondary dwell section.

Fig. 13-44. Scope patterns during a check of the secondary ignition voltage. (Courtesy of Sun Electric Corp., Sun Technical Services)

CONVENTIONAL IGNITION SYSTEM—PRIMARY SCOPE PATTERN INTERPRETATION

Figures 13-45 illustrates the scope patterns that would be viewed on the scope screen during a check of the primary ignition voltage. It is somewhat similar to that of the secondary scope pattern in that it is also divided into three distinct sections on the screen.

The reason for this test is to indicate the following ignition system conditions:

1. Allows scope tests to be conducted when secondary circuit connections are not possible.

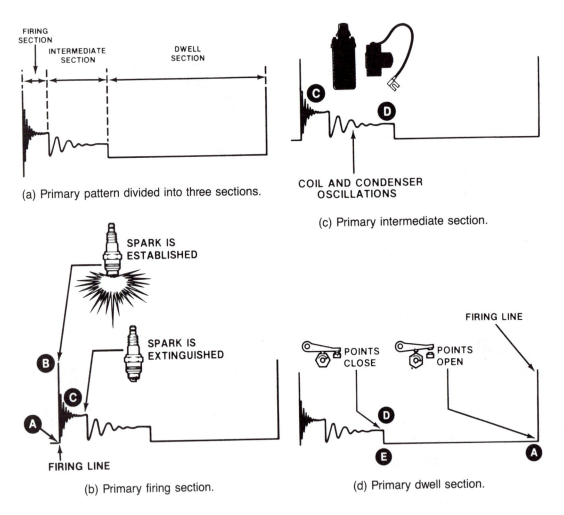

(a) Primary pattern divided into three sections.

(c) Primary intermediate section.

(b) Primary firing section.

(d) Primary dwell section.

Fig. 13-45. Scope patterns during a check of the primary ignition voltage. (Courtesy of Sun Electric Corp., Sun Technical Services)

2. Observance of contact breaker point condition and action.

3. Provides a means to observe dwell and cylinder timing problems.

Primary Firing Section

Illustrated in Fig. 13-45 (b) at point A is the initial contact breaker point opening which induces a magnetic field buildup within the ignition coil primary winding. The height of the vertical line from point A to point B represents the initial voltage rise. While the spark plug is firing, repeated charging and discharging of the condensor and induced voltage surges occur in the primary circuit. As the high tension spark jumps across or bridges the plug air gap, energy is dissipated from the coil; the amplitude of these oscillations will diminish until the spark is finally at a zero condition at point C.

Primary Intermediate Section

Illustrated in Fig. 13-45 (c), from point C to D is a series of gradually diminishing oscillations that end by the time the dwell section begins; therefore, at point C, any energy remaining in the ignition coil will simply dissipate itself as an oscillating current that drops to zero at point D.

Primary Dwell Section

Illustrated in Fig. 13-45 (d) from point D to point A is the ignition dwell section that begins when the contact breaker points close. This closure is represented by a faint downward line from point D to E while the actual dwell section is represented by a horizontal line that extends from point E to A.

OSCILLOSCOPE SCALES AND PATTERN SELECTION

The scales and patterns on the screen of the scope will vary depending on what tests are to be conducted; therefore, the following information is of a general nature to familiarize the reader with commonly selected scales and the resultant screen pattern.

Scope Scales

Illustrated in Fig. 13-46 are the commonly employed scope scales:

1. Vertical left scale divided into increments of 1 kilovolt (1000 volts) to provide a useable range of 0 to 25 KV (kilovolts) for secondary ignition circuit testing, while a lower range, 0 to 25 volts, is provided for primary ignition circuit testing.

2. Vertical right scale is provided to illustrate increments of 2 kilovolts (2000 volts); secondary circuit testing from 0 to 50 KV is provided; a range of 0 to 500 volts is provided for primary circuit testing.

3. At the bottom of the scope a horizontal percent of dwell scale is used for checking both the primary and secondary dwell angle. The dwell scale is divided into increments of two percentage points from 0 to 100.

4. Positioned across the screen is a horizontal millisecond (MS) scale on some oscilloscopes to measure time in milliseconds that the high tension spark actually jumps or bridges the spark plug air gap.

Scope Pattern Selection

Either the primary or secondary ignition circuits can be effectively monitored on the

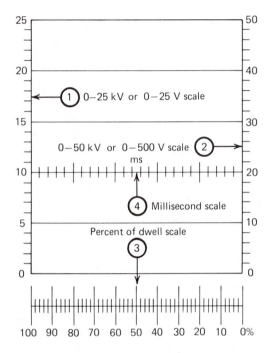

Fig. 13-46. Oscilloscope scales. (Courtesy of Sun Electric Corp., Sun Technical Services)

scope by the selection of one of the following positions:

1. Display position
2. Raster position
3. Superimposed
4. Millisecond

Illustrated in Fig. 13-47 is the scope pattern that will be provided when the display position is selected and the function selector is set to secondary. The scope presents a display of all of the engine cylinders starting at the extreme right, which is representative of the firing line for No. 1 cylinder. In Fig. 13-48, we see a primary display pattern with the function selector switch set to primary.

Note: In the display position, the scope will show the pattern for each cylinder's ignition cycle in the actual engine firing order. For a V8 engine with a firing order of 1-8-4-3-6-5-7-2, the scope will display the ignition cycles for each cylinder, as shown in Figs. 13-47 and 13-48.

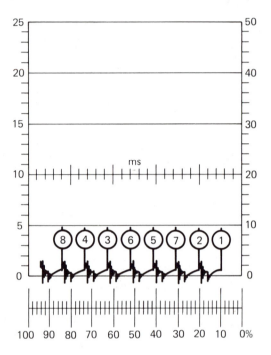

Fig. 13-47. Secondary display pattern. (Courtesy of Sun Electric Corp., Sun Technical Services)

Raster Pattern

Illustrated in Fig. 13-49 is a typical scope display of the individual patterns for each cylinder, vertically one above the other when the pattern selector switch is set to the raster position, and function switch to the secondary position.

With the function selector switch set to the primary position, a pattern such as that shown in Fig. 13-50 will appear on the scope screen.

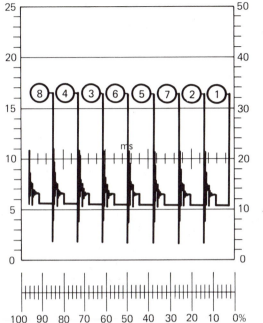

Fig. 13-48. Primary display pattern. (Courtesy of Sun Electric Corp., Sun Technical Services)

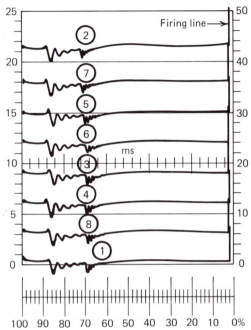

Fig. 13-49. Secondary raster pattern. (Courtesy of Sun Electric Corp., Sun Technical Services)

Note: In both Figs. 13-49 and 13-50, the engine's number one cylinder will appear at the bottom of the screen. Immediately above this will follow the other cylinders in firing order sequence.

Superimposed Pattern

Illustrated in Fig. 13-51 is the scope screen pattern displayed when the pattern selector switch is set to superimposed and the function selector is set to the secondary position. To obtain a primary superimposed scope reading (as shown in Fig. 13-52), simply place the function selector switch to the primary position.

The superimposed position is ideal for checking the ignition system for uniformity of firing lines and conditions since each cylinder's display is placed one on top of the other. This display can then be expanded horizontally to fill the space between the left and right vertical scale, thereby allowing you to analyze each cylinder's pattern and compare it with another.

Millisecond Pattern

On those scopes equipped with a millisecond (MS) sweep, a choice of scope pattern in a 5MS or 25MS time frame can be illustrated. Fig. 13-53 shows the display that appears on the scope screen if the 5MS position is selected, while in Fig. 13-54, the scope screen pattern appears as shown when the 25 MS position is selected.

Bear in mind that the scope screen can

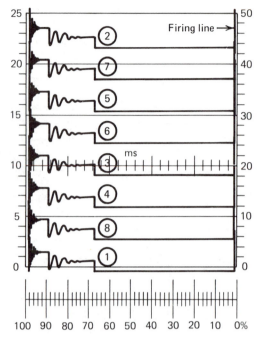

Fig. 13-50. Primary raster pattern. (Courtesy of Sun Electric Corp., Sun Technical Services)

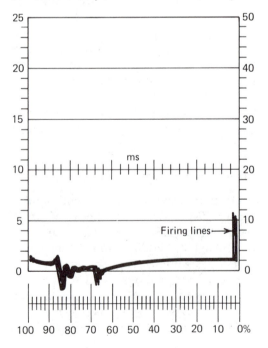

only show that portion of the ignition cycle that takes place within that time frame only for all of the cylinders.

SCOPE IGNITION DWELL

Ignition dwell was covered earlier in this book. However, to briefly review what it is we should remember—in a conventional contact breaker point ignition system, dwell is the period during the ignition cycle when the points remain closed. In an electronic ignition system the dwell period is controlled by the use of a transistor that is turned on and off.

Regardless of the type of ignition system used, the dwell period for an HEI system will show up on the scope screen in a similar manner to that for a conventional contact breaker point ignition system.

When we discussed Fig. 13-46 earlier dealing with the oscilloscope scales, we indicated that the dwell scale was divided into increments of two percentage points from 0 to 100. Therefore, the dwell period is read as a percentage of the total duration of one cylinder's firing cycle.

Since the scope screen illustrates the dwell as a percentage and we need to know the dwell in actual degrees to compare it to the manufacturer's specifications, the following procedure can be used to convert dwell percentage to dwell degrees:

1. Divide the number of engine cylinders into 360 degrees. For example, on a

Fig. 13-51. Secondary superimposed pattern. (Courtesy of Sun Electric Corp., Sun Technical Services)

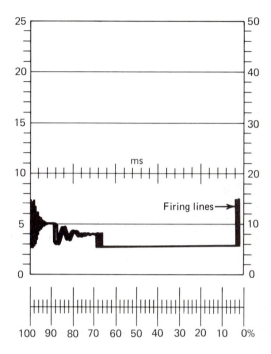

Fig. 13-52. Primary superimposed pattern. (Courtesy of Sun Electric Corp., Sun Technical Services)

six-cylinder engine the answer would be 60 degrees; this is representative of 100 percent dwell for one engine cylinder.

2. Multiply the degrees of dwell (60) by the percentage of dwell shown on the scope screen; this will provide the answer in degrees of dwell. For example, if the dwell were to read 60 percent, multiply 60 degrees by 0.60 (60%), which equals 36 degrees of dwell.

3. 100 percent dwell for any engine is arrived at simply by dividing the number of engine cylinders into 360 degrees.

Figure 13-55 shows the scope screen pattern that would be shown for the secondary circuit of an 8-cylinder engine with the pattern selector set at superimposed and the function selector to secondary.

Figure 13-56 shows the scope screen pattern with the switch set to the primary position.

Dwell Variation

The accuracy of the distributor cam establishes the ignition timing relationship of all engine cylinders. Cylinder timing variations for dwell are limited to the following percentages and degrees:

1. 4-cylinder engine—not to exceed 2 percent (2 degrees).

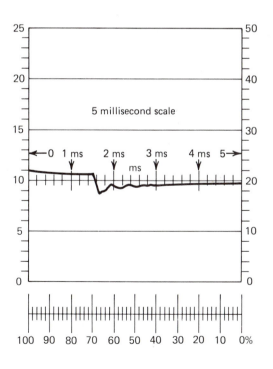

Fig. 13-53. Five-millisecond pattern. (Courtesy of Sun Electric Corp., Sun Technical Services)

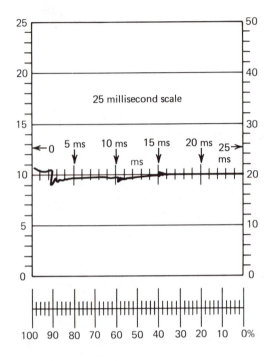

Fig. 13-54. Twenty-five millisecond pattern. (Courtesy of Sun Electric Corp., Sun Technical Services)

2. 6-cylinder engine—not to exceed 4 percent (2 degrees).
3. 8-cylinder engine—not to exceed 6 percent (2 degrees).

Should ignition dwell not be within specs, check the following areas:

Possible Cause	Suggested Correction
1. Improper point gap	Adjust points
2. Point rubbing block worn	Replace points
3. Worn distributor cam	Distributor tester

As a general rule, patterns on different scopes will vary slightly. The patterns shown in Fig. 13-57 are only used to illustrate typical waveforms.

In addition to the waveforms shown in Fig. 13-57, the waveform of the primary circuit is shown in Fig. 13-58 (b) and (c).

Due to the variety of oscilloscope testers on the market, and the large number of vehicles equipped with one of several types of ignition systems, many pages would be required to illustrate all of the possible waveforms and patterns that would be specific to a particular ignition system and its problems. The oscilloscope information given here is of a general nature only.

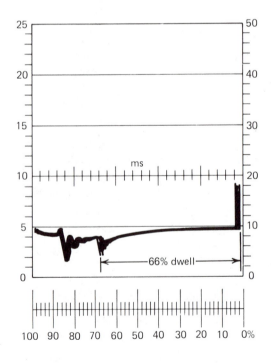

Fig. 13-55. Secondary dwell superimposed pattern. (Courtesy of Sun Electric Corp., Sun Technical Services)

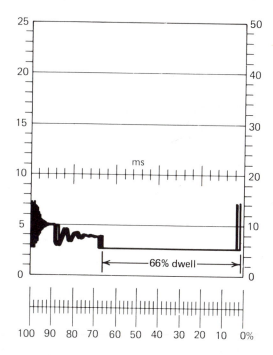

Fig. 13-56. Primary dwell superimposed pattern. (Courtesy of Sun Electric Corp., Sun Technical Services)

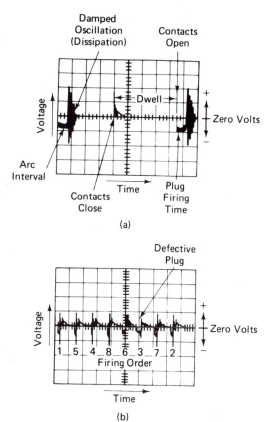

Fig. 13-57. (a) Normal high-tension waveform pattern; (b) parade display of a V8 engine with a firing order of 1, 5, 4, 8, 6, 3, 7, 2 showing a defective spark plug in number 3 cylinder.

Anytime that an oscilloscope is to be used, refer to the printed instructions or the engine manufacturer's service literature. No amount of theoretical knowledge on the interpretation and analysis of a waveform will make you an expert at ignition system diagnosis; however, if theory is combined with hands-on practical experience, in a reasonably short time, you will feel comfortable with the use of the oscilloscope and will be able to effectively pinpoint a problem area.

Apprentices can rely on the assistance of either a shop mechanic or tune-up technician, or the assistance of a college instructor during a training period to guide them through this phase of analysis. As with many other phases of your training and learning period, the effective use of the oscilloscope can only be achieved through a systematic sequence of tests, interpretation, and analysis. Continued exposure to this sequence of events will increase your knowledge and result in an appreciation of the proper use of ignition system test equipment.

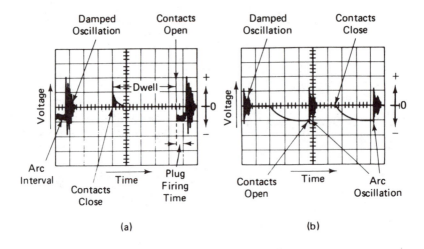

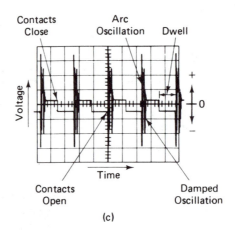

Fig. 13-58. (a) Normal secondary waveform; (b) normal primary waveform on the battery side of the ignition coil; (c) normal primary waveform on the switch contact side of the ignition coil.

GENERAL MOTORS VEHICLES—HEI SYSTEM DIAGNOSIS

Refer to Fig. 13-59 for typical procedural checks and tests.

GENERAL MOTORS HEI (HIGH ENERGY IGNITION) DIAGNOSIS WITH OSCILLOSCOPE

Figure 13-60 illustrates typical oscilloscope patterns that would be found with the HEI system and interpretation of the results.

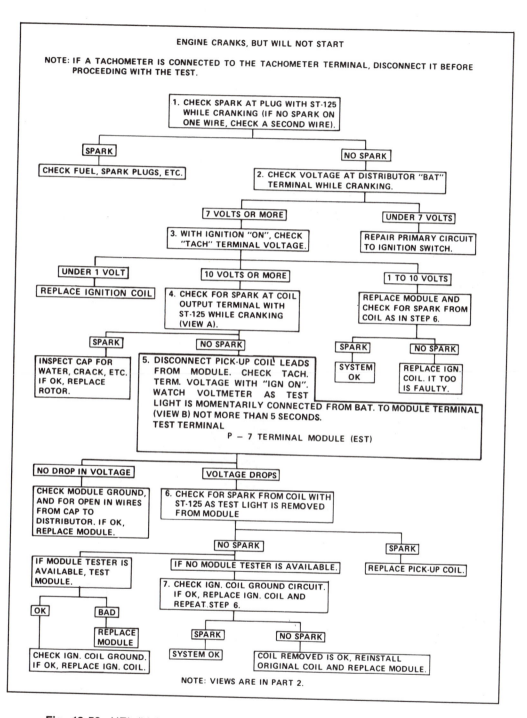

Fig. 13-59. HEI (high-energy ignition) system diagnosis chart. (Courtesy of Oldsmobile Div. of GMC) (continued on next page)

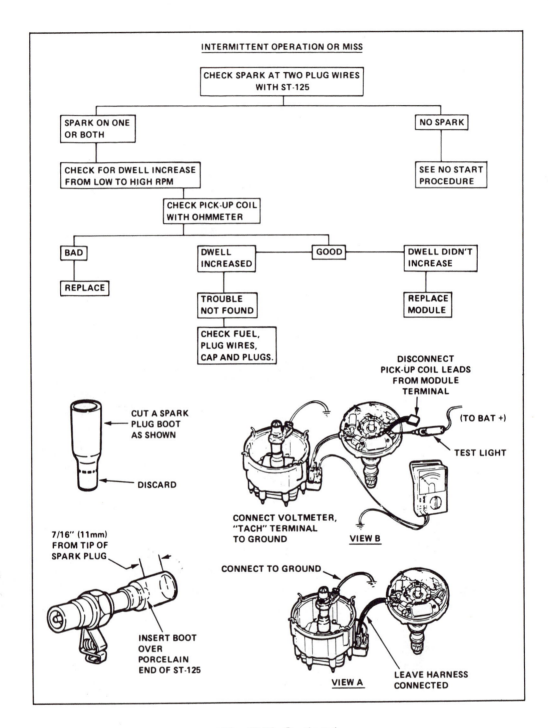

INTERMITTENT OPERATION OR MISS

CHECK SPARK AT TWO PLUG WIRES WITH ST-125

- SPARK ON ONE OR BOTH
- NO SPARK → SEE NO START PROCEDURE

CHECK FOR DWELL INCREASE FROM LOW TO HIGH RPM

CHECK PICK-UP COIL WITH OHMMETER

- BAD → REPLACE
- DWELL INCREASED → TROUBLE NOT FOUND → CHECK FUEL, PLUG WIRES, CAP AND PLUGS.
- GOOD
- DWELL DIDN'T INCREASE → REPLACE MODULE

CUT A SPARK PLUG BOOT AS SHOWN

DISCARD

7/16" (11mm) FROM TIP OF SPARK PLUG

INSERT BOOT OVER PORCELAIN END OF ST-125

DISCONNECT PICK-UP COIL LEADS FROM MODULE TERMINAL

(TO BAT +)

TEST LIGHT

CONNECT VOLTMETER, "TACH" TERMINAL TO GROUND

VIEW B

CONNECT TO GROUND

LEAVE HARNESS CONNECTED

VIEW A

Fig. 13-59. Continued.

HIGH ENERGY IGNITION DIAGNOSIS WITH OSCILLOSCOPE

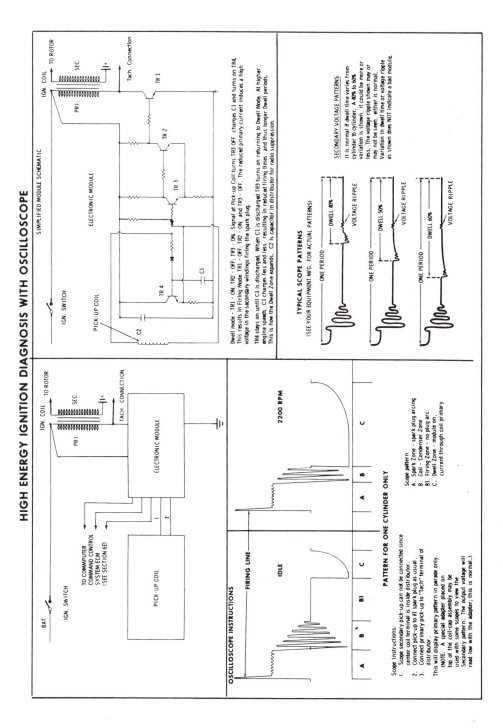

Fig. 13-60. Typical oscilloscope patterns found on an HEI system. (Courtesy of Oldsmobile Div. of GMC)

463

GLOSSARY OF TERMS

Alternator A device used in a vehicle charging system to produce current.

Alternating current (AC) An electric current that first flows one way in a circuit and then the other.

Ammeter An instrument used to measure current flow (in amperes).

Ampere A unit of measurement used in expressing the rate of current flow in a circuit.

Arcing Electricity bridging the gap between two electrodes.

Armature Used in electronic ignition systems, located in the distributor. As the distributor shaft rotates, the armature signals the control circuits to collapse the magnetic field in the primary circuit.

Available voltage The maximum secondary voltage an ignition system is able to produce whenever it attempts to fire an impossible gap.

Ballast Resistor Controls voltage applied to the coil.

Battery An electrochemical device that produces electricity.

Breaker Cam (Distributor Cam) Rotates with the distributor to close and open the breaker points at predetermined intervals (degrees) depending on the number of cylinders an engine has.

Breakerless Inductive Discharge (BID) An electronic ignition system used by AMC and IH.

Breaker Points A pair of movable points that are opened and closed to open and close the primary circuit.

Centrifugal Advance A unit designed to advance and retard the ignition timing through the action of centrifugal force.

Circuit A path that is used to direct electricity.

Coil (Ignition) A unit used to step up battery voltage to the point necessary to fire the spark plugs.

Compression The decrease in volume of a given quantity of air and fuel during the compression stroke.

Condenser A unit installed across the breaker points to minimize arcing. A condenser has the ability to absorb and retain surges of electricity.

Control Module A transistorized or computerized unit used in electronic ignition systems to switch the current in the primary circuit on and off.

Conventional Ignition An ignition system that utilizes breaker points, condenser and a distributor cam to close and open the primary circuit. Replaced in recent years by electronic ignition systems.

Corroded Ignition and/or electrical components gradually deteriorated by chemical action. Evident by pits, a buildup of a crusty substance, or material eaten away.

Current The movement of free electrons through a conductor.

Degree $\frac{1}{360}$ part of a circle.

Detonation The fuel charge firing or burning too violently, almost exploding.

Diaphragm A flexible cloth-rubber sheet that is stretched across an area, separating two different components.

Diode A unit having the ability to pass electricity readily in one direction but resisting current flow in the other.

Distributor (Ignition) A unit designed to make and break the ignition primary circuit and to distribute the high secondary voltage to the proper cylinder at the correct time.

Distributor Cap An insulated cap containing a center terminal with a series of terminals that are spaced in a circular pattern. The secondary voltage travels from the center terminal where it is then channeled to one of the outer terminals by means of a rotor.

Distributor Cap Adapter Used by Ford in their electronic ignition systems to accommodate large distributor caps.

Dura Spark Ignition A type of electronic ignition system used by the Ford Motor Company.

Dwell The number of degrees the breaker cam rotates from the time the breaker points close to the time the points open.

Electrode (Spark Plug) The center rod passing through the spark plug insulator, which forms one electrode. The rod welded to the shell of the spark plug forms another. They are referred to as the center and side electrodes.

Electronic Ignition An ignition system that electronically controls the current flow in the primary circuit instead of using breaker points, condenser and distributor cam as used in the conventional ignition system.

Electronic Ignition System (EIS) An electronic ignition system used by the Chrysler Corporation.

Electronic Spark Timing A term used with newer electronic ignition systems. A control module, or computer advances and/or retards the spark according to engine operation.

Engine Sensors Primarily used on electronic ignition systems with electronic spark control. The various sensors that are used send the changes in engine operation and signal the computer to adjust operating conditions.

Firing Line The firing line is part of the firing section in the primary, or secondary scope pattern. It represents the voltage required to overcome the rotor and spark plug gaps.

Firing Order The order in which the cylinders are fired.

Firing Voltage The voltage required to bridge the gap across the spark plug electrode to ignite the air/fuel mixture.

Fouled Usually pertains to a spark plug that is coated with a crusty substance which is caused by improper engine operation.

Gap A space between two objects.

Grounding Probe A tool used in testing ignition systems for high resistance and insulation breakdowns.

High Energy Ignition (HEI) An electronic ignition system used by the General Motors Corporation.

Ignition Coil See COIL.

Ignition Coil Output The amount of voltage produced in the secondary windings of the coil when the magnetic field in the primary collapses.

Ignition Timing The synchronization of the distributor to the engine so that ignition takes place at the proper time of the ignition cycle.

Insulation A non-conductive material used to cover or coat electrical components and wires.

Insulator (Spark Plugs) A non-conductive material made of porcelain to insulate the center electrode of the spark plug.

Ionization See FIRING VOLTAGE.

Kilovolt (KV) Equal to 1000 volts and used to measure the voltage levels in an ignition system.

Lean Burn A term used by Chrysler to describe its electronic ignition system.

Millisecond Equals one thousandth of a second. Used in conjunction with the millisecond scale of an oscilloscope.

Ohm A unit measurement used to indicate the amount of resistance to flow of electricity in a given circuit.

Ohmmeter An instrument used to measure the amount of resistance in a given unit or circuit (in ohms).

Open Circuit A circuit in which a wire is broken or disconnected.

Oscillations A flow of electricity changing periodically from maximum to minimum. Applied to the ignition system, these oscillations are the display of the voltage changes in the primary and secondary circuits.

Percent Equals one part in a hundred.

Pickup Part of the scope tester leads which senses the electrical pulses in a circuit so they can be displayed and measured on the scope.

Pickup Coil Used in an electronic ignition system to generate a voltage signal for the control module, or computer.

Polarity The particular state either positive or negative with reference to two poles of electrification.

Primary Circuit A low voltage circuit which is energized by the battery to begin the ignition process.

Primary resistance The resistance in the primary circuit.

Raster The display of all the individual cylinders one above the other, starting at the bottom of the scope screen with the No. 1 cylinder.

Reluctor See ARMATURE.

Required Voltage The amount of secondary voltage that must be produced to bridge the rotor and spark plug gaps.

Resistance A measure of a conductor's ability to retard the flow of electricity.

Rotor (Alternator) Consists of the field winding, two iron segments with interlacing fingers called poles, the shaft and two slip rings. When battery current flows through the field coil a magnetic field is generated. This flow of electrical energy through the field windings is called field current.

Rotor (Distributor) A cap-like unit fastened to the end of the distributor shaft. It is in constant contact with the distributor cap central terminal and as it turns, it will line up with the outer terminals to deliver the secondary voltage.

Rotor Air Gap The space between the rotor tip and distributor cap terminal.

Rotor Register The alignment of the rotor tip to the distributor cap terminal.

Rubbing Block The portion of the breaker points that rides against the distributor cam. When the rubbing block passes the highest portion of the cam lobe the breaker points open.

R.P.M. Revolutions Per Minute.

Scope Screen The portion of the scope that displays patterns.

Secondary Circuit The purpose of this circuit is to deliver the high voltage produced in the coil to the spark plugs at the correct time.

Secondary Resistance The amount of resistance in the secondary circuit.

Secondary Wires The wires that are connected from the coil high tension tower and to the distributor cap tower and from the outer terminals to the spark plugs.

Short or Short Circuit When electricity takes a shorter than desired path back to the electrical source.

Snap Acceleration The term used to define the rapid opening and closing of the throttle mechanism to apply a load on an engine for a very short time.

Spark The result of electricity bridging the gap between the spark plug electrodes.

Spark Advance Causes the spark to occur earlier in the engine cycle.

Spark Control Computer Used in electronic ignition systems to control engine operation.

Spark Duration The length of time a spark plug fires. Shown as the spark line in the firing section of the secondary scope pattern.

Spark Knock The result of the combustion chamber pressures building up too soon, resulting in uneven burning of the air-fuel mixture.

Spark Line The line in the firing section of the secondary scope pattern. The line represents the voltage required to maintain the spark.

Spark Plug A device containing two electrodes across which electricity jumps to produce a spark to fire the air-fuel mixture.

Spark Plug Gap The space between the center and side electrodes.

Spark Voltage The voltage required to maintain a spark for a predetermined amount of time under all operating conditions.

Stator A laminated iron frame and three output windings that are wound into slots of the frame.

Superimpose The display obtained on the scope by placing all the cylinders on top of one another.

Suppression A method of reducing or eliminating radio and TV interference generated by an ignition system. Typical ways of providing sup-

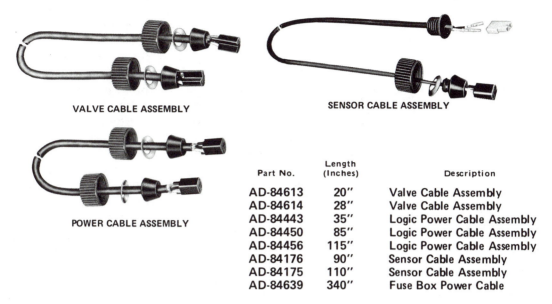

VALVE CABLE ASSEMBLY

SENSOR CABLE ASSEMBLY

POWER CABLE ASSEMBLY

Part No.	Length (Inches)	Description
AD-84613	20"	Valve Cable Assembly
AD-84614	28"	Valve Cable Assembly
AD-84443	35"	Logic Power Cable Assembly
AD-84450	85"	Logic Power Cable Assembly
AD-84456	115"	Logic Power Cable Assembly
AD-84176	90"	Sensor Cable Assembly
AD-84175	110"	Sensor Cable Assembly
AD-84639	340"	Fuse Box Power Cable

Fig. 31-9. Skid-control system cables and connectors. (Courtesy of Wagner Electric Corp.)

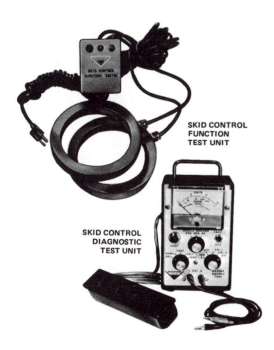

SKID CONTROL FUNCTION TEST UNIT

SKID CONTROL DIAGNOSTIC TEST UNIT

Fig. 31-10. Skid-control test equipment. (Courtesy of Wagner Electric Corp.)

With the coils placed over an axle hubcap, the tester is energized to simulate an 12.8 km/hr (8 mph) road speed condition from the wheel speed sensors. The brakes are then applied and power to the tester coils is quickly interrupted to simulate a wheel lock-up condition. If the skid-control system is operating correctly, service air pressure should exhaust from the air modulator valve preventing a wheel lockup condition each time that the tester pushbutton is depressed. The diagnostic tester unit includes a volt/ohmmeter connected into the sockets which mate with the cable plugs of the skid-control system. The tester can also be used for checking system components for shorts or grounds.

The tester operates on a 1.5 volt size AA battery; cables from the skid-control logic module are disconnected and temporarily connected to the test unit connections when trouble-shooting of the system is required. Wheel sensors, modulator valve solenoids and wiring continuity and resistance checks to ground can be monitored in this test hookup. Should no faults be found in any of these components, then the problem is in the logic module.

Although instructions are included with the test equipment, the following procedure will serve to illustrate the use of this equipment and why it is necessary to obtain such equipment if successful troubleshooting of the Wagner 121 system is to be concluded in a quick and efficient manner.

DIAGNOSTIC TESTER OPERATION

Always check first that power is being supplied to the skid-control system; blown fuses indicate a possible short or component damage. Also high circuit resistance can cause a low voltage condition to result; this check was described earlier for the fuse/junction box. To check the system voltage, plug a logic power lead into the diagnostic tester socket marked power and turn the tester polarity switch to the appropriate position for the particular system being checked, then energize the vehicle stop-light circuit. With the tester switch at SOL 1 position, there should be at least 9 volts which is what was obtained earlier at the fuse/junction box. A reading of less than 9 volts requires that you check the state of charge of the vehicle battery, electrical connections, etc. to establish the reason for a low reading.

When at least 9 volts exist in the system, plug the two sensor leads from the axle wheels into the diagnostic tester and turn the switch to SEN.L and SEN.R positions, with the function switch to the OHMS and CONT positions. With the switch at the OHMS position, the meter should read infinite ohms, while with the switch in the CONT position, the meter should read between 750 and 3000 ohms. Readings in ohms in excess of those stated generally indicate a faulty sensor or cable.

The solenoids in the air modulator valve are checked by plugging each valve cable individually into the tester socket labelled valve and turning the circuit switch to both SOL.1 and SOL.2 positions. With the function switch at CONT, a zero ohms reading indicates a shorted solenoid coil or cable, while an infinite reading indicates an open circuit. Readings other than infinite with the switch set at OHMS indicates a grounded coil or cable. By switching the selector circuit switch to EXT position, and connecting the test leads to a component, other electrical accessories can be checked on the vehicle.

To check the condition of the 1.5 volt tester battery, turn the function switch to CONT and the circuit switch to EXT; a reading of more than 400 ohms indicates a weak battery. Also included in this tester assembly is a convenient switch and indicator light for checking the skid-control fault indicator on the tractor unit. Within the tester are fuses for circuit protection.

BENDIX WHEEL SPEED SENSORS

The wheel speed sensors used by Bendix are illustrated in Fig. 31-11 in their assembled view. Figure 31-12 shows the unit in an exploded form. Note that the sensors shown in these first two figures are of the WS-1 and WS-2 type. Figure 31-13 shows the WS-3 wheel speed sensor which differs from that of the WS-1 and WS-2 type.

The WS-1 sensor is designed for use with 20 or 22 inch tires (rolling radius), while the WS-2 unit is designed for use with 15 inch tires (rolling radius) on a

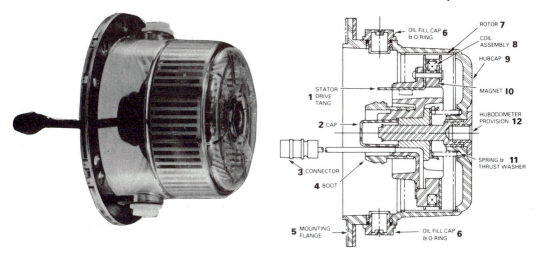

Fig. 31-11. WS-1 and WS-2 wheel speed sensors. (Courtesy of Bendix Heavy Vehicle Systems Group)

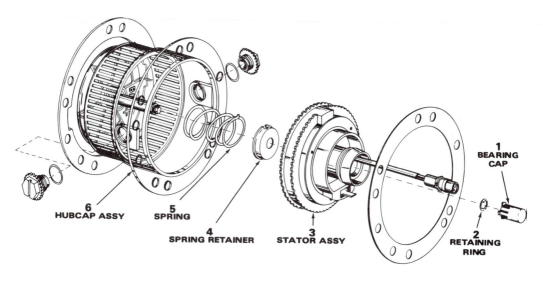

Fig. 31-12. Location of components of WS-1 and WS-2 wheel speed sensors. (Courtesy of Bendix Heavy Vehicle Systems Group)

trailer or rear non-driving axles on a tractor. Both sensors are installed on the spindle hub of the axle, are self-contained and self-adjusting.

Both the WS-1 and WS-2 are manufactured with two non-serviceable subassemblies, namely the hubcap sub-assembly which houses the rotor and oil filler caps, and the stator subassembly whose major components are the magnet, coil assembly, stator tang, and a wiring connector. The sensor is mounted to the wheel hub via a mounting flange, and a clear hubcap allows a visual check of the oil level. In order to connect the sensor to the skid-control system, an ITT cannon cable connector is provided.

In Fig. 31-11, the stator drive tang 1 engages the axle spindle keyway and the connector 3 is attached to the wiring harness. Therefore, as the wheel rotates, the stator tang 1 holds the stator motionless and the hubcap 9 and rotor 7 interrupt the magnetic field of the magnet 10, thereby producing an AC voltage.

SENSOR CONTINUITY TEST

In order to check out the condition of the wiring and coil proceed as follows: Locate the sensor wires at the anti-lock controller; then, with the wires removed from the controller terminals, connect an ohmmeter to the sensor wires and note the reading. An open or broken wire would be indicated with an infinite resistance reading; less than 1000 ohms indicates a shorted wire, and either of the two conditions above can also indicate that a sensor or the sensor lead wires or vehicle wiring harness has failed.

OPERATIONAL OUTPUT VOLTAGE CHECK

1. Identify the wires (2) at the anti-lock controller, then remove them and connect an AC voltmeter across them; with the vehicle wheel raised clear of the ground, spin the wheel and note the AC voltage output.

2. Minimum AC voltage should be more than 0.3 volts at 8 km/hr (5 mph) wheel speed, or 43 rpm for a 20 inch wheel, and 56 rpm for 15 inch wheels.

BENDIX WS-3 WHEEL SPEED SENSOR

This model sensor is constructed differently than the WS-1 and WS-3 types as can be readily seen in Fig. 31-13.

Replaceable parts in the WS-3 wheel speed sensor are the gauge blocks shown in Fig. 31-13 and the screw packs immediately above them. Should the sensor prove to be faulty after checking it out in accordance with the two checks listed for the WS-1 and WS-2 units, then replace the entire sensor assembly. The gauge blocks shown in Fig. 31-13 are replaced at every brake reline on the vehicle axle.

KELSEY HAYES SKID-CONTROL TROUBLESHOOTING

This explanation covers briefly the method used to effectively troubleshoot the antilock system; indeed, a separate book would be required to cover all of the checks and tests required on the system. Each individual antilock manufacturer can provide excellent reference material for the repair, maintenance, and effective troubleshooting of these systems through their own service literature departments.

Two main procedures are suggested and recommended for the troubleshooting approach to a skid-control system problem. One is by using a portable test unit number SE-2575 which is illustrated in Fig. 31-14. This unit is designed to allow an adapter to be installed into the system in place of the computer module cover. An

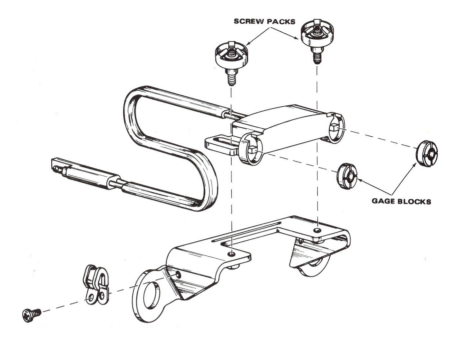

Fig. 31-13. Bendix WS-3 wheel speed sensor for anti-lock braking system. (Courtesy of Bendix Heavy Vehicle Systems Group)

(a)   (b)

Fig. 31-14. (a) Test unit SE-2575 anti-lock tester, (b) antilock tester installed on vehicle chassis. (Courtesy of International Harvester)

eight foot cord allows the mechanic to read the tester alongside the truck during a test procedure. Complete instructions for troubleshooting the antilock system are provided with the tester.

If the tester is not available, then use the second procedure: a volt/ohmmeter and a jumper wire fitted with test probes or alligator clips; install small nails into the alligator clips as test probes if necessary. A diagnostic troubleshooting guide is available either directly from a Kelsey Hayes dealer or from International-Harvester under number CTS1044 to assist you in quickly locating problems in the system.

Kelsey Hayes sensor continuity checks with an ohmmeter should provide resistance readings between 4000 and 6000 ohms. Sensor output should be checked with the wheel spinning at 35 to 45 rpm (one revolution every 2 seconds) with a minimum output of 0.3 volts. Another important check is that the exciter ring, shown in Fig. 31-2, when installed on the wheel should have a maximum runout not to exceed 0.635mm or (0.025 inches).

REVIEW QUESTIONS

Q1. What Federal Law in the USA identifies the need for an anti-skid system on heavy duty truck/trailers?

Q2. Name three major manufacturers of skid-control systems.

Q3. What components are used to monitor and activate the skid-control system?

Q4. When the electrical components, or an electrical fault exists in the skid-control system, how would the driver of the vehicle be aware of this condition?

Q5. What do the terms spin-down and spin-up mean?

Q6. At what road speed do the wheel sensors generate a voltage signal?

Q7. What amount of voltage is generated from the wheel speed sensors?

Q8. How can you check the condition of a wheel speed sensor?

Q9. What is the minimum voltage required through the fuse/junction box on a Wagner skid-control system?

Q10. What is a logic module?

Q11. What are the names of the test equipment available through Wagner Electric to monitor and test their skid-control systems?

Q12. How many wheel speed sensors types are used on Bendix anti-skid systems?

Q13. What would a resistance reading of less than 1000 ohms indicate to you when testing a wheel speed sensor?

Q14. How would you conduct an output voltage check of the wheel speed sensor on a Bendix skid-control system?

ANSWERS

A1. Federal Law FMVSS-121 (Federal Motor Vehicle Safety Standard).

A2. Wagner Electric, Bendix, and Kelsey-Hayes.

A3. Components used to monitor and activate the skid-control system are:

    (a) Wheel speed sensors to monitor wheel speed condition; rpm versus a lock-up condition.

    (b) A solid state logic monitor that receives voltage signals from the wheel speed sensors and compares them to preset frequencies; a signal is sent from the logic module to the solenoids of the air brake modulator valve to apply and release air pressure to the brakes.

(c) Air brake modulator valve which has service air directed through it to the brakes; this modulator contains solenoids that are energized and de-energized by a signal from the logic monitor.

A4. When a fault exists in the skid-control electrical system, a lamp monitor on the vehicle dash or instrument panel will illuminate to warn the driver of an electrical system fault.

A5. The terms spin-down and spin-up are related to the speed condition at the individual wheels.

A6. The wheel speed sensors generally will not generate a voltage signal at road speeds less than 8 km/hr (5 mph).

A7. Usually a voltage signal of not less than 0.3 volts is generated at the minimum road speed of 8 km/hr (5 mph), with a maximum value of 25 volts being generated at the vehicle's high speed end.

A8. By disconnecting its leads from the logic module and using an ohmmeter to measure its resistance relative to the manufacturer's specs.

A9. A minimum of 9 volts should be apparent when checking flow through the fuse/junction box of a Wagner skid-control system.

A10. The logic module is a solid state device that is programmed to monitor the signals from the wheel speed sensors and compare these signals to a preset frequency continually. A constant comparison through the logic module's memory bank is linked to so many vibrations per second or frequency in Hertz (Hz) from the wheel speed sensors. A constant comparison of these frequency signals through the logic module interfaces allows analogies which distinguish between the normal and the unusual situation at the road wheels to cause the logic module to control the solenoid activation within the air brake modulator valve thereby effectively applying and releasing the pressure to the individual wheel brakes to prevent a skidding condition.

A11. Wagner test equipment includes:

(a) The skid-control function test unit

(b) The skid-control diagnostic test unit

A12. Bendix identifies their wheel speed sensors by a designation of WS-1, WS-2, and WS-3.

A13. A resistance reading of less than 1000 ohms on a Bendix wheel speed sensor indicates a shorted wire.

A14. Disconnect wheel speed sensor wires, place a voltmeter (AC) across them; raise the wheel clear of the ground and spin it at least 8 km/hr (5 mph); voltage should be more than 0.3 volts.

Chapter

32

Trailer Wiring and Connections for Car and Truck

Many different styles and sizes of vehicle trailers are in use today; from the simple two wheel tag-along behind a car, to the single, double, or triple trailer concept now in use with Class 8 heavy-duty trucks on our nation's highways.

The recommended standards for plugs and receptacles for different types of trailers are discussed below.

FIVE-CONDUCTOR ELECTRICAL CONNECTORS FOR AUTOMOTIVE TYPE TRAILERS

The SAE standard for the wiring and connectors used with these types of trailers are for non-passenger carrying trailers with circuit loads not to exceed 7.5 amperes per circuit. Figure 32-1(a) shows the commonly recommended receptacle that is used with this system, while Fig. 32-2 shows the plug mated to this receptacle.

With this wiring arrangement, the wires should be securely attached to the trailer frame at distances no greater than every 18 inches (46 cm), with the receptacle leads

not to be smaller than 16 gauge (single), or smaller than 18 gauge (in multicolor cables) heavy duty SAE insulated automotive primary wire. The same specifications hold true for the plug leads.

FOUR- AND EIGHT-CONDUCTOR RECTANGULAR ELECTRICAL CONNECTORS FOR AUTOMOTIVE TYPE TRAILERS

The SAE standards for all trailers with a gross weight not in excess of 10,000 lbs (4540 kg) places these trailers in SAE classes 1 through 4 with running light circuit loads not to exceed 7.5 amperes per circuit. These circuits will provide power for such things as vehicle (trailer) lighting, electric brakes, trailer battery charging, and an auxiliary circuit. Figure 32-3 shows the recommended four and eight plug arrangements with receptacles, including recommended wiring color. The ground wire to the frame should be SAE wire size 16 or metric size 1.2 minimum for four circuit receptacles, while the ground wire

763

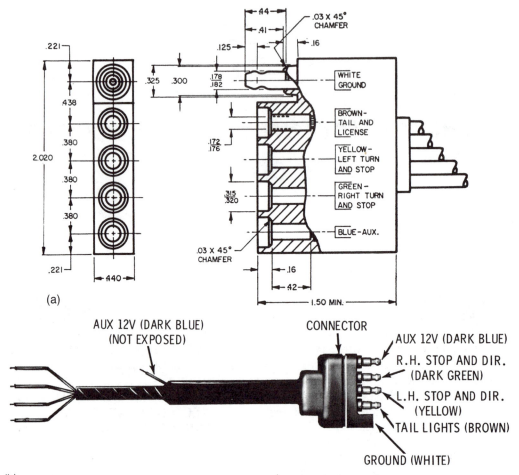

Fig. 32-1. (a) SAE recommended five-conductor trailer receptacle (courtesy of Society of Automotive Engineers); (b) five-wire trailer harness connector (trailer half) (courtesy of Oldsmobile Div. of GMC).

for the eight circuit receptacle should be direct to the battery negative with an SAE 12 gauge wire or metric size of 3.0 minimum. No receptacle leads for lighting systems should be smaller than SAE wire size 16 or metric size 1.2 for a single conductor, or smaller than SAE wire size 18 or metric size 0.8 for a multiconductor cable. For brake circuits, minimum SAE wire size 14 or metric size 2.0 should be used. Wires for

the trailer battery charge circuit or battery return circuit should be a minimum SAE number 12 or metric size 3.0.

SEVEN-CONDUCTOR TRAILER CORDS

The seven-conductor trailer cord is used on heavy-duty truck/tractor trailer wiring systems. Recommendations for the wiring

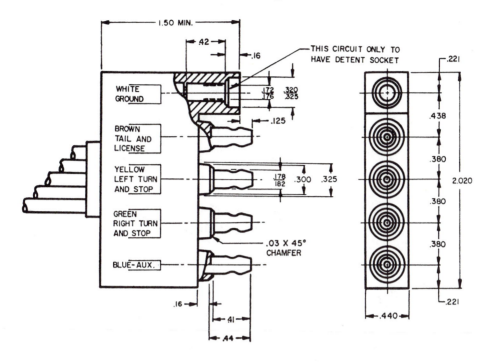

Fig. 32-2. SAE recommended five conductor plug. (Courtesy of Society of Automotive Engineers)

circuits for these heavy-duty units conform to the ATA (American Trucking Association), the SAE (Society of Automotive Engineers), and the TTMA (Truck Trailer Manufacturers Association).

Figure 32-4 shows a seven conductor electrical connector and cable plug for interchangeability with electrical connectors of different manufacture.

The receptacle socket and cable plug should contain a minimum wire size of number 8 gauge, since this is the ground wire circuit and should be white in color. All other terminal wires should be at least number 10 gauge wire. Both the plug and the receptacle are marked with identification letters to facilitate proper connection of the wiring to meet the industry standards.

The recommended industry standards for wire connection for a seven conductor connector and plug are shown in Table 32-1.

Seven-Cable Conductors

The conductors should be cabled together with a maximum lay of 6 inches (15.24 cm) and a wire configuration as shown in Fig. 32-5. The conductor wiring should also conform to the specifications shown in Table 32-5(b).

TRAILER WIRING GUIDE

The recommended trailer wiring guide as per the ATA, SAE and TTMA is shown in Fig. 32-6, which shows lamp placement and wire color.

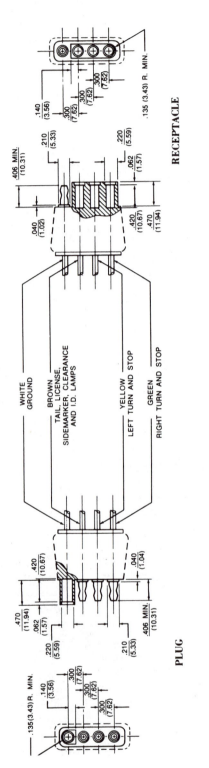

RECEPTACLE

.135 (3.43) R. MIN.

.140 (3.56)
.300 (7.62)
.300 (7.62)
.406 MIN. (10.31)
.210 (5.33)
.220 (5.59)
.062 (1.57)
.040 (1.02)
.420 (10.67)
.470 (11.94)

WHITE GROUND

BROWN
TAIL, LICENSE, SIDEMARKER, CLEARANCE AND I.D. LAMPS

YELLOW
LEFT TURN AND STOP

GREEN
RIGHT TURN AND STOP

(a)

.420 (10.67)
.040 (1.04)
.470 (11.94)
.062 (1.57)
.220 (5.59)
.406 MIN. (10.31)
.210 (5.33)

PLUG

.135 (3.43) R. MIN.

.140 (3.56)
.300 (7.62)
.300 (7.62)
.300 (7.62)

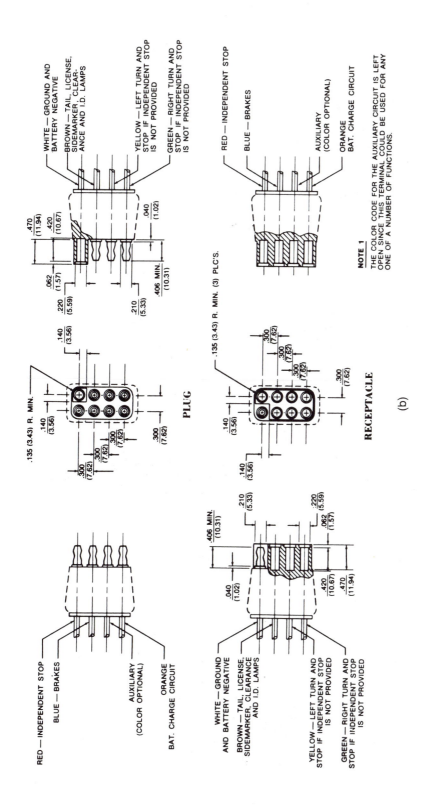

WHITE — GROUND AND
BATTERY NEGATIVE

BROWN — TAIL, LICENSE,
SIDEMARKER, CLEAR-
ANCE AND I.D. LAMPS

YELLOW — LEFT TURN AND
STOP IF INDEPENDENT STOP
IS NOT PROVIDED

GREEN — RIGHT TURN AND
STOP IF INDEPENDENT STOP
IS NOT PROVIDED

RED — INDEPENDENT STOP

BLUE — BRAKES

AUXILIARY
(COLOR OPTIONAL)

ORANGE
BAT. CHARGE CIRCUIT

.470
(11.94)
.420
(10.67)
.040
(1.02)
.062
(1.57)
.220
(5.59)
.210
(5.33)
406 MIN.
(10.31)

NOTE 1

THE COLOR CODE FOR THE AUXILIARY CIRCUIT IS LEFT
OPEN SINCE THIS TERMINAL COULD BE USED FOR ANY
ONE OF A NUMBER OF FUNCTIONS.

.135 (3.43) R. MIN.

.140
(3.56)

.300
(7.62)
.300
(7.62)
.300
(7.62)

PLUG

.135 (3.43) R. MIN. (3) PLC'S.

.300
(7.62)
.300
(7.62)
.300
(7.62)
.300
(7.62)

.140
(3.56)

.140
(3.56)

RECEPTACLE

(b)

RED — INDEPENDENT STOP

BLUE — BRAKES

AUXILIARY
(COLOR OPTIONAL)

ORANGE
BAT. CHARGE CIRCUIT

WHITE — GROUND
AND BATTERY NEGATIVE

BROWN — TAIL, LICENSE,
SIDEMARKER, CLEARANCE
AND I.D. LAMPS

YELLOW — LEFT TURN AND
STOP IF INDEPENDENT STOP
IS NOT PROVIDED

GREEN — RIGHT TURN AND
STOP IF INDEPENDENT STOP
IS NOT PROVIDED

.210
(5.33)
.220
(5.59)
.062
(1.57)
406 MIN.
(10.31)
.040
(1.02)
.420
(10.67)
.470
(11.94)

Fig. 32-3. (a) Four circuit receptacle and plug, (b) eight circuit receptacle and plug. (Courtesy of Society of Automotive Engineers)

767

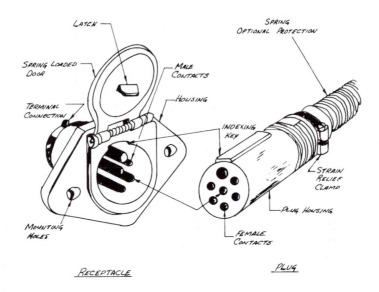

Fig. 32-4. Seven conductor electrical connector and cable plug. (Courtesy of Society of Automotive Engineers)

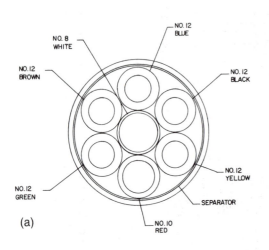

(a)

Fig. 32-5. (a) Conductor/cable arrangement, (b) Conductor dimensions. (Courtesy of Society of Automotive Engineers)

CONDUCTORS

SAE Wire[a] Size	No. of Wires	Nominal Size of Strand		Lay in.	Conductor Area Cir Mils	Max Dia of Stranded Conductor, in.
		AWG	in.			
12	65	30	.010 (.254 mm)	1.5 (38.1 mm)	6487	.100 (2.54 mm)
10	105	30	.010 (.254 mm)	1.5 (38.1 mm)	10479	.125 (3.18 mm)
8	168 or	30	.010 (.254 mm)	2.0 (50.8 mm)	16414	.175 (4.45 mm)
	427	34	.0063 (.160 mm)	2.0 (50.8 mm)		

(b)

[a]SAE wire size numbers indicate that the circular mil area of the stranded conductor approximates the circular mil area of American Wire Gage for equivalent gage size.

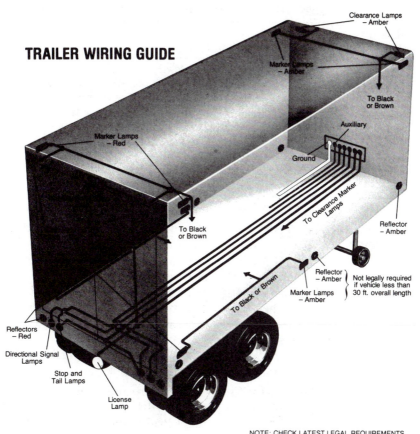

TRAILER WIRING GUIDE

NOTE: CHECK LATEST LEGAL REQUIREMENTS
FOR REQUIRED LOCATIONS AND
QUANTITIES OF LIGHTING DEVICES.
LIGHTING FUNCTIONS MAY BE COMBINED OR SEPARATED WHERE AND AS LEGALLY PERMITTED.

ATA, SAE & TTMA WIRE COLORS FOR 7 POLE CONNECTORS

FUNCTION	WIRE COLOR
GROUND RETURN	WHITE
LEFT TURN & HAZARD SIGNAL	YELLOW
RIGHT TURN & HAZARD SIGNAL	GREEN
STOP LAMPS & ANTILOCK DEVICES	RED
*TAIL, IDENTIFICATION, LICENCE, CLEARANCE & MARKER LAMPS	BROWN
*CLEARANCE, MARKER & IDENTIFICATION LAMPS	BLACK
AUXILIARY	BLUE
*IT IS DESIRABLE TO BALANCE THE CIRCUITS.	

TTMA RECOMMENDED WIRE GAUGES & VEHICLE INTERFACE

NUMBER OF TRAILERS (WHERE AND AS LEGALLY ALLOWED)	FOR GROUND CIRCUIT	FOR STOP LAMP CIRCUIT
SINGLE & DOUBLE TRAILERS	#10	#12
TURNPIKE DOUBLES & TRIPLES	#8	#10

Fig. 32-6. Trailer wiring guide. (Courtesy of Dominion Auto Accessories Ltd. Toronto, Canada)

Table 32-1 Wire Connection Standards

Conductor Identification	Wire Color	Lamp and Signal Circuits
WHT	White	Ground return to towing vehicle
BLK	Black	Clearance, side marker and identification lamps
YEL	Yellow	Left-hand turn signal and hazard signal
RED	Red	Stoplamps and anti-wheel lock devices
GRN	Green	Right-hand turn signal and hazard signal
BRN	Brown	Tail and license plate lamps
BLU	Blue	Auxiliary circuit

LIGHT LOCATIONS ON THE TRACTOR TRAILER

In addition to the trailer wiring and lamp locations shown in Fig. 32-6, Figs. 32-7, 32-8, and 32-9 show recommended lighting arrangements for truck/tractors as well as flat deck trailers, tank transporters, and buses.

The lamp locations shown for the bus are general; school buses will have a specific lamp arrangement that differs from that shown. The Code of Federal Regulations for Motor Carrier Safety Standard (108 Section 4.14) specifies this lighting arrangement. Figure 32-10 illustrates typical wiring lengths found in a heavy-duty trailer circuit, and also shows the maximum total lamp candlepower with a 12 volt circuit.

CABLE SELECTION

Selection of the proper wire cable size is a very important consideration that is often overlooked, therefore always consider the circuit load, length of wire, etc. that will be required in a circuit. For example, a 10 percent drop in battery voltage caused by wire resistance will result in a 30 percent loss in candlepower output at the lamp. In other words, voltage drop must be kept to a minimum through the proper selection of wire and cable.

In order to establish the correct wire gauge you must consider the following three main items:

1. Measure the length of the cable required.

2. Add up the total candlepower to be used in the circuit, or find the total amperes load of the circuit. Find this number in Fig. 32-11 to establish the correct wire size.

3. Determine the proper gauge of wire to minimize voltage drop in the circuit (from Fig. 32-11).

CABLE TIES

When it is necessary to wire either a truck or trailer with non-bundled or no-rubber sheathed pre-assembled wires, it is customary that these wires be supported at least every 18 inches (45.72 cm). A commonly employed industry practice is to use plastic cable ties, as shown in Fig. 32-12 which illustrates the various lengths and

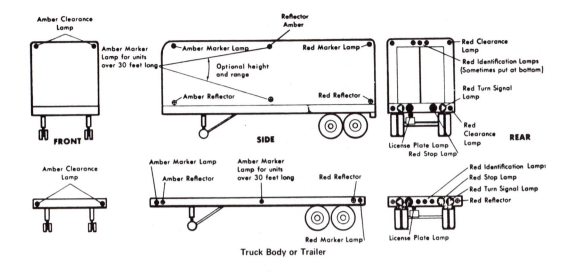

Truck Body or Trailer

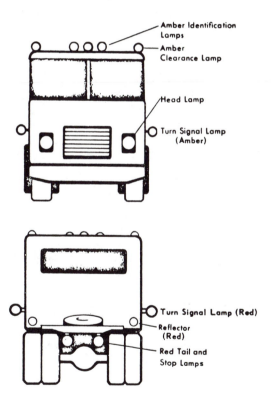

Truck Cab or Tractor

Fig. 32-7. (a) Box van and flat deck trailer lamp locations, (b) truck tractor lamp locations.

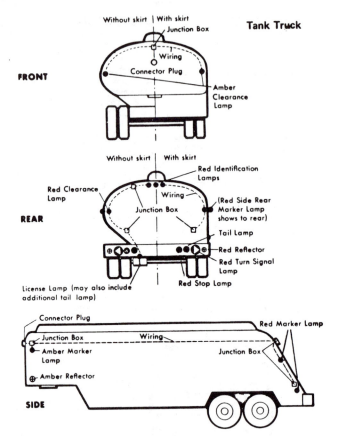

NOTE: Rear to be equipped with two stop lamps, two tail lamps and set of S.A.E., Class A, Type 1 directional signals. Any or all three of these type lamps may be in the same housing. All lamps required to conform to the requirements of 1964 S.A.E. Standards.

Fig. 32-8. Tanker trailer lamp locations.

widths commonly available from an automotive/truck electrical supplier.

TYPES OF CABLE TIES

Although Fig. 32-12 shows the available widths and lengths of cable ties commonly used, there are four general styles that are illustrated in Fig. 32-13.

1. **Type 1** is known as a Single-Unit Mounting Head style since its mounting clamp is an integral part of the tie head for quick attachment to the panel or chassis with a screw, rivet, or bolt.

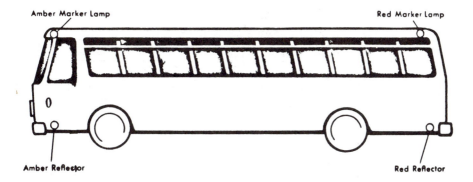

Amber Marker Lamp

Red Marker Lamp

Amber Reflector

Red Reflector

NOTE: Refer to C.F.R. "Motor Carrier Safety Standard" 108 Section 4.14 for school bus regulations.

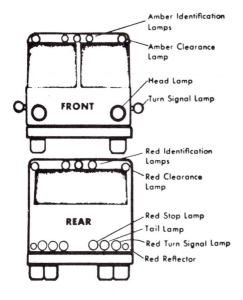

Amber Identification Lamps

Amber Clearance Lamp

Head Lamp

Turn Signal Lamp

FRONT

Red Identification Lamps

Red Clearance Lamp

Red Stop Lamp

Tail Lamp

REAR

Red Turn Signal Lamp

Red Reflector

Fig. 32-9. Passenger bus lamp locations.

2. **Type 2** is a Self-Locking Head for easy application by hand or with a tool. Once tightened, this style will not loosen.

3. **Type 3** is a Releasable Locating Tip style; the double bend tip locates around the wires for ease of insertion. The second

bend prevents snagging and the tip can be inserted in the head and later released, therefore facilitating easier positioning of the ties on bundled wire groups.

4. **Type 4** shows a tension-control application tool, part number 76-2824 Dominion Auto; this involves a three-step installation procedure as follows:

(a) Place the tie around the wire bundle with the double-bend tip located towards the locking head.

(b) Pull the tie through the head to tighten; the serrations on the tip are easy to grip.

(c) Lock the tie into place with the tension-control tool and cut it flush.

WIRE AND CABLE SHRINK TUBING

As a means of sealing out moisture, acting as a strain relief, and minimizing vibration at mechanical connections, a dual-wall Polyolefin tubing with a meltable inner wall can be used to encapsulate any electrical connection. In order to apply the shrink tubing, a shrink-tubing heatgun

TRACTOR CIRCUITS
Cable gauge recommendations for rewiring

CIRCUIT	12-Volt Gauge	6-Volt Gauge	CIRCUIT	12-Volt Gauge	6-Volt Gauge
AMMETER TO:			GENERATOR TO:		
Starter Motor	12	10	Regulator (Armature)	12	10
Ignition Switch	12	10	Regulator (Field)	12	10
Light Switch	12	10	Ground (Regulator)	18	16
Voltage Reg. (Batt.)	12	10	HEAD LAMPS TO:		
Horn Relay		10	Ground	18	16
BACK-UP LAMP	16	14	HEATER		
BATTERY CABLES (See Note Below)			HORN RELAY TO:		
COIL TO:			Feed	12	10
Ignition Switch	16	14	Horn	12	10
Distributor	16	14	Switch	18	16
CIGAR LIGHTER	16	14	LIGHT SWITCH TO:		
CLOCK	18	16	Parking Lights	18	16
DIMMER SWITCH TO:			Tail Lamps	16	14
			License Lamp	18	16
Light Switch	14	12	Instrument Lights	18	16
Low Beam Head Lamp	16	14	Stop Light Switch	16	14
High Beam Head Lamp	14	12	OIL PRESSURE GAUGE TO:		
High Beam Indicator	18	16	Feed	18	16
DIRECTIONAL SIGNAL SWITCH TO:			Sending Unit	18	16
Flasher	16	14	RADIO	16	14
Left Turn Signal Lamps	16	14	REAR SEAT SPEAKER	18	16
Right Turn Signal Lamps	16	14	SPARK PLUG CABLE		
Stop Lamp Switch	16	14	SPOT LAMP	16	14
DOME LAMP TO:			STARTER SWITCH TO SOLENOID	12	10
Feed	18	16	TEMPERATURE GAUGE TO:		
Switch	18	16	Ignition	18	16
Ground	18	16	Sending Unit	18	16
DIRECTIONAL SIGNAL FLASHER TO:			TRAILER-CONNECTOR CORD:		
Ignition	18	16	7 Conductor	(6/12	and 1/10)
Direction Indicator Lamps	18	16	6 Conductor	16	14
FUEL (GAS) GAUGE TO:			4 Conductor	16	14
Ignition	18	16	TRUNK LAMP	16	14-
Sending Unit	18	16	UNDER HOOD LAMP	16	14

NOTE: Battery Cable—Ampere draw of starter motor depends on many factors. It is advisable to use the same size cable recommended by the vehicle manufacturer.

tractor and trailer ampere and candlepower requirements

ELECTRICAL UNIT	12-VOLT UNITS			6-VOLT UNITS		
	Maximum Amperes	Design Voltage	Candlepower or Watts	Maximum Amperes	Design Voltage	Candlepower or Watts
Clearance and Marker Lamps	.5	12.5	3	.7	7.0	3
Coil	4.5	–	–	4.5	–	–
Directional Signal Lamps	2.1	12.8	32	3.0	6.4	21
Dome Lamps	1.0	12.8	15	2.0	6.5	15
Gas Gauge	.2	14.5	–	.3	7.2	–
Head Lamps — Upper	4.2	12.8	50 Watts	7.4	6.4	45 Watts
— Lower	3.4	12.8	40 Watts	5.8	6.4	35 Watts
Horn	7.0	–	–	10.0	–	–
Instrument Lamp	.3	14.0	2	.5	7.0	2
License Lamp	.5	12.5	3	.7	7.0	3
Parking Lamps	.6	14.0	4	.9	7.0	3
Spot Lamp	2.6	12.8	30 Watts	4.3	6.2	30 Watts
Stop Lamp	2.1	12.8	32	3.0	6.4	21
Tail Lamp	.6	14.0	4	.9	7.0	3

Fig. 32-10. Heavy-duty trailer circuit wiring lengths and maximum candlepower with a 12 volt circuit.

Length of Circuit**	Maximum Total Candlepower 12 Volts			
Feet	No. 10 Wire	No. 12 Wire	No. 14 Wire	No. 16 Wire
10	190*	119*	96*	32*
15	190*	119*	96*	32*
20	190*	119*	96*	32*
25	190*	119*	96*	32*
30	190*	119*	93	32*
35	190*	119*	79	32*
40	173	109	69	32*
45	154	97	62	32*
50	139	87	55	32*
55	126	79	50	31
60	116	73	46	29
65	107	67	43	26
70	99	62	40	25
75	93	58	37	23
80	87	55	35	21
85	82	51	33	20
90	77	49	31	19
95	73	46	29	18
100	69	44	28	17

Fig. 32-10 Continued.

Recommended cable sizes for replacement or additional electrical unit installations

Original equipment cable sizes on some vehicles may vary slightly from recommendations due to special electrical system design.

This chart applies to chassis grounded return systems. For two-wire circuits, use total length of both cables, or the double length to most distant electrical unit.

12-VOLT SYSTEM		Total Length of Cable in Circuit from Battery to most Distant Electrical Unit									
AMPERES (APPROX.)	CANDLE POWER	10 Feet	20 Feet	30 Feet	40 Feet	50 Feet	60 Feet	70 Feet	80 Feet	90 Feet	100 Feet
		Gge.	Gge.	Gge.	Gge.	Gge.	Gge.	Gge.	Gge.	Gge.	Gge.
1.0	6	18	18	18	18	18	18	18	18	18	18
1.5	10	18	18	18	18	18	18	18	18	18	18
2	16	18	18	18	18	18	18	18	16	16	16
3	24	18	18	18	18	18	16	16	16	14	14
4	30	18	18	18	16	16	16	14	14	14	12
5	40	18	18	18	16	14	14	14	12	12	12
6	50	18	18	16	16	14	14	12	12	12	12
7	60	18	18	16	14	14	12	12	12	10	10
8	70	18	16	16	14	12	12	12	10	10	10
10	80	18	16	14	12	12	12	10	10	10	10
11	90	18	16	14	12	12	10	10	10	10	8
12	100	18	16	14	12	12	10	10	10	8	8
15	120	18	14	12	12	10	10	10	8	8	8
18	140	16	14	12	10	10	8	8	8	8	8
20	160	16	12	12	10	10	8	8	8	8	6
22	180	16	12	10	10	8	8	8	8	6	6
24	200	16	12	10	10	8	8	8	6	6	6
36	—	14	10	8	8	8	6	6	6	4	4
50	—	12	10	8	6	6	4	4	4	2	2
100	—	10	6	4	4	2	2	1	1	0	0
150	—	8	4	2	2	1	0	0	00	00	00
200	—	6	4	2	1	0	00	000	000	000	0000

Fig. 32-11. Wire cable size chart. (Courtesy of Dominion Auto Accessories Ltd., Toronto, Canada)

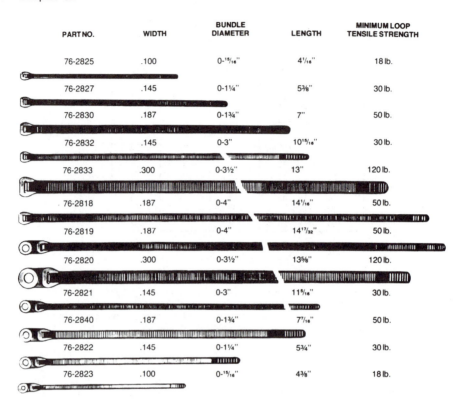

PART NO.	WIDTH	BUNDLE DIAMETER	LENGTH	MINIMUM LOOP TENSILE STRENGTH
76-2825	.100	0-$^{15}/_{16}$"	4$^1/_{16}$"	18 lb.
76-2827	.145	0-1¼"	5⅜"	30 lb.
76-2830	.187	0-1¾"	7"	50 lb.
76-2832	.145	0-3"	10$^{15}/_{16}$"	30 lb.
76-2833	.300	0-3½"	13"	120 lb.
76-2818	.187	0-4"	14$^1/_{16}$"	50 lb.
76-2819	.187	0-4"	14$^{17}/_{32}$"	50 lb.
76-2820	.300	0-3½"	13⅝"	120 lb.
76-2821	.145	0-3"	11$^5/_{16}$"	30 lb.
76-2840	.187	0-1¾"	7$^7/_{16}$"	50 lb.
76-2822	.145	0-1¼"	5¾"	30 lb.
76-2823	.100	0-$^{15}/_{16}$"	4⅜"	18 lb.

Fig. 32-12. Wire cable plastic ties. (Courtesy of Domionion Auto Accessories Ltd., Toronto, Canada)

① **Single-unit Mounting head**
Mounting clamp is integral part of tie head for quick attachment to panel or chassis with screw, rivet or bolt.

② **Self-locking Head**
Easy application by tool or by hand. Will not loosen when pulled tight.

③ **Releasable Locating Tip**
Double-bend tip locates around wires. Guides operator's hand for easy 90° insertion, even in confined areas. Second bend prevents snagging. Tip can be inserted in head and later released. Makes for easier positioning of ties on bundle.

④ **76-2824 Tension-control Application Tool**
Available on special order only. Easy, three step installation: 1 – Place tie around wire bundle. Double-bend tip locates toward locking head. Second bend prevents snagging. 2 – Pull tie through head to tighten. Serrations on tip are easy to grip. 3 – Lock into place with tension-control tool. Cuts flush.

Fig. 32-13. Four styles of cable ties. (Courtesy of Dominion Auto Accessories Ltd., Toronto, Canada)

must be used; the heatgun is shown in Fig. 32-14, along with examples of how the tubing can be applied to different wiring situations. The shrink tubing is designed so that when it is exposed briefly to temperatures of 135°C (275°F) the inner wall will melt and force its way into voids and around the connected parts to hermetically seal the area. The tubing is both chemical and solvent resistant. The shrink tubing can be used in the following basic applications:

1. Twisted-In-Line Splice as shown in Fig. 32-14 (b). Insert the tubing over one wire, then twist the stripped wires to-

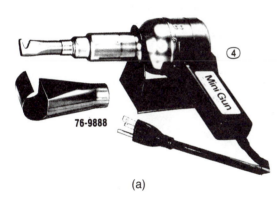

(a)

gether and bend the bare wire in-line with the wire as shown. Position the shrink tubing over the wire splice and center the reflector of the mini-gun on the splice. Switch the gun to the heat position and hold until the tubing shrinks, the wrinkles disappear, and the melted bead appears at each end of the tubing, then switch the blower to the cool position for a short period before removing the gun.

2. Twisted Pigtail Splice as shown in Fig. 32-14 (c). Twist the stripped wires together and position the shrink tubing so that it extends ¼ inch beyond the end of the wires. Heat and shrink with the mini-gun until wrinkles disappear. Squeeze the open-end shut with pliers and pinch the crotch with a pair of needle-nose pliers while still hot. Switch the blower to cool for a short period.

3. Battery Cable usage as shown in Fig. 32-14(c). The battery cable terminals can be sealed with the use of shrink tubing by sliding the tubing over the cable and applying the heat gun to it.

The shrink tubing is available in a variety of sizes as shown in Table 32-2.

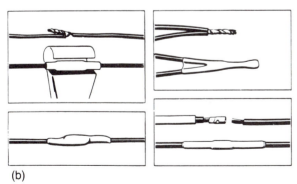

(b)

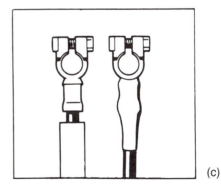

(c)

Fig. 32-14. (a) Shrink tubing heatgun, (b) twisted in-line splice, (c) twisted pigtail splice, (d) battery cable usage. (Courtesy of Dominion Auto Accessories Ltd., Toronto, Canada)

Table 32-2
Tubing Size Before and After Shrinkage

I.D. Before Shrinkage	I.D. After Shrinkage
³⁄₁₆ in (4.76 mm)	¹⁄₁₆ in (1.58 mm)
¼ in (6.35 mm)	⁵⁄₆₄ in (1.98 mm)
³⁄₈ in (9.52 mm)	⁹⁄₆₄ in (3.57 mm)
½ in (12.7 mm)	¹³⁄₆₄ in (5.15 mm)
¾ in (19 mm)	⁵⁄₁₆ in (7.93 mm)
1 in (25.4 mm)	¹³⁄₃₂ in (10.31 mm)

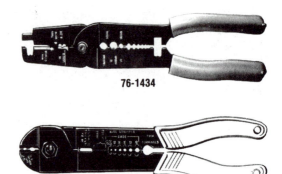

76-1434

76-1432

Fig. 32-15. Wire stripping pliers and crimpers.

WIRE STRIPPERS AND CRIMPERS

Although an insulated wire can be bared or stripped with side cutter pliers, a sharp knife, etc. the use of a wire stripper plier is recommended, since this is designed to allow all standard gauge wire to be stripped quickly and accurately. Generally a crimping tool is formed on the end of these wire stripper pliers as shown in Fig. 32-15.

REVIEW QUESTIONS

Q1. What are the common conductor connectors (number of) that are used in automotive trailer applications?

Q2. What is the recommended distance for securing trailer wires to the frame?

Q3. What are the recommended minimum wire sizes for four- and five-trailer connectors?

Q4. What is the recommended minimum wire gauge size for heavy-duty truck/tractor trailers?

Q5. What is the commonly used number of plug receptacles for heavy duty trailers?

Q6. Name the color-coded circuits that are recommended and accepted as an industry standard for heavy duty trailers.

ANSWERS

A1. Common trailer/plug connectors used in passenger car and light truck applications are usually of either the four or five connector type with a recommended circuit load not to exceed 7.5 amperes per circuit.

A2. Recommended wire support distance should not exceed 18 inches (46 cm).

A3. Recommended wire sizes for four- and five-trailer connectors are SAE 16 for single connectors, and SAE 18 for multi-conductor cable. Brake circuits should be SAE 14, while the ground wire should be SAE 16 for four circuit receptacles, and SAE 12 gauge for eight circuit receptacles. Wires for trailer battery charge or battery return circuits should be a minimum SAE 12 or metric size 3.

A4. The ground wire circuit should be SAE number 8, while all other terminal wires should be SAE number 10.

A5. A seven conductor plug receptacle trailer cord is standard on heavy duty trailers.

A6. Recommended conductor wire color coding for heavy duty trailers is as follows:

1. White: ground
2. Black: Clearance, side marker and identification lamps
3. Yellow: Left-hand turn signal and hazard
4. Red: Stoplamps and anti-wheel lock devices
5. Green: Right-hand turn signal and hazard
6. Brown: Tail and license lamps
7. Blue: Auxiliary circuit

Chapter
33

Oldsmobile/Chevrolet 5.7 and 6.2L Diesel Engine Electrics

The basic wiring of a vehicle equipped with a diesel engine is very similar to that of a unit with a gasoline engine. The major differences are in the following areas:

1. Because of the higher compression ratio of the diesel engine, two batteries are required to supply enough current to the starter motor as well as to the glow plugs for pre-heating of the combustion chamber especially in cold weather.

Figure 33-1 shows the two 12-volt batteries connected in parallel.

2. A larger starter motor is employed with the diesel engine because of the greater energy required to crank the diesel engine. A cranking speed of at least 100 rpm is necessary to start the diesel engine.

3. One glow plug per cylinder is employed to preheat the incoming air to the cylinder. The glow plugs are all 6 volt units, however, they are operated at normal system voltage or 12 volts in order to provide rapid heating. One of the main improvements that Oldsmobile made to the 1981 models was to improve the glow plugs so that they now operate to provide much faster preheat at freezing temperatures and below. Earlier engines using 12 volt glow plugs took up to 60 seconds before the start engine light would come on. Current engines fitted with 6 volt glow plugs, but operating on 12 volts have reduced this pre-heat time to 6 seconds.

The glow plugs are screwed into each cylinder and are located as shown in Fig. 33-2 just above the fuel injectors.

It is imperative that former and current glow plugs not be intermixed in an engine, since the earlier glow plugs were 12 volt units with steady current applied to them, whereas the current glow plugs are 6 volt units with controlled pulsing current applied to them. The former glow plugs were therefore known as slow glow plugs while the current ones are known as fast glow plugs. The former and current glow plugs can be identified by the size of the bayonet connection on the top of the glow plug as shown in Fig. 33-3.

To control both preglow and afterglow

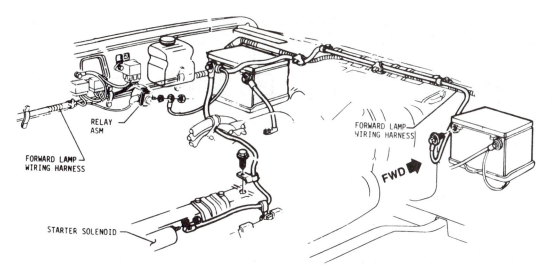

Fig. 33-1. Oldsmobile/GMC vehicle battery wiring and glow plug relay assembly. (Courtesy of Chevrolet Motor Div. of GMC)

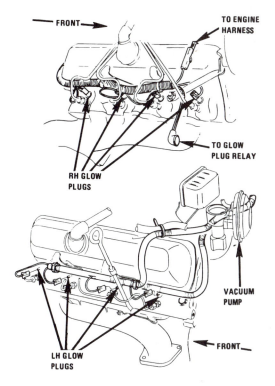

time periods, a controller located in a water passage (usually the front water passage) of the intake manifold senses coolant temperature and controls glow plug current. This controller also signals the cowl located lamp control relay to turn off the dash wait light, and when to start the engine.

4. The glow plug relay switches power on and off to the glow plugs as determined by the electronic module. The glow plug relay is shown on the fender panel in Fig. 33-1, which also shows the battery arrangement.

Caution: Do not attempt to bypass the relay of the glow plugs by using a jumper cable, since the glow plugs are designed for intermittent operation and not continuous. Supplying constant current to the

Fig. 33-2. Glow plug location. (Courtesy of Oldsmobile Div. of GMC)

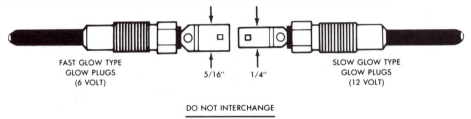

THE FAST GLOW DIESEL GLOW PLUG CONTROL SYSTEM USES 6 VOLT GLOW PLUGS WITH CONTROLLED PULSING CURRENT APPLIED TO THEM FOR STARTING. THE SLOW GLOW SYSTEM USED STEADY CURRENT APPLIED TO 12 VOLT GLOW PLUGS. IN EITHER CASE THE CORRECT GLOW PLUG SHOULD BE USED FOR PROPER STARTING. THE ILLUSTRATION SHOWS THE GLOW PLUG IDENTIFICATION.

FAST GLOW TYPE
GLOW PLUGS
(6 VOLT)

5/16″ 1/4″

SLOW GLOW TYPE
GLOW PLUGS
(12 VOLT)

DO NOT INTERCHANGE

Fig. 33-3. Former and current glow plugs. (Courtesy of Cadillac Motor Car Div. of GMC)

glow plugs through bypassing the relay will result in burning out the glow plugs' elements.

Figure 33-4 shows a simplified wiring diagram for the glow plug circuit.

Caution: If the ignition switch is left on (run position), without starting the engine, the glow plugs will continue to pulse on and off until the batteries are run down which takes about four hours when the coolant switch is open. Also do not use more than a 2-3 candle power test light when making circuit checks.

GLOW PLUG RESISTANCE CHECK

If a glow plug is suspected of being faulty, it can be removed from the vehicle and grounded on the body while battery voltage is applied to the connection terminal. Do not apply power for longer than 30 seconds to the glow plug in this manner; it can burn out (element damage). Compare the brilliance of the suspect plug with that of one known to be good or with a new one.

Glow plugs that fail to perform should be replaced. In addition to supplying preheat for starting purposes, a resistance check through the glow plugs can very effectively establish if one cylinder is producing more power than another, especially if a rough idle condition exists. Since the glow plugs are installed directly into the engine cylinder combustion chamber area along with the injector nozzle, they will be subjected to both the pressures and temperatures of combustion. A change in cylinder temperature will reflect a change in the resistance measurement through the glow plug when checked with an ohmmeter. This resistance method check is the recommended check by General Motors when a rough idle problem exists.

Note: The glow plug resistance check should only be undertaken once the idle roughness checks and adjustments have been done as per the systematic procedure found in all General Motors vehicle Service Manuals.

Once this has been done, the glow plug resistance check can be done as shown on page 784.

WATER-IN-FUEL DETECTOR

Because of the extremely fine tolerances of the injection pump components and

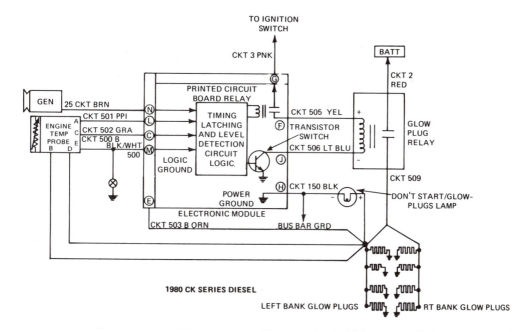

Fig. 33-4. Glow plug control schematic. (Courtesy of Chevrolet Motor Div. of GMC)

nozzles of the diesel engine, the presence of any water in the fuel system can do irreparable damage to these components. Therefore, a water-in-the-fuel detector is now used on current production vehicles fitted with the diesel engine.

Figure 33-5 shows the water-in-fuel detector which is located in the fuel tank, and Fig. 33-6 shows how this unit should be tested if it is suspected of being faulty.

If the water-in-fuel detector indicates that there is in fact water in the fuel system, then the fuel tank must be drained, removed from the vehicle and flushed clean.

In addition, all fuel lines should be blown clean with low pressure air towards the rear of the vehicle to prevent any dirt or water from being directed towards the fuel pump. The fuel filter should then be changed, and if not already done, the

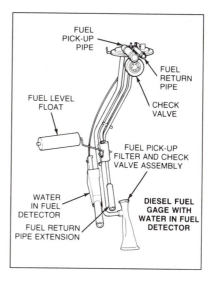

Fig. 33-5. Water in fuel detector. (Courtesy of Cadillac Motor Car Div. of GMC)

GLOW PLUG RESISTANCE PROCEDURE

1. Use the Kent-Moore High Impedence Digital Multimeter (Essential Tool J-29125) for resistance measurements.

2. Select scales as follows: LH Switch to "OHMS", RH Switch to full counterclockwise, "200Ω," Slide Center Switch to the left "DC.LO."

3. Start engine, turn on heater and allow engine to warm up. REMOVE all the feed wires from the glow plugs.

4. Using Mag-Tach J-26925, adjust engine speed by turning the idle speed screw on the side of the injection pump to the worst engine idle roughness, but do not exceed 900 RPM (860 is the most likely speed to get roughest idle).

5. Allow engine to run at worst idle speed for at least one minute. The thermostat must be open and the upper radiator hose hot.

6. Attach an alligator clip to the black test lead of the multimeter. This clip must be grounded to the engine lift strap on the left-hand side of the intake manifold. It must remain grounded to this point until all tests are completed.

7. On a separate sheet of plain writing paper write down the engine firing order — 1-8-3-26-5-7-3;

8. With engine still idling, probe each glow plug terminal and record the resistance values on each cylinder in firing sequence. Most readings will be between 1.8 and 3.4 OHMS. If these readings are not obtained, turn engine "OFF" for several minutes and recheck the glow plugs. The resistance should be .7 or .8 OHMS. If this reading is not obtained check meter for correct settings, check for low or incorrect battery in meter and check the meter ground wire to the engine.

9. The resistance values are dependent on the temperature in each cylinder, and therefore indicate the output of each cylinder.

10. If ohm reading on any cylinder is about 1.2 or 1.3 ohms, check to see if there is an engine mechanical problem. Make a compression check of the low reading cylinder and the cylinders whcih fire before and after the low cylinder reading. Correct the cause of the low compression before proceeding to the fuel system.

11. Examine the results of all cylinder glow plug resistance readings, looking for differences between cylinders. Normally, rough engines will have a difference of .3 ohms or more between cylinders in firing order. It will be necessary to raise or lower the reading on one or more of these cylinders by selection of nozzles.

12. Remove the nozzles from the cylinders in which you wish to raise or lower the ohm reading. Determine the pop off pressure of the nozzles as well as checking the nozzle for leakage and spray pattern. (Refer to Testing of Nozzles.)

   A. Install nozzles with a higher pop off pressure to lower the ohm reading, and nozzles with lower pop off pressure to raise an ohm reading. Normally, a change of about 30 psi in pressure will change the reading by .1 ohm. Nozzles normally will drop off in pop off pressure with miles. Use nozzles from parts stock or a new car. Use borken-in nozzles on a car with 1500 or more miles, if possible.

   B. After making a nozzle change, restart engine and check idle quality. If idle is still not acceptable, recheck glow plug resistance of each cylinder in firing order sequence. Record readings.

   C. Examine all glow plug resistance readings looking for differences of .3 ohms or more between cylinders.

   It will be necessary to raise or lower the reading on one or more of these cylinders as previously done.

   D. After making additional nozzle changes again check idle quality. Normally, after completing two series of resistance checks and nozzle changes, idle quality can be restored to an acceptable level.

13. An injection pump change may be necessary if the following occurs:

   A. If the problem cylinder moves from cylinder to cylinder as changes in nozzles are made.

   B. If cylinder ohm readings do not change when nozzles are changed.

   NOTE: It is important to always recheck the cylinders at the same RPM. Sometimes the cylinder readings do not indicate that an improvement has been made although the engine may in fact idle better.

(Courtesy of the Oldsmobile Div. of GMC)

water-in-fuel sending unit should also be removed from the fuel tank and cleaned. The fuel system must then be bled in order to start the engine.

The wiring circuit for the water in the fuel system does vary slightly between division vehicles of GMC. A typical system is shown in Fig. 33-7. In addition to water in the fuel, if for any reason the fuel tank is filled with gasoline, the tank should be drained and refilled with fresh diesel fuel, all lines blown clean, the filter replaced, and the system bled.

DIESEL FUEL HEATER

In order to reduce the possibility of the fuel filter plugging through wax crystal formation at low ambient temperatures, an in-line 12 volt electrical heater is used along with an engine coolant heater. When the ambient temperature drops to about 20°F the diesel fuel approaches what is known as the cloud point of the fuel. This is the temperature at which wax crystals start to separate out in the fuel due to the fact that the fuel has a paraffin wax base. The diesel fuel heater is a thermostatically controlled electrical resistance type heater which is designed to heat the fuel before it enters the fuel filter, and thereby prevent these wax crystals from settling out, which would subsequently plug the filter and prevent fuel flow.

When the ignition key is turned to the run position, battery voltage is applied to the heater which consists of a spiral strip wound around the fuel inlet pipe.

To control when the fuel heater is used, a bi-metallic thermal switch sensitive to ambient and fuel temperature closes the electrical circuit only when the fuel temperature drops to 20°F and opens it when the temperature reaches 50°F. Within the fuel tank filter sock, there is a bypass valve to allow fuel flow to the heater when wax crystals gather on the fuel tank filter. This wax will usually fall away after the pump has stopped.

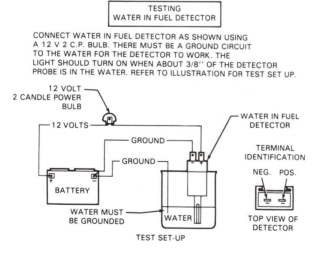

Fig. 33-6. Testing water in fuel detector assembly. (Courtesy of Cadillac Motor Car Div. of GMC)

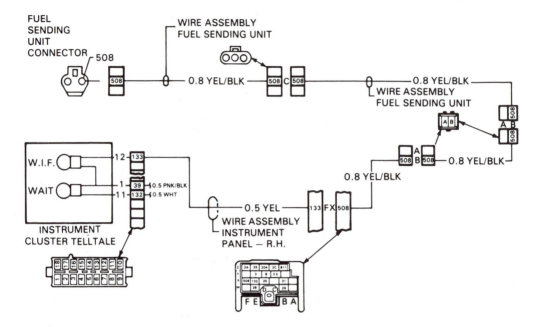

Fig. 33-7. Typical wiring circuit for water in fuel system. (Courtesy of Cadillac Motor Car Div. of GMC)

DIESEL FUEL IN-LINE HEATER

A recent introduction to heavy-duty Class 8 trucks, is the hotline fuel heater which eliminates cloud point or wax crystal formation in the fuel line that would normally restrict fuel flow at low temperatures and prevent engine operation.

This fuel-line heater is shown in Fig. 33-8 and can be specified as optional equipment on all new Peterbilt trucks, or installed on any Class 6, 7, or 8 diesel-powered vehicle.

The hotline heater is made from a specially formulated polymer that allows the heater to self-regulate its heat output. In other words, the heat increases as the temperature drops, and the heat drops as the fuel temperature increases.

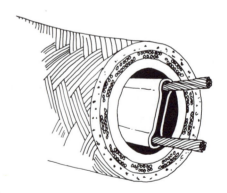

Fig. 33-8. Peterbilt Hotline fuel heater. (Courtesy of Peterbilt, Div. of PACCAR)

The heating element is activated by a thermostatic control to keep fuel in the line between the tank and primary filter above a pre-set minimum temperature. The unit is a 12 volt d.c. device.

REVIEW QUESTIONS

Q1. How does the basic starting system on the 350 diesel engine differ from that used on the gasoline 350?

Q2. Can all glow plugs be interchanged between all model year Oldsmobile 350 cu. in. diesel engines? Why or why not?

Q3. How are the glow plugs inserted into the engine?

Q4. How can you identify the former and current glow plugs?

Q5. What establishes the preglow time period of the actual glow plugs?

Q6. Do the glow plugs operate continuously?

Q7. What condition will occur should the ignition switch be left on in the run position?

Q8. When would a glow plug resistance check be taken?

Q9. When testing a glow plug for heating effectiveness, how long should battery current be applied to it?

ANSWERS

A1. The diesel starting system employs two 12-volt batteries plus a heavier duty starting motor, as well as glow plugs to aid starting.

A2. No! Earlier engines used a 12-volt glow plug system, while the current engines employ a 6-volt glow plug which is supplied with 12 volts to reduce glow plug preheat time.

A3. They are screwed into the cylinder head just above the injectors.

A4. They can be identified by the size of the bayonet connection on the top of the glow plug as shown in Fig. 33-3.

A5. The preglow time period is controlled by a controller located in the water passage at the front of the intake manifold to control glow plug current.

A6. No. The glow plugs are cycled on/off by a relay which is usually mounted on the fender panel and connected to the electronic control module.

A7. If the ignition switch is left in the run position, without starting the engine, the glow plugs will continue to pulse on/off until the batteries are run down.

A8. A glow plug resistance check can be taken when a rough idle condition exists, and after other idle roughness checks and adjustments have been made.

A9. Maximum time allowed is 30 seconds otherwise element damage can occur.

Chapter
34

Electrical Troubleshooting

The vehicle electrical and electronic system often scare people off because they are not familiar enough with the fundamentals of electricity. Many people have at one time or another received a minor shock from either an ignition circuit, or may even have connected a battery with the polarity reversed, especially when jump-starting another vehicle. The resultant shock or electrical system damage tends to create a hesitant approach. Others may not have had this type of experience, but because electricity cannot normally be seen, trained personnel who are excellent mechanics or technicians in other areas of the trade, shy away from this unseen system.

Although the electrical system is often compared to a basic water flow system, this analogy is not adequate for the current electronic componentry now in extensive use on both cars and trucks. In order to gain confidence and become an effective troubleshooter, the mechanic/technician must systematically establish an analytical approach to any problems encountered. Don't short out wires, disconnect wires, install jumper wires, or follow hapazard routines when unsure of the problem, because expensive and time consuming damage will invariably be the result.

Although the introduction of solid state electronic components may appear to have made the mechanic/technician's job harder; the availability of special tools and test equipment has removed a tremendous amount of trial and error in troubleshooting techniques. Pinpoint accuracy is now possible with these test machines. However, the test machines and special tools are only effective if you closely follow their directions for operation. You must also follow to the letter the vehicle manufacturer's test sequence; otherwise, you may be misled as to where the problem actually is.

In addition, many vehicles today are equipped with onboard diagnostic computers that facilitate the mechanic/technician's approach and effectively pinpoint problems in the electrical or electronic systems.

Within this book reference is often made to the use of these special test tools and equipment, therefore use these to advantage when required. Don't hope that you might be lucky enough to stumble upon the problem by a trial and error method of component parts replacement. This is not only expensive, but time-consuming; and, with today's rate for labor charges continually going up, the end result can be totally unacceptable.

The degree of experience of the individual obviously will determine to what degree of involvement he can tackle any given problem area. However, with diligence and patience, a study of this book coupled with hands-on shop exposure under the supervision of either a mechanic/technician, or vocational, trade school or college program instructor will bring success in understanding and effectively troubleshooting any part of the vehicle electrical/electronic system.

HOW TO FIND THE ELECTRICAL PROBLEM

When an electrical problem occurs, generally there is some sort of telltale warning prior to a failure that can indicate the problem area. If, however, no tell-tale sign is evident, then you should systematically approach the problem from the simplest possible cause before condemning or replacing a major component.

In many instances, problems can be caused by such simple items as a poor ground connection, or:

1. Loose connections or wire fittings

2. Corroded plug-in wire harnesses or snap-in connectors

3. High circuit resistance caused by corrosion, or a wire with too small a gauge size inserted or spliced into an existing circuit.

4. Circuit overload, too many accessories tied into the same circuit breaker or fuse. This is especially true of after-market add-on accessories.

5. A loose drive belt on an alternator or air conditioning system which causes slippage and low power output.

6. Light bulb burned out.

7. A faulty switch mechanism

8. Shorted wire (bared) caused by contact with hot engine parts

9. Fusible link melted

10. Corroded battery terminals

11. Low state of battery charge

In addition to the problem list given, use a voltmeter to systematically find out where the circuit is live and where it is not. In this way, you can establish specifically where the problem originates and progress from there.

In some particularly tricky situations, it is often necessary to simply substitute a suspected faulty component with another one known to be good to confirm your suspicions. Care should be exercised here, however, to ensure that you are not simply correcting a problem that will recur shortly. Often the replacement of a component will appear to have corrected the problem initially, but within a short time, the problem reappears.

These are just some of the more common areas that can create problems in the electrical system, although there can certainly be others. The key is to analyze the problem from a simple possible cause, and then to move towards the more difficult causes. Degree of experience will obviously prepare you to effectively troubleshoot any electrical system problem; however, even the experienced automotive electrician occasionally requires a reference to pinpoint a problem. Therefore, do not hesitate to refer to the vehicle manufacturer's system wiring diagrams found in the appropriate service manual, because with improvements and product change, a system that you were once familiar with may have been redesigned.

When an unusual problem exists, it is wise to spend a little time in tracing the print of the wiring circuit to be sure that you are on the right track. When a complaint is received, gather as much information as you can, then check and operate the suspected faulty circuit or component yourself to find out exactly what is not working, and if any other symptoms are apparent. Think through the wiring or controls that serve the circuit in question before attempting to repair the problem. Understand the complete problem, then proceed to systematically check it out, and once you have confirmed your suspicions, make the necessary repairs.

All vehicle service manuals list a number of possible complaint areas that should be checked and omitted one by one. In addition, with the great number of electronic items now used on vehicles, ensure that you are familiar with the location of each component.

When you feel that you have located the specific problem area and the repair has been made, always double check the repaired circuit and any other circuit that may be tied into this one to confirm that you have in fact corrected each and every problem that existed, and that you don't now have another problem that didn't exist before.

BASIC TROUBLESHOOTING TOOLS

Although many special tools and equipment are described in this book, the following general service tools are widely used by automotive electricians to effectively trace down faults.

Test Light

A test light can be purchased from any tool supplier. One end has a sharp probe, while the other end is connected to a wire lead with an alligator clip attached to it. Many people prefer to make up their own test light which can be done with a simple lamp socket and bulb, with two leads extending from the bulb holder in order to bridge a circuit, one to the live side and the other to a good ground. Figure 34-1 shows typical test light arrangements, with a 6, 12, 24, or 48 volt bulb. This method is commonly used to test for voltage or a short in a circuit.

Self-Powered Test Light

This test light differs from the one discussed earlier, in that it contains a light bulb, battery, and set of test leads which are wired in series. Therefore, when the test leads are connected to two points of any continuous circuit, the light bulb will glow.

Caution: To prevent damage to the circuit, no power should be flowing in the circuit when using the self-powered test light.

The self-powered test light is used to establish continuity in a circuit and also for a ground check. Figure 34-2 illustrates a typical arrangement for a self-powered test-light.

Jumper Wire

This is simply a length of wire that can be used to jump or connect across two points of a circuit. Although it can be used with bare ends, this can lead to arcing

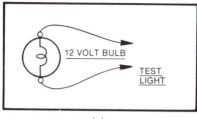

(a)

K-D 2646   NEW
Circuit Tester
6 & 12 Volt

Blister Packed

Tests for shorts or open circuits in 6 and 12 volt electrical systems. For car, home, boat, trailer, and aircraft. Quickly locates headlight, taillight, and turn signal circuits, faulty sockets, connections, fuses, and broken wires. Shock resistant with tough, durable plastic body. Use either end. Switch probe if bulb burns out. Cable approx. 36″.

(b)

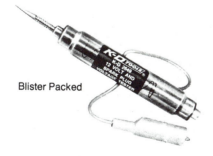

Blister Packed

K-D 2648   NEW
Circuit Tester
24 & 48 Volt

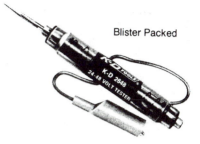

Blister Packed

Tests for shorts or open circuits in 24 and 48 volt electrical systems with power on. For car, home, boat, trailer, and aircraft. Quickly locates headlight, tail-light, and turn signal circuits, faulty sockets, connections, fuses, and broken wires. Shock resistant with tough, durable plastic body. Use either end. Switch probe if bulb burns out. Cable approx. 36″.

(c)

K-D 2649   NEW
Combination Circuit
(6 & 12 Volt) and
Spark Plug Tester

A shock proof combination electrical trouble-shooter and spark plug tester. Actually two testers in one. To change from spark plug voltage to low voltage test function, simply use opposite end of tester. Low voltage tester locates headlight, taillight and turn signals, circuits, faulty sockets, connections, fuses, and broken wires.

Checks 6 & 12 volt circuits with low voltage bulb. Check spark plug voltage with neon bulb. Cable approx. 36″.

(d)

Fig. 34-1. Typical 12-volt test light (courtesy of Chevrolet Motor Div. of GMC)

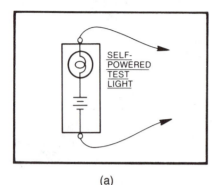

(a)

K-D 2647 NEW
Continuity Tester

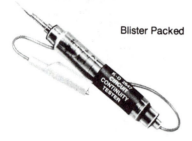

Blister Packed

Battery powered continuity tester. Safely tests circuits with power off. Ideal for testing fuses, grounds, shorts, contacts, checking diodes and open circuits, etc. Designed for heavy duty use by mechanics, electricians, and service repairmen. Cable approx. 36''.

(b)

Fig. 34-2. (a) Self-powered test light (courtesy of Chevrolet Motor Div. of GMC); (b) commercially available self-powered continuity tester (courtesy of KD Manufactruing Co., Lancaster, PA).

when one end is touched loosely to any live point; therefore, a proper jumper wire should be put together with an alligator

clip attached to each end. The main function of the jumper wire is to allow you to by-pass a suspected short area in a circuit or an open circuit, that may be open either because of a faulty circuit breaker or switch assembly.

Caution: Take care when using any jumper wire arrangement that the wire is not inserted into a load circuit such as a motor, or is connected between a hot portion of the circuit and ground; otherwise severe overheating, possible fire, and serious damage could result.

Figure 34-3 shows an example of where a jumper wire could be used. Also reference is made throughout this book to the insertion of a jumper wire for test purposes, such as in the alternator chapter.

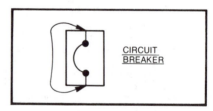

Fig. 34-3. Use of a jumper wire. (Courtesy of Chevrolet Motor Div.)

Multimeter or AVR

This multimeter or AVR (amps, volts, resistance) meter consists of a variety of switch knobs to allow it to be readily converted over for use in monitoring either the circuit amperage, voltage, or resistance. Many types of multimeters are readily available from the conventional expanded scale type shown in Fig. 34-4(a), to the microprocessor-digital type shown in (b).

Many multimeters, however, are limited to a fairly small current measurement. The

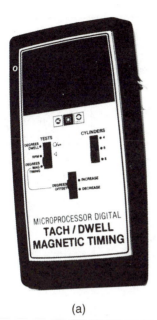

(a)

(b)

Fig. 34-4. (a) Expanded scale multimeter. (b) Microprocessor digital multimeter with dwell and RPM scales included (courtesy of AC Delco).

maximum allowable is stamped on the unit, or is limited by the reading on the scale of the face plate. Some of the newer type of microprocessor-digital units, however, are capable of measuring up to 300 amperes, such as the unit shown in Fig. 34-4(b).

Voltmeter

The voltmeter measures the circuit volt-age when the black lead is connected to either a negative (−) battery terminal or a ground point, and the red voltmeter lead is connected to the hot side or positive (+) battery terminal, or live wire of the circuit.

Ohmmeter

The ohmmeter scale is selected when you want to measure the resistance to flow in a wire, a circuit, or any switch or accessory item, when connected between two points. All ohmmeters have a choice of scale on the function switch that allows either 1, 10, 100, 1000, 10,000 or even 100,000 ohms to be measured.

The ohmmeter can also be used at any time to check continuity in a circuit (no breaks).

Some multimeters are known as a VOM or volt-ohm milliammeter which can be used to measure five things: D.C. volts, ohms, A.C. volts, D.C. current, and output which is basically an A.C. voltage-measuring function in which the instrument circuit passes alternating current and blocks direct current. This feature is used in certain checks, for example, on electronic ignition systems.

Ammeter

The ammeter is used to measure the current flowing in a circuit. Care must be exercised when this range is selected to ensure that the instrument is capable of handling the current flowing; otherwise, serious damage can occur to the test instrument. In addition, the ammeter should be connected into a circuit in series hookup.

VOLTMETER OR TEST LIGHT CONNECTIONS

Examples of where the voltmeter or test light leads would be connected into a circuit to establish if power is apparent in the circuit can be seen in Fig. 34-5 which is representative of typical areas where these test instruments could be employed.

In Fig. 34-5, if power is flowing, either the test light will illuminate or the voltmeter will register a voltage flow. Should you desire to check out a circuit for a short circuit condition, then the test light could

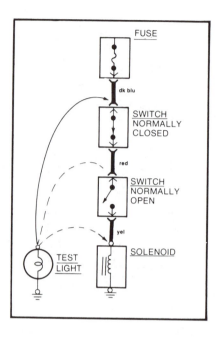

Fig. 34-5. Voltmeter or test light check points. (Courtesy of Chevrolet Motor Div. of GMC)

be used as shown in Fig. 34-6, whereby all power has been turned off to any accessories in the circuit that are receiving power through the fuse. The test light leads are then bridged across the fuse panel to establish if power is being fed to one side of the fuse holder. It may be necessary to turn the ignition switch to the run position to supply power to the particular fuse being tested. Some fuses are hot at all times without the ignition switch being on.

In Fig. 34-6, if you now disconnect the ground lead and connect it to the load side of the fuse, two things may happen; first, if the test light is not on, then the short exists in the disconnected equipment; or, if the test light illuminates, then the short is most likely in the wiring, and can be found by a process of elimination by working through the individual items in the circuit.

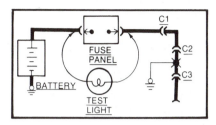

Fig. 34-6. Short circuit check. (Courtesy of Chevrolet Motor Div. of GMC)

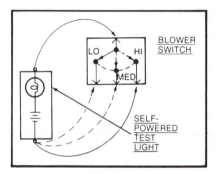

Fig. 34-7. Circuit continuity check. (Courtesy of Chevrolet Motor Div. of GMC)

When a lack of continuity is suspected in a circuit, connect a self-powered test light such as that shown in Fig. 34-2(b) or, if this is not available, select the ohmmeter scale on a multimeter and connect the test leads into the circuit or suspected faulty item as shown in Fig. 34-7, ONLY after turning off the power supply to the circuit. Any deflection of the ohmmeter needle on the multimeter scale or illumination of the test light is an indication that the circuit is closed; in other words, continuity exists between the two test points.

SUSPECTED POOR GROUND CHECK

A poor ground is one of the major reasons for many electrical system malfunctions. Although a wire connection may appear to be solid, it may in fact be poorly grounded. With a poor ground, the circuit is not connected with its source of supply, namely the battery, and no response will be apparent. A quick check for a poor ground can be made either by the use of an ohmmeter or a voltmeter, preferably by turning the power supply on to the circuit and connecting one test lead to the vehicle frame (clean surface) while the other lead is firmly held to the suspected bad ground area or wire connection. Since both are in effect battery negative or battery positive return (depending on type of grounded circuit), a good ground at the suspected connection would signify a no voltage condition. Should a voltage condition exist, then obviously the ground is bad (insulated from the frame).

A self-powered test light can be used, or an ohmmeter by first of all turning off the power to the suspected circuit, then connecting one test lead to the area in question and the other to a good ground. Illumination of the test light, or an ohmmeter reading, indicates that a good ground does exist.

SWITCH CIRCUIT CHECK

When a switch is used in a circuit in series with the load, connections as shown in Fig. 34-8 can be used to determine if a fault exists in what may be considered a faulty switch. With the jumper wire placed across the switch terminals as shown, the switch has no bearing on the current flow in the circuit. Therefore, if the illustration as shown resulted in the motor operating with the jumper wire in place, then the switch can be considered faulty.

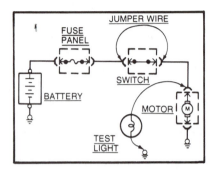

Fig. 34-8. Using a jumper wire to determine if a switch is faulty. (Courtesy of Chevrolet Motor Div. of GMC)

SPECIAL TOOLS FOR THE ELECTRICAL SYSTEM

With the use of solid state circuitry and the conventional wiring systems now employed on cars and trucks, it has become necessary to develop test instruments and tools that can be quickly adapted to the electrical system in order that the mechanic or technician can pinpoint the reason for a particular malfunction as quickly and accurately as possible. Each individual vehicle manufacturer offers through their distributor/dealer network, the necessary tools and special test equipment required for effective troubleshooting of these systems.

General Motors vehicles use either Delco or Kent-Moore special tools, while Ford vehicles specify their own, or Rotunda; Chrysler offers their own tools, and Volkswagen, Audi, Porsche, BMW and Mercedes-Benz usually recommend Robert Bosch test equipment; Datsun, Toyota, Mazda, Subaru, etc. generally recommend a variety of tools available through either their dealer network, or obtainable locally.

Many pages would be required to illustrate all of these special tools and test kits, since each company prints a tool catalogue illustrating all of these test items. However, within this book, you will notice that reference is drawn to the use of these special tools and equipment which should be used when and wherever possible to assist you in quickly and effectively troubleshooting the system. These tools remove the guesswork and will make you a much more productive and efficient technician.

General Motors Vehicles

Throughout this book several special test tools for use with the electrical system are shown. In addition to these units, Fig. 34-9 shows a Kent-Moore J-26426-01 Electest unit that is recommended for those vehicles equipped with the GM Diagnostic Plug-in receptacle.

Kent-Moore Steering Column Electrical Analyzer

Most vehicles today generally employ a variety of controls (electrical) mounted on the vehicle steering column. An example of a test instrument is shown in Fig. 34-10. This one is recommended for use with General Motors vehicles.

The J-23980-B analyzer can be used to check such items as the turn signal lights, horn, key buzzer, hazard warning system, and cornering lights. Use of the tester prevents premature disassembly of the steering column in order to pinpoint a problem area. The use of the tester allows the steering column switching mechanisms to be separated from the chassis wiring harness to effectively assist the technician in isolating the problem area.

Fig. 34-9. Kent-Moore J-26426-01 Electest set. (Courtesy of Kent-Moore Tool Div.)

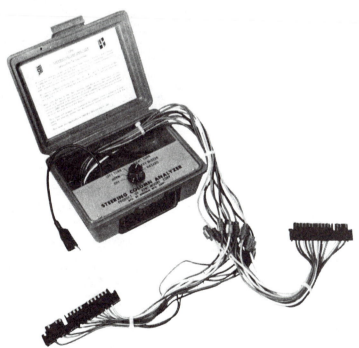

Fig. 34-10. Kent-Moore J-23980-B steering column electrical analyzer. (Courtesy of Kent-Moore Tool Div.)

Glossary of Automotive Electronic Terms

Active Element—A component capable of producing power gain such as a transistor, tunnel diode, thyristor, etc. Also active device, active component.

Active Filter—A device employing passive network elements and amplifiers used for transmitting or rejecting signals in certain frequency ranges or for controlling the relative output of signals as a function of frequency. (GRAF)

Ambient Conditions—The conditions (pressure, temperature, etc.) of the surrounding medium.

American Wire Gauge—Abbreviated AWG. System of numerical designations for wire size, based on specified ranges of circular mil area. American Wire Gauge starts with 4/0 (0000) at the largest size going to 3/0 (000), 2/0 (00), 1/0 (0), 1, 2, and up to 40 and beyond for the smallest sizes.

Ampere (A)—The standard unit for measuring the strength of an electric current. The rate of flow of a charge in a conductor or conducting medium of one coulomb per second.

Amplifier—A device, circuit, or component which produces as an output an enlarged reproduction of the essential features of its input.

Amplitude Modulation (AM)—Modulation in which the amplitude of a wave is the characteristic subject to variation. (GRAF)

Anode—The positive pole (+) in batteries, galvanic cells, or plating apparatus. In diodes, the positive lead.

Analog—Of or pertaining to the general class of devices or circuits in which the output varies as a continuous function of the input.

Analog Computer—A computer which represents numerical quantities as electrical and physical variables and manipulates these variables in accomplishing solutions to mathematical problems.

And Gate—A combinational logic element such that the output channel is in its one state, if and only if each input channel is in its *one* state.

Avalanche Breakdown—In a semiconductor diode, a nondestructive breakdown caused by the cumulative multiplication of carriers through field-induced impact ionization. (GRAF)

Avalanche Diode—Also called breakdown diode. A silicon diode that has a high ratio of reverse-to-forward resistance until avalanche breakdown occurs. After breakdown the voltage drop across the diode is essentially constant and is independent of the current. Used for voltage regulating and voltage limiting. Originally called zener diode before it was found that the Zener effect had no significant role in the operation of diodes of this type.

Bandwidth—The range within the limits of a band. The least frequency interval of a wave form. The range of frequencies of a device, within which its performance, with respect to some characteristic, conforms to a specified standard.

Bit—The smallest element of information in binary language. A contraction of BInary digiT. These characters in system (computer) language signify "on" and "off" (1 and 0). Word length, memory capacity, etc. can be expressed in number of "bits".

B-Multiplier—See Darlington Amplifier.

Barrier Layer—See Depletion Layer.

Base—(transistor) A region that lies between an emitter and a collector of a transistor and into which minority carriers are injected. (IEEE)

Base Resistance—Resistance in series with the base lead in the common T equivalent circuit of a transistor. (GRAF)

Battery—A DC voltage source which converts chemical, nuclear, thermal or solar energy into electrical energy. (GRAF)

Bidirectional Diode-Thyristor—A two-terminal thyristor having substantially the same switching behavior in the first and third quadrants of the principal voltage-current characteristic. (IEEE)

Bias—To influence or dispose to one direction, as, for example, with a direct voltage or with a spring. (IEEE)

Binary—A characteristic or property involving a selection, choice, or condition, in which there are but two possible alternatives.

Bipolar—Having to do with a device in which both majority and minority carriers are present. In connection with ICs, the term describes a specific type of construction; bipolar and MOS are the two most common types of IC construction. (GRAF)

Bleeder Resistor—A resistor used to draw a fixed current. Also used to discharge a filter capacitor after the circuit is de-energized. (GRAF)

Boolean Algebra—The Algebra of Logic named for mathematician George Boole using alphabetic symbols to stand for logical variables and "zero" and "one" to represent states. AND, OR, NOT, are the three basic logic operations in this algebra. NAND and NOR are combinations of the three basic operations.

Breakdown Voltage—See dielectric strength.

Capacitance (C)—In a system of conductors and dielectrics, that property which permits the storage of electrically separated charges when potential differences exist between the conductors. Its value is expressed as the ratio of a quantity of electricity to a potential difference (Q/V). (IEEE)

Capacitor—(condenser) A device consisting of two electrodes separated by a dielectric, which may be air, for introducing capacitance into an electric circuit. (IEEE)

Carrier—An AC voltage having a frequency suitably high to be modulated by electrical signals.

Cascade—An arrangement of two or more similar circuits or amplifying stages in which the output of one provides the input of the next. (GRAF)

Cathode—A general name for any negative electrode. (GRAF)

Cathode-Ray Tube—An electron-beam tube in which the beam can be focused to a small cross section on a luminescent screen and varied in position and intensity to produce a visible pattern. (IEEE)

Chip—A single substrate on which all the active and passive elements of an electronic circuit have been fabricated. A chip is not ready for use until it is packaged and provided with terminals for connection to the outside world. Also called a die. (GRAF)

Chip Sets—A term describing the microprocessor chip in addition to RAMs, ROMs, and interface I/O devices. Chip sets, mounted on a board, are also referred to as the CPU portion of the microcomputer.

Clock—A device that generates periodic signals used for synchronization. (IEEE)

Coil—See Inductor.

Collector—(transistor) A region through which primary flow of charge carriers leaves the base. (IEEE)

Common Collector Amplifier—A transistor amplifier in which the collector element is common to both the input and output circuit. Also known as an emitter-follower and a grounded-collector amplifier. (GRAF)

Common Mode Rejection—A measure of how well a differential amplifier ignores a signal which appears simultaneously and is in phase at both input terminals. Also, called in-phase rejection. (GRAF)

Complementary MOS—Pertaining to n- and p-channel enhancement-mode devices fabricated compatibly on a silicon chip and connected into push-pull complementary digital circuits. These circuits offer low quiescent power dissipation and potentially high speeds, but they are more complex than circuits in which only one channel type is used. Abbreviated CMOS. (GRAF)

Computer—Any device capable of accepting information, applying prescribed processes to the information, and supplying the results of the process.

Conductivity—The ability to transmit heat or electricity. Electrical conductivity is expressed in terms of the current per unit of applied voltage. The reciprocal of resistivity.

Constant Current Source—A regulated source which acts to keep its output current constant in spite of changes in load, line, or temperature while the output voltage changes by whatever amount is necessary to maintain the constant output current. (GRAF)

Continuous Rating—The rating applicable to specified operation for a specific uninterrupted length of time.

Central Processing Unit (CPU)—The section of a computer that contains the arithmetic, logic, and control circuits. In some systems it may also include the memory unit and the operator's console. Also called main frame.

Creep—A change in output occurring over a specific time period while the input and all environmental conditions are held constant.

Critical Damping—The value of damping which provides the most rapid transient response without overshoot. Operation between underdamping and overdamping. (GRAF)

Current Density—The amount of electric current passing through a given cross-sectional area of a conductor. (GRAF)

Damping—The transitory decay of the amplitude of a free oscillation of a system, associated with energy loss from the system. (IEEE)

Damping Ratio—The ratio of the degree of actual damping to the degree of damping required for critical damping. (GRAF)

Darlington Amplifier—A transistor circuit which, in its original form, consists of two transistors in which the collectors are tied together and the emitter of the first transistor is directly coupled to the base of the second transistor. Therefore, the emitter current of the first transistor equals the base current of the second transistor. This connection of two transistors can be regarded as a compound transistor with three terminals. (GRAF)

Darlington Pair—See Darlington Amplifier.

D'Arsonval Current—A high-frequency, low voltage current of comparatively high amperage. (GRAF)

Decibel—One-tenth of a bel, the number of decibels denoting the ratio of the two amounts of power being ten times the logarithm to the base 10 of this ratio. NOTE: The abbreviation dB is commonly used for the term decibel. With P_1 and P_2 designating two amounts of power and n the number of decibels denoting their ratio.

$$n = 10 \log_{10} [P_1/P_2] \text{ decibel}$$

When the conditions are such that ratios of currents or ratios of voltages (or analogous quantities in other field) are the square roots of the corresponding powers ratios, the number of decibels by which the corresponding powers differ is expressed by the following equations:

$$n = 20 \log_{10} [I_1/I_2] \text{ decibel}$$

$$n = 20 \log_{10} [V_1/V_2] \text{ decibel}$$

where I_1/I_2 and V_1/V_2 are the given current and voltage ratios, respectively. By extension, these relations between numbers of decibels and ratios of currents or voltages are sometimes applied where these ratios are not the square roots of the corresponding power ratios; to avoid confusion, such usage should be accompanied by a specific statement of this application. Such extensions of the term described should preferably be avoided. (IEEE)

Delay—(1) The amount of time by which an event is retarded. (2) The amount of time by which a signal is delayed. NOTE: It may be expressed in time (milliseconds, microseconds, etc.) or in number of characters (pulse times, word times, major cycles, minor cycles, etc.). (IEEE)

Delay Line—(electronic computers) (1) Originally, a device utilizing wave propagation for producing a time delay of a signal. (2) Commonly, any real or artificial transmission line or equivalent device designed to introduce delay. (IEEE)

Depletion Layer—In a semi-conductor, the region in which the mobile-carrier charge density is insufficient to neutralize the net fixed charge density of donors and acceptors. (GRAF)

Dielectric Constant—The property that determines the electrostatic energy stored per unit volume for unit potential gradient. NOTE: This numerical value usually is given relative to a vacuum. (IEEE)

Dielectric Strength—(material) (electric strength) (breakdown strength) The potential gradient at which electric failure or breakdown occurs. To obtain the true dielectric strength the actual maximum gradient must be considered, or the test piece and electrodes must be designed so that uniform gradient is obtained. The value obtained for the dielectric strength in practical tests will usually depend on the thickness of the material and on the method and conditions of test. (IEEE)

Digital Computer—A computer that processes information in numerical form. Electronic digital computers generally use binary or decimal notation and process information by repeated high speed use of the fundamental arithmetic processes of addition, subtraction, multiplication, and division.

Digital-to-Analog (D/A) Converter—A device which transforms digital data into analog data by translating digital magnitude to equivalent voltage level.

Diode—(electronic tube) A two electrode electron tube containing an anode and a cathode. (semi-conductor) A semi-conductor device having two terminals and exhibiting a non-linear voltage-current characteristic; in more restricted usage; a semi-conductor device that has the asymmetrical voltage-current characteristic exemplified by a single p-n junction. (IEEE)

Diode Transistor Logic—Abbreviated DTL. A logic circuit that uses diodes at the input to perform the electronic logic function that activates the circuit transistor output. In monolithic circuits, the DTL diodes are a positive level logic and function or a negative level or function. The output transistor acts as an inverter to result in the circuit becoming a positive NAND or a negative NOR function. (GRAF)

DIP—Abbreviation for dual in-line package. (GRAF)

Dipole Antenna—Any one of a class of antennas producing the radiation pattern approximating that of an elementary electronic dipole. NOTE: Common usage considers a dipole to be a metal radiating structure that supports a line current distribution similar to that of a thin straight wire, a half wavelength long, so energized that the current has two nodes, one at each of the far ends. (IEEE)

Drain (D)—In a field effect transistor, the element that corresponds to the collector of a transistor. (GRAF)

Drift—An undesired change in output over a period of time, which change is not a function of the input.

Duty Cycle—The ratio of the time "On" of a device or system divided by the total cycle time (i.e., "On" plus time "Off"). For a device that normally runs intermittently rather than continuously: the amount of time a device operates as opposed to its idle time.

Electromagnetic Compatability (EMC)—The ability of electronic communications equipment, sub-systems, and systems to operate in their intended environments without suffering or causing unacceptable degradation of performance as a result of unintentional electromagnetic radiation or response. (GRAF)

Electromagnetic Interference (EMI)—Electromagnetic phenomena which, either directly or indirectly, can contribute to the degradation in performance of an electronic receiver or system. (GRAF)

Electron—One of the natural elementary constituents of matter. It carries a negative electric charge of one electronic unit. (GRAF)

Electromotive Force (emf)—The force which may cause current to flow when there is a difference of potential between two points. (GRAF)

Electromagnetic Waves—The radiant energy produced by the oscillation of an electric charge. (GRAF)

Electroluminescence—Luminescence resulting from a high-frequency discharge through a gas or from application of an alternating current to a layer of phosphor. (GRAF)

Emitter—A region from which charge carriers that are minority carriers in the base are injected into the base. (IEEE)

Emitter-Coupled Logic—Abbreviated ECL. Nonsaturated bipolar logic in which the emitters of the input logic transistors are coupled to the emitter of a reference transistor. The basic gate circuit employs a long-tailed pair. Abbreviated ECL. (GRAF)

Exclusive OR—A logic operator having the property that if P is a statement and Q is a statement, then P exclusive ORQ is true if either but not both statements are true, false if both are true or both are false. (IEEE)

Feedback—The recycling of a portion of the output to the input of a system. Systems employing feedback are called closed-loop systems.

Feedback Amplifier—An amplifier that uses a passive network to return a portion of the output signal to modify the performance of the amplifier. (GRAF)

Ferrites—Chemical compounds of iron oxide and other metallic oxides combined with ceramic material. They have ferromagnetic properties but are poor conductors of electricity. Hence they are useful where ordinary ferromagnetic materials (which are good electrical conductors) would cause too great a loss of electrical energy. (GRAF)

Ferromagnetic Material—Material whose relative permeability is greater than unity and depends upon the magnetizing force. A ferromagnetic material usually has relatively high values of relative permeability and exhibits hysteresis. (IEEE)

FET—(field-effect transistor) A semi-conductor device in which the resistance between the source and drain terminals depends on a field produced by a voltage applied to the gate terminal. (GRAF)

Filter—A selective network of resistors, inductors, or capacitors which offers comparatively little opposition to certain frequencies or to direct current, while blocking or attenuating other frequencies. (GRAF)

Flat Pack—A flat, rectangular integrated circuit or hybrid-circuit package with coplanar leads. (GRAF)

Flux (Magnetic)—The sum of all the lines of force in a magnetic field crossing a unit area per unit time.

Flux Density—Flux per unit area perpendicular to the direction of the flux. (GRAF)

Forward Voltage—(V_F) The voltage across a semi-conductor diode associated with the flow of forward current. The p-region is at a positive potential with respect to the n-region.

Frequency Modulated Output—fm (frequency modulation) A scheme for modulating a carrier frequency in which the amplitude remains constant but the carrier frequency is displaced in frequency proportionally to the amplitude of the modulating signal. A frequency modulation broadcast system is practically immune to atmospheric and man-made interference.

Frequency Response—A measure of how the gain or loss of a circuit, device or system varies with the frequencies applied to it. Also, the portion of the frequency spectrum which can be sensed by a device within specified limits of error.

Gain—Any increase in power when a signal is transmitted from one point to another. Usually expressed in decibels. (GRAF)

GCS—Abbreviation for gate controlled switch. (GRAF)

Gate—(1) A device or element that, depending upon one or more specified inputs, has the ability to permit or inhibit the passage of a signal. (2) (electronic computers) (a) A device having one output channel and one or more input channels, such that the output channel state is completely determined by the contemporaneous input channel states, except during switching transients. (b) A combinational logic element having at least one input channel. (c) An AND gate. (d) An OR gate. (3) In a field effect transistor, the electrode that is analogous to the base of a transistor or the grid of a vacuum tube. (GRAF)

Hall Effect—The development of a transverse electric potential gradient in a current carrying conductor or semi-conductor upon the application of a magnetic field.

Hardware—(1) Mechanical, magnetic, electrical, or electronic devices; physical equipment (contrasted with software). (2) Particular circuits of functions built into a system. (IEEE)

Harmonic Distortion—The production of harmonic frequencies at the output by the nonlinearity of a system when a sinusoidal input is applied. (GRAF)

Heat Sink—A mounting base, usually metallic, that dissipates, carries away, or radiates into the surrounding atmosphere the heat generated within a semi-conductor device. (GRAF)

Hertz—The unit of frequency, one cycle per second. (IEEE)

High-Threshold Logic—Abbreviated HTL. Logic with a high noise margin, used primarily in industrial applications. It closely resembles DTL, except that in HTL a reverse-biased emitter junction is used as a threshold element operating as a zener diode. A typical noise margin is 6 volts with a 15-volt supply. (GRAF)

Hole—In the electronic valence structure of a semi-conductor, a mobile vacancy which acts like a positive electronic charge with a positive mass. (GRAF)

Hole Conduction—The apparent movement of a hole to the more negative terminal in a semi-conductor. Since the hole is positive, this movement is equivalent to a flow of positive charges in that direction.

Hybrid Circuit—A circuit which combines the thin-film and semi-conductor technologies. Generally, the passive components are made by thin-film techniques, and the active components by semi-conductor techniques. (GRAF)

Hysteresis—The difference between the response of a unit or system to an increasing and a decreasing signal. Hysteretical behavior is characterized by inability to *retrace* exactly on the reverse swing a particular locus of input/output conditions. (GRAF)

Impedance (Z)—The total opposition offered by a component or circuit to the flow of alternating or varying current. Impedance is expressed in ohms and is similar to the actual resistance in a direct current circuit. Impedance may be computed as $Z = E/I$, where E is the applied AC voltage and I is the resulting alternating current flow in the circuit.

Inductance—The property of an electric circuit by which a varying current in it produces a varying magnetic field that induces voltage in the same circuit or in a nearby circuit—measured in henrys.

Inductor—A device consisting of one or more associated windings, with or without a magnetic core, for introducing inductance into an electric circuit. (IEEE)

Integrated Circuit—A combination of interconnected circuit elements inseparably associated on or within a continuous substrate. NOTE: To further define the nature of an integrated circuit, additional modifiers may be prefixed. Examples are: (1) dielectric-isolated monolithic integrated circuit. (2) beam lead monolithic integrated circuit. (3) silicon-chip tantalum thin-film hybrid integrated circuit. (IEEE)

Input Impedance—The impedance a transducer presents to a source. The effective impedance *seen looking into* the input terminals of an amplifier; circuit details, signal level, and frequency must be specified. (GRAF)

Insulator—A high resistance device that supports or separates conductors to prevent a flow of current between them or to other objects. (GRAF)

Inverse Voltage—The effective voltage across a rectifier during the half-cycle when current does not flow. (GRAF)

Ion Implantation—A method of semi-conductor doping in which impurities that have been ionized and accelerated to a high velocity penetrate the semi-conductor surface and become deposited in the interior. (GRAF)

JFET—Abbreviation for Junction Field Effect Transistor.

Jump—(electronic computation) (1) To (conditionally or unconditionally) cause the next instruction to be obtained from a storage location specified by an address part of the current instruction when otherwise it would be specified by some convention. (2) An instruction that specifies a jump. (IEEE)

Latch—A feedback loop used in a symmetrical digital circuit (such as a flip-flop) to retain a state. (GRAF)

Large-Scale-Integration—Abbreviated LSI. (1) The simultaneous achievement of large area circuit chips and optimum density of component packaging for the express purpose of cost reduction by maximization of the number of system interconnections made at the chip level. (2) Monolithic digital ICs with a typical complexity of 100 or more gates or gate-equivalent circuits. The number of gates per chip used to define LSI depends on the manufacturer. The term sometimes describes hybrid ICs built with a number of MSI or LSI chips. (GRAF)

Lead Frame—A metal frame that holds the leads of a plastic encapsulated package (DIP) in place before encapsulation and is cut away after encapsulation. (GRAF)

Light-Emitting Diode—A pn junction that emits light when biased in the forward direction. (GRAF)

Linearity—The relationship between two quantities when a change in a second quantity is directly proportionate to a change in the first quantity. Also, deviation from a straight-line response to an input signal. (GRAF)

Logic—A mathematical approach to the solution of complex situations by the use of symbols to define basic concepts. In computers and information-processing networks, the systematic method that governs the operations performed on the information, usually with each step influencing the one that follows. (GRAF)

Magneto Resistive Effect—The change in the resistance of a conductor or semi-conductor due to the application of a magnetic field.

Memory—(electronic computation) See Storage.

Metalization—The deposition of a thin-film pattern of a conductive material onto a substrate to provide interconnection of electronic components or to provide conductive pads for interconnections. (GRAF)

Microcomputer—A complete system capable of performing minicomputer functions, through a much lower power range. It is a combination of the chip sets; inferface I/O along with the auxiliary circuits, power supply, and control console.

Micron—A unit of length equal to 10^{-6} metre.

Microprocessor—The digital processor on a chip which performs arithmetic logic and control logic. It is the basic building block of a microcomputer system.

Minority Carrier—The less predominate carrier in a semi-conductor. Electrons are the minority carriers in P-type semi-conductors since there are fewer electrons than holes. Holes are the minority carriers in N-types since they are outnumbered by electrons. (GRAF)

Monolithic—An integrated circuit which is built on a single slice of silicon substrate.

MOS—Abbreviation for Metal Oxide Semi-Conductor.

MNOS—Abbreviation for Metal-Nitride-Oxide Semi-Conductor. (GRAF)

Multiplexing—The process of combining several measurements for transmission over the same signal path. There are two widely used methods of multiplexing; time division, and frequency division. Time division utilizes the principle of time sharing among measurement channels. Frequency division utilizes the principle of frequency sharing among information channels where the data from each channel are used to modulate sinusoidal signals called subcarriers so that the resultant signal representing each channel contains only frequencies in a restricted narrow frequency range. Multiplex radio transmission, for instance, is the simultaneous transmission of two signals over a common carrier wave. (GRAF)

NAND Gate—A combination of a *not* function and an *and* function in a binary circuit that has two or more inputs and one output. (GRAF)

Negative Feedback—(degeneration) A process by which a part of the output signal of an amplifying circuit is fed back to the input. (GRAF)

NMOS (N-Type MOS)—MOS devices made on P-type silicon substrates where the active carriers are electrons flowing between N-type source and drain contacts.

Noise—Unwanted disturbances superposed on a useful signal that tend to obscure its information content.

Non-Volatile Memory—Electronic memory which is not lost during power off conditions.

NOR Gate—An *or* gate followed by an inverter to form a binary circuit in which the output is logic zero if any of the inputs is one, and vice versa. (GRAF)

NPN Transistor—A transistor with a P-type base and N-type collector and emitter. (GRAF)

Null—A condition (typically a condition of balance) which results in a minimum absolute value of output. Often specified as the calibration point when the least error can be tolerated by the associated control system.

N-Type Material—A crystal of pure semi-conductor material to which has been added an impurity so that electrons serve as the majority charge carriers. (GRAF)

Ohm—The unit of resistance. One ohm is the value of resistance through which a potential of one volt will maintain a current of one ampere. (GRAF)

Operational Amplifier—An amplifier that performs various mathematical operations. Also called OP-AMP. (GRAF)

OR Gate—A multiple-input gate circuit whose output is energized when any one or more of the inputs is in a prescribed state. Used in digital logic.

Oscillator—An electronic device which generates alternating current power at a frequency determined by the values of certain constants in its circuits. (GRAF)

Parallel Processing—Pertaining to the simultaneous execution of two or more sequences of instructions by a computer having multiple arithmetic or logic units. (IEEE)

Permeability—(μ) The measure of how much better a given material is than air as a path for magnetic lines or force. It is equal to the magnetic induction (B) in gausses, divided by the magnetizing force (H) in oersteds. (GRAF)

Phase Angle—(1) *general*. The measure of the progression of a periodic wave in time or space from a chosen instant or position. NOTES: (a) The phase angle of a field quantity, or of voltage or current, at a given instant of time at any given plane in a waveguide is [wt − Bz + θ], when the wave has a sinuosidal time variation. The term waveguide is used here in its most general sense and includes all transmission lines; for example, rectangular waveguide, coaxial line, strip line, etc. The symbol B is the imaginary part of the propagation constant for that waveguide, propagation is in the +z direction, and θ is the phase angle when z = t = 0. At a reference time t = 0 and at the plane z, the phase angle [− Bz + θ] will be represented by ϕ. (b) Phase angle is obtained by multiplying the phase by 360 degrees or by 2π radians. (2) *current transformer*. The angle between the current leaving the identified secondary terminal and the current entering the identified primary terminal. NOTE: This angle is conveniently designated by the Greek letter beta (β) and is considered positive when the secondary current leads the primary current. (3) *potential [voltage] transformer*. The angle between the secondary voltage from the identified to the unidentified terminal and the corresponding primary voltage. NOTE: This angle is conveniently designated by the Greek letter gamma (γ) and is considered positive when the secondary voltage leads the primary voltage. (4) (*instrument transformer*) Phase displacement, in minutes, between the primary and secondary values. (IEEE)

Photocell—*photoelectric cell* (1) A solid-state photosensitive electron device in which use is made of the variation of the current-voltage characteristic as a function of incident radiation. (2) A device exhibiting photovolatic or photoconductive effects. (IEEE)

Piezoelectric—The property of certain crystals, which: (1) produce a voltage when subjected to a mechanical stress, (2) undergo mechanical stress when subject to a voltage. (GRAF)

Plasma—A gas made up of charged particles. NOTE: Usually plasmas are neutral, but not necessarily so, as, for example, the space charge in an electron tube. (IEEE)

PMOS (P-Type MOS)—MOS devices made on an N-type silicon substrate where the active carriers are holes flowing between P-type source and drain controls.

PNP Transistor—A transistor consisting of two P-type regions separated by an N-type region. (GRAF)

PNPN Diode—A semi-conductor device which may be regarded as a two transistor structure with two separate emitters feeding a common collector. (GRAF)

Potential—The difference in voltage between two points of a circuit. Frequently one point is assumed to be ground which has zero potential. (GRAF)

Positive Feedback—*regeneration* The process by which the amplification is increased by having part of the power in the output returned to the input in order to reinforce the input power. (GRAF)

Potting—An embedding process for parts that are assembled in a container or can into which the insulating material is poured, with the container remaining an integral part as the outer surface of the finished unit. (GRAF)

P-Type Material—A semi-conductor material which has been doped with an excess of acceptor impurity atoms, so that free holes are produced in the material. (GRAF)

PROM—An acronym for Programmable Read Only Memory. An electronic memory which may be permanent (non-volatile) or semi-permanent (erasable electronically or with ultra-violet light) and therefore able to be reprogrammed one or more times.

RAM—An acronym for Random Access Memory. A memory that has stored information immediately available when addressed regardless of the previous memory address location. As the memory words can be selected in any order, there is equal access time to all.

rfi—*radio-frequency interference* Radio frequency energy of sufficient magnitude to have an influence on the operation of other electronic equipment. (GRAF)

Rectifier—A device which, by virtue of its asymmetrical conduction characteristic, converts an alternating current into a unidirectional current. (GRAF)

Regulated Power Supply—A unit which maintains a constant output voltage or current for changes in line voltage, output load, ambient temperature or time. (GRAF)

Regulation—*overall, power supplies* The maximum amount that the output will change as a result of the specified change in line voltage, output load, temperature, or time. NOTE: Line regulation, load regulation, stability, and temperature coefficient are defined and usually specified separately. (IEEE)

Relay—An electric device that is designed to interpret input conditions in a prescribed manner and after specified conditions are met to respond to cause contact operation or similar abrupt change in associated electric control circuits. NOTES: (1) inputs are usually electric, but may be mechanical, thermal, or other quantities. Limit switches and similar simple devices are not relays. (2) a relay may consist of several units, each responsive to specified inputs, the combination providing the desired performance characteristic. (IEEE)

Resistivity—The measure of the resistance of a material to electric current either through its volume or on a surface. (GRAF)

Resistor—A device the primary purpose of which is to introduce resistance into an electric circuit. NOTE: Resistor as used in electric circuits for purposes of operation, protection, or control, commonly consists of an aggregation of units. Resistors as commonly supplied consist of wire, metal ribbon, cast metal, or carbon compounds supported by or imbedded in an insulation medium. The insulating medium may enclose and support the resistance material as in the case of the porcelain-tube type, or the insulation may be provided only at the points of support as in the case of heavy-duty ribbon or cast iron grids mounted in metal frames. (IEEE)

Resistor-Capacitor-Transistor Logic—Abbreviated RCTL. A logic circuit design that employs a resistor and a speedup capacitor in parallel for each input of the gate. A transistor's base is connected to one end of the RC network. A positive voltage on the RC input will energize the transistor and turn it on, so that the output voltage is nearly zero volts. This circuit is a positive NOR or negative NAND when NPN transistors are used in the circuit. (GRAF)

Resistor-Transistor Logic—Abbreviated RTL. A form of logic that has a resistor as the input component that is coupled to the base of an NPN transistor. As in RCTL, the transistor is an inverting element that produces the positive NOR gate or the negative NAND gate function. (GRAF)

Resist Plating—Any material which, when deposited on a conductive area, prevents the areas underneath from being plated. (GRAF)

Resonant Frequency—The frequency at which a given system or object will respond with maximum amplitude when driven by an external sinusoidal force of constant amplitude. (GRAF)

Rise Time—The time required for the leading edge of a pulse to rise from 10–90% of its final value. It is proportionate to the time constant and is a measure of the steepness of the wavefront. Also, the measured length of time required for an output voltage of a digital circuit to change from a low voltage level (0) to a high voltage level (1) after the change has started. (GRAF)

ROM—An acronym for Read Only Memory. A memory which permits the reading of a predetermined pattern of *Zeros* and *Ones*. This predetermined information is stored in the ROM at the time of its manufacture. A ROM is analogous to a dictionary where a certain address results in predetermined information output.

Saturation—A circuit condition whereby an increase in the driving or input signal no longer produces a change in the output. (GRAF)

Saturation Voltage—Generally, the voltage excursion at which a circuit self-limits (i.e., is unable to respond to excitation in a proportional manner). (GRAF)

Schottky Barrier—A simple metal to semi-conductor interface that exhibits a nonlinear impedance. (GRAF)

Semi-conductor—An electronic conductor, with resistivity in the range between metals and insulators, in which the electric-charge-carrier concentration increases with increasing temperature over some temperature range. NOTE: Certain semi-conductors possess two types of carriers, namely, negative electrons and positive holes.

Semi-Conductor Controlled Rectifier (SCR)—An alternate name used for the reverse-blocking triode-thyristor. NOTE: The name of the actual semi-conductor material (selenium, silicon, etc.) may be substituted in place of the word *semi-conductor* in the name of the components. (IEEE)

Sensitivity—Measure of the ability of a device or circuit to react to a change in some input. Also, the minimum or required level of an input necessary to obtain rated output.

Serial-Parallel—Pertaining to processing that includes both serial and parallel processing, such as one that handles decimal digits serially but handles the bits that comprise a digit in parallel. (IEEE)

Serial Transmission—*data transmission, telecommunication* Used to identify a system wherein the bits of a character occur serially in time. Implies only a single transmission channel. Also called serial by bit. (IEEE)

Shift Register—(1) A logic network consisting of a series of memory cells such that a binary code can be caused to shift into the register by serial input to only the first cell. (2) A register in which the stored data can be moved to the right or left.

Signal—(1) A visual, audible, or other indication used to convey information. (2) The intelligence, message, or effect to be conveyed over a communication system. (3) A signal wave; the physical embodiment of a message. (4) *computing systems.* The event or phenomenon that conveys data from one point to another. (5) *control, industrial control.* Information about a variable that can be transmitted in a system. (IEEE)

Signal Generator—A shielded source of voltage or power, the output level and frequency of which are calibrated, and usually variable over a range. NOTE: The output of known waveform is normally subject to one or more forms of calibrated modulation. (IEEE)

Signal-To-Noise-Ratio—The ratio of the value of the signal to that of the noise. NOTES: (a) This ratio is usually in terms of peak values in the case of impulse noise and in terms of the root-mean-square values in the case of random noise. (b) Where there is a possibility of ambiguity, suitable definitions of the signal and noise should be associated with the terms; as, for example: peak-signal to peak-noise ratio; root-mean-square signal to root-mean square noise ratio; peak-to-peak signal to peak-to-peak noise ratio, etc. (c) This ratio may be often expressed in decibels. (d) This ratio may be a function of the bandwidth of the transmission system. (IEEE)

Silicon-On-Sapphire—Pertaining to the technology in which monocrystalline silicon films are epitaxially deposited onto a single-crystal sapphire substrate to form a structure for the fabrication of dielectrically isolated elements. Abbreviated SOS. (GRAF)

Software—(1) Computer programs, routines, programming languages and systems. (2) The collection of related utility, assembly, and other programs, that are desirable for properly presenting a given machine to a user. (3) Detailed procedures to be followed, whether expressed as programs for a computer or as procedures for an operator or other person. (4) Documents, including hardware manuals and drawings computer-program listings and diagrams, etc. (5) Items such as those in (1); (2), (3), and (4) as contrasted with hardware. (IEEE)

Solid-State—Pertaining to circuits and components using semi-conductors. (See solid-state devices.) (GRAF)

Solid State Device—Any element that can control current without moving parts, heated dilaments, or vacuum gaps. All semi-conductors are solid-state devices, although not all solid-state devices are semi-conductors (e.g., transformers). (GRAF)

Solid State Relay—A relay constructed exclusively of solid-state components.

Source(s) (or Source Electrode)—In a field effect transistor, the electrode that is analogous to the emitter of a transistor or the cathode of a vacuum tube. (GRAF)

Source Impedance—The impedance which a source of energy presents to the input terminal of a device. (GRAF)

Stability—The ability of a component or device to maintain its nominal operating characteristics after being subjected to changes in temperature, environment, current, and time. (GRAF)

Steady-State—A condition in which circuit values remain essentially constant, occurring after all initial transients or fluctuating conditions have settled down. (GRAF)

Storage—*electronic computation* (1) The act of storing information. (2) Any device in which information can be stored, sometimes called a memory device. (3) In a computer, a section used primarily for storing information. Such a section is sometimes called a memory or store (British). NOTES: (a) The physical means of storing information may be electrostatic, ferroelectric, magnetic, acoustic, optical, chemical, electronic, electric, mechanical, etc., in nature. (b) Pertaining to a device in which data can be entered, in which it can be held, and from which it can be retrieved at a later time. (IEEE)

Substrate—The supporting material on or in which the parts of an integrated circuit are attached or made. (GRAF)

Thermal Resistor—An electronic device which makes use of the change in resistivity of a semi-conductor with changes in temperature. (GRAF)

Thermal Runaway—A condition in which the dissipation in a transistor or other device increases so rapidly with higher temperature that the temperature keeps on rising. (GRAF)

Thermistor—A solid-state semi-conducting device, the electrical resistance of which varies with the temperature. Its temperature coefficient of resistance is high, nonlinear, and negative. (GRAF)

Thermocouple—Also called thermal junction. A device for measuring temperature where two electrical conductors of dissimilar metals are joined at the point of heat application and a resulting voltage difference, directly proportional to the temperature, is developed across the free ends and is measured potentiometrically. (GRAF)

Thick-Film—Pertaining to a film pattern usually made by applying conductive and insulating materials to a ceramic substrate by a silk-screen process. Thick films can be used to form conductors, resistors, and capacitors. (GRAF)

Thin-Film—A film of conductive or insulating material, usually deposited by sputtering or evaporation, that may be made in a pattern to form electronic components and conductors on a substrate or used as insulation between successive layers of components. (GRAF)

Thyristor—A bistable semi-conductor device comprising three or more junctions that can be switched from the *off* state to the *on* state or vice versa, such switching occurring within at least one quadrant of the principal voltage current characteristic. (IEEE)

Transducer—A device by means of which energy can flow from one or more transmission systems or media to one or more other transmission systems or media. NOTE: The energy transmitted by these systems or media may be of any form (for example, it may be electric, mechanical, or acoustical), and it may be of the same form or different forms in the various input and output systems or media. (IEEE)

Transformer—A device consisting of a winding with tap or taps, or two or more coupled windings with or without a magnetic core for introducing mutual coupling between electric circuits. (IEEE)

Transient—A phenomenon caused in a system by a sudden change in conditions, and which persists for a relatively short time after the change. Also a momentary surge on a signal or power line. It may produce false signals or triggering impulses and cause insulation or component breakdowns or failures. (GRAF)

Transistor—An active semi-conductor device with three or more terminals. (IEEE)

Transistor-Transistor Logic—Abbreviated TTL or T^{2}L. Also called multi-emitter transistor logic. A logic-circuit design similar to DTL, with the diode inputs replaced by a multiple emitter transistor. In a four-input DTL gate, there are four diodes at the input. A four-input TTL gate will have four emitters of a single transistor as the input element. TTL gates using NPN transistors are positive-level NAND gates or negative-level NOR gates. (GRAF)

Triac—A five-layer NPNPN device that is equivalent to two SCRs connected in antiparallel with a common gate. It provides switching action for either polarity of applied voltage and can be controlled in either polarity from the single gate electrode. (GRAF)

Unijunction Transistor—A three terminal semi-conductor device exhibiting stable open-circuit, negative resistance characteristics. (GRAF)

VAR—Abbreviation for Volt Ampere Reactive. The unit of reactive power, as opposed to real power in watts. One VAR is equal to one reactive volt-ampere. (GRAF)

Varistor—A two-electrode semi-conductor device with a voltage-dependent nonlinear resistance that drops markedly as the applied voltage is increased. (GRAF)

Volatile Memory—An electronic memory (RAM) which temporarily stores data that is lost when the power is turned off.

Volt—The unit of voltage or potential difference in SI units. The volt is the voltage between two points of a conducting wire carrying a constant current of one ampere, when the power dissipated between these points is one watt. (IEEE)

Waveguide—(1) Broadly, a system of material boundaries capable of guiding electro-magnetic waves. (2) More specifically, a transmission line comprising a hollow conducting tube within which electromagnetic waves may be propagated or a solid dielectric or dielectric filled conductor for the same purpose. (3) A system of material boundaries or structures for guiding transverse-electromagnetic mode, often and originally a hollow metal pipe for guiding electromagnetic waves. (IEEE)

Watt—A unit of the electric power required to do work at the rate of one joule per second. It is the power expended when one ampere of direct current flows through a resistance of one ohm. (GRAF)

Zener Diode—A two layer device that, above a certain reverse voltage (the Zener value), has a sudden rise in current. If forward-biased, the diode is an ordinary rectifier. But, when reversed-biased, the diode exhibits a typical knee, or sharp break, in its current-voltage graph. The voltage across the device remains essentially constant for any further increase of reverse current, up to the allowable dissipation rating. The Zener diode is a good voltage regulator, over voltage protector, voltage reference, level shifter, etc. True Zener breakdown occurs at less than six volts. (See also Avalanche Diode.) (GRAF)

Zener Effect—A reverse current breakdown due to the presence of a high electrical field at the junction of a semi-conductor or insulator. (GRAF)

Index